Cultural Anthropology

fourth canadian edition

Barbara Miller
George Washington University

Penny Van Esterik
York University

John Van Esterik
York University

Pearson Canada
Toronto

Library and Archives Canada Cataloguing in Publication

Miller, Barbara D., 1948–
    Cultural anthropology / Barbara D. Miller, Penny Van Esterik,
John Van Esterik.—4th Canadian ed.

    Includes bibliographical references and index.

    ISBN 978-0-205-57792-7

    1. Ethnology—Textbooks.   I. Van Esterik, Penny   II. Van Esterik,
John   III. Title.

    GN316.M34 2010   306   C2008-907490-4

ISBN-13: 978-0-205-57792-7
ISBN-10: 0-205-57792-X

Vice-President, Editorial Director: Gary Bennett
Editor-in-Chief: Ky Pruesse
Senior Acquisitions Editor: Laura Forbes
Marketing Manager: Arthur Gee
Senior Developmental Editor: Patti Altridge
Production Editor: Melissa Hajek
Copy Editor: Joe Zingrone
Proofreader: Susan McNish
Production Coordinator: Janis Raisen
Composition: Integra
Photo and Permissions Research: Sandy Cooke
Art Director: Julia Hall
Cover and Interior Design: Opus House Inc./Sonya Thursby
Cover Image: (Refugee from Darfur in a camp in Chad.) 2004 © Michal Safdie

4   13

Printed and bound in Canada.

Brief Contents

Contents

■ ■■ ■ I Introduction to Cultural Anthropology

1 Anthropology and the Study of Culture 3

2 Methods in Cultural Anthropology 33

▪■▪ II   Economic and Demographic Foundations ▬▬

3 Economies and Their Modes of Production   65

4 Consumption and Exchange   93

5 Birth and Death 121

6 Personality and Identity over the Life Cycle 147

■■■■ III Social Organization ■■■

7 Disease, Illness, and Healing 173

8 Kinship and Domestic Life 201

IV   Symbolic Systems

11 Religion   285

12 Communication   315

Boxed Features

Lessons Applied

Multiple Cultural Worlds

Ethnographic Profile

Critical Thinking

List of Maps

Preface from Barbara Miller

"I had no idea all those cultures were out there," said one of my students after taking my introductory cultural anthropology course. Another commented, "I'm a business major but I am going to keep the books from this course because they will help me in my career. I need to understand people."

Cultural anthropology opens up whole new worlds. Not just "out there," but here, there, and everywhere. The subject matter of cultural anthropology may seem distant, exotic, and "other"—jungle drumbeats and painted faces, for example. This book helps students to encounter those faraway cultures and to realize that their culture has its own versions of jungle drumbeats and painted faces. "Making the strange familiar" is essential learning in a globalizing world where cultural diversity may equal cultural survival for all of us. "Making the familiar strange" is a priceless revelation because it reduces the divide between "us" and the "other." "We"

become an "other" through the insights of cultural anthropology.

To achieve this double goal, *Cultural Anthropology*, Fourth Canadian Edition, delivers information about the world's cultures and promotes critical thinking and reflective learning. This book is rich in global examples of cultural diversity and change. Students will find many points at which they can connect with the material and reflect on their own culture—for example, hairstyles, food symbolism, sleep deprivation, doctor–patient dialogues, the meaning of gestures, and racism.

The book's organization and pedagogical features help ensure student engagement. Knowing that it is impossible to place culture in a linear series of chapters in a totally satisfactory way, I have organized the material in five parts. Within the five parts, each chapter presents findings from the latest, cutting-edge research in cultural anthropology, explained in clear and engaging prose.

Preface to the Fourth Canadian Edition

We are pleased with the reception of the first, second, and third editions of this textbook in Canadian schools from British Columbia to the Maritimes. The book entered the marketplace as the first Canadian edition of an introductory textbook in anthropology. In addition to updating and adding the work of more Canadian anthropologists in this fourth revised edition, we have added a special Ethnographic Profile box to illustrate particularly relevant societies from around the world. As in past editions, key questions open and close each chapter to help students focus on the most important issues in each chapter. In this edition, definitions of key concepts appear at the bottom of many pages to draw students' attention to these important ideas. A new map has been added at the beginning of the text to help students locate the peoples and places referred to in the book. Current interest in jobs for anthropologists outside of academia inspired the addition of profiles of anthropologists at work in non-academic settings at the beginning of each of the five sections of the book. We hope we have done justice to the work of the many colleagues whose work has inspired us, and to the generations of students taking courses in introductory anthropology.

In the 1960s, we were introduced to anthropology as students at the University of Toronto through American textbooks. As the subject was new to us, the content and approach seemed normal. Later, when we taught anthropology in Thai universities, we saw the same textbooks translated into Thai. In the 1970s we both taught Introduction to Anthropology at universities in the United States, so American texts fit the teaching contexts and indeed were normal. In the 1980s we returned to Canada and to teaching introductory anthropology. American textbooks were still being used, but their use seemed more problematic. By the 1990s we were teaching other courses in anthropology using texts by British, American,

and Canadian anthropologists that reflected the diversity of the discipline. Our colleagues still used American textbooks for teaching Introduction to Cultural Anthropology, but with growing dissatisfaction. It is appropriate to begin the new millennium with an anthropology textbook that includes Canadian experiences, research, and personalities.

Miller's text is an excellent choice for adaptation as it contains up-to-date materials on complex societies. Its strengths complement the interests of many Canadian anthropologists, and include a strong gender balance and focus, emphasis on the themes of social inequality and diversity, and a clear demonstration of applied anthropology and concern with contemporary issues such as health systems, migration, and development. Population and other statistical information now include Canadian data.

The practice and teaching of anthropology is shaped by context, both institutional and national. It matters to students and professors that Canadian anthropology is not the same as American anthropology. Its foundations were set in its long association with museums, First Nations research, anglophone and francophone dialogue, and ethnohistorical studies. In the first chapter we have made some adjustments to the theoretical stance of the book in keeping with the British, European, and American roots of Canadian anthropology. To orient the students to the unique history of anthropology in Canada, we have added material on the development of Canadian anthropology and sought out Canadian case studies—both new and classic—that may be more familiar to Canadian teachers and students, including references to First Nations groups, where appropriate. We have not included Canadian material gratuitously, nor have we removed all American examples. Rather, we have recontextualized American examples to become cross-cultural comparisons; American examples are no longer the benchmark defining "us" or "we." The suggested readings at the end of each chapter include the work of some Canadian anthropologists who have contributed to the field. In short, we have tried to highlight the significant contributions Canadians and Canadian institutions have made to the discipline and practice of anthropology.

Frank Manning (1983:2) began a volume reviewing Canadian ethnology by referring to a mythical plan that would see Canada incorporating British politics, American technology, and French culture, but, by accident, the country was left with French politics, British technology, and American culture. That story reveals something of the ironic and irreverent Canadian style, both self-deprecating and ambivalent toward our ancestors. A number of American anthropologists say they regularly participate in Canadian anthropology meetings because they enjoy the civility and the intellectual style of Canadian anthropology. This style is what makes the *Royal Canadian Air Farce* and *This Hour Has 22 Minutes* and the *Degrassi* series recognizable as Canadian television entertainment. It helps explain why clowns and magicians have been known to perform at Canadian anthropology meetings over the years. But, like all attempts at cultural generalization, this elusive sense of style is perhaps best conveyed by the Canadian anthropologists we hope will enjoy teaching from this book.

How This Book is Organized

Cultural Anthropology pursues its goal of promoting learning about the world's cultures in two ways, one that will be more familiar (the delivery of information) and another that may be unsettling and disturbing (asking questions about the information at hand that will make readers unsure of what they thought they knew).

Part I, Introduction to Cultural Anthropology, includes two chapters that provide the foundation for the rest of the book. They describe what anthropology is and how cultural anthropologists do research.

Part II, Economic and Demographic Foundations, includes chapters that explain how people make a living and provide for their needs, how people reproduce and raise children, and how different cultures deal with the inevitabilities of illness, suffering, and death.

Part III, Social Organization, provides chapters about how people around the world organize themselves into groups based on kinship and other forms of affiliation, how they form political alliances, and how they deal with conflict and the need for order.

Part IV, Symbolic Systems, presents chapters on religion, communication and language, and expressive culture and art.

Part V, Contemporary Cultural Change, looks at two of the most important topics in contemporary cultural change: migration and international development. These chapters explicitly put culture into motion and show how people are both affected by larger structures, such as globalization or violence, and exercise agency in attempting to create meaningful lives.

New Features of the Fourth Edition

Expanded Map Program

All chapters contain several maps. Each map is carefully designed to enhance the text material and all are clearly labelled. Cross-references throughout the book to maps located elsewhere encourage students to flip forward and backward in the book. This process facilitates review and helps readers make connections across chapters about the cultural groups and topics discussed.

Increased Number of Photographs

Each chapter has more photographs than the previous edition. They are selected to reinforce the material being discussed or take it in a new direction. Captions for all photographs are clear and concise.

Ethnographic Profile

All chapters include a one-page profile of a cultural group accompanied by a mini-panorama of two photographs and a map with captions. The summaries are brief, providing an enticing glimpse into the culture. At the end of each Ethnographic Profile, a list of resources (readings, videos, and websites) offers avenues for those who want to learn more. A good class assignment would be for students to do some independent research on one or more of the cultures in the Ethnographic Profile, or they might choose a different culture and compose their own Ethnographic Profile, with photographs (from Google.images, for example) and a map. For example:

- Chapter 1: "San Peoples of Southern Africa"
- Chapter 4: "The Kwakwaka'wakw of British Columbia"
- Chapter 5: "The Old Order Amish of the United States and Canada"

In-Text Glossary

Definitions for the Key Concepts are positioned on the bottom of the left page on the spread where the concept is first mentioned and defined. Key Concepts are also alphabetized in the Key Concepts list at the end of the chapter with page numbers included for easy cross-referencing.

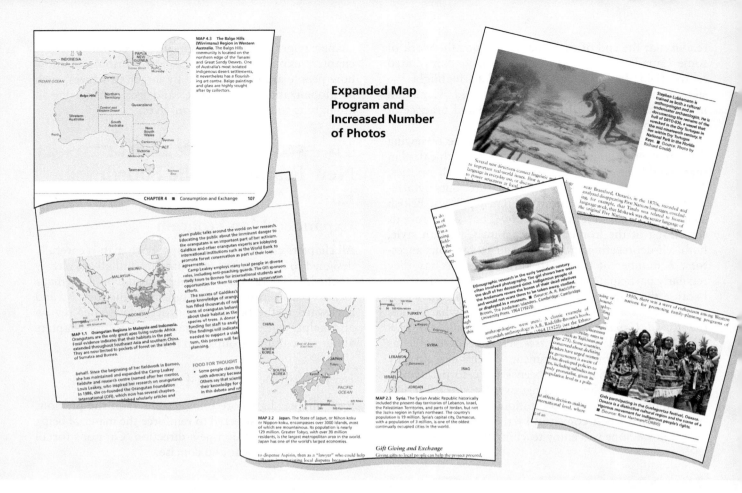

Expanded Map Program and Increased Number of Photos

Thinking Outside the Box

Another new feature, Thinking Outside the Box, prompts readers to relate an issue to their own cultural experiences or suggests ideas for further research. Each chapter contains three or four of these features. For example:

- Chapter 5: In your family, is there a preference about the desired number of sons and daughters? Is there a preference for their birth order?
- Chapter 12: Spend a week observing how people greet each other, both verbally and nonverbally. What are your major findings?

Anthropologists at Work

Each of the book's five parts opens with a profile of an applied anthropologist, someone who uses his or her anthropology training in non-academic settings. Profiles include a business anthropologist, a medical anthropologist, a forensic anthropologist, a development anthropologist, and a federal relations anthropologist.

Continuing Features

Several continuing features make this textbook distinctive and effective.

Key Questions

Three Key Questions are posed at the beginning of each chapter to alert readers to the chapter's overarching themes. They are carried through in the chapter outline as the three major headings. At the end of the chapter, Key Questions Revisited provides a helpful review of the key points related to each Key Question.

Boxed Features

Multiple Cultural Worlds boxes present material that demonstrates cultural variation and, often, but not always, inequalities by class, race, ethnicity, gender, and age. For example:

- Chapter 1: "Globalization and Tomato Production"
- Chapter 5 "A Preference for Sons"
- Chapter 6: "New Legal Rights for Gay and Lesbian Couples in Canada"

Critical Thinking boxes introduce an issue and show how it has been interpreted from two different, conflicting perspectives. Students are asked to consider how the researchers approached the issue, what kind of data they used, and how their conclusions are influenced by their

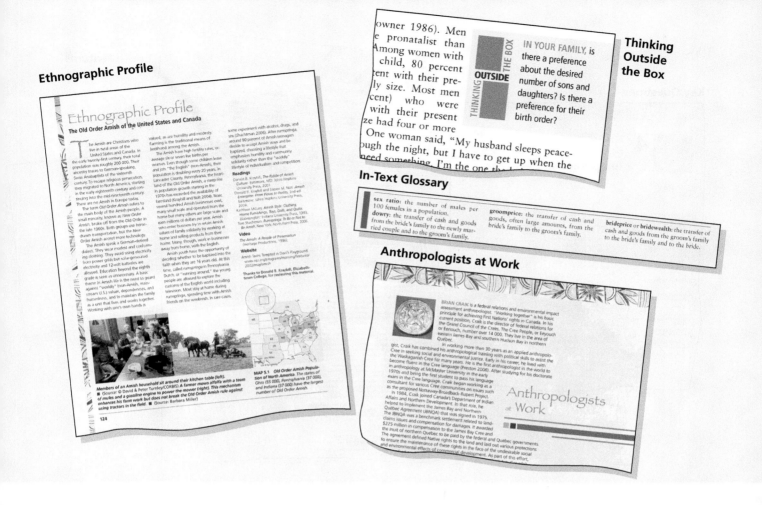

Ethnographic Profile

Thinking Outside the Box

In-Text Glossary

Anthropologists at Work

approach. Many of the boxes carry through on the three theoretical issues presented in Chapter 1 as characterizing contemporary cultural anthropology (biological determinism versus cultural constructionism, interpretive anthropology versus cultural materialism, and individual agency versus structure). For example:

- Chapter 6: "Cultural Relativism and Female Genital Cutting"

In other boxes, students are asked to reflect on "received wisdom" from a new angle:

- Chapter 3: "Was the Invention of Agriculture a Terrible Mistake?"

Lessons Applied boxes highlight how applied anthropologists work. Although students may appreciate the interesting material that cultural anthropology offers, they are still likely to ask, "Does this knowledge have any practical applications?" This fourth edition, even more than previous editions, shows the relevance of knowledge in cultural anthropology and the many ways it can be put into practice.

- Chapter 2: "Multiple Methods in a Needs Assessment Study"

- Chapter 13: "A Strategy for the World Bank on Cultural Heritage"
- Chapter 9: "Anthropology and Community Activism in Papua New Guinea"

In addition to the boxed features that add depth and richness to the text, *Suggested Readings* are listed at the end of each chapter. Each selection has a brief annotation to guide students who may be looking for resources for a class project or report.

Supplements

Along with this textbook come an array of supplements that will assist instructors in using the book and enriching the students' learning experience.

Supplements for Instructors

Accompanying this text is an array of supplements that will assist instructors in using the book. Contact your local Pearson Education Canada sales representative to obtain copies of the following items.

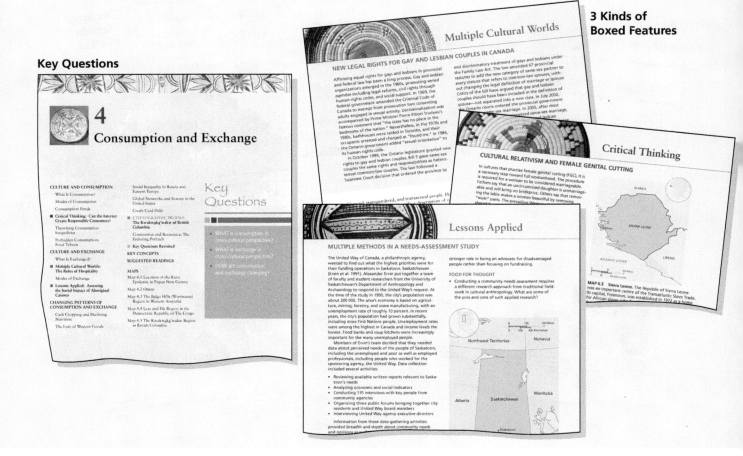

Instructor's Resource CD-ROM

This resource CD (ISBN 0-205-69316-4) includes the following instructor supplements:

- *Instructor's Manual* includes teaching tips and class-room exercises that can be used to teach cultural anthropology.
- *PowerPoint Presentations* combine graphics and text into chapter-based teaching modules.
- *Image Library* includes figures and tables from the text.
- *Pearson MyTest* from Pearson Education Canada is a powerful assessment generation program that helps instructors easily create and print quizzes, tests, exams, as well as homework or practice handouts. Questions and tests can all be authored online, allowing instructors ultimate flexibility and the ability to efficiently manage assessments at any time, from anywhere. MyTest for *Cultural Anthropology*, Fourth Canadian Edition, includes over 1000 questions in multiple-choice, true/false, short answer, and essay format. These questions are also available in Microsoft Word format on the Instructor's Resource CD-ROM.

Some of the supplements on the Instructor's Resource CD-ROM are also available for download from a password-protected section of Pearson Education Canada's online catalogue (vig.pearsoned.ca). Navigate to this book's catalogue page to view a list of those supplements that are available. Contact your local sales representative for details and access, or call Pearson's Faculty and Sales Service Department at 1-800-850-5813.

MyAnthroLab with peerScholar—Pearson Canada's online resource, MyAnthroLab, offers instructors and students all of their resources in one place, organized to accompany this text. With MyAnthroLab, you will be able to enliven your lectures with a variety of material. And your students will be able to "study smarter" with an ebook and a diagnostic test that creates a customized study plan to help them prepare for, and perform better on, exams. MyAnthroLab is available for instructors by going to www.myanthrolab.com and following the instructions on the page. Students get MyAnthroLab with an access code that is available with the purchase of a new text.

Bring thinking and writing assignments back into your anthropology course

- Do you regret that the economics and logistics of assessment make it impossible to grade first-year students other than by multiple-choice tests?

- Would you like a way to integrate writing assignments that give students the opportunity to develop critical thinking and communication skills in your course?
- Is lack of time and additional support your key challenge?

peerScholar is for you. Developed and successfully used for more than five years at University of Toronto—Scarborough, peerScholar provides a pedagogically powerful online tool that supports open-ended writing assignments in any size of class. Students write an abstract and a short essay in response to an article or other learning object and, after submitting it anonymously, receive the work of several peers to grade. Valuable learning takes place at both the writing stage and the grading stage, and results are distributed in a very timely manner. Ongoing research substantiates that the peer grading is similar in level and rank-order as that provided by "expert" graders. peerScholar saves TAs' and professors' time for more consultations and richer interactions with students.

Thought-provoking original articles, with suggested writing assignments and grading rubrics, are included in peerScholar. Use these preloaded assignments or create your own. Check out peerScholar for yourself in MyAnthroLab, or if you would like more information about how to use peerScholar, please contact your Pearson sales representative or technology specialist.

A student access code card for MyAnthroLab with peerScholar is packaged with every new copy of *Cultural Anthropology*, Fourth Canadian Edition. If a student purchases a used book, access code cards may be purchased at the campus bookstore.

Allyn &Bacon Interactive Video and User's Guide

This custom video covers a variety of topics, both national and global. The up-to-the-minute video segments are great to launch lectures, spark classroom discussion, and encourage critical thinking. The user's guide provides detailed descriptions of each video segment, specific tie-ins to the text, and suggested discussion questions and projects.

Allyn & Bacon Video Library

Qualified adopters may select from a wide variety of high-quality videos from such sources as Films for the Humanities and Sciences and Annenberg/CPB. Contact your Pearson Education Canada sales representative for a complete list of videos.

The Blockbuster Approach: A Guide to Teaching Anthropology with Film

This supplement guides the instructor on how to integrate feature films into an introductory course successfully and offers hundreds of film suggestions for topics covered in *Cultural Anthropology*, Fourth Canadian Edition.

Technology Specialists

Pearson's Technology Specialists work with faculty and campus course designers to ensure that Pearson technology products, assessment tools, and online course materials are tailored to meet your specific needs. This highly qualified team is dedicated to helping schools take full advantage of a wide range of educational resources, by assisting in the integration of a variety of instructional materials and media formats. Your local Pearson Education sales representative can provide you with more details on this service program.

CourseSmart

CourseSmart is a new way for instructors and students to access textbooks online any time from anywhere. With thousands of titles across hundreds of courses, Course-Smart helps instructors choose the best textbook for their class and give their students a new option for buying the assigned textbook as a lower-cost eTextbook. For more information, visit www.coursesmart.com.

Supplements for Students

myanthrolab MyAnthroLab with peerScholar—Supplied with every new copy of this text, MyAnthroLab provides students with access to a wealth of resources, including:

- Diagnostic tests that assess your understanding of the text
- A custom study program that creates a personalized study plan using the ebook and based on your diagnostic test results
- A media-enriched ebook, loaded with animations, videos, and additional resources
- Access to peerScholar, with written exercises assigned by your instructor

MyAnthroLab includes access to Research Navigator, Pearson's fully searchable online collection of academic and popular journals.

Get started with the personal access code packaged with your new copy of the text. Personal access codes for MyAnthroLab can also be purchased separately at www.myanthrolab.com.

The Anthropology Experience

This valuable multimedia resource for teaching and learning cultural anthropology includes a National Geographic video, an audio glossary, PowerPoint presentations, an illustrated supplementary cultural anthropology booklet, world-class anthropological photos in an accessible image bank, online activities, and more. Please visit www.pearsonhighered.com/educator and search for Anthropology Experience for more information on how to make use of these exciting media resources and how to make them available to your students or speak to your Pearson Canada sales representative.

Reader and Ethnographies

The following texts may be of interest to users of *Cultural Anthropology*. Instructors should contact a Pearson Canada sales representative for packaging information.

Reader

Conformity and Conflict: Readings in Cultural Anthropology, Thirteenth Edition, by James Spradley and David W. McCurdy (ISBN 0-20-564585-2)

Canadian Ethnography Series

Volume I: "Only God Can Own the Land": The Attawapiskat Cree, by Bryan D. Cummins and John L. Steckley (ISBN 0-13-177065-9)

Volume II: From American Slaves to Nova Scotian Subjects: The Case of the Black Refugees, 1813–1840, by Harvey Amani Whitfield, Bryan D. Cummins, and John L. Steckley (ISBN 0-13-177066-7)

Volume III: Ta'n teli-ktlamsi Tasit (Ways of Believing): Mi'kmaw Religion in Eskasoni, Nova Scotia, by Angela Robinson, Bryan D. Cummins, and John L. Steckley (ISBN 0-13-177067-5)

Cultural Survival Studies in Ethnicity and Change Series

Ariaal Pastoralists of Kenya: Studying Pastoralism, Drought, and Development in Africa's Arid Lands, Second Edition, Elliot M. Fratkin (ISBN 0-205-39142-7)

AlterNatives: Community, Identity, and Environmental Justice on Walpole Island, Robert M. Van Wynsberghe (ISBN 0-205-34952-8)

Indigenous Peoples, Ethnic Groups, and the State, Second Edition, David Maybury-Lewis (ISBN 0-205-33746-5)

Aboriginal Reconciliation and the Dreaming: Warramiri Yolngu and the Quest for Equality, Ian S. McIntosh (ISBN 0-205-29793-5)

Ethnicity and Culture Amidst New "Neighbors": The Runa of Ecuador's Amazon Region, Theodore Macdonald (ISBN 0-205-19821-X)

Defending the Land: Sovereignty and Forest Life in James Bay Cree Society, Ronald Niezen, (ISBN 0-205-27580-X)

Gaining Ground?: Evenkis, Land, and Reform in Southeastern Siberia, Gail A. Fondahl (ISBN 0-205-27579-6)

Forest Dwellers, Forest Protectors: Indigenous Models for International Development, Richard Reed (ISBN 0-205-19822-8)

Malaysia and the "Original People": A Case Study of the Impact of Development on Indigenous Peoples, Robert Knox Dentan, Kirk Endicott, Alberto G. Gomes, and M.B. Hooker (ISBN 0-205-19817-1)

In Thanks—from Barbara Miller

The breadth, depth, and quality of this edition are the result of many people's ideas, comments, corrections, and care. For the first edition, four anthropologists carefully reviewed multiple drafts of the book. I will always be grateful to them for their monumental contribution. They helped make this book what it is today: Elliot Fratkin, Pennsylvania State University; Maxine Margolis, University of Florida; Russell Reid, University of Louisville; and Robert Trotter II, University of Arizona.

The cultural anthropologists who served as reviewers for the second, third, fourth, and fifth editions helped me move the book forward in many ways: Warren D. Anderson, Southeast Missouri State University; Jason Antrosio, Albion College; Diane Baxter, University of Oregon; Monica L. Bellas, Cerritos College; Barbara Bonnekessen, University of Missouri–Kansas City; Peter Brown, University of Wisconsin, Oshkosh; Howard Campbell, University of Texas, El Paso; (the late) Charles R. de Burlo, The University of Vermont; Elizabeth de la Portilla, University of Texas at San Antonio; William W. Donner, Kutztown University; Lisa Pope Fischer, Santa Monica College; Pamela J. Ford, Mount San Jacinto College; Mary Kay Gilliland, Pima Community College; Nancy Gonlin, Bellevue Community College; Jeanne Humble, Bluegrass Community & Technical College; Ann Kingsolver, University of South Carolina; Leslie Lischka, Linfield College; William M. Loker, California State University, Chico; Martin F. Manalansan IV, University of Illinois; Corey Pressman, Mt. Hood Community College; Ed Robbins, University of Wisconsin; Jacquelyn Robinson, Albany State

University; Harry Sanabria, University of Pittsburgh; Kathleen M. Saunders, Western Washington University; G. Richard Scott, University of Nevada, Reno; Wesley Shumar, Drexel University; David Simmons, University of South Carolina; Kimberly Eison Simmons, University of South Carolina; Lori A. Stanley, Luther College; Jim Wilce, Northern Arizona University; and Peter Wogan, Willamette University; and Katrina Worley, Sierra College.

Many anthropologists and others have provided encouragement, suggestions, feedback, references, and photographs: Lila Abu-Lughod, Abigail Adams, Vincanne Adams, Catherine Allen, Joseph Alter, Matthew Amster, Myrdene Anderson, Donald Attwood, Christopher Baker, Isabel Balseiro, Nancy Benco, Marc Bermann, Alexia Bloch, Elson Boles, Lynne Bolles, John Bowen, Don Brenneis, Alison Brooks, Judith K. Brown, D. Glynn Cochrane, Jeffery Cohen, Carole Counihan, Brian Craik, Liza Dalby, Loring Danforth, Patricia Delaney, Alexander Dent, Linus Digim'rina, Timothy Earle, Daniel Everett, Johannes Fabian, Ilana Feldman, Elliot Fratkin, Martin Fusi, Maris Boyd Gillette, Richard A. Gould, David Gow, Richard Grinker, Daniel Gross, (the late) Marvin Harris, Tobias Hecht, Cornelia Mayer Herzfeld, Michael Herzfeld, Barry Hewlett, Danny Hoffman, Michael Horowitz, (the late) Robert Humphrey, Lanita Jacobs-Huey, Vicki Jensen, Anstice Justin, Barry D. Kass, Patty Kelly, Laurel Kendall, David Kideckel, Diane E. King, Stuart Kirsch, Dorinne Kondo, Conrad Kottak, Jennifer Kramer, Donald B. Kraybill, Ruth Krulfeld, Joel Kuipers, Takie Lebra, David Lempert, Lamont Lindstrom, Susan Orpett Long, Luisa Maffi, Beatriz Manz, Samuel Martínez, Catherine McCoid, Leroy McDermott, Kimber Haddox McKay, Jerry Milanich, Laura Miller, Madhushree Mukerjee, Kirin Narayan, Sarah Nelson, Gananath Obeyesekere, Ellen Oxfeld, Hanna Papanek, Michael G. Peletz, Deborah Pellow, Gregory Possehl, David Price, Joanne Rappaport, Jennifer Robertson, Nicole Sault, Joel Savishinsky, David Z. Scheffel, Nancy Scheper-Hughes, Pankaj Sekhsaria, Bob Shepherd, Richard Shweder, Jennie Smith-Pariola, Chunghee Soh, Kate Spilde Contreras, Anthony Stocks, Patricia Tovar, Sita Venkateswar, Martha Ward, James (Woody) Watson, Rubie Watson, Van Yasek, and Kevin Yelvington.

I thank "the Millers"—my parents, siblings, aunts and uncles, and nieces and nephews—for their interest and support. My father's two comments about the book were that it has an awful lot of long words, and how do I know so much about sex. "From reading, Dad," was my truthful reply. I am grateful to "the Heatons"—my former in-laws, including my ex-husband, (late) parents-in-law, brothers- and sisters-in-law, and nieces and nephews—for their enduring friendship.

I thank, especially, my son, Jack Heaton. He was a superb travelling companion on our trip around the world with the Semester at Sea Program in 1996 when I wrote much of the first edition. He continues to be excellent company during our many lunches and dinners in D.C. I dedicate this book to him.

Barbara Miller
Washington, D.C.

In Thanks—from Penny and John Van Esterik

The task of Canadianizing *Cultural Anthropology* was made possible by our being situated in York University's very vibrant department of anthropology. Students and colleagues generously provided references, suggestions, words of wisdom, and warning; we thank them all, and are particularly grateful for the assistance of Naomi Adelson, Kathryn Denning, Ruth King, Ken Little, David Lumsden, Kathy M'Closkey, Margaret MacDonald, Lynne Milgram, Lynne Phillips, and Daphne Winland. We give special thanks to Melissa Atkinson-Graham for research assistance on the fourth edition.

At Pearson Education Canada, we would like to thank Laura Forbes, Editorial Director, for guiding this undertaking. We thank Patti Altridge, Developmental Editor, for her patient efforts to keep us on schedule and focused; Joe Zingrone for his careful editing; Susan McNish for her meticulous proofreading; and Melissa Hajek, Production Editor, for integrating all the pieces into an outstanding product. We would also like to thank Arthur Gee, Marketing Manager, for directing our marketing campaign, and the members of the sales team, who have given this project such support.

We are most grateful to the reviewers who made valuable suggestions during the process of preparing the fourth Canadian edition. Thank you to Karen Hutton of University of New Brunswick, Brian Myhre of the University of Manitoba, Jacklyn Bate of Vancouver Island University, Diana French of UBC Okanagan, Clare Fawcett of St. Francis Xavier University, Sam Migliore of Kwantlen Polytechnic University, Terry Webb of the University of Western Ontario, Alexandre Enkerli of Concordia University, and Kathleen Gordon of Memorial University of Newfoundland. We regret the inevitable errors of omission and commission. Some of these we have been able to correct in this fourth Canadian edition.

Penny and John Van Esterik
Toronto, Ontario

Prologue

The Importance of Commitment: A Note on the Cover Image

Michal Ronnen Safdie was born in Jerusalem in 1951. Her mother was a Holocaust survivor. She is the author of *The Western Wall* (1997), a book of photographs. Her work has been exhibited worldwide.

During her 2004 trip to Chad on the border with Darfur, Sudan, she documented the situation of the so-called "lucky ones," those who had survived the years of violence and genocide to face hunger, disease, and the uncertainties of life as displaced persons. Her focus is on human beings trying to rebuild their lives in the aftermath of terrible pain and struggle.

Safdie's images of people, mainly women and children, living in a refugee camp in Bahai, Chad, on the border with Darfur, bring the truth of violence and its consequences into plain view as well as the dignity and hope of a child. Her photographs do not allow us to forget.

The Importance of Names: A Note about This Book

Since the beginning of modern humanity, people have been naming each other, naming other groups, and naming features of the places they inhabit. People of earlier times often referred to themselves in terms that translate roughly into The People. As far as they were concerned, they were The People: the only people on earth.

Things are more complicated now. European colonialism, starting in the fifteenth century, launched centuries of rapid contact between Europeans of named continents, countries, and regions, and thousands of indigenous groups around the world. The Europeans named and described these groups in their European languages. The names were not those that the people used for themselves, or if they were, the transliteration into a European language altered local names into something very different from the original.

The Spanish explorers' naming of all the indigenous peoples of North America as Indians is a famous example of erroneous naming. When conquerors rename people and claim their territory, they simultaneously erase much of the indigenous people's identity and heritage.

The challenge of using the preferred names for people and places of the world faces us today. Until recently, indigenous peoples of the present-day United States preferred to be called Native Americans, rejecting the pejorative term Indian. Now, they are claiming and recasting the term Indian. In Canada, preferred terms are First Nations, Native Peoples, and Northern Peoples.

From small-scale groups to entire countries, people around the world are attempting to revive precolonial group names and place names. Bombay is now Mumbai. Group names and place names are frequently contested. Is someone Hispanic or Latino? Is it the Persian Gulf or the Arabian Gulf? Is it Greenland or Kalaallit Nunaat? Does it matter? The answer is yes, resoundingly, yes.

This book seeks to provide the most currently accepted names for people, places, objects, activities, and ideas. But by the time this page is printed, some names and how they are spelled in English will have changed. It is part of our job, as citizens of the world, to pay attention to names, to keep track of changes, and to respect the motivations behind them.

About the Authors

BARBARA D. MILLER

Barbara Miller is Professor of Anthropology and International Affairs, and Director of the Culture in Global Affairs (CIGA) Research and Policy Program, at The George Washington University. She received her Ph.D. in anthropology from Syracuse University in 1978. Before coming to GW in 1994, she taught at the University of Rochester, SUNY Cortland, Ithaca College, Cornell University, and the University of Pittsburgh.

For 30 years, Barbara's research has focused mainly on gender-based inequalities in India, especially the nutritional and medical neglect of daughters in northern regions of the country. In addition, she has conducted research on culture and rural development in Bangladesh, on low-income household dynamics in Jamaica, and on Hindu adolescents in Pittsburgh. Her current interests include continued research on gender inequalities in health in South Asia, the role of cultural anthropology in informing policy issues, and cultural heritage and public policy, especially as related to women, children, and other disenfranchised groups. She teaches courses on introductory cultural anthropology, medical anthropology, development anthropology, culture and population, health and development in South Asia, and migration and mental health. In addition to many journal articles and book chapters, she has published several books: *The Endangered Sex: Neglect of Female Children in Rural North India,* 2nd ed. (Oxford University Press, 1997), an edited volume, *Sex and Gender Hierarchies* (Cambridge University Press, 1993), a co-edited volume with Alf Hiltebeitel, *Hair: Its Power and Meaning in Asian Cultures* (SUNY Press, 1998), and a text co-authored with Bernard Wood, *Anthropology* (Allyn & Bacon, 2006).

PENNY VAN ESTERIK

Penny Van Esterik is Professor of Anthropology at York University, Toronto. She graduated from the University of Toronto (BA) and the University of Illinois at Champaign–Urbana (MA, Ph.D.) and currently teaches nutritional anthropology, advocacy anthropology, and feminist theory. Her primary fieldwork has been done in Southeast Asia (Thailand, Indonesia, and Lao PDR). Past books include *Beyond the Breast–Bottle Controversy* (on infant feeding in Thailand), *Taking Refuge: Lao Buddhists in North America* (on the reintroduction of Buddhism by Lao refugees in North America), *Food and Culture: a reader*, edited with Carol Counihan (updated 2008 in a second edition), and *Food Culture in Southeast Asia* (Greenwood Press, 2008). Together with John Van Esterik, she established a CIDA-funded exchange program on gender and development in Thailand and has published jointly with him. She is a founding member of the World Alliance for Breastfeeding Action (WABA) and has been active in developing articles and advocacy materials on breastfeeding and women's work, breastfeeding and feminism, and contemporary challenges to infant feeding such as environmental contaminants and HIV/AIDS. In 2007, she received the Weaver-Tremblay award for applied anthropology from the Canadian Anthropology Society/ La Societé Canadienne d'Anthropologie (CASCA).

JOHN VAN ESTERIK

John Van Esterik is a retired senior scholar of anthropology at York University. He graduated from the University of Toronto (BA, MA) and from the University of Illinois at Champaign–Urbana (Ph.D.). For several years he taught in and managed programs for Southeast Asian refugees in Indiana and upstate New York. In 1985 he began teaching at York University and, with Penny Van Esterik, managed a linkage program on gender and development between York University and universities in Thailand. His research has been on changes in Thai Buddhist practice and Lao refugees in North America. He has published articles on refugee issues, Theravada Buddhism, and gender and development in Thailand including an edited volume with Penny Van Esterik entitled *Gender and Development in Thailand*.

AFGH. = Afghanistan
ALB. = Albania
ARM. = Armenia
AUS. = Austria
AZER. = Azerbaijan
BANG. = Bangladesh
BEL. = Belgium
B & H. = Bosnia and Herzegovina
BUL. = Bulgaria
BURK. FASO = Burkina Faso
C. AFR. REP. = Central African Republic
CAM. = Cameroon
CRO. = Croatia
C. V. = Cape Verde
CYP. = Cyprus
CZE. = Czech Republic
DEM. REP. OF THE CONGO =
    Democratic Republic of the Congo
DEN. = Denmark
EQ. GUINEA = Equatorial Guinea
EST. = Estonia
GAM. = Gambia
G.-B. = Guinea-Bissau
GER. = Germany
GUI. = Guinea
HOND. = Honduras
HUN. = Hungary
ISR. = Israel
KAMP. = Kampuchea
KRYG. = Kyrgyzstan
LAT. = Latvia
LEB. = Lebanon
LITH. = Lithuania
LUX. = Luxembourg
MAC. = Macedonia
MOL. = Moldova
MON. = Montenegro
MYAN. = Myanmar
NETH. = Netherlands
POL. = Poland
ROM. = Romania
RUS. = Russia
SER. = Serbia
SLO. = Slovakia
SLOV. = Slovenia
SWITZ. = Switzerland
SYR. = Syria
TAJIK. = Tajikistan
THAI. = Thailand
TURK. = Turkmenistan
UZBEK. = Uzbekistan
U.A.E. = United Arab Emirates

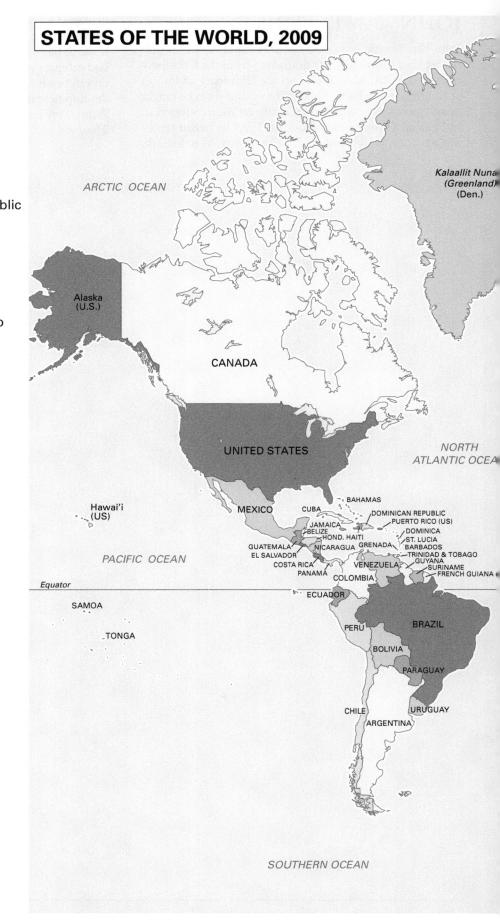

STATES OF THE WORLD, 2009

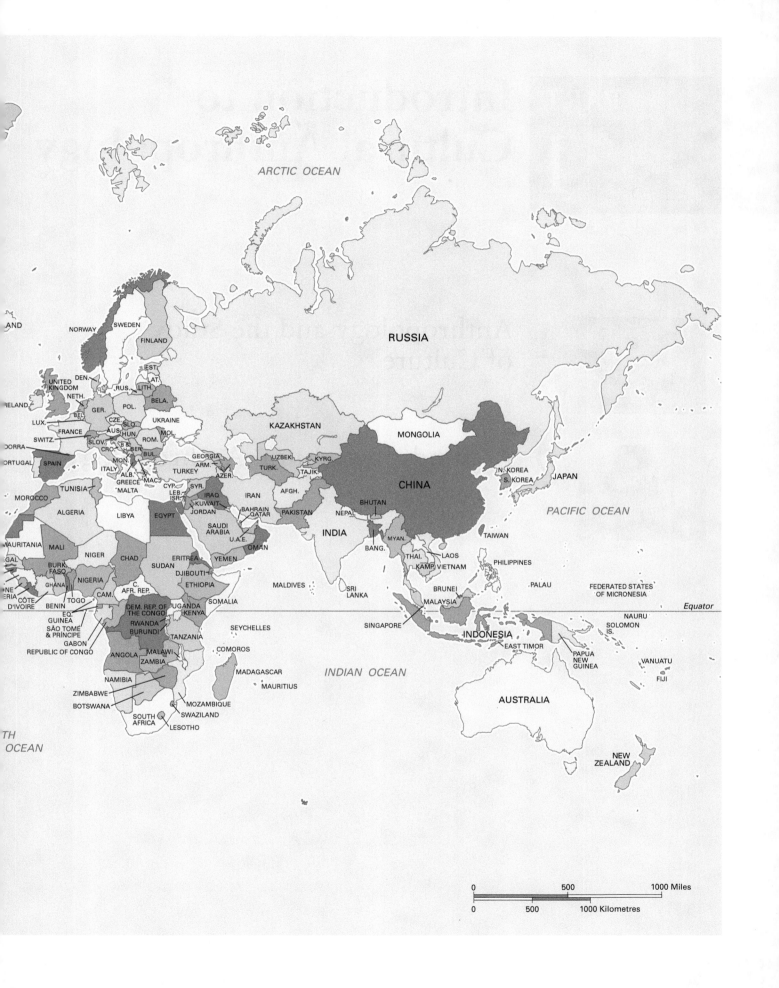

PART I

Introduction to Cultural Anthropology

 **1** Anthropology and the Study of Culture

 **2** Methods in Cultural Anthropology

BRIAN CRAIK is a federal relations and environmental impact assessment anthropologist. "Working together" is his basic principle for achieving First Nations' rights in Canada. In his current position, Craik is the director of federal relations for the Grand Council of the Crees. The Cree People, or Eeyouch or Eenouch, number over 14 000. They live in the area of eastern James Bay and southern Hudson Bay in northern Québec.

In working more than 30 years as an applied anthropologist, Craik has combined his anthropological training with political skills to assist the Cree in seeking social and environmental justice. Early in his career, he lived with the Waskaganish Cree for many years. He is the first anthropologist in the world to become fluent in the Cree language (Preston 2006). After studying for his doctorate in anthropology at McMaster University in the early 1970s and being the first student to pass his language exam in the Cree language, Craik began working as a consultant for various Cree communities on issues such as the proposed Nottaway-Broadback-Rupert Project.

Anthropologists at Work

In 1984, Craik joined Canada's Department of Indian Affairs and Northern Development. In that role, he helped to implement the James Bay and Northern Québec Agreement (JBNQA) that was signed in 1975. The JBNQA was a benchmark settlement related to land-claims issues and compensation for damages. It awarded $225 million in compensation to the James Bay Cree and the Inuit of northern Québec to be paid by the federal and Québec governments. The agreement defined Native rights to the land and laid out various protections to ensure the maintenance of these rights in the face of the undesirable social and environmental effects of commercial development. As part of this effort, Craik worked on the passage of the Cree/Naskapi (of Québec) Act, Canada's first Aboriginal local government act, and helped assure the approval of related funding.

In 1987, Craik left the government to return to private consulting. He worked with the Lubicon Crees of Alberta, the Inuit of northern Québec, the Micmac of Conn River, and the Mohawks of Kahnawake. In 1989, he advised the James Bay Cree on relations with the federal government and on the environmental and social issues related to the Great Whale Project. The Cree People appointed him to two of the environmental committees that reviewed the project. Craik played a central role in the 1989–1994 campaign that stopped the Great Whale River hydroelectric project. From 1997 to 1999, he negotiated an agreement between the Crees and the federal government on Canada Manpower Services and has worked to implement the 2002 New Relationship Agreement between the Crees and Québec's government—Craik also helped to review the Eastmain 1A–Rupert Diversion Project that the New Relationship Agreement contains.

The Cree People have faced many threats to their lifeway, culture, and environment. The Grand Council of the Crees was formed in 1974 in response to the James Bay Hydroelectric Project (see www.gcc.ca/gcc/fedrelations.php). Their political mobilization was inspired by the need to "stand in the way of development projects designed to serve others" (Craik 2004). With Craik's long-term assistance in their struggle, they have sharpened their political and economic power and skills. They now choose when to block a destructive project or when to work to change the terms of a project in order to mitigate damage to their culture and land and to reap some of the benefits for their own group-defined development goals.

1

Anthropology and the Study of Culture

Key Questions

- WHAT is anthropology?
- WHAT is cultural anthropology?
- HOW is cultural anthropology relevant to a career in the world of work?

Folk dancers in Oaxaca, southern Mexico. *(Source: Bob Krist/CORBIS)*

Old bones, *Jurassic Park*, cannibalism, hidden treasure, *Indiana Jones and the Kingdom of the Crystal Skull*. The popular impression of anthropology is based mainly on movies and television shows that depict anthropologists as adventurers and heroes. Many anthropologists do have adventures, and some discover treasures such as ancient pottery, medicinal plants, and jade carvings. But most of their research is not glamorous. Some anthropologists spend years in difficult physical conditions searching for the earliest fossils of our ancestors. Others live among, and study first-hand, how people work and organize family life in a setting permeated by modern technology. Some anthropologists conduct laboratory analyses of the contents of tooth enamel to reveal where an individual once lived. Others study designs on prehistoric pottery to learn what the symbols mean, or observe nonhuman primates such as chimpanzees or orangutans in the wild to learn how they live.

Anthropology is the study of humanity, including our prehistoric origins and contemporary human diversity. Compared to other disciplines that study humanity (such as history, psychology, economics, political science, and sociology), anthropology is broader in scope. Anthropology covers a much greater span of time than these disciplines and it encompasses a broader range of topics.

Introducing Anthropology

The breadth of topics in anthropology matches its breadth in research methods, which range from scientific to humanistic. Some anthropologists consider anthropology to be a *science*: a form of inquiry that involves first the formulation of a hypothesis, or hunch, about the way things work and then observation or testing to see whether the hypothesis is correct. Other anthropologists pursue a *humanistic approach*, which is a subjective way of understanding humanity through the study of people's art, music, poetry, language, and other forms of symbolic expression. This approach avoids working from a pre-set hypothesis but instead seeks insight through culturally informed understanding.

No matter whether it is pursued from a more scientific or a more humanistic perspective, anthropology seeks to produce new knowledge, and this is its primary goal as an academic field of inquiry. But its findings are also relevant to significant real-world issues and therefore to the public at large. Anthropologists' research findings can influence government policy-makers, businesses, technology developers, health-care providers, teachers, and the general public. You will learn more about these contributions in this chapter and throughout the book.

In North America, anthropology is divided into four fields (see Figure 1.1 on page 6) that focus on separate, but connected, subject matter related to humanity:

- **Biological anthropology** (or **physical anthropology**): the study of humans as biological organisms, including their evolution and contemporary variation.
- **Archaeology** (or **prehistory**): the study of past human cultures through their material remains.
- **Linguistic anthropology**: the study of human communication, including its origins, history, and contemporary variation and change.
- **Cultural anthropology** (or **social anthropology**): the study of living peoples and their cultures, including variation and change. **Culture** refers to people's learned and shared behaviours and beliefs.

Some anthropologists argue that a fifth field, applied anthropology, should be added. **Applied anthropology** (also called **practising anthropology** or **practical anthropology**) is the use of anthropological knowledge to prevent or solve problems or to shape and achieve policy goals. The authors of this book take the position that the application of knowledge, just like theory, is an integral part of each of the four fields and should be integrated within each of them.

The sheer amount of knowledge in the various fields has increased over time, and apparently greater differences in theory, methods, and subject matter have emerged, making interchange across fields less frequent or useful. At least two Canadian universities have split their departments into anthropology and archaeology. Only about one-third of the departments of anthropology in Canada include the four

---

anthropology: the study of humanity, including our prehistoric origins and contemporary human diversity.
biological anthropology or **physical anthropology**: the study of humans as biological organisms, including their evolution and contemporary variation.
archaeology or **prehistory**: the study of past human cultures through their material remains.

linguistic anthropology: the study of human communication, including its origins, history, and contemporary variation and change.
cultural anthropology or **social anthropology**: the study of living peoples and their cultures, including variation and change.

culture: people's learned and shared behaviour and beliefs.
applied anthropology or **practising anthropology** or **practical anthropology**: the use of anthropological knowledge to prevent or solve problems or to shape and achieve policy goals.

subfields within one department. Linguistics is most likely to be omitted, reflecting the British university pattern of considering linguistics outside the scope of anthropology (Darnell 1998). The distinctly Canadian triad of archaeology, ethnology, and folklore may have its roots in government-supported museums rather than U.S. departments of anthropology (Preston 1983:288).

Archaeology

The field of archaeology is devoted to studying the lifeways of past cultures by examining material remains. Data include stone and bone tools, skeletal material, remains of buildings, and refuse such as pot shards (broken pieces of pottery) and coprolites (fossilized fecal matter). Since its beginnings in the mid-eighteenth century, archaeology has contributed knowledge about towns and villages, as well as the emergence of the great early states of Egypt, Phoenicia, the Indus Valley, and Mexico. New research is questioning some previous conclusions about "kingdoms." For example, excavations at a royal burial site of the Old Silla Kingdom of Korea, which extended from 57 BCE (Before Common Era) to 668 CE (Common Era), reveal that queens were often the rulers (Nelson 1993). This finding challenges the earlier generalization that centralized state systems always involve male political dominance.

An example of a relatively new area of research is archaeologists' examination of European colonialism and its impact on pre-colonial states (Graham 1998). In the Maya area, for example, where an interest in the civilization of the Classic Maya period has dominated research, archaeologists have documented intensive occupation from the time of the so-called Maya collapse, in the ninth century, to the end of the seventeenth century (Pendergast, Jones, and Graham 1993). This long sequence has enabled them to chart the changes that took place as the Spanish administrators and priests colonized the Maya world, and the result has been documentation of the continuity of cultural, social, and technological traditions from the ancient past to the modern times.

The archaeology of the recent past or social archaeology is another important research direction; an example is the "Garbage Project," which is being conducted by archaeologists at the University of Arizona at Tucson (Rathje and Murphy 1992). The "Garbage Archaeologists" excavated the Fresh Kills landfill on Staten Island, near New York City. Its mass is estimated at over 90 million tonnes and its volume at 82 million cubic metres. Thus, it is one of the largest human-made structures in North America. Through excavation of artifacts such as pop-top can tabs, disposable diapers, cosmetic containers, and telephone books, the Garbage Archaeologists are learning about recent consumption patterns. These findings also provide lessons for the future. They reveal how long it takes for contemporary goods to decompose. Urban planners and other people interested in recycling may be surprised to learn that the kinds of garbage that people often blame for filling up landfills, such as fast-food packaging, polystyrene foam, and disposable diapers, are less serious problems than paper. Paper, especially newspaper, is the major culprit because of sheer quantity. This kind of information can help improve recycling efforts in North America.

Biological or Physical Anthropology

Biological anthropology encompasses three subfields. The first, *primatology*, is the study of the nonhuman members of the order of mammals called primates, which includes a wide range of animals from very small, nocturnal creatures to gorillas, the largest members. Primatologists study nonhuman primates in the wild and in captivity. They record and analyze how the animals spend their time, collect and share food, form social groups, rear offspring, develop leadership patterns, and experience conflict and conflict resolution. Primatologists are well known for their pioneering work in studying nonhuman primates in their natural habitats. Jane Goodall's (1971, 1986) research on Tanzanian chimpanzees revealed rich details about their social relationships. Linda Fedigan (1992) has shown how females play significant roles in the social structure of primate groups, and provided a feminist critique of theories of primate and human evolution.

The second subfield is *paleoanthropology*, the study of human evolution on the basis of the fossil record. One important activity is the search for fossils to increase the amount and quality of the evidence related to the way human evolution occurred. Discoveries of new fossils provide "ah-hah!" moments and arresting photographs for the covers of popular magazines. A less glamorous but equally important activity is *paleopathology*, the study of diseases in prehistory. Analysis of trace elements in bones, such as strontium, provides surprisingly detailed

Primatologist Dian Fossey interacts with a gorilla during fieldwork in Rwanda. ■ (Source: Richard Wrangham/ AnthroPhoto)

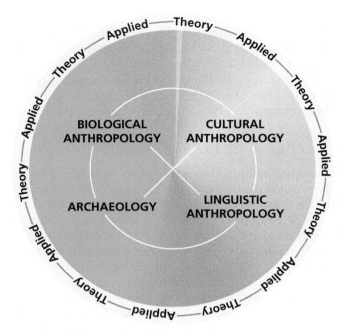

FIGURE 1.1   The Four Fields of Anthropology

information about the diets, activities, and health of prehistoric people, including whether they were primarily meat eaters or vegetarians and how their diets affected their health. Stress marks on bones provide information on work patterns—for example, skeletons of nineteenth-century voyageurs from a fur trade post in Alberta show evidence of arthritis of the spine, shoulder, and elbow, and robust muscle attachments compatible with paddling heavy freight canoes (Lovell and Lai 1994). We can also learn age at death, age at birth of first child for a woman, and birth rate per woman. Data from several time periods provide clues about how the transition to agriculture altered people's health and longevity (M.N. Cohen 1989; Cohen and Armelagos 1984; Cohen and Bennett 1993).

The third subfield is the study of *contemporary human biological variation.* Anthropologists working in this area define, measure, and seek to explain differences in the biological makeup and behaviour of contemporary humans. In the past, biological anthropologists defined what they perceived as significant differences among modern humans as "racial" (quotation marks indicate that the meaning of this term is contested). Early anthropologists in the late nineteenth and early twentieth centuries used the term "race" to refer to social categories defined on the basis of skin colour, hair texture, head shape, and facial features. These biological markers were supposedly associated with in-born ways of behaving and thinking. The controversial book, *The Bell Curve: Intelligence and Class Structure in American Life* (Herrnstein and Murray 1994), is an example of such thinking in the United States in its assertion that "race" determines intelligence and class position. In fact, DNA evidence clearly demonstrates that "races," defined on the basis of external physical features,

Maya people watch as forensic anthropologist Francisco de Leon conducts an exhumation of more than 50 bodies in a highland Guatemalan village in 1997.
■ (Source: AP/Wide World Photos)

are not scientifically valid categories; they lack internal consistency and clear boundaries. Anthropologists do, however, recognize the reality of racism and that many people in many contexts worldwide discriminate against people on the basis of their imputed race.

Linguistic Anthropology

Linguistic anthropology is devoted to the study of communication, mainly (but not exclusively) human languages. Linguistic anthropology has three subfields: *historical linguistics,* the study of language change over time and how languages are related; *descriptive linguistics* or structural linguistics, the study of the structure of languages; and *sociolinguistics,* the study of the relation between language and social interaction, including non-verbal communication.

Linguistic anthropology is integral to cultural anthropology since language is the primary means for transmitting culture. How we classify relatives, honour our ancestors, and describe beauty make visible beliefs and values.

Stephen Lubkemann is trained as both a cultural anthropologist and an underwater archaeologist. He is documenting the remains of the hull of DRTO-036, a vessel that wrecked in the Dry Tortugas in the mid-nineteenth century. It lies within Dry Tortugas National Park in the Florida Keys. ■ (Source: Photo by Richard Gould)

Several new directions connect linguistic anthropology to important real-world issues. First is a trend to study language in everyday use, or discourse, and how it relates to power structures at local, regional, and international levels (Duranti 1997a). In some contexts, powerful people speak more than less powerful people, whereas sometimes the more powerful people speak less. Power relations may also be expressed through intonation, word choice, and such nonverbal forms of communication as posture and dress. Second is increased attention to the role of information technology in communication, especially the Internet and cell phones. Third is attention to the increasingly rapid extinction of indigenous languages worldwide.

Early philologists such as Horatio Hale (1817–1896), who worked with the elders in the Six Nations Reserve near Brantford, Ontario, in the 1870s, recorded and analyzed disappearing First Nations languages, concluding, for example, that Tutelo was related to Siouan language stock, that Mohawk was the senior language of the original Five Nations, and that Huron was nearer proto-Iroquoian than Mohawk. Today, most "disappearing" languages have either been recorded or lost, and most previously unwritten languages have been transferred into written form.

Cultural Anthropology

Cultural anthropology is the study of contemporary people and their cultures. It considers variations and similarities across cultures, and how cultures change over

Iron Bridge, England, is an important site of industrial archaeology. Considered the "birthplace of industry," the site includes the world's first iron bridge and remains of factories, furnaces, and canals. Take a virtual tour of the site by going to www.ironbridge. org.uk. ■ (Source: Barbara Miller)

ORANGUTAN RESEARCH LEADS TO ORANGUTAN ADVOCACY

Primatologist Biruté Galdikas (pronounced Beer-OO-tay GAL-dee-kas) first went to Indonesia to study orangutans in 1971 (Galdikas 1995). She soon became aware of the threat to the orangutans from local people who, as a way of making a lot of money, capture them for sale to zoos around the world. These poachers separate the young from their mothers, often killing the mothers in the process. Sometimes local police locate and reclaim these captured orphans. They try to return them to the rainforest, but the transition into an unknown niche is extremely difficult and many do not survive.

Orangutan juveniles are highly dependent on their mothers, maintaining close bodily contact with them for at least two years and nursing until they are eight. Because of this long period of orangutans' need for maternal contact, Galdikas set up her camp to serve as a way station for orphans and she became the maternal figure. Her first "infant" was an orphaned orang, Sugito, who clung to her for years as if she were its own mother.

Now, the survival of orangutans on Borneo and Sumatra (their only habitats worldwide) is seriously endangered by massive commercial logging and illegal logging, population resettlement programs, cultivation, and other pressures on the forests where the orangutans live.

Galdikas is focusing her efforts on orangutan preservation. She says, "I feel like I'm viewing an animal holocaust and *holocaust* is not a word I use lightly. . . . The destruction of the tropical rainforest is accelerating daily. And if orangutans go extinct in the wild, paradise

Biruté Galdikas in Indonesia. She has been studying the orangutans for over three decades and is an active supporter of conservation of their habitat. ■ (Source: © Spooner/Redmond-Callow/Gamma Press)

is gone" (Dreifus 2000:D3). Across all ranges, it is estimated that during the twentieth century the orangutan population experienced a huge decrease, from 315 000 in 1900 to 44 000 in 2000 (IUCN/SSC Conservation Breeding Specialist Group 2004). Aerial surveys (Ancrenaz et al. 2005) and DNA analysis of living orangutans (Goossens et al. 2006) confirm recent and dramatic declines that, if not halted, will lead to extinction in the next few decades.

Galdikas has studied orangutans longer than anyone else. She links her knowledge of and love for the orangutans with applied anthropology and advocacy on their

time. Cultural anthropologists learn about culture by spending extended periods of time living with the people they study (discussed in Chapter 2).

Since World War II, cultural anthropology has grown dramatically in North America. This growth has brought about the development of many specialties within the field. Prominent areas of specialization include economic anthropology, political anthropology, medical anthropology, psychological anthropology, and development anthropology (the study of the effects and patterns of international development policies and plans in crosscultural perspective). In the rest of this book, we cover these and other topics.

Applied Anthropology: Separate Field or Crosscutting Focus?

Applied anthropology, or practising anthropology, involves the application of anthropological knowledge to help solve social problems. Richard Salisbury (1983), who developed applied anthropology at McGill University in Montréal, saw applied work as the growth point of anthropology in Canada, and trained many Canadian anthropologists to put their research to practice in fields such as Native land claims, health care, and ethnic diversity. Active engagement with First Nations peoples and rural communities characterized the work of

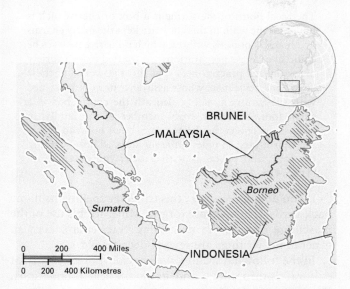

given public talks around the world on her research. Educating the public about the imminent danger to the orangutans is an important part of her activism. Galdikas and other orangutan experts are lobbying international institutions such as the World Bank to promote forest conservation as part of their loan agreements.

Camp Leakey employs many local people in diverse roles, including anti-poaching guards. The OFI sponsors study tours to Borneo for international students and opportunities for them to contribute to conservation efforts.

The success of Galdikas's activism depends on her deep knowledge of orangutans. Over the decades, she has filled thousands of notebooks with her observations of orangutan behaviour, along with such details about their habitat as the fruiting times of different species of trees. A donor recently gave software and funding for staff to analyze the raw data (Hawn 2002). The findings will indicate how much territory is needed to support a viable orangutan population. In turn, this process will facilitate conservation policy and planning.

MAP 1.1   Orangutan Regions in Malaysia and Indonesia. Orangutans are the only great apes living outside Africa. Fossil evidence indicates that their habitats in the past extended throughout Southeast Asia and southern China. They are now limited to pockets of forest on the islands of Sumatra and Borneo.

FOOD FOR THOUGHT

- Some people claim that science should not be linked with advocacy because it will create biases in research. Others say that scientists have an obligation to use their knowledge for good causes. Where do you stand in this debate and why?

behalf. Since the beginning of her fieldwork in Borneo, she has maintained and expanded the Camp Leakey fieldsite and research centre (named after her mentor, Louis Leakey, who inspired her research on orangutans). In 1986, she co-founded the Orangutan Foundation International (OFI), which now has several chapters worldwide. She has published scholarly articles and

francophone anthropologists in the 1960s. Many anthropologists in small colleges and universities engaged in community-based applied research. One of the defining features of Canadian anthropology is the integration of basic and applied research. From the earliest work of nineteenth-century ethnologists to the expert witnesses in current land claim issues, we find the widely shared assumption that anthropological research should not be morally or ethically neutral (Darnell 1998:155). Advocacy roles, however, require sensitivity to complex moral and political contexts.

Applied anthropology is an important thread that weaves through the entire discipline of anthropology

(Rylko-Bauer, Singer, and van Willigen 2006). Application of knowledge to help solve particular social problems is, and should be, part of all four fields. Just like theory, application is a valid aspect of every branch of the discipline. Many archaeologists in Canada are employed, for example, in *cultural resource management* (CRM), undertaking professional assessments of possible archaeological remains before construction projects such as roads and buildings can proceed. Biological anthropology has many applied aspects. For example, *forensic anthropologists* participate in criminal investigations through identifying bodily remains. Others work in the area of primate conservation (see the Lessons Applied box).

Applied linguistic anthropologists consult with educational institutions about how to improve standardized tests for bilingual populations, or they may do policy research for governments. Development anthropology refers to an aspect of applied anthropology concerned with how so-called developing countries change and how knowledge in anthropology can play a role in formulating and implementing more appropriate kinds of change.

Many anthropologists are concerned that applied anthropology should be addressing more directly and with greater force the effects of globalization, particularly some of its negative consequences such as the increasing wealth gap between powerful industrialized countries and less powerful, less industrialized countries (Hackenberg 2000). This need takes anthropologists in a challenging direction since it involves the study of global-local interactions and change over time, both important parts of cultural anthropology's focus. Moreover, it asks that cultural anthropologists abandon an attitude of non-involvement in change. One anthropologist goes so far as to ask, "Can anthropology in the 21st century be anything except applied anthropology?" (Cleveland 2000:373).

Introducing Cultural Anthropology

Cultural anthropology is devoted to studying human cultures worldwide, both their similarities and differences. Ultimately, cultural anthropology decentres us from our own cultures, teaching us to look at ourselves from the "outside" as somewhat "strange." Cultural anthropology makes "the strange familiar and the familiar strange" (Spiro 1990). A good example of making the familiar strange is the case of the Nacirema, a culture first described in 1956:

> They are a North American group living in the territory between the Canadian Cree, the Yaqui and the Tarahumare of Mexico, and the Carib and the Arawak of the Antilles. Little is known of their origin, though tradition states that they came from the east. According to Nacirema mythology, their nation was originated by a culture hero, Notgnihsaw, who is otherwise known for two great feats of strength—the throwing of a piece of wampum across the river Pa-To-Mac and the chopping down of a cherry tree in which the Spirit of Truth resided. (Miner 1965 [1956]:415)

The anthropologist goes on to describe the Nacirema's intense focus on the human body and their many private rituals. He provides a detailed account of a daily ritual performed within the home in a specially constructed shrine area:

> The focal point of the shrine is a box or chest which is built into the wall. In this chest are kept the many charms and magical potions without which no native believes he could live. These preparations are secured from a variety of specialized practitioners. The most powerful of these are the medicine men, whose assistance must be rewarded with substantial gifts. . . . Beneath the charm box is a small font. Each day every member of the family, in succession, enters the shrine room, bows his head before the charm-box, mingles different sorts of holy water in the font, and proceeds with a brief rite of ablution. (1965:415–416)

If you do not recognize this tribe, try spelling its name backwards. (*Note:* Please forgive Miner for his use of the masculine pronoun in describing Nacirema society in general; his writings are several decades old.)

In the following section, we provide a brief history of cultural anthropology and its theoretical foundations. We also include discussion of the concept of culture; important cultural categories based on gender, race and ethnicity, and age; some distinctive features of cultural anthropology; and an overview of three major debates in cultural anthropology.

A Brief History of Cultural Anthropology

The distant origins of cultural anthropology go back to writers such as Herodotus (fifth century BCE, or Before the Common Era), Marco Polo (thirteenth to fourteenth centuries), and Ibn Khaldun (fourteenth century), who travelled extensively and wrote reports about cultures they encountered. More recent conceptual roots are found in writers of the French Enlightenment, such as philosopher Charles Montesquieu, who wrote in the first half of the eighteenth century. His book, *The Spirit of the Laws*, published in 1748 [1949], discussed the temperament, appearance, and government of various people around the world. Montesquieu explained cultural differences as due to the differing climates in which people lived (Barnard 2000:22ff). European colonial expansion prompted Enlightenment thinkers to question the

---

functionalism: the theory that a culture is similar to a biological organism, in which parts work to support the operation and maintenance of the whole.

holism: the perspective in anthropology that cultures are complex systems that cannot be fully understood without paying attention to their different components, including economics, social organization, and ideology.

cultural relativism: the perspective that each culture must be understood in terms of the values and ideas of that culture and should not be judged by the standards of another.

FIGURE 1.2   Key Figures in
Cultural Anthropology

Late Nineteenth Century

Sir Edward Tylor	Armchair anthropology, first definition of culture
Sir James Frazer	Armchair anthropology, comparative study of religion
Lewis Henry Morgan	Kinship, cultural evolution, comparative method

Early Twentieth Century

Bronislaw Malinowski	Functionalism, holism, participant observation
Franz Boas	Cultural relativism, historical particularism, advocacy
Margaret Mead	Personality and culture, cultural constructionism, public anthropology
Ruth Benedict	Personality and culture, national character studies
Zora Neale Hurston	Black culture, women's roles, ethnographic novels

Mid- and Late Twentieth Century and Early Twenty-First Century

Claude Lévi-Strauss	Symbolic analysis, French structuralism
Joan Ryan	First Nations ethnography and advocacy
Eleanor Leacock	Anthropology of colonialism and indigenous peoples
Marvin Harris	Cultural materialism, comparison, theory building
Richard Lee	Hunters and gatherers, advocacy
Mary Douglas	Symbolic anthropology
Michelle Rosaldo	Feminist anthropology
Clifford Geertz	Interpretive anthropology, thick description of local culture
Laura Nader	Legal anthropology, "studying up"
George Marcus	Critique of culture, critique of cultural anthropology
Gilbert Herdt	Gay anthropology
Nancy Scheper-Hughes	Critical medical anthropology
Sally Engle Merry	Globalization and human rights

accuracy of the biblical narrative of human origins. The Bible, for example, does not mention the existence of people in the New World.

In the latter half of the nineteenth century, the discovery of the principles of biological evolution by Charles Darwin and others had a major impact on anthropology by offering a scientific explanation for human origins and contemporary human variation. Biological evolution says that early forms evolve into later forms through the process of natural selection, whereby the most biologically fit organisms survive to reproduce while those that are less fit die out. Darwin's model is, thus, one of continuous progress of increasing fitness through struggle among competing organisms.

The most important founding figures of cultural anthropology of the late nineteenth and early twentieth centuries include Sir Edward Tylor and Sir James Frazer in England and Lewis Henry Morgan in the United States (see Figure 1.2). Inspired by the concept of biological evolution, they developed a model of cultural evolution whereby all cultures evolve from lower to higher forms over time. This view placed non-Western peoples at a "primitive" stage and Euro-American culture as "civilization" and assumed that non-Western cultures would either catch up to the level of Western civilization or die out.

Polish-born Bronislaw Malinowski is a major figure of early cultural anthropology. In the first half of the twentieth century, he established a theoretical approach called **functionalism**: the view that a culture is similar to a biological organism, in which parts work to support the operation and maintenance of the whole. Religion and family organization, for example, contribute to the functioning of the whole culture. Functionalism is linked to the concept of **holism**, the view that one must study all aspects of a culture in order to understand the whole culture.

Franz Boas is considered the founder of North American cultural anthropology. Born in Germany and educated in physics and geography, he came to the United States in 1887 (Patterson 2001:46ff). He brought with him a skepticism toward Western science gained from a year's study with the Inuit, the indigenous people of Baffin Island (see Map 1.2 on page 12). The Inuit experience taught him that people in different cultures have different perceptions of even basic physical substances, such as water. Boas recognized the individuality and validity of different cultures. He introduced the now widely known concept of **cultural relativism**, or the view that each culture must be understood in terms of the values and ideas of that culture and not be judged by the standards of another. According to Boas, no culture is more advanced than another. His position, thus, contrasted

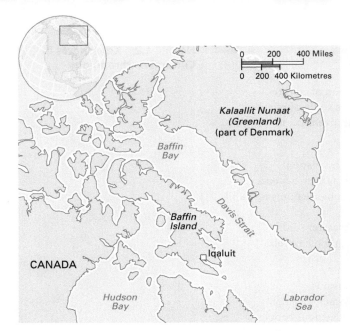

MAP 1.2   Baffin Island in the Canadian Arctic and Kalaallit Nunaat (Greenland). Baffin Island is the largest island in the Canadian Arctic. Iqaluit, a town of about 3000 people, is the capital of the Nunavut territory. Kalaallit Nunaat, meaning "The Humans' Land," is the world's largest island and a self-governed Danish territory. Its population of 56 000 people is mainly of mixed descent between the indigenous Kalaallit (Inuit) and Danish people.

Franz Boas is an important figure in the history of anthropology for many reasons, including his emphasis on a four-field approach and the principle of cultural relativism. ■ (Source: © Bettmann/CORBIS)

markedly with that of the nineteenth-century cultural evolutionists.

Boas promoted the detailed study of individual cultures within their own historical contexts. This approach is called *historical particularism*, or the view that individual cultures must be studied and described on their own terms and that cross-cultural comparisons and generalizations ignore the realities of individual cultures.

Boas helped to institutionalize North American anthropology as a discipline. While a professor at Columbia University, he trained many students who became prominent anthropologists. He founded several professional organizations, and he supported the development of anthropology museums. Boas was also engaged in debates about civil rights and social justice, and he carried out policy research related to these issues (Patterson 2001: 48–50). His socially progressive philosophy sometimes embroiled him in controversy. One study, commissioned by U.S. President Theodore Roosevelt, was to examine the effects of the environment (in the sense of a person's location) on immigrants and their children. At this time, some

leaders of the U.S. government were seeking justifications for limiting the numbers of immigrants. Boas and his research team measured the height, weight, head size, and other features of over 17 000 adults and children who had migrated to the United States. The researchers found substantial differences in the measurements of the older and younger generations. Boas concluded that body size and shape can change quickly in response to a different environment. The U.S. Immigration Commission, however, dismissed his findings, and Congress passed the Immigration Restriction Act in 1924. Through this study and many more, Boas left a legacy to anthropology that biology is not destiny and that no populations are innately inferior.

Margaret Mead, whose work is discussed in Chapter 6, was Boas's most famous student. She contributed to knowledge of South Pacific cultures, gender roles, and the impact of child-rearing practices on personality. Her scholarly works as well as her columns in popular magazines had wide influence on U.S. child-care patterns in the 1950s. Mead was, thus, an early *public anthropologist* who took seriously the importance of bringing cultural anthropology knowledge to the general public in order to create positive social change.

The roots of Canadian anthropology are anchored in both the British/European tradition of social anthropology

cultural materialism: a theoretical position that takes material features of life, such as the environment, natural resources, and mode of production, as the bases for explaining social organization and ideology.

interpretive anthropology or **interpretivism:** the view that cultures can be understood by studying what people think about, their ideas, and the meanings that are important to them.

FIGURE 1.3   Canadian Museum Timeline

Canadian anthropology developed in close relationship to its national and regional museums.

1841	1877	1910	1927	1968	1986
Queen Victoria granted £1500 for a geological survey of the provinces of Canada.	The Geological Survey was mandated to make botanical, zoological, and ethnological collections.	The Geological Survey began a linguistic and ethnological survey of First Nations communities in Canada.	The National Museum of Canada was established.	The National Museum of Man was established as an amalgamation of other museums of natural sciences and technology.	The National Museum of Man became the Canadian Museum of Civilization, and opened to the public in 1989.

and U.S. cultural anthropology. Canadian anthropology was shaped by ethnohistorical and advocacy work with First Nations peoples and strong relations with museums (see Figure 1.3). Many people contributed to the institutional development of a distinguished independent anthropological tradition in Canada.

One very interesting figure was Sir Daniel Wilson, a Scottish archaeologist appointed professor of English literature and history at University College, Toronto, in 1853. He introduced the term *prehistory* into the English language, and offered courses in comparative societies (what we discuss later as ethnology) as early as 1855.

Following World War II, cultural anthropology expanded substantially in terms of the number of trained anthropologists and departments of anthropology in colleges and universities. Along with this growth came increased theoretical diversity. Several anthropologists developed theories of culture based on environmental factors. They suggested that similar environments (for example, deserts, tropical rainforests, or mountains) would predictably lead to the emergence of similar cultures. This approach pursued cross-cultural generalizations, and so it came into direct conflict with Boasian historical particularism (which we defined earlier). At the same time, French anthropologist Claude Lévi-Strauss was developing a quite different theoretical perspective, which became known as *French structuralism*. He maintained that the best way to understand a culture is to collect its myths and stories and analyze the underlying themes in them. (Later chapters in this book provide more details about the work of Lévi-Strauss.) French structuralism inspired the development of *symbolic anthropology*, or the study of culture as a system of meanings, which was especially prominent in the later part of the twentieth century.

In the 1960s, Marxist theory emerged in anthropology, stating the importance of people's access to the means of production. It inspired the emergence of a new theoretical school called **cultural materialism**. Cultural materialism is an approach to studying culture by emphasizing the

Sir Daniel Wilson of the University of Toronto, the first lecturer on ethnology in Canada. ■ (Source: University of Toronto Archives)

material aspects of life, especially the natural environment and how people make a living. Also arising in the 1960s was the theoretical position referred to as **interpretive anthropology**, or **intepretivism**. This perspective developed from both symbolic anthropology and French structural anthropology. It says that understanding culture should focus on what people think about, their ideas, and the symbols and meanings that are important to them. These two positions will be discussed further later in this section.

Since the 1990s, two other theoretical directions have gained prominence. Both are influenced by *postmodernism*, an intellectual pursuit that asks whether modernity is truly progress and that questions such aspects of modernism as the scientific method, urbanization, technological change, and mass communication. For the purposes of discussion in this book, the first theory is termed **structural**, the view that powerful structures such as economics, politics, and media shape cultures and create entrenched systems of inequality and oppression. The second theory emphasizes human **agency**, or free will, and the power of individuals to create and change culture by acting against structures. These two contrasting positions also will be discussed later in this section.

Cultural anthropology continues to be rethought and refashioned. Over the past few decades, several new theoretical perspectives have transformed and enriched the field. *Feminist anthropology* is a perspective that emphasizes the need to study female roles and gender-based inequality. Starting in the 1970s, early feminist anthropologists realized that anthropology had largely bypassed women since its beginning. To address this gap, feminist anthropologists undertook research that explicitly focused on women and girls. A related area is *gay and lesbian anthropology*, or queer anthropology, a perspective that emphasizes the need to study gay people's cultures and discrimination based on sexual identity and preferences.

The Concept of Culture

Although cultural anthropologists are united in the study of *culture,* the question of how to define it has been debated for decades. This section discusses definitions of culture today, characteristics of culture, and bases for cultural identity.

Definitions of Culture

Culture is the core concept in cultural anthropology, so it might seem likely that cultural anthropologists would agree about what it is. In the 1950s, an effort to collect definitions of culture produced 164 different ones (Kroeber and Kluckhohn 1952). Since then, no one has tried to count the number of definitions of culture used by anthropologists.

British anthropologist Sir Edward Tylor proposed the first definition in 1871. He stated, "Culture, or civilization . . . is that complex whole which includes knowledge, belief, art, law, morals, custom, and any other capabilities and habits acquired by man as a member of society" (Kroeber and Kluckhohn 1952:81). The phrase "that complex whole" has been the most durable feature of his definition. Two other features of Tylor's definition have not stood the test of time. First, most anthropologists now avoid using the word *man* to refer to all humans; instead, they use generic words such as *people* and *humans.* One may argue that the word *man* can be used generically according to its linguistic roots, but this usage can be ambiguous. Second, most anthropologists no longer equate culture with civilization. The word *civilization* implies a sense of "highness" versus noncivilized "lowness" and sets up a distinction placing "us" (people of the so-called civilized regions) in a superior position to "them."

In contemporary cultural anthropology, the theoretical positions of interpretive anthropologists and cultural materialists correspond to two different definitions of culture. Interpretive anthropologists argue that culture includes symbols, motivations, moods, and thoughts. This definition focuses on people's perceptions, thoughts, and ideas, and does not focus on behaviour as a part of culture but, rather, seeks to explain behaviour. Interpretive anthropologists stress the idea that culture is contested and negotiated, and not always shared or imposed. Cultural materialist Marvin Harris states that "A culture is the total socially acquired life-way or lifestyle of a group of people. It consists of the patterned repetitive ways of thinking, feeling, and acting that are characteristic of the members of a particular society or segment of society" (1975:144). Like Tylor's definition of over 100 years ago, Harris's definition pays attention to both behaviour and ideas (beliefs). The definition of culture used in this book follows this more comprehensive approach.

Culture exists among all human beings. It is something that all humans have. Some anthropologists refer to this universal concept of culture as *Culture* with a capital C. Culture also exists in a more specific way. **Local culture**, refers to distinct patterns of learned and shared behaviour and ideas that are found in local regions and among particular groups and are based on ethnicity, gender, age, and more.

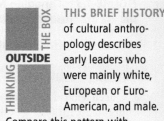

THINKING OUTSIDE THE BOX THIS BRIEF HISTORY of cultural anthropology describes early leaders who were mainly white, European or Euro-American, and male. Compare this pattern with the history of some other discipline you have studied. What are the similarities and differences?

---

structural: a theoretical position concerning human behaviour and ideas that says "free choice" is an illusion since the choices themselves are determined by larger forces such as the economy, social and political organization, and ideological systems.
agency: the ability of humans to make choices and exercise free will.

local culture: a distinct pattern of learned and shared behaviour and thinking found within larger cultures.

Characteristics of Culture

Understanding of the complex concept of culture can be gained by looking at its characteristics. This section discusses some characteristics of culture.

Culture Is Not the Same as Nature The relationship between nature and culture is of great interest to cultural anthropologists in their quest to understand people's behaviour and thinking. This book emphasizes the importance of culture (most of you will already have taken several courses on biology, which emphasizes the importance of human nature). Obviously, culture and nature are intertwined and often difficult to separate in terms of their effects. For example, certain aspects of biology affect people's behaviour and lifestyle, such as being HIV-positive. But it is impossible to predict how a person who is HIV-positive will fare in Culture A versus Culture B. Different cultural contexts shape matters such as labelling and negative stereotypes and access to care and support.

A good way to see how culture diverges from, and shapes, nature is to consider basic natural demands of life within different cultural contexts. The universal human functions that everyone must perform to stay alive are

- Eating
- Drinking
- Sleeping
- Eliminating

You may wonder about requirements for shelter and clothing. They vary, depending on the climate, so they are not included on this list. You may also wonder about sexual intercourse. It is not necessary for individual survival, so it is not included on this list, but it is discussed elsewhere in this book.

Given the primary importance of these four functions in supporting a human being's life, it seems logical that people would fulfill them in similar ways everywhere. But that is not the case.

Eating Culture shapes what people eat, how they eat, when they eat, and the meanings of food and eating. Culture also defines foods that are acceptable and unacceptable. In China, most people think that cheese is disgusting, but in France, most people love cheese. Throughout China, pork is a widely favoured meat. The religions of Judaism and Islam, in contrast, forbid consumption of pork. In many cultures where gathering wild plant foods, hunting, and fishing are important, people value the freshness of food. They would consider a package of frozen food on a grocery store shelf as way past its time.

Perceptions of taste vary dramatically. Western researchers have defined four supposedly universal taste categories: sweet, sour, bitter, and salty. Cross-cultural research disproves these as universals. For example, the Weyéwa people of the highlands of Sumba, Indonesia (see Map 1.3 on page 16), define seven categories of flavour: sour, sweet, salty, bitter, tart, bland, and pungent (Kuipers 1991).

How to eat is also an important aspect of food behaviour. Rules about proper ways to eat are one of the first things a person needs to learn when living in another culture. Dining rules in India require using only the right hand. The left hand is considered polluted because it is

Colombian anthropologist Patricia Tovar (middle) at an anthropology conference in Colombia. In much of Central and South America, applied anthropology is an integral part of cultural anthropology.
■ (Source: Patricia Tovar)

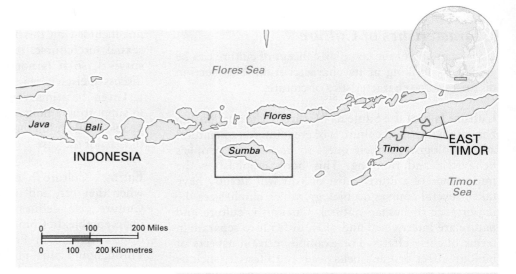

MAP 1.3 Weyéwa Region in Indonesia. Sumba, one of Indonesia's many islands, is seventy-five miles (120 kilometres) long. The Weyéwa people number about 85 000 and live in small settlements on grassy plateaus. They grow rice, maize, and millet, and raise water buffaloes and pigs.

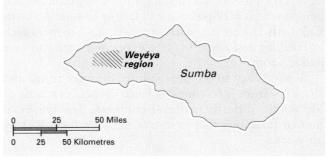

used for personal cleansing after elimination. A person's clean right hand is the preferred eating utensil. Silverware that has been touched by others, even though it has been washed, is considered unclean. In some cultures, it is important to eat only from one's own plate, whereas in others, eating from a shared central platter is considered proper.

Another area of cultural variation involves who is responsible for cooking and serving food. In many cultures, domestic cooking is women's responsibility, but cooking for public feasts is more often something that men do. Power issues may arise about who cooks what for whom.

Drinking The cultural elaboration of drinking is as complex as for eating. Every culture defines the appropriate substances to drink, when to drink, and with whom. French culture allows for consumption of relatively large amounts of wine with meals. In Canada, water is commonly consumed during meals, but in India, one takes water after the meal is finished. Different categories of people drink different beverages. In cultures where alcoholic beverages are consumed, men tend to consume more than women.

Coffee is the liquid of choice among homemakers in North America, while martinis might be the choice for male corporate executives. The meaning of particular drinks and the style of drinking and serving them are heavily influenced by culture. If you were a guest and the host offered you water, you might think it odd. If your host then explained that it was "sparkling water from France," you might be more impressed. Social drinking, whether the beverage is coffee, beer, or

Two Ethiopian women dining at an Ethiopian restaurant. The main meal consists of several meat and vegetable dishes, cooked with special spices and laid out on *injera* bread, a soft, flat bread that is torn into small pieces and used to wrap bite-sized bits of meat and vegetables. The entire meal can be eaten without utensils. ■ (Source: © Michael Newman/PhotoEdit)

symbol: an object, word, or action with culturally defined meaning that stands for something else; most symbols are arbitrary.

vodka, creates and reinforces social bonds. In Canada, for example, beer is closely identified with national identity.

Sleeping Going without sleep for an extended period would eventually lead to insanity and even death. Common sense might say that sleep is the one natural function that is not shaped by culture, because people tend to do it within every 24 hours, everyone shuts their eyes to do it, everyone lies down to do it, and most everyone sleeps at night. But there are many cultural aspects to sleep, including the question of who sleeps with whom. Cross-cultural research reveals varying rules about where infants and children should sleep: with the mother, with both parents, or by themselves in a separate room. Among indigenous cultures of the Amazon, mothers and babies share the same hammock for many months, and breastfeeding occurs whenever the baby is hungry, not on a schedule. Culture often shapes the amount of time a person sleeps. In rural India, women sleep fewer hours than men since they have to get up earlier to start the fire for the morning meal. In fast-track, corporate North America, "A-type" males sleep relatively few hours and are proud of that fact—to have slept too much is to be a wimp. A new disorder in Japan, called *excessive daytime sleepiness* (EDS) (Doi and Minowa 2003), is especially common in Tokyo and other cities. Excessive sleepiness is correlated with more accidents on the job, more absenteeism, decreased productivity, deteriorated personal and professional relationships, and increased rates of illness and death. Women are almost twice as likely as men to experience EDS, and married women are especially vulnerable.

Elimination This subject takes the discussion into more private territory. How does culture affect the elimination process? Anyone who has travelled internationally knows that there is much to learn about elimination when you leave familiar territory. The first question is, Where to eliminate? Differences emerge in the degree to which elimination is a private act or can be done in more or less public areas. Public options include street urinals for males but not for females, as in Paris. In most villages in India, houses do not have interior bathrooms. Instead, early in the morning, groups of women and girls leave the house and head for a certain field where they squat and chat. Men go to a different area. No one uses toilet paper; instead everyone carries in their left hand a small brass pot full of water with which they splash themselves clean. This practice has ecological advantages because it adds fertilizer to the fields and leaves no paper litter. Westerners may consider the village practice unclean, but village Indians would think that the Western system is unsanitary because paper does not clean one as well as water.

In many cultures, the products of elimination (urine and feces) are considered dirty, polluting, and disgusting. People do not try to keep such things, nor do they in any way revere them. In Papua New Guinea, in the South Pacific, people take great care to bury or otherwise hide their fecal matter. They fear that someone will find it and use it for magic against them. A negative assessment of the products of elimination is not universal, however. In some cultures, these substances are believed to have positive effects. Among First Nations cultures of the Pacific Northwest, urine, especially women's urine, was believed to have medicinal and cleansing properties and was considered the "water of life" (Furst 1989). In certain death rituals, it was sprinkled over the corpse in the hope that it might rejuvenate the deceased. People stored urine in special wooden boxes for ritual use, including the first bath that a baby was given (the urine was mixed with water for this purpose).

THINKING OUTSIDE THE BOX THINK ABOUT your everyday drinking patterns (no matter what the liquid) and then think about your drinking patterns on special occasions, including weekends, holidays, or special events such as weddings. What beverages do you consume, with whom, and what are the meanings and wider social implications involved?

Culture Is Based on Symbols Making money, creating art, and practising religion all involve symbols. A **symbol** is an object that has a range of culturally significant meanings. Symbols are arbitrary (bearing no necessary relationship with that which is symbolized), unpredictable, and diverse. Because symbols are arbitrary, we cannot predict how a particular culture will symbolize any particular thing. Although we might predict that people who are hungry would have an expression for hunger involving their stomach, no one could predict that in Hindi, the language of much of northern India, a colloquial expression for being hungry says that "rats are jumping in my stomach." It is through symbols that culture is shared, stored, and transmitted over time.

Culture Is Learned Because culture is based on arbitrary symbols, it cannot be predicted, but must be learned. Cultural learning begins from the moment of birth, if not before (some people think that an unborn baby takes in and stores information through sounds heard from the outside world). A large but unknown amount of people's cultural learning is unconscious, occurring as a normal part of life through observation. Schools, in contrast, are a formal way to learn culture. Not all cultures throughout history have had formal schooling. Instead, children learned appropriate cultural patterns through guidance from elders and observation and practice. Hearing stories and seeing performances of rituals and dramas are other long-standing forms of *enculturation*.

Cultures Are Integrated To state that cultures are internally integrated is to assert the principle of holism.

In India, a white sari (women's garment) symbolizes widowhood. To these women, the Western custom of a bride wearing white would seem inauspicious.
■ (Source: Barbara Miller)

Consider what would happen if a researcher were to study intertribal warfare in Papua New Guinea (see Map 1.4) and focused only on the actual practice of warfare without examining other aspects of culture. A key feature of highland New Guinea culture is the exchange of pigs at political feasts. To become a political leader, a man must acquire many pigs. Pigs eat yams, which men grow, but pigs are cared for by women. This division of labour means that a man with more than one wife will be able to produce more pigs and rise politically by giving more feasts. Such feasting enhances an aspiring leader's status and makes his guests indebted to him. With more followers attracted through feasting, a leader can gather forces and wage war on neighbouring villages. Success in war brings gains in territory. So far, this example focuses mainly on economics, politics, and marriage systems. But other aspects of culture are involved, too. Supernatural powers affect the success of warfare. Painting spears and shields with particular designs helps increase their power. At feasts and marriages, body decoration, including paint, shell ornaments, and elaborate feather headdresses, is an important expression of identity and status. Looking at warfare without attention to its wider cultural context yields an extremely narrow view.

The fact of cultural integration is also relevant to applied anthropologists who are involved in analyzing cultural change. Attempting to introduce change in one aspect of culture without giving attention to what its effects will be in other areas is irresponsible and may even be detrimental to the survival of a culture. For

Thus, studying only one or two aspects of culture provides understanding so limited that it is more likely to be misleading or wrong than more comprehensively grounded approaches.

MAP 1.4 Papua New Guinea. The Independent State of Papua New Guinea gained its autonomy from Australia in 1975. Mostly mountainous with coastal lowlands, PNG is richly endowed with gold, copper, silver, natural gas, timber, oil, and fisheries. Its population is around 5 700 000. Port Moresby, the capital, has a high rate of HIV/AIDS infection among the working-age population.

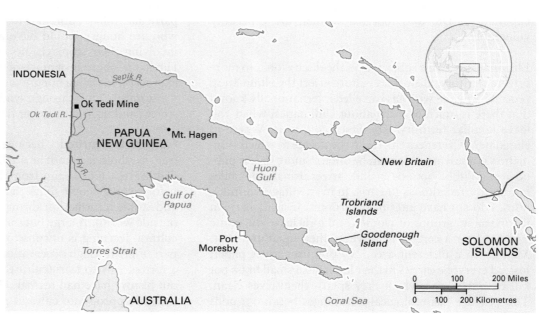

globalization: increased and intensified international ties related to the spread of Western, especially United States, capitalism that affects all world cultures.

localization: the transformation of global culture by local cultures into something new.

class: a way of categorizing people on the basis of their economic position in society, usually measured in terms of income or wealth.

example, Western missionaries and colonialists in parts of Southeast Asia banned the practice of headhunting. This practice was embedded in many other aspects of culture, including politics, religion, and psychology (a man's sense of identity as a man sometimes depended on the taking of a head). Stopping headhunting might seem like a good thing, but its cessation had disastrous consequences for the cultures in which it was practised.

Cultural Interaction and Change

Cultures interact with each other and change each other through contact. Trade networks, international development projects, telecommunications, education, migration, and tourism are just a few of the factors that affect cultural change through contact. **Globalization**, the process of intensified global interconnectedness and movement of goods, information, and people, is a major force of contemporary cultural change. It has gained momentum through recent technological change, especially the boom in information and communications technologies (Pieterse 2004).

Globalization does not spread evenly, and its interactions with and effects on local cultures vary substantially from positive change to cultural destruction and extinction. Four models of cultural interaction capture some of the variation (see Figure 1.4). The *clash of civilizations* argument says that the spread of Euro-American capitalism and lifeways throughout the world has created disenchantment, alienation, and resentment among other cultural systems. This model divides the world into the "West and the rest."

The *McDonaldization* model says that under the powerful influence of U.S.-dominated corporate culture, the world is becoming culturally homogeneous. "Fast-food culture," with its principles of mass production, speed, standardization, and impersonal service, is taken to be at the centre of this new global culture.

Hybridization is the third model. Also called *syncretism*, *creolization*, and *cultural crossover*, hybridization occurs when aspects of two or more cultures are mixed to form something new—a blend. In Japan, for instance, a grandmother might bow in gratitude to an automated banking machine. In the Amazon region and in the Arctic, indigenous people use satellite imagery to map and protect the boundaries of their ancestral lands.

A fourth pattern is **localization**, the transformation of global culture by local cultures into something new. Consider the example of McDonald's restaurants. In many Asian settings, people resist the pattern of eating quickly and insist on leisurely family gatherings (Watson 1997). The McDonald's managers accommodate and alter the pace of service to allow for a slower turnover of tables. In Riyadh, Saudi Arabia, McDonald's provides separate areas for families and for "couples." In another example, Western-style department stores in Japan have played a major role in introducing Western goods into Japanese society by cleverly contextualizing them within Japanese customs. One such item is the diamond engagement ring, which has been promoted not as a sign of emotional love between the two engaged people but as part of *yuinōhin*, a series of gifts from the groom's household to the bride that symbolize a long and happy life together (Creighton 1992).

Many more examples of cultural localization exist, throwing into question the notion that a form of Western "mono-culture" is taking over the entire world and erasing cultural diversity. In some contexts, Western culture is localized in ways that make it difficult for a Westerner to comprehend (see the Multiple Cultural Worlds box on page 20).

Multiple Cultural Worlds

Many local cultures exist within every culture. Much of this internal cultural differentiation is structured by the categories of class, race, ethnicity, gender, age, region, and institutions. A particular individual fits into several categories, but may identify more or less strongly with one, say, a teenager, a woman, or a member of a visible minority. Memberships may overlap or they may be related to each other hierarchically. The contrast between difference and hierarchy is important. People and groups can be considered different from each other on a particular criterion, but not unequal. For example, people with blue or brown eyes might be recognized as different, but this difference does not entail unequal treatment or status. In other instances, such differences do become the basis for inequality.

Class

Class is a category based on people's economic position in society, usually measured in terms of income or wealth and exhibited in terms of lifestyle. Class societies may be divided into upper, middle, and lower classes. An earlier definition of class associated with Karl Marx and Friedrich Engels says that class membership is determined by a group's relationship to ownership of the means of production, or how groups

FIGURE 1.4 Four Models of Cultural Interaction

Clash of civilizations	Conflict model
McDonaldization	Takeover and homogenization model
Hybridization	Blending model
Localization	Local cultural remaking and transformation of global culture

GLOBALIZATION AND TOMATO PRODUCTION

Every food item creates complex relations of production and consumption. Consider the tomato. The Tomasita Project (Barndt 1999) traced the journey of a tomato from the Mexican field to a Canadian fast food restaurant. The tomato was chosen as a symbol of globalization and the shifting roles of women as producers and consumers of food. With collaborators from Canada, Mexico, and the United States, women told their stories about making and producing food. One story told of the members of a Canadian family working at McDonald's, often on different shifts, so that they seldom ate together; other stories tell of the peasant and indigenous labourers working on tomato plantations in Mexico, making CDN$3.50 a day, barely able to afford their traditional tortillas and beans. These stories bring out a North–South contradiction: while fresh tomatoes come north, fast food restaurants like McDonald's are moving south, and at a faster rate since NAFTA was implemented in January 1994. Tomatoes have complex metaphorical meanings and fit into culturally constructed recipes and meals. When multinational corporations control food production, tomatoes also become commodities.

FOOD FOR THOUGHT

- Provide another example of how a food product you regularly eat illustrates globalization.

A view into the yard of a house of a low-income neighbourhood of Kingston, Jamaica. People in these neighbourhoods prefer the term *low-income* to *poor*.
■ (Source: Barbara Miller)

of people make a living. Separate classes are, for example, the *working class* (people who trade their labour for wages) and the *landowning class* (people who own land on which they or others labour). Classes are related in a hierarchical system, with certain classes dominating others. According to Marx and Engels, class struggle is inevitable as those at the top seek to maintain their position while those at the bottom seek to improve theirs. People at the bottom of the class structure may attempt to improve their place in the hierarchy by gaining access to resources and by adopting aspects of upper-class symbolic behaviours vis-à-vis speech, dress, leisure, and recreation.

Class is a key basis of cultural stratification in most contemporary states, but it is a relatively recent social development in human history. For example, in precontact groups in the Amazonian region, all members had roughly equal wealth. In complex and large capitalist states, however, classes are prominent forms of cultural differentiation. Some scholars say that global systems of cultural integration now mean that indigenous groups, which themselves have little internal class differentiation, have become part of a global class structure, with their position being at the bottom.

race: a classification of people into groups on the basis of supposedly homogeneous biological traits.
ethnicity: a shared sense of identity among a group based on a heritage, language, or culture.

indigenous peoples: groups who have a long-standing connection with their home territory that predates colonial or outside societies that prevail in that territory.

gender: culturally constructed and learned behaviours and ideas attributed to males, females, or blended genders.

Race, Ethnicity, and Indigenous People

Race refers to groups of people with supposedly homogeneous biological traits. However, race is a culturally constructed category, not a biological reality. In South Africa, race is mainly defined on the basis of skin colour. In pre-twentieth-century China, however, the basis of racial classification was body hair (Dikötter 1998). Greater amounts of body hair were associated with "barbarian" races and the lack of "civilization." Chinese writers described male missionaries from Europe, with their beards, as "hairy barbarians." Even in the twentieth century, some Chinese anthropologists and sociologists divided humans into evolutionary stages on the basis of their body hair. One survey of humankind provided a detailed classification on the basis of types of beards, whiskers, and moustaches.

Physical features do not explain or account for behaviour or ideas, as Franz Boas proved a century ago. Instead, the fact of being placed in a particular racial category and the status of that category in society are what explain racial behaviours and ideas. Rather than being a biological category, race in the anthropological view is a cultural or social category just like class. People's perceptions about race and their use of racial differences may result in racism, discrimination and marginality of certain groups. Racial differentiation has been the basis for some of the most invidious oppression and cruelty throughout history. A concept of racial purity inspired Nazi leader Adolf Hitler to pursue his program of exterminating Jews and others who were not of the Aryan "race." Racial apartheid in South Africa denied citizenship, security, and a decent life to all those labelled non-white (including, for example, "blacks" and "coloureds").

Ethnicity refers to a sense of group affiliation based on a distinct heritage or worldview as a "people," for example, Caribbean Canadians or Italian Canadians, the Croats of Eastern Europe, and the Han people of China. This sense of identity can be vigorously expressed through political movements or more quietly stated. It can be a basis for social ranking, claimed entitlements to resources such as land or artifacts, and a basis for defending or retrieving those resources.

Compared to the term *race*, *ethnicity* is often used as a more neutral or even positive term. But ethnicity has often been a basis for discrimination, segregation, and oppression. The "ethnic cleansing" campaigns conducted in the early 1990s by the Serbs against Muslims in the former Yugoslavia are an extreme case of ethnic discrimination. Expression of ethnic identity has been politically suppressed in many cultures, such as that of the Tibetans in China. Tibetan refugees living outside Tibet are struggling to keep their ethnic heritage alive. Among First Nations groups in contemporary Canada, a shared ethnicity is one basis for cultural and spiritual revival.

Indigenous peoples, following guidelines laid down by the United Nations, are defined as groups who have a long-standing connection with their home territory predating colonial or other societies that prevail in their territory (Sanders 1999). They are typically a numerical minority and often have lost the rights to their original territory. The United Nations distinguishes between indigenous peoples and *minority ethnic groups* such as the Roma, the Tamils of Sri Lanka, and African Americans. This distinction is more useful in some contexts than others (Maybury-Lewis 1997b). The San peoples of southern Africa, and their several subgroups, are an important example of indigenous peoples whose way of life was dramatically affected by colonialism and now by globalization (see the Ethnographic Profile on page 22).

Gender

Gender refers to patterns of culturally constructed and learned behaviours and ideas attributed to males, females, or sometimes a blended or "third gender." Thus, gender variability can be contrasted to sex, which uses biological markers to define the categories of male and female. Sex determination relies on genital, chromosomal, and hormonal distributions and, thus, depends on Western science to determine who is male or female. Cultural anthropology shows that a person's biological makeup does not necessarily correspond to gender. A simple example is that in the West, people tend to associate the activity of sewing with women, but in many other areas of the world, sewing (or tailoring) is mainly

A drawing of an Ainu (indigenous) person of Japan in a Chinese anthropology textbook published in 1918.

Ethnographic Profile

San Peoples of Southern Africa

San is a cluster name for many groups of southern Africa who speak related languages, all having glottal click sounds. Around 2000 years ago, the San were the only people living in southern Africa, but today they are restricted to scattered locations throughout the region. European colonialists referred to San people as Bushmen, a derogatory term at the time but one that San people now prefer over what some locals call them. Some San also refer to themselves with the English language term *First People*.

For many centuries, the San supported themselves through collecting food such as roots and birds' eggs and by hunting eland, giraffe, and other animals. Now, pressure from African governments, farmers, ranchers, game reserves, diamond companies, and international tourism has greatly reduced the San's access to their ancestral land and their ability to survive. Some have been arrested for hunting on what they consider their land.

The Ju/'hoansi ("True People") are a subgroup of San who live in a region crossing the borders of Namibia, Botswana, and Angola and numbering between 10 000 and 15 000 people. As described by Richard Lee in the early 1960s, they were highly mobile food collectors and quite healthy (1979). Today, many have been forced from their homeland and live as poor, urban squatters or in government-built resettlement camps. Many work as farm labourers or in the international tourist industry, serving as guides and producing and selling crafts.

The specifics of their situation now depend on government policy toward indigenous foragers in the particular country where they live. Conditions are most difficult for them right now in Botswana due to forced sedentarization.

Transnational advocacy organizations, including Working Group of Indigenous Minorities in Southern Africa (WIMSA) and First People of the Kalahari (FPK), are making progress in protecting the rights of San peoples. Recently, WIMSA waged an international legal case with a large pharmaceutical company and succeeded in ensuring that the San receive a portion of the profits from the commercial development of hoodia (*Hoodia gordonia*). Hoodia is extracted from a cactus indigenous to the Kalahari region. An effective appetite suppressant, it is now widely available in North America and on the Internet as a diet pill.

Readings

Richard Katz, Megan Biesele, and Verna St. Denis. *Healing Makes Our Hearts Happy: Spirituality and Cultural Transformation among the Kalahari Ju/'hoansi*. Rochester, VT: Inner Traditions, 1997.

Sidsel Saugestad. *The Inconvenient Indigenous: Remote Area Development in Botswana, Donor Assistance, and the First People of the Kalahari*. Uppsala, Sweden: The Nordic Afrika Institute, 2001.

Marjorie Shostak. *Nisa: The Life and Times of a !Kung Woman*. Cambridge, MA: Harvard University Press, 1981.

Video

Bushmen of the Kalahari: A Bushman Story (National Geographic Videos, 1973).

Website

The Kalahari Peoples Fund: www.kalaharipeoples.org.

Thanks to Alison Brooks, George Washington University, for reviewing this material.

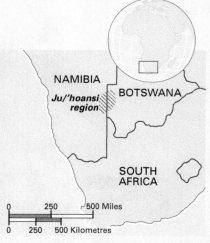

Richard Lee (left) asks Ju/'hoansi men about food plants of the Kalahari Desert. This photograph was taken in 1968. Lee, and many other researchers affiliated with the Harvard Kalahari Research Project, learned to speak the Ju/'hoansi language and make glottal clicks using the upper part of the larynx. ■ (Source: Stan Washburn/AnthroPhoto) *San peoples have long consumed parts of the hoodia plant to suppress hunger and thirst when on long trips in the desert (right). Now, they cultivate it for commercial use in a diet pill.* ■ (Source: Louise Gubb/CORBIS)

MAP 1.5 Ju/'hoansi Region in Namibia and Botswana. *Before country boundaries were drawn, the Ju/'hoansi freely ranged across their traditional territory (shaded area), depending on the seasonal availability of food and water. Now, they must show a passport when crossing from one country to another.*

men's work. The task, in other words, has nothing to do with biology. Only a few tasks are related to biology, such as nursing babies.

Cross-culturally, gender differences vary from societies in which male and female roles and worlds are largely shared, with few differences, to those in which genders are sharply differentiated. In much of rural Thailand, males and females are about the same size, their clothing is quite similar, and their agricultural tasks are complementary and often interchangeable (P. Van Esterik 2000). Among the Hua of the New Guinea Highlands, extreme gender segregation exists in almost all aspects of life (Meigs 1984). The *rafuri*, or men's house, physically and symbolically separates the worlds of men and women. The men live in strict separation from the women, and they engage in rituals seeking to purge themselves of female influences and substances: nose or penis bleeding, vomiting, tongue scraping, sweating, and eye washing. Men possess the sacred flutes, which they parade through the village from time to time. If women dare to look at the flutes, however, men have the right to kill them for that transgression. Strict rules also govern the kinds of food that men and women may eat.

In many cultures, the lives of gay and lesbian people are adversely affected by discrimination based on gender identity and sexual preferences. Other societies are less repressive, such as Thailand, Indonesia, and many First Nations groups in Canada.

Age

The human life cycle, from birth to old age, takes a person through cultural stages for which appropriate behaviour and thinking must be learned anew. Special rituals marking physical maturation, marriage, or the end of a period of learning are found in all societies, with varying degrees of elaboration. In many African herding societies, elaborate age categories for males define their roles and status as they move from being boys with few responsibilities and little status, to young men who are warriors and live apart from the rest of the group, to finally becoming adult men who are allowed to marry, have children, and become respected elders.

In many cultures, adolescents are in a particularly powerless category since they are neither children, who have certain well-defined rights, nor adults. Given this "threshold" position, many adolescents behave in ways of which the larger society disapproves and defines as deviance, crime, or even psychopathology (Fabrega and Miller 1995). Many youth gangs in North America are examples of situations in which adolescents have a marginal social position associated with signs of psychological deviance. Concerning women, cross-cultural research shows that in many pre-industrial societies, middle-aged women have the highest status in their life cycle if they are married and have children (J. Brown 1982).

Institutions

Institutions, or enduring group settings formed for a particular purpose, have their own cultural characteristics. Institutions include hospitals, boarding schools and universities, and prisons. Anyone who has entered such an institution has experienced that feeling of strangeness. Until you gain familiarity with the often unwritten cultural rules, you may do things that offend or puzzle people, that fail to get you what you want, and that make you feel marginalized and insecure.

Hospitals are excellent examples of institutions with their own cultural rules. Melvin Konner, an anthropologist who had studied among a group of indigenous hunting-gathering people of southern Africa and had taught anthropology for many years, decided to become a doctor. In his book, *Becoming a Doctor* (1987), Konner reports on his experience in medical school, providing an anthropologist's insights about the hospital as a particular kind of cultural institution. One of his most striking conclusions is that medical students undergo training that in many ways functions to dehumanize them, numbing them to the pain and suffering that they will confront each day. Medical training involves, for example, the need to memorize massive amounts of material, sleep deprivation, and the learning of a special form of humour and vocabulary that seems crude and even cruel. Some special vocabulary items are *boogie*—a verb meaning to move patients along quickly in a clinic or emergency room (as in "Let's boogie!"); a *dud*—a patient with no interesting findings; and a *gomer*—an acronym for Get Out of My Emergency Room, referring to an old, decrepit, hopeless patient whose care is guaranteed to be a thankless task, usually admitted from a nursing home.

Relationships of power and inequality exist within institutions and between different institutions. These relationships crosscut other criteria, such as gender. Recent claims by women prisoners in North America of rape and abuse by prison guards are an example of intra-institutional inequality linked with gender inequality. Within and between universities, rivalries are played out in the area of competition for large research grants as well as in athletics. Within the classroom, studies document that many professors are not egalitarian in the way they call on and respond to students, depending on their gender, race, or "looks." In the Kilimanjaro region of north Kenya, a lesson about proper sexual behaviour directed to secondary school students advised boys to "preserve your bullets" and girls to "lock your boxes" (Stambach 2000:127–30). The surface message is that boys should learn to control their mental processes and girls should look after their possessions, which they keep in a metal trunk beneath their bed. The underlying message is that boys should learn to control their sexual desire and that girls should protect their bodies. The separate metaphors, bullets and boxes, for the boys and the girls, reflect and reinforce gender differences in moral codes and expected behaviour.

Distinctive Features of Cultural Anthropology

Several features of cultural anthropology have traditionally distinguished it from other disciplines. Scholars in other disciplines, however, have been adopting anthropological approaches. Thus, while cultural anthropology's traditional characteristic features may no longer be unique to the field, they are still part of its identity and character.

Ethnography and Ethnology

Cultural anthropologists approach the study of contemporary human life in two basic ways. The first is in-depth study of one culture. This approach, **ethnography**, meaning "culture writing," provides a first-hand, detailed description of a living culture based on personal observation. Ethnography is usually presented in the form of a full-length book.

In the first part of the twentieth century, ethnographers wrote about "exotic" cultures located far from the homes of European and North American anthropologists. Classics of this phase of ethnography include A.R. Radcliffe-Brown's *The Andaman Islanders* (1922), a study of people living on a group of small islands off the coast of Burma; Bronislaw Malinowski's *Argonauts of the Western Pacific* (1922), concerning a complex trade network linking several islands in the South Pacific; and Reo Fortune's *Sorcerers of Dobu* (1932), which describes a culture in the Western Pacific islands, with a focus on its social and religious characteristics. Although early Canadian ethnographies were not considered classics, it is interesting that the mammoth ethnography, *The Bella Coola Indians* by T.F. McIlwraith (the first professional anthropologist to hold an academic position at a Canadian university), was ready in draft form in 1925, but not published until 1948 because the editors judged the material to be obscene (Barker 1987).

For several decades, ethnographers tended to treat a particular tribal group or village as a bounded unit. The era of "village studies" in the ethnography of India, extending from the 1950s through the 1960s, is an example of this trend. Dozens of anthropologists went to India for fieldwork, and each typically studied in one village and then wrote an ethnography describing that village. These anthropologists were inspired by the perspective of holism, the view that says cultures consist of integrated features, such as economy and religion, and one must study all of the features to have a complete picture. Examples of village studies include Adrian Mayer's *Caste*

and Kinship in Central India (1960), S.C. Dube's *Indian Village* (1967), and Gerald Berreman's *Hindus of the Himalayas* (1963). The topics of concern were caste, agricultural practices, kinship, and religion. Little attention was given to exploring links between villages, or to determining the effects of world forces such as nineteenth-century colonialism or twentieth-century post-colonialism on the villagers' lives. Berreman's book is an exception. It includes a detailed chapter entitled, "The Outside World: Urban Contact and Government Programs."

Recent ethnographies, from 1980 onward, differ from earlier ethnographies in several ways. First, they are more likely to treat local cultures as embedded within regional and global forces. Francis Henry's *Victims and Neighbors: A Small Town in Nazi Germany Remembered* (1984) examines social relations between Jews and Christians in a town in Germany where Henry grew up during the 1930s. The ethnography combines extensive interviews in 1979 about events in the 1930s to document acts of kindness in the context of state-encouraged hatred. This study demonstrates the importance of local context in understanding events of global importance such as World War II. Second, many contemporary ethnographies are focused on one topic of interest and avoid a more holistic approach. Cultural anthropologists in this category feel that holism is an impossible goal, since no one can perceive cultures from all their complex angles. A third trend is incorporating history into ethnography. Philip Gulliver and Marilyn Silverman's *Merchants and Shopkeepers: A Historical Anthropology of an Irish Market Town* (1995) examines a town in southeast Ireland that has been a site of commerce for nearly 800 years. As a regional trade centre, the location provides an opportunity to analyze shopkeeping and entrepreneurial strategies over a long duration. A fourth trend is for an increasing number of ethnographic studies to be situated in Western, industrialized cultures. Philippe Bourgois's research in New York's East Harlem for his book, *In Search of Respect: Selling Crack in El Barrio* (1995), explores how people in one neighbourhood cope with poverty and dangerous living conditions. Daniel Wolf's research on a biker gang in Alberta, *The Rebels: A Brotherhood of Outlaw Bikers* (1991), provides another example of urban ethnographic work close to home.

While these topics may superficially resemble something that a sociologist might study, the approach of a cultural anthropologist provides a unique perspective that is more richly detailed from the everyday perspective of the people.

---

ethnography: a first-hand, detailed description of a living culture, based on personal observation.

ethnology: the study of a particular topic in more than one culture using ethnographic material.

ethnocentrism: judging other cultures by the standards of one's own culture rather than by the standards of that particular culture.

In contrast to ethnography, **ethnology** is cross-cultural analysis, or the study of a particular topic in more than one culture using ethnographic material. Ethnologists have compared such topics as marriage forms, economic practices, religious beliefs, and child-rearing practices in order to examine patterns of similarity and variation and possible causes for them. For example, some ethnologists examine the amount of time caretakers spend with infants and how contact time may shape personality. Anthropologists also contribute ethnological insights to help improve public policy (Fox and Gingrich 2002). Taking a comparative or internationalist approach prompts a wide view of issues such as human rights, family organization, and religious beliefs and opens up more options for thinking about the quality of life today and in the future.

Ethnography and ethnology are mutually supportive. Ethnography provides rich, culturally specific insights. Ethnology, by looking beyond individual cases to wider patterns, provides a comparative view and raises new questions that prompt future ethnographic research and can provide policy insights.

Cultural Relativism

Most people grow up thinking that their culture is *the* way of life and that other ways of life are strange, perhaps even inferior. Other cultures may even be considered less than human. Cultural anthropologists have labelled this attitude **ethnocentrism**: judging other cultures by the standards of one's own culture rather than by the standards of that particular culture.

Penny Van Esterik interviewing the manager of a tourist park in Suphanburi Province, Thailand. ■ (Source: John Van Esterik)

Ethnocentric views have fuelled centuries of efforts at changing "other" people in the world, sometimes in the guise of religious missionizing and sometimes in the form of secular colonial domination. Looking back to the era of European colonial expansion beginning in the fifteenth century, it is clear that exploration and conquest were intended to extract wealth from the colonies. In addition to plundering their colonies, the Europeans also imposed their culture on indigenous groups. The British poet, Rudyard Kipling, reflected the dominant view when he said that it was "the white man's burden" to spread Western culture throughout the world. Many contemporary world powers hold similar attitudes, making foreign policy decisions that encourage the adoption of their economic, political, and social systems.

The opposite of ethnocentrism is cultural relativism, the idea that each culture must be understood in terms of the values and beliefs of that culture and should not be judged by the standards of another culture. Cultural relativism assumes that no culture is better than any other. How does a person gain a sense of cultural relativism? The best way is to be able to spend substantial amounts of time living with people outside your own culture. Studying abroad and socially engaged travel help. More locally, you can experience aspects of other cultures by reading about them, learning about them in anthropology classes, doing Internet research, cooking and eating "foreign" foods, listening to "world music," reading novels by authors from other cultures, making friends who are "different" from you, and exploring the multicultural world on your campus.

One way that some anthropologists have interpreted cultural relativism is to use *absolute cultural relativism*, which says that whatever goes on in a particular culture must not be questioned or changed because no one has the right to question any behaviour or idea anywhere—it would be ethnocentric to do so. The position of absolute cultural relativism can lead, however, in dangerous directions. Consider the example of the Holocaust during World War II, in which millions of Jews and other minorities in much of Eastern and Western Europe were imprisoned and murdered as part of the German Nazis' Aryan supremacy campaign. The absolute cultural relativist position becomes boxed in, logically, to saying that since the Holocaust was undertaken according to the values of the culture, outsiders have no business questioning it. Can anyone feel truly comfortable with such a position?

Critical cultural relativism offers an alternative view that poses questions about cultural practices and ideas in terms of who accepts them and why, and who they might be harming or helping. In terms of the Nazi Holocaust, a critical cultural relativist would ask, "Whose culture supported the values that murdered millions of people on the grounds of racial purity?" Not the cultures of the Jews, Roma, and other victims. It was the culture of Aryan supremacists, who were one subgroup among many. The situation was far more complex than a simple absolute cultural relativist statement takes into account because there was not "one" culture and its values involved. Rather, it was a case of *cultural imperialism*, in which one dominant group claims supremacy over minority cultures and proceeds to change the situation in its own interests and at the expense of the subjugated cultures. Critical cultural relativism avoids the trap of adopting a homogenized view. It recognizes internal cultural differences and winners/losers, oppressors/victims. It pays attention to the interests of various power groups. Critical cultural relativism can be applied to illuminate recent and contemporary conflict situations, such as those in Yugoslavia, Rwanda, and Afghanistan.

Many cultural anthropologists seek to *critique* (which means to probe underlying power interests, not just to offer negative comments as in the general usage of the term *criticism*) the behaviour and values of groups from the standpoint of some set of generally agreed-on human rights. But they recognize how difficult it is to generate a universal list of what all cultures view as good and right. As Claude Lévi-Strauss once commented, "No society is perfect" (1968:385). While considering the "imperfections" of any and all cultures, cultural anthropologists, like people in general, should be open about their own positions and biases and try to view all cultures with an equally "critical" eye.

Valuing and Sustaining Diversity

Anthropologists value and are committed to cultural diversity just as environmentalists value and are committed to biological diversity. Thus, cultural anthropologists contribute to the preservation of cultural diversity and knowledge by describing cultures as they have existed, as they now exist, and as they change. Many have become activists in the area of cultural survival.

Since 1972, an organization named Cultural Survival has been helping indigenous people and ethnic minorities to interact as equals with others in society. Cultural Survival's guiding principle is printed on the inside cover of this book. Cultural Survival sponsors programs to help indigenous peoples and ethnic minorities protect and manage natural resources, claim land rights, and diversify their means of livelihood.

Three Theoretical Debates

Within cultural anthropology, enduring theoretical debates both divide the discipline and provide threads that give it coherence. Contemporary theoretical approaches include interpretive, symbolic, political ecology, political economy, and postmodernism. Although different departments of anthropology in Canada often have specific theoretical orientations, Canadian anthropologists in general tend to avoid extremely deterministic interpretations of human behaviour. They seek to explain difference as well as similarity, and address questions that crosscut theoretical (and national) borders. Three important contemporary debates, explained briefly here, will resurface throughout the book. Each is concerned with cultural anthropology's basic question of why people behave and think the way they do.

Biological Determinism versus Cultural Constructionism

Biological determinism seeks to explain why people do and think what they do by considering biological factors such as people's genes and hormones. Thus, biological determinists search for the gene or hormone that might lead to certain forms of behaviour such as homicide, alcoholism, or adolescent stress (see the Critical Thinking box on page 28). They examine cultural practices in terms of how they contribute to the "reproductive success of the species," or how they contribute to the gene pool of subsequent generations through promoting the numbers of surviving offspring produced in a particular population. Behaviours and ideas that have reproductive advantages logically are more likely than others to be passed on to future generations. Biological determinists, for example, have provided an explanation for why human males apparently have "better" spatial skills than females. They say that these differences are the result of evolutionary selection because males with "better" spatial skills would have an advantage in securing both food and mates. Males with "better" spatial skills impregnate more females and have more offspring with "better" spatial skills.

Cultural constructionism, in contrast, maintains that human behaviour and ideas are best explained as products of culturally shaped learning. In terms of the example of "better" male spatial skills, cultural constructionists

---

biological determinism: a theory that explains human behaviour and ideas mainly as a result of biological features such as genes and hormones.

cultural constructionism: a theory that explains human behaviour and ideas as being mainly the results of learning.

would provide evidence that such skills are passed on culturally through learning, not genes. They would say that parents socialize their sons and daughters differently in spatial skills and that boys are more likely to gain greater spatial skills through learning than girls, in general. Anthropologists who favour cultural construction and learning as an explanation for behaviours such as homicide and alcoholism also point to the role of childhood experiences and family roles as being more important than genes or hormones. Most cultural anthropologists are opposed to biological determinism and support cultural constructivism. However, some of them connect biology and culture in their work.

Interpretive Anthropology versus Cultural Materialism

Interpretive anthropology considers how people use symbols to make sense of the world around them, and how these meanings are negotiated. Interpretive anthropologists view culture as a contested domain, not a given. They favour an approach to ethnography that constructs a rich, complex description emerging from the insider's point of view. Interpretive anthropology tries to communicate this complexity, and rejects approaches that are reductionistic. For example, if Hindus in India say they don't eat cows because cows are sacred, interpretive anthropologists would explore the meaning of food and eating within the Hindu religion. Similarly, an interpretive anthropologist like Mary Douglas argues that pigs cannot be eaten by Jews because of their taxonomical definition in Jewish belief as defined in the rules of Leviticus. The pig is a hoofed animal that does not chew its cud, unlike cows and sheep, and is categorized as anomalous and, thus, impure. Materialists have rejected such reasoning because the rules of Leviticus are untestable (Harris and Ross 1987:60).

Cultural materialism emphasizes the importance of material conditions in studying and explaining human behaviours and ideas. Cultural materialists take as basic the material features of life, such as the environment, natural resources, and ways of making a living. *Infrastructure* is the term that refers to these crucial material factors. Infrastructure largely shapes the other two domains of culture: *structure* (social organization, kinship, and political organization) and *superstructure* (ideas, values, and beliefs). Cultural materialists seek explanations for behaviour and ideas by looking first and primarily at infrastructural factors. For example, a materialist explanation for a taboo restricting the eating of a particular animal first considers the possibility that such an animal plays a more important role alive, such as cows' utility in agricultural work in India.

The debate between interpretive anthropology and cultural materialism has a long history in cultural anthropology, and its philosophical roots can be traced back to Plato (who emphasized that the only reality is ideas) and Aristotle (who emphasized that there is some sort of reality that can be learned about through observation). These days, most cultural anthropologists take an approach that combines the best of interpretive anthropology and cultural materialism.

Individual Agency versus Structural

The individual agency versus structural debate concerns the question of how much individual will, or agency, has to do with why people behave and think the way they do, versus the power of forces, or "structures," that are beyond individual control. Western philosophical thought gives much emphasis to the role of agency. The individual is supposed to be able to choose how to behave and think. In contrast, analysts who emphasize the structural argue that "free choice" is an illusion since choices are structured by larger forces, such as the economy, social and political institutions, and ideological systems.

A prime example is the study of poverty. Those who emphasize agency focus their research on how individuals attempt to act as agents, even in situations of extreme poverty, in order to change their situation as best they can. Theorists who see the world controlled by structures would emphasize that the poor are trapped by large and powerful forces. They would describe how the political economy and other forces provide little room for agency for those at the bottom. An increasing number of cultural anthropologists seek to blend a structural perspective with attention to agency.

Beyond the Debates: Holism at Heart

Cultural anthropologists often take different theoretical positions. Some apply their work while others follow academic pursuits. But it is fair to say that cultural anthropologists are united in their interest in and care about humanity and its richly varied cultures.

Cultural Anthropology and Careers

Some of you reading this book may take only one anthropology course to satisfy a requirement. Others may become interested in the subject matter and take a few more. Some will decide to major or minor in anthropology. Even just one course in anthropology can change your way of

Critical Thinking

ADOLESCENT STRESS: BIOLOGICALLY DETERMINED OR CULTURALLY CONSTRUCTED?

Margaret Mead, one of the first trained anthropologists of North America, went to Eastern Samoa in 1925 to spend nine months studying child-rearing patterns and adolescent behaviour. She sought to answer these questions: "Are the disturbances which vex our adolescents due to the nature of adolescence itself or to the civilisation? Under different conditions does adolescence present a different picture?" (1961:24). Mead observed and interviewed 50 adolescent girls of three different villages. Her conclusion, published in the famous book, *Coming of Age in Samoa* (1961 [1928]), was that, unlike the typical experience in the United States, children in Samoa grew up in a relaxed and happy atmosphere. As young adolescents, they made a sexually free and unrepressed transition to adulthood. These findings had a major impact on thinking about child-rearing in North America, prompting attempts at more relaxed forms of child-rearing in the hope of raising less-stressed adolescents.

In 1983, five years after Mead's death (at which point she had no chance for response), Derek Freeman, an Australian anthropologist, published a strong critique of Mead's work on Samoa. Freeman said that Mead's findings on adolescence were wrong. Freeman, a biological determinist, believes that, universally, adolescents are driven by hormonal changes that cause social and psychological upheavals. He claims that Mead's work was flawed in two major ways. First, he says her fieldwork was inadequate because Mead spent a relatively short time in the field and she had insufficient knowledge of the Samoan language. Second, he says that her theoretical bias against biological determinism led her to overlook or under-report evidence that was contrary to her interests. In addition, he marshals statistical evidence against Mead's position. He compares rates of adolescent delinquency in Samoa and England and finds that they are similar in both cultures. On the basis of this result, he argues that sexual puritanism and social repression also characterized Samoan adolescence. In other words, Samoa is not so different from the West with its supposedly pervasive adolescent problems.

Because of Mead's reputation, Freeman's critique prompted a vigorous response from scholars, mostly in defence of Mead. One response in defence of Mead came from Eleanor Leacock, an expert on how colonialism affects indigenous cultures. Leacock (1993) claimed that Freeman's position failed to take history into account: Mead's findings apply to Samoa of the 1920s while Freeman's analysis is based on data from the 1960s. By the 1960s, Samoan society had gone through radical cultural change due to the influence of World War II and intensive exposure to Western influences, including Christian missionaries. Freeman's data, in her view, do not contradict Mead's because they are from a different period.

CRITICAL THINKING QUESTIONS

- Mead felt that finding one "negative case" (no adolescent stress in Samoa) was sufficient to disprove the view that adolescent stress is a cultural universal. Do you agree that one negative case is sufficient?
- If an anthropologist found that a practice or pattern of behaviour was universal to all cultures, does that necessarily mean that it is biologically driven?

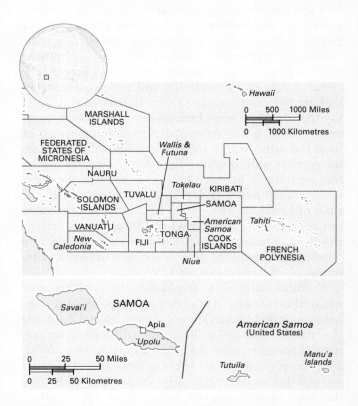

MAP 1.6 Samoa, American Samoa, and the South Pacific. Samoa, or the Independent State of Samoa, was known as German Samoa (1900–1919) and Western Samoa (1914–1997) until it was recognized by the United Nations as a sovereign country. Its population is around 177 000. American Samoa, or Amerika Samoa in Samoan English, is a territory of the United States with a population of roughly 57 000. During World War II, U.S. Marines in American Samoa outnumbered the local population and had a strong cultural influence. Unemployment rates are now high and the U.S. military is the largest employer.

thinking about the world and your place in it. On top of that, it can add to your ability to get a job that values the kinds of thinking and skills that anthropology provides.

Majoring in Anthropology

An anthropology B.A. is a liberal arts degree. It is not, however, a professional degree, such as a business degree or a degree in physical therapy. It provides a solid education relevant to many career directions that are likely to require further study, such as law, criminal justice, medicine and health services, social services, education, humanitarian assistance, international development programs, and business. Students interested in pursuing a B.A. major in anthropology should know that a degree in this discipline is at least as useful as other liberal arts majors for either graduate study or a professional career.

Anthropology has several clear advantages over other liberal arts majors, and employers and graduate schools are increasingly recognizing these features. Cultural anthropology provides knowledge about the world's people and diversity. It offers insights about a variety of specialized research methods. Cross-cultural awareness and communication skills are valuable assets sought by business, government, health-care providers, and nongovernmental organizations.

The question students always ask is this: "Is it possible to get a good job, especially one related to anthropology, with a B.A. in anthropology?" The answer is yes, but it takes planning and hard work. Do the following: Gain expertise in at least one foreign language, study abroad, do service learning during your undergraduate years, and conduct an independent research project and write up the results as a professional report or conference paper. Package these skills on your resumé so that they appear relevant to employers. Do not give up. Good jobs are out there, and coursework and skills in anthropology are increasingly valued.

Anthropology can also be an excellent minor. It complements almost any other area of study by adding a cross-cultural perspective. For example, if you are majoring in music, courses about world music will greatly enrich your primary interest. The same applies to subjects such as interior design, psychology, criminal justice, international affairs, economics, political science, and more.

Graduate Study in Anthropology

Some of you may go on to pursue a master's degree (M.A.) or doctorate degree (Ph.D.) in anthropology. If you do, here is some advice: Be passionate about your interest but also be aware that full-time jobs as a professor or as a professional anthropologist are not easy to get. To expand possibilities of a good job, it is wise to consider combining a professional skill with your degree program in anthropology, such as a law degree, an M.A. degree in project management, a master's of public health (M.P.H.), a certificate in disaster relief, or participation in a training program in conflict prevention and resolution.

Useful skills will make your anthropology degree more powerful. In biological anthropology, it may be course work in anatomy that helps you get a job working in a forensics lab or teaching anatomy in a medical school. In archaeology, it may be your experience on a summer dig that helps you get a job with a firm that investigates building sites before construction begins to check for the presence of fossils or artifacts. In cultural anthropology, cross-cultural experiences or knowledge of a foreign language may get you a position with an international aid organization. In linguistic anthropology, your knowledge of bilingualism means that you can help design a more effective program for teaching English to refugees or immigrants.

Living an Anthropological Life

Studying cultural anthropology makes for smart people and people with breadth and flexibility. In North America, university graduates are likely to change careers (not just jobs, but careers) several times in their lives. You never know where you are going to end up working, or in what endeavour. So it pays to be broadly informed about the world. Cultural anthropology will help you to ask original and important questions about the world's people and their relationships with one another and to provide original and important answers. It will enrich your daily life by increasing your exposure to the world's cultures. When you pick up a newspaper, you will invariably find articles that connect with what you have learned in your anthropology classes. You will be able to view your own everyday life as culturally constructed in interesting and meaningful ways.

Key Questions Revisited

WHAT is anthropology?

Anthropology is an academic discipline, like history or economics. It comprises four interrelated fields in its attempt to explore all facets of human life from its very beginnings until the present: archaeology, physical or biological anthropology, linguistic anthropology, and cultural anthropology.

Each field contributes a unique but related perspective. The perspective of this book is that applied anthropology, just like theoretical anthropology, should be an integrated and important part of all four fields, rather than a separate, fifth field. Examples of applied anthropology in the four fields include forensic anthropology, nonhuman primate conservation, assisting in literacy programs for refugees, and advising businesses about consumer preferences.

WHAT is cultural anthropology?

Cultural anthropology is the field within general anthropology that focuses on the study of contemporary human culture—that is, on patterned and learned ways of behaving and thinking. It has several distinctive features that set it off from both the other fields of general anthropology and other academic endeavours. It uses ethnographical and ethnological approaches, supports the view of cultural relativism, and values cultural diversity.

Culture is the key concept of cultural anthropology. Some anthropologists define culture as both shared behaviour and ideas, while others equate culture with ideas alone and exclude behaviour as a part of culture. Important characteristics of culture are that it is adaptive, related to nature but not the same as nature, based on symbols, and learned. Cultures are integrated within themselves. They also interact with other cultures and change. Several models of cultural interaction involve varying degrees of conflict, blending, and resistance. People participate in cultures of different levels, including local cultures shaped by such factors as class, race/ethnicity/indigeneity, gender, age, and institutions.

HOW is cultural anthropology relevant to a career in the world of work?

Taking just one course in cultural anthropology expands awareness of the diversity of the world's cultures and the importance of cross-cultural understanding. Employers in many fields—such as public health, humanitarian aid, law enforcement, business, and education—increasingly value a degree in cultural anthropology. In today's diverse and connected world, being culturally informed and culturally sensitive is essential.

Graduate degrees in cultural anthropology, either at the M.A. or Ph.D. level, are even more likely to lead to professional positions that directly use your anthropological education and skills. Combining graduate course work in anthropology with a professional degree, such as master's degree in public health or public administration, or a law degree, is a successful route to a meaningful career outside academia.

KEY CONCEPTS

agency, p. 14
anthropology, p. 4
applied anthropology, p. 4
archaeology, p. 4
biological anthropology,
   p. 4
biological determinism,
   p. 26
class, p. 19
cultural anthropology, p. 4
cultural constructionism,
   p. 26

cultural materialism,
   p. 13
cultural relativism,
   p. 11
culture, p. 4
ethnicity, p. 21
ethnocentrism, p. 25
ethnography, p. 24
ethnology, p. 25
functionalism, p. 11
gender, p. 21
globalization, p. 19

holism, p. 11
indigenous peoples, p. 21
interpretive anthropology,
   p. 13
linguistic anthropology,
   p. 4
local culture, p. 14
localization, p. 19
race, p. 21
structural, p. 14
symbol, p. 17

To reinforce your understanding of this chapter, and to identify topics for further study, visit MyAnthroLab at www.myanthrolab.com for diagnostic tests and a multimedia ebook.

SUGGESTED READINGS

William I. Adams, *The Philosophical Roots of Anthropology*. Stanford, CA: CSLI Publications, 1998. Adams considers five ideas as roots of North American anthropology: progressivism, primitivism, natural law, Indianology (the study of First Nations), and German idealism. These ideas help explain why North American anthropology, compared with British anthropology, for example, retained the four-field structure.

Thomas J. Barfield, ed. *The Dictionary of Anthropology*. Malden, MA: Blackwell Publishing, 1997. This reference work contains hundreds of brief essays on concepts in anthropology, such as evolution, myth, functionalism, and applied anthropology, and on important anthropologists.

Stanley Barrett, *Anthropology: A Student's Guide to Theory and Method*. Toronto: University of Toronto Press, 1996. This helpful handbook for undergraduate anthropology students provides a useful overview of the development of the discipline, and links methods to past and present theories.

Merryl Wyn Davies and Piero (illus.), *Introducing Anthropology*. Cambridge, UK: Icon Books, 2002. This book offers snappy insights on key thinkers, developments, and arguments in anthropology. Each page is illustrated with cartoon-like drawings that make for lively reading.

Marvin Harris, *Our Kind: Who We Are, Where We Came From and Where We Are Going*. New York: HarperCollins, 1989. This book contains 100 thought-provoking essays on topics in general anthropology's four fields, including early human evolution, tool making, Neanderthals, food preferences, sex, sexism, politics, animal sacrifice, and thoughts on the survival of humanity.

F. Manning, ed., *Consciousness and Inquiry: Ethnology and Canadian Realities*. Ottawa: National Museum of Man, 1983. CES paper 89e. In this edited volume, eminent Canadian anthropologists present overviews or historical perspectives on their areas of specialization, including applied anthropology in Canada.

R. Bruce Morrison and C. Roderick Wilson, eds. *Native Peoples: The Canadian Experience*, 3rd ed. Toronto: Oxford University Press, 2004. This sourcebook on northern peoples contains 26 chapters with sections divided by region. Chapters about various cultural groups provide historical context and updates on the current situation.

Pearl T. Robinson and Elliott P. Skinner, eds., *Transformation and Resiliency in Africa: As Seen by Afro-American Scholars*. Washington, DC: Howard University Press, 1983. Framed by an introductory essay on black scholarship on Africa and a conclusion that looks toward the future, nine chapters explore different areas of African culture, including labour migration in Kenya, politics and government in Nigeria, religion in the Ivory Coast, religion and popular art in urban Africa, and the transformation of African music.

George W. Stocking, Jr., *The Ethnographer's Magic and Other Essays in the History of Anthropology*. Madison, WI: University of Wisconsin Press, 1992. The author provides a detailed examination of the emergence of cultural anthropology from Tylor through Boas and Mead, with a summary chapter on major paradigms in the history of general anthropology.

Eric R. Wolf, *Europe and the People without History*. Berkeley, CA: University of California Press, 1982. In this book, Wolf examines the impact since 1492 of European colonial expansion on the indigenous cultures with which they came into contact. He also traces various phases of trade relationships, including the slave trade and goods such as fur and tobacco, and the emergence of capitalism and its effects on the movement of people and goods between cultures.

2

Methods in Cultural Anthropology

Key Questions

- HOW do cultural anthropologists conduct research on culture?

- WHAT does fieldwork involve?

- WHAT are some important issues in cultural anthropology research today?

During the course of winter travels with the Hare Indians in Canada, anthropologist Joel Savishinsky holds an 11-kilogram lake trout. His dog team is resting behind him. *(Source: © Joel Savishinsky)*

This chapter is about how cultural anthropologists do research. In the first section, we describe the evolution of methods in cultural anthropology since the late nineteenth century. The second section covers the steps involved in a research project. We conclude the chapter by addressing two urgent topics in cultural anthropology research: fieldwork ethics and safety during fieldwork. Throughout the chapter, you might consider the similarities and differences between research in cultural anthropology and research in other disciplines, such as biology, psychology, political science, economics, and history.

Ethnographic research in the early twentieth century often involved photography. The girl shown here wears the skull of her deceased sister. Indigenous people of the Andamans revere the bones of their dead relatives and would not want them to be taken away, studied, or displayed in a museum. ■ (Source: A. R. Radcliffe-Brown, The Andaman Islanders. Cambridge: Cambridge University Press, 1964 [1922])

Changing Research Methods in Cultural Anthropology

Today's methods in cultural anthropology are different in several ways from those used during the nineteenth century. Most cultural anthropologists now gather data by doing **fieldwork**, going to the *field*, which is wherever people and cultures are, to learn about culture through direct observation (Robson 1993). They also use a variety of specialized research techniques discussed in this section.

From the Armchair to the Field

The term *armchair anthropology* refers to how early cultural anthropologists conducted research by sitting and reading about other cultures. They read reports written by travellers, missionaries, and explorers but never visited those places or had any kind of direct experience with the people. Sir Edward Tylor, who proposed the first definition of culture in 1871, as we noted in Chapter 1, was an armchair anthropologist. Sir James Frazer, another famous founding figure of anthropology, was also an armchair anthropologist. He wrote *The Golden Bough* (1978 [1890]), a multivolume collection of myths, rituals, and symbols that he compiled from his wide reading.

In the late nineteenth and early twentieth centuries, anthropologists hired by European colonial governments moved a step closer to learning directly about the people of other cultures. They travelled to colonized countries in Africa and Asia where they lived near—but not with—the people they were studying. This approach is called *verandah anthropology*; typically, the anthropologist would send out for "natives" to come to his verandah for interviewing (verandah anthropologists, like armchair

anthropologists, were men). A classic example of verandah anthropology is A.R. Radcliffe-Brown's book, *The Andaman Islanders* (1964 [1922]) (see the Ethnographic Profile in Chapter 3 on page 71). At the time of Radcliffe-Brown's research on Great (now South) Andaman Island at the turn of the twentieth century, the indigenous population had been decimated by diseases brought in by the British colonizers and by the effects of direct colonial violence. Radcliffe-Brown's assignment was to do *salvage anthropology*, to collect what data he could from the remaining people in order to document their language, social life, and religious beliefs.

A bit earlier, during the mid-nineteenth century, Lewis Henry Morgan had taken steps toward learning about people through direct observation. Morgan, a lawyer from Syracuse, New York, made observations of Iroquoian groups. Less well known, Horatio Hale, a lawyer from Brantford, Ontario, did the same for Iroquoian groups in his hometown. Both made short trips to Iroquois settlements. This experience, though brief, provided important insights into the lives of the Iroquois and formed the basis for Morgan's book, *The League of the Iroquois* (1851), and Hale's *Iroquois Book of Rites* (1883). The books helped dismantle the prevailing Euro-American perception of the Iroquois as "dangerous savages."

fieldwork: research in the field, which is any place where people and culture are found.
participant observation is a research method for learning about culture that involves living in a culture for an extended period while gathering data.
multisited research: fieldwork conducted in more than one location in order to understand the behaviours and ideas of dispersed members of a culture or the relationships among different levels such as state policy and local culture.

Participant Observation

A major turning point in how cultural anthropologists do research occurred in the early twentieth century, during World War I. It laid the foundation for the current cornerstone method in cultural anthropology: fieldwork combined with **participant observation.**

The "father" of participant observation is Bronislaw Malinowski. He adopted an innovative approach to learning about culture in the South Pacific's Trobriand Islands during World War I (see the Ethnographic Profile on page 40). "For two years, he set his tent in their midst, learned their language, participated as much as he could in their daily life, expeditions, and festivals, and took everything down in his notebooks" (Sperber 1985:4). As established by Malinowski, the key elements of participant observation are

- Living with the people
- Learning the language
- Participating in their everyday life

By living with the people of the Trobriand Islands, Malinowski could learn about their culture in context, rather than through second-hand reports. By learning the local language, Malinowski could talk with the people without the need for interpreters.

The benefits of this new approach are evident in Malinowski's many writings about the Trobriand Islanders, including his most famous book, *Argonauts of the Western Pacific* (1961 [1922]). When the war ended, Malinowski returned to Europe and established the tradition of participant observation in the new university programs for training anthropologists.

In this early phase of fieldwork and participant observation, a primary goal was to record as much as possible of a people's language, songs, rituals, and social life because many cultures were disappearing. Most early cultural anthropologists did fieldwork in small, relatively isolated cultures. They thought they could study everything about such cultures; those were the days of holism (defined in Chapter 1). Typically, the anthropologist (a white man) would go off with his notebooks to collect data on a standardized list of topics including economics, family life, politics, religion, language, art and crafts, and more.

Today, few if any such seemingly isolated cultures remain. Cultural anthropologists have now devised new research methods so that they can study larger-scale cultures, global–local connections, and cultural change. One methodological innovation of the late twentieth century is especially important in addressing these new issues: **multisited research**, which is fieldwork conducted on a topic in more than one location (Marcus 1995). While especially helpful in studying migrant populations in both their place of origin and their new location (see Chapter 14, "People on the Move"), multisited research is useful for studying many topics.

Lanita Jacobs-Huey's fieldsites include hairstyling competitions throughout the United States and London, England. Here, a judge evaluates the work of a student stylist at the Afro Hair & Beauty Show in London, England. ■ (Source: Lanita Jacobs-Huey)

Lanita Jacobs-Huey conducted multisited fieldwork in order to learn about the language and culture of hairstyles among English-speaking African American women (2002). She chose a range of sites throughout the United States and in London, England, in order to explore the many facets of this far-from-simple topic: beauty salons, regional and international hair expos and training seminars, Bible study meetings of a nonprofit group of Christian cosmetologists, stand-up comedy clubs, a computer-mediated discussion about the politics of black hair, and a cosmetology school in Charleston, South Carolina.

Canadian anthropologist and novelist Camilla Gibb (2002) studied the Harari, a dispersed community of Muslim Ethiopians, in the city of Harar and in Toronto. Since a third of the Harari are scattered across the globe, a key component of her study included discussions taking place on H-Net, an email-based discussion group where aspects of community and identity were defined and debated. Use of this new media revealed differences among diasporic generations about an eventual return to Ethiopia.

Other examples of contemporary ethnographies demonstrate the simultaneous attention to local patterns and wider cultural links. Albert Schrauwers's study, *Colonial 'Reformation' in the Highlands of Central Sulawesi, Indonesia, 1892–1995*, shows the complex effects of a Dutch Protestant mission on the religion and culture of the To Pamona people, and the role of the church in Dutch and Indonesian affairs of state. He combined archival research in the Netherlands with ethnographic observations in Sulawesi to explore the contemporary dynamics of religious practice in the region.

Margaret Lock explored the cultural construction of death in *Twice Dead*: *Organ Transplants and the Reinvention of Death* (2002). In her book, Lock argues that dying is as culturally constructed as living. Using comparative materials from Japan and North America, she explores the moral uncertainty around the culture of dying and the politics of human body parts. The ethnography is based on historical analysis combined with long-term ethnographic fieldwork.

Doing Fieldwork in Cultural Anthropology

Conducting research in cultural anthropology is challenging, exciting, sometimes frustrating, and full of

Visitors walk past a giant Coca-Cola logo at a slogan launch party in Shanghai, China. The market leader in ready-to-drink soft drinks in China, Coca-Cola brought pop stars to the party to entertain guests and promote its new slogan: "No Compromise on Real Refreshment, Coca-Cola!" ■ (Source: Qilai Shen/epa/epa/CORBIS)

surprises. No doubt all cultural anthropologists would agree that their fieldwork experiences have altered their own lives immeasurably. Here, we explore all the stages of a fieldwork research project, from the initial planning to the concluding analysis and write-up of the findings.

Beginning the Fieldwork Process

Two important activities characterize the first stage of cultural anthropology research: project selection and funding, and preparing for the field.

Project Selection and Funding

Finding a topic for a research project is a basic first step. The topic should be important and feasible. Cultural anthropologists often find a topic to research by carrying out a *literature review*, or reading what others have already written. Conducting a literature review often exposes a gap in previous research. For example, cultural anthropologists realized during the 1970s that anthropological research had bypassed women and girls, and this is how feminist anthropology began (B. Miller 1993).

Notable events sometimes inspire a research topic. The HIV/AIDS epidemic and its rapid spread continue to prompt research. The recent rise in the numbers of international migrants and refugees is another pressing area for study. The fall of state socialism in Russia and Eastern Europe shifted attention to that region; it also meant that cultural anthropologists could conduct fieldwork in previously closed countries. Conflicts in Ireland, Rwanda, the former Yugoslavia, Sudan, and other places spur cultural anthropologists to ask what keeps states together and what makes them fall apart (Harris 1992) and to contribute to their knowledge about conflict prevention and postconflict resolution (Lubkemann 2005).

Some cultural anthropologists find a focus for their research by choosing a particular material item, such as sugar (Mintz 1985), cars (D. Miller 2001), beef (Caplan 2000), money (Foster 2002), shea butter (Chalfin 2004), wedding dresses (Foster and Johnson 2003), coca (Allen 2002), and cocaine (Taussig 2004). The material items provide a focus for understanding the social relations surrounding their production and trade and what they mean in terms of people's changing identities.

Another fruitful avenue for research is a *restudy*, fieldwork conducted in a previously researched community. Many decades of previous research provide a baseline of

informed consent: an aspect of fieldwork ethics requiring that the researcher inform the research participants of the intent, scope, and possible effects of the study and seek their consent to be in the study.

John Van Esterik continues his restudy in a Thai village. Here he is asking his informant about pictures taken at a housewarming ritual. ■ (Source: Penny Van Esterik)

information on which later studies can build. For example, John and Penny Van Esterik returned to their fieldsite, a village in Central Thailand, to see how the community had changed in 30 years. It makes sense to examine changes that have occurred or to look at the culture from a new angle. For her doctoral dissertation research, Annette Weiner (1976) decided to go to the Trobriand Islands, following in the footsteps of Malinowski, to learn what people's lives were like over 50 years after his fieldwork. What Weiner discovered prompted her to alter her original research plans (see the Critical Thinking box on page 39 and the Ethnographic Profile on page 40).

Even luck can lead to a research topic. While conducting fieldwork in southwestern Ontario on contemporary Mennonite efforts to articulate a renewed vision of peoplehood, Daphne Winland came across a small congregation of Hmong refugees from Laos who had been sponsored by the Mennonite community in Kitchener-Waterloo, Ontario. These refugees, who had decided to convert to Christianity (specifically Mennonitism), not only provided Winland with a fascinating example of the role of religion in refugee adjustment but also a perfect case study through which to examine the central theme of her research, Mennonite struggles over their long-established identity as an ethno-religious enclave (Winland 1992).

Over the past several decades, the regional focus of research in cultural anthropology has shifted. These changes are not random, but occur in response to underlying factors such as funding sources or security interests (Shankman and Ehlers 2000). Some funding sources support domestic research by applied anthropologists on issues such as homelessness and HIV/AIDS. But when the research site is more "foreign" and "exotic," the researcher gains more status and prestige (Gupta and Ferguson 1997). Nevertheless, some of the most significant and policy-relevant anthropological research in Canada is conducted "at home." (See, for example, Scott 2001; Asch 1997; Glasser and Bridgeman 1999; Winland 1992; Davis 1989; Culhane Speck 1987; and Adelson 2000.) Private or government foundations provide research funding on a competitive basis. A research proposal is usually required for consideration by the funding source. It describes the project; explains why it is important; and provides information about how the research will be conducted, how much it will cost, and what the results will be—a book, scholarly papers, a film, or a detailed report. Canadian funding for anthropological research comes primarily from the Social Science and Humanities Research Council (SSHRC), Canadian International Development Agency (CIDA) awards programs, and area-specific foundations, such as the Shastri Indo-Canadian Institute and the Japan Foundation.

Preparing for the Field

Once the project is defined and funding secured, it is time to begin preparing to go to the field.

If the project involves international travel, the host government may require a visa and an application for permission to conduct research. These formalities may take a long time and may even be impossible to obtain. The government of India, for example, is highly restrictive about research by foreigners. Research permission for "sensitive" topics such as tribal people, border areas, and family planning is unlikely to be granted. China's restrictions against allowing foreign anthropologists to do research there have been lifted only in the past 15 years or so, and Russia's restrictive policies have changed even more recently.

Some research topics are more sensitive than others are (Lee and Renzetti 1993). Sexual behaviour is a potentially sensitive research issue, more from the point of view of research participants than from the host governments. Typically, it is even more difficult to research homosexuality than heterosexuality, because of mainstream norms, laws, and social stigma (see the Multiple Cultural Worlds box on page 37).

Many countries and institutional review boards (IRBs) now also require that researchers follow official guidelines for *protection of human subjects*. **Informed consent** is an aspect of research ethics requiring that the researcher inform the research participants of the intent, scope, and possible effects of the study and seek their agreement to be in the study. Obtaining such consent of research participants is reasonable and feasible in many anthropological research projects. However, written

TALKING ABOUT SEX

It is likely that all cultures define certain topics as out of bounds for public discussion within the group or for discussion with an outsider. Sex, as in sexual intercourse, is a frequently avoided area. Heterosexual societies are likely to limit talk about homosexuality even more. How does, and can, an anthropologist learn about sexuality, especially homosexuality? Here, you'll find an expert's insights into how an anthropologist stumbled into learning about homosexuality in Brazil.

Richard Parker, a U.S. anthropologist, went to Brazil to study the historical and political aspects of *carnaval*, a popular public celebration that occurs at the beginning of the Christian period of Lent (1991). Parker became aware of how closely linked the celebration is to sexual symbolism and sexuality, both heterosexual and homosexual, and he realized how important these topics are to understanding Brazilian culture in general. As his research continued, he gained the trust of heterosexuals, gay men, and lesbians. The quality of his personal relationships with his more than 30 participants was the key factor in the success of the study.

It may seem surprising, but Parker's research focus on sexual culture had a positive effect on his study by creating rapport through a shared sense of breaking the rules of social decorum. This kind of rapport would not develop from study of a less sensitive topic, such as employment or family life. Parker found that his research participants

> often seemed to take a certain pleasure in being part of a project which seemed to break the rules of proper decorum . . . while they often resisted, understandably, speaking too directly about their own sexual lives, they seemed to enjoy (and, at times, to take a positive

A participant in *carnaval* in Rio de Janeiro, Brazil. This springtime celebration is an occasion of heightened merriment and display of sexuality. ■ (Source: © AFP/CORBIS)

> delight in) the opportunity to speak freely about the question of sex more generally. (1991:177)

Parker's rapport with his research participants is evident in the rich data that he collected on such topics as masturbation, oral sex, and anal sex. One lesson about fieldwork is that the sheer sensitivity of a topic does not always prevent its study. The researcher, however, has to be sensitive, too.

FOOD FOR THOUGHT

- How would you feel about discussing sexual behaviour in your community with an anthropologist from Brazil?

---

consent is not always reasonable or feasible in oral-based cultures where most people are not literate. In these cases, it is possible to request a waiver of informed written consent and obtain informed oral consent instead.

Preparation may involve buying equipment, such as a tent, arctic sleeping bag, or special clothing. Health preparations may involve having a series of shots for immunization against contagious diseases such as yellow fever. For research in malaria-endemic areas, individuals are advised to start taking anti-malaria pills weeks before arrival to build up immunity. If the project is to take place in a remote area far from adequate medical care, a

---

kula: a trading network linking many of the Trobriand Islands in which men have long-standing partnerships for the exchange of everyday goods, such as food as well as highly valued necklaces and armlets.

Critical Thinking

SHELLS AND SKIRTS IN THE TROBRIAND ISLANDS

A lasting contribution of Bronislaw Malinowski's ethnography, *Argonauts of the Western Pacific* (1961 [1922]), is its detailed examination of the **kula**, a trading network linking many islands in the region in which men have long-standing partnerships for the exchange of everyday goods such as food as well as highly valued necklaces and armlets.

More than half a century later, Annette Weiner (1976) travelled to the Trobriand Islands to study woodcarving. She settled in a village less than a mile from where Malinowski had done his research. She immediately began making startling observations: "On my first day in the village, I saw women performing a mortuary [death] ceremony in which they distributed thousands of bundles of strips of dried banana leaves and hundreds of beautifully decorated fibrous skirts" (xvii).

Nowhere in Malinowski's voluminous writings did these women's activities appear. Weiner was intrigued and decided to change her research project to investigate women's goods, exchange patterns, and prestige. Men, as Malinowski showed, exchange shells, yams, and pigs. Women, as Weiner learned, exchange bundles of banana leaves and intricately made skirts. Power and prestige derive from both exchange networks.

Reading Malinowski alone informs us about the world of men's status systems and describes them in isolation from half of the islands' population: women. Weiner's book, *Women of Value, Men of Renown* (1976), provides an account of women's trading and prestige activities as

Bronislaw Malinowski during his fieldwork in the Trobriand Islands, 1915–1918. ■ (Source: Pearson Education)

well as how they are linked to those of men. Building on the work of her predecessor, Weiner shows how a full understanding of one domain requires knowledge of the other.

CRITICAL THINKING QUESTIONS

- How is it possible that Malinowski overlooked women's exchange patterns?
- Do Weiner's findings simply provide another one-sided view?
- What might a cultural anthropologist discover in the Trobriand Islands now?

---

well-stocked medical kit is essential. Research equipment and supplies are other important aspects of preparation. Cameras, video recorders, tape recorders, and laptop computers are becoming basic field equipment, reflecting technological changes in doing fieldwork from the days of the simple notebook and pen.

If a researcher is unfamiliar with the local language, intensive language training before going into the field is a necessity. If a particular language is not taught anywhere in the anthropologist's home country, intensive language study should be started on arrival in the country where the research will be done. Even with language training in advance, cultural anthropologists often find

that they need to learn the local version of the more standardized language they studied in a classroom. Many cultural anthropologists rely on help from a local interpreter.

THINKING OUTSIDE THE BOX

WHAT RESEARCH projects in anthropology are funded at your university?

Working in the Field

Fieldwork in cultural anthropology is a difficult and long process that involves the researcher coming to terms with an unfamiliar culture. The anthropologist attempts to

---

Ethnographic Profile

The Trobriand Islanders of Papua New Guinea

The Trobriand Islands are named after eighteenth-century French explorer Denis de Trobriand. They include 22 flat coral atolls east of the island of New Guinea. The indigenous Trobriand population lives on four main islands. Kiriwina is by far the most populated, with roughly 28 000 people (digim'Rina, personal communication 2006). The Papua New Guinea (PNG) district office and an airstrip are located on Kiriwina at Losuia.

The islands were first colonized by Britain and then ceded to Australia in 1904 (Lawton 1987; Weiner 1988). The British attempted to stop local warfare and change many other aspects of Trobriand culture. Christian missionaries introduced the game of cricket as a substitute for warfare (see Chapter 13 on expressive culture for further discussion). In 1943, Allied troops landed as part of their Pacific operations. In 1975, the islands became part of the state of Papua New Guinea.

Island-to-island cultural differences exist. Even within one island population, people may speak different dialects, although everyone speaks a version of the language called Kilivila (Weiner 1988). The Trobrianders grow much of their own food, including root crops such as yams, sweet potatoes, and taro; beans and squash; and bananas, breadfruit, coconuts, and betel nut. Pigs are the main animal raised for food and as prestige items. In the later part of the twentieth century, Trobrianders were increasingly dependent on money sent to them by relatives working elsewhere in PNG. Current development projects are encouraging people to plant more fruit trees, such as mango (digim'Rina 2005).

Kinship emphasizes the female line, meaning that mothers and daughters form the core of co-residential groups. Fathers, while not co-residential, are nonetheless important family members and spend as much time at child care as women do (Weiner 1988). Fathers of political status give their babies and children, both boys and girls, highly valued shell earrings and necklaces to wear. Mothers give daughters prized red skirts. Trobriand children attend Western-style schools on the islands, and many go to mainland PNG and beyond for further studies.

Today, elders worry that young people do nothing but dream about money and fail to care for the heritage of their ancestors. Another concern is that the coral reefs are being endangered by commercial overfishing.

Readings

Shirley F. Campbell. *The Art of Kula*. New York: Berg, 2002.
Bronislaw Malinowski. *Argonauts of the Western Pacific*. New York: E. P. Dutton & Co. 1961 [1922].
Linus S. digim'Rina. "Food Security through Traditions: Replanting Trees and Wise Practices." *People and Culture in Oceania, 20*, 13–36, 2005.
Annette B. Weiner. *The Trobrianders of Papua New Guinea*. New York: Holt, Rinehart and Winston, 1988.

Video

The Trobriand Islanders of Papua New Guinea (Disappearing World, 1990).

Website

Promotion of Indigenous Wise Practices: Food Security, Trobriand Islands, Milne Bay Province, Papua New Guinea, www.unesco.org.

Thanks to Linus S. digim'Rina, University of Papua New Guinea, and Robert Foster, University of Rochester, for reviewing this material.

TROBRIAND ISLANDS

Trobriand men's coveted trade goods include this shell necklace and armlet (left). ■ (Source: Irven Devore/AnthroPhoto) *A Trobriand girl wears a valued skirt at a dance in honour of the ancestors on Kiriwina Island. She and other female participants coat their skin with coconut oil and herbs and wear decorative flowers (right).* ■ (Source: © Albrecht G. Schaefer/CORBIS)

MAP 2.1 *Trobriand Islands of Papua New Guinea. Also known as the Kiriwina Islands, these islands are an archipelago of coral atolls lying off the eastern coast of the island of New Guinea.*

learn the language of the people, live as they do, understand their lives, and be a friend. Before embarking on those activities, the project needs a site (or sites) and the anthropologist needs a place to live.

Site Selection

A research *site* is the place where the research takes place, and sometimes a project involves more than one site. The researcher often has a basic idea of the area where the fieldwork will occur—for example, a *favela* (shanty town) in Rio de Janeiro or a village in Scotland—but it is difficult to know exactly where the project will be located until after arriving.

Selecting a research site depends on many factors. For example, it may be necessary to find a large village if the project involves looking at social class differences in work patterns and food consumption, or a clinic if the study concerns health-care behaviour. Locating a place where the people welcome the researcher and the project, that offers adequate housing, and that fits the requirements of the project may not be easy.

Jennifer Robertson's (1991) selection of Kodaira as a research site in Japan for her study of urban residents and immigrants (see Map 2.2 on page 42), was based on a combination of good advice from a Japanese colleague available housing, a match with her research interests, and the happy coincidence that she already knew the area:

> I spent my childhood and early teens in Kodaira [but] my personal past did not directly influence my selection of Kodaira as a fieldsite and home. . . . A colleague, Matsumura Mitsuo of the Institute for Areal Studies in Tokyo, suggested that the Mutashine region in central Tokyo prefecture would be an ideal locus for a historical anthropological study of village-making (mura-zakuri), the substance of my initial research proposal. That I wound up living in my old neighborhood in Kodaira was determined more by the availability of a suitable apartment than by a nostalgic curiosity about my childhood haunts. As it turned out, I could not have landed at a better place at a better time. (1991:6)

Gaining Rapport

Rapport is a trusting relationship between the researcher and the study population. In the early stages of research, the primary goal is to establish rapport, probably first with key leaders or decision-makers in the community who may serve as *gatekeepers* (people who formally or informally control access to human or material resources to the group or community). Gaining rapport involves trust on the part of the study population, and their trust depends on how the researcher presents herself or

Jennifer Robertson (far left) celebrates the publication of her book, *Native and Newcomer* (1991), with several administrators from Kodaira City Hall. This informal gathering at a local restaurant followed a formal ceremony at the City Hall, where Robertson presented her book to the mayor of Kodaira, an event covered by city and regional newspapers. ■ (Source: Jennifer Robertson)

himself. In many cultures, local people will have difficulty understanding why a person would come to "study" them, since they may not know about universities and research and cultural anthropology. They may provide their own often inaccurate explanations, based on previous experience with outsiders whose goals differed from those of cultural anthropologists, such as tax collectors, missionaries, family-planning promoters, and law-enforcement officials.

Much has been written about the problem of how the anthropologist presents herself or himself in the field and how the local people interpret "who" the anthropologist is and why the anthropologist is there at all. Stories about such role assignments can be humorous. Richard Kurin (1980) reports that in the earliest stage of his research among the Karan in the Punjab region of northwest Pakistan, the villagers thought he was a spy—from the United States, Russia, India, or China. After he convinced them that he was not a spy, the villagers came up with several other acceptable roles for him—first as a "teacher" of English because he was tutoring one of the village boys, then as a "doctor" because he was known

rapport: a trusting relationship between the researcher and the study population.

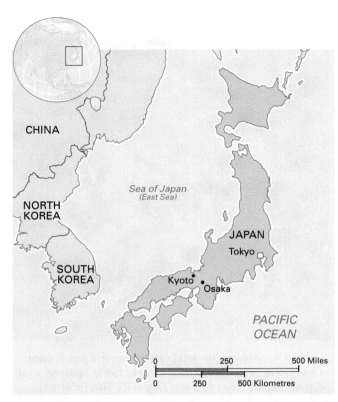

MAP 2.2 **Japan.** The State of Japan, or Nihon-koku or Nippon-koku, encompasses over 3000 islands, most of which are mountainous. Its population is nearly 129 million. Greater Tokyo, with over 30 million residents, is the largest metropolitan area in the world. Japan has one of the world's largest economies.

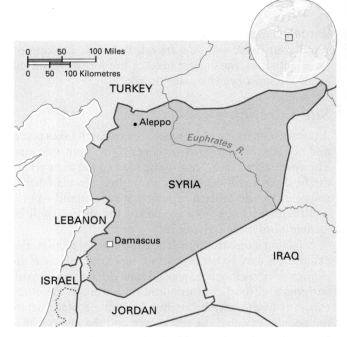

MAP 2.3 **Syria.** The Syrian Arabic Republic historically included the present-day territories of Lebanon, Israel, the Palestinian Territories, and parts of Jordan, but not the Jazira region in Syria's northeast. The country's population is 19 million. Syria's capital city, Damascus, with a population of 3 million, is one of the oldest continually occupied cities in the world.

to dispense Aspirin, then as a "lawyer" who could help villagers in negotiating local disputes because he could read court orders. Jean Briggs was adopted as a daughter in an Inuit community in the Canadian Arctic. Briggs's new role raised problems, in that she lost her outsider status, suffered a depletion of her supplies, and no longer had privacy.

Being labelled a spy is still a serious issue for anthropologists. Many people worldwide have no concept of what a cultural anthropologist is and why a person would want to, or be able to, spend a year or more living with them and learning about their everyday lives. Christa Salamandra, a Western-trained doctoral student in anthropology, went to Damascus, Syria (see Map 2.3), for her dissertation research (2004). Damascus is a city with a long history and is increasingly cosmopolitan. Damascenes, however, have little exposure to anthropology. Syria has no university with a department of anthropology, and there are no Syrian anthropologists. Salamandra's research interests in popular culture (movies, cafés, and fashion) perplexed the Damascenese, who decided she must be a spy. One person said to her, "Your question is CIA, not academic" (2004:5).

Gift Giving and Exchange

Giving gifts to local people can help the project proceed, and they are sometimes an expected part of exchange relationships in the culture. Gifts should be culturally and ethically appropriate. Many cultural anthropologists working in developing countries have provided basic medical care, such as wound dressing, as a regular part of their interactions. Some have taught in the local school part-time. Others have helped support individuals in obtaining a higher education degree outside their homelands.

Learning the local rules of exchange is important, including what constitutes an appropriate or inappropriate gift, how to deliver the gift (timing, in private or public, wrapped or unwrapped), and how to behave as a gift giver (for example, should one be modest and emphasize the smallness of the gift?).

Richard Lee, who conducted fieldwork among the !Kung San Bushmen (Ju/wasi), wrote on the complexities of gift giving and reciprocity. After a year in the field, he used the custom of slaughtering a huge, fat ox at Christmas to partially repay the community for their hospitality. Because of the disparity between his inventory of canned food and the Bushmen's scant supplies of food, he fell open to accusations of being stingy, a hard-hearted miser:

> As I read it, their message was this: There are no totally generous acts. All "acts" have an element of calculation. One black ox slaughtered at Christmas does not wipe out a year of careful manipulation of gifts given to serve your own ends. After all, to kill an animal and share the meat with people is really no more than Bushmen do for each other every day and with far less fanfare. (Lee 1969:29)

Factors Influencing Fieldwork

An anthropologist's class, race, gender, and age all affect how he or she will be interpreted by local people. An anthropologist who is a young, unmarried female studying child-rearing practices may not be taken seriously since she is not herself a mother. In the rest of this section, we offer some examples of how class, race/ethnicity, gender, age, and other factors can influence the rapport an anthropologist is able to achieve with the population.

Class In most fieldwork situations, the anthropologist is more wealthy and powerful than the people studied. This difference is obvious to the people. They know that the anthropologist may have spent hundreds or thousands of dollars on education and travel to the research site. They see the expensive equipment (camera, tape recorder, video recorder, even a vehicle) and valuable trade items (stainless steel knives, cigarettes, flashlights, canned food, medicines). This class difference affects how people in the field relate to the researcher. When Ernestine Friedl (1986) and her husband did fieldwork in a Greek village, their status as "professors" influenced people's behaviour. Village men would refrain from telling sexual jokes or swearing when they were present (213).

Laura Nader urged that anthropologists should also "study up" by doing research among powerful people such as members of the business elite, political leaders, and government officials (1972). As one example of this approach, research on the high-fashion industry of Japan placed the anthropologist, Dorinne Kondo, in touch with members of the Japanese elite—influential people capable of taking her to court if they felt she wrote something defamatory about them (1997). "Studying up" has contributed to awareness of the need, in all fieldwork situations, for recognition of the anthropologist's accountability to the people being studied.

Race/Ethnicity For most of its history, cultural anthropology has been dominated by Euro-American white researchers who have studied "other" cultures, most often non-white and non-Euro-American. The effects of "whiteness" on role assignments range from the anthropologist being labelled as a god or ancestor spirit to his or her being reviled as a representative of a colonialist past. While doing research in Jamaica, Tony Whitehead (1986) learned how race and status interact. For Whitehead, an African American, being essentially the same "race"—of African descent—did not automatically create solidarity between him and the African-descent residents of Haversham, Jamaica. The people of Haversham have a complex status system that relegated Whitehead to a higher social status position that he did not predict. Similarly, David Murray working in Martinique recognized that his "presence as a 'white' man may have censured the expression of other beliefs, feelings or opinions among both gay and straight Martinican men as the white/black racial dyad has a major structuring influence on Martinican social life" (Murray 2002:12).

Gender If a female researcher is young and unmarried, she is likely to face more difficulties than a young unmarried man or an older woman, married or single, because people in most cultures consider a young unmarried female on her own as extremely unusual. Rules of gender segregation may dictate that a young unmarried woman should not move about freely without a male escort, and her status may prevent her from attending certain events or being in some places. Gender boundaries exist cross-culturally to varying degrees, and a researcher probably can never fully overcome them. A woman researcher who studied a secretive male gay community in the United States comments,

> I was able to do fieldwork in those parts of the setting dedicated to sociability and leisure—bars, parties, family gatherings. I was not, however, able to observe in those parts of the setting dedicated to sexuality—even quasi-public settings such as homosexual bath houses. . . . Thus my portrait of the gay community is only a partial one, bounded by the social roles assigned to females within the male homosexual world. (Warren 1988:18)

Gender segregation limits male researchers from gaining access to a full a range of activities as well, especially in the domestic domain. In an unusual study, Liza Dalby (1983) lived with the geishas of Kyoto, Japan, and trained to be a geisha. Through this, she learned more about the inner workings of this local culture than a man ever could.

Age Typically, adult anthropologists are responsible for studying people in all age categories. Although some children and adolescents readily welcome the participation

Liza Dalby in full geisha formal dress in the person of Ichigiku. ■ (Source: Liza Dalby)

of a friendly adult in their daily lives and respond to questions openly, others are much more tentative. Margaret Mead (1986) commented that "ideally, a three-generation family, including children highly trained to understand what they experience, would be the best way to study a culture" (321). She recognized that each age category has its own cultural rules and age-specific language, and needs to be studied on its own terms. Although Mead paid a great deal of attention to children and adolescents, few contemporary anthropologists consider children except in discussions of the family and motherhood. Recently, a number of Canadian anthropologists explored the complexity of children's lives, including the media depiction of children, the intimacy of children's play, and the cultural politics revealed in postwar parliamentary debates about family allowances and "the right kind of children"

(Helleiner 2001). Virginia Caputo (2001) studied children's musical practices in Toronto and showed how their play allowed them to resist adult definitions of childhood. When Pamela Downe asked children to choose a research name for themselves, she learned about how important names are to children's identity. Seven-year-old Kizzy from Bridgetown, Barbados, explains, "Sometimes I feel very tiny . . . Like I [could] fit in a thimble, like the tooth fairy— but all's I gotta do is imagine someone calling my name and I be feeling big again. That is why I like thinking about what name you should call me in your notes" (Downe 2001:167).

Ethnographies of children also demonstrate how clichés like "the innocent child" mask differences among children according to age, gender, race, class, and location.

Other Factors   The fieldworker's role is affected by many more factors than the characteristics listed above, including language, dress, and religion. Being the same religion as the elderly Jewish people at the Aliyah Center in California helped Barbara Myerhoff (1978) in establishing rapport in her first meeting with the members there. This is evident in her conversation with one elderly woman named Basha:

> "So, what brings you here?"
> "I'm from the University of Southern California. I'm looking for a place to study how older Jews live in the city." At the word *university*, she moved closer and nodded approvingly. "Are you Jewish?" she asked.
> "Yes, I am."
> "Are you married?" she persisted.
> "Yes."
> "You got children?"
> "Yes, two boys, [ages] four and eight," I answered.
> "Are you teaching them to be Jews?" (14)

Myerhoff was warmly accepted into the lives of people at the Aliyah Center, and her plan for one year of research grew into a long-standing relationship.

In a study of women who were denied the *get*, or Jewish divorce document, Lisa Rosenberg (1996) was aware that although she was a Jewish woman, as a non-Orthodox woman she might be perceived as an outsider by those within the Orthodox community. She was often subject to scrutiny that was, at times, quite overt. More than once she was asked, "What synagogue do you belong to?" It was also common for

---

culture shock: persistent feelings of uneasiness, loneliness, and anxiety that often occur when a person has shifted from one culture to a different one.

deductive approach (to research): a research method that involves posing a research question or hypothesis, gathering the empirical data related to the question, and then assessing the findings in relation to the original hypothesis.

inductive approach (to research): a research approach that avoids hypothesis formation in advance of the research and instead takes its lead from the culture being studied.

her to have to speak about her Jewish education and her knowledge of Jewish law.

Culture Shock

Culture shock consists of persistent feelings of uneasiness, loneliness, and anxiety that often occur when a person has shifted from one culture to a different one. The more "different" the two cultures are, the more severe the shock is likely to be. Culture shock happens to many cultural anthropologists, no matter how much they have tried to prepare themselves for the field. Culture shock can happen to students who study abroad, overseas volunteers (CUSO, WUSC), or anyone who spends a significant amount of time living and participating in another culture. It can range from problems with food to the language barrier. Food differences were a major adjustment problem for a Chinese anthropologist who came to the United States (Shu-Min 1993)—the food there never gave him a "full" feeling.

One psychological aspect of culture shock is the feeling of reduced competence as a cultural actor. At home, the anthropologist is highly competent. Everyday tasks like shopping, talking with other people, mailing a letter, or sending an email can be done without thinking. In a new culture, the most simple task becomes difficult and one's sense of self-efficacy is undermined. In extreme cases, an anthropologist may have to abandon a project because of an inability to adapt to the fieldwork situation. For most, however, culture shock is a temporary affliction that subsides as the person becomes more familiar with the new culture.

Reverse culture shock can occur on returning home. Alan Beals (1980) describes his feelings on returning to San Francisco after a year of fieldwork in a village in India:

> We could not understand why people were so distant and hard to reach, or why they talked and moved so quickly. We were a little frightened at the sight of so many white faces and we could not understand why no one stared at us, brushed against us, or admired our baby.
>
> We could not understand the gabble of voices on the television set. When we could understand people, they seemed to be telling lies. The trust and warmth seemed to have gone out of life to be replaced by coldness and inhumanity. People seemed to have no contact with reality. All of the natural human processes—eating, sleeping together, quarreling, even playing—seemed to be divorced from earth and flesh. Nowhere could we hear the soft lowing of cattle or the distant piping of the shepherd boy. (119)

Fieldwork Techniques

The goal of fieldwork is to collect *data*, or information, about the research topic. In cultural anthropology, variations exist about what kinds of data to emphasize and the best ways to collect data.

Deductive and Inductive Research Approaches

A **deductive approach** is a form of research that starts from a research question or *hypothesis*, and then involves collecting data related to the question through observation, interviews, and other methods. An **inductive approach** is a form of research that proceeds without a hypothesis and involves gathering data through

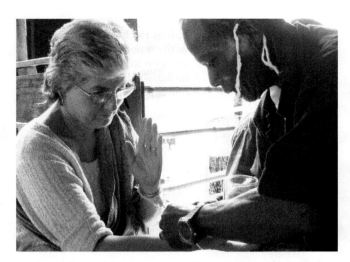

Anthropologist Penny Van Esterik participates in a "spirit calling" ceremony in northern Laos. ■ (Source: John Van Esterik)

unstructured, informal observation, conversation, and other methods. Deductive methods are more likely to collect **quantitative data**, or numeric information, such as the amount of land in relation to the population or numbers of people with particular health problems. The inductive approach in cultural anthropology tends to avoid quantitative data and emphasizes **qualitative data**, or nonnumeric information, such as recordings of myths, conversations, and filming of events. Most anthropologists, however, operate somewhere between these two extremes, combining deductive and inductive approaches and quantitative and qualitative data.

Cultural anthropologists have labels for data collected in each approach. **Etic** (pronounced like the last two syllables of *phonetic*) refers to data collected according to the researcher's questions and categories, with the goal of being able to test a hypothesis. In contrast, **emic** (pronounced like the last two syllables of *phonemic*) refers to data collected that reflect what insiders say and understand about their culture, and insiders' categories of thinking.

Participant Observation

Most cultural anthropologists will tell you that participant observation is essential in order to learn about a culture.

The phrase *participant observation* includes two processes: *participating*, or being part of the people's lives, while carefully *observing*. These two activities may sound simple, but they are actually quite complex.

Being a participant means that the researcher adopts the lifestyle of the people being studied, living in the same kind of housing, eating similar food, wearing similar clothing, learning the language, and participating in the daily round of activities and in special events. The rationale is that participation over a long period improves the quality of the data. The more time the researcher spends living among the people, the more likely it is that the people will live their "normal" lives. In this way, the researcher is able to overcome the **Hawthorne effect**, a research bias that occurs when participants change their behaviour to conform to the perceived expectations of the researcher. The Hawthorne effect was discovered in the 1930s during a study of an industrial plant in the United States. During the study, research participants altered their behaviour in ways they thought would please the researcher.

Although participant observation is often equated with the casual term "hanging out," in fact, it means constant choices about where to be on a particular day at a particular time, what one observes, with whom, and what, by default, one misses. Depending on the research topic, participant observation may focus on who lives with whom, who interacts with whom in public, who are leaders and who are followers, what work people do, how people organize themselves for different activities, rituals, arguments, festivals, funerals, and far more.

No matter how well accepted into everyday life the anthropologist becomes, however, the very nature of anthropological research and the presence of the anthropologist will have an effect on the people involved. Since the 1980s, anthropologists have increasingly considered how their presence affects their fieldwork and their findings, an approach called reflexive anthropology or reflexivity. An emphasis on reflexivity involves "constant awareness, assessment, and reassessment by the researcher of the researcher's own contribution [to and] influence [on] intersubjective research and the consequent research findings" (Salzman 2002:806). This approach is a good corrective for the assumption that an anthropologist can go to the field and conduct research

---

quantitative data: research that emphasizes gathering and analyzing numeric information and using tables and charts when presenting results.
qualitative data: research that emphasizes generating descriptive information.
etic: an analytical framework used by outside analysts in studying culture.

emic: what insiders do and perceive about their culture, their perceptions of reality, and their explanations for why they do what they do.
Hawthorne effect: research bias due to participants changing their behaviour to conform to expectations of the researcher.

interview: a research technique that involves gathering of verbal data through questions or guided conversation between at least two people.
questionnaire: a formal research instrument containing a pre-set series of questions that the anthropologist asks in a face-to-face setting, by mail, or by email.

just as a scientist can in a lab. Working closely with real people in their everyday lives is a highly interactive and mutually influencing process: Everyone is changed in some way through the anthropological enterprise because it is a social process itself.

Talking with People

Common sense tells you that participating and observing are important, but what about talking to people and asking questions, such as, "What is going on here?" "What does that mean?" "Why are you doing that?" The process of talking to people and asking them questions is such an important third component of participant observation that the method should actually be called *participant observation and talking*. Cultural anthropologists use a variety of data-collection techniques that rely on talking with people, from informal, casual, and unplanned conversations to more formal methods.

An **interview** is a technique for gathering verbal data through questions or guided conversation. It is more purposeful than a casual conversation. An interview may involve only two people, the interviewer and the interviewee, or several people in what are called *group interviews* or *focus groups*. Cultural anthropologists use varying interview styles and formats, depending on the kinds of information they seek, the amount of time they have, and their language skills. The least structured type of interview is an *open-ended interview*, in which the respondent (interviewee) takes the lead in setting the direction of the conversation, topics to be covered, and the amount of time devoted to a particular topic. The interviewer does not interrupt or provide prompting questions. In this way, the researcher discovers what themes are important to the person.

A **questionnaire** is a formal research instrument containing a pre-set series of questions that the anthropologist asks in a face-to-face setting, or by mail or email. Cultural anthropologists who use questionnaires usually favour a face-to-face setting. Like interviews, questionnaires vary in the degree to which the questions are *structured* (close-ended) or *unstructured* (open-ended). Structured questions limit the range of possible responses—for example, by asking research participants to rate their positions on a particular issue as "very positive," "positive," "negative," "very negative," or "no opinion." Unstructured interviews generate more emic responses.

When designing a questionnaire, the researcher should have enough familiarity with the study population to be able to design questions that make cultural sense (Fitchen 1990). Researchers who take a ready-made questionnaire to the field with them should ask another researcher who knows the field area to review it in advance to see

Marjorie Shostak (right) during fieldwork among the Ju/wasi of Botswana in 1975. Shostak focused her research on women's lives and wrote about Nisa, a Ju/wasi woman. ■ (Source: © Mel Konner/AnthroPhoto)

whether it makes cultural sense. Further revisions may be required in the field to make the questionnaire fit local conditions. A *pilot study* using the questionnaire among a small number of people in the research area can expose areas that need further revision.

Combining Observation and Talking

Many cultural anthropologists agree that formal interviews and questionnaires must be complemented by observational data on what people actually do (Sanjek 2000). Consider this example of a study that relied on interview data alone to examine the relationship between personal characteristics and participation in a fishing cooperative in Newfoundland and Labrador (Jentoft and Davis 1993). The Canadian and Norwegian researchers conducted formal interviews with a questionnaire among 51 members of the fishing cooperative. Questions probed such issues as whether members were willing to donate their time to cooperative projects, and what they valued most about the cooperative. On the basis of their responses, the researchers categorized the members into two basic groups: "rugged individualists" and "utilitarians." The people in the first group tended to be older and less educated than those in the latter group. According to the questionnaire responses, the rugged individualists were more willing to donate time to cooperative activities compared to the utilitarians. Since observational studies were not conducted, however, there is no way to know whether the respondents' self-reported participation in the cooperative corresponded to their actual involvement. Other research on the Canadian fishing industry examines the discourse of fishing. Adlam's study of "fish talk" among Mi'kmaq fishers of the Miramichi River, New Brunswick (2002), contrasts the traditionalist with the modernist conception of the rapidly changing fishing economy.

Specialized Methods

Cultural anthropologists also use a variety of more specific research methods. The choice depends on the anthropologist's research goals.

Life History   A *life history* is a qualitative, in-depth description of an individual's life as narrated to the researcher. Anthropologists differ in their views about the value of the life history as a method in cultural anthropology. Early in the twentieth century, Franz Boas rejected this method as unscientific because research participants might lie or exaggerate (Peacock and Holland 1993). Others disagree, saying that a life history reveals rich information on individuals and how they think, no matter how "distorted" their reports are. For example, some anthropologists have questioned the accuracy of parts of *Nisa: The Life and Times of a !Kung Woman* (Shostak 1981), probably the most widely read life history in anthropology. It is a book-length story of a Ju/'hoansi woman of the Kalahari Desert of southern Africa (review the Ethnographic Profile on page 22 in Chapter 1). Presented in Nisa's voice, it includes rich details about her childhood and several marriages. The value of the narrative is not so much whether it is all "true" or not; rather, the value is that we learn from Nisa what she wants to tell us, her cultural construction of her experiences. That counts as "data" in cultural anthropology, for it is "truly" what she reported to Marjorie Shostak.

In the early days of life history research, anthropologists tried to choose an individual who was somehow typical, average, or representative. It is not possible, however, to find one person who is representative of an entire culture in the scientific sense. Instead, anthropologists now seek individuals who occupy particularly interesting social niches. For example, Gananath Obeyesekere (pronounced Oh-baya-SEKa-ra) wrote a book, *Medusa's Hair: An Essay on Personal Symbols and Religious Experience* (1981), which presents the life histories of four Sri Lankan people—three women and one man. Each became a Hindu religious devotee and ascetic, distinguished by their thickly matted hair, twisted into coils like a snake. Their snaky hair is permanently matted and

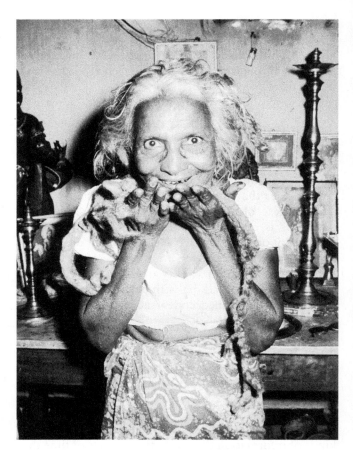

One of the Sri Lankan women whose life story Gananath Obeyesekere analyzed, a priestess to the deity Kataragama, stands in the shrine room of her house holding her long, matted hair. ■ (Source: Gananath Obeyesekere)

impossible to comb. According to the devotees, a deity is present in their matted hair. Analyzing the four life histories, Obeyesekere suggests that all four people had suffered deep psychological afflictions, including sexual anxieties. Their matted hair symbolizes their suffering and provides them with a special status as holy, thus beyond the rules of married life and conjugal sexual relations.

Life histories of several people in a similar situation can reveal both individual experiences and shared patterns. James Freeman's book, *Hearts of Sorrow* (1989), is an example of this approach with attention to refugees. It presents short "cuts" from several life stories of Vietnamese refugees living in southern California. These "cuts" portray a range of adaptive individual experiences and the overarching theme of sadness of all the refugees about the loss of their homeland.

triangulation: research technique that involves obtaining information on a particular topic from more than one person or perspective.

The ability of people to present a story of their lives varies, depending on the cultural context. An attempt to gather life histories from women on Goodenough Island, Papua New Guinea (see Map 1.4 on page 18), was difficult because telling one's life story is a masculine style of presentation, and the women were reluctant to adopt it (Young 1983). Marjorie Shostak, in contrast, found a willing and extremely expressive narrator in Nisa (1981).

Time Allocation Study   A *time allocation study* is a quantitative method that collects data on how people spend their time each day on particular activities. This method relies on standard time units as the basic matrix and then labelling or coding the activities that occur within certain time segments (Gross 1984). Activity codes must be adapted to fit local contexts. For example, activity codes for various kinds of work would not be useful in a time allocation study in a retirement home. Data can be collected through observation that may be continuous, at fixed intervals (for instance, every 48 hours), or on a random basis. Continuous observation is extremely time-consuming and means that the number of people observed is limited. Spot observations help increase the number of observations but may inadvertently miss important activities. Another option for data collection is to ask people to keep daily time logs or diaries.

Texts   Many cultural anthropologists collect *textual material*, a category that includes written or oral stories, myths, plays, sayings, speeches, jokes, and transcriptions of people's everyday conversations. In the early twentieth century, Franz Boas collected thousands of pages of texts from Aboriginal groups on British Columbia's coast; these included myths, songs, speeches, and accounts of how to perform rituals. The collections provide valuable records of cultures that have changed since the time of Boas's fieldwork. Surviving tribal members have consulted them in order to recover forgotten aspects of their culture.

Archival and Historical Sources   Many cultural anthropologists who work in cultures with a written history gain important insights about the present from records of the past preserved in archives maintained in institutions such as libraries, churches, and museums. Ann Stoler (1985, 1989) made excellent use of archival resources in her study of Dutch colonialism in Java. Her research has exposed rich details about colonial strategies, the culture of the colonizers themselves, and their impact on indigenous Javanese culture. Most countries have libraries and historical archives in which written records of the past are maintained. Local official archives are rich sources of information about land ownership, agricultural production, religious practices, and political activities. London, Paris, and Amsterdam contain records of colonial contact and relations.

The National Archives of Canada, provincial archives, and mission reports provided valuable evidence on the development of residential schools for Native peoples in Canada (D. Smith 2001). Meticulous record keeping in France meant that Harriet Rosenberg (1988) had access to information about dowries, wills, marriage contracts, court cases, land survey registers, tax rolls, and family histories for reconstructing the history of a village in the French Alps.

Important information about the past can also come from fieldwork among living people through an approach called the *anthropology of memory*. Anthropologists study patterns of what people remember and what they don't, how culture shapes their memories, and how their memories shape their culture. Information on how memory is shaped exists in collections of letters, diaries, and family photograph albums. The importance of memory, not simply as a record of history but as interpretive reconstruction, is increasing in anthropology (Antze and Lambek 1996) and in the public domain.

Multiple Research Methods and Team Projects
Most cultural anthropologists use several different methods for their research because just one would not provide all the varieties of data necessary to understand a given topic. For example, consider what interviews with people in 100 households would provide in terms of breadth of coverage, and then add what you could learn from life histories collected from a subset of five men and five women to provide depth.

Another way to add richness is the use of **triangulation**, a technique that involves seeking information on a particular topic from more than one angle or perspective (Robson 1993:290). Asking only one person provides information from only that person's viewpoint. Asking two people about the same thing doubles the information and often reveals that perspectives differ. The researcher may then want to check other sources, such as written records or newspaper reports, for additional perspectives.

In Canada, team research may also involve several anthropologists and students working together with members of First Nations communities to document land claims or to assess the consequences of new hydroelectric development projects for their communities. The James Bay Cree Project, which began in 1971 at McGill University in Montréal, trained graduate students in anthropology to do research for local agencies representing indigenous groups, providing information useful in settling the James Bay land claim (Trigger 1997; Salisbury 1986). (See the Lessons Applied box on page 50 for another example of team research in Canada.)

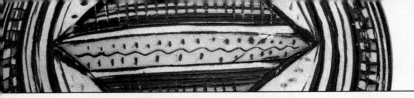

Lessons Applied

MULTIPLE METHODS IN A NEEDS-ASSESSMENT STUDY

The United Way of Canada, a philanthropic agency, wanted to find out what the highest priorities were for their funding operations in Saskatoon, Saskatchewan (Ervin et al. 1991). Alexander Ervin put together a team of faculty and student researchers from the University of Saskatchewan's Department of Anthropology and Archaeology to respond to the United Way's request. At the time of the study in 1990, the city's population was about 200 000. The area's economy is based on agriculture, mining, forestry, and some manufacturing, with an unemployment rate of roughly 10 percent. In recent years, the city's population had grown substantially, including more First Nations people. Unemployment rates were among the highest in Canada and income levels the lowest. Food banks and soup kitchens were increasingly important for the many unemployed people.

Members of Ervin's team decided that they needed data about perceived needs of the people of Saskatoon, including the unemployed and poor as well as employed professionals, including people who worked for the sponsoring agency, the United Way. Data collection included several activities:

- Reviewing available written reports relevant to Saskatoon's needs
- Analyzing economic and social indicators
- Conducting 135 interviews with key people from community agencies
- Organizing three public forums bringing together city residents and United Way board members
- Interviewing United Way agency executive directors

Information from these data-gathering activities provided breadth and depth about community needs and opinions as well as agency priorities and interests.

The research team produced a report that included a list of over 200 identified needs. It organized this extensive list into 17 sectors, including general health, mental health, the senior population, First Nations issues, racism and discrimination, and immigrant and refugee resettlement. One of the most pressing community needs involves eliminating hunger, especially among children. The report recommended the provision of more food banks and attention to preventive health care for children. Another high priority is improving access to public transportation for economically disadvantaged people and for the elderly. The research revealed the need for better communication among nonprofit organizations in the city that seek to improve living standards. The report suggested that the United Way take a stronger role in being an advocate for disadvantaged people rather than focusing on fundraising.

FOOD FOR THOUGHT

- Conducting a community-needs assessment requires a different research approach from traditional fieldwork in cultural anthropology. What are some of the pros and cons of such applied research?

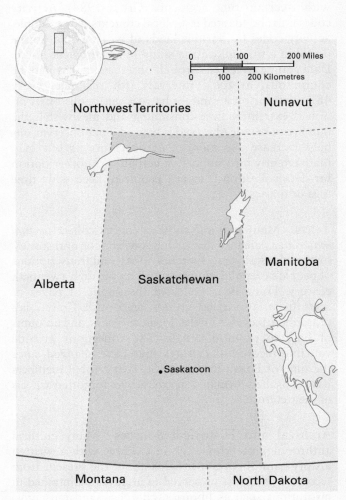

MAP 2.4   Saskatoon, Saskatchewan. Saskatoon is the largest city in Saskatchewan—a province with a population of over 200 000. After an economic slump in the 1980s and 1990s, it launched several new industrial parks in 2005. Corporate headquarters of industries involved in uranium and potash are located in Saskatoon. Food processing and information technology are important sources of employment.

Another way of gaining a more complex and complete view is through team projects that involve cultural anthropologists and researchers from other disciplines who provide additional skills. A research project designed to assess the effects of constructing a dam on the agricultural and fishing practices of people in the Senegal River Valley, West Africa, included cultural anthropologists, hydrologists, and agronomists (Horowitz and Salem-Murdock 1993). In another project, a cultural anthropologist and a nutritionist worked together to study the effects of adopting new agricultural practices in the Amazon (Gross and Underwood 1971).

Recording Culture

How does an anthropologist keep track of all the information collected in the field and record it for future analysis? As with everything else about fieldwork, things have changed since the early days when a notebook and typewriter were the major recording tools. Yet, there is continuity, in that taking notes is still the trademark method of recording data for a cultural anthropologist.

Field Notes

Field notes include daily logs, personal journals, descriptions of events, and notes about those notes. Ideally, researchers should write up their field notes each day.

A multidisciplinary team consisting of anthropologists, engineers, and agricultural experts from North America and Senegal meet to discuss a resettlement project.
■ (Source: Michael Horowitz)

Otherwise, a backlog accumulates of daily "scratch notes," or rough jottings made on a small pad or note cards (Sanjek 1990a:95–99). Trying to capture, in the fullest way possible, the events of even a single day is a monumental task and can result in dozens of pages of handwritten or typed field notes. Laptop computers now enable anthropologists to enter many of their daily observations directly into a database.

Tape Recording, Photography, Videos, and Films

Tape recorders are a major aid to fieldwork. Their use may raise problems, however, such as research participants' suspicions about a machine that can capture their voices, and the ethical issue of protecting the identity of people whose voices are preserved on tape.

In order to be useful for analysis, tape recordings have to be transcribed (typed up), either partially or completely. Each hour of recorded talk takes between five and eight hours to transcribe.

Like tape recordings, photographs, films, or videos may catch and retain more detail than rough notes. Any researcher who has watched people doing a ritual, taken rough notes, and then tried to reconstruct the details of the ritual later on in more detailed field notes knows how much of the sequencing and related activity is lost to memory within just a few hours. Reviewing photographs or a video recording of the ritual provides a surprising amount of forgotten, or missed, material. But there is a trade-off. Using a camera or video recorder precludes taking notes simultaneously. Since field notes are invaluable, even if the video is also available, it is best to use a team approach. Kirsten Hastrup (1992) provides an insightful description of her use of photography—and its limitations—in recording the annual ram exhibition in Iceland (see Map 2.5 on page 52) that celebrates the successful herding in of the sheep from mountain pastures. Hastrup took many photographs. After they were developed, she was struck by how flat they were and how little of the totality of the event they conveyed. Photographs and films, just like field notes and other forms of recorded culture, provide only partial images of a cultural event.

Rosalind Morris (1994a) examined ethnographic films of the Northwest Coast of Canada. From the earliest films made of the Northwest Coast (1914), the Kwakwaka'wakw, Nootka, Tsimshian, and Haida, in addition to other First Nations peoples, have been represented by outsiders who made films that drew attention to potlatches, feasts, totem poles, and wood carvings. More recently, films have been made by and for First Nations communities, and they focus more on land-claim disputes and other struggles with provincial

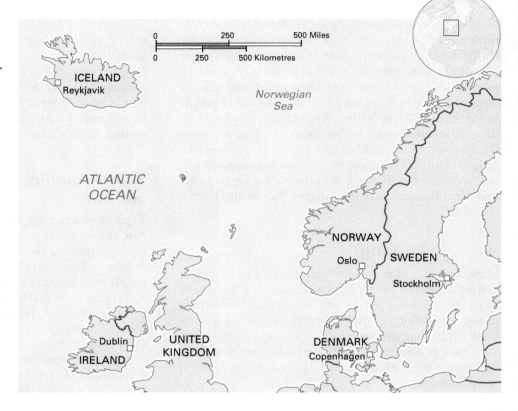

MAP 2.5 Iceland. The Republic of Iceland has a population of 300 000. A volcanic island, Iceland is the fifth richest country in the world, according to GDP (gross domestic product) per capita. It has a high quality of life and ranked second in the 2005 United Nations Human Development Index. Iceland's economy comprises exporting fish and fish products, technology, and tourism.

and federal governments (Morris 1994a:118). Clearly, films are no more objective than any other form of recorded culture since it is the researcher who selects what the camera will capture.

Textbooks in anthropology use illustrations to draw the eyes and interests of students (and to break up the text), to illustrate abstract principles in the discipline, and to provide visual images of the people discussed in the text. Photographs relate to textual arguments in distinctive ways; they may supplement, complement, or even contradict written accounts (see Figure 2.1). They may be arranged in groups to suggest comparison, or juxtaposed in a striking manner to illustrate change. They often document a technical process or a material object that may be unfamiliar to the reader and difficult to describe in words.

Data Analysis

During the research process, a vast amount of data in many forms is collected. The question is how to use these data to increase our understanding of human societies. Ethnographic research mostly entails qualitative, prose-based analysis in combination with quantitative (numeric) data where appropriate. Qualitative data can be rendered in quantitative terms, and reporting on quantitative results necessarily requires descriptive analysis of local conditions to accompany graphs, charts, and computations.

Analyzing Qualitative Data

Qualitative data include descriptive field notes, informants' narratives, myths and stories, and songs and sagas. Relatively few set guidelines exist for undertaking qualitative analysis of qualitative data. One general procedure of qualitative analysis is to search for themes, or regularities, in the data. This approach involves exploring the data, or "playing" with the data, either "by hand" or with the use of a computer. Jennifer Robertson's analysis of her Kodaira data was inspired by author Gertrude Stein's approach to writing "portraits" of individuals, such as *Picasso* (1959). Robertson says that Stein was a superb ethnographer who was able to illuminate the nature of her subjects and their worlds through a process that Stein

THINKING OUTSIDE THE BOX

HAVE YOU ever had the experience of taking photographs of a place, event, or people and then being terribly disappointed because the results did not capture the essence of your experience? What was missing from the photographs? (Do not include discussion of photographs that turned out badly due to technical reasons.)

FIGURE 2.1   Photographs in Anthropology

Photographs may be "worth a thousand words," but they never speak for themselves. Their meanings are shaped by the interaction between the producer of the image, the subject of the image, and the viewer. You may have a personal response to a photograph that is quite unlike the response the photographer intended. For example, the choice of photographs used in this textbook represents a selection of what the authors think is instructive. Even captions draw attention to how you are expected to analyze photographs. Thus, the photograph is never a snapshot of reality, but something that must be interpreted.

To improve your *visual literacy*, consider each of the photographs used in this textbook:

- What questions does the photograph raise for you?
- How might the presence of the camera alter the event recorded in the photo?
- How do you think the community or subject of the photograph would react to the use of the photo in a textbook of anthropology?
- What ethical issues are raised by the use of this photograph?

Select a photograph that illustrates rapport, ethnocentrism, gender inequity, racism, globalization, acculturation, or another concept.

- Suggest an alternative caption for the photograph.
- What does the photograph say about the culture portrayed and the representing culture?

---

called "condensation." To do this, "she scrutinized her subjects until, over time, there emerged for her a repeating pattern of their words and actions. Her literary portraits . . . were condensations of her subjects' repeatings" (Robertson 1991:1). Like Stein, Robertson reflected on all that she had experienced and learned in Kodaira, beginning with the years when she lived there as a child. Emerging from all this was the dominant theme, *furusato*, which literally means "old village." References to *furusato* appear frequently in people's accounts of the past, conveying a sense of nostalgia for a more "real" past.

Many qualitative anthropologists use computers to help sort for *tropes* (key themes). Computer scanning of data offers the ability to search vast quantities of data more quickly and perhaps more accurately than is possible using the human eye. The range of software available for such data management—for example, ETHNO and The Ethnograph—is expanding. Of course, the quality of the results depends on, first, careful and complete inputting of the data and, second, an intelligent coding scheme that will tell the computer what it should be scanning for in the data.

The ethnographic presentation of qualitative data relies heavily on the use of quotations of informants—their stories, explanations, and conversations. Although most ethnographies also include analytical

commentary, some provide just the informants' words. Lila Abu-Lughod followed this approach in her book, *Writing Women's Worlds* (1993). She presents Bedouin women's stories and conversations within a light authorial framework that organizes the stories into thematic clusters such as marriage, production, and honour. Although she provides a rather traditional, scholarly introduction to the narratives, Abu-Lughod offers no conclusion. In her view, a conclusion would give a false sense of authorial control over the narratives. She prefers to prompt readers to think for themselves about the meanings of the stories and what they say about Bedouin life.

Some anthropologists question the value of interpretive analyses because, in their view, they lack verifiability or reliability. Too much depends on the individual selection process of the anthropologist, and too much is built around too few cases. Most anthropologists would respond that verifiability in the scientific sense is not their goal and it is not a worthwhile goal for cultural anthropology in general. Instead, they seek to provide a plausible interpretation, an evocation, or new understanding that has detail and richness as its strengths rather than replicability. They would criticize purely quantitative research for its lack of richness and depth of understanding, even though it has the appearance of validity.

Analyzing Quantitative Data

Analysis of quantitative, or numeric, data can proceed in several directions. Some of the more sophisticated methods require knowledge of statistics, and many require the use of a computer and a software package that can perform statistical computations. In Barbara Miller's (1987a) research on low-income household budgeting patterns in Jamaica, she used computer analysis first to divide the sample households into three income groups (lower, medium, higher). She then used the computer to calculate percentages of expenditures in the three categories on individual goods and groups of goods, such as food, alcohol, dry goods, housing, and transportation (see Table 2.1). Because the number of households in the study was relatively small (120), the analysis could have been done "by hand." However, using the computer helped Miller's analysis proceed more quickly and accurately.

Writing about Culture

Ethnography, or descriptive writing about a culture (defined in Chapter 1), is the main way that cultural anthropologists present their findings about culture. In the early phase of cultural anthropology, in the first half of the twentieth century, ethnographers wrote about "exotic" cultures located far from their homes in Europe and North America. Two classic ethnographies of this period are A. R. Radcliffe-Brown's *The Andaman Islanders* (1964 [1922]), a study of indigenous people living on several islands off the coast of Burma (also known as Myanmar) (see the Ethnographic Profile in Chapter 3 on page 71), and Bronislaw Malinowski's *Argonauts of the Western Pacific* (1961 [1922]), concerning men's trade networks linking several islands in the South Pacific (see the Ethnographic Profile on page 40).

The early ethnographers tended to treat a particular local group or village as a unit unto itself with clear boundaries. Since the 1980s, ethnographies have changed in several ways:

- Ethnographers now treat local cultures as embedded within regional and global structures and forces. For example, Janice Boddy studied female circumcision in colonial Sudan and linked the campaigns against the practice to British political and economic policies. Her book, *Civilizing Women: British Crusades in Colonial Sudan* (2007), explores efforts to end this "barbarous custom." In Edward Fischer's book, *Cultural Logics and Global Economics: Maya Identity in Thought and Practice* (2001), he takes the topic of Mayan political activism in Guatemala as its focus, setting it within the context of changing economic structures, family life, and individual action.

TABLE 2.1   Mean Weekly Expenditure Shares (Percentage) in Eleven Categories by Urban and Rural Expenditure Groups, Jamaica, 1983–1984

Item	Urban				Rural			
	Group 1	Group 2	Group 3	Total	Group 1	Group 2	Group 3	Total
Number of Households	26	25	16	67	32	30	16	78
Food	60.5	51.6	50.1	54.7	74.1	62.3	55.7	65.8
Alcohol	0.2	0.4	1.5	0.6	0.5	1.1	1.0	0.8
Tobacco	0.8	0.9	0.9	0.9	1.1	1.7	1.2	1.4
Dry Goods	9.7	8.1	8.3	8.7	8.8	10.2	14.3	10.5
Housing	7.3	11.7	10.3	9.7	3.4	5.7	3.9	4.4
Fuel	5.4	6.0	5.0	5.6	3.7	3.9	4.1	3.9
Transportation	7.4	8.2	12.4	8.9	3.0	5.3	7.6	4.9
Health	0.3	0.6	0.7	0.5	1.5	1.4	1.7	1.5
Education	3.5	2.8	3.1	3.2	1.2	2.1	3.0	1.9
Entertainment	0.1	0.9	1.1	0.6	0.0	0.1	0.3	0.2
Other	5.2	8.3	6.9	6.8	2.1	6.0	6.9	4.6
Total*	100.4	99.5	100.3	100.2	99.4	99.8	99.7	99.9

*Totals may not add up to 100 due to rounding.

Source: From "Social Patterns of Food Expenditure Among Low-Income Jamaicans" by Barbara D. Miller in *Papers and Recommendations of the Workshop on Food and Nutrition Security in Jamaica in the 1980s and Beyond*, ed. by Kenneth A. Leslie and Lloyd B. Rankine (Kingston, Jamaica: Caribbean Food and Nutrition Institute, 1987).

- *Reflexive ethnographies* explore the research experience itself, in addition to generating or presenting wider theoretical arguments and analysis: "The story itself . . . is a representational means of cracking open the culture and the fieldworker's way of knowing it" (Van Maanen 1988:103). Reflexive ethnographies are distinguished by the degree to which the authors include their fieldwork experience as an important part of the ethnography. They are thus characterized by highly personalized styles and findings. In contrast to earlier ethnographies, reflexive ethnographers frequently use the word *I* in their writings. Reflexive ethnographers offer more poetically insightful perspectives that might not be perceived or grasped by anyone except the particular anthropologist involved. Anne Meneley has captured some of the complexity around reflexive work in her edited collection, *Autoethnographies* (2005).

- Ethnographers often are situated in Western, industrialized cultures. Philippe Bourgois's research in New York's East Harlem for his book, *In Search of Respect: Selling Crack in El Barrio* (1995), explores how people in one neighbourhood cope with poverty and dangerous living conditions. This topic resembles something that a sociologist might study, but a cultural anthropologist will provide rich details about the everyday perspectives and experiences of the people.

Urgent Issues in Cultural Anthropology Research

In this section, we consider two urgent issues in cultural anthropology research: fieldwork ethics and safety during fieldwork.

Ethics and Collaborative Research

Anthropology was one of the first disciplines to devise and adopt a code of ethics. Two major events in the 1950s and 1960s led U.S. anthropologists to reconsider their role in research in relation to both the sponsors (or funders) of their research and the people whom they were studying. The first was the infamous "Project Camelot" of the 1950s. Project Camelot was a plan of the United States government to influence political leadership and stability in South America (Horowitz 1967). To further this goal, the U.S. government employed several anthropologists, who were to gather detailed information on political events and leaders in particular countries without revealing their purpose, and then report back to their sponsor (the government) about their findings. It is still unclear whether the anthropologists involved were completely informed about the purposes to which their data would be put.

The second major event was the Vietnam War (or the "American War," as it is called in Vietnam). This brought to the forefront conflicts about government interests in ethnographic information, the role of the anthropologist, and the protection of the people studied. American anthropologists were recruited and funded to provide information that could help subvert communism in Vietnam and Thailand (Wakin 1992). The Vietnam War affected Canadian anthropology, as many anthropologists participated in teach-ins and anti-war protests, and many departments of anthropology absorbed U.S. draft resistors as graduate students and professors, aligning some Canadian departments more closely with U.S. ones.

In 1971, a standard code of ethics was adopted by the American Anthropological Association (AAA) (see Figure 2.2 on page 57). This code states that the anthropologist's primary responsibility is to ensure the safety of the people being studied. A related principle is that cultural anthropology does not condone covert or "undercover" research. The people being studied should be informed that they are being studied, and the purposes for which they are being studied should be explained. Long a practice in biomedical research, the principle of informed consent requires that the researcher fully inform the research participants of the intent, scope, and possible effects of the study and seek their consent to be in the study. Anthropologists have adapted the concept of informed consent to make it applicable to the varied contexts in which cultural anthropologists work (Fluehr-Lobban 1994).

Canadian anthropologists face new ethical demands as they must now conform to the ethics policies of cross-disciplinary research agencies, in addition to meeting university and anthropology standards. Many anthropologists say that the nature of anthropological research often makes it difficult to apply the strict standards of informed consent that are used in medical settings. For example, people in non-literate societies may be frightened by being asked to sign a typed document of consent that they cannot read. Given that the intent of informed consent is a good one—people should be aware of the purpose and scope and possible effects of a study involving them—each anthropologist should consider some way to achieve this goal. Holding a "town meeting" with all community members present and explaining the research project is one approach.

In presenting the results of one's research, whether in a book or a film, all efforts should be made to protect the anonymity of the people in the study unless they give permission for their identities to be revealed. The usual practice in writing ethnographies has been to change the name of the specific group, area, or village, blur the location, and use made-up names for individuals mentioned.

Some topics are more sensitive than others, and some topics are sensitive to some groups but not others (Lee and Renzetti 1993). Governments may decree that certain subjects are simply off limits for research by foreigners. Strictly speaking, an anthropologist should abide by the ethical guideline stating that rulings of host governments are to be respected. Sometimes, such rules can be highly restrictive. For example, the Indian government allows no foreigners to visit the Nicobar Islands, and it has strict regulations that limit how long foreigners—tourists or anthropologists—can spend in the Andamans (only 30 days). Major factors influencing the extreme sensitivity of the Indian government about foreigners in the Andaman and Nicobar Islands include the islands' strategic location near Burma and Indonesia, and the need to protect the indigenous peoples from unwanted contact.

Collaborative Research

A new direction in methods explicitly seeks to involve members of the study population in collaborative research—from data collection to analysis and presentation. **Collaborative research** is an approach to learning about culture that involves the anthropologist working with members of the study population as partners and teammates rather than researcher and "subject." This strategy, from the start, forces reconsideration of how anthropologists refer to the people being studied, especially the long-standing term *informant*. The term sounds hauntingly and negatively related to espionage or war, and implies a passive role on handing over information to someone else. As we noted earlier in this chapter, institutional review boards (IRBs) use the term *human subject*, which cultural anthropologists reject for similar reasons. Some cultural anthropologists now use the term *consultant*, which implies work for hire. Perhaps the least objectionable term is *research participant*.

Luke Eric Lassiter is a pioneer in collaborative methods, first in research with Native Americans and later with African Americans (2004). During his doctoral studies at the University of North Carolina at Chapel Hill, Lassiter explored ways to conduct his dissertation research as a collaborative project. He developed a close working relationship with about a dozen Kiowa people in Oklahoma who were especially helpful to him in understanding and writing about Kiowa songs. They insisted that Lassiter's book should not be just another academic dissertation but should be for "normal" people. In response to this advice, Lassiter wrote for an audience that included both his professors at the university and the Kiowa people. Beyond learning came the benefits of sharing, as Lassiter says: "A collaborative ethnography opens up the possibility that ethnography can matter for people beyond the academy. This was brought home to me most powerfully when a sixteen-year-old Kiowa singer revealed to me that *The Power of Kiowa Song* was the first book he had actually read from cover to cover" (2004:8).

Lassiter's next project was even more widely collaborative. He involved his anthropology students in ethnographic collaboration with members of the African American community of Muncie, Indiana. This project resulted in a book with shared authorship (2004).

Anthropologists researching First Nations communities in Canada must follow stringent guidelines and be approved by band councils. Research is conducted in partnership with the council and community, and the results of research are expected to be shared with the community, although individuals retain the right to privacy.

Cultural anthropologists are working to find better ways to share the benefits of research with the people and places we study. Research methods in cultural anthropology have come a long way from the armchair to new strategies for nonhierarchical research.

The collaborative research team led by Luke Eric Lassiter includes Muncie, Indiana, community members as well as students and faculty from Ball State University. ■ (Source: © Danny Gawlowski)

---

collaborative research: an approach to learning about culture that involves anthropologists working with members of the study population as partners and teammates rather than as researchers and "subjects."

Research

1. Primary ethical obligations are to the people, species, and materials they study and to the people with whom they work. These obligations can supersede the goal of seeking new knowledge:

   - Avoid harm or wrong, understanding that the development of knowledge can lead to change, which may be positive or negative for the people or animals worked with or studied.

   - Respect the well-being of humans and nonhuman primates.

   - Work for the long-term conservation of the archaeological, fossil, and historical records.

   - Consult actively with the affected individuals or group(s), with the goal of establishing a working relationship that can be beneficial to all parties involved.

2. Ensure that anthropological research does not harm the dignity or privacy of the people with whom they conduct research, or harm the safety, well-being, and survival of animals with which they work.

3. Determine in advance whether human research participants wish to remain anonymous or receive recognition. Informed consent of persons being studied must be obtained in advance. Informed consent does not necessarily imply or require a written or signed form, but involves the quality of consent that is provided on the basis of a clear understanding of possible effects of participation in the research.

4. Recognize their obligations to individuals, groups, and host institutions that participated in or otherwise facilitated the research.

Responsibility to Scholarship and Science

1. Anticipate possible ethical dilemmas and raise these issues in their research proposals.

2. Assume responsibility for the integrity and reputation of the discipline and abide by general moral rules of science:

   - Do not deceive.

   - Do not knowingly misrepresent.

   - Do not prevent reporting of misconduct.

   - Do not obstruct the research of others.

3. Preserve opportunities for future fieldworkers.

4. Use findings in an appropriate fashion and, whenever possible, disseminate findings to the scientific and scholarly community.

5. Consider all reasonable requests for access to data and ensure preservation of data for posterity.

Responsibility to the Public

1. Make findings appropriately available to sponsors, students, decision-makers, and other nonanthropologists and ensure that such information is well understood and properly utilized.

2. It is possible to move to a position of advocacy, but this is an individual decision rather than an ethical responsibility.

Teaching

1. Do not discriminate on the basis of sex, marital status, "race," social class, political convictions, disability, religion, ethnic background, national origin, sexual orientation, age, or other criteria irrelevant to academic performance.

2. Strive to improve teaching, availability, counselling, and helping students obtain professional placement.

3. Impress upon students the ethical challenges in every phase of anthropological work.

4. Publicly acknowledge student assistance in research and preparation of work and compensate students justly for their participation in all professional activities.

5. Avoid sexual liaisons with students for whose education they are in any way responsible.

Application

1. Follow the same ethical guidelines in all anthropological work, be open with funders, and make carefully considered decisions about what types of work in which to be involved.

2. Be honest with employers about qualifications, capabilities, and aims and do not accept conditions contrary to professional ethics.

3. Be alert to dangers of compromising anthropological ethics and understand that contributions to public or private sector actions and policies may include both proactive participation and noncooperation, depending on circumstances.

Note: The AAA code does not dictate behaviour or include sanctions. It is designed to promote discussion and provide general guidelines for ethically responsible decisions.

Source: Adapted from www.aanet.org by permission of the American Anthropological Association from the Code of Ethics of the American Anthropological Association, approved June 1998.

Safety in the Field

Fieldwork can involve serious physical and psychological risks to the researcher and to members of his or her family if they are also in the field. The image of "the anthropologist as hero" has muffled, to a large degree, both the physical dangers and psychological risks of fieldwork. An inquiry into the hazards faced by anthropologists while conducting fieldwork—including mental health problems—has brought more attention to fieldwork safety. Some university departments in Canada require students to submit a form indicating that they are aware of possible risks in the field and have taken precautions to ensure that their fieldwork will be as safe as possible.

Dangers from the physical environment can be fatal. The slippery paths of the highlands of the Philippines caused the death in the early 1980s of Michelle Zimbalist Rosaldo, one of the major figures in contemporary cultural anthropology. Disease is another major risk factor. Many anthropologists have contracted contagious diseases, such as malaria and typhoid, which stay with them throughout their lives.

Social violence figures prominently in some recent research experiences. During the five years that Philippe Bourgois lived in East Harlem, New York, he witnessed the following: a shooting outside his window; a bombing and machine-gunning of a numbers joint; a shootout and police car chase in front of the pizza parlour where he was eating; the aftermath of a fire-bombing of a heroin house; a dozen serious fights; and "almost daily exposure to broken-down human beings, some of them in fits of crack-induced paranoia, some suffering from delirium tremens, and others in unidentifiable pathological fits of screaming and shouting insults to all around them" (1995:32). He was roughly handled by the police several times because they did not believe that he was "just a professor" doing research. Bourgois was once mugged for the sum of $8. Although his research placed him in danger, it also enabled him to gain an understanding, from the inside, of everyday violence in the lives of desperately poor and addicted people.

Anthropological research increasingly involves danger from public violence, such as political mobs or actual battles. This kind of research requires skills and judgment that anthropology classes or research methods books do not typically address (Nordstrom 1997; Kovats-Bernat 2002). A new area of study, *war zone anthropology*, or research conducted within zones of violent conflict, can provide important insights into topics such as the militarization of civilian lives, civilian protection, the cultural dynamics of military personnel,

and the prospects for postconflict reconstruction (Hoffman 2003; Hoffman and Lubkemann 2005). Anthropologists doing research in war zones require special training and experience in how to behave and survive. Previous experience in conflict zones as workers in international aid organizations or the military is helpful.

Based on the fieldwork experiences of anthropologists, specific recommendations were made about how fieldworkers can prepare themselves more effectively for risks they might face. After her son died in the field, anthropologist Nancy Howell received financial support from the American Anthropological Association to undertake a detailed inquiry into fieldwork hazards in anthropology. Howell drew a sample of 311 anthropologists listed as employed in the American Anthropological Association's Guide to Departments. She sent them a questionnaire asking for information on gender, age, work status, health status, and work habits in the field; and she asked for information on health problems and other hazards they had experienced. She received 236 completed questionnaires, a high response rate indicating strong interest in the study. She found regional variation in risk and danger. The highest rates

The food ration queue at an emergency clinic near Buedu, Sierra Leone. While conducting his dissertation research in war-torn Sierra Leone in 2001, Danny Hoffman combined traditional fieldwork techniques such as participant observation and interviews. But he also had to be alert to sudden danger and other risks specific to research during war. He believes anthropologists must be willing to take such risks in order to provide essential knowledge about the complex causes and consequences of war that are overlooked by war correspondents writing for the media. ■ (Source: © Danny Hoffman)

FIGURE 2.3   Recommendations
for Improving Fieldwork Safety

General

Raise awareness of the dangers of fieldwork:

• Overcome the tradition of denial of problems.

• Share information on risks and strategies for risk reduction more widely.

For fieldworkers

Anticipate potential risks at the chosen site.

Obtain appropriate medical training.

Locate medical care facilities in the country and region.

For colleges and universities

Train anthropology students in fieldwork safety.

Ensure that university policies on safety extend to fieldwork situations.

Source: Adapted with permission of the American Anthropological Association from Nancy Howell, *Surviving Fieldwork: A Report of the Advisory Panel on Health and Safety in Fieldwork*, American Anthropological Association, 1990.

were in Africa, followed by India, the Asia/Pacific region, and Latin America. Howell provides recommendations about how anthropologists can prepare themselves more effectively for preventing and dealing with fieldwork risks (see Figure 2.3). They include increasing risk awareness, training in basic medical care, and learning about fieldwork safety in anthropology classes.

Key Questions Revisited

HOW do cultural anthropologists conduct research on culture?

Cultural anthropologists conduct research by doing fieldwork and using participant observation. In the nineteenth century, early cultural anthropologists conducted what we now call armchair anthropology, meaning that they learned about other cultures by reading reports written by explorers and other untrained observers. The next stage was verandah anthropology, in which an anthropologist went to the field but did not live with the people. Instead, the anthropologist would interview a few members of the study population where the anthropologist lived, typically on that person's verandah. Fieldwork and participant observation became the cornerstones of cultural anthropology research only after Malinowski's innovations in the Trobriand Islands during World War I. His approach emphasized the value of living for an extended period in the field, participating in the daily activities of the people, and learning the local language. These features are still the hallmarks of research in cultural anthropology today. New techniques continue to develop to respond to changing times. One of the most important is multisited research in which the anthropologist studies a topic at more than one location.

WHAT does fieldwork involve?

Research in cultural anthropology involves several stages. The first is to have a research topic. A good topic is timely, important, and feasible. Ideas for topics can come from literature review, restudies, current events and pressing issues, and even sheer luck. Once in the field, the first steps include selecting sites, gaining rapport, and dealing with culture shock. The community studied will affect how the anthropologist will gain rapport and will shape access of the anthropologist to particular cultural domains. Participating appropriately in the culture involves learning local forms of gift giving and other exchanges to express gratitude for people's hospitality, time, and trust.

Specific research techniques may emphasize gathering quantitative or qualitative data. Cultural materialists tend to focus on quantitative data, whereas interpretive anthropologists gather qualitative data. When in the field, anthropologists take daily notes, often by hand but now also using a computer. Several other methods of documenting culture include photography, audio recording, and video recording. The anthropologist's theoretical orientation and research goals affect the approach to data analysis and presentation. Quantitative data may involve statistical analysis and presentation in graphs or tables. The presentation of qualitative data is more likely to be descriptive.

WHAT are some important issues in cultural anthropology research today?

Questions of ethics have been paramount to anthropologists since the 1950s. In 1971, U.S. anthropologists adopted a set of ethical guidelines for research to address their concern about what role, if any, anthropologists should play in research that might harm the people being studied. The first rule listed in the American Anthropological Association code of ethics states that an anthropologist's primary responsibility is to maintain the safety of the people involved. Thus, anthropologists should never engage in covert research and should always explain their purpose to the people in the study and preserve the anonymity of the location and of individuals. Collaborative research is a recent development that responds to ethical concerns by pursuing research that involves the participants as partners rather than as subjects.

Safety during fieldwork is another urgent issue. Danger to anthropologists can come from physical sources such as infectious diseases and from social sources such as political violence. A survey of anthropologists in the 1980s produced several recommendations about increasing safety during fieldwork: raising awareness of possible risks, providing training in basic medical care, and teaching about fieldwork safety in anthropology classes.

KEY CONCEPTS

collaborative research, p. 56
culture shock, p. 45
deductive approach
  (to research), p. 45
emic, p. 46
etic, p. 46
fieldwork, p. 34

Hawthorne effect, p. 46
inductive approach
  (to research), p. 45
informed consent, p. 37
interview, p. 47
kula, p. 39
multisited research, p. 35

participant observation,
  p. 35
qualitative data, p. 46
quantitative data, p. 46
questionnaire, p. 47
rapport, p. 41
triangulation, p. 49

myanthrolab

To reinforce your understanding of
this chapter, and to identify
topics for further study,
visit MyAnthroLab at
www.myanthrolab.com for
diagnostic tests and a
multimedia ebook.

SUGGESTED READINGS

Michael V. Angrosino. *Projects in Ethnographic Research*. Long
  Grove, IL: Waveland Press, 2005. This brief manual provides
  students with ideas about what doing research in anthropology is
  like. The author discusses the fundamental stages of three projects
  with insights about how students can conduct their own research.

H. Russell Bernard, *Research Methods in Cultural Anthropology:
  Qualitative and Quantitative Approaches*. 2nd edition. Newbury
  Park, CA: Sage Publications, 1995. This is a sourcebook of
  anthropological research methods—from how to design a
  research project to data analysis and presentation.

Sidney C. H. Cheung, *On the South China Track: Perspectives on
  Anthropological Research and Teaching*. Hong Kong: Hong Kong
  Institute of Asia-Pacific Studies, 1998. Thirteen chapters explore
  aspects of anthropological research and teaching in Chinese
  cultures including Hong Kong, China, Taiwan, and Singapore.

S. Cole and L. Phillips, *Ethnographic Feminisms*. Ottawa: Carleton
  University Press, 1995. This book of readings explores how
  feminist anthropologists have approached ethnography, and
  includes experimental approaches to writing ethnography in
  innovative ways.

Kathleen M. DeWalt and Billie R. DeWalt, *Participant Observation:
  A Guide for Fieldworkers*. New York: AltaMira Press, 2002. This
  book is a comprehensive guide to doing participant observation.
  It covers research design, taking field notes, data analysis, and
  theoretical issues.

Alexander Ervin. *Applied Anthropology: Tools and Perspectives for
  Contemporary Practice*. Boston: Allyn and Bacon, 2005. Chapters
  discuss links between anthropology and policy, the history of
  applied anthropology, ethics, and specialized methods.

Peggy Golde, ed., *Women in the Field: Anthropological Experiences*.
  2nd edition. Berkeley: University of California Press, 1986. This
  reader provides 15 chapters on fieldwork by women anthropologists, including Margaret Mead's fieldwork in the Pacific, Laura
  Nader's fieldwork in Mexico and Lebanon, Ernestine Friedl's
  fieldwork in Greece, and Jean Briggs's fieldwork among the Inuit
  of the Canadian Arctic.

Bruce Grindal and Frank Salamone, eds., *Bridges to Humanity:
  Narratives on Anthropology and Friendship*. Prospect Heights,
  IL: Waveland Press, 1995. The 14 chapters of this text explore
  the humanistic dimension of fieldwork, in which the anthropologist reflects on the friendships established in the field, how they
  contributed to the fieldwork, and how or if they can be continued
  once the anthropologist leaves the field.

Joy Hendry, *An Anthropologist in Japan: Glimpses of Life in the
  Field*. London, UK: Routledge, 1999. This book is a first-person
  account of the author's third research project in Japan, including
  information on her original research design, how the focus
  changed, and how she reached unanticipated conclusions.

Carolyn Nordstrom and Antonius C. G. M. Robben, eds., *Fieldwork
  under Fire: Contemporary Studies of Violence and Survival*.
  Berkeley, CA: University of California Press, 1995. After an introductory chapter discussing general themes, examples are provided
  of fieldwork experiences in dangerous situations including Palestine, China, Sri Lanka, United States, Croatia, Guatemala, and
  Ireland.

Sarah Pink, *Doing Visual Ethnography: Images, Media and Representation in Research*. Thousand Oaks, CA: Sage Publications,
  2001. The author considers a wide variety of topics in visual
  ethnography, including the role of subjectivity, the usefulness
  of visual methods, ethics, photography, video, and electronic
  texts.

Tom Ric with Mette Louise Berg, eds. *Future Fields*, special issue of
  the online journal, *Anthropology Matters*, Volume 6, No. 2,
  2004. This issue includes eleven articles that address a range of
  methodological issues that cultural anthropologists are facing
  today, including emotional, financial, and ethical challenges as
  well as how to cope in situations of physical danger. The journal
  is accessible at no charge at www.anthropologymatters.com.

Roger Sanjek, ed., *Fieldnotes: The Makings of Anthropology*.
  Ithaca, NY: Cornell University Press, 1990. This reader includes
  16 chapters by cultural anthropologists on taking and using field
  notes in ethnographic research in diverse settings.

LARA TABAC, MEDICAL ANTHROPOLOGIST, works at the New York City Department of Health and Mental Hygiene, along with another cultural anthropologist and 6000 other employees. Her responsibilities with the DOHMH's Epidemiology Services require that she collect qualitative information from New Yorkers about how certain health issues affect their lives.

Tabac describes her job as an "unusual joint venture of words and numbers." She explains that the department is traditionally highly quantitative; it uses statistics to determine health-action agendas. The numbers "tell how many, but they do not tell why. In order to be responsive to the health needs of New Yorkers, the DOHMH needs to know why. This is where I come in."

Formal anthropological training reinforced and shaped Tabac's natural tendency to observe and ask questions. She now puts these skills and interests to work by listening to and talking with people who are affected by various health initiatives.

Anthropologists at Work

"I do a lot of listening on a wide range of topics, and I need only a MetroCard to reach far-flung and eclectic neighborhoods peopled with individuals who share their health dilemmas and life struggles with me, as well as their suggestions for improving the services and programs that will ultimately affect them."

One project that Tabac has been working on is an analysis of the sexual behaviours of men who have sex with men. Noting an increase in recent years of syphilis cases in this population, the DOHMH believes that the safe-sex message has lost its urgency. Tabac is consequently trying to determine what situations affect whether individuals in this group use condoms and for what reasons they do or do not do so.

To gather qualitative information about the issue, Tabac has spent many hours participating in Internet chat rooms and conducting open-ended, face-to-face interviews. "As a technique, interviewing is crucial for gaining a deep understanding of sensitive issues. . . . People tend to be more honest when they don't feel as though they are going to be judged by their peers." She notes that every interview for this project has been valuable.

Another project she has collaborated on involves interviewing injection drug users about unsafe injection practices, which often cause HIV, and other sexually transmitted diseases. Many public health experts believed that if people know how to protect themselves, they will do so, and considerable effort was put into educating individuals at risk. But recent research has disproved this assumption. Tabac's assignment was to discover when and why this assumption fails and to create alternative programs that might have more success in encouraging individuals to protect themselves from infectious disease.

Tabac finds her job with the DOHMH challenging and socially relevant. She took it because she wanted to contribute to improving the quality of people's lives. She has not been disappointed.

3

Economies and Their Modes of Production

Key Questions

- WHAT is the scope of economic anthropology?

- WHAT are the characteristics of the five major modes of production?

- WHAT are some directions of change in the five modes of production?

A woman pounding millet in Agadez in Niger, West Africa. Wild millet, a kind of grass, was first domesticated in Africa. Millet is now, after sorghum, the second most important food grain in Africa. It is typically combined with meat and vegetables in a stew, and it is also used for brewing beer. (*Source: © Charles Cecil*)

During the many thousands of years of human prehistory, people made their living by collecting food and other necessities from nature. All group members had equal access to life-sustaining resources. Most people throughout the world now live in economies much different from this description.

Economic anthropology is the subfield of cultural anthropology that studies economic systems cross-culturally. The term *economic system* includes three areas: *production,* or making goods or money; *consumption,* or using up goods or money; and *exchange,* or the transfer of goods or money between people or institutions (see Table 3.1). In this chapter, we first lay out the basic objectives of economic anthropology. Next, we turn to the subject of production and introduce the concept of **mode of production,** or the dominant way of making a living in a culture. Ethnographic examples illustrate each of five major modes of production. In the chapter's last section, we discuss a case of economic change in each mode of production.

Culture and Economies

Economic anthropology differs from the discipline of economics in several ways. First, the subject matter of economic anthropology is much wider. It covers the entire range of ways that people make a living, not just modern capitalism. Second, economic anthropologists' methods are different. They often collect qualitative data and quantitative data, as we discussed in Chapter 2, and they rely on fieldwork and participant observation rather than analyzing "canned" statistical datasets or census information. Third, economic anthropologists believe that it is important to gather emic data in order to understand people's own concepts and categories related to making a living, rather than simply applying Western concepts and categories. If you have taken an economics course, try to recall how much you learned about people from various world cultures.

In spite of these differences between economics and economic anthropology, some shared territory also exists. Researchers in both disciplines are interested in production, consumption, and exchange. Some economists do learn a foreign language and some try to learn about economic behaviour and thought by conducting fieldwork. Some economic anthropologists analyze large, quantitative datasets. Also, some economists and some economic anthropologists are working together on research and policy issues.

Many years of ethnographic research on economic systems has produced a rich set of knowledge on diverse ways of making a living. Anthropologists attempt to organize all this information by sorting it into categories, called modes. In this chapter, we focus on modes of

TABLE 3.1 Three Components of Economic Systems

Production	Making goods or money
Consumption	Using up goods or money
Exchange	Transfer of goods or money

production, and in Chapter 4, we cover modes of consumption and exchange.

Creating Typologies: Modes of Production

Categorizing a certain society as having a particular mode of production implies an emphasis on that type of production; it does not mean that it is the only kind of production undertaken. In a given society, some people will be involved in the prevailing mode of production while others will not. Also, a particular individual may be involved in more than one kind of production—for example, a person could be both a farmer and a herder. Another point to keep in mind is that the five modes of production, in reality, blend with and overlap each other. Therefore, it is possible that some cultures do not fit well within any one mode. Real life is always more complicated than the categories researchers create.

Globalization and the World Economy

Although economic anthropologists focus on local economic systems, they are increasingly involved in researching how global and local systems are linked. The spread of Western capitalism in recent centuries has had, and continues to have, massive effects on other modes of production that it meets.

The intensification of global trade in the past few decades has created a global division of labour, or *world economy,* in which countries compete unequally for a share of the wealth (Wallerstein 1979). In this view, the modern world economy is stratified into three major areas: *core, periphery,* and *semiperiphery. Core areas* monopolize the most profitable activities, such as the high-tech service, manufacturing, and financial activities. They have the strongest governments, which play a dominating role in the affairs of other countries. *Peripheral areas* are relegated to the least profitable activities, including production of raw materials, foodstuffs, and labour-intensive goods, and they must import high-tech goods and services from the core. They tend to have weak governments and are dominated, either directly or indirectly, by core states. *Semiperipheral areas* stand in the middle.

mode of production: the dominant pattern of making a living in a culture.

foraging: collecting food that is available in nature, by gathering, fishing, or hunting.

Monterrey, Mexico, is the second-most important city in Mexico after the capital. Because of its strong steel industry, it is called "the Pittsburgh of Mexico." It has several major beer breweries and is home to the Mexican Baseball Hall of Fame. The city centre has monuments of both Spanish colonialism and cosmopolitan modernity.
■ (Source: Barbara Miller)

According to this model, economic benefits are highly unequal across regions, with core areas profiting most.

Modes of Production

While reading this section, bear in mind that most anthropologists are uneasy about typologies because they often don't reflect the rich reality that ethnographic research presents. This scheme is presented as a way to help you organize the vast amount of ethnographic information we present to you in the book.

Foraging

Foraging involves using food that is available in nature, provided by gathering, fishing, or hunting. It is the oldest way of making a living, having existed since the appearance of *Homo sapiens* roughly 100 000 years ago, perhaps earlier. Foraging has thus survived as the predominant mode of production for 90 percent or more of human existence, but it is now in danger of extinction.

Only around 250 000 people support themselves predominantly from foraging now. Most contemporary foragers live in what are considered marginal areas, such as deserts, tropical rainforests, and the circumpolar region. These areas, however, often contain material resources that are in high demand in core areas, such as oil, diamonds, gold, and expensive tourist destinations.

Foragers collect food items available in nature. Depending on the environmental context, foragers' food sources include nuts, berries and other fruits, and surface-growing vegetables such as melons, roots,

A Ju/'hoansi traditional shelter. ■ (Source: © Irven DeVore/AnthroPhoto)

THE IMPORTANCE OF DOGS

Dogs were the first domesticated animal, with evidence of their domestication from sites in Eastern Europe and Russia dating to around 18 000 years ago. In spite of their long-standing importance to humans around the world, few cultural anthropologists have focused their attention on humans and their dogs. One of the rare ethnographies to do so provides insights about the economic, social, and psychological importance of dogs among a group of circumpolar foragers.

Under 100 Hare Indians constitute the community of Colville Lake in the Northwest Territories (Savishinsky 1974). They live by hunting, trapping, and fishing in one of the harshest environments in the world. Joel Savishinsky went to Colville Lake with the intention of studying stress, tension, and anxiety among this isolated group and how people cope. Environmental stress factors include extremely cold temperatures, long and severe winters, extended periods of isolation, and hazardous travel conditions along with the constant need for mobility during the harshest periods of the year, and sometimes food scarcity. Social and psychological stress factors also exist, including contact with white fur traders and missionaries.

Savishinsky discovered the importance of dogs to the Hare people early in his research:

> Later in the year when I obtained my own dogteam, I enjoyed much greater freedom of movement, and was able to camp with many people whom I had previously not been able to keep up with. Altogether I travelled close to 600 miles by dogsled between

Hare First Nations children use their family's sled and dogs to haul drinking water to their village from Colville Lake, Northwest Territories. ■ (Source: Joel Savishinsky)

mid-October and early June. This constant contact with dogs, and the necessity of learning how to drive, train and handle them, led to my recognition of the

honey, insects, and eggs. They trap and hunt a wide variety of birds, fish, and animals. Successful foraging requires sophisticated knowledge of the natural environment and seasonal changes in it. Most critical is knowledge about the location of water sources and of various foods, how to follow animal tracks, how to judge the weather, and how to avoid predators. This unwritten knowledge is passed down over the generations.

Foragers rely on a diverse set of tools used for gathering, transporting, and processing wild foods. Tools include digging sticks for removing roots from the ground and for penetrating the holes dug by animals in order to get the

animals out, bows and arrows, spears, nets, and knives. Baskets are important for carrying food. For processing raw materials into edible food, foragers use stones to mash, grind, and pound. Meat can be dried in the sun or over fire, and fire is used for cooking either by boiling or by roasting. These activities involve few nonrenewable fuel sources beyond wood or other combustible substances for cooking. Foraging is an **extensive strategy,** a mode of production requiring access to large areas of land and unrestricted population movement. Cultural anthropologists distinguish two major varieties of foraging that are related to different environmental contexts: *temperate-climate foraging* and *circumpolar foraging* (see Table 3.2).

---

extensive strategy: a form of production involving temporary use of large areas of land and a high degree of spatial mobility.

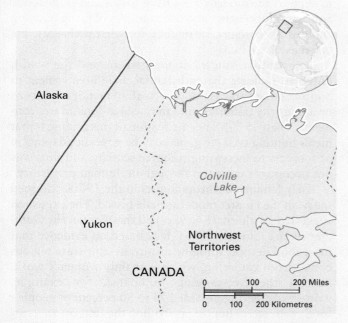

MAP 3.1   Hare Region Near Colville Lake in the North-west Territories. Early European colonialists named the local people Hare because of their reliance on snowshoe hares for food and clothing. The Hare people became involved in the wage-labour economy and were afflicted by alcoholism, tuberculosis, and other diseases. Efforts to re-establish claims to ancestral lands began in the 1960s.

social and psychological, as well as the ecological, significance of these animals in the lives of the people. (1974:xx)

Among the 14 households, there are a total of 224 dogs. Some households have as many as four teams, with an average of 6 dogs per team, corresponding to people's estimation that 6 dogs are required for travel. More than being economically useful, dogs play a signifi-cant role in people's emotional lives. They are a frequent topic of conversation: "Members of the community constantly compare and comment on the care, condition, and growth of one another's animals, noting special qualities of size, strength, colour, speed, and alertness" (1974:169). Emotional displays, uncommon among the Hare, are significant between people and their dogs:

The affectionate and concerned treatment of young animals is participated in by people of all ages, and the nature of the relationship bears a striking resem-blance to the way in which people treat young chil-dren. Pups and infants are, in essence, the only recipients of unreserved positive affect in the band's social life, all other relationships being tinged with varying degrees of restraint and/or negativism. (1974:169–170)

FOOD FOR THOUGHT

- Think of another culture (perhaps yours) in which dogs or some other domesticated animals are a focus of intense human interest. How do people and the animals in question interact? Are there age and gender differences in human relationships with domesticated animals?

TABLE 3.2   Temperate and Circumpolar Foraging Systems Compared

	Temperate-Region Foragers	Circumpolar-Region Foragers
Diet	Wide variety of nuts, tubers, fruits, small animals, and occasional large game	Large marine and terrestrial animals
Gender division of labour in food procurement	Men and women forage; men hunt large game	Men hunt and fish
Shelter	Casual construction, nonpermanent, little maintenance	Time-intensive construction and maintenance, some permanent

The Ju/'hoansi people of southern Africa, as studied in the early 1960s, moved several times during a year, depending on the seasonal availability of water sources. Each cluster of families would regularly return to "their" territory, reconstructing or completely rebuilding their shelters with sticks for frames and leaf or thatch coverings. Shelters are sometimes attached to two or three small trees or bushes for support. The amount of time involved in gathering and processing food and constructing shelters is modest.

In contrast to foragers of temperate climates, those living in the circumpolar regions of North America, Europe, and Asia must devote more time and energy to obtaining food and providing shelter. The specialized technology of circumpolar peoples includes spears, nets, and knives, as well as sleds and the use of domesticated animals to pull them. Dogs or other animals used to pull sleds are an important aspect of circumpolar peoples' technology and social identity (see the Multiple Cultural Worlds box on pages 68–69). Considerable amounts of labour are needed to construct and maintain igloos or log houses. Protective clothing, including coats, gloves, and boots, is another feature of circumpolar foraging that is time-intensive in terms of making and maintaining.

Division of Labour

Among foraging peoples, a *division of labour,* or occupational specialization (assigning particular tasks to particular people) depends mainly on gender and age. Among temperate foraging cultures, a minimal gender-based division of labour exists. Temperate foragers get most of their food by gathering roots, berries, grubs, small birds and animals, and fish, and both men and women collect these basic foods. Hunting large animals, however, tends to involve only men, who go off together in small groups on long-range expeditions. Large game provides a small and irregular part of the diets of temperate-climate foragers. In circumpolar groups, in contrast, hunting large animals (including seals, whales, and bears) and capturing large fish provide a significant part of the diet, require more time and labour, are dangerous activities, and tend to involve only men. Among circumpolar foragers, therefore, the gender division of labour is marked.

The issue of large game hunting connects to a long-standing theoretical debate in anthropology. Many anthropologists support a *Man the Hunter model* for explaining how humans evolved in prehistory (Lee 1979; Stanford 1999). This model says that early humans relied heavily on animal meat in their diets; that men were responsible for providing the meat, which explains men's high status in many societies relative to women; and that the need to hunt in groups formed the basis for social life, including the evolution of verbal language. This model gives much importance to meat and masculinity in explaining key features of humanity. Some of the scientific evidence used to support the model comes from fossils and stone tools. Some anthropologists also use examples of living foraging cultures as analogies, or models, for what prehistoric life may have been like.

Comparative studies of foragers around the world, however, indicate that substantial male involvement in hunting large game is not universal. In fact, it appears to be a minority pattern found in resource-limited environments (Hiatt 1970). The implication of this finding is that men's hunting of large game may be a recent adaptation of foragers to increasing resource scarcity and thus was not necessarily common throughout human prehistory.

Early feminist anthropologists in the 1970s critiqued the Man the Hunter model as male biased. Their research suggested an alternate view called the *Woman the Gatherer model* (Slocum 1975). It is based on evidence that most food in most foraging groups in temperate regions comes from gathering, which is mainly women's work. Among the free-ranging Ju/'hoansi, for example, women's gathering provided 75 to 80 percent of people's food, with men's hunting providing the rest, on an irregular basis. To complicate matters further, in some foraging societies, women hunt. Among the Agta of eastern Luzon, the Philippines, a group of women go hunting while other women stay at the camp caring for the small children (Estioko-Griffin 1986). Most cultural anthropologists now agree that the Man the Hunter model should be abandoned. The Man the Hunter model, however, lives on in much popular thinking, perpetuated through textbook images and museum displays of prehistoric peoples which depict men hunting and carrying dead animals while women carry babies or squat in front a fire, cooking (Gifford-Gonzalez 1993).

Age is a basis for task allocation in all modes of production, including foraging. Young boys and girls help collect food. Elderly people tend to stay at the camp area where they are often responsible for caring for children who are too young to go with their parents to collect food.

Property Relations

The concept of *private property,* in the sense of owning something that can be sold to someone else, is not found in foraging societies. Instead, the term **use rights** is more appropriate. It means that a person or group has socially recognized priority in access to particular resources, such as gathering regions, hunting and fishing areas, and water holes. This access, however, is willingly shared

---

use rights: a system of property relations in which a person or group has socially recognized priority in access to particular resources such as gathering, hunting, and fishing areas and water holes.

Ethnographic Profile

The Andaman Islanders of India

The Andaman Islands are a string of islands in the Bay of Bengal (off the coast of Burma [Myanmar]) that belong to India. For unknown numbers of centuries, many of the islands were inhabited by people who fished, gathered, and hunted for their livelihood. During the eighteenth century, when European countries were expanding trade routes to the Far East, the Andaman Islands were of major strategic importance as a stopping place.

At the time of the first, small settlements of the British in the late eighteenth century, the total indigenous population was estimated at between 6000 and 8000 (Miller 1997). Today, over 400 000 people live on the islands, mostly migrants from the Indian mainland. The total number of indigenous people is about 400. British colonialism brought contagious diseases and increased death from violence among disrupted Andaman groups and between the Andaman people and the British.

There are now four surviving clusters of indigenous Andamanese. The smallest group, just a few dozen people, consists of the remnants of the so-called Great Andamanese people. They live on a small island near Port Blair, the capital, in what is essentially a reservation area. Several groups of Great Andamanese people formerly lived throughout North and Middle Andaman Islands, but no indigenous people inhabit these islands now. The so-called Jarawa, numbering perhaps 200, live in a reserved area on the southwest portion of South Andaman. Currently, no outsider knows their language or what name they use for themselves. *Jarawa* is a term that the Great Andamanese people use for them. The Onge, around 100 in number, live in one corner of Little Andaman Island. Another 100 people or so live on North Sentinel Island. Outsiders call them the "Sentinelese." No one has established communication with them, and almost no one from the outside has gotten closer than arrow-range of their shore.

The 2005 tsunami disrupted much of the Andaman Island topography, particularly areas that had been cleared of mangroves and other trees. As far as anyone knows, none of the indigenous people died as a direct result of the tsunami, though many of the immigrant settlers did (Mukerjee 2005). The future of the indigenous people is more endangered by culture, in the form of immigration and development, than from nature.

Readings

Madhusree Mukerjee. *The Land of Naked People: Encounters with Stone Age People.* New York: Houghton Mifflin, 2003. www.samarmagazine.org/archive/article.

A. R. Radcliffe-Brown. *The Andaman Islanders: A Study in Social Anthropology.* New York: The Free Press. 1964 [1922].

Sita Venkateswar. "The Andaman Islanders." *Cultural Survival,* 280 (5), 82–88, 1999.

Website

www.andaman.org.

Thanks to Madhusree Mukerjee, independent scholar and activist, and Sita Venkateswar, Massey University, for reviewing this material.

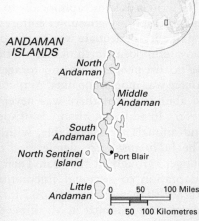

A Jarawa woman receives a handout from a passenger bus driver on the Andaman Trunk Road (ATR) (left). Part of the ATR passes through the Jarawa reservation on South Andaman Island. ■ (Source: Pankaj Sekhsaria) *Government officials from Pt. Blair make periodic visits by boat to the Jarawa area to attempt to build Jarawa trust. This landmark incident (right), of getting some Jarawa to board a government boat, occurred in 1998. The Jarawa occupy land that is rich in resources, such as ancient hardwood trees. Rumours are that the administration wants to remove the Jarawa from their territory and exploit it for logging, tourism, and other commercial interests.* ■ (Source: Pankaj Sekhsaria)

MAP 3.2 *Andaman Islands of India. The 576 islands are geologically part of Burma and Southeast Asia. The British Empire controlled them until India's independence in 1947.*

ANDAMAN ISLANDS

North Andaman
Middle Andaman
South Andaman
North Sentinel Island
Port Blair
Little Andaman

0   50   100 Miles
0   50   100 Kilometres

with others by permission. Among the Ju/wasi, certain family groups are known to control access to particular water holes and the territory surrounding them (R. B. Lee 1979:58–60). Visiting groups are welcome and will be given food and water. In turn, the host group, at another time, will visit other camps and be given hospitality there. In India's Andaman Islands (see the Ethnographic Profile on page 71), family groups each control known offshore areas for fishing. Again, sharing is a common practice if permission has been given. Encroaching on someone else's area without permission is a serious misdemeanour that could result in violence. In foraging groups, use rights are generally invested in the collective group and passed down equally to all children who are members of the group.

Foraging as a Sustainable System

When untouched by outside influences and with abundant land available, foraging systems are sustainable, meaning that crucial resources are regenerated over time in balance with the demand that the population makes on them. North Sentinel Island, one island in the Andaman Islands, provides a clear case because its inhabitants have lived in a "closed" system. So far, the few hundred indigenous people live in almost complete isolation from the rest of the world, other than the occasional helicopter flying overhead and the occasional attempt by outsiders to land on their territory.

One reason for the sustainability of foraging is that foragers' needs are modest. Anthropologists have typified the foraging lifestyle as the original *affluent* society because needs are satisfied with minimal labour efforts. This term is used metaphorically to remind people living in contemporary consumer cultures that foraging is not a pathetic, inadequate way to make a living, contrary to most ethnocentric thinking. In the 1960s, when the Ju/'hoansi people were still foragers, their major food source was mongongo nuts. At that time, these nuts were so abundant that there was never a shortage (Howell 1986). In addition, hundreds of species of edible plants and animals were available, with seasonal variations. The Ju/'hoansi were slender and often complained of hunger throughout the year. Their thinness may be an adaptation to seasonal fluctuations in food supply. Rather than maximizing food intake during times of plenty, they minimize it. Mealtime is not an occasion for stuffing oneself. Ju/'hoansi culture taught that it is good to have a hungry stomach, even when food is plentiful.

Because foragers' needs for goods are not great, minimal labour efforts are required to satisfy them. Foragers typically work fewer hours a week than the average employed North American. In traditional (undisturbed) foraging societies, people spend as few as five hours a week collecting food and making and repairing tools. They have much time for storytelling, playing games, and resting. Foragers also traditionally enjoyed good health. During the early 1960s, the age structure and health status of the Ju/'hoansi compared well with people in the United States of around 1900 (Lee 1979:47–48). They had few infectious diseases or degenerative diseases (related to aging such as arthritis).

Horticulture

Both horticulture and pastoralism are recent modes of production, having emerged only as recently as 12 000 years ago in the Middle East and then later in Africa, Asia, Europe, and the western hemisphere. Both of these modes of production depend on the *domestication* of plants and animals—that is, the process by which human selection causes genetic changes in plants and animals and leads to their greater control by humans in terms of their location and their reproduction.

Cassava, also called manioc, is a root crop grown extensively in western Africa. This man displays a cassava plant grown in Niger. Cassava and millet are the staple foods for many West Africans. ■ (Source: © Charles O. Cecil)

horticulture: a mode of production based on growing domesticated crops in gardens using simple hand tools.

Horticulture is a mode of production based on cultivating domesticated plants in gardens using hand tools. Garden crops are often supplemented by foraging and by trading with pastoralists for animal products. Horticulture is still practised by many thousands of people throughout the world. Prominent horticultural regions are found in sub-Saharan Africa, South Asia, Southeast Asia and the Pacific, Central America, South America, and the Caribbean islands. Major horticultural crops include yams, corn, beans, grains such as millet and sorghum, and several types of roots, all of which are rich in protein, minerals, and vitamins.

Horticulture involves the use of hand-held tools, such as digging sticks, hoes, and carrying baskets. Rain is the sole source of moisture. Horticulture requires rotation of garden plots in order to allow used areas to regenerate. Thus, another term for horticulture is *shifting cultivation*. Average plot sizes are less than 0.4 hectares, and just over 1 hectare can support a family of five to eight members for a year. Yields can support semipermanent villages of 200 to 250 people. Overall population density per square mile is low because horticulture, like foraging, is an extensive strategy. Horticulture is more labour intensive than foraging because of the energy required for plot preparation and food processing. Anthropologists distinguish five stages in the horticultural cycle (see Figure 3.1).

Surpluses in food supply are possible in horticulture. These surpluses enable trade relationships and can lead to greater wealth for some people. In the past, horticulture has been the foundation for complex and rich civilizations,

such as the Maya civilization of Mexico and Central America of between 200 and 900CE (Common Era).

Division of Labour

Gender and age are the key factors structuring the division of labour, with men's and women's work roles often being clearly differentiated. Most commonly, men clear the garden area while both men and women plant and tend the staple food crops. This pattern exists in Papua New Guinea, much of Southeast Asia, and parts of West and East Africa. Food processing involves women often working in small groups while men more typically form small groups for hunting and fishing for supplementary food. Among horticultural groups in rural Malawi, in southern Africa, women are responsible for food crops and men are responsible for hunting game animals (Morris 1998). A common pattern among horticulturalists is for women to grow the staple food crops while men grow the "prestige foods" used in ritual feasts. In these contexts, men have higher public status than women.

Two unusual horticultural cases involve extremes in terms of gender roles and status. The first involves the pre-contact Iroquois of central New York State (Brown 1975) (see Map 3.3 on page 74). Iroquois women cultivated maize, the most important food crop, and they controlled its distribution. This control meant that they were able to decide whether the men would go to war, because a war effort depended on the supply of maize to support it. A contrasting example is that of the Yanomami of the Venezuelan Amazon (see Map 3.4 on page 74) (Chagnon 1992). Yanomami men clear the fields and tend and harvest the crops. They also do much of the cooking for ritual feasts. Yanomami women, though, are not idle. They play an important role in providing the staple food that comes from manioc, a starchy root crop that requires substantial processing work—it has to be soaked for a long time to remove toxins and then scraped into a mealy consistency. Among the Yanomami, however, men are the dominant decision-makers and have more social power than Yanomami women do.

Anthropologists cannot explain the origins of different divisions of labour in horticulture, but the differences have implications for men's and women's status (Sanday 1973). Cross-cultural analysis of many horticultural societies shows that women's contribution to food production is a necessary but not sufficient basis for women's high status. In other words, if women do not contribute to producing food, their status will be low. If they do contribute, their status may, or may not, be high. The critical factor appears to be control over the distribution of what is produced, especially public distribution beyond the family. Slavery is a clear example of how a major role in production does not bring high status because slaves have no control over the product and its distribution.

FIGURE 3.1 Five Stages in Horticulture

Clearing: A section of the forest is cleared, partially or completely, by cutting down trees and brush and then setting the area on fire to burn off other growth. The fire creates a layer of ash that is rich fertilizer. The term *slash and burn cultivation* refers to this stage of clearing.

Planting: People use digging sticks to loosen the soil. They place seeds though the broadcasting method (scattering the seeds by hand) or place slips of plants by hand into the loose soil.

Weeding: Horticulture involves little weeding because the ash cover and shady growing conditions keep weed growth down.

Harvesting: This phase requires substantial labour to cut or dig crops and carry them to the residential area.

Fallowing: Depending on the soil and the crop grown, the land must be left unused for a specified number of years so that it regains its fertility.

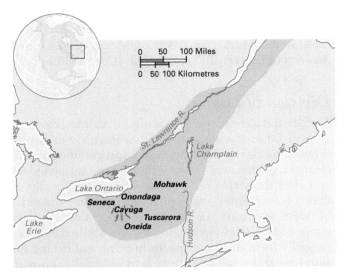

MAP 3.3 Pre-colonial Iroquois Region. At the time of the arrival of the European colonialists, the Haudenosaunee, or People of the Longhouse, extended over a wide area. The Mohawk stood guard over the eastern door of the confederacy's symbolic longhouse, and the Seneca guarded the western door. Six nations worked out a peace treaty among them and established a democracy. A great orator named Hiawatha promoted the plan throughout the tribes, and a Mohawk woman was the first to approve it.

Children do more productive work in horticultural societies than in any other mode of production (Whiting and Whiting 1975). *The Six Cultures Study* is a research project that examined children's behaviour in horticultural, farming, and industrial settings. Children among a horticultural group, the Gusii of western Kenya, performed the most tasks at the youngest ages. Gusii boys and girls care for siblings, collect fuel, and carry water. Among the Gusii and in other horticultural societies, children do so many tasks because adults, especially women, are busy working in the fields and markets. Children's work in the domestic domain fulfills what would be adult roles in other economic systems.

Property Relations

Private property, as something that an individual can own and sell, is not characteristic of horticultural societies. Use rights are typically important, although they are more clearly defined and formalized than among foragers. By clearing and planting an area of land, a family puts a claim on it and its crops. The production of surplus goods allows the possibility of social inequality in access to goods and resources. Rules about sharing within the larger group decline in importance as some people gain higher status.

Horticulture as a Sustainable System

Fallowing is crucial in maintaining the viability of horticulture. It allows the plot to recover lost nutrients and improves soil quality by promoting the growth of weeds whose root systems keep the soil loose. The benefits of a well-managed system of shifting cultivation are clear as are the two major constraints involved: the time required for fallowing and the need for access to large amounts of land so that some of it is in use while other land is fallowed. Using a given plot for too many seasons or reducing fallowing time quickly results in the depletion of soil nutrients, decreased crop production, and soil erosion. The following conditions are linked with such harmful practices and their negative consequences (Blaikie 1985):

- Pressure on access to land as a consequence of encroachment by outsiders such as loggers, miners, farmers, ranchers, tourists; creating conservation areas; and development projects such as dams
- Government policies that force horticulturalists to increase production for cash in order to pay taxes
- Interest of horticulturalists in increasing production for cash in order to buy manufactured commodities
- Pressure on land from internal population growth when outmigration is not an option

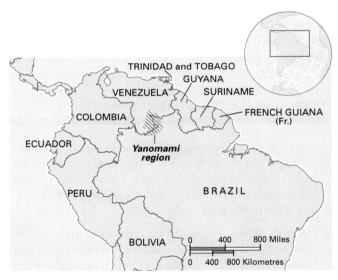

MAP 3.4 Yanomami Region in Brazil and Venezuela. The Yanomami region is supposedly protected from outsiders. But miners, ranchers, loggers, and other commercial developers have encroached on the reserve, extracting material resources and sexually exploiting women and children.

---

pastoralism: a mode of production based on keeping domesticated animal herds and using their products, such as meat and milk, for most of the diet.

The last factor, population growth, is often blamed as the sole culprit for soil degradation and erosion in horticultural contexts, but often it is not involved at all. Ethnographic studies indicate, instead, that the major threats to horticultural sustainability worldwide are external factors.

Pastoralism

Pastoralism is a mode of production based on the domestication of animal herds and the use of their products, such as meat and milk, for 50 percent or more of the pastoral society's diet. Pastoralism has long existed in the Middle East, Africa, Europe, and central Asia, especially in regions where rainfall is limited and unpredictable. In the western hemisphere, before the arrival of the Spanish in the fifteenth century, the only indigenous herding system existed in the Andean region and involved llamas. Sheep, goats, horses, and cattle became prominent after the Spanish conquest (Barfield 2001). Some First Nations groups, especially in the southwestern United States, still rely on herding animals.

Pastoralists raise a limited variety of animals. Worldwide, the six most popular species are sheep, goats, cattle, horses, donkeys, and camels. Three others have more restricted distribution: yaks at high altitudes in Asia, reindeer in northern sub-Arctic regions, and llamas in highland South America. Many pastoralists keep dogs for protection and for help with herding. Pastoralism can succeed in a variety of environments, depending on the animal involved. For example, reindeer herding is popular in the circumpolar regions of Europe and Asia, and cattle and goat herding is common in India and Africa.

In terms of food, pastoralism provides primarily milk and milk products with occasional slaughtering of animals for meat. Thus, pastoralists typically form trade links with foragers, horticulturalists, or farmers in order to obtain food and other goods that they cannot produce themselves.

Among the Ariaal, herders of Kenya, men are in charge of herding camels. Here, an Ariaal herder watches over two baby camels. ■ (Source: Elliott Fratkin)

Prominent trade items are food grains and manufactured items, such as cooking pots, for which they offer milk, animals, hides, and other animal products. Pastoralism may seem to resemble contemporary large-scale ranching, but, in fact, ranches resemble modern industry more than traditional pastoralism (Fratkin, Galvin, and Roth 1994; Loker 1993). The primary purpose of ranching is to provide meat for sale, whereas pastoralism provides many animal products. Also, pastoralism involves the movement of animals to pasture, whereas ranching moves the fodder to the animals.

A common problem for all pastoralists is the continued need for fresh pasture for their animals. This need makes pastoralism, like foraging and horticulture, an extensive form of economic adaptation. Herds must move or else the pasture area will become depleted. A useful distinction is made between pastoralists depending on whether they move their herds for short or long distances (Fratkin, Galvin, and Roth 1994).

The Nuer are an example of short-distance herders. E. E. Evans-Pritchard's (1947) classic study describes the Nuer, cattle herders of Sudan, in the late 1930s. Depending on the availability of water, the Nuer would spend part of the year in settled villages and part in temporary camps. Cattle and cows provided food for the Nuer from their milk, meat, and blood (the Nuer, and other East African pastoralists, extract blood from the cow's neck, which they drink). Cattle also furnished hides, horn, and other materials for everyday use and were the medium of exchange for marriage and payment of fines. The economic and social importance of cattle is reflected in the Nuer's detailed vocabulary which elaborates on their colours and markings.

The Qashqai of Iran are long-distance sheep herders and camel drivers (Beck 1986). Iran offers a varied and rich natural resource base that supports pastoralsim, agriculture and large urban centres, including the important city of Shiraz (see Map 3.5). The nomadic pastoralism of the Qashqai involves seasonal migration to remote pastures, separated by roughly 500 kilometres. Long-distance herding makes the Qashqai vulnerable to raids and requires negotiation with settlements along the way for permission to cross their land. This vulnerability prompted them to develop a confederacy of tribes into a centralized political organization for protection. The Qashqai thus show how ecology, economy, and political organizations are linked within an environment well endowed with resources and with many settled communities.

Division of Labour

Families and clusters of related families are the basic unit of production. Gender and age are, again, key factors in the allocation of work. In many pastoralist cultures, gender roles are clearly divided. Men are often in charge of the herding activities—moving the animals from place to place. Women tend to be responsible for processing the

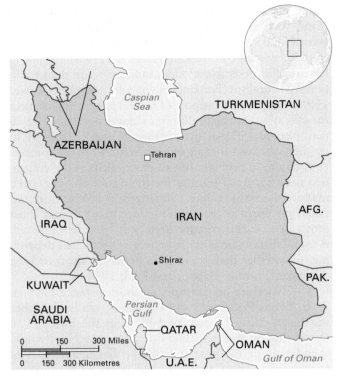

MAP 3.5 Iran. The Islamic Republic of Iran is one of the world's most mountainous countries. Its economy is based on oil, family farming, and small-scale trading. Iran is OPEC's second-largest oil producer and has the second-largest natural gas reserves in the world after Russia. The population of Iran is over 70 million. Its urban population is one of the fastest-growing worldwide. The official language is Persian (Farsi) and Shi'a Islam is the official state religion.

These girls are in charge of herding water buffaloes to the Ganges River, in Banaras, India. ■ (Source: Barbara Miller)

herd's products, especially the milk. A cultural emphasis on masculinity characterizes many herding populations. Reindeer herding among the Saami of Finland is closely connected to male identity to the extent that the definition of being a man is to be a reindeer herder (Pelto 1973). In contrast, women are the herders among the Navajo of the American Southwest. Navajo men's major work role is crafting silver jewellery.

The size of the animal involved is sometimes, but not always, related to the gender division of herding. Girls and women are often herders of smaller animals, perhaps because smaller animals need to graze less widely and can be kept penned near the house. Boys and men tend the animals that are pastured farther away. Children play important roles in tending herds. Among the cattle-herding groups of eastern Africa, for example, parents want to have many children to help out with the herds.

Property Relations

The most important forms of property among pastoralists are, by far, animals, followed by housing (such as tents or yerts) and domestic goods (rugs and cooking ware). Depending on the group, ownership of animals is inherited through males, most commonly, or, less frequently, through females, as among the Navajo. A concept of private property exists for animals, which the family head may trade for other goods. A family's housing materials are also their own. Use rights, however, regulate pasture land and migratory routes, and these rights tend to be informally regulated through an oral tradition.

Pastoralism as a Sustainable System

Pastoralists have developed sustainable cultures in extremely varied environments, from the relative lushness of Iran to the more depleted situation of Mongolia. Pastoralism can be a highly successful and sustainable economic system that functions in complementarity with other economic systems. The Mongolian empire, one of the world's most powerful empires, was based on herding animals, along with pillaging. As with foraging and horticulture, however, when outside forces squeeze

---

agriculture: a mode of production that involves growing crops with the use of plowing, irrigation, and fertilizer.
intensive strategy: a form of production that involves continuous use of the same land and resources.

indigenous knowledge (IK): local knowledge about the environment, including plants, animals, and resources.

family farming (formerly termed *peasant agriculture*): a form of agriculture in which farmers produce mainly to support themselves but also produce goods for sale in the market system.

the space available for population movements, over-exploitation of the environment results. A major external constraint on pastoralism is the goal of many governments to *sedentarize* (settle down) pastoralists. States want pastoralists to stay in one place so that the people will be easier to keep track of and tax. States do not like pastoralists to move across state lines, as they have done long before state boundaries were created.

Agriculture

Agriculture is a mode of production that involves growing crops on permanent plots with the use of plowing, irrigation, and fertilizer; it is also called *farming*. In contrast to foraging, horticulture, and pastoralism, agriculture is an **intensive strategy**. Intensification involves the use of techniques that allow the same plot of land to be used repeatedly without losing its fertility. Crucial inputs include substantial amounts of labour for weeding, use of natural and chemical fertilizers, and control of water supply. The earliest agricultural systems are documented from the time of the Neolithic period, beginning around 12 000 years ago in the Fertile Crescent region in present-day Iraq. Agricultural systems now exist worldwide, on all continents except Antarctica.

Agriculture relies on the use of domesticated animals for plowing, transportation, and organic fertilizer either in the form of manure or composted materials. It is highly dependent on artificial water sources such as irrigation channels or terracing the land. Like the modes of production already considered, agriculture involves complex local forms of knowledge about the environment, including plant varieties, pest management, precipitation patterns, and soil types. Anthropologists refer to this knowledge as **indigenous knowledge (IK)** to distinguish it from Western, scientific knowledge. Long-standing agricultural traditions are now being increasingly displaced by methods introduced from the outside, and so the world's stock of indigenous knowledge is declining rapidly. In many cases, it has become completely lost, along with the cultures and languages associated with it. Many applied anthropologists are actively involved in recording indigenous knowledge as a resource for the future (see the Lessons Applied box on page 78).

Occupational specialization increases in agricultural societies. Instead of people repairing their own tools and weapons, some people take on this work as a full-time job and no longer grow their own food, trading their skills for food with farmers. Other specializations that emerge as full-time occupations are political leaders, religious leaders or priests, healers, artisans, potters, musicians, and traders. Three major types of agriculture are discussed next (also see Table 3.3).

Family Farming

One variety of agriculture is **family farming** (formerly termed *peasant agriculture*) in which production is geared to support the family and to produce goods for sale. Thus, family farming is always part of a larger market economic system (E. Wolf 1966). Today, more than 1 billion people, or about one-sixth of the world's population, make their living from family farming. Found throughout the world, family farming is more common in countries such as Mexico, India, Poland, and Italy than in more industrialized countries. Family farmers exhibit much cross-cultural variety. They may be full-time or part-time farmers; they may be more or less closely linked to urban markets; and they may be poor and indebted or wealthy and powerful. Major activities in family farming include plowing, planting seeds and cuttings, weeding, caring for irrigation systems and terracing, harvesting crops, and processing and storing crops.

Division of Labour The family (or household) is the basic unit of production, and gender and age are important in organizing work. Most family farming societies have a marked gender-based division of labour. Cross-cultural analysis of gender roles in 46 cultures revealed that men perform the "bulk" of the labour in more than three-fourths of the sample (Michaelson and Goldschmidt 1971). Anthropologists have proposed various theories to explain why productive work on so many family farms is male dominated (see Figure 3.2 on page 78). The remaining one-fourth of the sample includes cultures in which men's and women's roles are balanced and cultures in which women play the dominant role. These three variations on the gender division of labour in family farming are the subject of much anthropological research.

	Family Farming	Industrial Capital Agriculture	Industrial Collectivized Agriculture
Labour Inputs	Kin-based	Hired, impersonal	Communal
Capital Inputs	Low–Moderate	High	Moderate–High
Sustainability	High	Low	Low–Moderate

TABLE 3.3 Characteristics of Three Forms of Agriculture

PRESERVING INDIGENOUS KNOWLEDGE ABOUT FARMING THROUGH DATA BANKS

In 1992, the United Nations Conference on Environment and Development, held in Rio de Janeiro, first promoted global awareness of the complementary relationships between indigenous knowledge (IK) about the environment and biodiversity (Warren 2001). Scholars had long recognized the links (Scott 1998), but its official recognition in 1992 led to action directed at preserving and promoting IK in order to prevent loss of biodiversity. Cultural anthropologists have documented IK about agriculture in matters such as emic classification of soil types, what kinds of foods grow best in what contexts, how to mix crop plantings effectively, and how to prevent pests from destroying crops.

Studies also reveal that IK is culturally variable: Men know some things, women know other things, and the young and old have different kinds of IK, as do members of different economic niches within the same cultural area. All these varying "knowledges" should be documented as part of indigenous cultural/agricultural heritage, because they have local specificity and validity that outside systems often lack.

An effort is now under way to link universities and agricultural research laboratories worldwide in order to support IK data collection and documentation. Over 30 IK resource centres exist, housing computerized databases of case studies and ethnographic reports. Coordination among the centres is leading to improved guidelines and recommendations about data recording, archiving, and sharing. All of these practices are aimed at both preserving the knowledge for the future and providing wider access to it. Although the primary goal of the project is to support biodiversity, it will have the effect of supporting cultural diversity as well.

For examples of the Global Network of Indigenous Knowledge Resource Centers, visit this website: www.ciesin.org/IC/cikard/Indigcenters.html.

FOOD FOR THOUGHT

- This global information network will clearly help inform agricultural policy-makers, but how will it benefit the people whose knowledge is being recorded and preserved in the data banks?

Analysis of time allocation data for men and women in horticultural and agricultural societies reveals that both men's and women's work hours are substantially higher in agricultural economies, but in differing proportions to inside and outside work (Ember 1983). Women's contribution to production is not less in agriculture. Instead, the shares of time devoted to particular activities shift. Women's inside work hours increase

---

FIGURE 3.2   Three Hypotheses to Explain Male Dominance in the Gender Division of Labour in Family Farming

Men and Plowing Hypothesis
This hypothesis is based on the importance of plowing fields in preparation for planting and on the fact that plowing is almost exclusively a male task (Goody 1976). Some anthropologists say that men plow because they are stronger than women and have the advantage of greater aerobic capacity. In southern India, for example, weather patterns require that plowing be accomplished in a very narrow time period (Maclachlan 1983). Assigning the task to the physically stronger gender ensures that the work is done more quickly and is thus an adaptive cultural strategy because it increases the chances for a good crop.

Women and Child Care Hypothesis
This hypothesis says that women are not involved in plowing and other agricultural field labour as much as men because such tasks are incompatible with child care (J. K. Brown 1970).

Women and Food-Processing Hypothesis
This hypothesis notes that agriculture increases the demand for labour within and near the house (Ember 1983). Winnowing, husking, grinding, and cooking agricultural products are extremely labour-intensive processes. Linked to women's primary roles in child care and increased fertility in farm families, these labour demands restrict women to the household domain.

---

public–private dichotomy: gender division in society that emerged with agriculture, whereby men are more involved with the nondomestic domain and women are more involved in activities in or near the home.

Family farming in highland Ecuador. A man plows while women in the family follow, planting seed potatoes. ■ (Source: © Jeremy Horner/ CORBIS)

absolutely and relatively (compared to men's), and their outside work hours increase absolutely, but decline relative to those of men.

In farming systems where men play the major role in agriculture, women are likely to work in or near the home, processing food, maintaining the household, and caring for children (Ember 1983). This division of labour results in the **public–private dichotomy** in family farm societies, in which men are more involved with the outside, public world and women are more involved in the domestic domain. In this variety of family farming, men work more hours per week than in foraging, horticultural, and pastoralist systems. Women's work hours, in contrast, are as high as they are in horticultural and pastoralist systems.

In family farms in North America, men typically have the main responsibility for daily farm operations; women's participation ranges from equal to minimal involvement (Barlett 1989:271–273)—they do run farms, but generally only when divorced or widowed. Women are usually responsible for managing the domestic domain. On average, women's daily work hours are 25 percent more than those of men. A trend is for family-farm women to take salaried jobs off-site to help support the farm.

Balanced work roles between men and women in family farming frequently involve a pattern in which men do the agricultural work and women do marketing. This gender division of labour is common among highland indigenous groups of Central and South America. For example, among the Zapotec Indians of Mexico's southern state of Oaxaca (pronounced wah-HAKA), men

grow maize, the staple crop, and cash crops such as bananas, mangoes, coconuts, and sesame (Chiñas 1992). Zapotec women sell produce in the town markets, and they make tortillas, which they sell from their houses. The family thus derives its income from the labour of both men and women working interdependently. Male status and female status are quite equal in such contexts.

THINKING OUTSIDE THE BOX

ON THE BASIS of your personal experience and observations, how would you describe the gender division of labour in your culture, both in the domestic domain and in outside work?

Family farms in which females play the major role in production are called *female farming systems*. They are found mainly in southern India and Southeast Asia where *wet rice agriculture* is practised. This is a highly labour-intensive way of growing rice that involves starting the seedlings in nurseries and transplanting them to flooded fields. Men are responsible for plowing the fields using teams of water buffaloes. Women own land and make decisions about planting and harvesting. Women's labour is the backbone of this type of farming. Standing calf-deep in muddy water, they transplant rice seedlings, weed, and harvest the rice. Why women predominate in wet rice agriculture is an intriguing question but impossible to answer. Its consequences for women's status, however, are clear. In female farming systems, women have relatively high status. They own land, play a central role in household decision-making, and have substantial personal autonomy (Stivens et al. 1994).

This farmer works near a highly urbanized area of Kyoto, in Japan, where farming combines elements of industrial mechanization with intensive labour.

■ (Source: Barbara Miller)

Children's roles in agricultural societies range from being prominent to rather minor, depending on the context (Whiting and Whiting 1975). The *Six Cultures Study,* mentioned earlier in the chapter, found lower rates of child work in the North Indian and Mexican agricultural villages, compared to the horticultural Gusii in Kenya. But in some agricultural societies, children's work rates are very high, as shown through detailed observations of children's activities in two Asian villages, one in Java and the other in Nepal. In these villages, an important task of children, even as young as six to eight years old, was tending the farm animals (Nag, White, and Peet 1978), and children spent more time caring for animals than adults did. In both villages, girls aged six to eight spent more time than adults in child care. Some of the Javanese children in the six- to eight-year-old group worked for wages. In general, girls did more hours of work daily than boys at all ages.

Property Relations   The investments in land that agriculture requires, such as clearing, terracing, and fencing, are linked to the development of firmly delineated and protected property rights. Rights to land, the most important resource, can be acquired and sold. Clear guidelines exist about inheritance and transfer of rights to land through marriage. Social institutions such as law and police emerge to protect private rights to resources. The more marked gender division of labour in many family farming systems often means that men have access to the more highly valued tasks and to goods that have value in the outside world. The women are more involved with food processing, child-bearing and child-rearing, and family maintenance, tasks that generate no income and have no exchange value.

In family farming systems where male labour and decision-making predominate, women and girls tend to be excluded from land rights and other forms of property control. Conversely, in female farming systems, inheritance rules tend to regulate the transmission of property rights more often through females. In Malaysia, gender inequality was less severe than in many parts of the world. Daughters traditionally inherited land equally with sons. In terms of labour force participation, women again ranked high. Women's economic rights produced a significant degree of autonomy for rural women. Over time, however, this has changed. Both colonialism and international development programs have brought disadvantages to Malay women that did not exist before. For example, British colonial officials registered land in the name of men only, regardless of whether the property was owned by a woman or jointly owned by a husband and wife. With independence from British colonial rule, agricultural development programs in Malaysia, as elsewhere, have been aimed at males. The Green Revolution promoted mechanized rice farming and displaced thousands of female workers from their jobs. Rodolphe De Koninck (1992) studied the impact of the Green Revolution in Malaysia and reports how men have become entrepreneurs, borrowing money and purchasing mechanized harvesters. One man used land owned by his sisters and mother without compensation to support his harvester rental business (128). In 100 years, the gender division of labour and women's economic rights and status have been steadily transformed from one in which women had high status to one in which men now have dominant roles.

Industrial Agriculture

Industrial capital agriculture produces crops through capital-intensive means using machinery and purchased inputs such as processed fertilizers for human and animal labour (Barlett 1989:253). It is mostly practised in the United States, Canada, Germany, Russia, and Japan and is increasingly adopted in developing nations such as India and Brazil as well as in socialist countries such as China.

---

industrial capital agriculture: a form of agriculture that is capital-intensive, substituting machinery and purchased inputs for human and animal labour.

industrial collectivized agriculture: a form of industrialized agriculture that involves state control of land, technology, and goods produced.

Industrial agriculture has brought with it *corporate farms,* huge agricultural enterprises that produce goods solely for sale and are owned and operated by companies entirely reliant on hired labour. Industrial agriculture has major social effects (see Figure 3.3).

Much of the labour demand in industrial agriculture is seasonal, creating an ebb and flow of workers, depending on the task and time of year. Crop harvesting is a high-demand point. Leo Chavez (1992) studied the lives of undocumented (illegal) migrant labourers from Central America who work in the huge tomato, strawberry, and avocado fields owned by corporate farms in southern

California. Many of these migrants are Indians from Oaxaca, Mexico. They sneak across the border to work in the United States as a way of making ends meet. In the San Diego area, they live temporarily in shantytowns, or camps that Chavez describes as resembling Third World living conditions (63). Here is what a camp, where all male workers live, is like on Sunday when the men do not go out to work in the fields:

> On Sundays, the campsites take on a community-like appearance. Men bathe, and wash their clothes, hanging them on trees and bushes, or on lines strung between the trees. Some men play soccer and basketball, using a hoop someone has rigged up. Others sit on old crates or tree-stumps as they relax, talk, and drink beer. Sometimes the men talk about fights from the night before. With little else to do, nowhere to go, and few outsiders to talk to, the men often drink beer to pass the time on Saturday nights and Sundays. Loneliness and boredom plague them during nonworking hours. (65)

Another recent change in corporate agriculture has been the introduction of genetically engineered crops. A few large agribusiness corporations and government agencies encouraged this change in Canada. This process has been largely hidden from the bulk of the Canadian population, who are now consuming great quantities of genetically altered food, especially in processed items using canola and soybeans. Brewster Kneen, a former farmer and food activist, has been concerned about the consequences of industrial agriculture in Canada for many years. He argues that there are substantial differences between the ways farmers selected plants and animals in the past, and the use of genetic technology. He argues that farmers were not imposing genetic uniformity, but rather required diversity. He writes:

> We were not violently forcing plants or microorganisms to conform to our model of what they should be in order to maximize our profits. We were encouraging transformations to be sure, but they were gradual, subtle ones that we could only observe after the fact. . . . we do not really know what the long-term consequences of genetic engineering will be, and are not prepared to move slowly and take the time to find out, [this] means that a grand experiment is taking place, and the outcome is anyone's guess. (Kneen 1999:5–8)

Industrial Collectivized Agriculture Industrial collectivized agriculture is a form of industrialized agriculture that involves nonprivate control of land, technology, and goods produced. Mao Tse-tung undertook a massive effort to establish collective production in China. Collectivism's basic goal was to provide for greater economic equality and a greater sense of group welfare than is possible under competitive capitalism. A variety of collective agriculture arrangements have been used in places such as Russia and Eastern Europe, China, Vietnam, Laos, Cambodia, Tanzania, Ethiopia, and Nicaragua.

FIGURE 3.3   Three Features of Industrial Agriculture and Their Social Effects

- Increased use of complex technology (including machinery, chemicals, and genetic research) on new plant and animal varieties.

  Social effects: This feature results in displacement of small landholders and field labourers. For example, replacing mules and horses with tractors for plowing in the U.S. South during the 1930s led to the eviction of small-scale sharecroppers from the land because the landowners could cultivate larger units. Similarly, the invention of mechanical cotton pickers displaced field labourers.

- Increased use of capital (wealth used in the production of more wealth) in the form of money or property.

  Social effects: The high ratio of capital to labour enables farmers to increase production but reduces flexibility. If a farmer invests in an expensive machine to harvest soybeans and then the price of soybeans drops, the farmer cannot simply switch from soybeans to a more profitable crop. Capitalization creates opportunities and risks for farmers. It is most risky for smaller farms, which cannot absorb losses easily.

- Increased use of energy (primarily gasoline to run the machinery and nitrates for fertilizer) to grow crops. This input of energy often exceeds the calories of food energy yielded in the harvest. Calculations of how many calories of energy are used to produce a calorie of food in industrial agricultural systems reveal that some 2.5 calories of fossil fuel are invested to harvest 1 calorie of food—and more than 6 calories are invested when processing, packaging, and transport are taken into account.

  Social effects: This energy-heavy mode of production creates farmers' dependence on the global market of energy supplies.

Source: Adapted from "Industrial Agriculture" by Peggy F. Barlett in *Economic Anthropology,* ed. by Stuart Plattner. Copyright © 1989. Published by Stanford University Press.

Migrant workers picking broccoli in Salinas, California.
■ (Source: © Morton Beebe/CORBIS)

This Romanian collective farm work team is sorting potatoes. Note the feminization of agricultural labour. Teams were composed of close friends, relations, and neighbours so that farms could take advantage of local social relations to satisfy their labour needs. ■ (Source: David Kideckel)

Cultural anthropology studies of collectivized agriculture are rare. This section presents findings from research conducted in Romania, specifically its Olt Land region, which comprises about 65 villages and a high degree of social homogeneity (Kideckel 1993) (see Map 3.6). David Kideckel conducted fieldwork in two periods: first in 1974, during a period of optimism for socialism, and later in 1990, after the revolution that brought socialism's end.

Socialism in Romania involved an extensive state plan with the most comprehensive and centralized system in Eastern Europe. The state oversaw nearly every aspect of society, from university enrollments to the production of steel and tractors. With the completion of agricultural collectivization in the early 1960s, about 30 percent of the land was in state farms, 60 percent in collectives, and 10 percent privately held. Workers on state farms were employees and were paid wages. They received a small garden for their own use. The state farm provided services such as child care facilities and shopping centres. Collective farms, in contrast, were ostensibly "owned" and controlled by their members, who pooled land, labour, and resources. Their earnings were determined by total farm production, and their wages tended to be lower than state farm worker wages. Collective farm workers were entitled to a "use plot" of the collective land. These plots could provide up to three-fourths of subsistence needs. Most of the private land existed in mountain zones where ecology limited the feasibility of collectivization.

In spite of the socialist rhetoric proclaiming equality between all workers, there were economic distinctions between males and females. Women were relegated to agricultural and reproductive labour, while rural men moved into industry. Women were the mainstay of collective farm labour, but they were under-represented among the leadership. Nevertheless, women's increased involvement in wage-earning, and their roles in cultivating household use plots, strengthened their influence in the household and the community. Overall, the gender division of labour involved substantial overlap between male and female roles in the rural sector.

After the revolution of 1989, the policy of returning land to private ownership had mixed results. State farms gave up land reluctantly. Many collective farmers thought that privatized farming was not worth the effort and risk because they were accustomed to shorter working days and shared risk. Some younger people welcomed the idea of private farming but lacked the necessary knowledge to succeed. With Romania's likely membership in the EU, agriculture in the country may go through yet another transition.

The Sustainability of Agriculture

Agriculture requires more in the way of labour inputs, technology, and the use of nonrenewable natural resources than the other systems discussed earlier. The ever-increasing spread of corporate agriculture is displacing other long-standing economic systems, including

industrialism: a mode of production in which goods are produced through mass employment in business and commercial operations.

formal sector: salaried or wage-based work registered in official statistics.

informal sector: work that is outside the formal sector, not officially registered, and sometimes illegal.

MAP 3.6   Olt Region in Romania. The Olt region, or Olt Land, is near the Olt River in central Romania. Romania's geography comprises mountainous, hilly, and lowland terrains. Its population is over 22 million. Romania is the most economically developed country of southeastern Europe with strong agricultural and industrial sectors. The official language is Romanian and the major religion is Romanian Orthodox Christianity.

foraging, horticulture, and pastoralism. It is resulting in the destruction of important habitats, notably rainforests, in its search for agricultural land (along with commercial ranching and other aspects of industrialism, discussed next), and for water and other energy sources to support its enterprises. Intensive agriculture itself is nonsustainable. It is also undermining the sustainability of other systems. Anthropologists have pointed to some of the social costs of agriculture as well (see the Critical Thinking box on page 84).

Industrialism and Post-Industrialism

Industrialism is the production of goods through mass employment in business and commercial operations. In industrial capitalism, the form of capitalism found in most industrialized nations, the bulk of goods are produced not to meet basic needs but to satisfy consumer demands for nonessential goods. Employment in agriculture decreases while jobs in manufacturing and the service sector increase. In some industrialized countries, the number of manufacturing jobs is declining, with more people being employed in service occupations and in the growing area of *information processing* (such as computer programming, data processing, communications, and teaching). Some experts feel that Canada, for example, is moving out of the industrial age and into the information age.

An important distinction exists between the **formal sector**, which is salaried or wage-based work registered in official statistics, and the **informal sector**, which includes work that is outside the formal sector, not officially registered, and sometimes illegal. If you have done babysitting and were paid cash that was not formally recorded by your employer (for tax-deduction purposes) or by you (for income tax purposes), then you have participated in the informal sector. Informal sector activities that are illegal are referred to as being part of the *underground economy,* a huge and uncounted part of global and local economies worldwide.

The Formal Sector

The formal sector comprises a wide array of occupations, ranging from stable and lucrative jobs to unstable or part-time and less lucrative jobs (Calhoun, Light, and Keller 1994). Cultural anthropologists have focused on small-scale workplaces, especially factories.

In one factory study, a team of cultural anthropologists and university graduate students studied the role of ethnicity in social relationships in a Miami clothing factory (Grenier et al. 1992). The clothing plant, a subsidiary of the largest U.S. clothing manufacturer, employs about 250 operators, mainly women. The majority of employees are Cuban women who, fleeing from the Castro regime, immigrated to Miami many years ago. As these employees have begun to retire, they are being replaced by new immigrants from Central America as well as Haitians and African Americans.

The workers are organized into a union, but members of the different ethnic groups have more solidarity with each other than with people in the union. Interethnic rivalry exists around the issue of management's treatment of members of different groups. Many non-Cuban workers claim that management favours Cuban employees. Some supervisors and managers expressed ethnic stereotypes, but not always consistent ones: "Depending on whom one listens to, Haitians are either too slow or too fast; Cubans may talk too much or be extraordinarily dedicated workers" (1992:75). Managers see ethnic-based competition and lack of cooperation as a key problem that they attempt to deal with in various ways. For example, management banned workers from playing personal radios and installed a system of piped-in music by a radio station that supposedly alternates between "American" and "Latino" songs.

The Informal Sector

Studying the informal sector presents several challenges. People who work in the informal sector may not be "organized" in one location, like a factory. Often, workers are involved in illegal activities, which means they are even less willing than other people to be "studied." In general, it is easier to do research on aspects of people's lives of which they are proud. Informal economy work may yield a sense of pride less often than formal economy

Critical Thinking

WAS THE INVENTION OF AGRICULTURE A TERRIBLE MISTAKE?

Most Euro-Americans have a "progressivist" view that agriculture is a major advance in cultural evolution because it brought with it so many things that westerners admire—cities, centres of learning and art, powerful state governments, and monumental architecture:

> Just count our advantages. We enjoy the most abundant and varied foods, the best tools, and material goods, some of the longest and healthiest lives, in history. . . . From the progressivist perspective on which I was brought up, to ask "Why did almost all our hunter-gatherer ancestors adopt agriculture?" is silly. Of course they adopted it because agriculture is an efficient way to get more food for less work. (Diamond 1994:106)

Another claim about the advantage of agriculture is that it allows more leisure time, so art could flourish. Why would one rather be a hunter-gatherer, struggling every day to make ends meet?

On the other hand, many scholars raise serious questions about the advantages of agriculture. These "revisionists" argue that agriculture may be "the worst mistake in the history of the human race . . . a catastrophe from which we have never recovered" (Diamond 1994:105–106). Some of the "costs" of agriculture include

social inequality; disease; despotism; and destruction of the environment from soil exhaustion and chemical poisoning, water pollution, dams and river diversions, and air pollution from tractors, transportation, and processing plants.

With agriculture, life did improve for many people, but not all. Elites emerged with distinct advantages, but the gap between the haves and the have-nots increased. Health improved for the elites, but not the landless poor and labouring classes. With the vast surpluses of food created by agricultural production, elaborate state systems developed with new forms of power exercised over the common people.

CRITICAL THINKING QUESTIONS

- What is your definition of the "good life"?
- Given your definition, how does life in pre-agricultural societies compare to life in contemporary agricultural and industrial societies?
- What are the benefits and costs of achieving the good life among the Ju/wasi compared to contemporary agricultural and industrial societies?
- Who gets the good life in each type of economy?

---

work. On the other hand, some research advantages also arise. People involved in the informal economy, compared to a CEO of a multinational corporation, may

A street vendor in Kingston, Jamaica. In many modernizing countries, city planners are taking steps to make street vending illegal on the grounds that such informal stands are unsightly. ■ (Source: Barbara Miller)

have more time to share with the anthropologist. This is not always the case, however, since many informal sector workers are involved in more than one enterprise in an attempt to make ends meet, as well as being responsible for child care.

The illegal drug industry is an important part of the globalized informal economy. Neither international drug dealers nor street sellers pay income tax on their profits, and their earnings are not part of the official GNP of any nation. In the United States and Canada, many young males are drawn into the drug economy as sellers. Their lives are fractured with danger and violence. Some anthropologists have undertaken research in such settings, including Philippe Bourgois (1995), who reports on his findings about Hispanic crack dealers in Harlem:

> Regular displays of violence are necessary for success in the underground economy—especially at the street-level drug-dealing world. Violence is essential for maintaining credibility and for preventing rip-off by colleagues, customers, and hold-up artists. Indeed, upward mobility in the underground economy requires a systematic and effective use of violence. . . . Behaviour that appears

irrationally violent and self-destructive to the middle class (or the working class) outside observer, can be reinterpreted according to the logic of the underground economy, as a judicious case of public relations, advertising, rapport building, and long-term investment in one's "human capital development." (29)

In many parts of the world, prostitution is illegal but exists as part of the informal sector. In Thailand, the sex industry, although illegal, is the leading sector of the economy (Skrobanek, Boonpakdee, and Jantateero 1997). In 1990, Thailand's sex industry accounted for about 10 percent of Thailand's GNP, following closely behind income from all agricultural imports. Much of the income derives from Thailand's international popularity as a place for "sex tourism," which is travel that includes a "sex package." Thai prostitutes are also part of the international "export" sex industry. Over 200 000 Thai prostitutes live in Europe, while many others live in Japan, Hong Kong, Taiwan, Singapore, Canada, the United States, Saudi Arabia, and Kuwait.

Child sex work in Thailand is an increasingly important part of this informal economy. The number of child prostitutes under 16 years old is estimated to be about 800 000, or 40 percent of the total prostitute labour force. Recent changes, especially the fear of AIDS, have stepped up the demand for ever-younger prostitutes, since people associate child sex with safe sex. Health risks are high for prostitutes. In Thailand, statistics show that AIDS is increasing rapidly among child prostitutes. Many international organizations have become involved in focusing attention on the issue of child prostitution in Thailand.

How do children become involved in commercial sex work? Family poverty is a major part of the answer in Thailand. Low and declining incomes in rural northern Thailand continue to prompt parents to send children into sex work. Within the context of severe and increasing

Child labour is prominent in many modes of production. In this photograph, a girl picks coffee beans in Guatemala.
■ (Source: © Sean Sprague/Stock Boston, LLC)

poverty in northern Thailand, however, a village-based study provides further details about how culture shapes family decisions about sending daughters into sex work (Rende Taylor 2005). In northern Thailand generally, and in the study village, daughters are valued members of the family. Along with their value come obligations to the family. From an early age, the eldest daughter is expected to assume major household responsibilities, including care of her younger siblings. The youngest daughter will inherit the house and, with it, the obligation to care for her aging parents. Middle daughters are the ones most likely to be sent outside to earn an income, often in commercial sex work. Parents are more concerned about the welfare of the family than about a daughter's involvement in commercial sex work. They say, "The problem here isn't that our daughter sells her body . . . it's that we have no food to eat" (2005:416).

The views and voices of the children themselves are also important (Montgomery 2001). Research in a small slum community on the edge of a tourist town, frequented mainly by Europeans, reveals that the children reject the view of child prostitutes as mere victims, a view promoted by international organizations concerned with child welfare and rights. They believe the work they do is moral because it is done in support of their family. The child sex workers and their pimps, also children, exercise some choice in deciding which clients to accept and which to reject. These insights do not deny the fact that the child sex workers are exploited and often seriously harmed. They do, however, provide a fuller picture by showing how the children define their work as related to family obligations, and how they seek to protect themselves within a context of limited options.

This study, and other research on child labour worldwide, raises important questions about what childhood is, what a good childhood is, and what child rights are and should be (Panter-Brick and Smith 2000). The voices and views of the children must be heard. But scholars and activists must look beyond the children's emic worlds to the global structures that generate and support the people who pay for sex with children and the poverty in the communities that send children into sex work.

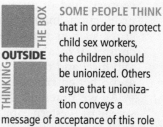

OUTSIDE THE BOX | THINKING

SOME PEOPLE THINK that in order to protect child sex workers, the children should be unionized. Others argue that unionization conveys a message of acceptance of this role for children. Where do you stand on this issue and why?

Changing Modes of Production

This section looks at changes that have occurred in recent times in the five modes of production. Most notably, European colonialism, starting in the fifteenth century, had dramatic effects on indigenous people's production, mainly through the introduction of cash crops such as tea, coffee, and cotton; co-optation and control of local labour through slavery, indentureship, and hire; and taking over land for colonial plantations and other enterprises.

As we noted at the beginning of this chapter, the spread of Western capitalism in recent times continues to have far-reaching effects on the local economies with which it comes in contact. In the later part of the twentieth century, major economic growth in Asia, the demise of socialism in the former Soviet Union, and the increasing economic power of the United States throughout the world have combined to move everyone, everywhere into the global economy. The term *global economy* refers to the interconnectedness of all aspects of international, transnational, national, and local economies: raw materials, labour supply, transportation, finance, and marketing (Robins 1996).

This interconnectedness is also characterized by its instantaneity. Electronic forms of communication mean, more than ever, that when a world economic power centre sneezes, the rest of the world will catch a cold. Social scientists vigorously debate the effects of economic globalization on poverty and inequality (Ravaillon 2003). Economists, who tend to rely on national figures about changing income levels and distribution, have often espoused the view that economic globalization is beneficial overall, because it increases economic activity. Cultural anthropologists, who work with localized data and a more "on the ground" view, tend to emphasize the negative effects of capitalist expansion into noncapitalist settings (Blim 2000). They point to three major transformations:

- Increases in commercial production in local and periphery regions in response to the demands of a global market
- Recruitment of former foragers, horticulturalists, pastoralists, and family farmers to work in the industrialized sector and their exploitation in that setting
- Dispossession of local people of their land and other resource bases and substantial growth in the numbers of unemployed, displaced people

Examples exist of some foraging-horticultural groups choosing to become involved in the global economy on their own terms (Godoy et al. 2005). Far more often, however, these cultures have been destroyed by the intrusion of Western economic interests, their local knowledge has been lost, and the people have become demoralized, distressed, ill, and suicidal. The following examples illustrate ways that small-scale cultures have dealt with Western capitalism and globalization.

Foragers: The Tiwi of Northern Australia

The Tiwi live on two islands off the north coast of Australia (see Map 3.7) (Hart, Pilling, and Goodale 1988). As foragers, the Tiwi gathered food, especially vegetables (such as yams) and nuts, grubs, small lizards, and fish. Women provided the bulk of the daily diet with their gathered vegetables and nuts that were ground and cooked into a porridge. Occasionally men hunted kangaroos, wildfowl, and other game such as *goanna*, larger lizards. Vegetables, nuts, and fish were abundant year-round. The Tiwi lived a more comfortable life than Aboriginal groups of the mainland, where the environment was less hospitable.

The Tiwi have long been in contact with different foreign influences, beginning in the 1600s with the arrival of the Portuguese, who were attracted to the islands as a

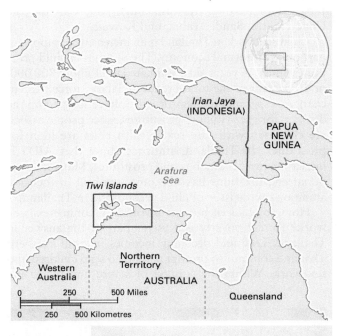

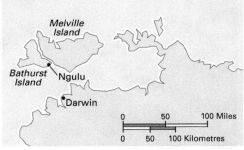

MAP 3.7 Tiwi Region in Northern Australia. The Tiwi Islands consist of Bathurst and Melville Islands. The total number of Tiwi is about 2500 people. Most Tiwi live on Bathurst Island. In 2001, the Tiwi Islands Local Government Area was established, launching a new era of local government with statutory authority.

source of iron. Later, in 1897, an Australian buffalo hunter named Joe Cooper came to the islands and kidnapped two Native women to train as mainland guides in the Tiwi language. Cooper and his group greatly changed the Tiwi by introducing a desire for Western goods, especially tobacco. Later, Japanese traders arrived, offering Tiwi men manufactured goods in return for Tiwi women. In the early 1900s, the French established a Catholic mission on one island. The mission disapproved of the traditional Tiwi marriage pattern of polygamy (multiple spouses, in this case a man having more than one wife) and promoted monogamy instead. The year 1942 brought World War II to the Tiwi, as the Japanese bombed and strafed a U.S. airstrip. Military bases were prominent on the islands. Tiwi dependency on Western manufactured goods increased.

Tiwi residence patterns have changed substantially. The Tiwi have become settled villagers living in houses built of corrugated iron sheets. Tiwi men now play football (soccer) and water polo and engage in competitive javelin throwing. Tiwi art, especially carving and painting, is widely recognized in Australia and, increasingly, internationally.

The Tiwi are active in public affairs and politics, including the Aboriginal rights movement. Another major factor of change is international tourism, a force that the Tiwi are managing with dignity and awareness. One Tiwi commented that tourism may mean "that white people too will learn to live with and survive in the country" (Hart, Pilling, and Goodale 1988:144–145).

Horticulturalists: The Mundurucu of the Brazilian Amazon

Outside economic and political factors have major effects on horticultural societies. The rubber industry's impact on indigenous peoples of the Amazon ranges from maintenance of many aspects of traditional life to the complete loss of traditional life-ways. Like the Tiwi, the Mundurucu illustrate the complexities of change that are neither complete cultural retention nor complete loss (Murphy and Murphy 1985). After the arrival of Brazilians who were commercial rubber producers in the Amazon in the late nineteenth century, many Indians began to work for the Brazilians as latex tappers. For over a century, Mundurucu men combined their traditional horticultural life with seasonal work in the rubber area collecting latex. Marked cultural change occurred when many Mundurucu opted to leave their traditional villages, migrating to live in the rubber area year-round.

In the traditional villages, men still live in a separate house at one side of the village, with husbands visiting wives and children in their group houses. In the rubber settlement, husbands and wives live in their own houses and there is no separate men's house. In the traditional

Aboriginal artist Eymard Tungatalum retouches a traditional Tiwi carving in an art gallery in Australia's Northern Territory. Tungatalum's carvings, along with songs and poems, are an important part of the Aboriginal people's efforts to revive their culture.
■ (Source: © Reuters/Megan Lewis/Archive Photos)

villages, women's communal work groups shared water-carrying tasks. Such groups do not exist in the rubber settlement villages. The husbands have taken over the task of carrying the water, so men work harder than in the traditional village. Although women in the settlement area work more hours per day than men, they believe that life is better because they like living in the same house with their husbands.

Pastoralists: The Herders of Mongolia

In the early 1990s, cultural anthropologist Melvyn Goldstein and physical anthropologist Cynthia Beall (1994) were allowed to do fieldwork among herders in Mongolia, a landlocked and mountainous country located between Russia and China. The Mongolian rural economy has long been, and still is, heavily dependent on animal herds. The "big five" animals are sheep, goats, cattle (mostly yak), horses, and camels. As one herder said, "The animals are our food and money. They give us our dairy products and meat to eat, dung to warm our *ger* [tent], and wool and skins to make our felt and clothes . . . " (38). Sheep and goats provide meat and clothing and some milk, yaks are most important for dairy products because they give milk all year, and horses and camels provide transportation. Goldstein and Beall wanted to study how the transformation from a socialist, collectivized, pastoral economy to a capitalist, market system was affecting the people.

Since the 1950s, the former USSR ruled Mongolia and sought to transform it into an agricultural and industrial state. As urban centres were established, the urban population began to grow and the rural population declined. The state provided all social services, such as health and education. There was no homelessness or unemployment.

The official policy regarding pastoralism was to ban private ownership and collectivize the herds. The transition was not smooth or easy. Collectivization resulted in a 30 percent reduction of livestock, as owners chose to slaughter animals rather than collectivize them (Barfield 1993). Subsequently, policy was altered and the people were allowed to control some of their own animals.

Starting in the late 1980s, the transition away from socialist economic policies spread to Mongolia. By the early 1990s, privatization, a process of transferring the collective ownership and provision of goods and services to a system of private ownership, was the government's policy guideline. Collective ownership of herds was abandoned, and family-organized production was reinstated.

Goldstein and Beall (1994) selected a more traditional region for their research: the Moost district in the Altai Mountain area in the southeastern part of the country. The district includes over 26 000 square kilometres (10 000 square miles) of mountain and valley land, of which 99.9 percent is pasture. The area contains about 4000 people and about 115 000 head of livestock. Goldstein and Beall set up their *ger* and were immediately welcomed by an invitation to have milk-tea, a hot drink made of tea, water, milk, butter, and salt. During their stay, they spoke with many of the nomads, participated in their festivals, and learned about perceptions of economic change.

Changes in the wider Mongolian economy during privatization created serious problems for the herders. Their standard of living declined markedly in the early 1990s. Goods such as flour, sugar, candy, and cooking oil were no longer available. Prices for meat fluctuated widely, and the herders, who had become accustomed to the security of state-controlled prices, had to adjust to market fluctuations. Lower meat prices meant fewer herd animals were slaughtered. Larger herd sizes exceeded the carrying capacity of the grasslands.

External political and economic policies and events have had major effects on Mongolian herders' lifestyle. They have had to adjust to dramatic restructuring of their economy, from private family herding to collectivized herding and then back to private herding, in the space of a few decades. Along with these changes, social services such as health care and schools, which were relatively easy to access during the collective period, became less readily available with privatization. We can only wonder how individual agency and choice have played a part within these massive structural changes. One scholar of central Asian pastoralists comments in an upbeat way that the cultural identity and pride of the descendants of Genghis Khan will endure (Barfield 1993:176) even though their numbers have dwindled, their standard of living has declined, and their herding practices are now part of the global economy.

Even the most remote areas of Mongolia are now connected to the wider world through satellite dishes.
■ (Source: © Adrian Arbib/CORBIS)

Family Farmers: The Maya of Chiapas, Mexico

Some applied anthropologists and other development specialists have said that family farmers in closed communities are "risk averse" because they avoid adopting innovations such as new techniques for cultivation, new seed varieties, and new forms of fertilizer. Economic anthropologists have shown, in contrast, that such conservatism may be adaptive. Family farmers have intimate knowledge of the systems within which they work, and they are capable of assessing costs and benefits of innovations. These two perspectives both emphasize the farmers' agency as decision-makers, determining whether they should change in certain directions. In contrast, development projects such as the construction of roads, global patterns in demand for certain products, and labour opportunities shape the options that farmers have to consider.

Economic anthropologist Frank Cancian first studied production among the Mayan Indians of Zinacantán, located in the Chiapas region of Mexico's southern region, in 1960. He returned in 1983 to conduct a restudy and thus gained insight into changes that had taken place in the intervening 20 years (1989). At the time of his first research, most Zinacantecos earned their livelihood by growing corn and selling some of their crops in a nearby city. They were largely independent of outside forces in terms of their own food supply. The community was closely knit, its social boundaries defined by people's commitment to community roles and ceremonies. Twenty years later, both the local economy and the social system had changed, reflecting the much greater effects of the world system economy on the region. Zinacantán's economy had become much more connected with forces beyond its borders.

The major direct cause of change was the massive increase in public spending by the government in the

1970s. This spending supported the construction of roads, dams, schools, and housing throughout the Chiapas region. The government also sponsored outreach programs to promote agricultural change, mainly crop diversification and ways to increase production. Another important factor was the oil boom in northern Chiapas and nearby Tabasco province, which brought huge amounts of cash into the local economy.

By 1983, 40 percent of the households had no land at all and planted no corn. The majority of the population had become involved in wage work, and unemployment, rather than a bad farming season, was the major threat to food security. Wage work included the new opportunities in road construction, government jobs, transportation (of people, food goods, and flowers), and full-time trading in urban markets reachable by the new roads.

This story, in its general outlines, is similar to that of many family farmers throughout the world, especially in developing countries. It involves transformation from production for own-use to production for sale within a monetized system of trade for profit. Having sold the family farm, self-employed farmers enter the wage economy and become dependent on it for their livelihood. Many Zinacantecos raised their income level substantially during this period, and a clear income gap emerged among different categories of people. Being able to buy one or more trucks and take advantage of the new opportunities for urban trade created by the new roads was the most reliable way to become richer. In contrast, households with the least access to cash were left behind; these households were characteristically headed by a woman on her own.

Overall, the area became more prosperous, more monetized, and more dependent on the outside economy. Internally, social differentiation increased, and social solidarity within the community declined.

Industrialists: Factory Workers in Ohio

Increased mechanization is another major aspect of change in industry worldwide, and it has marked impacts on labour. Unemployment and manufacturing declines in the U.S. Rust Belt are well-known trends in industrial lifeways. Gregory Pappas (1989) studied unemployment in Barberton, a working-class Ohio town. A tire company that had been Barberton's major employer closed in 1980, eliminating 1200 jobs. Pappas lived in Barberton for a year, interviewing many people and sending a questionnaire to over 600 displaced workers for further information. His work sheds light on how unemployed workers coped either by migrating or by finding new ways to spend their time in Barberton. These people are

faced with having to construct a new identity for themselves: "For factory workers the place of employment is crucial; their identities are bound up in a particular place, and plant shutdowns compromise their ability to understand themselves" (83). As one unemployed man commented, "I don't know who I am anymore." In this context of decline, levels of stress and mental disorder have increased for many people.

Global Capitalism: Taiwanese in South Africa

In South Africa during the 1990s, after the dismantling of apartheid, political leaders adopted a neoliberal economic policy (Hart 2002). One step toward expanding production and trade was to forge links with Taiwanese businesses in hopes of transferring to South Africa the Asian economic "miracle." Several Taiwanese industries were established outside major urban areas. Although there is no simple explanation for the so-called Asian economic miracle, one component was family-based production in which power structures governed by age and gender ensured compliance among workers.

Taiwanese managers tried to use such a hierarchical family system in South Africa in order to bring about a smoothly functioning labour force. Research in Taiwanese knitwear factories in KwaZulu-Natal province in western South Africa reveal substantial worker resentment against the Taiwanese managers. Women workers were especially vocal. Taiwanese patterns of communicating with women workers by using an idiom of family did not work with the South Africans. The women said they felt as though they were being treated like animals. The Taiwanese industrialists were separated from the workers by a wide racial, economic, and social divide. Imposing hierarchical family metaphors failed to create a cooperative workforce in South Africa. Many of the Taiwanese industrialists found themselves a focal point of local political conflict. In one town, a Chinese welcome monument was removed.

Although Karl Marx predicted that capitalism would wither away, it has not yet done so. In its latest aspect, global incorporation, its effects are ever more powerfully felt in localities worldwide. Marx would be interested to observe how the Tiwi are developing international tourism, how the Maya people in Chiapas took up road construction for cash, and how Taiwanese knitwear manufacturers in KwaZulu-Natal encountered problems in cross-cultural labour management. Marx would perhaps be surprised to see how, at the same time, cultural anthropologists are trying to document and understand these changes.

Key Questions Revisited

WHAT is the scope of economic anthropology?

Economic anthropology is the study of production, consumption, and exchange cross-culturally. Economic anthropologists classify cross-cultural data on production, or ways of making a living, into five modes: foraging, horticulture, pastoralism, agriculture, and industrialism.

The current world system economy is increasingly competitive and unequal, placing some countries in the core where their strong governments protect and expand their economic interests. Some countries are in the semiperiphery, and many are in the periphery. Economic anthropologists mainly study local economic practices and beliefs but they increasingly realize that they must also study regional and global factors that affect local economies.

WHAT are the characteristics of the five major modes of production?

Foraging involves collecting food that is available in nature. In foraging societies, the division of labour is based on gender and age, with temperate foragers having more gender overlap in tasks than circumpolar foragers. All group members have equal rights to resources. Foraging has long-term sustainability when not affected by outside pressure.

Horticulture and pastoralism are extensive strategies that depend on domesticated plants (horticulture) and animals (pastoralism). Horticulture requires fallowing, and pastoralism requires the constant movement of animals to fresh pastures. The division of labour varies, including situations in which men do more productive work, those where women do more work, and those in which workloads are shared equally between men and women. *Use rights* are the prominent form of property relations. Both horticulture and pastoralism have long-term sustainability when not affected by encroachments.

Family-farming systems produce crops for the family's use and for sale in the market. Most family-farming systems involve more male labour in the fields and more female labour in the domestic domain. Socialist states created a form of labour organization for farming through the collective. Agriculture's sustainability is limited by the need to replenish the land.

In industrialism, the division of labour is highly differentiated by class, gender, and age. Widespread unemployment is found in many industrial economies. In capitalist societies, private property is the dominant pattern. Socialist societies have attempted to distribute property among all people, but most attempts have not been successful. Industrialism lacks sustainability.

WHAT are some directions of change in the five modes of production?

Foragers are being incorporated into settled economies as their access to land is constricted by outside forces and as governments force them to sedentarize. Many former foraging people now work as farm labourers and in other jobs of low status in the mainstream cash economy. Others are advocating for the revitalization of their culture in the new global economy, producing art for sale on the world market, developing cultural tourism opportunities for outsiders, or gaining a share in profits related to commercialization of their indigenous knowledge.

Horticulture and pastoralism are under great pressure from the competing economic forms of agriculture and industrialism. Many former horticulturalists have migrated to plantations or urban areas and become part of the cash economy. States have pressured pastoralism to settle down or (in communist systems) to become collectivized and then (with the decline of communism) decollectivized. Family farms are declining worldwide in number as corporate farms increase. The labour supply has changed from being family based to including a high proportion of migrant labourers.

Capitalism increasingly involves international investments and location of production sites in countries where wages are low. Such situations implicate culture in complex ways, including managerial issues and cross-cultural communication.

KEY CONCEPTS

agriculture, p. 77
extensive strategy,
    p. 68
family farming, p. 77
foraging, p. 67
formal sector, p. 83
horticulture, p. 73

indigenous knowledge (IK),
    p. 77
industrial capital agriculture,
    p. 80
industrial collectivized
    agriculture, p. 81
industrialism, p. 83

informal sector, p. 83
intensive strategy, p. 77
mode of production, p. 66
pastoralism, p. 75
public–private dichotomy,
    p. 79
use rights, p. 70

SUGGESTED READINGS

Anne Allison, *Nightwork: Sexuality, Pleasure and Corporate Masculinity in a Tokyo Hostess Club.* Chicago: University of Chicago Press, 1994. Based on the author's participant observation, this book explores what it is like to work as a hostess in a club that caters to male corporate employees and discusses how that culture is linked to men's corporate work culture.

Jans Dahl, *Saqqaq: An Inuit Hunting Community in the Modern World.* Toronto: University of Toronto Press, 2000. This ethnography of Saqqaq, a hunting community located on Disko Bay, eastern Greenland, is based on fieldwork carried out at several times since 1980 in order to provide a diachronic perspective. Hunting beluga is a central activity and still forms the basis of community identity, even though commercial fishing and other economic activities have gained importance in recent times.

J. A. English-Lueck. *Cultures@SiliconValley.* Stanford, CA: Stanford University Press, 2002. A team of professors and anthropology students at San Jose State University have been conducting research for over a decade in Silicon Valley, and this book is the result of that work. The focus is on describing what life is like for people in a "technology-saturated" environment, from working to shopping to family life.

Elliot Fratkin, *Ariaal Pastoralists of Kenya: Surviving Drought and Development in Africa's Arid Lands.* Boston: Allyn and Bacon, 1998. Based on several phases of ethnographic research among the Ariaal beginning in the 1970s, this book provides insights about pastoralism in general and the particular cultural strategies of the Ariaal, including attention to social organization and family life.

John G. Galaty and Pierre Bonte, eds., *Herders, Warriors, and Traders: Pastoralism in Africa.* Boulder, CO: Westview Press, 1991. This collection of readings examines the ability of pastoralists in Africa to maintain their way of life despite years of droughts and war.

David Uru Iyam, *The Broken Hoe: Cultural Reconfiguration in Biase Southeast Nigeria.* Chicago: University of Chicago Press, 1995. Based on fieldwork among the Biase people by an anthropologist who is a member of a Biase group, this book examines changes since the 1970s in the traditional forms of subsistence—agriculture, fishing, and trade—and related issues such as environmental deterioration and population growth.

Richard Lee and Richard Daly, eds., *The Cambridge Encyclopaedia of Hunters and Gatherers.* Cambridge, UK: Cambridge University Press, 1999. This comprehensive book, written by recognized leaders in the field, outlines and evaluates anthropological knowledge on hunters and gatherers worldwide.

Heather Montgomery, *Modern Babylon? Prostituting Children in Thailand.* New York: Bergahn Books, 2001. The author conducted fieldwork in a tourist community in Thailand where parents frequently commit their children to prostitution. She sought to gain a view of this system from the perspective of the children and the parents. She found that these insiders' views are far more complex than the monolithic "victim" picture painted by international agencies.

Brian Morris, *The Power of Animals: An Ethnography.* New York: Berg, 1998. This book is an ethnography of Malawi in southern Africa. It is based on in-depth fieldwork in one region, supplemented by travel and study throughout the country. It focuses on men's roles in animal hunting and women's roles in agriculture as crucial to understanding wider aspects of Malawian culture, including diet and food preparation, marriage and kinship, gender relations, and attitudes about nature.

Katherine S. Newman, *Falling from Grace: The Experience of Downward Mobility in the American Middle Class.* New York: The Free Press, 1988. Newman provides ethnographic research on the downwardly mobile of New Jersey as a "special tribe," with attention to loss of employment by corporate managers and blue-collar workers, and the effects of downward mobility on middle-class family life, particularly among women.

Richard H. Robbins, *Global Problems and the Culture of Capitalism.* Boston: Longman, 1999. Robbins takes a critical look at the role of capitalism and global economic growth in creating and sustaining many world problems such as poverty, disease, hunger, violence, and environmental destruction. The last section includes extended case studies to support the argument.

Michael K. Steinberg, Joseph J. Hobbs, and Kent Mathewson, eds. *Dangerous Harvest: Drug Plants and the Transformation of Indigenous Landscapes.* New York: Oxford University Press, 2004. Various contributors address opium and the people of Laos, opium production in Afghanistan and Pakistan, struggles over coca in Bolivia, marijuana growing by the Maya, use of kava in the Pacific, and policy questions.

4

Consumption and Exchange

Key Questions

- WHAT is consumption in cross-cultural perspective?

- WHAT is exchange in cross-cultural perspective?

- HOW are consumption and exchange changing?

A scene at the annual camel fair in Pushkar, in Rajasthan, India. Every year, 200 000 people gather to trade and admire camels and other animals. Herding people set up camp and are joined by food vendors, carousel operators, and tourists. Camel races and cattle beauty contests are high points. (*Source:* © *Brian A. Vikander/CORBIS*)

Imagine that it is the late eighteenth century and you are a member of the Kwakwa̲ka'wakw (pronounced: KWA kwuh kyuh' wakw) of British Columbia (see the Ethnographic Profile on page 116). You and your tribal group are invited to a **potlatch**, a feast in which the host lavishes the guests with abundant quantities of the best food and many gifts (Suttles 1991). The most honourable foods are fish oil, high-bush cranberries, and seal meat, and they will be served in ceremonial wooden bowls. Gifts include embroidered blankets, household articles such as carved wooden boxes and woven mats, canoes, and items of

Villagers assemble gifts in preparation for a potlatch, held before 1914 in Alert Bay, Vancouver Island.
■ (Source: J. Welsh/Royal British Columbia Museum 2307b)

food. The more the chief gives, the higher his status rises and the more his guests are indebted to him. Later, when it is the guests' turn to hold a potlatch, they will give away as much as, or more than, their host did.

The Pacific Coast region is rich in fish, game, berries, and nuts, among other foods. Nonetheless, given regional climatic variation, food supplies were often uneven, with some groups each year having surpluses while others faced scarcity. The potlatch system helped to smooth out these variations: Groups with a surplus would sponsor a potlatch and those experiencing a leaner year were guests. In this way, potlatching established a *social safety net* across a wide area of the Northwest.

This brief sketch of potlatching shows the linkages among the three economic processes of production, consumption, and exchange. Potlatches are related to production, are opportunities for consumption, and involve exchange. Chapter 3 began the discussion of economic systems with the subject of production. This chapter provides cross-cultural examples of the other two components of economic systems:

■ **Mode of consumption:** the dominant way, in a culture, of using up goods and services.

■ **Mode of exchange:** the dominant way, in a culture, of transferring goods, services, and other items between and among people and groups.

In the chapter's last section, we provide examples of contemporary change in consumption and exchange.

Culture and Consumption

In this section, we examine the concept of consumption, cross-cultural patterns of consumption budgets, consumption inequalities, and two theoretical positions on *food taboos* (forbidden food).

What Is Consumption?

Consumption has two senses: First, it is a person's "intake" in terms of eating or other ways of using things; second, it is "output" in terms of spending or using

potlatch: a grand feast in which guests are invited to eat and to receive gifts from the hosts.
mode of consumption: the dominant pattern, in a culture, of using things up or spending resources in order to satisfy demands.
mode of exchange: the dominant pattern, in a culture, of transferring goods,

services, and other items between and among people and groups.
minimalism: a mode of consumption that emphasizes simplicity, is characterized by few and finite (limited) consumer demands, and involves an adequate and sustainable means to achieve them.
consumerism: a mode of consumption in which people's demands are many and

infinite and the means of satisfying them are insufficient and become depleted in the effort to satisfy these demands.
levelling mechanism: an unwritten, culturally embedded rule that prevents an individual from becoming wealthier or more powerful than anyone else.

resources to obtain those things. Thus, for example, "intake" is eating a sandwich; "output" is spending money at the store to buy a sandwich. Both activities fit within the term of consumption.

People consume many things. Food, beverages, clothing, and shelter are the most basic consumption needs in most cultures. People also may acquire tools, weapons, means of transportation, computers, books and other items of communication, art and other luxury goods, and energy for heating and cooling their residence. In cashless economies, such as foragers, people "spend" time or labour in order to provide for their needs. In money-based economies, such as industrialized contexts today, most consumption depends on having cash or some virtual form of money.

Modes of Consumption

In categorizing modes of consumption, it makes sense to consider two contrasting modes, with mixed modes in the middle (see Figure 4.1). They are based on the relationship between *demand* (what people want) and *supply* (the resources available to satisfy demand):

- **Minimalism**: a mode of consumption characterized by few and finite (limited) consumer demands and an adequate and sustainable means to achieve them. It is most characteristic of free-ranging foragers but is also found to some degree among horticulturalists and pastoralists.

- **Consumerism**: a mode of consumption in which people's demands are many and infinite, and the means of satisfying them are never sufficient, thus driving colonialism, globalization, and other forms of expansionism. Consumerism is the distinguishing feature of industrial/informatic cultures. Globalization is spreading consumerism throughout the world.

The social organization and meaning of consumption varies cross-culturally. As we noted in Chapter 3, foragers are generally egalitarian, whereas social inequality characterizes most agricultural and industrial/informatic societies. Among foragers, sharing within the group is the norm, and everyone has equal access to all resources. Among the Ju/'hoansi: "Even though only a fraction of the able-bodied foragers go out each day, the day's return of meat and gathered foods are divided in such a way that every member of the camp receives an equitable share" (Lee 1979:118). Among the Hadza of northern Tanzania, people prize meat and eagerly anticipate the arrival of a hunting group with large game to share. The man who brings home large game will abide by unwritten rules of sharing and give 90 percent or more of the meat to everyone in the camp group, keeping only a small share for himself and his immediate family (Hawkes et al. 2001).

The distribution of personal goods such as clothing, beads, musical instruments, or smoking pipes is also equal. **Levelling mechanisms** are unwritten, culturally embedded

FIGURE 4.1 Modes of Production, Consumption, and Exchange

Foraging	Horticulture	Pastoralism	Agriculture	Industrialism/Informatics
Mode of Consumption				**Mode of Consumption**
Minimalism				Consumerism
Finite needs				Infinite needs
Social Organization of Consumption				**Social Organization of Consumption**
Equality/sharing				Class-based inequality
Personalized products are consumed				Depersonalized products are consumed
Primary Budgetary Fund				**Primary Budgetary Fund**
Basic needs				Rent/taxes, luxuries
Mode of Exchange				**Mode of Exchange**
Balanced exchange				Market exchange
Social Organization of Exchange				**Social Organization of Exchange**
Small groups, face-to-face				Anonymous market transactions
Primary Category of Exchange				**Primary Category of Exchange**
The gift				The sale

Well-stocked and brightly lit candy shops are a prominent part of urban nightlife in Valencia, Spain. Sugarcane was introduced into Spain by the Arabs. Later, the Spanish established the first sugarcane plantations on Madeira and the Canary Islands using enslaved labourers from Africa. ■ (Source: Barbara Miller)

rules that prevent an individual from becoming wealthier or more powerful than anyone else. They are maintained through social pressure and gossip. An important levelling mechanism among the Ju/'hoansi requires that any large game animal killed be shared with the group, and its killer must be modest, insisting that the meat is meagre and there is no fat at all (Lee 1969). Ju/'hoansi hunters gain no social status or power through their provision of meat. The same applies to other foragers. Levelling mechanisms are important in horticultural and pastoralist societies, too. For example, when someone's herd grows "too large," that person will be subject to social pressure to sponsor a large feast in which many of the herd animals are eaten.

At the other end of the consumption continuum is consumerism, with the United States as the primary example, being the major consumerist country of the world. Since the 1970s, consumption levels in the United States have been the highest of any society in human history, and they show no sign of decline. The mass media send out seductive messages promoting consumerism as the way to happiness. Since China began to adopt some features of capitalism, it has quickly become a consumerist giant. In the world's poorest countries, too, rising numbers of middle- and upper-class people pursue consumerism. One

estimate is that around 800 million people in "developing" and "transition" countries earn enough to be part of the consumerist economy (Myers 2000).

The growth of consumerism worldwide has some major costs:

- *The environment and biological species diversity:* natural features such as rivers and lakes, forests, mountains, and beaches; nonhuman primates and hundreds of other species; and substances such as oil, gold, and diamonds
- *The world's cultural diversity:* people who live in environments being destroyed by consumerism (these people currently occupy the tropical rainforests, circumpolar regions, deserts, and mountain areas)
- *The poor, everywhere:* people whose real and relative incomes place them in poverty and who experience an ever-widening gap between themselves and the well-off and the super-rich

Minimalism was sustainable over hundreds of thousands of years, for most of humanity's time on earth. The amount of goods that the world's population consumed in the past 50 years equals what was consumed by all previous generations in human history.

consumption fund: a category of a personal or household budget used to provide for consumption demands.

A view of Toronto. The demand for electricity in urban centres worldwide has prompted the building of many high dams to generate power. Food must be shipped to urban markets. In general, cities have high energy costs compared with rural areas. ■ (Source: Dick Loek/Canadian Press/Toronto Star)

In the United States, the attention given to the negative effects of consumerism tends to focus on the natural environment (especially "unspoiled" places for vacations) rather than on consumerism's endangerment of indigenous peoples and other nonindustrialized people, minimalists who "tread lightly on the land." The tragic irony is that more people in the United States probably know about an endangered bird species, the spotted owl, than about any single endangered human group—and there are many. Some countries have policies that seek to control consumerism and its negative effects. The government of Sweden has invested in public transportation and bicycle paths in cities in order to reduce the use of cars (Durning 1993). London recently placed a tax on cars entering the city. San Francisco is working on a plan to recycle dog waste and use it to create energy.

As consumerism spreads through globalization, a change in the social relations involved in consumption also occurs. In small-scale societies—such as those of foragers, horticulturalists, and pastoralists—consumption items are typically produced by the consumers themselves for their own use. If not, they are likely to be produced by people with whom the consumer has a personal, face-to-face relationship—in other words, *personalized consumption*. Everyone knows where products came from and who produced them. This pattern contrasts markedly with consumption in our contemporary globalized world, which is termed *depersonalized consumption*. Multinational corporations manage the production of most of the goods that people in industrialized countries consume. These products often are multisourced, with parts assembled in diverse parts of the world by hundreds of unknown workers. Depersonalized consumption, by distancing consumers from workers who actually produce goods, makes it more possible for workers to be exploited.

Even in the most industrialized contexts, depersonalized consumption has not completely replaced personalized consumption. The popularity of farmers' markets in urban centres is an example of personalized consumption in which the consumer buys apples from the person who grew them and with whom the consumer may have a friendly conversation, perhaps while sampling one of the apples. A reaction against depersonalized consumption supports regional markets in southern France where, even though many of the products come from far away, the marketers create a pretense of personalized production in order to satisfy their customers' preferences (de la Pradelle 2006).

Consumption Funds

Anthropologists define a **consumption fund** as a category within a person's or household's budget used to provide for his or her needs and demands. Cross-cultural analysis reveals five categories that appear to be relevant universally. The five funds are

- *Basic needs fund:* for food, beverages, shelter, clothing, fuel, and the tools involved in producing or providing for them
- *Recurrent costs fund:* for maintenance and repair of tools, animals, machinery, and shelter
- *Entertainment fund:* for leisure activities
- *Ceremonial fund:* for social events such as rituals
- *Rent and tax fund:* for payments to landowners or governments for use of land, housing, or civic responsibilities

CAN THE INTERNET CREATE RESPONSIBLE CONSUMERS?

One important feature of increasingly globalized production is that the role of the producer is hidden from the consumer. Furthermore, many products are assembled with parts from all over the world, created by many invisible workers. Daniel Miller says that such labour invisibility and product depersonalization make it all too easy for consumers to be irresponsible and to support practices that are harmful to the distant, unseen labourers (2003). Most consumers are happy enough to blame the higher profits of multinational corporations for the poor treatment of producers. Miller points out, however, that the major responsibility lies with us, the consumers. It is our search for the cheapest possible goods that drives the commercial competition that results in further exploitation of workers. Consumers must be persuaded to pay more in order to facilitate better conditions for producers.

If consumers were educated about the actual dynamics of production and the role of the labourers, they would be more likely to make wiser and more responsible choices about which products to buy. For example, they would avoid products made by the more exploitative companies or by less ecologically responsible companies. And they might be willing to pay higher prices to discourage abuse of workers and of the environment.

Miller sees a lack of attention to consumer education in the school curriculum in his home country, the United Kingdom. It is extraordinary, he says, that we call people "educated" who know more about ancient Rome or physics than about the products they consume every day. Most students will never use the higher math or physics that they study in school, he says, but they will be consumers for the rest of their lives. So why not provide consumer education for students?

Miller devised an Internet education project for schoolchildren that would teach them about the role of workers in relation to the products the children consume in order to link the human faces of producers with the commodities. Having discovered the importance of "interactivity" from his earlier fieldwork on people's use of the Internet in Trinidad, Miller created a plan for an interactive narrative about a product. The Internet could enable students to talk in real time with actual producers going about their work. To avoid a power differential between workers and viewers, the producers should be able to question the students (the consumers) about their lives as well. This interaction would include, in the case of a relatively simple product like a banana, not just the plantation worker but also the wider process of banana production and marketing: plantation managers, packers, and transporters. The students would choose a banana company, webcams would be supplied to the workers, and both students and workers would be connected online once a week. In order to push the reality of production all the way, Miller hopes that students would actually end up eating the same bananas that they saw being produced.

This is a big project, even for just a single commodity. Miller is well aware that people cannot, within reason, learn all the details about the production of every product they consume. He suggests that three exemplary products be more complex to illustrate multiple sourcing. The third product might be locally produced by a small-scale firm.

Miller sought government funding for his project but was denied. Undaunted, he published an article in a journal in order to share his idea and inspire others to develop similar consumer-education projects elsewhere. We ask you, the students of cultural anthropology, to consider Miller's project.

CRITICAL THINKING QUESTIONS

- Is Miller's idea of enhancing the school curriculum in this way important?
- Is it feasible?
- What suggestions do you have for two products in addition to bananas?

The categories apply universally, but the proportion of the budget allocated to each category varies widely and in relation to the mode of consumption. Remember: The "spending" involved may be in time, labour, or money, depending on the cultural context.

In the budget of free-ranging foragers, the largest share of expenditures goes into the basic needs fund. Foragers in temperate climates, however, spend far fewer hours per week collecting food than those in circumpolar climates. The next most important consumption fund among

---

entitlement: a culturally defined right to life-sustaining resources.

foragers is the recurrent costs fund, which supports repair and maintenance of tools and baskets, weapons, and shelter. Smaller shares are devoted to the entertainment fund and the ceremonial fund. Nothing goes into the rent and tax fund, because access to all land and other resources is free.

Consumption budgets in consumerist cultures differ in several ways from those in foraging, minimalist cultures. First, the absolute size of the budget is larger. People in agricultural and industrial societies work longer hours (unless they are unemployed), so they "spend" more of their time and labour providing for their consumption than foragers. Depending on their class position, they may have weekly cash budgets that are worth far more than their earnings due to stored wealth. Second, the relative size of the consumption funds varies in household budgets cross-culturally. Taking as an example an imagined middle-class person in North America, his or her consumption funds might look like this, compared to a forager's: The basic needs fund is a small portion of the total budget, given the increased overall size of the budget. This finding is in line with the economic principle that budgetary shares for food and housing (basic needs) decline as income rises. For example, someone who earns a total of $1000 a month and spends $800 on food and housing spends 80 percent of his budget in that category. Someone who makes $10 000 a month and spends $2000 a month on food and housing spends only 20 percent of her budget in this category, even though she spends more than twice as much as the first person, in an absolute sense. The largest share of the budget is the rent and tax fund. In some agricultural contexts, tenant farmers have to pay one-third to one-half of their crops to the landlord as rent. Income taxes claim well over 50 percent of personal income in countries such as Japan, Sweden, the Netherlands, and Italy. The entertainment fund receives a large share, larger than the ceremonial fund.

Theorizing Consumption Inequalities

Amartya Sen, an economist and a philosopher, proposed the theory of entitlements in order to explain why some groups suffer more than others during a famine (1981). An **entitlement** is a culturally defined right to provide for one's life needs. According to Sen, everyone has a set, or "bundle," of entitlements. For example, a person might own land, earn cash from a job, be on welfare, or live off an inheritance. Some entitlements are more secure and lucrative than others. *Direct entitlements* are the most secure form. In an agricultural society, for example, owning land that produces food is a direct entitlement. *Indirect entitlements* depend on exchanging something in order to obtain consumer needs: labour, animal hides, money,

or food stamps. Because indirect entitlements involve dependency on other people or institutions, they are riskier bases of support than direct entitlements are. When a factory shuts down, animal hides drop in value, or a food stamp program ends, a person depending on those entitlements is in trouble. During times of economic decline, scarcity, or disaster, people with indirect entitlements are the most vulnerable to impoverishment, hunger, and forced displacement.

THINKING OUTSIDE THE BOX — ESTIMATE YOUR MONTHLY EXPENDITURES in terms of the five funds. What proportion of your total expenditures goes to each fund? Do your expenditures fit well within the five categories or are different categories needed?

Entitlements Cross-Culturally

Entitlements vary depending on the type of economic system. In foraging societies, everyone has the same entitlement bundle. Entitlements are mainly direct, with the exception of infants and very old people who depend on sharing from group members for food and shelter. In industrial capitalist societies, entitlements are mainly indirect. People who grow all their own food are a small proportion of the total population. Even they depend on indirect entitlements for electricity and inputs required for maintaining their lifestyles. In highly monetized economies, the most powerful entitlements are those that provide a large and steady cash income, such as a good job. Other strong entitlements include home ownership, savings, stocks and bonds, and a retirement fund.

Internationally, entitlement theory exposes contrasts between countries that have secure and direct access to life-supporting resources and those that do not. Countries that produce food surpluses have a more secure entitlement to food than nations that are dependent on imports, for example. Replacing food crops with **cash crops**, or plants grown primarily for sale, such as coffee or tobacco, rather than for own-use, shifts a country from having mainly direct food entitlements to having mainly indirect entitlements. The same applies to access to energy sources that may be important for transportation to work or for heating homes. Direct access to energy resources is preferable to indirect access. This formula, however, leaves out the important factor of political power as exercised by the core countries of today's global economy. Many core countries lack direct access to critical resources, notably oil, yet they use political force to maintain access to such resources.

At the state level, governments affect people's entitlements through policies related to employment, welfare programs, health care, and tax structures, among others. Political leaders and powerful policy-makers decide how many people will live in poverty and how many will be allowed to become rich, or even super-rich. They decide on whether or not to fund programs that transfer wealth from the rich to the poor or, the opposite, as is the case with regressive tax structures that tax lower-income people at higher rates than the rich.

The entitlement concept can also be applied to intra-household entitlements. Households do not always provide equal entitlements for all members. A household member who is employed and earns wages, for example, has a more secure position than someone who does not. Commonly, men have more secure entitlements than women. Inheritance practices may ensure that certain children, often sons, receive assets such as land or the family business, while others, often daughters, are excluded. Intra-household entitlements may also affect the distribution of food and health care.

During crises, entitlement structures often become glaringly clear. Famines are a good example. *Famine* is defined as massive levels of death resulting from food deprivation in a geographically widespread area. Most people think that famines are caused by overpopulation or by natural disasters such as droughts and floods. Comparative analyses of many famine situations prove, however, that neither overpopulation nor natural disasters are sufficient explanations for famine (Sen 1981). Calculations of world food supply in relation to population prove that there is enough food produced every year to

Homeless children rest by a storefront grate in Ho Chi Minh City, Vietnam. The transition from socialism to capitalism has altered people's entitlement bundle in Vietnam. ■ (Source: Edward Kellar III)

Civil war in southern Sudan in 1998 contributed to the spread of famine. Here, a sister and brother await medical treatment in a Doctors Without Borders relief compound. ■ (Source: Brennan Linsey/Canadian Press)

feed the world's population. Furthermore, although natural factors are often catalysts of famine, they do not always cause famine.

Hurricane Andrew of 1992 devastated much of Florida, but state and federal agencies rushed aid to the stricken area. In Louisiana and Mississippi, the hurricanes of 2005 caused many deaths, massive loss of private and commercial property, and displacement of thousands of people. But they did not cause a famine. Anthony Oliver-Smith, an anthropologist who specializes in disasters, has said that there is no such thing as a purely natural disaster (2002). His point is that culture always shapes the patterns of suffering and loss. The social structure of suffering following the 2005 hurricanes in Louisiana and Mississippi had clear lines according to "race"/ethnicity and class, with low-income African Americans being the hardest hit in every respect.

Entitlement analysis can help improve the effectiveness of humanitarian aid during famines and other crises (Harragin 2004). During the famine in southern Sudan in 1988, relief workers failed to understand the local

THINKING OUTSIDE THE BOX

WHAT IS IN YOUR personal entitlement bundle? Conduct a self-analysis of your daily consumption needs (food, shelter, entertainment, and other things) and how you provide for them. Then, imagine how you would provide for these needs if, starting today, your usual entitlements no longer had any value.

cash crop: a plant grown primarily for sale rather than own-use.

cultural pattern of sharing, which extends to the last cup of rice. As food supplies decreased, local people continued to share whatever food was available. The result was that many people were surviving, but barely. When the food supply declined even more, the social safety net was unable to stretch further, and suddenly hundreds of people were dying. If relief workers had known about the culture of sharing until death, they might have been able to forecast the breaking point before it happened and to bring in food aid sooner.

Consumption Categories

People's consumption patterns are also shaped by class, gender, race, and age. These intersecting categories influence entitlement bundles and ways of consuming resources. People's consumption patterns are rarely the consequences of just one factor but, rather, are shaped by affiliation with multiple and intersecting groups that determine entitlement bundles and ways of consuming resources.

Class and the Game of Distinction in Israeli Birthday Parties

Class differences, defined in terms of levels of income, are reflected in distinctive consumption patterns. Although class differences in consumption may seem too obvious to be worth studying, they constitute an important and growing area in anthropology.

A landmark study about consumer preferences, or "tastes," was conducted by a team of French researchers led by French anthropologist/sociologist Pierre Bourdieu (1984). They sent questionnaires to several thousand people, based on a national sample, and received 1000 responses. Statistical analysis of the responses revealed clear class patterns in, for example, choice of favourite painters or pieces of music. Preferences corresponded with educational level and father's occupation. An overall pattern of *distance from necessity* in tastes and preferences characterized members of the educated upper classes, who were more likely to prefer abstract art. Their goal was to keep "necessity" at a distance. In comparison, the working classes were closer to "necessity," and they preferred realist art. Bourdieu provides the concept of the game of distinction in which people of the upper classes continually adjust their preferences to distance themselves from the lower classes, whereas members of the lower classes tend to adopt aspects of upper-class preferences in order to gain status.

Cross-culturally, events such as weddings, funerals, and children's birthday parties are often occasions requiring large expenditures that send messages about the status (real or aspired) of the hosts. Children's birthday parties are a less-studied topic but one with much

potential, especially since such parties are becoming increasingly popular in cultures around the world. In Israel, children's birthday parties have recently become expensive events among middle-class and upper-class urbanites (Goldstein-Gidoni 2003). Parents hire birthday party professionals to create special themes. "Around the World" themes are popular, especially those drawing on Japanese, Spanish, South American, and Middle Eastern motifs. A current craze for Japanese culture, such as gardens and food, means that the Japanese theme is one of the most popular. "Around the World" birthday party themes are ostensibly to help the children learn about other places and people. At the same time, they make a statement about how cosmopolitan, well-off, and stylish the hosts are.

Not everyone, everywhere, buys into the game of distinction. Many individuals and wider social movements actively resist the spread of upper-class consumption patterns and promote alternative cultural practices.

Gender and Deadly Food in Papua New Guinea

Consumption patterns are often marked by gender and related to discrimination and inequality. Specific foods may be considered "men's food" or "women's food." Beverage consumption is often related to gender, too. In cultures where alcoholic beverages are consumed, the general pattern is that men drink more than women, and certain types of alcoholic beverages are more likely to be consumed by men or women. Gender may play into what are considered appropriate quantities of food.

An example of lethal gender inequalities in food consumption comes from highland Papua New Guinea (see Map 4.1). The story begins with the eruption of a mysterious disease, with the local name of *kuru*, among the Fore (pronounced FOR-AY), a horticultural people

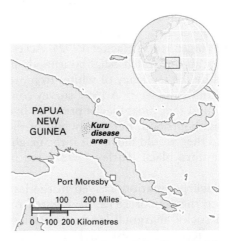

MAP 4.1 Location of the Kuru Epidemic in Papua New Guinea.

(Lindenbaum 1979). Between 1957 and 1977, roughly 2500 people died of kuru. A marked gender pattern in the deaths emerged: Most victims were women. The first signs of kuru are shivering tremors, followed by a progressive loss of motor ability along with pain in the head and limbs. People with kuru could walk unsteadily at first but would later be unable to get up. Death occurred about a year after the first symptoms appeared.

Medical researchers revealed that kuru was a neurological disease. Australian cultural anthropologist Shirley Lindenbaum pinpointed the cultural cause of kuru: cannibalism. Kuru victims had eaten the flesh of deceased people who had died of kuru. Most of the kuru victims were women. Lindenbaum sought to explain the gender bias in the disease. She learned that among the Fore, it was considered acceptable to cook and eat the meat of a deceased person, although it was not a preferred food. The preferred source of animal protein is meat from pigs, and men receive preferential access to the best food. Fore women had begun to eat human flesh more often because of increased scarcity of pigs. Population density in the region had risen, more land was being cultivated, and forest areas had decreased. Pigs live in forest areas, so as their habitat became more restricted, their numbers declined. The Fore could not move to more pig-abundant areas because they were bounded on the east, west, and north sides by other groups. The south was a harsh and forbidding region. These factors, combined with the Fore's male-biased system of protein consumption, forced women to turn to the less-preferred protein source of human flesh. By eating the flesh, including brains, of kuru victims, they contracted the disease.

Race and Living in Africville   In North America racial differences in consumption and welfare exist. One area in which racial discrimination affects consumption is access to housing, a subject that has been studied by cultural anthropologists and other social scientists (B. Williams 1988; Yinger 1995; Hacker 1992). Access by blacks to housing in integrated neighbourhoods in U.S. cities is limited by the tendency of whites to move out as more black families move in. A 1992 survey conducted in Detroit found that most blacks prefer to live in an integrated neighbourhood, but nearly half of the whites surveyed said they would move out if the neighbourhood were one-third black (Farley 1993, cited in Yinger 1995:7).

Nova Scotia's black population arrived in the late 1700s and following the war of 1812. Segregated on small farm lots on rocky, marginal land, the settlers formed Canada's earliest and largest black settlement, Africville. The community had no plumbing, sewage, running water, or paved roads, and was identified as early as 1917 as a slum requiring clearance. It was cleared in the 1960s, with property owners compensated or rehoused. Today, the descendants of Africville view the destruction of their community as racially motivated and seek redress for the injustices of community destruction and relocation (Millward 1996). On July 5, 2002, Africville was designated a national heritage site as a reminder of the need for racial respect.

Age and Consumption Patterns   Age categories often have characteristic consumption patterns that are culturally shaped. Certain foods are believed appropriate for infants, young children, adolescents, adults, or the aged. Consider the category of "the aged." Biologically, the elderly have "more critical and unique nutritional needs" than other age groups (Shifflett and McIntosh 1986–1987). In spite of these special needs, in many cultures the very old fall into a category with declining entitlements and declining quality of consumption. In North America, the elderly tend to decrease their physical activities, and they tend to omit important food groups, especially fruits and vegetables. Little exercise and inadequate diet lead to increased obesity and reduced resistance to disease. Elderly men or women living alone may eat junk food and meals prepared with the least effort.

Aging affects everyone, regardless of class level, but wealth can protect the elderly from certain kinds of marginalization and deprivation. The class effects of aging are somewhat reduced in Canada by community care programs that gear community-based care and long-term institutionalized care to income and the Canada Pension Plan, as well as universal access to health care.

Forbidden Consumption: Food Taboos

Cultural anthropologists have a long-standing interest in trying to explain culturally specific food taboos, or rules about prohibited foods. This interest has generated several conflicting theories, with the strongest difference between cultural materialists and those who favour symbolic or meaning-centred theories.

Marvin Harris and Food Taboos

Marvin Harris (1974) asks why there are Jewish and Muslim taboos on eating pig when pig meat is so enthusiastically consumed in many other parts of the world. He says, "Why should gods so exalted as Jahweh and Allah have bothered to condemn a harmless and even laughable beast whose flesh is relished by the greater part of mankind?" (36). Harris proposes that we consider the role of environmental factors during early Hebrew times and the function of this prohibition in terms of its fit to the local ecology:

> Within the overall pattern of this mixed farming and pastoral complex, the divine prohibition of pork constituted a sound ecological strategy. The nomadic Israelites could not raise pigs in their arid habitats, while for the semi-sedentary and village farming populations, pigs were more of a threat than an asset. . . . The pig has a further disadvantage of not being a practical source of milk, and of being notoriously difficult to herd over long distances. . . . Above all, the pig is thermodynamically ill-adapted to the hot, dry climate of the Negev, the Jordan Valley, and the other lands of the Bible and the Koran. Compared to cattle, goats, and sheep, the pig has an inefficient system for regulating its body temperature. Despite the expression "To sweat like a pig," it has recently been proved that pigs can't sweat at all. (41–42)

Raising pigs in this context would be a luxury. On the other hand, in "pig-loving" cultures of Southeast Asia and the Pacific, climatic factors including temperature, humidity, and the presence of forest cover (good for pigs) promote pig raising. There, pigs offer an important protein source in people's diets that complements yams, sweet potatoes, and taro. In conclusion, Harris acknowledges that not all religiously sanctioned food practices can be explained ecologically, and he allows that food practices do have a social function in promoting social identity. But first and foremost, analysis of food consumption should consider ecological and material factors of production.

Preparations for a feast in the highlands of Papua New Guinea, where people place much value on consuming high-status foods such as roasted pig meat. ■ (Source: © David Austen/Stock Boston LLC)

Food Taboos as Systems of Meaning

Mary Douglas (1966) argues that what people eat has to do with the value of food as a way of communicating symbolic meaning as well as with the material conditions of life, including hunger. For Douglas, people's mental categories provide a psychological ordering of the world. Anomalies, or things that don't fit into the categories, become reminders to people of moral problems or things to avoid.

She uses this approach of ordered categories and disordered anomalies in her analysis of food prohibitions in the Old Testament book of Leviticus. One rule is that people may eat animals with cloven hoofs and that chew a cud. Several tabooed animals are said to be unclean, such as the camel, the pig, the hare, and the rock badger. Among a pastoral people, she says, it is logical that the model food animal would be a ruminant (a cloven-hoofed, cud-chewing, four-footed animal such as a cow, bison, goat, and sheep). In contrast, a pig is a four-footed animal with cloven hoofs, but it does not chew a cud; thus, the pig is an anomaly and taboo as food. In this way, Leviticus sets up a system that contrasts sacred completeness and purity (the animals one can eat) with impurity and sinfulness (the animals one cannot eat) to remind people of God's holiness and perfection and people's responsibility toward God.

Anthropologists studying food systems try to consider both the material aspects of food practices and the communicative, symbolic meaning of food in order to explain food prohibitions and preferences, acknowledging that there is more to food than just eating.

Culture and Exchange

Exchange is the transfer of something that may be material or immaterial between at least two persons, groups, or institutions.

Cultural anthropologists have done much research on gifts and other forms of exchange, starting with the early twentieth century studies by Malinowski of the *kula* of the Trobriand Islands and Boas's research on the potlatch. In all economic systems, individuals and groups exchange goods and services with others, so exchange is a cultural universal. But cultural variations arise in several areas: in what is exchanged, in how exchange takes place, and in when exchange takes place.

What Is Exchanged?

The items that people exchange range from seashells to stocks and bonds and may be purely utilitarian (see Table 4.1 on page 104). Items of exchange may carry

THE RULES OF HOSPITALITY

In much of the Middle East, where women spend most of their time in the domestic domain, social visits among women are eagerly anticipated and carefully planned events with complex rules about what foods and drinks should be served (Wikan 1982). In Oman, when women go outside the home, they wear head veils, face masks, and full-length gowns. Their main social activity consists of visits to other women in their homes. A typical visit involves sitting, chatting, and eating snacks.

Social etiquette dictates what should be served and how. Coffee and dates are the traditional entertainment foods offered to close neighbours. Biscuits (cookies), inexpensive caramels, and popcorn are increasingly favoured snacks. The number of dishes offered is important. Between neighbours who interact on a daily basis a single dish is typical. All other visitors should be offered at least two plates, with different contents, or else the hostess will be considered stingy. In the case of many guests, the number of plates must be increased, with a minimum of four plates, and the variety of snacks must be greater. If a hostess wishes to honour one or two guests, she may offer them three or four plates of different snacks. Another rule of visitor etiquette requires that approximately half of the food served should be left for the hostess' household (1982:130–132).

Cooked food, such as meat and sweets, is served when one entertains guests at weddings, seasonal feasts, and burials. With cooked food, the hosts may never eat with their guests: "Even if the consequence is that the guest must eat all alone, in a separate room, it would be disrespectful to arrange it otherwise" (1982:133).

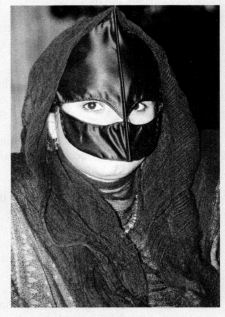

A Bedu (Bedouin) woman of Muscat, Oman, wearing traditional face covering. ■ (Source: © Charles O. Cecil)

FOOD FOR THOUGHT

• How do these Omani rules of hospitality resemble or contrast with rules of hospitality you know?

meanings and have a history, or "social life," of their own, as prized kula items do (Appadurai 1986).

In contemporary industrial societies, money is the major item of exchange, and such economies are referred to as *monetized.* In *nonmarket economies,* money plays a less important role, and time, labour, and goods are prominent exchange items. As nonmarket economies are connected, through globalization, they are confronted

TABLE 4.1   Items of Exchange

Category	Selected Examples
Material Goods	Food to family and group members Gifts for special occasions such as weddings Money
Nonmaterial Goods	Myths, stories, rituals Time, labour
People	Offspring in marriage Slavery

Omani biotech scientist, Ms. Wahida al-Amri, at work in her lab in the Omani Marine Science and Fisheries Center. ■ (Source: © Charles O. Cecil)

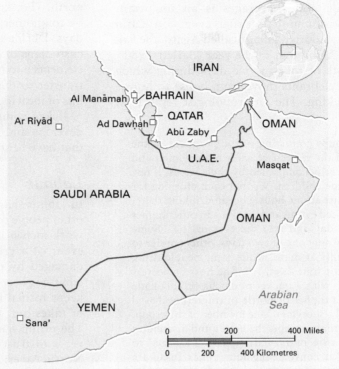

MAP 4.2 **Oman.** The Sultanate of Oman is mainly a vast desert plain with a hot and dry climate. The population of nearly 3 million includes over 500 000 non-nationals who are immigrant labourers. The economy is based mainly on crude oil. The major religion is Ibādī Islam, a more liberal version of Islam than Sunni or Shi'a Islam. Arabic is the official language, with English a widely spoken second language. Several local dialects are spoken including the Omani dialect of Arabic.

with the (to them) peculiar and mysterious meaning of Western money. Often, they localize the meanings of money, by treating particular bills as more special than others. In many cultures, money has completely replaced other valued items of exchange, such as shell wealth in Papua New Guinea.

Nonmonetary exchange exists in contemporary industrial societies, too. Hosting dinner parties, exchanging gifts at holiday times, and sharing a bag of potato chips with a friend are examples of common forms of nonmonetary exchange. Some scholars would even include caresses, kisses, loyalty, and glances (Blau 1964).

Material Goods

Food is one of the most common exchange goods in everyday life and on ritual occasions. Marriage arrangements often involve complex stages of gifts and countergifts exchanged between the groom's family and the bride's family. Wedding exchanges among the Nias of northern Sumatra, Indonesia, provide a good illustration. From the betrothal onward to the actual marriage, there is a scheduled sequence of events at which gifts are exchanged between the families of the bride and groom (Beatty 1992). At the first meeting, the prospective groom expresses his interest in a betrothal. He and his party visit the bride's house and are fed: "The guests are given the pig's lower jaw (the portion of honour) and take away with them raw and cooked portions for the suitor's father" (121). Within the next week or two, the groom brings a gift of three to twelve pigs to confirm the betrothal. He also returns the container used for the pig meat given to him on the previous visit, filled with a certain kind of nut. The groom gives pigs and gold as the major gift that seals the marriage. Gifts will continue to be exchanged between the two families over many years. Exchanges of food are important in signalling and reaffirming friendships.

Exchanging alcoholic beverages is an important feature of many communal, ritual events in Latin America. In an Ecuadorian village called Agato, the San Juan fiesta is the high point of the year (Barlett 1980). The fiesta consists of four or five days during which small groups of celebrants move from house to house, dancing and drinking. The anthropologist reports on the event:

> I joined the groups consisting of the president of the community and the elected *alcaldes* (councilmen and police), who were accompanied by their wives, a few friends, and some children. We met each morning for a hearty breakfast at one house, began drinking there, and then continued eating and drinking in other homes throughout the day and into the evening. . . . Some people drink for only one or two days, others prefer to make visits mainly at night, while some people drink day and night for four days. . . . The host or hostess greets the group with a bucket of chicha (home-made corn beer) and a dipper or bottle of trago (purchased cane liquor) and a shotglass. One member of the group, often the oldest man, accepts the liquor and distributes drinks to the entire party. Participants are urged to "do their share" to consume the liquor, but refusals are also accepted easily. After several rounds of drink, the server returns the empty bottle or bucket to the host, the group choruses goodbyes and hurries into the street. (118–119)

Guests who drink at someone's house will later serve their former hosts alcohol in return. Functional theorists would view this ritual exchange as contributing to social cohesion.

Symbolic Goods

Intangible valuables such as myths (sacred stories) and rituals (sacred practices) are sometimes exchanged in ways similar to material goods. In lowland areas of Papua New Guinea, men trade myths, rituals, dances, flutes, costumes, and styles of body decoration for the pigs of highland men (Harrison 1993). Certain secret spells were some of the most prestigious trade items. In the Balgo Hills region of Australia (See Map 4.3), long-standing exchange networks transfer myths and rituals among groups of women (Poirier 1992). Throughout the region, the women may keep important narratives and rituals only for a certain time and then must pass them on to other groups. One such ritual is the *Tjarada*, a love-magic ritual with an accompanying narrative. The *Tjarada* came to the women of Balgo Hills from the north. They kept it for about 15 years and then passed it on to another group in a ceremony that lasted for three days. During the time that the Balgo Hills women were custodians of the *Tjarada*, they incorporated some new elements into it. These elements are retained even after its transfer to the next group. Thus, the *Tjarada* contains bits of local identity of each group that has had it. A sense of linked community and mutual responsibility thereby develops and is sustained among the different groups that have held the *Tjarada*.

Labour

In labour-sharing groups, people contribute labour to other people on a regular basis (for seasonal agricultural work such as harvesting) or on an irregular basis (in the event of a crisis such as the need to rebuild a barn damaged by fire). Labour-sharing groups are part of what has been called a "moral economy," since no one keeps formal records on how much any family puts in or takes out. Instead, accounting is socially regulated. The group has a sense of moral community based on years of trust and sharing. In Amish communities of North America, labour sharing is a major factor of production, infrastructure maintenance, and social cohesion. When a family needs a new barn or faces repair work that requires group labour, a barn-raising party is called. Many families show up to help. Adult men provide manual labour, and women provide food for the event. Later, when another family needs help, they call on the same people.

Money

For most of humanity's existence, people did not purchase things. They collected or made things they needed themselves, shared, or exchanged items for other things. The invention of money is recent, only a few thousand years ago. **Money** refers to a medium of exchange that can be used for a variety of goods (Godelier 1971:53). Money exists cross-culturally in such diverse forms as shells, salt, cattle, furs, cocoa beans, and iron hoes.

Modern money, in the form of coins and paper bills, has the advantages of being portable, divisible, uniform, and recognizable (Shipton 2001). On the other hand, modern money is vulnerable to economic changes

---

money: a medium of exchange that can be used for a variety of goods.

such as inflation, which reduce its value. The use of modern money is spreading throughout the world. Nonmonetary cultures, however, often adopt modern money in limited ways. They may prohibit its use in religious exchanges or in life-cycle rituals such as marriages. All forms of money, even modern money, are symbolic. They have meaning to the user, and they are associated with the user's identity and sense of self. The colour and design of a credit card, for example, may signify status, such as "platinum" for the biggest spenders. As the European Union was forming, lengthy discussion was devoted to what the new currency would look like. As e-money becomes increasingly used, it will be interesting to see what kinds of meaning are attached to it.

People

Exchange in human beings relegates humans to objects. Throughout history, some people have been able to gain control of other people and treat them as items of exchange, as in slavery and human trafficking. The enslavement of people from many regions of Africa during European colonialism from the fifteenth to nineteenth centuries stands as one of the most heinous processes of treating humans as commodities in the full light of day, with no legal sanctions involved for slave traders or owners. This process cruelly transformed thousands of people into property that could be bought and sold, used and abused, and even murdered.

A long-standing debate in anthropology concerns women as objects of exchange in marriage. Lévi-Strauss proposed many years ago that the exchange of women between men is one of the most basic forms of exchange among humans (1969 [1949]). He based his assertion on the universality of some sort of *incest taboo*, which he defined as a rule preventing a man from marrying or cohabiting with his mother or sister (Chapter 8 provides the current definition). Such a rule, he says, is the logic driving the exchange of women among men: "The fact that I can obtain a wife is, in the final analysis, the consequence of the fact that a brother or father has given her up" (1969:62). Thus, the avoidance of incest forces men to develop exchange networks with other men and, by extension, leads to the emergence of social solidarity more widely. For Lévi-Strauss, the incest taboo provides the foundation for human social organization.

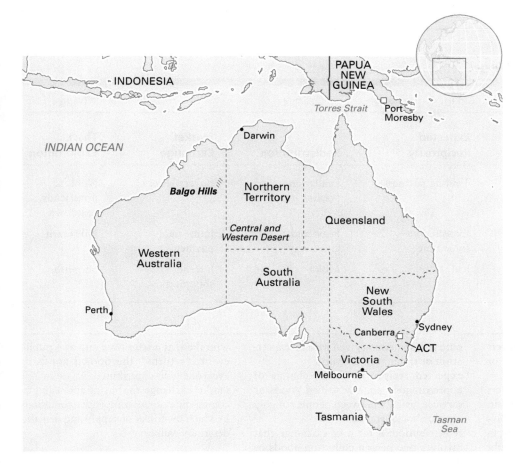

MAP 4.3 The Balgo Hills (Wirrimanu) Region in Western Australia. The Balgo Hills community is located on the northern edge of the Tanami and Great Sandy Deserts. One of Australia's most isolated indigenous desert settlements, it nevertheless has a flourishing art centre. Balgo paintings and glass are highly sought after by collectors.

Feminist anthropologists say that this theory overlooks much ethnographic evidence to the contrary. Men do not have rights over women in many foraging societies; instead, women make their own choices

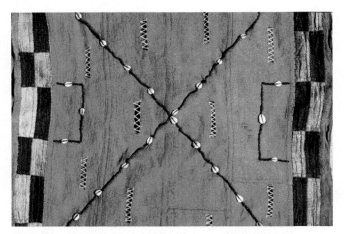

This raffia cloth, from the Democratic Republic of Congo, is woven from palm fibres. Throughout central Africa, raffia cloth functions as limited-purpose money, or money that can be used only for specific purposes, such as marriage or compensation for wrongdoing. It cannot be used for commercial transactions such as buying food, a house, or a car. ■ (Source: J. Marshall—Tribaleye Images/Alamy)

about partners (Rubin 1975). In many horticultural and agricultural societies of Southeast Asia, men do not exchange women (Peletz 1987). Instead, women select grooms for daughters. This pattern turns Lévi-Strauss on his head because it involves women organizing the exchange of men.

Modes of Exchange

Parallel to the two contrasting modes of consumption described earlier (minimalism and consumerism) two distinct modes of exchange can be delineated (see Table 4.2). They are

■ **Balanced exchange:** a system of transfers in which the goal is either immediate or eventual balance in value.

■ **Unbalanced exchange:** a system of transfers in which one party attempts to make a profit.

Balanced Exchange

The category of balanced exchange contains two subcategories based on the social relationship of the two parties involved in the exchange and the degree to which a "return" is expected. **Generalized reciprocity** is a transaction that involves the least conscious sense of interest in material gain or thought of what might be received in return, and when. Such exchanges often involve goods and

TABLE 4.2   Keeping Track of Exchange

	Balanced Exchange			Unbalanced Exchange	
	Generalized Reciprocity	**Expected Reciprocity**	**Redistribution**	**Market Exchange**	**Theft, Exploitation**
Actors	Kin, friends	Trading partners	Leader and pooling group	Buyers/sellers	Nonkin, nonfriends, unknown
Return	Not calculated or expected	Expected at some time	Feast and give-away	Immediate payment	No return
Example	Buying coffee for a friend	Kula	Moka	Internet shopping	Shoplifting

balanced exchange: a system of transfers in which the goal is either immediate or eventual equality in value.
unbalanced exchange: a system of transfers in which one party seeks to make a profit.
generalized reciprocity: exchange involving the least conscious sense of interest in material gain or thought of what might be received in return.

pure gift: something given with no expectation or thought of a return.
expected reciprocity: an exchange of approximately equally valued goods or services, usually between people roughly equal in social status.
redistribution: a form of exchange that involves one person collecting goods or money from many members of a group

who then, at a later time and at a public event, "returns" the pooled goods to everyone who contributed.

market exchange: the buying and selling of commodities under competitive conditions in which the forces of supply and demand determine value.

services of an everyday nature, such as a cup of coffee. Generalized reciprocity is the main form of exchange between people who know each other well and trust each other. Therefore, it is the main form of exchange in foraging societies. It is also found among close kin and friends cross-culturally.

A **pure gift** is something given with no expectation or thought of a return. The pure gift is an extreme form of generalized reciprocity. Examples of a pure gift include donating money for a food drive, or making donations to famine relief, blood banks, and religious organizations. Some people say that a truly pure gift does not exist because one always gains something, no matter how difficult to measure, in giving—even if it is just the good feeling of generosity. Parental care of children is said to be a pure gift by some, but others do not agree. Those who say that parental care is a pure gift argue that most parents do not consciously calculate how much they have spent on their children with the intention of "getting it back" later on. Those who do not consider parental care a pure gift say that even if the "costs" are not consciously calculated, parents have unconscious expectations about what their children will "return" to them, whether the return is material (care in old age) or immaterial (making the parent feel proud).

Expected reciprocity is the exchange of approximately equally valued goods or services, usually between people of roughly equal social status. The exchange may occur simultaneously between both parties, or it may involve an understanding about the time period within which the exchange will be completed. This aspect of timing contrasts with generalized reciprocity, in which there is no fixed time limit for the return. In expected reciprocity, if the second party fails to complete the exchange, the relationship will break down. Balanced reciprocity is less personal than generalized reciprocity and, according to Western definitions, more "economic."

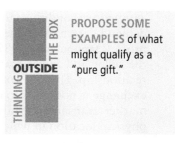

THINKING OUTSIDE THE BOX

PROPOSE SOME EXAMPLES of what might qualify as a "pure gift."

The kula is an example of a system of expected reciprocity. Men exchange necklaces and armlets, giving them to their exchange partners after keeping them for a while. Partners include neighbours as well as people on far-away islands who are visited via long canoe voyages on high seas. Trobriand men are distinguished by the particular armlets and necklaces that they exchange, and certain armlets and necklaces are more prestigious than others. One cannot keep one's trade items for long because the kula code dictates that "to possess is great, but to possess is to give." Generosity is the essence of goodness, and stinginess is the most despised vice. Kula exchanges should involve items of equivalent value. If a man trades a very valuable necklace with his partner, he expects to receive in return a very valuable armlet as a *yotile* (equivalent gift). At the time, if one's partner does not possess an equivalent item, he may have to give a *basi* (intermediary gift). The basi stands as a token of good faith until a proper return gift can be given. The *kudu* ("clinching gift") will come later and balance the original gift. The equality of exchange ensures a strong bond between the trading partners and is a statement of trust. When a man arrives in an area where it may be dangerous because of previous raids or warfare, he can count on having a friend to give him hospitality.

Redistribution is a form of expected reciprocity in which one person collects goods or money from many members of a group and provides a social return at a later time. At a public event, even several years later, the organizer "returns" the pooled goods to everyone who contributed by sponsoring a generous feast. Compared to the two-way pattern of exchange involved in reciprocity, redistribution involves some "centricity." It contains the possibility of inequality because what is returned may not always equal, in a material sense, what each individual contributed. The pooling group may continue to exist, however, because it benefits from the leadership skills of the person who mobilizes contributions. If a neighbouring group threatens a raid, people turn to their redistributive leader for political leadership (discussed further in Chapter 10).

Shell ornaments are important items to be worn at ceremonial events, as shown on this man of the Sepik River area of Papua New Guinea. ■ (Source: Chuck Fishman/Woodfin Camp)

Unbalanced Exchange

Market exchange, a prominent form of unbalanced exchange, is the buying and selling of commodities under competitive conditions in which the forces of supply and demand determine value and the seller seeks to make a profit (Dannhaeuser 1989:222). In market transactions, the seller and buyer may or may not have a personal relationship. They may or may not be social equals. Their exchange is not likely to generate social bonding. Many market transactions take place in a *marketplace,* a physical location in which buying and selling occur. The market system evolved from other, less formal contexts of **trade,** formalized exchange of one thing for another according to set standards of value.

The market system is associated with regional specialization in producing particular goods and trade between regions. Certain products are often identified with a town or region. In Oaxaca, Mexico (see Map 5.4 on page 129), some villages are known for their blankets, pottery, stone grinders, rope, and chili peppers (Plattner 1989). In Morocco, the city of Fez (see Map 5.3 on page 128) is famous for its blue-glazed pottery, whereas the Berber people of the Atlas Mountains are known for their fine wool blankets and rugs. Specialization develops with illegal commodities, too. For example, Jamaican marijuana is well known for its high quality, and many tourists travel to Jamaica, especially the Negril beach area, in order to buy this product.

Marketplaces range from informal, small stands that appear in the morning and disappear at night to huge multistoried shopping centres. One variety found in many parts of the world is a *periodic market,* a site for buying and selling that takes place on a regular basis (for example, monthly) in a particular location but without a permanent physical structure. Sellers appear with their goods and set up a table with perhaps an awning. In contrast, *permanent markets* are built structures situated in fixed locations. Marketplaces, however, are more than just places for buying and selling. They involve social interactions and even performances. Sellers solicit customers, shoppers meet and chat, government officials drop by, religious organizations may hold services, and traditional healers may treat toothaches. The particularities of how markets are structured, spatially

The weekly market in Pistoia, a small town near |Firenze (Florence), Italy, is set up each Saturday next to the main church. According to government regulations, all food items are supposed to have labels that identify where they were grown. ■ (Source: Barbara Miller)

In China, many marketers are women. These two women display their wares in a regular neighbourhood food market in a city about an hour from Shanghai. ■ (Source: Barbara Miller)

trade: the formalized exchange of one thing for another according to set standards of value.

and socially, and how culture shapes market transactions are rich topics for ethnographic research.

Other Forms of Unbalanced Exchanges

Several forms of unbalanced exchange exist that involve the transfer of goods from one person or institution to another without an equivalent return. In extreme instances, no social relationship is involved; in others, sustained unequal relationships are maintained over time between people. These forms range from the extreme example of giving something with no expectation of return to taking something with no expectation of return. These forms of unbalanced exchange can occur anywhere along the continuum of economic systems, but they are more likely to be found in large-scale or culturally complex societies where more options for other than face-to-face, balanced exchange exist.

Gambling   *Gambling,* or gaming, is the attempt to make a profit by playing a game of chance in which a certain item of value is staked in hopes of acquiring the much larger return that one receives if one wins the game. If one loses, that which was staked is lost. Gambling is an ancient practice and is common cross-culturally. Ancient forms of gambling involved games such as dice throwing and card playing. Risky investing in the stock market can be considered a form of gambling, as can gambling of many sorts through the Internet. Although gambling may seem an odd category within unbalanced exchange, its goals of making a profit seem to justify its placement here. The fact that gambling within "high" capitalism is on the rise justifies anthropological attention to it. In fact, some scholars have referred to the present stage of Western capitalism as *casino capitalism,* given the propensity of investors to play very risky games on the stock market (Klima 2002).

Gambling casinos established by First Nations and Native American groups have mushroomed in recent years in both the United States and Canada. These casinos are so financially successful that they are perceived as an economic threat to other casinos and government lotteries. Through gaming, some aboriginal groups have become successful capitalists. An important question is what impact these casinos will have on both Native and non-Native communities (see the Lessons Applied box on page 112).

Theft   *Theft* is taking something with no expectation or thought of returning anything to the original owner for it. It is the logical opposite of a pure gift. The study of theft has been neglected by anthropologists, perhaps because it might involve danger.

One rare study of theft focused on food stealing by children in West Africa (Bledsoe 1983). During fieldwork among the Mende people of Sierra Leone, Caroline Bledsoe learned that children in town stole fruits such as mangoes, guavas, and oranges from neighbourhood trees. Bledsoe at first dismissed cases of food stealing as rare exceptions, but then she realized that she "rarely walked through town without hearing shouts of anger from an adult and cries of pain from a child being whipped for stealing food" (1983:2). Deciding to look into children's food stealing more closely, she asked several children to keep diaries. Their writings were dominated by themes of *tiefing,* the local term for stealing. Fostered children, who are temporarily placed in the care of friends or relatives, do more food tiefing than children living with their birth families do. Such food stealing can be seen as children's attempts to compensate for their less-than-adequate food shares in their foster homes.

Stealing as a conscious attempt to alter an unfair entitlement system underlies an analysis of the looting that occurred in Los Angeles in 1992 following the announcement of the infamous Rodney King verdict (Fiske 1994). This looting was an outcome of the economic inequities faced by the African American community of South Central Los Angeles.

> Between 1982 and 1989, 131 factories closed in LA with the loss of 124,000 jobs. . . . The jobs that were lost were ones that disproportionately employed African Americans . . . in the four years before 1982, South Central, the traditional industrial core of LA, lost 70,000 blue-collar jobs. In Black eyes, this pattern is produced not by a raceless free market, but by racism encoded into economics: To them the 50 percent Black male unemployment in South Central does not look like the result of neutral, let alone natural, economic laws. (1994, 469–470)

How is this context related to exchange? One interpretation is that the looting expressed deep-seated resentment about economic discrimination. It was a form of political protest. The media's use of the word *looting* linked the uprising to the domain of crime, leaving prison as the only solution. Framing the uprising as a law-and-order issue diverted the public's attention from its roots in severe economic discrimination.

Much theft worldwide is motivated by greed. Cultural anthropologists, for obvious reasons, have not done research on high-level theft involving expensive commodities such as drugs, gems, and art, nor have they examined corporate financial malpractice as a form of theft. Given the ethical principle of informed consent, it is highly unlikely that any anthropologist would be given permission to study such criminal activity, even if the researcher was willing to risk his or her life by entering such dangerous domains.

Exploitation   *Exploitation* is getting something of greater value for less in return; it is extreme and persistent

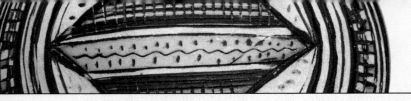

Lessons Applied

ASSESSING THE SOCIAL IMPACT OF ABORIGINAL CASINOS

In 2006, the Center for California Native Nations (CCNN) at the University of California at Riverside released an evaluation of the effects of Indian gaming in California (Spilde Contreras 2006). Kate Spilde Contreras, applied cultural anthropologist, directed the multidisciplinary team that included anthropologists, political scientists, economists, and historians.

The research objective was to evaluate the social and economic effects of Indian gaming operations on tribal and local governments in California. The study relies mainly on public data, especially the 1990 and 2000 U.S. Censuses, to supply a "before" and "after" picture during the initial growth phase of Indian gaming in the state. To learn about more recent changes, the research team conducted surveys of tribal and local government officials and in-depth case studies of individual tribal governments.

Findings indicate two important factors that shape the effects of Indian gaming in California: gaming establishments are owned by tribal governments, and gaming establishments are located on existing tribal trust lands. Therefore, gaming revenues support community and government activities of the tribal communities, and employment generation is localized within the tribal communities.

Indian reservations in California are more economically heterogeneous than elsewhere in the United States. Since the development of gaming, it similarly has a larger inequality across gaming and nongaming reservations than in the rest of the country. By 2000, the fastest average income growth on California reservations occurred on gaming reservations. A policy response to this situation is a tribal-state gaming contract, the Revenue Sharing Trust Fund (RSTF) that provides for sharing of gaming revenue with nongaming communities.

Spilde Contreras's team also considered the effects on gaming beyond the reservation. They found that areas within ten miles (16 kilometres) of gaming reservations experienced significant employment increases, greater income growth, and more educational expansion than those farther away. Given the fact that reservations in California are located in the poorest regions, this location effect is progressive.

Although the income and other effects of gaming in California are clearly substantial for Indians and their neighbours, Spilde Contreras points to the large gaps that still exist between conditions on Indian reservations and those for most U.S. citizens.

FOOD FOR THOUGHT

- Consider the development of First Nations and Native American casinos from the theoretical perspective of structure versus agency. (Review the discussion of these perspectives in Chapter 1.)

---

unbalanced exchange. Slavery is a form of exploitation in which people's labour power is appropriated without their consent and with no recompense for its value. Slavery is rare among foraging, horticultural, and pastoral societies. Social relationships that involve sustained unequal exchange do exist between members of different social groups that, unlike pure slavery, involve no overt coercion and a certain degree of return by the dominant member to the subdominant member. Some degree of covert compulsion or dependence is likely to be present, however, in order for relationships of unequal exchange to endure.

Relationships between the Efe, who are "pygmy" foragers, and the Lese, who are farmers, in the Democratic Republic of the Congo (formerly Zaire) exemplify sustained unequal exchange (Grinker 1994). The Lese live in small villages located along a dirt road. The Efe are semi-nomadic, and they live in temporary camps near Lese villages. Men of each group maintain long-term hereditary exchange partnerships with each other. Members of the two groups describe their relationship simply: The Lese give cultivated foods and iron to the Efe, and the Efe give meat, honey, and other forest goods to the Lese.

Each Efe partner is considered a member of the "house" of his Lese partner, although he lives separately. Their main link is the exchange of food items, a system conceptualized by the Lese not as trade, per se, but as sharing of co-produced goods, as though the two partners were a single unit with a division of labour and a subsequent division or co-sharing of the goods produced. Yet there is evidence of inequality in these trading relationships, with the Lese having the advantage. The Efe provide much-wanted meat to the Lese, but this role gives them no status, for it is the giving of cultivated foods by the Lese to the Efe that conveys status. In fact, the Lese claim that the Efe are *their* dependents, denying that their interest in Efe meat supplies

---

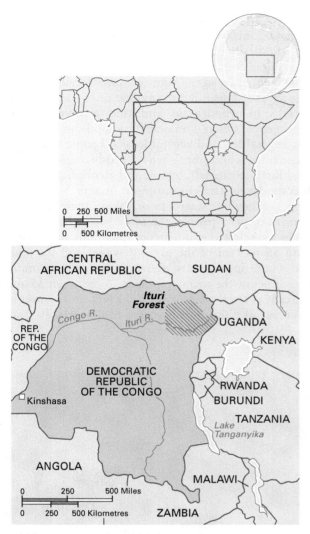

MAP 4.4 Lese and Efe Region in the Democratic Republic of the Congo. The Lese and Efe live in the Ituri Forest, a dense tropical rainforest in the northern part of the Congo River Basin. Cultural Survival supports the Ituri Forest Peoples Fund, which promotes the health and education of Efe foragers and Lese farmers.

actually makes them dependent. Another area of inequality is in marital and sexual relationships. Lese men may marry Efe women, and sometimes do, and the children are considered Lese. Efe men, however, cannot marry Lese women.

Changing Patterns of Consumption and Exchange

Several trends are notable in the transformation of consumption and exchange. The powerful market forces of the First World are the predominant shapers of global change. At the same time, local cultures variously adopt and adapt to global patterns of consumption and exchange, and sometimes resist them outright.

Cash Cropping and Declining Nutrition

Increasing numbers of horticultural and agricultural groups have been persuaded to change over from growing crops for their own use to cash crop production. Intuition might tell you that cash cropping should lead to a rising standard of living. Some studies show, to the contrary, that often people's nutritional status declines with the introduction of cash cropping. A carefully documented analysis of how people's nutritional status was affected by introducing sisal (a plant that has leaves used for making rope) as a cash crop in Brazil is one such case (Gross and Underwood 1971). Around 1950, sisal was widely adopted in arid parts of northeastern Brazil. The traditional economy was based on some cattle raising and subsistence farming. Many poor subsistence farmers gave up farming and took up work in the sisal processing plants. They thought that steady work would be preferable to being dependent on the unpredictable rains in this dry region.

Processing sisal leaves for rope is an extremely labour-consuming process. One of the most demanding jobs is being a "residue man," whose tasks include shovelling soggy masses of fibre, bundling fibre, and lifting bundles for weighing. In families that contained a "residue man," the amount of money required for food was as much as what the sisal worker earned. In one case-study household, the weekly budget was completely spent on food. The greatest share of the food goes to the sisal worker himself because of his increased energy output in his work. Analysis of data on the nutritional status of several hundred children in sisal-processing areas showed that: "Some sisal workers in northeastern Brazil appear to be forced systematically to deprive their dependents of an adequate diet . . . if they did not they could not function as wage earners. In those cases where the workers' dependents are growing children, the deprivation manifests itself in attenuated growth rates" (736).

The Lure of Western Goods

There is now scarcely any human group that does not engage in exchanges beyond its boundaries to acquire new consumer goods (Gross et al. 1979). The northern Cree have embraced many technological changes in the last few decades: "Satellite dishes, fax machines, computers and websites are as much a part of northern living as skidoos, rifles, and the ubiquitous Northern

Stores (formerly the Hudson's Bay Company Posts)" (Adelson 2000:11). Forest-living foraging groups in the Brazilian Amazon also embraced manufactured goods with amazing enthusiasm. They appreciated the efficacy of a steel machete, axe, or cooking pot. In the early decades of the twentieth century, when the Brazilian government sought to "pacify" Amazonian groups, they used manufactured goods. They placed pots, machetes, axes, and steel knives along trails or hung them from trees. Once the Indians have grown accustomed to these new items, the next step is to teach them that these gifts will not be repeated. The Indians are now told that they must work to earn money or must manufacture goods for trade so that they can purchase new items. Unable to contemplate returning to life without steel axes, the Indians begin to produce extra arrows or blowguns or hunt additional game or weave baskets beyond what they normally need so that this new surplus can be traded. Time that might, in the past, have been used for other tasks—subsistence activities, ceremonial events, and so on—is now devoted to production of barter goods (Milton 1992:40).

Adoption of Western foods has negatively affected the nutrition and health of indigenous peoples. Cree health and strength is intimately connected to eating Cree bush food. Now that there is a greater variety of processed foods available for sale, it is often consumed to excess (Adelson 2000:103). In the Amazon, "The moment manufactured foods begin to intrude on the indigenous diet, health takes a downward turn" (Milton 1992:41). The Amazonian Indians have begun to use table salt, which they have been given by outsiders, and refined sugar. Previously, they consumed small quantities of salt made by burning certain leaves and collecting the ash. The sugar they consumed came from wild fruits, in the form of fructose. Sucrose tastes "exceptionally sweet" in comparison, and the Indians get hooked on it. As a result, tooth decay, obesity, and diabetes become new health risks.

Social Inequality in Russia and Eastern Europe

As the countries of the former Soviet Union entered the global market economy, income inequality within those countries grew dramatically. The new rich own mansions and Mercedes-Benz cars. The influx of Western goods, including sugared soft drinks and junk food, has been nicknamed "pepsistroika" by an anthropologist who did fieldwork in Moscow around the time of the transition to capitalism (Lempert 1996). Advertising messages encourage people to adopt new diets that include unhealthy amounts of rich food.

From 1961 to 1988, consumption of calories, proteins, and fats in what are now Russia and Eastern Europe were above the level recommended by the World Health Organization (WHO) and exceeded those of most middle-income countries worldwide (Cornia 1994). These countries had full employment and little income inequality, so the high consumption levels were widely shared. This is not to say that diets were perfect. Especially in urban areas and among lower-income groups, people's diets contained less good-quality meat, fruits, vegetables, and vegetable oils. People tended to overconsume cholesterol-heavy products (eggs and animal fats), sugar, salt, bread, and alcohol.

Income levels and consumption quality have fallen among the newly created poor. Now, there are two categories of poor people: the *ultra-poor* (those whose incomes are below the subsistence minimum, or between 25 and 35 percent of the average wage) and the *poor* (those whose incomes are above the subsistence minimum but below the social minimum, or between 35 and 50 percent of the average wage). The largest increases in the number of ultra-poor occurred in Bulgaria, Poland,

A member of the Kayapo tribe of Brazil eats a Popsicle during a break in a meeting of indigenous peoples to protest a dam-building project. Changing worldwide consumption patterns are increasing the incidence of tooth decay, diabetes, and obesity among indigenous people.
■ (Source: © Wilson Melo/CORBIS)

An upscale car dealer in Moscow uses a cell phone to communicate with customers. His car lot stands on what was a sports ground during the Soviet era. ■ (Source: © Caroline Penn/CORBIS)

Romania, and Russia, where between 20 and 30 percent of the population are ultra-poor and another 20 to 40 percent are poor. Overall calorie and protein intake fell significantly. People in the ultra-poor category substitute less expensive sources of nutrients. They now consume more animal fats and starch, and less milk, animal proteins, vegetable oils, minerals, and vitamins. Rates of low-birth-weight babies have risen in Bulgaria and Romania, reflecting the deterioration in maternal diets, and the rate of childhood anemia has risen dramatically in Russia.

Global Networks and Ecstasy in the United States

In the late 1990s, a sharp increase in the use of ecstasy occurred in the United States (Agar and Reisinger 2003). Ecstasy, or MDMA (an abbreviation for its long chemical name), is an illicit drug that produces a high without, apparently, leading to clinical dependence. Fieldwork and interviews in Baltimore, Maryland, revealed that ecstasy use took off in the late 1990s as the drug of choice among youth. As one research participant commented, "A lot of people I know like rolling, taking a pill of ecstasy and going to like a club or going to a school dance. I mean, alcohol is up and coming among like teenagers, like it's always been, but I think ecstasy's making a pretty powerful fight" (2003:2).

Official statistics confirmed this rise: In 1998, 10 percent of Baltimore County high school seniors reported that they had tried ecstasy; in 2001, the number had increased to nearly 20 percent. Nationwide statistics on reported use, arrests of distributors, and numbers of MDMA-related seizures reveal a similar pattern of increased use during this period. What accounts for this change? Two anthropologists conducted research to assess their hypothesis that there was a major change in the systems that produced and delivered the drug, leading to increased availability.

The standard story of the supply chain goes like this: Ecstasy is produced in the Netherlands and Belgium, distributed to the United States by Israelis, with a fuzzy role for Russian organized crime along the way. Two anthropologists studied websites and media reports in 2000 and discovered a much more complicated story. They found a network of multiple and shifting production sites all over the world, including the largest illicit drug lab ever reported in Canadian history. Distribution channels are also highly diffuse. Although the simpler story may have been true in 1998, it was no longer true two years later. Perhaps as demand rose in the United States and elsewhere, this rise prompted the development of a wider network of production and distribution.

Credit Card Debt

Some markets, worldwide, have long allowed buyers to purchase goods on *credit,* which involves payment over time. Informal credit is usually based on personal trust and face-to-face interaction. Only recently did the invention of the credit card make credit purchasing a widespread and growing phenomenon. Credit card companies in the United States have created astounding new levels of debt across many social and economic levels: "New electronic technology in the 1970s and deregulation in the 1980s offered retail bankers exciting opportunities to experiment with credit as a commodity, and they did experiment, wildly, at 'penetrating the debt capacity' of varied groups of Americans" (B. Williams 1994:351).

The primary users of credit cards are between 25 and 44 years old with flat or falling incomes. Many people use credit cards to pay for their college education, or set up a household, or buy a car or major household appliances. Charging the costs of leisure activities, such as a vacation trip, is another major use of credit cards. Maintaining a running debt to credit card companies has become an expected part of life for many people and a habit not easily changed. Attitudes about credit card debts vary. Some people express feelings of guilt similar to having a drug dependency. One woman in a study of credit card debt in the Washington, D.C., area said, "Last year I had a charge-free Christmas. It was like coming away from drug abuse" (B. Williams 1994:354). Another expressed gratitude: "I wouldn't be able to go to college without my credit card" (1994:355).

Ethnographic Profile

The Kwakwaka'wakw of British Columbia

Several First Nations peoples recently adopted the name Kwakwaka'wakw to refer to a cluster of 20 linguistically related groups of British Columbia's coastal region (Macnair 1995). It means "the people who speak Kwak'wala." It replaces the earlier term *Kwakiutl*, which refers to only one of the several groups and is insulting to members of the other groups to be so named.

Their territory includes many islands as well as the waterways and deep inlets penetrating the Coast Mountains, a region of dense forests and sandy beaches. In earlier times, travel was mainly by canoe. Families moved seasonally with all their belongings packed in the canoe (Macnair 1995).

The Kwakwaka'wakw are famous for aspects of their material culture, including tall, carved wooden totem poles, canoes, masks, and serving bowls, as well as richly decorated capes, skirts, and blankets.

Cedar is vital to the Kwakwaka'wakw. They use its wood for the objects just mentioned and the inner bark for garments. Women pounded the bark strips with a whalebone beater until the fibres separated and became soft. They wove the strips on a loom or hand-wove them into mats used for sleeping on.

The first contact with whites occurred in 1792, when explorer Captain George Vancouver arrived (Macnair 1995). At that time, the Kwakwaka'wakw population was perhaps 8000. Franz Boas arrived in 1886 and carried out research with the help of George Hunt, born of an English father and a high-ranking Tlingit (Northwest Coast) mother.

In the late nineteenth century, colonial authorities and missionaries disapproved of matters such as marriage arrangements and the potlatch, and enacted legislation to promote change, including a ban on potlatching from 1884 to 1951. The people continued, however, to potlatch in secret.

The Royal British Columbia Provincial Museum (RCBM) in Victoria worked closely with Kwakwaka'wakw communities to document their potlatches and promote cultural revitalization (Kramer, personal communication 2006). The first legal potlatch of recent times, hosted by Mungo Martin in 1953, was held outside the RCBM.

Readings

Boas, Franz. *Ethnology of the Kwakiutl.* Washington, DC: Government Printing Office, 1921.

Audrey Hawthorn, *Kwakiutl Art.* Seattle: University of Washington Press, 1979.

Bill Holm, *Smoky Top: The Art and Times of Willie Seaweed.* Seattle: University of Washington Press, 1983.

Videos

In the Land of the War Canoes: A Drama of Kwakiutl Life in the Northwest (1914; rereleased by Milestone Film & Video, 1992).

Raven Tales: How Raven Stole the Sun (Simon James, producer; NMAI, 2004).

Website

Museum of Anthropology, University of British Columbia, First Nations Collections; www.moa.ubc.ca/collections

Thanks to Jennifer Kramer, University of British Columbia, for reviewing this material.

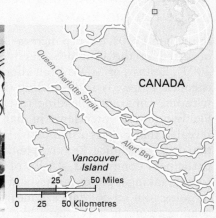

Canoes and their crews from other Kwakwaka'wakw villages gather at Alert Bay in 1999 to help celebrate the opening of the newly built Big House (left). ■ (Source: © Vickie Jensen) *Kwakwaka'wakw students practise the hamat'sa dance at a school in Alert Bay, under the tutelage of K'odi Nelson (right).* ■ (Source: © Vickie Jensen)

MAP 4.5 The Kwakwaka'wakw Region in British Columbia. *The total number of Kwakwaka'wakw is over 5000 people.*

Continuities and Resistance: The Enduring Potlatch

Potlatching among Native peoples of the Northwest Coast of Canada and the United States was subjected to decades of opposition from Europeans and Euro-Americans (Cole 1991). The missionaries opposed potlatching as an un-Christian practice. The government thought it was wasteful and excessive, out of line with their goals for the "economic progress" of the Indians. In 1885, the Canadian government outlawed the potlatch. Of all the Northwest Coast tribes, the Kwakwaka'wakw (see the Ethnographic Profile) resisted this prohibition most strongly and for the longest time. In Canada, potlatches are no longer illegal. But it took a long battle to remove restrictions.

Reasons for giving a potlatch today are similar to those in the past: naming children, mourning the dead, transferring rights and privileges, celebrating marriages, and raising totem poles (Webster 1991). The length of time devoted to planning a potlatch, however, has changed. In the past, several years were involved compared to about a year now. Still, it takes much organization and work to accumulate enough goods to ensure that no guest goes away empty-handed, and the guest list may include between 500 and 1000 people. Another change is in the kinds of goods exchanged. Typical potlatch goods now include crocheted items (such as cushion covers, blankets, and potholders), glassware, plastic goods, manufactured blankets, pillows, towels, articles of clothing, and sacks of flour and sugar. The potlatch endures but changes.

Key Questions Revisited

WHAT is consumption in cross-cultural perspective?

Consumption includes a person's "intake" in terms of eating or other ways of using things and "output" in terms of spending or using resources to obtain those things. Anthropologists delineate two major modes of consumption. The first is minimalism, which is characterized by finite needs, the means of satisfying them, and sustainability. The second is consumerism, the mode of consumption with infinite needs, the inability to satisfy all needs, and lack of sustainability. Foraging societies typify the minimalist mode of consumption. Horticulture, pastoralism, and farming are associated with mixed patterns of consumption, with a rising trend toward consumerism. The consumerist mode of consumption is most clearly associated with industrialism.

In nonmarket economies, most consumers either produce the goods they use themselves or know who produced them. This is called personalized consumption. In market economies, consumption is largely depersonalized through globalized mass production. The increase in depersonalized consumption may put workers at greater risk of exploitation because consumers are alienated from producers.

Anthropologists define five consumption funds the proportions of which vary in different economic systems. Factors such as race/ethnicity, class, and gender are linked to specific consumption patterns. Such patterns may involve inequalities that affect human welfare.

A long-standing area of interest in cultural anthropology is cross-cultural patterns of food taboos and why such taboos exist. Cultural materialists provide interpretations that consider the ecological and environmental contexts of such food taboos and how taboos make sense to people's material lives. Symbolic/interpretive anthropologists interpret food taboos as systems of meaning that give people a sense of identity and communicate that identity to others.

WHAT is exchange in cross-cultural perspective?

Exchange refers to the transfer of goods, both material and intangible, or services between people, groups, or institutions. Cross-culturally, people and groups exchange a wide variety of goods and services. Nonmarket exchange long existed without the use of money. Modern money is now found throughout most of the world, though some groups restrict its use.

Anthropologists define two major modes of exchange. The first is balanced exchange in which items of roughly equal value are exchanged over time between people who have a social relationship. Balanced exchange reinforces social ties. In unbalanced exchange, the value of items transferred is unequal and there may or may not be a social relationship between the seller and buyer.

Market exchange, the main form of unbalanced exchange, is a transaction in which the seller's goal of making a profit overrides social relationships. Markets exist in many forms. Some are impermanent and irregular; some are impermanent and regular, as in a weekly farmer's market; and others are permanent. Recent technological developments have led to the creation of virtual marketplaces in which buyers and sellers never meet face to face.

HOW are consumption and exchange changing?

Globalizing capitalism is leading to many changes in consumption and exchange around the world. Globalization appears to differentially benefit securely entitled people in core countries.

Many indigenous peoples are attracted by Western goods, such as steel knives and processed food. In order to obtain these goods, they have to have cash, so they are lured into the cash economy and subject to the fluctuations of the world labour market. The nutritional and health status of many such groups has declined with the adoption of Western-style foods, especially large amounts of sugar and salt in food.

The transition following the break-up of the USSR created vast disparities in income and human well-being. Throughout the post-Soviet world, average health and nutrition levels fell.

A prominent trend in consumption and exchange is credit card shopping. More people are buying on credit, accumulating large debts, and struggling to keep up with high interest payments.

KEY CONCEPTS

balanced exchange, p. 108
cash crop, p. 100
consumerism, p. 95
consumption fund, p. 97
entitlement, p. 99
expected reciprocity,
    p. 109

generalized reciprocity,
    p. 108
levelling mechanism, p. 95
market exchange, p. 109
minimalism, p. 95
mode of consumption, p. 94
mode of exchange, p. 94

money, p. 106
potlatch, p. 94
pure gift, p. 109
redistribution, p. 109
trade, p. 110
unbalanced exchange,
    p. 108

myanthrolab

To reinforce your understanding of this chapter, and to identify topics for further study, visit MyAnthroLab at www.myanthrolab.com for diagnostic tests and a multimedia ebook.

SUGGESTED READINGS

Denise Brennan. *What's Love Got to Do With It? Transnational Desires and Sex Tourism in the Dominican Republic.* Durham, NC: Duke University Press, 2004. This account of global sex tourism is located in the town of Sosúa, Dominican Republic, where Afro-Dominican and Afro-Haitian women sell sex to foreign, white tourists.

Michael F. Brown. *Who Owns Native Culture?* Cambridge, MA: Harvard University Press, 2003. This book documents the efforts of indigenous peoples to redefine heritage as a resource over which they claim proprietorship. It considers specific cases and proposes strategies for defending the rights of indigenous people within a market system.

Jane I. Guyer, ed., *Money Matters: Instability, Values and Social Payments in the Modern History of West African Communities.* Portsmouth, NH: Heinemann/James Currey, 1995. A collection of chapters by historians and cultural anthropologists examining topics such as why people in rural Gambia do not save money in banks, money as a symbol among the Yoruba, and the impact of colonial monetization in Nigeria and elsewhere.

Dwight B. Heath, *Drinking Occasions: Comparative Perspectives on Alcohol and Culture.* New York: Taylor & Francis, 2000. This book provides an ethnological review of drinking. The author focuses on several questions: When do people drink alcohol? Where do people drink? Who drinks and who doesn't? How do people drink? What do people drink? And why do people drink? He asks, in conclusion, where do we go from here with this topic?

Bill Maurer. *Mutual Life, Limited: Islamic Banking, Alternative Currencies, Lateral Reason.* Princeton, NJ: Princeton University Press, 2005. This comparison of Islamic bankers who seek to avoid interest with local currency proponents who seek to provide an alternative to capitalist financial mechanisms shows how both resist and sometimes replicate Western capitalism.

Grant McCracken, *Culture and Consumption.* Bloomington, IN: Indiana University Press, 1988. This book examines consumption in history, theory, and practice in relation to different consumer goods, including a consideration of clothing as language.

Daniel Miller, *The Dialectics of Shopping.* Chicago: University of Chicago Press, 2001. First delivered as the Lewis Henry Morgan lecture series at the University of Rochester, this book is the result of the author's interest in studying shopping as a clue to social relations. He discusses how shopping is related to kinship, community, ethics and identity, and the political economy. He draws on his own ethnographic research in several locations.

Sidney W. Mintz, *Sweetness and Power: The Place of Sugar in Modern History.* New York: Penguin Books, 1985. Combining historical and anthropological techniques, this book traces an important part of the story of world capitalism: the transformation of sugar from a luxury item to a staple of consumption worldwide.

Lidia D. Sciama and Joanne B. Eicher, eds., *Beads and Bead Makers: Gender, Material Culture and Meaning.* New York: Berg, 1998. Over a dozen articles on beads including early international trade in Venetian beads, the relationship between beads and ethnicity in Malaysia, beads and power at the New Orleans Mardi Gras, and rosaries in the Andes, all providing insights about gender roles and meanings.

James L. Watson, ed., *Golden Arches East: McDonald's in East Asia.* Stanford: Stanford University Press, 1997. This book contains five case studies, preceded by an introduction written by the editor and an afterword by Sidney Mintz, noted cultural anthropologist of food and food-ways. Case studies are focused on China, Taiwan, Korea, and Japan, and address topics such as how McDonaldized U.S. culture becomes localized, dietary effects on children, eating etiquette, and how food choices relate to national identity.

5

Birth and Death

Key Questions

- HOW is reproduction related to modes of production cross-culturally?

- HOW does culture shape fertility in different contexts?

- HOW does culture shape mortality in different contexts?

Two sisters of the Tarahumara people of northern Mexico. The Tarahumara once occupied most of the present-day state of Chihuahua but retreated to the Copper Canyon area in the mountains after the arrival of the Spanish colonialists. (*Source:* © William Coupon/*CORBIS*)

- A common belief among Hindus in India is that men are weakened by sexual intercourse because semen is a source of strength, and it takes a long time to replace even a drop. Yet, India has a high rate of population growth.

- The Chinese government policy of urging parents to have only one child significantly decreased the population growth rate. It also increased the death rate of female infants to the extent that there is now a shortage of brides.

- The highest birth rates in the world are found among the Mennonites and Hutterites in the United States and Canada. In these Christian groups, women on average bear nine children.

Such population puzzles can be understood using anthropological theories and methods. Population dynamics, along with many other examples of human variation in births and deaths, are culturally shaped and change over time in response to changing conditions. This chapter looks at some aspects of **demography**, the study of population dynamics in cross-cultural perspective.

While demographers compile statistical reports, cultural anthropologists contribute understanding of what goes on behind the numbers and provide insights about the causes of demographic trends. For example, demographers may find that fertility rates are falling more rapidly in one nation than in another. They may be able to correlate certain factors with it, such as changing literacy rates or economic growth. Cultural anthropologists studying these issues would take a closer look at the causes and processes involved in the declining birth rates, including some that might not be included in official censuses or other statistical sources. For example, they would collect information about people's values about children, their aspirations for their children, and the source of changing values.

Demography includes three areas: **fertility** (births, or rate of population increase from reproduction), **mortality** (deaths, or rate of population decline in general or from particular causes), and **migration** (movement of people from one place to another). When cultural anthropologists examine these processes, they often focus on small populations and samples and examine the relationships between population dynamics and other aspects of culture, such as gender roles, social inequality, sexual beliefs and behaviour, marriage, household structure, child care, and health and illness.

In this chapter, we first discuss how the modes of production (see Chapter 3) relate to reproduction. We then examine how and to what extent culture shapes the processes of birth and death.

Culture and Reproduction

Every human population, at all times, has had culturally constructed ways to either promote or limit population growth. Archaeologists and cultural anthropologists have enough data to allow the construction of general **modes of reproduction** (the predominant patterns of fertility in a culture) corresponding roughly with different means of livelihood. Three general models of reproduction are proposed. The foraging model of reproduction, which lasted for most of human prehistory, had low population growth rates because of a combination of moderate birth rates and moderate death rates. The agricultural model emerged with sedentarization (permanent settlement). As increased food surpluses became available to support more people, birth rates increased over death rates, and high population densities were reached in agricultural societies such as India and China. Children's labour was highly valued. Horticulturalists and pastoralists exhibit some features of the foraging and agricultural models of reproduction, depending on specific conditions. In the industrialized model of reproduction, exemplified by Europe, Japan, and North America, population growth rates declined because of falling birth rates and declining death rates.

Reproduction in Foraging Societies

Foraging societies' daily and seasonal spatial mobility calls for a relatively small number of children to facilitate movement. It is difficult for adults to carry more than one infant. Nancy Howell (1979) conducted a classic study on the demography of the Ju/wasi that sheds light on

demography: the study of population dynamics in cross-cultural perspective.
fertility: the rate of births in a population, or the rate of population increase in general.
mortality: deaths in a population, or the rate of population decline in general or from particular causes.

migration: the movement of a person or people from one place to another.
modes of reproduction: the predominant patterns of fertility in a culture.
pronatalism: an ideology promoting the birthing of many children.
replacement-level fertility: in which the number of births equals the number of

deaths, leading to maintenance of current population size.
below-replacement-level fertility: in which the number of births is less than the number of deaths, leading to population decline.

how population homeostasis is achieved. (Review the Ethnographic Profile in Chapter 1 on page 22) She found that *birth intervals* (the time between one birth and a subsequent birth) among the Ju/wasi are often several years in duration. What accounts for these long birth intervals? Two factors are most important: breastfeeding and women's low levels of body fat. Frequent and long periods of breastfeeding inhibit progesterone production and suppress ovulation. Also, a certain level of body fat is required for ovulation. Ju/wasi women's diets contain little fat, and their regular physical exercise as foragers keeps their body fat level low, further suppressing ovulation. Thus, diet and work are key factors underlying Ju/wasi population dynamics. Ju/'hoansi women, during the time of the study, typically had between two and three live births of which two children survived into adulthood.

This model of reproduction is highly adaptive to the Ju/wasi environment and sustainable over time. Among the Ju/wasi who have given up foraging and become sedentarized farmers or labourers, fertility levels have increased, because of higher consumption levels of grains and dairy products and less physical activity.

Reproduction in Agricultural Societies

Settled agriculture promotes and supports the highest fertility rates of any model of production. **Pronatalism**, an ideology promoting the birthing of many children, emerges as a key value of farm families. It is prompted by the need for a large labour force to work the land, care for animals, process food, and do marketing. In this context, having many children is a rational reproductive strategy related to the model of production. Thus, people living in family farming systems cross-culturally have their own "family planning"—which is to have many children.

The groups with the highest fertility rates worldwide are the Mennonites and Hutterites, European-descent Christians of the United States and Canada (Stephenson 1999). Women in these groups typically have between eight and ten children who survive into adulthood. A closely related religious cultural group, the Amish (see the Ethnographic Profile box on page 124), also have high fertility rates.

Global variation in fertility in farming populations does exist, however, partly because of recent declines due to reduced demands for family labour. High rates of seven or more children per woman exist in several low-income, agricultural countries of Africa, such as Niger (8.0 births per woman), Guinea-Bissau (7.1 births per woman), Mali (7.1 births per woman), and Somalia (7.0 births per woman) (Population Reference Bureau

2005). Lower rates, of two or three children per woman, are found in many agricultural countries in South America, such as Venezuela, Chile, and Argentina.

Within countries, significant variation often exists in different regions, between urban and rural areas, and among different ethnic and class groups. In the Kilimanjaro region of northern Tanzania (see Map 5.2 on page 125), East Africa, fertility is lower than in the country as a whole, perhaps because the region has an unusually active family-planning program (Larsen and Hollos 2003). Within the Kilimanjaro region, fertility is lower among women who are economically better-off, have more years of education, choose their husbands, and have an equitable marital relationship. This study is just one of many that demonstrate the importance of women's status in shaping fertility.

In rural North India, sons are especially important, given the gender division of labour. Men provide the crucial work of plowing the fields and protecting the family in the case of village quarrels over land rights and other matters. When Western family-planning agents first visited the village of Manupur in northern India in the late 1950s to promote small families, the villagers expressed dismay (Mamdani 1972). To them a large family is a sign of wealth and success, not poverty and failure. Having many children in a family farming system makes sense.

Reproduction in Industrial Societies

In industrial societies, either capitalist or socialist, reproduction declines to the point of **replacement-level fertility** in which the number of births equals the number of deaths, leading to maintenance of current population size or **below-replacement-level fertility**, in which the number of births is less than the number of deaths, leading to population decline. Some countries with below-replacement-level fertility include Canada; Japan; Cuba; Thailand and several European countries such as Austria, Belgium, Hungary, Denmark, and Norway. Children are considered less useful in production because of the reduced labour demands of industrialism. Furthermore, children are required to attend school and cannot work for their families as much. Parents respond to these changes by having fewer children and by investing more resources in them.

Population changes during the industrial mode of reproduction correspond to what demographers call the

THINKING OUTSIDE THE BOX

CHOOSE A COUNTRY and do Internet research to locate fertility data about internal patterns, such as state-by-state, regional, ethnic, class, urban–rural, education levels, or other variables.

Ethnographic Profile

The Old Order Amish of the United States and Canada

The Amish are Christians who live in rural areas of the United States and Canada. In the early twenty-first century, their total population was roughly 200 000. Their ancestry traces to German-speaking, Swiss Anabaptists of the sixteenth century. To escape religious persecution, they migrated to North America, starting in the early eighteenth century and continuing into the mid-nineteenth century. There are no Amish in Europe today.

The term *Old Order Amish* refers to the main body of the Amish people. A small minority, known as *New Order Amish,* broke off from the Old Order in the late 1960s. Both groups use horse-drawn transportation, but the New Order Amish accept more technology.

The Amish speak a German-derived dialect. They wear modest and conforming clothing. They avoid using electricity from power grids but solar-generated electricity and 12-volt batteries are allowed. Education beyond the eighth grade is seen as unnecessary. A basic theme in Amish life is the need to guard against "worldly" (non-Amish, mainstream U.S.) values, dependencies, and hurriedness, and to maintain the family as a unit that lives and works together. Working with one's own hands is

valued, as are humility and modesty. Farming is the traditional means of livelihood among the Amish.

The Amish have high fertility rates, on average six or seven live births per woman. Even though some children leave and join "the English" (non-Amish), their population is doubling every 20 years. In Lancaster County, Pennsylvania, the heartland of the Old Order Amish, a steep rise in population growth starting in the 1970s has exceeded the availability of farmland (Kraybill and Nolt 2004). Now, several hundred Amish businesses exist, many small scale and operated from the home but many others are large scale and earn millions of dollars per year. Amish who enter business try to retain Amish values of family solidarity by working at home and selling products from their home. Many, though, work in businesses away from home, with the English.

Amish youth have the opportunity of deciding whether to be baptized into the faith when they are 16 years old. At this time, called *rumspringa* in Pennsylvania Dutch, or "running around," the young people are allowed to explore the customs of the English world including television. Most stay at home during rumspringa, spending time with Amish friends on the weekends. In rare cases,

some experiment with alcohol, drugs, and sex (Shachtman 2006). After rumspringa, around 90 percent of Amish teenagers decide to accept Amish ways and be baptized, choosing a lifestyle that emphasizes humility and community solidarity rather than the "worldly" lifestyle of individualism and competition.

Readings

Donald B. Kraybill, *The Riddle of Amish Culture.* Baltimore, MD: Johns Hopkins University Press, 2001.

Donald B. Kraybill and Steven M. Nolt. *Amish Enterprise: From Plows to Profits,* 2nd ed. Baltimore: Johns Hopkins University Press, 2004.

Kathleen McLary. *Amish Style: Clothing, Home Furnishings, Toys, Dolls, and Quilts.* Bloomington: Indiana University Press, 1993.

Tom Shachtman. *Rumspringa: To Be or Not to Be Amish.* New York: North Point Press, 2006.

Video

The Amish: A People of Preservation (Heritage Productions, 1996).

Website

Amish Teens Tempted in Devil's Playground. www.npr.org/programs/morning/features/2002/may/amish

Thanks to Donald B. Kraybill, Elizabethtown College, for reviewing this material.

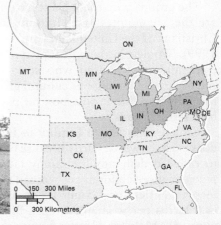

Members of an Amish household sit around their kitchen table (left).
■ (Source: © David & Peter Turnley/CORBIS) *A farmer mows alfalfa with a team of mules and a gasoline engine to power the mower (right). This mechanism enhances his farm work but does not break the Old Order Amish rule against using tractors in the field.* ■ (Source: Barbara Miller)

MAP 5.1 *Old Order Amish Population of North America. The states of Ohio (55 000), Pennsylvania (37 000), and Indiana (37 000) have the largest number of Old Order Amish.*

MAP 5.2   **Tanzania.** The United Republic of Tanzania is named after its mainland region, Tanganyika, and Zanzibar off its east coast. Its population is nearly 37 million. The capital city moved from Dar es Salaam to Dodoma in 1996, but many government offices remain in "Dar." Agriculture is the basis of the economy, and over 80 percent of the population is rural. Tanzania has substantial natural resources, especially gold. More than 120 different ethnic groups live in Tanzania. The national language is Swahili, a Bantu language, with English as a second official language. Many local languages are also spoken.

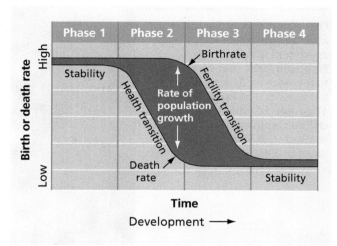

FIGURE 5.1   **Model of the Demographic Transition**
(*Source:* Nebel and Wright, *Environmental Science: The Way the World Works,* 7th ed. © 2000. Adapted by permission of Pearson Education, Inc. Upper Saddle River, NJ.)

demographic transition, a process of change from the high fertility and high mortality in agricultural societies to the low fertility and low mortality of industrialized societies. There are two phases in the demographic transition model (see Figure 5.1). In the first phase, mortality declines because of improved nutrition and health, so population growth rates increase. The second phase occurs when fertility also declines. At this point, low rates of population growth occur.

Cultural anthropologists have critiqued the demographic transition model as being too narrowly focused on the role of industrialism and not allowing for alternative models (Ginsberg and Rapp 1991). They claim that industrialism, with its reduced need for labour, is not the only factor that reduces pronatalism. China, for example, began

to reduce its population growth rate before widespread industrialism (Xizhe 1991). Instead, strong government policies and a massive family-planning program caused China's demographic transition.

The industrial mode of reproduction has three distinguishing features. First, social inequality is reflected in population patterns, referred to as *stratified reproduction*. Typically, middle-class and upper-class people tend to have few children, with high survival rates.

Among the poor, however, both fertility and mortality rates are high. Brazil, a newly industrializing state, has the world's most extreme income inequality. Parallel to its economic inequality is extremely stratified reproduction (discussed later in this chapter's section on mortality). Increasing international migration to core countries adds to variation in population dynamics within them. In France, the government promotes pronatalism to address its population deficit, but pronatal messages and programs are aimed at the "authentic" French population. In contrast, low-income immigrants from Mali, West Africa, living in Paris, receive antinatalist messages in clinics (Sargent 2005). Immigrant fertility, rather than being desired by the French government, is a matter of concern, as it strains public resources such as schools and hospitals. The fact that the immigrants are poor, black, and Muslim, with a culture that values many children, places them in stark contrast to the "authentic" French people who are relatively well-off, white, and have few children.

---

demographic transition: a process of change from the high fertility and high mortality   in agricultural societies to the low fertility and low mortality of industrialized societies.

Firefighters survey the scene after a fire in a six-story apartment building in Paris, France, in 2005, that was home to low-income African immigrants. The fire killed 17 people, of whom half were children, and injured 30 more.
■ (Source: © Victor Tonelli/Reuters/CORBIS)

A second characteristic of industrial contexts is population aging. In Japan, the total fertility rate declined to replacement level in the 1950s and later reached the below-replacement level (Hodge and Ogawa 1991). Japan is currently experiencing a decline in population growth of about 15 percent per generation and, simultaneously, rapid aging of the population. As many people enter the senior category, they create a population bulge that is not balanced by the number of younger people (see Figure 5.2). A population projection for the year 2050 suggests that the bulge will increase.

A third distinguishing feature of industrial demographies is the high level of involvement of scientific (especially medical) technology in all aspects of pregnancy: prevention, termination, and becoming pregnant in the first place (Browner and Press 1995, 1996). This trend is accompanied by increasing levels of specialization in providing the new services.

FIGURE 5.2 Changes in the Population Pyramid of Japan
(*Source:* Adapted from *Statistical Handbook of Japan*, Statistics Bureau, MIC, Japan.)

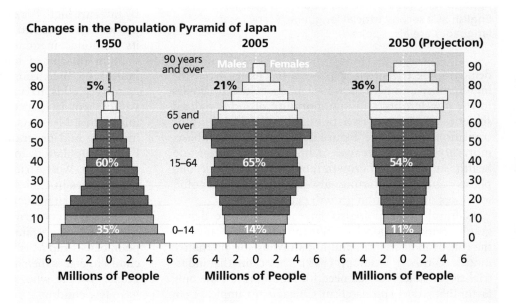

menarche: the onset of first menstruation.
menopause: the final cessation of menstruation.

Culture and Fertility

Cultures shape human reproduction from its very beginning, sexual intercourse itself or some other form of fertilization of an ovum. Cultural practices and beliefs about pregnancy and birth affect the viability of the fetus during its gestation as well as the infant's fate after birth.

Sexual Intercourse

Anthropological research on sexuality and sexual practices is particularly difficult to undertake. Sexuality involves private, sometimes secret, beliefs and behaviours. The ethics of participant observation disallow intimate observation or participation, so data can be obtained only indirectly. Biases in people's reports about their sexual beliefs and behaviour are likely for several reasons. People may be too shy to talk about sex in the first place, too boastful to give accurate information, or simply unable to answer questions such as, "How many times did you have intercourse last year?" If people do provide detailed information, it might be inappropriate for an anthropologist to publish it because of the need to protect confidentiality.

Malinowski (1929) wrote the first anthropological study of sexuality, based on his fieldwork in the Trobriands (review the Ethnographic Profile in Chapter 2 on page 40). He discusses the sexual lives of children; sexual techniques; love magic; erotic dreams; husband-wife jealousy; and a range of topics related to kinship, marriage, exchange, and morals. Since the late 1980s, cultural anthropologists have paid more attention to the study of sexuality, especially practices related to sexually transmitted diseases (STDs), including HIV/AIDS.

When to Begin Having Intercourse?

Sexual intercourse between a fertile female and fertile male is normally required for human reproduction, although artificial insemination is an option in some contexts. Biology, interacting with environment and culture, defines the time span within which a female is fertile: from **menarche** (the onset of first menstruation) to **menopause** (the final cessation of menstruation). Globally, average age at menarche is between 12 and 14 years (Thomas et al. 2001). Generally, girls in richer countries reach menarche a few years earlier than girls in poorer countries do. For example, the estimated age at menarche in Japan is 12.5 years, but in Haiti it is 15.5 years. Worldwide, a trend is for the age at menarche to become earlier. The reasons for this change are not completely clear. Diet and activity patterns are likely factors involved. The underlying assumption is that today's diets and lifestyles are a sign of "progress" and thus earlier age at menarche is an indicator of social well-being.

Average age at menopause varies more widely, from the 40s to the 50s, with later ages in richer countries (Thomas et al. 2001). According to a review of studies worldwide, in France, the latest average age at menopause is 52 years. Diet and activity level, again, are accepted as causes for regional differences. A woman's lifetime fertility also appears to be involved: Women who have more children reach menopause earlier than women who have few or no children.

Cultures socialize children about the appropriate time to begin sexual intercourse. Guidelines for initiating sexual intercourse may differ by gender, class, race, and ethnicity. In many cultures, sexual activity should begin only with marriage. This rule often applies more strictly to females than to males. In Zawiya, a traditional Muslim town of northern Morocco, as in much of the Middle East, the virginity of the bride—but not the groom—is highly valued (Davis and Davis 1987). The majority of brides conform to the ideal. Some unmarried young women do engage in premarital sex, however, and if they choose to have a traditional wedding, then they must somehow deal with the requirement of producing blood-stained wedding sheets. How do they do this? If the bride and the groom have been having premarital sexual relations, the groom may assist in the deception by nicking a finger with a knife and bloodying the sheets himself. Another option is to buy fake blood in the drugstore.

In many societies, young women are married immediately after menarche, making "teenage pregnancy" a desired condition instead of a "social problem," as perceived by many experts in North America (Ginsberg and Rapp 1991:320). The concept of a 30-year-old first-time mother would shock many people worldwide, as to both its physical possibility and its social advisability. Commonly in South Asia, Africa, and elsewhere, a married woman's status depends on her having children. The longer she delays, the more her spouse and in-laws might suspect her of being infertile. In that case, they might send her back to her parents or bring in a second wife.

Intercourse Frequency and Fertility

Cross-cultural studies indicate a wide range in frequency of sexual intercourse, confirming the role of culture in shaping sexual desire. However, the relationship between sexual intercourse frequency and fertility is not simple. A common assumption is that people in cultures with high fertility rates must have sexual intercourse frequently. Without modern birth control, such as condoms, birth control pills, and the intrauterine device (IUD), intercourse frequency would seem to lead logically to high rates of fertility.

A classic study of reported intercourse frequency for Euro-Americans in the United States and Hindus in India reveals that Indians had intercourse far less frequently (less than twice a week) than the Euro-Americans did

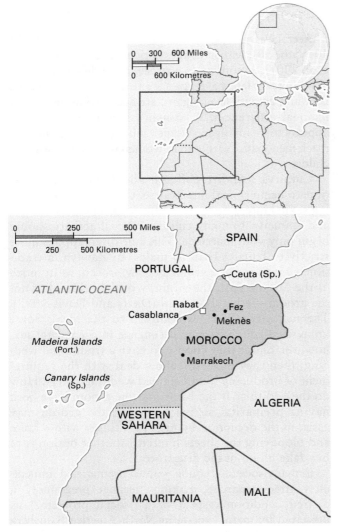

MAP 5.3 **Morocco.** The Kingdom of Morocco is the westernmost country of the Arab world. A border dispute continues with the Western Sahara, which Morocco has administered since 1975. Morocco's population is 30 million people. The terrain ranges from coastal lowlands to rugged interior mountains. Morocco's economy is based on mining phosphates, remittances, and tourism. It is one of the world's largest producers and exporters of cannabis and the world's largest per capita consumer of sugar. Most Moroccans are Sunni Muslims of Arab, Berber, or mixed Arab-Berber descent. The official language is classical Arabic but a dialect, Moroccan Arabic, is widely spoken. Over 40 percent of the people speak a variety of Berber.

(two to three times a week) in all age groups (Nag 1972). Several features of Indian culture limit sexual intercourse. The Hindu religion teaches the value of sexual abstinence, thus providing ideological support for limiting sexual intercourse. Hinduism also suggests that one should abstain from intercourse on many sacred days: the first night of the new moon, the first night of the full moon, and the eighth day of each half of the month (the light half and the dark half), and sometimes on Fridays. As many as 100 days each year could be observed as non-sex days.

A bride wearing traditional wedding clothing in the city of Meknès, Morocco. ■ (Source: © Stephanie Dinkins/ Photo Researchers, Inc.)

A more subtle psychological factor may be what Morris Carstairs (1967) termed the "lost semen complex" to explain the beliefs of Gujerati men in North India:

> "Everyone knew that semen was not easily formed; it takes forty days and forty drops of blood to make one drop of semen. . . . Semen of good quality is rich and viscous, like the cream of unadulterated milk. . . . Celibacy was the first requirement of true fitness, because every sexual orgasm meant the loss of a quantity of semen, laboriously formed." (83–86, quoted in Nag 1972:235)

The fact remains, however, that fertility is higher in India than in many other parts of the world where such restrictions on sexual intercourse do not exist. Obviously, sheer frequency of intercourse is not the explanation. It takes only one act of sexual intercourse at the right time of the month to create a pregnancy. The point of this discussion is to show that "reverse reasoning" (assuming that high fertility means that people have nothing better to do than have sex) is wrong. The cultural dynamics of sexuality in India function to restrain sexual activities and thus may keep fertility lower than it otherwise would be.

Fertility Decision-Making

This section explores decision-making about fertility at three levels: the family level, the national level, and the global level. Within the family, decision-makers weigh factors influencing why and when to have a child. At the national level, governments seek to plan their overall population objectives on the basis of particular goals that are sometimes *pronatalist* (favouring many births) and sometimes *antinatalist* (opposed to many births). At the global level, we can see that powerful economic and political interests are at work influencing the reproductive policies of individual nations and, in turn, of families and individuals within them.

At the Family Level

Within the family, parents and other family members consider, consciously or unconsciously, the value and costs of children (Nag 1983). Four factors are most important in affecting the desire for children:

- Children's labour value
- Children's value as old-age support for parents
- Infant and child mortality rates
- Economic costs of children

The first three factors have a positive effect on fertility: When children's value is high in terms of labour or old-age support, fertility is likely to be higher; when infant and child mortality rates are high, fertility rates tend to be high in order to "replace" offspring who do die. In the case of child costs—including direct costs (for food, education, clothing) and indirect costs (employment opportunities that the mother gives up)—the relationship is negative. Higher costs reduce the desire for children. Industrialism raises child costs and lowers their value dramatically because it tends to avoid using child labour. Mandatory school attendance also pulls children out of the workforce and may involve direct costs for fees, uniforms, and supplies. States that provide old-age security and pension plans further reduce the need for children.

In a highland village in the Oaxacan region of southern Mexico (see Map 5.4), men and women have different preferences about the number of children they wish to have (Browner 1986). Men are more pronatalist than women. Among women with only one child, 80 percent were content with their present family size. Most men (60 percent) who were satisfied with their present family size had four or more children. One woman said, "My husband sleeps peacefully through the night, but I have to get up when the children need something. I'm the one the baby urinates on; sometimes I have to get out of bed in the cold and change both our clothes. They wake me when they're sick or thirsty; my husband sleeps through it all." (1986: 714)

Depending on the gender division of labour and other social features related to gender, sons or daughters may be relatively more valued. Son preference is widespread, especially in Asia and the Middle East, but it is not universal. In Southeast Asia, people prefer a balanced sex ratio in their offspring. Daughter preference is found in some Caribbean populations, in Venezuela, and some parts of Africa south of the Sahara.

In Tokugawa, Japan, during the eighteenth and nineteenth centuries, husbands and wives had different fertility preferences about the gender of their first child (Skinner 1993). Tokugawa wives, as is still common in Japan, preferred to have "first a girl, then a boy." This preference is related to the benefit in having a girl to help the

THINKING OUTSIDE THE BOX

IN YOUR FAMILY, is there a preference about the desired number of sons and daughters? Is there a preference for their birth order?

MAP 5.4 Mexico. The United Mexican States is the most populous Spanish-speaking country in the world. It was subjected to Spanish rule for three centuries before gaining independence. Its population is 107 million, and the capital has a population of 20 million people. Mexico has a mixed economy of industry, agriculture, and trade, and is the fourth largest oil producer in the world. Ethnically, the population consists of mestizos (60 percent), Indians (30 percent), and whites (9 percent). Southern states have the highest proportion of Indians.

mother in her work and to care for subsequent children, especially the boy it was hoped would come next. Husbands prefer a son-first strategy since a son helps them with their work. Husbands and wives each tried to achieve their goals with the one method available: **sex-selective infanticide**, or the killing of offspring on the basis of sex. Depending on their relative power, either the husband or wife would be able to dominate the decision-making about whether a child born would be kept. But how could one assess the relative power of spouses? Age differences in Japan are a key status index. Seniority commands deference, respect, and obedience. Three categories of marital power can be defined, based on age differences at the time of marriage:

- *Low husband power:* The wife is older than the husband (5 percent of marriages).
- *Intermediate husband power:* The ages of husband and wife are about equal (60 percent).
- *High husband power:* The husband is older than the wife (35 percent).

In households with high husband power, 84 percent of first-born children kept alive were boys, compared to 34 percent in households with low husband power (see Figure 5.3). Households with more balanced marital power had a roughly equal number of first-born boys and girls (53 percent).

At the National Level

National governments play major roles in decreasing or increasing rates of population growth within their boundaries. Governments are concerned about providing employment and public services, maintaining the tax base, filling the ranks of the military, maintaining ethnic and regional proportions, and dealing with population aging. The former Soviet Union faced significant planning challenges created by the contrasts between the below-replacement fertility of the "European" areas and high fertility rates in the central Asian and Muslim regions such as Tajikistan and Kyrghizstan (see Map 10.3 on page 275). Some countries, including Japan and France, are concerned about declining population growth rates. Their leaders have urged women to have more babies. The Quebec government is aware of the province's low birth rate and has developed policies to provide extra supports for families, including subsidies and low-cost child care. Israel is openly pronatalist, given its interest in boosting its national population level as a political statement of strength.

At the Global Level

The most far-reaching layer that affects decision-making about fertility occurs at the international level, where

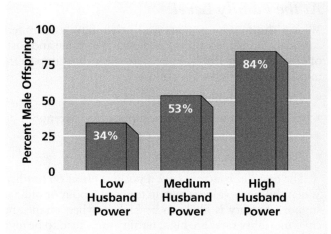

FIGURE 5.3 Gender of First-Born Child According to Spouse Power in the Household, Tokugawa, Japan
(*Note:* Under normal conditions, one would expect roughly equal percentages of male and female births.) (Source: From "Conjugal Power in Tokugawa Japanese Families: A Matter of Life or Death" by William G. Skinner, in *Sex and Gender Hierarchies*, edited by Barbara D. Miller. Copyright © 1993. Reprinted by permission of Cambridge University Press.)

global power structures such as the World Bank, pharmaceutical companies, and religious leaders influence national and individual priorities about fertility. In the 1950s, there was a wave of enthusiasm among Western nations for promoting family-planning programs of

Girls participating in the Guelaguetza festival, Oaxaca. Oaxaca is a distinctive cultural region and the scene of a vigorous movement for indigenous people's rights.
■ (Source: Rose Hartman/CORBIS)

sex-selective infanticide: the killing of an infant or child because of its sex.

many types. In the 1990s, the United States adopted a more restricted policy toward family planning, withdrew support for certain features such as abortion, and began to promote abstinence as the foundation of population control (see the Critical Thinking box on page 132). The policy of the Canadian International Development Agency (CIDA) is to support women's reproductive health programs in developing countries in the context of family health, safe motherhood, women's nutrition, and quality family-planning services. Population policies of the governments of donor countries may affect the welfare of people in developing countries.

Fertility Control

People in all cultures throughout history have had ways of influencing fertility, including ways to increase it, reduce it, and regulate child spacing. Some ways are direct, such as using certain herbs or medicines that induce abortion. Others are indirect, such as long periods of breastfeeding, which reduce chances of conception. In Indonesia, for example, breastfeeding probably accounts for more child spacing than all other forms of contraception combined (Rohde 1982).

Hundreds of indigenous fertility-control methods are available cross-culturally. One study conducted in Afghanistan in the 1980s found about 500 fertility-regulating techniques in just one region of the country (Hunte 1985). In Afghanistan, as in most pre-industrial societies, it is women who possess this information. Specialists, such as midwives or herbalists, provide further guidance and expertise. Of the total number of methods in the Afghanistan study, 72 percent were aimed at increasing fertility, 22 percent were contraceptives (preventing fertilization of the ovum by the sperm), and 6 percent were used to induce abortion. Most methods involve plant and animal substances prepared in different ways. Herbs are made into tea and taken orally, some substances are formed into pills, some steamed and inhaled as vapours, some vaginally inserted, and others rubbed on the woman's stomach.

The next section considers two methods of family planning: induced abortion, which is a long-standing form of family planning, and, the most recent, the *new reproductive technologies* (NRTs).

Induced Abortion

Direct intervention in a pregnancy may be resorted to in order to prevent fetal development and lead to abortion (expulsion of the fetus from the womb). Induced abortion, in its many forms, is probably a cultural universal. A review of ethnographic literature on about 400 societies indicates that it was practised in virtually all societies (Devereaux 1976). It is usually done either

by the woman herself or with assistance from another woman, perhaps a midwife. Attitudes toward abortion range from acceptability to conditional approval (abortion is acceptable under specified conditions), to tolerance (abortion is regarded with neither approval nor disapproval), to opposition and punishment for offenders. Methods of inducing abortion include hitting the abdomen, starving oneself, taking drugs, jumping from high places, jumping up and down, lifting heavy objects, and doing hard work.

Economic and social factors usually explain why women induce abortion (Devereaux 1976:13–21). Nomadic pastoral women, for example, work hard and frequently carry heavy loads, sometimes for long distances. This lifestyle does not allow women to care for many small children at one time. Poverty is another motivating factor: When a woman is faced with another birth in the context of limited resources, abortion may appear to be the best option. Culturally defined "legitimacy" of a pregnancy, along with possible social penalties for bearing an illegitimate child, has been a prominent reason for abortion in Western societies.

Some governments have intervened in family decisions to regulate access to abortion in varying ways, sometimes promoting it, and other times forbidding it. Since the late

Women waiting for their turn at the clinic in Bazarak, eastern Afghanistan. Patriarchal norms prevent women from going to clinics, and the geographical terrain and distance make it impossible to get to a clinic in cases of emergency. Rates of maternal mortality in remote areas of Afghanistan are probably the highest in the world.
■ (Source: © Reza Webistan/CORBIS)

Critical Thinking

FAMILY-PLANNING PROGRAMS IN BANGLADESH

Beginning in the 1980s, criticism of Western family-planning programs in relation to reproductive rights emerged from several directions. In the United States, the conservative Reagan administration opposed support of abortion and other forms of population control at home and abroad. (In November 1999, the United States government again refused to pay its estimated $1.5 billion in unpaid United Nations dues, an estimated 80 percent of all unpaid dues, because of Republican demands for conditions that ban spending any U.S. funds to support family-planning clinics offering abortions in other countries.) At the same time, critics on the left claimed that the Western-supported and Western-styled family-planning programs in developing countries were a form of neo-colonialism. Areas of concern included sterilization of women and the use of incentives such as cash payments, radios, or clothing to attract people to being sterilized.

Betsy Hartmann, an early critic of Western family-planning promotion in developing countries, wrote an influential book called *Reproductive Rights and Wrongs* (1987). In the mid-1970s, she did fieldwork in a village in Bangladesh. Two key lessons about women's reproductive freedom emerged. First, in one area, there were women who were satisfied with the number of children they had, and they wanted to adopt some form of "modern" contraception, but none was available. Second,

> In other areas of Bangladesh, population control programs were vigorously promoting various methods

including the pill, the injectable Depo-Provera, and IUDs without adequate medical screening, supervision, or follow-up. Many women experienced negative side-effects and became disillusioned with family planning. The government's response was not to reform the program to meet women's needs, but instead to further intensify its population control efforts by promoting female sterilization. In both contexts, women were denied control over their reproduction. (x–xi)

In addition, Hartmann became involved in exposing the United States' involvement in sterilization abuse in Bangladesh, arguing that sterilization was targeted at the poorest women and involved "coercive" incentives. The incentive given to a man or woman for sterilization was Taka 175, equivalent to several weeks' wages. Women also received a *sari* (women's clothing worth about Taka 100), and men received a *lungee* (men's clothing worth roughly Taka 50). In some cases, food incentives were given. Poor women who approached local government officials for wheat as part of a special food aid program were told that they would get wheat if they had the "operation." Food aid was withheld from women who refused. The number of sterilizations increased during the autumn months when food was scarcest. Doctors and clinic staff received a bonus for each sterilization. Some family-planning workers who failed to meet the sterilization quota for the month suffered pay cuts. However, others have argued that the

1980s, China has pursued one of the most rigorous campaigns to limit population growth (Greenhalgh 2003). Its One-Child per Couple Policy, announced in 1978, allowed most families to have only one child. It involved strict surveillance of pregnancies, strong group pressure toward women pregnant for the second time or more, and forced abortions and sterilizations. This policy inadvertently led to an increase in female infanticide, as parents, in their desire for a son, killed or abandoned infant daughters.

Religion and abortion are often related, but there is no simple relationship between what a particular religion teaches about abortion and what people actually do. Catholicism forbids abortion, but thousands of Catholic women have sought abortions throughout the world. Catholic countries have laws making induced abortion illegal. This is the case in Brazil where, in spite of the law

and Catholic beliefs, many women, especially poor women, resort to abortion. In one impoverished shantytown in the city of Recife (see Map 10.1 on page 260), one-third of the women said that they had aborted at least once (Gregg 2003:71–72). Illegal abortions are more likely to have negative effects on women's health than safe, legal abortion services. Although solid statistics are difficult to obtain, one estimate for Bahia is that at least one-fourth of all maternal deaths were due to complications of abortion (McCallum 2005:222).

Islamic teachings forbid abortion and female infanticide, yet sex-selective abortion of female fetuses is practised covertly in Pakistan and by Muslims in India. Hinduism teaches *ahimsa*, or nonviolence toward other living beings, including a fetus whose movements have been felt by the mother ("quickening"). Yet thousands of Hindus seek abortions every year, and many are specifically to abort a female.

A family-planning clinic in Egypt. Throughout much of the world, provision of Western-style family-planning advice is controversial because it may conflict with local religious and other beliefs about the value of having many children and women's duty to be child bearers.
■ (Source: © Barry Iverson/Woodfin Camp & Associates)

"compensation payment does not appear to be an important influence on the decision as to whether or not to get sterilized" (Pillsbury 1990:181).

In the mid-1980s, over 60 health-advocacy groups formed a coalition to block the approval of the injectable hormone Depo-Provera for use as a contraceptive in Canada. An effective contraceptive when injected every three months, activists were concerned that Depo-Provera had been used for years in family-planning programs in developing countries and refugee camps before having been approved for use in Canada. They raised concerns over safety issues, including considerations of risk–benefit for women, and informed consent, since Depo-Provera had been administered to mentally handicapped women, women with disabilities, First Nations women, addicted women, and women prisoners, often without informed consent, screening, or follow-up care. Because of the potential for abuse and concerns about safety, the coalition managed to delay approval of the drug's use as a contraceptive in Canada until 1997 (Tudiver 1997). Depo-Provera is currently used successfully in Canada and in overseas programs, but in 2005, new warnings suggested that it should be used only as a last resort and for a short period of time.

CRITICAL THINKING QUESTIONS

- How might anthropological fieldwork provide more information on the role of individual decision-making concerning family-planning choices?

- If you were a population policy-maker for CIDA, would you support family-planning programs using incentives such as cash payments or the use of Depo-Provera without informed consent? How would you justify your position?

- Was the delay in approving Depo-Provera use as a contraceptive in Canada justified considering its widespread and effective use today in Canada and in developing countries?

In contrast, Buddhism provides no overt rulings against abortion. In fact, Japanese Buddhism teaches that all life is fluid and that an aborted fetus is simply "returned" to a watery world of unshaped life and may, some time later, come back to live with humans (LaFleur 1992). This belief is compatible with the fact that abortion has, in recent years, been the most commonly used form of birth control in Japan.

The New Reproductive Technologies

Women's reproductive rights are an important contemporary issue worldwide. These rights range from the choice of seeking abortion to the right to bear a second child (in China). They include the issue of the right to decide to abort a fetus on the basis of its gender, physical disabilities, or other characteristics. Since the early 1980s, new forms of reproductive technology have been developed and have been made available in many places around the world.

One recent development is the ability to gain genetic information about the fetus, which can be used by parents in decision-making about whether to continue or stop the pregnancy. In North America and some European countries, amniocentesis is a legal test used to reveal certain genetic problems in the fetus, such as Down syndrome or spina bifida. Anthropologists have begun to question the social justice involved in this testing and the ethical issues related to the growing role of technology in birth and reproduction. For example, Rayna Rapp's research (1993) among poor women on Medicare in New York City demonstrated that new technology such as amniocentesis overpowered rather than empowered women.

After four years of research and public hearings, the Royal Commission on New Reproductive Technologies released its report on the social, ethical, and medical implications of these new technologies in 1993. The committee recommended banning surrogate motherhood; sex-selection procedures for non-medical purposes; the buying and selling of human eggs, sperm, embryos, and fetal tissue; and genetic alteration such as the creation of human–animal hybrids. Procedures such as artificial insemination and in vitro fertilization should only be performed in public, non-profit clinics. The commission also upheld the rights of a pregnant woman over the rights of her fetus; no woman should face civil liability for harm done to her fetus during pregnancy. Since 2000, Health Canada has been reviewing possible new legislation for dealing with reproductive and genetic technologies.

In vitro fertilization (IVF) procedures are another important feature of the new reproductive technologies; IVF is designed to bypass infertility in a woman or couple and thus promote fertility. This technique is highly sought after by many couples in Western countries, especially middle- and upper-class couples, among whom infertility is inexplicably high. It is also increasingly available in urban centres around the world (Inhorn 2003). As this new technology spreads throughout the world, people reframe it within their own cultural logics. In much of North America and the United Kingdom, where in vitro fertilization first became

available, people tend to view it as "reproduction gone awry," because it is non-natural and a sign of one's natural inadequacy and failure (Jenkins and Inhorn 2003). In Athens, Greece, women who seek in vitro fertilization see it as natural because it helps them realize a key aspect of their feminine nature through pregnancy and birth (Paxson 2003). Husbands feel less positive about IVF because they believe that their important role in conception is bypassed by the process. A study of male infertility in two Middle Eastern cities, Cairo in Egypt and Beirut in Lebanon, reveals how closely linked masculine identity is with male fertility (Inhorn 2004). In these cities, infertile men face serious social stigma and feelings of deep inadequacy. In addition, a third-party donation of sperm is not acceptable according to Islam.

Medical institutions also vary worldwide in terms of their attitudes toward IVF. In the Canada and the United States, it is medically acceptable to provide IVF services, and some, in Canada, are covered by medical insurance. In Japan, a doctor who performed an IVF procedure was expelled by the leading obstetric society there in 1998 (M. Jordan 1998). Japanese societal values in relation to reproduction are complicated: They oppose surgery because it cuts the body, but they allow abortion. There is, however, growing public demand in Japan for new reproductive techniques—a demand that is opposed by the medical profession.

People in Japan regularly visit and decorate statues in memory of their aborted or "returned" fetuses. ■
(Source: © Bettmann/CORBIS)

---

direct infanticide: the killing of an infant or child from actions such as beating, smothering, poisoning, or drowning.

indirect infanticide: the killing of an infant or child via a more subtle process, such as food deprivation, failure to take

a sick infant to a clinic, or failure to provide warm clothing in winter.

Culture and Death

Cultural anthropologists have studied mortality less than fertility (Bledsoe and Hirschman 1989). Mortality is more difficult to research in a typical fieldwork period. In a year, several births might occur in a village of 1000 people, while fewer infant deaths will occur and perhaps no murders or suicides. Another reason for the difference in research emphasis between fertility and mortality is the greater availability of funding for fertility studies, given the worldwide concern with population growth and family planning.

Cultural factors often put certain people more at risk of dying from a certain cause and at a particular age than others. Consider patterns on deaths from car accidents. The rate of severe car accidents is higher among men, and is associated with more high-risk driving behaviour, such as driving at high speeds and driving under the influence of alcohol (Hakamies-Blomqvist 1994). For older drivers in Finland, an increase in fatal accidents occurs among females. The analysis found that older women drivers had substantially less driving experience because men have jobs to which they commute. Women's relative lack of driving experience places them at a disadvantage when it comes to coping with the effects of aging on driving.

Causes of death can be analyzed on several levels. For example, if an infant living in a poor, tropical country dies of dehydration, what might be the cause? Levels of causality considered in population studies are *proximate, intermediate,* and *ultimate* causes. A proximate cause is the one that is closest to the actual outcome. In the case of the infant death, dehydration was the proximate cause of death and one that might be written on the death certificate. Why was the baby dehydrated? A closer look into the situation might show that the baby was malnourished. Malnutrition leads to diarrhea and subsequent dehydration. Malnutrition could be considered the intermediate cause of death. Why was the baby malnourished? This question takes us down a complex pathway of inquiry—perhaps the baby was not breastfed, and the family was poor and tried to bottle feed using expensive breast milk substitutes that were over-diluted with dirty water (P. Van Esterik 1989); perhaps the baby died during a period of extreme food scarcity in the area; or maybe the baby was an unwanted third daughter and was fed less than she needed in order to thrive. The question of ultimate causation entails an analysis of the deeper economic, political, and social factors that put a particular individual at increased risk of dying. In the next sections, we review how culture shapes death.

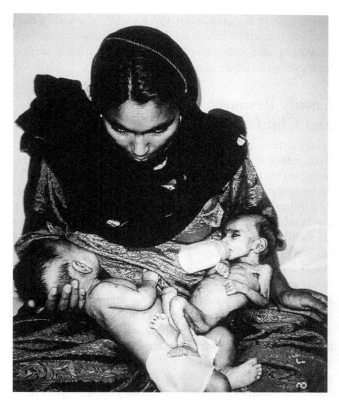

This Pakistani mother allowed her twin son exclusive access to her breast milk, while not breastfeeding her twin daughter. The girl died the day after this photo was taken. The mother told her doctor to use the picture if it would help others avoid making the same mistake.
■ (Source: Courtesy of UNICEF)

Infanticide

Infanticide, or the deliberate killing of offspring is widely practised, although rarely a frequent or common practice. **Direct infanticide** is the death of an infant or child resulting from actions such as beating, smothering, poisoning, or drowning. **Indirect infanticide,** a more subtle process, may involve prolonged practices such as food deprivation, failure to take a sick infant to a clinic, or failure to provide warm clothing in winter. The most frequent motive for direct infanticide reported in the cross-cultural record is that the infant was "deformed" or very ill (Scrimshaw 1984:490–91). Other motives for infanticide include sex of the infant, an adulterous conception, an unwed mother, the birth of twins, too many children in the family already, and poverty. Psychologists Martin Daly and Margo Wilson (1984) offered a sociobiological explanation for 148 cases of

THINKING OUTSIDE THE BOX

THINK OF a context where it would be feasible for an anthropologist to study mortality.

infanticide in Canada from 1961 to 1979, arguing that mothers convicted of killing their offspring were likely to be young and unmarried, and may thus have lacked financial and family resources to help them.

Family Resource Constraints and Child "Fitness"

In all cultures, parents have expectations for their children. If an infant appears to be unable to meet these expectations, parental disappointment and detachment might occur and may result in lethal neglect or direct infanticide.

Culturally accepted infanticide has long existed among the Tarahumara, (pronounced tara-oo-MAR-a) a group of about 50 000 indigenous peoples living in a rugged mountainous area of northern Mexico (see Map 5.4 on page 129) (Mull and Mull 1987). Most live in log houses with dirt floors and no running water or electricity. They grow corn and beans and raise sheep and goats, mainly for their own use. Human strength is valued in adults as well as in children, since children begin helping with herding and child care early in their lives. Dorothy and Dennis Mull first learned of the possible existence of culturally sanctioned infanticide when Dennis was working as a volunteer physician in a hospital. A 12-month-old girl who had been admitted several months earlier developed a complication necessitating the amputation of half her foot. During her recovery in hospital, her mother's visits became less frequent. In conversations with the medical staff, the mother expressed a restrained but deep anger about the fact that her daughter had lost half her foot. After the child had been released from the hospital, she died. It was generally understood in the community that the child was a victim of indirect infanticide. One person explained: "Well, after all, with only half a foot she'd never be able to walk right or work hard. She might never find a husband" (116–117).

Among the poor of northeastern Brazil, indirect infanticide is also related to harsh conditions and poverty (Scheper-Hughes 1992). Life is hard for the poor residents of the shantytown called Bom Jesus. Available data on infant and child mortality rates in Bom Jesus since the 1960s led anthropologist Nancy Scheper-Hughes to coin the ironic phrase the *modernization of mortality*. The modernization of mortality in Brazil refers to a deep division between mortality patterns of the rich and the poor. Recent economic growth in Brazil has brought rising standards of living for many. The national **infant mortality rate** (deaths of children under the age of one year per 1000 births) declined substantially in recent decades, but the declines have been unevenly distributed. High infant death rates are concentrated among the poorest classes of society. Poverty forces mothers to selectively (and unconsciously) neglect babies that seem sickly or weak, sending them to heaven as "angel babies" rather than trying to keep them alive with the inadequate resources available. People's

These Tarahumara women of Chihuahua state, Mexico, are making tesgüino. Tesgüino is an alcoholic beverage made from fermented maize (corn). It is of central importance in the secular and religious lives of the Tarahumara. The Tarahumara region often experiences extended drought and food shortages and poverty is prevalent. ■
(Source: © Lindsay Hebberd/ CORBIS)

infant mortality rate: deaths of children under the age of one year per 1000 births.

religious beliefs, a form of Catholicism, provide ideological support for this practice of indirect infanticide since it allows mothers to believe that their dead babies are now safe in heaven (this ethnographic case is discussed further in Chapter 6).

When the infant's sex is the basis for infanticide, females tend to be the target (Miller 1997:42–44). Among foraging groups, sex-selective infanticide is rare, found among some circumpolar groups of North America. While early ethnographers such as Boas and Rasmussen attribute high rates of female infanticide among the Inuit to the need to reduce the number of nonfood producers, more recent reports emphasize the decline in infant mortality rates among the Inuit as health care improved (Frideres 1998:401). Among horticultural societies, a correlation exists between the level of intergroup warfare and the practice of female infanticide (Divale and Harris 1976). Warfare puts a premium on raising males, and diverts care and resources from females.

Son preference, discussed earlier in this chapter, is linked to direct female infanticide in contemporary times in much of China, the Republic of Korea, Hong Kong, India, Pakistan, and parts of the Middle East (see the Multiple Cultural Worlds box on page 138). In these countries, female infanticide is related to a complex set of factors, including the gender division of labour and marriage practices and costs.

Suicide

Suicide occurs in all societies, but whether it is viewed as a positive or negative act varies. In some contexts, suicide is considered a crime. Catholicism defines suicide as a sin, and suicide rates tend to be lower in Catholic countries than in Protestant countries (Durkheim 1951:152). Buddhism does not consider attempted suicide a punishable crime. Indeed, Buddhists have sometimes resorted to suicide as a political statement, as in the suicides of Buddhist priests and nuns by self-immolation during the Vietnam War.

Suicide terrorism is a term that has become prominent in the United States since the September 11, 2001, attacks. Those attacks, as well as many others carried out in the Middle East and elsewhere by people of several different religious and political persuasions, involve the suicide of one or more people with the intention of killing other people as well (Andriolo 2002). Many religions put a positive value on martyrdom, or a person facing and accepting death for a sacred cause. Linking personal martyrdom with killing others is also found in some religions and secular political movements. The young Tamil woman who in 1991 blew herself up, along with India's then prime minister Rajiv Gandhi (Indira Gandhi's eldest son), is an example of a political martyr–assassin. Her cause was ethnic Tamil

separatism in Sri Lanka. Islam condemns suicide and teaches that hell awaits those who commit it. But certain reinterpretations, among Philippine Muslims, for example, see purposeful suicide killings as being outside Islamic teachings but nonetheless justifiable on other grounds. A few pages in the manual that the September 11 hijackers had with them related their actions to raids that the prophet Muhammad conducted to consolidate his position, thus portraying their actions as acceptable and even heroic and the end for them as entry into paradise instead of hell. Many Islamic scholars, however, reject this reasoning.

Throughout much of Asia and the South Pacific, suicide is considered a noble and honourable act. When Cheyenne Brando, daughter of Marlon Brando and Tahitian actress Tarita, committed suicide in Tahiti, the local mayor called her suicide "a beautiful gesture" (Gliotto 1995:70). Honourable suicide is also found in Japan, where it seems to result from a strong commitment to group goals and a feeling of failure to live up to those goals (Lebra 1976). In this way, suicide is a way of "saving face."

Sati (pronounced "SUT-TEE"), or the suicide of a wife upon the death of her husband, has been practised in parts of India for several hundred years and, on occasion, into the present. According to Hindu scriptures, a woman whose husband dies does an act of great personal and group honour if she voluntarily joins his corpse on the funeral pyre and thus burns to death. No one knows for sure how common this was in the past, but its ideal is still upheld by conservative Hindus. The most recent reported *sati* occurred in the northern state of Rajasthan in 1987 by a young widow named Roop Kanwar. Historians and social scientists have debated the degree of agency involved in such suicides, as there is evidence of direct coercion in some cases—for example, when a widow was drugged, or physically forced onto the pyre. Indirect coercion is also culturally embedded in the belief that a woman whose husband dies is to blame for his death. Perhaps she didn't serve him with enough devotion, pray or fast for him enough, or she ate too much and didn't give him enough food. The life of surviving widows is difficult, involving loss of status, shame, and material deprivation. Knowing this, a new widow may decide she would be better off dead. The film *Water* (2005; the final instalment in her Elements trilogy—*Fire* and *Earth* being the first two) by Canadian director Deepa Mehta is a dramatic representation of the lives of young Hindu widows.

Since the mid-1950s, suicide rates have increased by 60 percent worldwide (Buvinic and Morrison 2000). Around 1 million people take their own lives each year, and that number continues to rise. Suicide has long been most prevalent in the industrialized, urbanized societies of Europe. In the late twentieth century, however, suicide

A PREFERENCE FOR SONS

Prospective parents in all cultures may ask themselves questions such as: Will my baby be healthy? Will I have a girl or a boy? Throughout South and East Asia, the baby's gender is often as important as the health of the baby. The preference for sons is especially strong in northern India.

The population of India has 55 million fewer females than males. Much of this gap is caused by indirect female infanticide and sex-selective abortion (Miller 1997 [1981]). These practices cause the **sex ratio**, or the number of males per 100 females in a population, to become unbalanced. The scarcity of girls is most extreme in northern India. In this region, it is common for mothers to breastfeed infant daughters less often and for a shorter period of time than they do their sons. Hospitals admit twice as many boys as girls, not because more boys are sick than girls but because family decision-makers are more willing to allocate time and money to the health of boys than of girls.

The regional pattern corresponds with two features of the economy: production and marriage exchanges. The northern plains are dominated by *dry-field wheat cultivation,* which requires intensive labour inputs for plowing and field preparation and then moderate amounts of field labour for sowing, weeding, and harvesting, with women assisting in the latter tasks as unpaid family labour. Production in southern and eastern India relies more on *wet rice cultivation,* in which women form the bulk of the paid agricultural labour force. In much of southern India, women sometimes participate equally with men in agricultural planning and decision-making.

Paralleling this regional difference in the gender division of labour is a contrast in costs related to marriage. In the north, marriage typically requires, especially among the propertied groups, a **dowry**, or **groomprice**—the transfer of money and goods from the bride's family to the groom's family. Marriage costs in the south among both propertied and unpropertied groups may involve **brideprice** or **bridewealth**—the transfer of money and goods from the groom's side to the bride's father, along with a tradition of passing gold jewellery through the female line from mother to daughter. In recent years, however, dowry has been spreading throughout India.

From a parent's perspective, the birth of several daughters in the northern system is a financial drain. In the

A low-income, itinerant vendor in a small town in India's Himalayan region proudly displays her son. Son preference is spreading from the North Indian plains region throughout India. ■ (Source: Barbara Miller)

north, the more sons per daughter in the household the better: More dowries coming in will finance a "better" marriage of a daughter. In the south, a daughter is considered a valuable labourer and source of wealth. Importantly, much of northern dowry and southern brideprice circulates. In the north, an incoming dowry can be used to finance the marriage of the groom's sister; in the south, cash received at the marriage of a daughter can be used for the marriage of her brother.

---

sex ratio: the number of males per 100 females in a population.
dowry: the transfer of cash and goods from the bride's family to the newly married couple and to the groom's family.

groomprice: the transfer of cash and goods, often large amounts, from the bride's family to the groom's family.

brideprice or **bridewealth:** the transfer of cash and goods from the groom's family to the bride's family and to the bride.

The economic costs and benefits to a household of having sons versus daughters in India also vary by class. Middle-class and upper-class families, especially in the north, tend to keep girls and women out of the paid labour force. Thus, daughters are a greater economic liability among them. Among the poor, where girls, as well as boys, may earn money in the informal sector (such as doing piece-work at home), daughters are less of a burden. This class difference is mirrored in marriage costs. Among the poor, marriage costs are lower than among the middle and upper classes. They often involve balanced transfers between the bride's and groom's families.

Thus, poverty is not the major cause of son preference and daughter disfavour in India. Instead, the cause is the desire to maximize family status and wealth. If parents have two sons and one daughter in the north Indian marriage system, then two dowries come in with the brides of the sons and only one dowry will be paid out. The incoming dowries can be used to finance an impressive outgoing dowry of one's daughter that will attract a high-status husband. If northern parents have two daughters and one son, the ratio of incoming to outgoing wealth changes dramatically. This situation will impoverish a family.

FOOD FOR THOUGHT

• Have you experienced, or has anyone you know experienced, a feeling of being less valued as a child than other children in the family? If you are an "only child," you will need to ponder experiences you may have heard from friends. Have you seen or experienced preferential treatment among siblings? How can you account for this partiality?

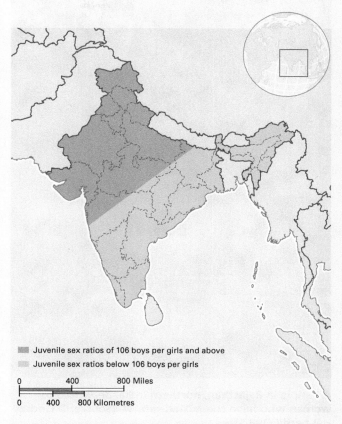

Juvenile sex ratios of 106 boys per girls and above

Juvenile sex ratios below 106 boys per girls

0	400		800 Miles
0	400	800 Kilometres	

MAP 5.5 India's Regional Pattern of Unbalanced Child Sex Ratios. The number of sons per daughters is distinctly higher in the northwestern region than in the south and east.

Sania Mirza of India lunges for a return from Marion Bartoli of France during the U.S. Open tennis tournament in Flushing Meadows, New York, in 2005. A Muslim and world-class tennis player, Mirza is the poster girl for India's public education campaign to promote awareness of the value of daughters. Slogans urge parents to have daughters and to care for them because their daughter may be the next Sania Mirza. At the same time, some conservative Islamic groups criticize Mirza for wearing immodest clothing. ■ (Source: © Brian Snyder/Reuters/CORBIS)

A temple in Rajasthan, northern India, dedicated to women who have committed *sati.* ■ (Source: © Lindsey Hebberd/CORBIS)

rates rose steeply in several developing nations, such as Sri Lanka and Samoa (Kearney and Miller 1985). This rise appears to be driven by a widening gap between aspirations, especially of youth, and limited ways of achieving these aspirations due to economic constraints. Even more recently, suicide among youth in many Amazonian tribal groups has risen steeply (Jeter 2004). Forcibly displaced from their traditional territories, these people live on reservations that are squeezed more and more each year by encroaching development. They are impoverished, grieving for their lost heritage and lifestyle, and despairing. The only available work in sugar cane refineries and alcohol processing plants is extremely arduous and pays little. Faced with a bleak future, many young people end their lives, usually by hanging. One man commented, "It is a curse to have to cut your children down . . . we are living in a time of a great plague" (2004:A22)

In Canada and the United States, the highest suicide rates occur among Indian or First Peoples' populations, especially among youth (EcoHawk 1997). In the recently created Nunavut Territory of Canada's eastern Arctic (see Map 1.2 on page 12), suicide among the native Inuit people is the most serious problem facing the new government (Tester and McNicoll 2004). Suicide rates in Nunavut are six times higher than in the southern provinces, and males aged 15 to 29 are most likely to commit suicide (Frideres 1998:182). A compelling interpretation of this situation is that four aspects of *colonial* stress are related to the high suicide rates: stress of identity and self-definition, stress of isolation, and stress of changing intergenerational relations. In this region, colonialism refers to domination by the Canadian state, with the 1960s and 1970s being a particularly intense period. During this time, the government attempted to repress Inuit identity through various assimilation strategies, including imposition of the English language. One result was loss of Inuit self-esteem, or *inuusittiaqarniq,* a process that affected young men the most, given intergenerational expectations for them and their inability to fulfill these expectations.

Epidemics

Epidemics are diseases that spread rapidly and widely throughout populations. Throughout humanity's evolution, major epidemics such as the European plague dramatically affected population numbers and challenged people's social and psychological coping mechanisms. The major epidemic of modern times, HIV/AIDS, has been identified only since the 1980s. It has had a substantial mortality effect over the past two decades.

Currently, sub-Saharan countries are the most affected by the HIV epidemic, with most of the deaths occurring among adults (Nyambedha, Wandibba, and Aagaard-Hansen 2003). These deaths are tragic in themselves, but they also create huge numbers of orphaned children. Global estimates are that 10 million children under the age of 15 years have lost their mother or both parents to AIDS. In Kenya alone, it is estimated that there are 1.5 million orphaned children. Some families in Kenya are now headed by children as young as 10 to 12 years old. Community-based interventions to help these disadvantaged children would benefit from attention to local cultural factors (see the accompanying Lessons Applied box).

Violence

Violent death can be the result of private, interpersonal conflict or it can occur in a public arena, either through informal conflict between individuals or groups, such as gang fights, or formal conflict, such as war. Violent death can be direct, as when someone kills someone else with a weapon, or indirect, as when a government fails to provide food for people during a disaster. Often, culture shapes the victim pattern of violent death.

Lessons Applied

LOCAL CULTURAL PATTERNS FOR IMPROVED ORPHAN CARE IN KENYA

The steep rise in the numbers of orphans in Africa—due to the AIDS epidemic—calls for new thinking about how to care for these children. Traditional kin-based support systems are breaking down under the strain. Child care in many African societies involves parents, grandparents and other family members. But now, even this social safety net is not enough.

Many nongovernmental agencies are helping to design community-based services for AIDS orphans. Cultural anthropologists can help make these services more effective by offering insights about local cultural practices and beliefs so that programs can be tailored to fit particular communities. Anthropologists have long known that "one-size-fits-all" programs, designed by outsiders without attention to local culture, are less effective than they could be or, at worst, fail disastrously.

One anthropological study undertaken to provide such needed cultural information was conducted in western Kenya in an area bordering Lake Victoria (Nyambedha, Wandibba, and Aagaard-Hansen 2003) (see Map 6.2 on page 159). The Luo are the predominant ethnic group in the region. The area is poor, and most Luo practise small-scale farming and obtain some additional income from fishing, migrant labour, and informal gold mining. Recurrent droughts lead to frequent crop failures. Children are important in the local economy: They work on farms planting, weeding, and harvesting and doing other important tasks such as collecting firewood, herding animals, fetching water, and fishing. Clean water is scarce. Health services provided by a Christian mission and the government are of poor quality and not affordable for most people.

The Luo define an orphan as someone under the age of 18 years who has lost either one or both parents; thus they refer to single and double orphans. (The Luo definition differs from the usual international definition: someone under the age of 15 years who has lost both parents.) The Luo say that the neediest are double orphans.

The large and sudden increase in the number of orphans creates larger strains on the community as people come to realize that their traditional pattern of caring for orphans within the kinship structure is not adequate. The traditional generosity of kin seems to be declining. At the same time, a long-standing pattern of spending a lot of money on funerals means that resources that could go to orphans instead go to burial and after-burial rituals.

Community-based organizations such as churches and women's groups in this region are doing little to help the orphans, although in other areas they are more active. The study provides a baseline of the population of orphans, information about their specific needs and coping strategies, and insights about community views of the problem. It points to the particular needs of different types of orphans and the varying strengths of different family structures in caring for orphans.

The authors reject the idea of constructing an orphanage as a way of dealing with the problem. They offer no specific suggestions for community-based programs, but it is easy to see that the following would help: financial support to single-parent and grandparent caregivers, waiving or community funding of the school fees for orphans, and a social movement to divert some of the money used for funerals to orphan care.

FOOD FOR THOUGHT

- Has the issue of AIDS orphans in Africa come to your attention before? If so, how? Via television? newspapers? How was the issue presented? If it had not come to your attention, what might explain its relative invisibility as a globally significant issue?

Private Violence: Wife Killing

Throughout the world, private violence resulting in death is all too common. One example, infanticide, was discussed earlier. Lethal spousal violence is known to exist throughout most of the world in varying degrees, although dependable statistics are unavailable. In the case of spouses, far more women are killed by husbands or male partners than vice versa. Anecdotal evidence suggests that in much of the Middle East, a husband may kill his wife or daughter with a fair amount of impunity, as if it is within his rights in terms of protecting family honour. In Canada in 1997, one in eight women living with a man was abused at some time, according to the federal Department of Justice.

In India, beginning in the 1980s, many cases of *dowry death* were reported in the media. Such murders were characteristically committed by a husband, often in collusion with his mother, and often carried out by throwing a flammable substance over the victim and then lighting her on fire. These murders are especially prevalent in northern cities, among the middle and upper classes. They are motivated by an obsessive material interest in extracting wealth from the wife's family through a continuing stream of demanded gifts. If the bride's family cannot comply the bride is endangered. This form of **femicide** or murder of a person based on being female is related to the low value of women in India, especially in the North and among the status-aspiring middle and upper classes.

Public Violence

Two forms of lethal public violence that anthropologists study are warfare and genocide. These topics are discussed further in Chapter 10. This section focuses on their effects on mortality. The few studies that have addressed mortality from warfare cross-culturally reveal that, among horticultural societies, warfare is the leading cause of male deaths (Divale and Harris 1976). Horticulture's requirement for large territories puts many groups in conflict with one another. In recent decades, conflicts with outsiders have increased; for example, the Yanomami of the Brazilian and Venezuelan Amazon region (see Map 3.4 on page 74) are squeezed by outsiders such as cattle ranch developers and miners (R. Ferguson 1990). This external pressure impels them to engage in intergroup raids that often result in the deaths of male fighters and also sometimes women, who may be captured and killed. In some especially vulnerable groups of Yanomami, up to one-third of all adult males die as a result of intergroup raids and warfare.

In contrast, in industrialized societies, the death rates of males actively involved in warfare are a much smaller proportion of the total death rate, being replaced by such causes as automobile accidents or heart disease. Canadian casualties totalled 138 166 in World War I, 53 145 in World War II, and 516 in the Korean War. Since then, most Canadian military casualties, numbering less than 150, have come during UN and NATO peacekeeping operations, according to the Department of National Defence. By fall 2008, more than 100 Canadian soldiers had died in Afghanistan. The Vietnam–American War of the 1960s and 1970s resulted in the death of roughly 60 000 Americans in Vietnam (mostly males) and of many times that number of Vietnamese.

Some scholars distinguish **ethnocide**, destruction of a culture without physically killing its people, from **genocide**, the destruction of a culture and its people through physical extermination. The Chinese occupation of Tibet, the Khmer Rouge's massacres in Cambodia, the Serbian-Bosnian conflict, the Hutu–Tutsi conflict in Rwanda, and the Indonesian government's actions in East Timor are examples of politically motivated genocide.

Refugees from the late 1990s violence in Rwanda on their way to neighbouring Democratic Republic of the Congo (Zaire). Many refugees did not survive the ordeal, although adequate statistics are not available to assess the mortality rate of refugees. ■ (Source: Allan Tannenbaum/ Image Works)

The legacy of mistreatment, forced relocation, and discriminatory policies experienced by Native Americans in the United States and First Peoples in Canada continues to play out in much higher rates of mortality in these

Shanawdithit, the last known Beothuk, captured in 1823. She died of tuberculosis in St. John's, Newfoundland. ■ (Source: The Rooms Corporation of Newfoundland and Labrador)

---

femicide: the murder of a person based on the fact of her being female.

ethnocide: the destruction of a culture without physically killing its people.

genocide: the destruction of a culture and its people through physical extermination.

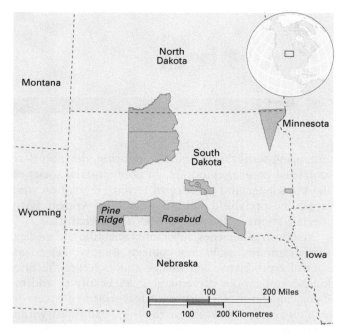

MAP 5.6 Indian Reservations in South Dakota. South Dakota has a total population of 755 000 of which 88 percent are white and 8 percent are Native American. The geography consists of prairie, low-lying hills, and the Black Hills. Before European colonialism, the region was inhabited by the Sioux and Northern Cheyenne. South Dakota is nicknamed "The Mount Rushmore State" because of the massive stone carving of four U.S. presidents in the Black Hills, the state's major tourist attraction. Indian tribes in the area object to the sculpture since it is carved into one of their most sacred sites.

populations compared to the general population (Brave Heart 2004). The situation among the Lakota and Dakota/Nakota peoples (see Map 5.6) living on reservations is grim. Mortality rates are three times higher than the U.S. average. Tuberculosis death rates are more than six times higher. Alcoholism mortality rates are 29 percent higher. Suicide rates for the northeastern part of South Dakota are the second highest in the Indian Health Service areas, exceeded only by those in Alaska. These rates should be viewed in the context of unemployment levels of over 70 percent, cumulative losses of resources and culture over generations, and the breakdown of spiritual and social supports. Native American and First People leaders are working hard to devise programs to help alleviate despair, substance abuse, and the intergenerational transfer of suffering.

In another example of genocidal destruction, the Beothuk, the Aboriginal inhabitants of Newfoundland, were actively hunted and killed primarily by British farmers, fishers, and trappers who settled on the bays that had been the Beothuk's summer camps. The Beothuk had been pushed further inland, away from their resources, from the time of the island's discovery in 1497. With no intermediaries such as traders or missionaries interested in interacting with them, and weakened by diseases such as bubonic plague, smallpox, and tuberculosis, the population decreased from approximately 345 in 1768, to 72 in 1811; the "last" Beothuk, Shanawdithit, was captured and brought to St. John's in 1823, where she died of tuberculosis in 1829 (J. Price 1979; I. Marshall 1996).

Genocide against indigenous peoples has been occurring for centuries as imperialist powers and profit-seeking explorers and settlers have intentionally brought about the extinction of entire peoples (Maybury-Lewis 2002). During the nineteenth century, British settlers in Tasmania, an island off the southern coast of Australia (see Map 4.3 on page 107) carried out an overt campaign to exterminate the indigenous Tasmanians. In other cases, mass killings were used as means of terrorizing survivors into performing forced labour, as, for example, in the rubber plantations of Peru and the Democratic Republic of Congo. These historical examples of imperialist genocide were driven by greed and supported by a racist ideology that considered indigenous people less than human. Today, greed-driven and carelessly planned development projects such as large dams (Chapter 15) often prove to be an indirect form of genocide when they completely disrupt where indigenous people live, force them to resettle, and subject them to new diseases and suicidal despair.

Public policies can be instruments of indirect violence, or *structural violence,* which lead to "excess" deaths. One such case is documented in Mongolia (Janes and Chuluundorj 2004). Beginning in 1990, Mongolia put into place several economic reforms as it transitioned from a socialist state to market capitalism: removal of restrictions on international trade, lifting of price controls, decollectivation of herds, privatization of state-run enterprises, and marked reduction in government services. The immediate consequences were food shortages to near-famine, widespread unemployment, rising urban crime, increase in alcoholism, emergent social inequality, and the collapse of the health-care system. During the early 1990s, the *maternal mortality rate* (measured as deaths of women related to pregnancy and birth per 100 000 live births) rose steeply. In 1990, the maternal mortality rate in Mongolia, as a whole, was 119. By 1994, it rose to its peak of 240. Since then, the maternal mortality rate began to decline. In 1999, it was around 180, still far higher than it was before the reforms. Mongolian women paid a heavy price for the postsocialist transition policies.

Key Questions Revisited

HOW is reproduction related to modes of production cross-culturally?

Cultural anthropologists study how culture shapes fertility, or the number of births in a population. They classify the cross-cultural data on fertility into three models of reproduction, or the dominant pattern of fertility in a culture. These models relate to three modes of production: foraging, agriculture, and industrialism. For thousands of years, foragers maintained a balanced level of population through direct and indirect means of fertility regulation.

With farming and sedentarization, a different model of reproduction emerged. Farming provided different foods, especially more starchy foods, and increased food availability. The effect of sedentarization means that people are not constantly moving, and they can manage to raise more children. The highest rates of population growth in human history are found among settled agriculturalists. The contemporary Amish of North America are an example of high-fertility farmers.

In industrial economies, fertility rates are generally low or at a below-replacement level. Within many countries, both rich and poor, economic inequalities are linked to different patterns of fertility among well-off people and low-income people.

HOW does culture shape fertility in different contexts?

Cultural anthropologists find that, in all cultures, fertility is not purely "natural." No woman, anywhere, bears as many children as her biological capacity allows. Cross-culturally, many techniques exist for increasing fertility, reducing it, and regulating its timing. Anthropological studies of indigenous fertility-regulating mechanisms reveal hundreds of different methods, including the use of herbs and other natural sources for inhibiting or enhancing fertilization and for inducing abortion if an undesired pregnancy occurs. In nonindustrial societies, the knowledge and practice of fertility regulation were largely unspecialized and available to all women. Early specializations included midwives and herbalists.

In industrial societies, substantial scientific and medical specialization exists. In these contexts, most women do not control reproductive knowledge and expertise. Technological innovations are emerging, especially to address increasing rates of infertility. Class-stratified access to fertility-regulating methods exists globally and within countries. Artificial insemination and in vitro fertilization are challenging religions to develop new policies.

HOW does culture shape mortality in different contexts?

Population growth and change are also affected through the cultural shaping of death. The practice of infanticide, or the deliberate killing of a child, is of ancient origin, and it still exists today. In some cases, people resort to infanticide because of limited family economic resources. In others, motivating factors appear to be perceptions about the "fitness" of the child or gender preferences. Infanticide can be direct or indirect. Both types of infanticide exist in parts of India, China, and elsewhere in Asia where people strongly prefer sons. This practice results in highly unbalanced sex ratios in these populations, and many activists and politicians are concerned about these situations. Deaths from suicide, from epidemics, and from public and private violence are also culturally patterned. Suicide rates are rising worldwide. No longer mainly a European practice, suicide is rising dramatically among young people in colonized contexts and many developing countries. Birth and death—far from being random, natural events—are cultural events to a large extent.

KEY CONCEPTS

below-replacement-level
  fertility, p. 123
brideprice or bridewealth,
  p. 138
demographic transition,
  p. 125
demography, p. 122
direct infanticide, p. 135
dowry or groomprice, p. 138

ethnocide, p. 142
femicide, p. 142
fertility, p. 122
genocide, p. 142
indirect infanticide, p. 135
infant mortality rate, p. 136
menarche, p. 127
menopause, p. 127
migration, p. 122

modes of reproduction,
  p. 122
mortality, p. 122
pronatalism, p. 123
replacement-level fertility,
  p. 123
sex ratio, p. 138
sex-selective infanticide,
  p. 130

myanthrolab

To reinforce your understanding of this chapter, and to identify topics for further study, visit MyAnthroLab at www.myanthrolab.com for diagnostic tests and a multimedia ebook.

SUGGESTED READINGS

Kamran Asdar Ali, *Planning the Family in Egypt: New Bodies, New Selves.* Austin: University of Texas Press, 2002. This ethnographic study, conducted by a Pakistani doctor and anthropologist, examines the policies and practices of family-planning programs in Egypt to see how this elitist, Western-influenced state creates demographically compliant citizens. Ali's findings reveal the dilemma created for women as family-planning programs pressure them to think of themselves as individual decision-makers acting in their own and the nation's interest by limiting their fertility, even though they are still bound by their wider families and religion to pronatalism.

Caroline Bledsoe and Barney Cohen, eds., *Social Dynamics of Adolescent Fertility in Sub-Saharan Africa.* Washington, DC: National Academy Press, 1993. An anthropologist and a demographer examine national survey data on cultural factors related to high fertility rates among adolescents in sub-Saharan Africa. Attention is given to patterns of adolescent sexuality, attitudes toward marriage, women's status, knowledge and practice of contraception, and the role of education in change.

Nadia Taysir Dabbagh. *Suicide in Palestine: Narratives of Despair.* London: Hurst & Company, 2005. The author, who is the daughter of a Palestinian refugee, studied the rising rates of suicide in Ramallah, the West Bank. She examines recent trends in the context of Arab values, the family, and the political economy. In-depth examination of several cases of suicide by men and women reveal no simple pattern.

John D. Early and Thomas N. Headland, *Population Dynamics of a Philippine Rain Forest People: The San Ildefonso Agta.* Gainesville: University of Florida Press, 1998. This comprehensive study of population dynamics of an Agta group living on Luzon Island in the Philippines draws on a 44-year quantitative database on fertility, mortality, and migration from the time when the Agta were forest foragers to the present (they are now small-scale farmers in rural Philippine society). It profiles a minority people without economic and political power and documents the impact of international logging interests on their lives.

Thomas E. Fricke, *Himalayan Households: Tamang Demography and Domestic Processes.* New York: Columbia University Press, 1994. An example of demographic anthropology, this is a local study of population patterns and change in one region of Nepal. The book includes chapters on the subsistence economy, fertility and mortality, the life course, household dynamics, and recent changes.

Jessica L. Gregg. *Virtually Virgins: Sexual Strategies and Cervical Cancer in Recife, Brazil.* Stanford, CA: Stanford University Press, 2003. Research in a favela, or shantytown, in northeast Brazil, and in a maternity clinic, as well as interviews with many impoverished women of the favela, show how they attempt to deal with racism, sexism, poverty, and violence. The women establish relationships with men in order to be able to feed their children.

W. Penn Handwerker, ed., *Births and Power: Social Change and the Politics of Reproduction.* Boulder, CO: Westview Press, 1990. An overview chapter by the editor is followed by 11 case studies, including studies of the Inuit of Canada, the Bariba of West Africa, the Mende of Sierra Leone, teen pregnancies in the United States, and people who have AIDS in Africa.

Nancy Howell, *Demography of the Dobe !Kung.* New York: Academic Press, 1979. This classic book describes the demography of a group of South African foragers before they were sedentarized. The text considers how anthropological methods contribute to demographic analysis of small-scale societies, causes of illness and death, fertility and sterility, and population growth rates.

Marcia C. Inhorn, *Infertility and Patriarchy: The Cultural Politics of Gender and Family Life in Egypt.* Philadelphia: University of Pennsylvania Press, 1996. Based on fieldwork in Alexandria, this book uses narratives from several infertile Egyptian women to show the different ways these women and their families deal with cultural pressures to bear children.

Jennifer Johnson-Hanks. *Uncertain Honor: Modern Motherhood in an African Crisis.* Chicago: University of Chicago Press, 2005. Educated women among the ethnic Beti people of southern Cameroon delay motherhood as a modern form of honour. This strategy is related to their formal education, their Catholicism, and the uncertain economic context in the region.

Leith Mullings and Alaka Wali, *Stress and Resilience: The Social Context of Reproduction in Central Harlem.* New York: Kluwer Academic, 2001. Documenting the daily efforts of African Americans to contend with oppressive conditions, this ethnography focuses on the experiences of women especially during pregnancy and details the strategies they use to address the strains that their economic and social contexts place on them.

Nancy Scheper-Hughes, *Death without Weeping: The Violence of Everyday Life in Brazil.* Berkeley: University of California Press, 1993. This book is a landmark "ethnography of death," based on fieldwork in a Brazilian shantytown over several periods of time. The author argues that poverty drives a demographic system of very high infant mortality rates and high fertility.

Nancy Scheper-Hughes and Carolyn Sargent, eds., *Small Wars: The Cultural Politics of Childhood.* Berkeley: University of California Press, 1998. Following an introduction by the co-editors, 18 chapters explore aspects of infant and child mortality and health in a wide array of contexts, including Japan, Ecuador, the United States, Israel, Mexico, Portugal, the Dominican Republic, Cuba, England, Croatia, and Brazil.

Andrea S. Wiley. *An Ecology of High-Altitude Infancy: A Biocultural Perspective.* New York: Cambridge University Press, 2004. Ladakh is a district in India's far north, high in the Himalayas. Wiley's several years of fieldwork there focused on the links among biology and culture in birth, infant health and survival, and women's reproductive health. A final section considers the relevance of the findings for policies to improve infant survival and women's health.

6

Personality and Identity over the Life Cycle

Key Questions

- WHAT is the scope of psychological anthropology?

- HOW does culture shape personality and identity from birth through adolescence?

- HOW does culture shape personality and identity in adulthood through old age?

Young boys of the Shan people, Thailand, participating in the Poi Sang Long festival. This annual event culminates in the initiation of young boys into the Buddhist monkhood for a minimum of two years. (*Source: Kevin R. Morris/CORBIS*)

Psychological anthropology addresses many of the topics of contemporary Western psychology: personality, identity, learning, memory, the emotions, sexuality and gender, and so-called mental health problems. Anthropological evidence from cultures around the world suggests that Western psychological concepts are not universally valid, including the definition of what is "normal." As always, an anthropological approach reveals richly varying local ways of being a person.

In this chapter, we focus on individuals within their cultural context. A major area of interest is how cultures shape **personality**, an individual's patterned and characteristic way of behaving, thinking, and feeling. Another interest is how culture shapes a person's *identity:* a person's sense of self and relations with others. Much of the subject matter of this chapter is referred to as **ethnopsychology**, the study of how various cultures define and create personality, identity, and mental health. In this chapter, we consider "normal" human development, and, in Chapter 7, we provide material on what Western psychologists define as mental illnesses.

Culture, Personality, and Identity

Most cultural anthropologists assume that personality is formed through **enculturation**, or socialization, the process of transmitting culture to infants and other new members of society through both informal and formal processes. They study how various cultures enculturate their members into having different personalities and identities. Cultural anthropologists also investigate how personalities vary according to cultural context, and some ask why such variations exist. Others study how changing cultural contexts affect personality, identity, and well-being over the life cycle. In the following discussion, we situate contemporary psychological anthropology in the context of its historical development in North America.

The Culture and Personality School

Psychological anthropology is rooted in the so-called Culture and Personality School, an intellectual movement that began in the United States in the 1930s and persisted through the 1970s. Culture and personality studies began with Franz Boas's interest in the individual, developed through his fieldwork on the Northwest Coast and the

central Arctic. The school was further developed through Boas's students. Members of the school adopted some aspects of Freudian theories, including the importance of childhood experiences in shaping personality and identity, and the symbolic analysis of dreams. Boas's student Edward Sapir shared his interest in the relation between language and culture. In spite of Boas and Sapir's important role in institutionalizing Canadian anthropology, culture and personality as a "school" was never strongly developed in Canada, partly because of the influence of British social anthropology in the country. American influence on Canadian anthropology was strongest in the 1960s when many U.S. professors taught in Canadian anthropology departments. By that time, culture and personality was no longer an important theoretical orientation in the United States. Instead, Canadian anthropologists began collaborating with psychologists and psychiatrists to explore transcultural psychiatry. In 1955, a department

Margaret Mead, during some of her later years of fieldwork, observes children's interactions in Sicily.
■ (Source: © Ken Heyman/Woodfin Camp & Associates)

---

personality: an individual's patterned and characteristic way of behaving, thinking, and feeling.
ethnopsychology: the study of how various cultures define and create personality, identity, and mental health.

enculturation: the process of transmitting culture to infants and other new members of society through both informal and formal processes.
cultural configuration: Ruth Benedict's theory that cultures are formed through

the unconscious selection of a few cultural traits that interweave to form a cohesive pattern shared by all members of the culture.

devoted to transcultural psychiatric studies was established at McGill University to explore the effects of culture on psychiatric disorders.

Two directions that the Culture and Personality School took were, first, understanding how child-rearing practices affect personality and, second, describing national-level personality patterns. The first of these is still accepted, whereas the second is largely discredited.

Personality and Child-Rearing

In the early 1930s, Margaret Mead went with her husband, anthropologist Reo Fortune, to the Sepik River area of northern New Guinea. Her subsequent publication, *Sex and Temperament in Three Primitive Societies* (1935), revealed striking differences in male and female personalities and behaviour in three different groups. Among the Arapesh, both men and women had nurturant and gentle personalities. Both valued parental roles and both participated equally in child care. All Arapesh males and females behaved according to what is stereotypically defined as "feminine" in Western cultures. Among the Mundugumor, in contrast, both males and females corresponded to the Western stereotype of "masculine" behaviour. In general, adults were assertive, aggressive, loud, and even fierce. Both parents treated their children with indifference. The situation among the Tchambuli was equally surprising to Mead and her readers: The men fussed about their looks, gossiped with each other most of the day, and did little in the way of productive work. The women were competent and responsible, providing most of the food through fishing and gardening, and managing the household. Among the Tchambuli, women played a dominant role in the culture, and their personalities reflected their position.

Since all three groups Mead studied share similar biological traits, her findings indicate that gender is culturally defined and constructed rather than being inborn. Mead's research showed that differences in tenderness or neglect when holding, breastfeeding, and bathing infants led to different personalities. This view had an enormous impact on changing people's thinking about the best way to care for babies in North America during the mid-twentieth century and is still prominent in psychological anthropology today.

Cultural Patterns and National Character

Ruth Benedict, a leading figure of the Culture and Personality School, argued that cultures promote distinct personality types. In her book *Patterns of Culture* (1959), she proposed that cultures are formed through the unconscious selection of a few cultural traits from the "vast arc" of potential traits. For example, one culture may emphasize monetary values while another overlooks them. The selected traits interweave to form a

cultural configuration, a cohesive pattern shared by everyone in that culture. Benedict formulated her theories while doing research on Native American cultures. In her view, the Pueblo Indians of the American Southwest had personalities that exemplified a "middle road," involving moderation in all things and avoiding excess and violence. She termed the Pueblo an "Apollonian" culture, after the Greek deity Apollo. In contrast, she labelled the Kwakwaka'wakw (the group Franz Boas called Kwakiutl) of the Pacific Northwest "Dionysian," after the Greek god of revelry and excess. She chose this term because of their potlatches, high levels of expressive emotionality, and colourful art, architecture, and textiles (review the Ethnographic Profile in Chapter 4 on page 116).

THINKING OUTSIDE THE BOX

CHOOSE A CULTURAL CONTEXT with which you are familiar: your hometown, your university or college, or whatever culture with which you most closely identify. Assume that you are Ruth Benedict. What term(s) will you use to label your cultural group?

Benedict's portrait of the Kwakwaka'wakw has been criticized for its overreliance on Boas's data on just one group of southern nobility after European contact; its selective ignoring of the amiable, playful side of their life; and for ignoring ecological factors. Similar criticisms have been levelled against Ruth Landes, a student of Boas and Benedict, for her portrayal of the Ojibwa of northwestern Ontario. Her work stressed the extreme individualism and atomistic behaviour of the Ojibwa, their lack of political organization, and severe anxiety neuroses manifested in cannibalism and violence. Anthropologists have criticized her work for questionable ethnographic accuracy and for failing to place the Ojibwa in historical context by noting their changed economic conditions after government suppression of political and religious organizations (Lovisek, Holzkamm, and Waisberg 1997).

During World War II, the United States Office of War Information commissioned Benedict to analyze the Japanese personality and submit reports to the government that might be used to help defeat the Japanese. Because she could not do fieldwork during the war, Benedict consulted secondary sources (newspapers, magazines, movies) and interviewed Japanese Americans. Her book, *The Chrysanthemum and the Sword* (1946), lists what she saw as essential features of Japanese personality and character: the importance of *on* (obligation, the necessity to repay gifts and favours), the concept of virtue, the value of self-discipline, the importance of keeping one's name honourable, and the significance of maintaining rules of etiquette. Her interpretations influenced U.S. policy toward Japan during the postwar occupation.

Following Benedict's work on Japan, national character studies that defined personality types and core values of nations declined in importance. Such studies suffer from being:

- *Ethnocentric:* They classify cultures according to Western psychological values and features.
- *Reductionist:* They emphasize only one or two features.
- *Totalizing:* They obscure internal and local variation in their construction of a monolithic national character such as "the French," "the English," or "the Japanese."

Nonetheless, psychological anthropologists still consider it valid to typify localized cultures in terms of valued personality traits so long as a more scientific research approach is employed. One such study is based on fieldwork in three areas of Wales (see Map 6.1). This project combined methods of interviewing people about what is true "Welshness" along with observations of behaviour in everyday situations (Trosset and Caulkins 2001). Results show a high degree of consensus among the interviewees that was confirmed by the observations. Five characteristics are the most important: egalitarianism, martyrdom, emotionalism, performance, and nostalgia (see Table 6.1). Welsh people in this study perceive many of these characteristics as providing a distinction between themselves and "the English."

Class and Personality

Pursuing a different line of thinking, two cultural anthropologists of the mid-twentieth century looked at how poverty shapes personality. George Foster's research among low-income family farmers in Mexico led him to propose a model called the **image of the limited good** (1965). In this worldview, people believe that the resources or wealth available within their group are finite, or limited. If someone becomes wealthier, other people necessarily become poorer. The analogy of a pie illustrates how the image of the limited good works. If a group of eight people divides a pie equally into eight pieces, everyone gets the same size piece. But if one person takes two pieces, only six pieces remain for everyone else to share. The image of the limited good, according to Foster, coexists with personality traits such as jealousy and suspiciousness, as people guard against anyone taking a larger piece of the pie.

Oscar Lewis (1966) proposed a related concept, the **culture of poverty**, to explain the personality and behaviour of the poor and why poverty persists. He typified poor

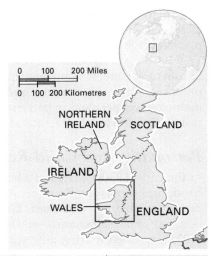

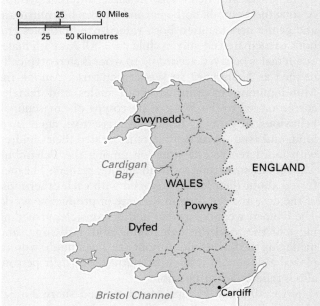

MAP 6.1   Wales. Wales, or Cymru (prounounced COME-ree) is one of the four countries of the United Kingdom. Its population of 3 million is 96 percent white British with Asian-origin residents constituting another 2 percent. Mining has been a large part of the economy since the eighteenth century. Given the natural beauty of much of Wales, tourism is important and growing. Welsh and English are the official languages. The main religion is Christianity, with the Presbyterian Church of Wales the largest denomination.

---

image of the limited good: George Foster's theory that in nonindustrial cultures, people have a characteristic worldview of finite resources or wealth such that if someone in the group increases his or her wealth, other people will necessarily lose out.

culture of poverty: Oscar Lewis's theory that the personality characteristics of the poor trap them in poverty.
person-centred ethnography: anthropological research that focuses on the individual and how the individual's

psychology and subjective experience both shape and are shaped by the wider culture.

TABLE 6.1 Five Characteristics of Welsh Personhood

Value		Behaviour
Egalitarianism	All people are equal and personal ties are more important than status.	Social introductions and interactions emphasize personal ties.
Martyrdom	The best acts are done on behalf of the group and may involve self-sacrifice.	Mothers labour for the family; protestors go to jail.
Emotionalism	Interactions with people should show emotion.	Anger is preferable to detachment; arguing is from the heart.
Performance	Differences exist between private and public self, with the public self more performative.	An aspiring community leader disclaims interest in the position.
Nostalgia	Sadness is shown for something lost.	Feels homesick; returns home to visit the graves of parents each year.

Source: Trosset and Caulkins (2001:66–68, 71–73).

Mexican people as, among other things, lacking a future time-orientation, and sexually promiscuous. He argued that because of these personality traits, poor people are trapped in poverty and cannot change their situation.

Today, these theories appear to be ethnocentric products of their time. During the period of mid-twentieth-century capitalist growth in North America, valued personality characteristics included self-assertion, aggressive competitiveness, and a forward-thinking mindset, along with a belief in infinite resources and an ever-expanding "pie" of wealth. At the time that Foster and Lewis were doing research, anthropologists did not highlight either structural factors or human agency in relation to people's wealth or poverty. In spite of the limits of these theories, Lewis and Foster are still remembered as major figures in North American anthropology. Lewis wrote valuable ethnographies about people living in poverty in Mexico, Puerto Rico, and the United States, and Foster played an important role in building the subfield of medical anthropology.

Recent ethnopsychology studies attempt to be less ethnocentric by emphasizing the terms and meanings important in other cultures. They also bring attention to structural factors that affect personality and identity as well as to the importance of human agency such as active resistance among poor and marginalized people, completely reversing the models proposed by Foster and Lewis about passivity.

At the opposite end of the class spectrum, psychological anthropologists are beginning to "study up" the class structure. Allison's ethnographic work in Japan (1994) shows how corporate culture shapes the personality and identity of middle- and upper-class urban "salarymen" in Japan, and how child-care patterns based on total control by mothers fit with the demands of the corporate business world to create compliant male workers.

Person-Centred Ethnography

The newest direction in psychological anthropology is called **person-centred ethnography**; it is research that focuses on the individual and how the individual's psychology and subjective experience both shape and are shaped by her or his culture (Hollan 2001). Gaining an

Japanese salarymen singing karaoke. ■ (Source: © Barry Lewis/Alamy)

emic view about individual people and their perceptions is the paramount goal. Thus, person-centred ethnographic research focuses on what people say about their perceptions and experiences. Like Western psychology and psychiatry, it is fundamentally discourse-based rather than observation-based. Yet most person-centred ethnographies situate details about individuals and what they say about their experience within the wider cultural context, because individuals and cultures are interactive.

One such contextualized study considers notions of the self and selfhood in a mountainous village in eastern Nepal (Hardman 2000) (see Map 7.3 on page 194). In this region, family farming is the major occupation and an egalitarian principle of exchange prevails. In opposition to many broad statements from non-anthropologists about "Asian mentalities" and the lack of a concept of an autonomous self in "Asian societies," this study found clear evidence of a concept of individuality and interpersonal difference in *niwa*. As one villager commented, there are as many different niwa as there are faces. But people do not express their individual niwa in public.

With increasing social change, however, niwa is beginning to be exhibited in public more often. For example, some women are demonstrating their niwa as initiative and agency by selling beer and liquor. Young people are expressing opinions in public. So far, the prevailing view is that such expressions of individuality should not go so far as to upset accepted views of propriety, which include frugality, charitable giving, and feelings of conscience and shame. In this cultural context, the self and individualism can exist but within cultural bounds.

As many psychological anthropologists direct their attention to the details of individual perceptions and experience, others insist on the value of the comparative, ethnological method (Moore and Mathews 2001). They ask, for example, how does the Nepali villager's concept of *niwa* compare to notions of the self in other societies? Are there private/public notions of self elsewhere, and, if so, how does that distinction play out? The study of the individual provides a clear example of the fruitful tension between ethnography (analysis of a single group of people) and ethnology (placing detailed local cases into a wider comparative frame).

Personality and Identity Formation from Infancy through Adolescence

In Euro-American culture, commonly accepted life stages include infancy, childhood, adolescence, middle age, and old age (psychologists and other experts concerned with human development construct even finer substages). These life-cycle stages are based on biological features such as the ability to walk, puberty, and capacity for parenthood (Bogin 1988). However, these stages are not universals. Cultural anthropologists find striking variations in how different cultures construct life stages and how such stages are quite unrelated to biology (Johnson-Hanks 2002). For example, one might think that the biological fact of having a baby places a female into the life stage of "mother," but such is not always the case. The cross-cultural construction of life stages sometimes uses markers that Western biology recognizes, and sometimes not. The following sections consider personality formation and identity according to Western life-cycle categories.

Birth and Infancy

In this section, we first consider the social context of birth itself. We then discuss cultural variations in infant care and how they may shape personality and identity. Last, we take up the topic of gender identity formation in infancy.

The Birth Context

The cultural context of birth affects an infant's psychological development. Brigitte Jordan (1983), a pioneer in the cross-cultural study of birth, conducted research on birth practices in Mexico, Sweden, Holland, and the United States. She studied the birth setting, including its location and who is present, the types of attendants and their roles, the birth event, and the post-partum period. Among Mayan women in Mexico, the midwife is called in the early stages of labour. One of her tasks is to give a *sobada* (massage) to the mother-to-be. She also provides psychological support by telling stories, often about other women's birthing experiences. The husband is expected to be present during the labour, so that he can see "how a woman suffers." The woman's mother should be present, along with other female kin such as her mother-in-law, godmother and sisters, and her friends. Thus, the Mayan mother is surrounded by a large group of supportive people.

In North America, hospital births are the norm. In hospitals and birth centres, the newborn infant is generally taken to a nursery where it is wrapped in cloth, placed in a crib under bright lights, and fed with sugar water rather than being left with the mother to be fed. Some critics argue that the hospital-based system of highly regulated birth is extremely technocratic and too managed, alienating the mother—as well as other members of the family and the wider community—from the birthing process and the infant (Davis-Floyd 1992). A study exploring natural childbirth in Toronto, including Lamaze preparation as an alternative to medical control, showed that mothers wanted more control over the childbirth experience and less dependence on technological interventions such as induced labour, anesthesia, episiotomies, and fetal heart monitoring (Romalis 1981). This critique has led to consideration of how to improve the way birth is conducted.

Lessons Applied

THE ROLE OF CULTURAL KNOWLEDGE IN CONFLICT MEDIATION

Many North American hospitals are concerned about how to provide services for their rapidly growing immigrant populations. In a new suburban hospital that Lynn Deitrick (2002) studied, most of the nurses on staff were long-time residents of the community and had graduated from a local community college, where their training included no attention to cultural differences.

Cultural conflict arose upon the birth of a baby to a Turkish immigrant family. The infant had not yet been brought to the mother's room, and members of her family arrived to welcome the new baby. Along with them came a Muslim religious leader to administer the usual honey blessing to the infant before his first feeding. This ritual ensures a sweet life for the baby.

The nurse in charge denied the family access to the baby, saying that he first must have a medical examination and that unpasteurized honey could not be given to him. The baby's father was upset and claimed that the blessing must be administered because whatever the baby first tastes determines the quality of its life.

Fortunately, a nurse who also had training in cultural anthropology, Deitrick, entered into the discussions and was able to act as a **cultural broker**, a person—often but not always an anthropologist—who is familiar with the practices and beliefs of two different cultures and can promote cross-cultural understanding to prevent or mediate conflicts. She listened to the views of the Turkish family and learned that only a tiny amount of honey would be placed on the baby's tongue for the blessing. She suggested a compromise to the medical staff whereby the baby would be taken for 10 minutes to the mother's room, where the family would be present and the Muslim cleric could administer the blessing. The attending physician agreed, saying that she was not "on record" as approving the blessing but that she understood its importance. Deitrick took the baby to the family and returned 10 minutes later to find a smiling mother and father. The baby then underwent blood tests and other medically mandated procedures and was discharged in good health—*and* assured of a sweet life—two days later.

FOOD FOR THOUGHT

- Did Lynn Deitrick do the right thing by acting as a cultural broker in this case, or should the medical model have been followed with no compromise?

The Western medical model of birth contrasts sharply with non-Western practices. Sometimes they come into serious conflict. In a Western hospital birthing situation where immigrant families have views on proper infant care, providing an anthropological perspective on their culture may serve to mediate conflict between the medical culture and the immigrant people's culture (see the accompanying Lessons Applied box).

Criticism of the Western birth process and the subsequent physical separation of the infant from the mother has led to consideration of how to improve the way birth is conducted and the condition it sets for maternal support and infant bonding. For example, the Baby-Friendly Hospital Initiative supported by the United Nations Children Fund (UNICEF), the World Health Organization (WHO), and many nongovernmental organizations (NGOs) identifies hospital practices that will encourage mother–infant bonding and successful breastfeeding, including initiating breastfeeding immediately after birth, allowing mothers and infants to room together, discouraging the use of pacifiers, and refusing monetary donations and free supplies from the infant formula industry. In 1999, the Brome-Missisquoi-Perkins Hospital in Cowansville, Quebec, became the first Canadian hospital to be designated as "baby-friendly," joining over 15 000 baby-friendly hospitals worldwide.

Bonding

Many Western psychologists argue that early parent–infant contact and bonding at the time of birth is crucial for setting in motion parental attachment to the infant. Western specialists say that if this bonding is not established at the time of the infant's birth, it will not develop later. Explanations for juvenile delinquency or other unfavourable child-development problems often include

---

cultural broker: a person who is familiar with the practices and beliefs of two or more cultures, and can promote cross-cultural understanding to prevent or mediate conflicts.

In Bom Jesus, a shantytown in northeastern Brazil, this mother was told by a doctor at the local clinic that her son was dying of anemia and that she needed to feed him red meat. The mother said, "Now where am I going to find the money to feed my hopeless son rich food like that?" Western mother–infant bonding theory does not appear to apply in all cultures. ■ (Source: Nancy Scheper-Hughes)

adaptive in low-mortality/low-fertility societies in which strong maternal attachment is reasonable because infants are likely to survive.

Caregiver–Infant Proximity

Across cultures, wide differences exist in how much time an infant spends in close contact with caregivers. Euro-American cultures stand at one extreme, with infants spending much of their time not in physical contact with a caregiver (Keller et al. 2005). In a city in northern Germany, spot-check observations of families with infants from two to three months old found that the babies were on their own, with no caregiver in view, 40 percent of the time. In contrast, in research sites in rural northern India and Cameroon, infants spend less than 10 percent of their time away from physical contact with caregivers. In these cultural settings, caregivers spend much time rocking babies, holding and feeding them, massaging them, and bouncing them. Typical German personalities are, in fact, more autonomous than in cultures that focus on group connectedness.

Sleeping Patterns

In most societies, it is common for parents to let their children sleep beside them. Recent research by physical anthropologist James McKenna (1993) demonstrates the advantages of sleeping in close contact with at least one other person, including possible protection against SIDS (sudden infant death syndrome). His research demonstrates the importance of a co-sleeping environment, rather than a solitary environment, for infant well-being.

Where and with whom the infant sleeps may also be related to the development of connected or autonomous personalities. The underlying hypothesis motivating research on sleeping patterns is the following: Little or no infant–parent co-sleeping promotes "strong ego formation" (in other words, an autonomous self with a high degree of independence), whereas long periods of parent–infant co-sleeping foster "weak ego formation" (a person with little sense of autonomous selfhood and a high degree of interpersonal connectedness).

This hypothesis is confirmed by data from Japan, where mothers and infants co-sleep for several years—longer, on average, than other world cultures (Caudill and Plath 1966). The long period of infant co-sleeping seems to match the high degree of social connectedness of Japanese people. The hypothesis, however, is not confirmed in a study of personality formation among the Basque people of Spain (Crawford 1994). Most of the Basque women interviewed had slept in their parents' room for two to three years. The women who had been co-sleepers had both greater ego strength and a stronger sense of social connectedness than women who

reference to lack of proper infant bonding at birth. In spite of these theories, many Western-based hospital practices separate infants from mothers immediately after birth.

Nancy Scheper-Hughes (1992), whose research in a Brazilian shantytown appeared in Chapter 5, questions Western bonding theory. She argues that bonding does not necessarily have to occur at birth to be successful. Her observations in Brazil show that many low-income mothers do not exhibit bonding with their infants at birth. Bonding occurs later, if the child survives infancy, when it is several years old. She proposes that this pattern of later bonding is related to the high rate of infant mortality among poor people of northeast Brazil. If women were to develop strong bonds with their newborn infants, they would suffer untold amounts of grief. Western bonding is

had not been co-sleepers. Thus, co-sleeping does not necessarily prevent the development of an autonomous ego and sense of self.

Gender in Infancy

Anthropologists distinguish between *sex* and *gender* (review the definitions in Chapter 1). Sex is something that everyone is born with. In the view of Western science, it has three biological markers: genitals, hormones, and chromosomes. A male has a penis, more androgens than estrogens, and the XY chromosome. A female has a vagina, more estrogens than androgens, and the XX chromosome. Increasingly, however, scientists know that these two categories are not definitive. In all populations, some people are born with indeterminate genitals, similar proportions of androgens and estrogens, and chromosomes with more complex distributions than simply XX or XY. Thus, a continuum model of gender is more accurate than a strictly binary model.

Gender is a cultural construction and is highly variable across cultures (B. Miller 1993). Gender refers to the learned behaviour and beliefs associated with maleness and femaleness.

Two major problems arise in testing for innate gender characteristics: First, one needs data on infants before they are subject to cultural influences. But culture starts shaping the infant from the moment of birth through handling and treatment by others (some scholars say that socialization could begin even in the womb through exposure to sound and motion). Second, studying and interpreting the behaviour of infants is fraught with potential bias on the part of observers.

Studies of infants have focused on assessing the potential innateness of three major Euro-American personality stereotypes: whether infant males are more aggressive than infant females, whether infant females are more social than infant males, and whether males are more independent. What is the evidence? Boy babies cry more than girl babies, and some people believe this is evidence of higher levels of inborn aggression in males. An alternative interpretation is that baby boys on average tend to weigh more than girls at birth. They therefore are more likely to have a difficult delivery from which it takes time to recover, so they cry more, but not out of aggressiveness. In terms of sociability, baby girls smile more often than boys. Does this mean girls are born to be people pleasers? Evidence of caregivers smiling more at baby girls shows that the more frequent smiling of girls is a learned, not innate response. In terms of independence or dependence, studies thus far reveal no clear gender differences in how upset babies are when separated from their caregivers. Overall, studies seeking to document innate gender differences through the behaviour of infants are not convincing. In the next section, we explores cultural constructions of gender at various stages of the life cycle.

Socialization during Childhood

The concept of "the child" as a special age category may have emerged first in Europe in recent centuries. In art, portraits of children became commonplace only in the seventeenth century. Other changes occurred at the same time: new interests in children's habits, more elaborate terminology about children and childhood, and special clothing for children instead of small-sized versions of adult clothing. The special focus on the child is associated with the emergence of industrial capitalism's need for an ever-expanding market. Children became a new niche for sales and prompted the production of clothes, books, and toys specifically for them. In many nonindustrialized societies, a child is not regarded as having such specialized needs. Children are expected to take on adult tasks at an early age.

Mode of Production and Child Personality

The *Six Cultures Study* (mentioned in Chapter 3) is a classic cross-cultural research project designed to provide comparative data on how children's activities and tasks shape their personalities (Whiting and Whiting 1975). Researchers used parallel methods at six sites (see Figure 6.1), observing children between the ages of 3 and 11 years. They recorded behaviour, such as caring for and being supportive of other children; hitting other children; and performing tasks such as child care, cooking, and errands. The data collected were analyzed in terms of two major personality types: nurturant-responsible and dependent-dominant. A *nurturant-responsible personality* is characterized by caring and sharing acts toward other children. The *dependent-dominant personality* involves fewer acts of caregiving, more acts that assert dominance over other children, and more need for care by adults.

Of all six cultures, the Gusii children of southwestern Kenya (see Map 6.2 on page 159) had the highest frequency of a nurturant-responsible personality type. Gusii children were responsible for the widest range of

FIGURE 6.1 Groups in the *Six Cultures Study*

Horticultural Groups
Gusii people of Kenya
Maya people of Oaxaca, Mexico
Tarong people, Philippines

Intensive Agriculture or Industrial Groups
Taira village, Okinawa, Japan
Rajput people, village in North India
Middle-class Euro-Americans in Orchard Town, New England, United States

Source: Whiting and Whiting (1975).

tasks and at earlier ages than children in any other culture in the study, often performing tasks that an Orchard Town, United States, mother does. Although some children in all six cultures took care of other children, Gusii children (both boys and girls) spent the most time doing so. They began taking on this responsibility at a very young age, between 5 and 8 years old.

In contrast, Orchard Town children had the highest frequency of the dependent-dominant personality type. The differences correlate with the mode of production. The people in Kenya, Mexico, and the Philippines all had more nurturant-responsible children and their economies are reliant on horticulture. The study sites in Japan, India, and the United States were based on either intensive agriculture or industry. How do these different modes of production influence child personality? The key underlying factor is women's work roles. In the horticultural societies, women are an important part of the labour force and spend much time working outside the home. Their children take on many family-supportive tasks and thereby develop personalities that are nurturant-responsible. When women are mainly occupied in the home, as in the second group of cultures, children have fewer tasks and less responsibility. They develop personalities that are more dependent-dominant.

This study has many implications for Western child development experts. For one thing, what happens when the dependent-dominant personality develops to an extreme level—into a *narcissistic personality?* A narcissist is someone who constantly seeks self-attention and self-affirmation, with no concern for other people's needs. Consumerism supports the development of narcissism via its emphasis on identity formation through ownership of self-defining goods (clothing, electronics, cars) and access to self-defining services (vacations, therapists, fitness salons). The *Six Cultures Study* suggests that involving children more in household responsibilities might result in less self-focused personality formation and more nurturant-responsible people.

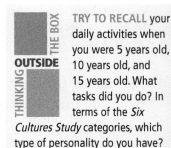

THINKING OUTSIDE THE BOX

TRY TO RECALL your daily activities when you were 5 years old, 10 years old, and 15 years old. What tasks did you do? In terms of the *Six Cultures Study* categories, which type of personality do you have?

Left: A Yanomami boy acquires skills necessary for hunting and warfare through play. ■ (Source: © Napoleon A. Chagnon/AnthroPhoto) **Right: A North American boy playing a video game.** ■ (Source: © Bill Varie/CORBIS)

Informal Learning

Toys and games shape children's personalities universally, though in different ways and with different effects. Among the Yanomami, young boys learn to be future hunters by shooting small arrows from small bows at small targets such as beetles. They learn to kill animals without sentimentality. In contrast, caring for animals as pets is a prominent part of child socialization in the West, where many animals are taboo as food. Some games, such as chess, teach strategic thinking that appears to be correlated with social-political patterns of hierarchy and obedience.

Charles James Nowell is a Kwakwaka'wakw man born in 1870 at Fort Rupert, in what is now British Columbia. When he was interviewed in English in 1940, he recalled giving play potlatches of small canoes to imitate the potlatches of older people, taught by his fathers and brothers (Hirschfelder 1995:103–104).

The media play an important role in child socialization and personality acquisition. Generations of Canadian children watched the *Polka Dot Door* and *Mr. Dressup*, shows that attempted to break down gender and racial stereotypes. Cartoon shows from the United States are also aired on Canadian television. One study examined children's cartoon shows aired on U.S. television in the 1980s and how they support stereotypical Euro-American gender roles (B. Williams 1991). Content analysis reveals two types of shows, one featuring interpersonal relationships aimed at little girls and one featuring battles that toy companies intended for little boys.

Formal Schooling

Schools have important effects on personality and identity formation. Worldwide, schools vary in terms of their accessibility and quality. For example, not all countries provide for universal primary education. Even in those that do provide universal schooling, there may be wide gaps in quality for different children. Within countries, poorer children are more likely to face problems enrolling and remaining in school. Beside the fact of an inadequate number of schools, poor families may need their children to work and contribute to the household income. Malnourished and exhausted children have difficulty concentrating in class, and their level of achievement is likely to be lower than that of better-off children. Teachers, however, may interpret their performance as a sign of bad attitude or laziness rather than the result of poverty.

School systems that offer inadequate learning experiences, home situations that are unsupportive of girls' achievement, and conservative political elements in the wider society often combine to constrain girls' achievements in school. Furthermore, "tracking" female students into domestic roles characterizes formal education throughout much of the world. In Israel, all-girl Zionist-Orthodox boarding schools aim to strengthen the religiosity of girls and prepare them for married life. But they also emphasize academic excellence, and the girls are highly motivated to achieve. The curriculum includes lectures, lessons, religious activities, and volunteer community work. Religious study excludes the canonic texts, promoting instead everyday religious practice and emphasis on morality, wifehood, child-rearing, and purity. A study of girls in such schools takes into account the interplay of religion and gender (Rapoport, Garb, and Penso 1995). Close supervision of the girls is maintained by teachers, peers, and older girls who serve as "big sisters." Even during free time, the girls are supposed to discuss religion. According to the school teachings, a woman's modesty is part of her essence. The ideal is invisibility and muteness in the public world. Girls learn that their sexuality is a secret, hidden treasure to be guarded with self-restraint, a key virtue that contrasts with how secular girls behave. One student commented, "For example, I walk by some [secular] girl with exposed legs, so she has no value, she simply presents herself as an object, she doesn't say, first look for my character . . . and I feel very proud that I am modest" (1995:54). Some girls, however, described the dilemma created by the Zionist-Orthodox emphasis on women's family roles, the pressure for academic achievement, and personal aspirations for a career.

Schoolchildren in Japan exhibiting eagerness to participate in class. ■ (Source: © Nichol Katz/Woodfin Camp & Associates)

Their only options are relinquishing aspirations for academic excellence or finding a career that accommodates family responsibilities and modesty rules.

Oppressed minority groups often find that formal schooling in the mainstream society is another context for discrimination and marginalization. Standard curricula reflect mainstream values and exclude or denigrate those of minority groups. Native Americans and First Nations people of Canada are developing community-based schools with curricula that combine standard subjects such as mathematics with learning that is necessary for true personhood in their local community (Manuelito 2005). Students learn their native language, kinship system, history, and skills such as telling stories, cooking, hunting, and weaving. Some are adapting the teaching of such subjects as mathematics in culturally meaningful ways (Lipka et al. 2005). Such a program has substantial implications for students' learning and for strengthening their sense of identity and self-esteem.

Schools and social inequality are intimately related. Schools may be places where social barriers are reduced and opportunities for marginalized students enhanced. Or they may reinforce existing social gaps. No simple story exists for any cultural context but, clearly, schools possess the potential for social progress as well as for social control and maintenance of conformity.

Adolescence and Identity

The transition from "childhood" to "adulthood" involves both biological and cultural events. In this section, we provide ethnographic insights into the cultural construction of this transition to adulthood.

Is Adolescence a Universal Life-Cycle Stage?

Puberty is a time in the human life cycle that occurs universally and involves a set of biological markers. In males, the voice deepens and facial and body hair appear; in females, menarche and breast development occur; in both males and females, pubic and underarm hair appear and sexual maturation is achieved. **Adolescence**, in contrast, is a culturally defined period of maturation from around the time of puberty until the attainment of adulthood, usually marked by becoming a parent, getting married, or becoming economically self-sufficient.

Some scholars say that all cultures define a period of adolescence. A comparative study using data on 186 societies argues for the universality of a culturally defined phase of adolescence (Schlegel 1995; Schlegel

Two schoolgirls of Oman. The female literacy rate in Oman is about 50 percent, whereas the male literacy rate is 75 percent. Gender inequality in literacy is not, however, universal in Arab countries. ■ (Source: © Charles O. Cecil)

and Barry 1991). People in cultures as diverse as the Navajo and the Trobriand Islanders have special terms comparable to *adolescent* to refer to a person between puberty and marriage. Sociobiologists have generated a model that views adolescence as a response to the biological onset of reproductive capacity and as biologically adaptive because it provides training for parenthood and thus contributes to enhanced reproductive success and survival of parents' genes (Schlegel 1995:16).

Other anthropologists view adolescence as culturally constructed and as highly variable, and thus impossible to explain solely on biological grounds. They point out that people in many cultures recognize no period of

puberty: a time in the human life cycle that occurs universally and involves a set of biological markers and sexual maturation.

adolescence: a culturally defined period of maturation from the time of puberty until adulthood.

Ethnographic Profile

The Maasai of Kenya and Tanzania

The Maasai (sometimes spelled Masai), before recent changes, made their living mainly as cattle herders. Their ancestral lands cover a large area crossing from Kenya into Tanzania, but far less than what they had before European colonialism. During the colonial era, they lost 75 percent (over 15 million acres) of their ancestral land (Oloi-Dapash 2002). Since then, the governments of Kenya and Tanzania continued to claim Maasai land. In the last two decades of the twentieth century, the Maasai lost over 1 million acres of land to white farmers, development projects, national parks, and game reserves. The Maasai now come into frequent conflict with outsiders who are fencing the land, preventing the free movement of wildlife, and disturbing what was a more stable lifestyle. Several indigenous and international nongovernmental organizations are advocating for the return of land to the Maasai.

The Maasai population is roughly 500 000. Most live in the traditional Maasai region, but many have migrated to cities in Kenya and Tanzania for work. Many have obtained prominent positions, as head of Kenya Airways, for example. Some have travelled to Europe and North America to attend college.

For many Maasai men, the traditional rite of passage is now augmented by the need to go to the city and earn money, or to go abroad and gain a Ph.D. in order to prove one's manhood.

Maasai life revolves around cattle, although the people also keep sheep and goats. Property rights invest cattle ownership in men only, though in the past, before the concept of "ownership" existed, men and women had overlapping rights in livestock. Elder men occupy leadership positions. A married woman manages her husband's cattle and has rights to its products, notably milk and hides, for household consumption. Ownership of the cattle passes from father to sons. Women build and maintain the houses, which were formerly low, dome-shaped, earthen constructions but are now taller and with thatched roofs. They have a say in who enters the house, thus giving them some domestic status (Hodgson 2004). Modern houses are made from commercial materials obtained with cash. Women's domestic status related to control of the house has declined. Maasai women are increasingly involved in beadwork for sale to tourists.

The Maasai share much with each other, including food and sexual partners.

Young Maasai men and women are free to have sexual liaisons with multiple partners. Young married women, whose husbands are much older than they, frequently have lovers. The increase in urban migration has brought HIV/AIDS to the Maasai (May 2003). Their relatively free sexual relations mean that the disease could spread rapidly. Nongovernmental organizations are working hard to raise awareness of the risk of HIV/AIDS among the Maasai and to urge young Maasai in the cities to abstain from sex or to use condoms.

Readings

Elizabeth Gilbert. *Broken Spears: A Maasai Journey.* New York: Atlantic Monthly Press, 2003.
Dorothy L. Hodgson. *Once Intrepid Warriors: Gender, Ethnicity, and the Cultural Politics of Maasai Development.* Bloomington: Indiana University Press, 2001.

Videos

The Masai Today: Changing Traditions (Films Media Group, 2003).
Masai Women (Disappearing World, 1994).

Thanks to Dorothy L. Hodgson, Rutgers University, for reviewing this material.

A Maasai warrior's mother shaves his head during part of his initiation ceremony into adulthood (left). This ritual validates her status as a mother as well as her son's adulthood. ■ (Source: © Robert Caputo/National Geographic Image Collection) *Maasai women own no land and no animals (right). Their hand-made jewellery is theirs, however, to have, to give, and to sell.* ■ (Source: © Barry D. Kass)

MAP 6.2 Maasai Region of Kenya and Tanzania. *An estimated 350 000 Maasai live in Kenya and 150 000 in Tanzania. Sixteen major sections of Maasai exist throughout the region. The climate is semi-arid and arid.*

adolescence. In some others, identification of an adolescent phase is recent. Moroccan anthropologist Fatima Mernissi (1987), for example, states that adolescence became a recognized life-cycle phase for females in Morocco only in the late twentieth century. "The idea of an adolescent unmarried woman is a completely new idea in the Muslim world, where previously you had only a female child and a menstruating woman who had to be married off immediately so as to prevent dishonorable engagement in premarital sex" (1987:xxiv).

Another line of evidence supporting a constructionist view is that, in different cultures, the length of the period of adolescence varies for males and females. In many horticultural and pastoral societies where men are valued as warriors, as among the Maasai, a long period between childhood and adulthood is devoted to training in warfare and developing solidarity among males (see the Ethnographic Profile on page 159). This adolescent period has nothing to do with training for parenthood. Maasai females, on the other hand, move directly from being a girl to being a wife, and have no culturally marked adolescent period. They learn adult roles when they are children.

Long periods of male initiation among some highland groups in Papua New Guinea that involve institutionalized homosexual relationships also do not fit within the sociobiological interpretation. Gilbert Herdt conducted research with the Sambia, highland horticulturalists, and learned about their secret male initiation practices (1987). The Sambia believe that, in order for a young boy to mature into a healthy adult, he must join a secret, all-male initiation group. A boy becomes a partner of a senior male who regularly transfers his semen to the youth orally. The Sambia believe that the youth is nourished by ingesting semen. After a period of time in the initiation group, the "grown" youth rejoins society as a man. At that time he will marry a woman and raise children.

In some cultures, females have long adolescent phases during which they live separated from the wider group and gain special knowledge and skills (J. Brown 1978). After this period of seclusion, they re-emerge as full-fledged women and marry.

A cultural explanation exists for why gender affects whether a young person has an adolescent phase of life. Cultural materialism (Chapter 1) offers an explanatory framework that accounts for variation. In this perspective, a prolonged and marked period of adolescence is likely to be preparation for any of several culturally valued adult roles: worker, warrior, or parent. Confirmation comes from the finding that extended adolescence for females in many nonindustrial societies occurs in cultures where adult females are important as food producers (J. Brown 1978).

Globalization is spreading Western patterns of adolescence to the middle and upper classes around the world. Globally, the age at marriage has risen steadily in the past few decades as young people attend college or university and then find employment before starting a family. At the same time, class differences in the adolescent phase of the life cycle are widening. Those who are poor have short periods of adolescence, or none at all. They spend little, if any, time in formal education, and they are likely to become parents when young.

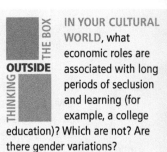

THINKING OUTSIDE THE BOX

IN YOUR CULTURAL WORLD, what economic roles are associated with long periods of seclusion and learning (for example, a college education)? Which are not? Are there gender variations?

Coming of Age and Gender Identity

Margaret Mead made famous the phrase "coming of age" in her book *Coming of Age in Samoa* (1960 [1928]). It can refer generally to the period of adolescence or specifically to a ceremony or set of ceremonies that marks the boundaries of adolescence. What are the psychological aspects of such special events for the children that go through them? Some of the ceremonies have a sacrificial element, with symbolic death and rebirth (Ingham 1996:183–184). Most coming of age ceremonies are gender specific, highlighting the importance of adult roles of men and women. These ceremonies often involve marking the body of the initiate in some way. Such marking may include scarification, tattooing, and genital surgery. In many societies, adolescent males undergo genital surgery that involves removal of part of the skin around the tip of the penis. Without this operation, the boy would not become a full-fledged male. In others, girls undergo genital cutting of various types which, similarly, is the only way to become a real woman.

A young Maasai male, in a first-person account of his initiation into manhood, describes the "intolerable pain" he experienced following the circumcision, as well as his feeling of accomplishment two weeks later when his head was shaved and he became a warrior: "As long as I live, I will never forget the day my head was shaved and I emerged a man, a Maasai warrior. I felt a sense of control over my destiny so great that no words can accurately describe it" (Saitoti 1986:71).

---

female genital cutting (FGC): a term used for a range of genital cutting procedures, including the excision of part or all of the clitoris, excision of part or all of the labia, and sometimes infibulation, the stitching together of the vaginal entry.

berdache: an early term for blurred gender category among Native Americans, usually referring to a person who is biological male but who assumes a female gender role. Today the term is considered derogatory.

two-spirit person: refers to gay, lesbian, bisexual, transgendered, and transsexual people among First Nations, emphasizing the spiritual nature of non-binary gender identities.

Less common worldwide is **female genital cutting** (**FGC**), a Western term referring to several forms of genital surgery practised on females (Gruenbaum 2001). These practices may involve the excision of part or all of the clitoris, part or all of the labia, and (the least common practice) *infibulation,* the stitching together of the vaginal entry, leaving a small aperture for drainage of menstrual blood. These procedures are performed when the girl is between 7 and 15 years of age. Many people practise some form of female genital cutting in the Sahelian countries extending from Africa's west to east coast (see Map 15.6 on page 416). It is also found in Egypt, in some groups of the Middle East (particularly among Bedu tribes), and among some Muslim groups in South and Southeast Asia. In terms of religion, FGC is often, but not always, associated with people who are Muslim. In Ethiopia, some Christian groups practise it. Genital cutting occurs in many groups in which female labour participation is high, but in others where it is not.

Scholars have yet to provide an explanation for the regional and social distribution of female genital cutting. Anthropologists who study this practice ask the people involved for their views. Many young girls say they look forward to the ceremony so that they will be free from childhood tasks and can take on the more respected role of an adult woman. In other cases, anthropologists have reported hearing statements of resistance (Fratkin 1998:60). Fewer issues force the questioning of cultural relativism more clearly than female genital cutting (see the Critical Thinking box on page 162).

Consider what happens, in different cultural contexts, to the biological universal of menarche, or first menstruation. In some cultures, menarche is a time of elaborate celebration and community feasting. In other, more male-dominated cultures, there is no public mention of it. For example, in rural Turkey, parents do not discuss menstruation with young girls, and the girls are shocked at menarche (Delaney 1988:79). Menstruation for Turkish girls is a matter of shame and embarrassment. Islamic teachings say that menstruation is the result of Eve's disobedience against Allah. Eve allowed herself to be persuaded by Satan to eat a forbidden fruit, so she was punished by being made to bleed monthly. In contrast, Hindus in southern India celebrate a daughter's menarche with a family gathering, special food, and songs (Miller 1997 [1981]). In the absence of studies on the psychological impact of these differences, one can only speculate that being honoured at a celebration would have positive effects on a girl's sense of self-esteem, whereas linking menstruation with shamefulness would have the opposite effect.

Sexual Identity and Gender Pluralism

Scholars have long debated whether sexual preferences and gender identity are biologically determined (ruled by genetic or hormonal factors) or culturally constructed and learned. Biological anthropologist Melvin Konner (1989) takes a middle position, saying that both factors play a part, but simultaneously warning that no one has a simple answer to the question of who is gay. Science has yet to produce a clear answer.

Lesbian feminist poet Adrienne Rich's (1980) approach combines attention to both biology and culture in her view that all people are biologically bisexual, but that patriarchal cultures try to mould them into being heterosexual. This "compulsory heterosexual project," she says, will never be completely successful in overcoming innate bisexuality, and so some people will always opt out of the heterosexual mould and become either homosexual or bisexual. (See the Multiple Cultural Worlds box on page 163).

The cultural constructionist position emphasizes socialization and childhood experiences as more powerful than biology in shaping sexual orientation. These anthropologists find support for their position in the cross-cultural record and its cases in which people change their sexual orientation once, or sometimes more than once, during their lifetimes. The Sambia of Papua New Guinea are one example. In the Gulf state of Oman, the *xanith* is another example (Wikan 1977) (see Map 4.2 on page 105). A xanith is a man who, for a time, becomes more like a woman, wears female clothing, and has sex with other men. Later, the xanith returns to a standard male role, marries a woman, and has children. Thus, given the same biological material, some people assume different sexual identities over their lives.

No matter what theoretical perspective one takes on the causes of sexual preferences, it is clear that homosexuals are discriminated against in many cultural contexts where heterosexuality is the norm of mainstream society. Gays and lesbians in North America have frequently been victims of violence, housing discrimination, and legal biases. They often suffer from being stigmatized by parents, other students, and the wider society. The psychological damage done to their self-esteem is reflected in the fact that homosexual youths in North America have substantially higher suicide rates than heterosexual youths.

Some cultures allow for a third gender, which is neither purely "male" nor "female," according to a particular culture's definition of those terms. As with the xanith of Oman, these gender categories offer ways for "males" to cross gender lines and assume more "female" behaviours, personality characteristics, and dress. In some Native American groups, a male (in terms of genitals) who opts to wear female clothing, may engage in sexual relations with a man or a woman, and performs female tasks such as basket-weaving and pottery-making (W. Williams 1992). Early ethnographers called such an individual, a **berdache**, a word of Persian origin. Since the 1990s, First Nations have begun to use **two-spirit person** to refer to gay, lesbian,

CULTURAL RELATIVISM AND FEMALE GENITAL CUTTING

In cultures that practise female genital cutting (FGC), it is a necessary step toward full womanhood. The procedure is required for a woman to be considered marriageable. Fathers say that an uncircumcised daughter is unmarriageable and will bring no brideprice. Others say that removing the labia makes a woman beautiful by removing "male" parts. The prevailing Western view, increasingly shared by many people who have long practised female genital cutting, is that FGC is both a sign of low female status and an unnecessary cause of women's suffering.

Female genital cutting is linked with several health risks, including those related to the surgery itself (shock, infection) and future genito-urinary complications (Gruenbaum 2001). Infibulation scars the vaginal canal and may lead to problems during childbirth, sometimes causing the death of the infant and mother. Having a new bride's husband "open" her, using a stick or knife to loosen the aperture, is both painful and an opportunity for infection. After giving birth, a woman is usually reinfibulated, and the process begins again. Health experts say that repeated trauma to the woman's vaginal area increases the risk of contracting HIV/AIDS.

The Western view argues that the effects of both clitoridectomy and infibulation on a woman's sexual enjoyment are highly negative—for one thing, clitoral orgasm is no longer possible. Some experts also say that FGC is related to the high level of infertility in many African countries, although a comparative study of fertility data from the Central African Republic, Côte d'Ivoire, and Tanzania found no clear relationship between FGC and infertility (Larsen and Yan 2000).

Outsiders often view these practices in oversimplified terms and in the most extreme forms. What are the views of insiders? Is there any evidence for agency? Or is it all structure and should anthropologists support FGC liberation movements? One voice that transcends insider/outsider divisions is that of Fuambai Ahmadu, who was born and raised in Washington, D.C. She is descended from a prominent Kono lineage in Sierra Leone and has done research for her doctorate in anthropology on female genital cutting in the Gambia (2000).

In 1991, Ahmadu travelled to Sierra Leone with her mother and other family members for what she refers to as her "circumcision." Upon her return, she wrote about her initiation experience and what it meant to her. Although the physical pain was excruciating (in spite of the use of anaesthetics), "the positive aspects have been much more profound" (2000:306). Through the initiation she became part of a powerful female world. Her analysis

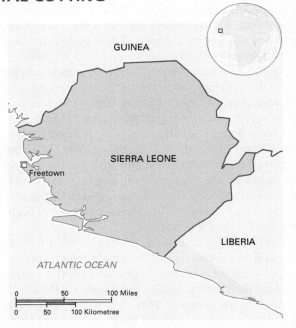

MAP 6.3   Sierra Leone. The Republic of Sierra Leone was an important centre of the Transatlantic Slave Trade. Its capital, Freetown, was established in 1972 as a home for African slaves who fought with the British during the American Revolution. Sierra Leone's coast is covered with mangrove swamps while the interior is plateau, forests, and mountains. The population is 6 million people. Sierra Leone suffered a terrible civil war from 1991 to 2002, causing thousands of deaths and the displacement of 2 million people. It has the lowest per capita income in the world. English is the official language, but most people speak tribal languages.

addresses the effects of genital cutting on health and sexuality. Ahmadu argues that westerners exaggerate these issues by focusing on infibulation (which she says is rarely practised) rather than on the less extreme forms. She adds, however, that if global pressures against the practice continue, she will go along with that movement and support "ritual without cutting" (2000:308).

CRITICAL THINKING QUESTIONS

- Why do you think FGC is a prominent issue in human rights debates in the West, whereas male circumcision and other forms of initiation (such as fraternity and sorority hazing) are condoned?

- Where do you stand on FGC and why?

- What kinds of cultural remodelling of the female body are practised in your community?

NEW LEGAL RIGHTS FOR GAY AND LESBIAN COUPLES IN CANADA

Affirming equal rights for gays and lesbians in provincial and federal law has been a long process. Gay and lesbian organizations emerged in the 1960s, promoting varied agendas including legal reforms, civil rights through human-rights codes, and social support. In 1969, the federal government amended the Criminal Code of Canada to exempt from prosecution two consenting adults engaged in sexual activity. Decriminalization was accompanied by Prime Minister Pierre Elliott Trudeau's famous comment that "the state has no place in the bedrooms of the nation." Nevertheless, in the 1970s and 1980s, bathhouses were raided in Toronto, and their occupants arrested and charged as "found-ins." In 1986, the Ontario government added "sexual orientation" to its human-rights code.

In October 1999, the Ontario legislature granted new rights to gay and lesbian couples. Bill 5 gave same-sex couples the same rights and responsibilities as heterosexual common-law couples. The law followed a Supreme Court decision that ordered the province to end discriminatory treatment of gays and lesbians under the Family Law Act. The law amended 67 provincial statutes to add the new category of same-sex partner to every statute that refers to common-law spouses, without changing the legal definition of *marriage* or *spouse*. Critics of the bill have argued that gay and lesbian couples should have been included in the definition of *spouse*—not separated into a new class. In July 2002, the Ontario courts ordered the provincial government to recognize same-sex marriage. In 2005, after most other provinces had also recognized same-sex marriage, the federal government legalized gay and lesbian marriage, making Canada the fifth country to recognize same-sex marriage.

FOOD FOR THOUGHT

- What effect do you think legal changes are having on attitudes toward same-sex relationships and sexual identity in your community?

---

bisexual, transgendered, and transsexual people. However, two-spirit is not primarily a description of one's sexual orientation, but rather a term to emphasize the spiritual nature of non-binary gender identities.

During decades of contact with Euro-American colonizers, including Christian missionaries, the outsiders viewed two-spirit individuals with disapproval and ridicule (Roscoe 1991). Under the influence of the negative reactions of the Euro-Americans, many Native American cultures began to suppress these traditions. In the 1980s, as Native American cultural pride began to grow, the open presence of the two-spirited individuals has returned. Native American cultures in general remain accepting of gender role fluidity and the contemporary concept of being gay: "Younger gay Indians, upon coming out to their families, will sometimes have an elderly relative who takes them aside and tells them about this tradition. A part-Choctaw gay man recalls that his full-blooded Choctaw grandmother realized he was gay and it was totally acceptable . . . This respectful attitude eliminates the stress felt by families that harbor homophobia" (1991:225). First Nations in general continue to be more tolerant of homosexuality than mainstream Euro-American society.

In India, **hijras** dress and act like women, but are neither truly male nor truly female (Nanda 1990). Many hijras were born with male genitals, or with genitals that were not clearly male or female. Hijras have the traditional right to visit the home of a newborn, inspect its genitals, and claim it for their group if the genitals are neither clearly male nor female. Some evidence exists that hijras may forcibly claim or steal babies in order to increase their population. Hijras born with male genitals may opt to go through an initiation ceremony that involves cutting off the penis and testicles. Hijras roam large cities of India, earning a living by begging from store to store (and threatening to lift their skirts if not given money). Because women rarely sing or dance in public, the hijras play an important role as performers in public events, especially as dancers or musicians. Given this public role and the hijra's association with prostitution, people in the mainstream do not admire or respect hijras, and no family would be delighted to hear that their son has decided to become a hijra. In contrast to the

---

hijra: term used in India to refer to a blurred gender role in which a person, usually biologically male, takes on female dress and behaviour.

A Zuni two-spirit person or "berdache," We'wha, wearing the ceremonial costume of Zuni women and holding a pottery bowl with sacred cornmeal. ■ (Source: © The National Anthropological Archive/Smithsonian Institution)

The South Korean transgender musical group "Lady" includes four transsexuals. ■ (Source: © Kim Kyung-Hoon/Reuters/CORBIS)

situation among First Nations peoples, hijras are a stigmatized group, separated from mainstream society.

In mainland and island Southeast Asia (see Map 6.4), the situation is even more complex, with a wide range of gender options, or **gender pluralism**. Gender pluralism is the existence in a culture of multiple categories of femininity, masculinity, and androgyny which are tolerated and legitimate (Peletz 2006:310). In Thailand, three basic gender categories have long co-existed: *phuuchai* (male), *phuuying* (female), and *kathoey* (transvestite/transsexual/ hermaphrodite) (Morris 1994b; P. Van Esterik 2000). Like the hijra, a kathoey is "originally" a male who crosses into the body, personality, and dress defined as

female. Kathoeys represent a "third gender," and may be heterosexual, homosexual, or bisexual in orientation. In contemporary Thailand, sexual orientation does not confer a fixed gender identity, nor is it legally regulated. The discourse on HIV/AIDS is shaping the way sexual identities are talked about and labelled, and terms derived from English are appearing. For example, the words for lesbian include *tom* (from the word *tomboy*) and *dee* (from *lady*). As in many parts of the world, reflecting the widespread presence of patriarchal norms, lesbianism is a more suppressed form of homosexuality than male homosexuality, and there has been less research on women's same-sex relationships.

gender pluralism: the existence within a culture of multiple categories of femininity, masculinity, and androgyny that are tolerated and legitimate.

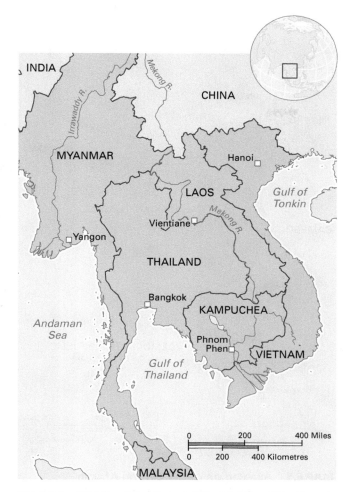

MAP 6.4 Mainland Southeast Asia. Mainland Southeast Asia comprises Myanmar (Burma), Thailand, Laos, Vietnam, Cambodia, and Malaysia. Although each country has a distinct history, the region shares a tropical monsoon climate, emphasis on wet-rice agriculture, and ethnic contrasts between highlanders and lowlanders. Many national and ethnic languages exist. Theravada Buddhism, Islam, and Christianity are major religions. Growth in industry and informatics has created an economic upsurge in many parts of the region.

Personality and Identity in Adulthood

Adulthood for most people means entering into some form of marriage, or long-term domestic relationship, and having children. In this section, we discuss the psychological aspects of parenthood and the senior years.

Becoming a Parent

More studies have been done of how cultures shape maternal roles than paternal roles. Biologically, a woman becomes a mother when she gives birth to an infant: She is transformed from a pregnant woman to a mother. Like adolescence, the cultural definition of motherhood varies in terms of duration and meaning. In some cultures, a woman is transformed into a mother as soon as she thinks she is pregnant. In others, she becomes a mother and is granted full maternal status only when she delivers an infant of the "right" sex, a male in much of northern India.

Among the Beti people of southern Cameroon, West Africa, motherhood is not simply defined by having a child (Johnson-Hanks 2002). The Beti are both an ethnic group and a social status group of educated professionals. "School girl" is one category of young Beti women. If a school girl becomes pregnant, it is a matter of great shame, and the girl is not considered to have entered a phase of motherhood even though she has borne a child. In this case, a biological marker does not bring about movement into a new life stage but instead creates ambiguity.

In many nonindustrial societies, becoming a mother occurs in the context of supportive family members. Some cultures promote prenatal practices such as abiding by particular food taboos. Such rules make the pregnant woman feel that she has some role in helping to make the pregnancy turn out well. In the West, medical experts have increasingly defined the prenatal period as an important phase of becoming a mother, and they have issued many scientific and medical rules for potential parents, especially mothers (Browner and Press 1995, 1996). Pregnant women are urged to seek prenatal examinations; be under the regular supervision of a doctor who monitors the growth and development of the fetus; follow particular dietary and exercise guidelines; and undergo a range of tests such as ultrasound scanning. Some anthropologists think that such medicalized pregnancies lead to the greater likelihood of post-partum depression among mothers as a result of their lack of control in the birthing process.

Fear is the predominant feeling that poor, young Afro-Brazilian mothers expressed in their narratives of birth-giving in a public hospital in the northeastern city of Salvador (McCallum and dos Reis 2005). For these women, giving birth in a run-down hospital where the medical staffers are middle class and white, the lack of social support is one cause of their fear. The mother-to-be enters the hospital alone to confront an unfamiliar environment. The labour ward is full of women shrieking with pain. Any friendly interaction with the hospital staff is a source of uplift. Most women said that they missed their mothers and felt lonely. All the women's narratives, however, contained the theme of personal growth by learning to become stronger. Giving birth, in difficult circumstances, was a kind of ritual of transformation.

Becoming a father is usually less socially noted than becoming a mother. One exception to this generalization is the **couvade**, beliefs and customs applying to a father during his wife's pregnancy and delivery (Broude 1988:902). In some cases, the father takes to his bed before, during, or after the delivery, and may experience pain and exhaustion. Couvade often involves rules for the expectant father. For example, he may not hunt a certain animal, eat certain foods, or cut objects. Early theories of why couvade exists relied on Freudian interpretations that men were seeking cross-sex identification (with the female role) in contexts where the father role was weak. But cross-cultural data on the existence of couvade indicates the opposite: Couvade occurs in societies where fathers have prominent roles in child care. This interpretation views couvade as one phase of men's participation in parenting: Their proper behaviour as expectant fathers helps ensure a good delivery and a healthy baby. Another interpretation of couvade is that it offers support for the mother. In Estonia, some people believe that a woman's birth pains will be less if her husband bears some of them (Oinas 1993).

The widespread pattern of women being the major caregivers for infants and children has led many people to

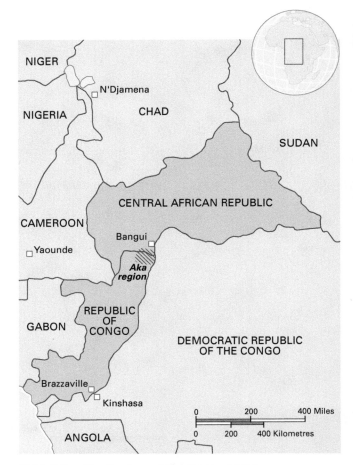

MAP 6.5   Aka Region of the Central African Republic and the Democratic Republic of the Congo. The 30 000 Aka are tropical forest foragers who know hundreds of forest plants and animals. They eat roots, leaves, nuts, fruits, mushrooms, honey, grubs, caterpillars, and meat from monkeys, rats, mongooses, and porcupines. They trade meat to farmers for manioc and other cultivated foods. They are socially egalitarian, and their religious beliefs are indigenous. Diaka, their main language, is tonal. The Aka territory is seriously endangered by commercial loggers.

An Aka father and his son. Aka fathers are affectionate caregivers to infants and small children. Compared to mothers, they are more likely to kiss and hug children.
■ (Source: Barry Hewlett)

think there is something biologically innate about females that makes them especially suited to caregiving roles. Most cultural anthropologists agree that child care is predominately the responsibility of women worldwide—but not universally. While breastfeeding is exclusively a female act of nurturance and care, other aspects of child care can be taken over by caregivers besides the biological mother. In many cultures of the South Pacific, child care

couvade: customs applying to the behaviour of fathers during and shortly after the birth of their children.

iatrogenic: an affliction caused by medical definition or intervention.

is shared across families, and women breastfeed other women's babies. Paternal involvement varies as well. Among the Aka pygmy hunter-gatherers of central Africa (see Map 6.5), paternal child care is prominent (Hewlett 1991). The Aka are an exceptional case, perhaps even unique, in comparison with other societies because of the high involvement of fathers in child care. Aka fathers are intimate, affectionate, and helpful, spending about half of their time each day holding or within arm's reach of their infants. While holding their infants, they are more likely to hug and kiss them than mothers are. Good fatherhood among the Aka means being affectionate toward children and assisting the mother when her workload is heavy. Among the Aka, a prevailing ideology of gender equality exists and violence against women is unknown; the high level of paternal involvement in child care probably helps explain this pattern.

Middle Age

In industrial and post-industrial countries, the lower and upper boundaries of "middle age" are typically defined as being 30 and 70 years of age (Shweder 1998). A major turning point is now the fortieth birthday. Stanley Brandes explores the meanings of turning age 40 to U.S. middle-class men in a book entitled *Forty: The Age and the Symbol* (1985). The "40 syndrome" comprises feelings of restlessness, rebelliousness, and unhappiness that often lead to family breakups. One possible reason behind this emphasis on age 40 as a turning point for males is that it is the current midpoint of a "typical" lifespan for a middle-class North American man. In cultures with shorter lifespans, a so-called midlife crisis would necessarily occur at some point other than the age of 40 years, if it were to happen at all. Such a "crisis" seems strongly embedded in contemporary North American culture and its pervasive fear and denial of death (Shore 1998:103).

Menopause is a significant aspect of middle age for women in some, but not all, cultures. A comparative study examined differences in perception and experience of menopause among Mayan women of Mexico and rural Greek women (Beyene 1989). Among the Mayan women, menopause is not a time of stress or crisis. They consider menstruation an illness and look forward to its end. Menopause among these women is not associated with physical or emotional symptoms. In fact, none of the women reported hot flashes or night sweats. No role changes were associated with menopause. In contrast, the rural Greek women recognized menopause as a natural phenomenon that

all women experience and one that causes temporary discomfort, *exapi*, which is a phase of hot flashes, especially at night, that may last about a year. The women did not think *exapi* was terribly serious, certainly nothing worthy of medical attention.

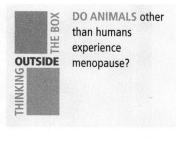

THINKING OUTSIDE THE BOX

DO ANIMALS other than humans experience menopause?

Postmenopausal women emphasized the relief and freedom they felt. Postmenopausal women can go into cafés by themselves, something they would never do otherwise, and they can participate more fully in church ceremonies. In Japan, also, menopause is a minimally stressful experience and is rarely considered something that warrants medical attention (Lock 1993).

In Canada, debates about surgical menopause and the safety of hormone replacement therapy confirm the medicalization of an event that is physiologically universal, but that carries diverse cultural meanings. Patricia Kaufert (1986) studied the transition to menopause in women in Manitoba, and found that the rate of estrogen use was low, and that it was used intermittently and possibly with reluctance. These variable findings raise the question of how much perceived suffering from menopause in North America is **iatrogenic**, that is, an affliction caused by medical definition or intervention.

The Senior Years

The "senior" life-cycle stage may be a development of contemporary human society because, like most other mammals, our early ancestors rarely lived beyond their reproductive years (Brooks and Draper 1998 [1991]). Cross-culturally, the category of the aged is variably recognized, defined, and valued. In many cultures, elders are highly revered, and their life experiences are valued as the greatest wisdom. In others, aged people become burdens to their families and to society.

In general, the status and well-being of the elderly cross-culturally is higher where they continue to live with their families (Lee and Kezis 1979). This pattern is more likely to be found in nonindustrial societies than in industrialized ones, where the elderly are increasingly experiencing a shift to "retirement homes." In such age-segregated settings, people have to create new social roles and ties and find new ways of gaining self-esteem and personal satisfaction. Being allowed to have pets seems to have a positive effect on people's adjustment to retirement homes (Savishinsky 1991).

Throughout Asia, it is the responsibility of children to care for their parents in their old age. But the numbers of the elderly are growing, while reduced fertility means fewer family caregivers. ■ (Source: Barbara Miller)

Compared with the elderly of East Asia, many aged people in North America have no family support and end up living on the street or in shelters. ■ (Source: © Douglas Kirkland/CORBIS)

The Final Passage: Death and Dying

It may be that no one in any culture welcomes death, unless he or she is in very poor health and suffering greatly. Contemporary North America, with its dependence on medical technology, appears to be particularly active in resisting death, often at very high financial and psychological cost. In many other cultures, a greater degree of acceptance prevails.

A study of attitudes toward death and dying among Alaskan Inuit revealed a pervasive feeling that people are active participants in their death rather than passive victims (Trelease 1975). The usual pattern for a person near death is that the person calls friends and neighbours together, is given a Christian sacrament, and then, within a few hours, dies. The author comments, "I do not suggest that everyone waited for the priest to come and then died right away. But the majority who did not die suddenly did some degree of planning, had some kind of formal service or celebration of prayers and hymns and farewells" (1975:35).

Terminally ill people, especially in industrial societies with a high level of medical technology, are likely to be faced with choices about how and where they should die: at home or in a hospital? Prolong life with "unusual means" or opt for "physician-assisted suicide"? Depending on the cultural context, the options are affected not only by the degree of medical technology and health-care services available but also by matters of kinship and gender role ideals (Long 2005). In urban Japan, terminally ill people have clear ideas of what is a "good death" and multiple "scripts" exist for a "good death." A modern script of dying in a hospital is widely accepted, because it reduces burdens on family members. But a value on dying surrounded by one's family members still prevails; this practice reassures the dying person that he or she will be remembered.

Proper treatment of the corpse is another important cultural aspect of death. Archaeological evidence suggests that the practice of burying corpses is only a few hundred thousand years old and likely originated in the Middle East. Since then, rituals associated with death have been elaborated around the world.

In many cultures, the inability to perform a proper burial and funeral for the deceased person is a cause of serious social suffering. Among refugees from Mozambique living in neighbouring Malawi, the greatest cause of stress was being forced to leave behind deceased family members without providing a proper burial for them (Englund 1998). Such improperly treated deaths mean that the unhappy spirit of the deceased will haunt the living. This belief is related to

On December 6, 1989, 14 women students were murdered at the École Polytechnique at the Université de Montréal. A visitor offers flowers at the memorial that marks the anniversary of the Montreal massacre.
■ (Source: CP PHOTO/Ryan Remiorz)

the high rates of mental-health problems among the refugees. A culturally informed recommendation for reducing anxiety among the refugees is to provide them with money to travel home and to perform a proper funeral for their deceased relatives. In that way, the living may carry on in greater peace.

Anthropologists know little about people's grief at the death of a loved one or close community member. It might seem that sadness and grief, and a period of mourning, are only natural. But the outward expression of grief varies from extended, dramatic, public grieving that is overtly emotional to no visible sign of grief at all. The latter pattern is the norm in Bali, Indonesia (see Map 1.3 on page 16), where people's faces remain impassive at funerals and no vocal lamenting occurs (Rosenblatt, Walsh, and Jackson 1976). Do impassive faces and silence mean that the Balinese feel no sadness? Such different modes of expression of loss may be related to the healing process for the survivors by providing socially accepted rules of behaviour—in other words, a script for loss. Either highly expressive public mourning or repressed grief may be equally effective, depending on the context.

Key Questions Revisited

WHAT is the scope of psychological anthropology?

Psychological anthropology is the study of individuals and their personalities and identities, within particular cultural contexts. In North American anthropology, psychological anthropology has its roots in the Culture and Personality School that emerged in the early part of the twentieth century. These anthropologists studied child-rearing patterns and their effect on personality, national patterns of personality, and the relationship between poverty and personality. More recently, psychological anthropologists have begun studying personality formation in Western and industrial cultures. The latest turn in psychological anthropology is an emphasis on person-centred ethnography and close attention to individual perceptions and experiences.

Compared to the Western discipline of psychology, psychological anthropology takes a much wider view of concepts such as personality and the self—a perspective gained through ethnographic research.

HOW does culture shape personality and identity from birth through adolescence?

Human psychological development begins from the moment of birth, if not before. Margaret Mead was a pioneer in showing how child-care practices such as breastfeeding, how the baby is held, and how much contact the infant has with others can affect personality formation, including gender identity. Her study of the Arapesh, Mundugumor, and Tchambuli peoples of Papua New Guinea showed that gender is a "plastic" (or malleable) aspect of human personality. Cross-cultural studies indicate that children's work roles and family roles correspond to personality patterns. Depending on cultural context, informal and formal learning shape young people's sense of identity in various ways.

Adolescence, a phase of the life cycle around puberty and before adulthood, varies cross-culturally from being nonexistent to being long in duration and involving detailed training and elaborate ceremonies. "Coming of age" ceremonies may involve bodily cutting, which denotes membership of the initiate in a particular gender. In contrast to the clear distinction between "male" and "female" defined by Western science, many cultures have long-standing traditions of third-gender identities, especially for males or people of indeterminate biological sex markers, and gender pluralism.

HOW does culture shape personality and identity in adulthood through old age?

Reflecting the fact that women tend to be more involved than males in child care, cultures generally provide more in the way of enculturation of females for this role. In nonindustrial societies, learning about motherhood is embedded in other aspects of life, and knowledge about birthing and child care is shared among women. In industrialized cultures, science and medicine play a large part in defining the maternal role. This change reduces women's autonomy and fosters their dependence on external, nonfamily-based structures.

In general, the senior years are shorter in nonindustrialized societies than in industrial societies, in which lifespans tend to be longer. Elder men and women in nonindustrial cultures are treated with respect, are considered to be highly knowledgeable, and retain a strong sense of their place in the culture. Increasingly, in industrial societies, elderly people either remove themselves or are removed from their families and spend many years in age-segregated institutions. This transition tends to have negative implications for their psychological well-being.

Anthropologists know relatively little about how people in different cultures experience and express grief at the loss of a loved one. In some cultures, grief is openly expressed, whereas in others, it is repressed.

KEY CONCEPTS

adolescence, p. 158
berdache, p. 161
couvade, p. 166
cultural broker, p. 153
cultural configuration,
  p. 149
culture of poverty, p. 150
ethnopsychology, p. 148

enculturation, p. 148
female genital cutting
  (FGC), p. 161
gender pluralism, p. 164
hijra, p. 163
iatrogenic, p. 167
image of the limited good,
  p. 150

person-centred ethnography,
  p. 151
personality, p. 148
puberty, p. 158
two-spirit person, p. 161

SUGGESTED READINGS

Evalyn Blackwood, ed., *The Many Faces of Homosexuality: Anthropological Approaches to Homosexual Behavior.* New York: Harrington Park Press, 1986. This text contains chapters on anthropological writings about lesbianism, and case studies of ritualized male homosexuality in Irian Jaya, the berdache in North America, hijiras of India, lesbian relationships in Lesotho, and Mexican male homosexual interaction patterns in public.

Jean Briggs, *Never in Anger.* Cambridge, MA: Harvard University Press, 1970. This classic study explores the ethnographer's experience with the Inuit of the Canadian Arctic through a perceptive and reflective examination of family life.

Jean Briggs, *Inuit Morality Play.* New Haven, CN: Yale University Press, 1998. A wonderful introduction to the use of psychoanalytic anthropology, this book details the "dramas" in the life of a three-year-old Inuit girl. (Winner of the Boyer Prize in psychoanalytic anthropology for 1999).

Sally Cole, *Ruth Landes: A Life in Anthropology.* Omaha: University of Nebraska Press, 2003. In this book, Canadian anthropologist Sally Cole reconsiders the life and work of Ruth Landes, whose work among the Ojibwa is considered today an early and exemplary study of gender relations.

Robbie E. Davis-Floyd. *Birth as an American Rite of Passage,* 2nd ed. with a new preface. Berkeley: University of California Press, 2003. This book provides a cultural critique of the dominant U.S. model of birth as "technocratic" and patriarchal. The last two chapters consider the future of birthing in the United States and the increasing role of computers in obstetrics.

Ellen Gruenbaum. *The Female Circumcision Controversy: An Anthropological Perspective.* Philadelphia: University of Pennsylvania Press, 2001. The author draws on her more than five years of fieldwork in Sudan and discusses how change is occurring through economic development, the role of Islamic activists, health educators, and educated African women.

Charlotte E. Hardman. *Other Worlds: Notions of Self and Emotion among the Lohorung Rai.* New York: Berg, 2000. The author conducted fieldwork in a mountainous region of eastern Nepal to learn about one community's perception of what it means to be a person.

Susan Orpett Long. *Final Days: Japanese Culture and Choice at the End of Life.* Honolulu: University of Hawai'i Press, 2005. An increasing array of choices about how to die a "good death" now exists in Japan, mainly due to technological innovations. This study, conducted in an urban area, shows how people make end-of-life choices within the context of universal health care, kinship, and gender roles.

Susan McKinnon. *Neo-Liberal Genetics: The Myths and Moral Tales of Evolutionary Psychology.* Chicago: University of Chicago Press, 2005. Cuturally based analysis of U.S.-based evolutionary psychology, as defined by such prominent scholars as Steven Pinker and David Buss, reveals that it is ethnocentric, myth creating, and linked to contemporary U.S. capitalist values. Evolutionary psychology's understandings of sex, gender, kinship, and social relations are at the centre of the critique.

Judith Schachter Modell. *Ruth Benedict: Patterns of a Life.* Philadelphia: University of Pennsylvania Press, 1983. This biography provides insights into Benedict's development as an anthropologist, her research and writings, and her role in the Culture and Personality School.

Michael Moffatt. *Coming of Age in New Jersey: College and American Culture.* New Brunswick: Rutgers University Press, 1991. Based on a year's participant observation in a college dormitory in a university in the eastern United States, this study discusses sexuality, race relations, and individualism.

Mimi Nichter. *Fat Talk: What Girls and Their Parents Say About Dieting.* Cambridge, MA: Harvard University Press, 2000. The author collected and analyzed interview data with adolescent girls in the United States, focusing on perceptions of weight, attachment to dieting, and the influence of their mothers' views and comments on weight.

Richard Parker. *Bodies, Pleasures and Passions: Sexual Culture in Contemporary Brazil.* Boston: Beacon Press, 1991. This ethnographic study of contemporary sexual culture in Brazil addresses such topics as sexual socialization, bisexuality, sadomasochism, AIDS, prostitution, samba, the symbolism of breasts, courting, and carnival.

Richard K. Reed. *Birthing Fathers: The Transformation of Men in American Rites of Birth.* New Brunswick, NJ: Rutgers University Press, 2005. The author interviewed 50 U.S. fathers, collected their narratives about birthing, and attended birthing classes. This book relates its findings to both classic and new themes in cultural anthropology such as the couvade, rites of passage, and ideas about the human body.

Jennifer Robertson, ed. *Same-Sex Cultures and Sexualities: An Anthropological Reader.* Malden, MA: Blackwell Publishing, 2004. The chapters in this book explore theory, biology and sexuality, language and sexuality, transsexuality, modernity and desire, and the globalization of gay sexual identity. Cultural contexts include North America, Japan, West Sumatra, South Africa, Bolivia, and more.

Joel S. Savishinsky. *Breaking the Watch: The Meanings of Retirement in America.* Ithaca, NY: Cornell University Press, 2000. Fieldwork in a nursing home in a small town in central New York state sheds light on the retirees themselves through vivid portraits of several, along with their own words on friendship in the home, finding purpose in life, and dealing with finances.

Joseph J. Tobin, David Y. H. Wu, and Dana H. Davidson. *Preschool in Three Cultures: Japan, China, and the United States.* New Haven, CT: Yale University Press, 1989. This book offers comparative insights about parents' reasons for sending children to preschool, including a concern that children learn cooperation in all three contexts and a contrast between the emphasis on academic learning in the United States and social learning in Japan.

John W. Traphagan. *Taming Oblivion: Aging Bodies and the Fear of Senility in Japan.* Albany: State University of New York Press, 2000. The author conducted fieldwork in a small town north of Tokyo to investigate people's attitudes and practices related to old age, especially as aging people attempt to prevent the onset of the *boke* condition, or what westerners call senility.

7

Disease, Illness, and Healing

Key Questions

- WHAT is ethnomedicine?

- WHAT are the major theoretical approaches in medical anthropology?

- HOW are disease, illness, and healing changing during globalization?

Mentawai healers treat a woman suffering from a toothache on Siberut Island, Indonesia. *(Source: B. & C. Alexander, Photo Researchers)*

Primatologist Jane Goodall once witnessed the consequences of a polio epidemic among the chimpanzees she was studying in Tanzania (Foster and Anderson 1978:33–34). A group of healthy animals watched a stricken member try to reach the feeding area but did not help him. Another badly paralyzed chimpanzee was simply left behind when the group moved on. Humans also sometimes resort to isolation and abandonment of those who are ill and dying. But compared to our nonhuman primate relatives, humans have created more complex ways of interpreting health problems and highly creative methods of preventing and curing them.

Medical anthropology is one of the most rapidly growing areas of research in anthropology. In this chapter, we present a selection of findings from this subfield. We first describe how people in different cultures think and behave regarding health, illness, and healing. In the second section, we consider different theoretical approaches in medical anthropology. The chapter concludes with a discussion about how globalization is affecting health.

Ethnomedicine

Medical anthropologists have long been interested in studying **ethnomedicine**, or cross-cultural health systems. A health system encompasses many areas: perceptions and classifications of health problems, prevention measures, diagnosis, healing (magical, religious, scientific, healing substances), and healers. Ethnomedicine has expanded its focus to new topics such as the anthropology of the body, culture and disability, and change in indigenous or "traditional" healing systems—especially change resulting from the effects of globalization.

In the 1960s, when the term *ethnomedicine* first came into use, it referred only to non-Western health systems and was synonymous with *folk medicine, popular medicine,* or the abandoned term *primitive medicine.* Two major problems exist with using *ethnomedicine* in this way. First, it is totalizing—that is, excessively generalizing. Labelling all non-Western medicine as "folk" or "popular," in contrast to "scientific" or "professional" Western medicine, overlooks such highly developed and specialized non-Western systems as those of India and China. It also implies that all Western health systems are professional and, thus, overlooks much thinking and practice in the West that could well be labelled "folk" or "popular." Second, the early meaning of ethnomedicine is ethnocentric, because Western medicine is an

South African healer Magdaline Ramaota speaks to clients in Durban. In South Africa, few people have enough money to pay for AIDS drugs. The role of traditional healers in providing psychological and social support for victims is extremely important. ■ (Source: © AFP/CORBIS)

ethnomedical system, too, intimately bound to Western culture and its values. With the increasing spread of Western culture and science globally, Western biomedicine (WBM) is more appropriately termed a global or cosmopolitan system. Thus the current use of the term *ethnomedicine* embraces all health systems.

Perceptions of the Body

Cultural perceptions of the body have implications for how people maintain health, respond to illness, and approach healing. The highland Maya of Chiapas, southern Mexico, have a detailed vision of the exterior body, but do not focus much attention on internal organs, a fact related to the absence of surgery as a healing technique among them

---

ethnomedicine: expands on conventional medicine, with a focus on new topics such as the anthropology of the body, culture and disability, and change in indigenous or "traditional" healing systems, especially change resulting from the effects of globalization

(Berlin and Berlin 1996). Western logic of mind–body dualism has long pervaded popular and scientific thinking about health and illness. Thus, Western medicine has a special category called "mental illness," which addresses certain health problems as if they were located only in the mind. In many cultures where such a mind–body distinction does not exist, there is no category of "mental illness."

Cross-cultural variation exists in perceptions of which bodily organs are most critically involved in the definition of life versus death. In the West, a person may be declared dead while the heart is still beating if the brain is judged "dead." In Japan, organ transplant from a brain-dead donor remains an unacceptable medical practice (Lock 1996). The definition of *brain-dead* is not accepted in Japan, perhaps an indication of the relatively great value accorded to the brain in Western culture (Ohnuki-Tierney 1994).

In Japan, the concept of *gotai* refers to the ideal of maintaining bodily intactness in life and death, to the extent of not piercing one's ears (Ohnuki-Tierney 1994:235). When Crown Prince Naruhitao was considering who to marry, one criterion for the bride was that she not have pierced ears. Underlying the value on intactness is the belief that an intact body ensures rebirth. Historically, a warrior's practice of beheading a victim was the ultimate form of killing because it violated the integrity of the body and prevented the enemy's rebirth. Gotai is an important reason for the low rates of surgery in Japan—compared to North America—and the widespread popular resistance to organ transplantation.

Ideals about the female body are implicated in the high rate of Caesarean births in Brazil (McCallum 2005).

Ethnographic research in the city of Salvador, northeastern Brazil, reveals that vaginal childbirth is considered more "primitive," painful, and destructive of a woman's sexuality than Caesarean delivery. One doctor said that "more and more, the vulva and the vagina are becoming the organs of sexuality and not parturition. . . . No worse thing can happen to a woman than that her husband take a mistress because (her vagina) is slack" (2005:226). When a pregnant woman asks how to avoid such problems, the doctor recommends a Caesarean delivery as safe, practical, and having no "aesthetic damage."

Another area of interest for medical anthropologists is the relationship between the physical body and the social body in matters of health, illness, and healing. Western biomedicine typically treats only the physical body or only the mind, as they are thought to be completely separate from each other and from the social and cultural milieu of the patient. In contrast, many non-Western healing systems encompass the social context within which an individual's body is situated.

Health is also closely related to the body politic. The Cree from northern Quebec translate *miyupimaatisiiu* as "being alive well." The term encompasses practices of Cree daily living such as hunting, eating the right foods, keeping warm, and balancing human relationships. Naomi Adelson's research (2000) with the Whapmagoostui Cree living along the Great Whale River demonstrated that understanding health means understanding what it is to be Cree in a rapidly changing political and economic environment.

Most medical systems recognize a relationship between mind and body, and between individuals and their social

People in Laos gathered around an offering to the spirits in preparation for a *sukhwan* ritual. ■ (Source: Penny Van Esterik)

contexts. Strained social relations—including those with supernatural beings—may cause illness; healing is intended to address and alleviate problems in the social body as well as the physical body. A cure is brought about by holding a family or community ritual that seeks to regain correct social relations or that will appease the deities. For example, the Lao residing in Laos and those who settled as refugees in North America perform a communal ritual called *sukhwan* to "tie" the 32 components of an individual's spirit essence permanently into the body with sacred strings tied around the wrist. This ritual draws the individual, who may have been ill or frightened, more tightly into the community (P. Van Esterik 1992).

Defining Health Problems

Emic diversity in labelling health problems presents a challenge for medical anthropologists and health-care specialists. Western labels, which biomedically trained experts accept as true, accurate, and universal, often do not correspond to the labels in other cultures. One set of concepts that medical anthropologists use to sort out the many cross-cultural labels and perceptions is the *disease/illness dichotomy*. In this model, **disease** refers to a biological health problem that is objective and universal, such as a bacterial or viral infection or a broken arm. **Illness** refers to culturally specific perceptions and experiences of a health problem. Medical anthropologists study both disease and illness, and they show how both must be understood within their cultural contexts. Arthur Kleinman, medical anthropologist and physician, says that Western biomedicine focuses too narrowly on disease and neglects illness (1995). He advocates that biomedicine should pay more attention to the findings of medical anthropologists and broaden the understanding of health problems and their cultural construction.

A first step in ethnomedical research is to learn how people label, categorize, and classify health problems. Depending on the culture, the following may be bases for labelling and classifying health problems: cause, *vector* (the means of transmission, such as mosquitoes), affected body part, symptoms, or combinations of these. Often, knowledgeable elders are the repositories of this knowledge, and they pass it down through oral traditions. Among Native Americans of the Washington–Oregon region, many popular stories refer to health (Thompson and Sloat 2004). The stories convey messages about how

to prevent health problems, avoid bodily harm, relieve afflictions, and deal with old age. For example, here is the story of Boil, a story for young children:

THINKING OUTSIDE THE BOX

IN YOUR SUBCULTURE, what are the prevailing perceptions about the body and how are they related to medical treatment?

> Boil was getting bigger.
> Her husband told her to bathe.
> She got into the water.
> She disappeared. (2004:5).

Other, longer stories about Boil add complexities about the location of the boil and how to deal with particular boils, revealing indigenous patterns of classification.

A classic study among the Subanun people focused on their categories of health problems (Frake 1961). The Subanun, in the 1950s, were horticulturalists living in the highlands of Mindanao, in the Philippines (see Map 7.1). An egalitarian people, all Subanun, even young children, had substantial knowledge about health problems. Of their 186 labels for health problems, some are a single term, such as "itch," which can be expanded on using two words such as "splotchy itch."

This young man is carrying his teenage sister, Geralda, to a clinic in rural Haiti. She has tuberculosis. Tuberculosis worldwide now often exists in strains that are resistant to treatment with the usual drugs.
■ (Source: © Gilles Peress)

---

disease: in the disease/illness dichotomy, a biological health problem that is objective and universal.

illness: in the disease/illness dichotomy, culturally specific perceptions and experiences of a health problem.

culture-specific syndrome: a collection of signs and symptoms that is restricted to a particular culture or a limited number of cultures; also called "folk illness."

somatization: the process through which the body absorbs social stress and manifests symptoms of suffering.

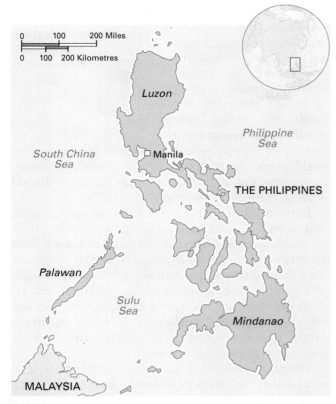

MAP 7.1 The Philippines. The Republic of the Philippines comprises over 7000 islands of which around 700 are occupied. The population is over 85 million with two-thirds living on Luzon. The economy is based on agriculture, light industry, and a growing business processing outsourcing (BPO) industry. Over 8 million Filipinos work overseas and remit more than US$12 billion a year, a large part of the GDP. Although Filipino and English are the official languages, more than 170 languages are spoken. The Philippines has the world's third-largest Christian population, with Roman Catholicism predominant.

In Western biomedicine, panels of medical experts have to agree about how to label and classify health problems according to scientific criteria. Classifications and descriptions of thousands of afflictions are published in thick manuals that physicians consult before they give a diagnosis. In countries where medical care is privatized, the code selected may determine whether the patient's costs are covered by insurance or not. The *International Classification of Diseases* (ICD), now in its tenth edition (1993), is a major source for coding health problems according to Western biomedical standards. Even though it contains abundant details on many health problems and is carefully arranged according to a complex coding system, its categories often prove to be inadequate. For example, following the September 11, 2001, attacks on the United States, medical personnel who had to classify the cause of death of those who perished at the four sites and the health problems of survivors found the *ICD-10* codes of little help.

Another weakness of the *ICD-10* is that it is biased toward diseases that Western biomedicine recognizes and ignores health problems of many other cultures. Anthropologists have discovered the existence of many health problems around the world, first referred to as culture-bound syndromes. Now called **culture-specific syndrome**, the term refers to health problems with a set of symptoms associated with a particular culture. Social factors such as stress, fear, or shock often are the underlying causes of culture-specific syndromes. Biophysical symptoms may be involved, and culture-specific syndromes can be fatal. **Somatization** refers to the process through which the body absorbs social stress and manifests symptoms of suffering.

For example, *susto,* or "fright/shock disease," is found in Spain and Portugal and among Latino people wherever they live. People afflicted with susto attribute it to events such as losing a loved one or having a terrible accident (Rubel, O'Nell, and Collado-Ardón 1984). In Oaxaca, southern Mexico (see Map 5.4 on page 129) a woman reported that her susto was brought on by an accident in which pottery she had made was broken on its way to market. A man said that his susto came on after he saw a dangerous snake. Susto symptoms include appetite loss, lack of motivation, breathing problems, generalized pain, and nightmares. The researchers analyzed many cases of susto in three villages. They found that the people most likely to be afflicted were those who were socially marginal or experiencing a sense of role failure. For example, the woman with the broken pots had also suffered two spontaneous abortions and was worried that she would never have children. In Oaxaca, people with susto have higher mortality rates than other people. Thus, social marginality, or a deep sense of social failure, can place a person at a higher risk of dying. It is important to look at the deeper causes of susto and susto deaths.

Medical anthropologists first studied culture-specific syndromes in non-Western cultures. This focus created a bias in thinking that they exist only in "other" cultures. Now, anthropologists recognize that Western cultures also have culture-specific syndromes. Anorexia nervosa and a related condition, bulimia, are culture-bound syndromes found mainly among white middle-class adolescent girls in North America, although some cases have been documented among African American girls in the United States and among young males (Fabrega and Miller 1995). Perhaps as a result of Western globalization, since the 1990s, cases have been documented in cities in Japan, Hong Kong, and India (Fabrega and Miller 1995; Nasser, Katzman, and Gordon 2001). Anorexia nervosa's cluster of symptoms includes self-perceptions of fatness, aversion to food, hyperactivity, and, as the condition progresses, continued wasting of the body and often death. Fat phobias or self-perceptions of fatness are often absent in Asian patients, a reminder that there are many routes to anorexia.

No one has found a biological cause for anorexia nervosa, and thus it can be interpreted as a culturally constructed affliction. Eating disorders are difficult to cure with either medical or psychiatric treatment (Gremillion 1992). Pinpointing the cultural causes has not proved easy. Many experts cite the societal pressures on young girls in North America toward excessive concern with their looks, especially body weight. Others feel that anorexia is related to girls' unconscious resistance to overcontrolling parents. To such girls, food intake may appear to be the one thing they can control. This need for self-control through food deprivation becomes addictive and entrapping. The highly controversial Montreux Clinic in Victoria, British Columbia, proposed a causal model of psychological negativity that "forbade" sufferers to eat. Although the primary cause of anorexia may be rooted in culture, the affliction becomes intertwined with the body's biological functions. Extreme fasting leads to the body's inability to deal with ingested food. A starving anorexic literally may no longer be able to eat and derive nourishment from food. Some medical treatments therefore include in-hospital monitored feeding or intravenous feeding to override the biological block. Other interventions by Canadian hospitals and advocacy groups include the following: support groups for parents of children with eating disorders; out-patient treatment programs to develop coping strategies and improve self-acceptance; individual psychotherapy focusing on issues such as control or body image; family counselling; publicity concerning the early signs of eating disorders; public education such as National Eating Disorders Week (first week of February) and Internet resources.

Ethno-etiologies

People in all cultures, everywhere, attempt to make sense of health problems and try to understand their cause, or etiology. Following anthropological practice, the term **ethno-etiologies** refers to cross-cultural variations in causal explanations for health problems and suffering.

Among the urban poor of northeastern Brazil, people consider several causal possibilities when they are sick (Ngokwey 1988). In Feira de Santana, the second largest city in the state of Bahia, ethno-etiologies can be natural, socioeconomic, psychological, or supernatural. Natural causes include exposure to the environment—for example: "Too much cold can provoke gripe; humidity and rain cause rheumatism; excessive heat can result in dehydration. . . . Some types of winds are known to provoke *ar do vento* or *ar do tempo,* a condition characterized by migraines . . ." (1988:795).

Other natural explanations for illness take into account the effects of aging, heredity, personal nature (*natureza*), and gender. Contagion is another natural explanation, as are the effects of certain foods and eating habits. People also recognize the lack of economic resources, proper sanitation, and health services as structural causes of health problems. In the words of one person: "There are many illnesses because there are many poor" (1988:796).

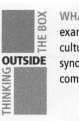

THINKING OUTSIDE THE BOX

WHAT IS an example of a culture-specific syndrome in your community?

In the psychosocial domain, emotions such as anger and hostility cause certain health problems. In the supernatural domain, spirits and magic can cause health problems. The African-Brazilian religious systems of the Bahia region encompass many spirits who can inflict illness. They include spirits of the unhappy dead and devil-like spirits. Some spirits cause specific illnesses; others bring general misfortune. In addition, envious people with the evil eye (*ohlo grosso*) cast spells on people and cause much illness.

The people of Feira de Santana recognize several levels of causality. In the case of stomachache, they might blame a quarrel (*underlying cause*), which prompted the aggrieved party to seek the intervention of a sorcerer (*intermediate cause*), who cast a spell (*immediate cause*), which led to the resulting illness. The multilayered causal understanding opens the way for many possible avenues of treatment (see Figure 7.1).

The multiple understandings of etiology in Bahia contrast with the more narrowly scientific understandings of causality in Western biomedicine. The most striking difference is the tendency for biomedical etiologies to exclude as causal the many kinds of problems related to structural issues and social inequality. In contrast to the more narrow biomedical approach to causality, medical anthropologists use the term **structural suffering,** or social suffering, which refers to health problems that powerful forces such as poverty, war, famine, and forced migration cause. Structural conditions affect health in many ways, with effects ranging from anxiety and depression to death. An example of a culture-specific syndrome that clearly implicates structural factors as causal is *sufriendo del agua,* or "suffering from water" (Ennis-McMillan 2001).

Research in a poor community in the Valley of Mexico, located in the central part of the country reveals that "suffering from water" is a common health problem, especially among women. The cause is the lack of water for drinking, cooking, and washing. Women, who are

---

ethno-etiologies: culturally specific causal explanations for health problems and suffering.

structural suffering: human health problems caused by such economic and political situations as war, famine, terrorism,

forced migration, and poverty. Also called *structural affliction.*

FIGURE 7.1   Three Levels of Causation for Morbidity and Mortality

▬ ▬ ▬

Ultimate	Poverty
Intermediate	Lack of food, malnutrition
Immediate	Dehydration, diarrhea

responsible for cooking and doing the washing, cannot count on water coming from their taps on a regular basis. This insecurity makes the women feel anxious and constantly in a state of nervous tension. The lack of access to water also means that the people are at higher risk of cholera, skin and eye infections, and other biophysical problems. The development of piped water systems in the Valley of Mexico bypassed low-income communities in favour of servicing wealthier urban neighbourhoods and supplying water for irrigation projects and the industrial sector. In Mexico, as a whole, nearly one-third of the population has inadequate access to water, in terms of quantity or quality.

Prevention

Many practices, based in either religious or secular beliefs, exist cross-culturally for preventing misfortune, suffering, and illness. Among the Maya of Guatemala (see Map. 7.2), *awas* is a common childhood illness (Wilson 1995). Children born with awas have lumps under the skin, marks on the skin, or albinism. People say that awas is caused by events that happen to the mother during her pregnancy: She may have been denied food she desired or have been pressured to eat food she did not want, or she may have encountered a rude, drunk, or angry person (usually a man). To prevent awas in babies, the Maya are extremely considerate of pregnant women. A pregnant woman, like land before planting, is sacred. People make sure to give her the food she wants, and they behave with respect in her presence. The ideal is that a pregnant woman should be content. Proper social behaviour is necessary for the health of the mother and baby.

Common forms of ritual health protection include charms, spells, and strings tied around parts of the body. After visiting a Buddhist temple in Japan, for example, one might purchase a small band to tie around the wrist to prevent future problems related to health and fertility. Wrist ties are commonly placed on infants in rural areas in India, especially by Hindus. Recall the *sukhwan* rituals among the Lao who often use protective wrist strings to strengthen children.

In Thailand, spirits (*phii*) are a recognized source of illness, death, and other misfortunes. One variety of *phii*, a widow ghost, is the sexually voracious spirit of a woman who has met an untimely and perhaps violent death. When a seemingly healthy man dies in his sleep, a widow

MAP 7.2   Central America. The countries of Central America share a similar geography as part of a long isthmus with a mountainous spine, active volcanoes, and rich soil. A federation that linked much of the region into the United Provinces of Central America existed from 1824 to 1838. The population of the region, around 40 million people, includes indigenous peoples and people of mixed indigenous and European ancestry. European colonialism has left a strong mark on the region, which is now heavily influenced by the United States and its interests in hemispheric hegemony.

SELECTED CULTURE-SPECIFIC SYNDROMES

Some medical anthropologists have been concerned about labelling locally specific complaints as culture-bound syndromes or culture-specific syndromes because the label may reinforce stereotypes and result in dismissing the complaints of women, refugees, or First Nations patients. A focus on static categorization may also obscure how meanings are linked to larger social and political contexts, and how diseases and disorders may be a form of resistance. The following work relevant to Canadian medical anthropology demonstrates some of the debates about whether a label names a unique cultural product or a local manifestation of a more general disease process.

- **"Old Hag"—Newfoundland and Labrador:** The "Old Hag" is a local term for a condition of sleep paralysis and hallucinations accompanied by the feeling that a great weight is pressing on the chest. Attacks of the "Old Hag" are not considered manifestations of mental illness, but rather normal occurrences, possibly caused by occupationally derived sleeplessness related to the demands of family fishing in Newfoundland (Firestone 1985).
- **Anfechtung—Hutterites in Manitoba:** *Anfechtung* is identified as a culture-bound syndrome characterized by a withdrawal from social contact, a feeling of having sinned, and concerns with religious unworthiness. Through the Hutterite baptism of

blood, disciples experience the suffering of Christ as an inner suffering of doubt and despair (Stephenson 1991:28). Stephenson reminds us that the stereotypes of Hutterites as dour, sober-faced authoritarians struggling under religious oppression influence the way illnesses are interpreted by health professionals.

- ***Pibloktoq* (Arctic hysteria)—Inuit:** Arctic hysteria is widely cited as a culture-bound syndrome characterized by brooding, depressive silences followed by convulsive hysterical seizures, followed by collapse and recovery with amnesia for the experience. Possible explanations for the syndrome include the ecology of long, dark, cold days; crowded conditions in confined houses; shamanistic beliefs; and dietary conditions such as calcium and vitamin D deficiency, and hypervitaminosis A. Marine animals contain high, toxic concentrations of vitamin A in their livers, kidneys, and fat, which are then consumed in large quantities by Inuit (Landy 1985). Landy argues that biological and cultural factors are inseparable, and taken together, may offer a biocultural approach to explaining emotional disturbances.
- **Windigo—Cree and Ojibwa:** "Windigo psychosis," long identified as a classic culture-bound syndrome, is described as a condition characterized by depression, nausea, distaste for usual foods, and

ghost is blamed. The wooden phalluses hung on the houses were protection against a possible sudden attack or death. Mary Beth Mills, an anthropologist working in northeastern Thailand, learned of the display of these carved wooden phalluses (see photo) as protection against this form of sudden death among men (Mills 1995):

> [I]nformants described these giant penises as decoys that would attract the interest of any *phii mae maai* which might come looking for a husband. The greedy ghosts would take their pleasure with the wooden penises and be satisfied, leaving the men of that household asleep, safe in their beds. (251)

In 1990, fear of a widow ghost attack spread throughout a wide area of northeastern Thailand. The fear was based on national news and radio reports of

unexplained deaths among Thai migrants working in Singapore. Local people, many of whom had family and friends employed in Singapore, interpreted these sudden deaths as caused by widow ghosts. Widow ghosts are known to roam about, searching for men whom they take as their "husbands." Mary Beth Mills returned to Baan Naa Sakae village at the time of the fear:

> I returned to Baan Naa Sakae village after a few days' absence to find the entire community of two hundred households festooned with wooden phalluses in all shapes and sizes. Ranging from the crudest wooden shafts to carefully carved images complete with coconut shell testicles and fishnet pubic hair, they adorned virtually every house and residential compound. The phalluses, I was told, were to protect residents, especially boys and

community healing: emphasizes social context as crucial to healing.

feelings of being possessed by a cannibalistic spirit. The condition is attributed to the Cree, Ojibwa, and other subarctic First Nations groups in northeastern Canada. Early reports hypothesized that the condition developed as a result of the stress of a diminishing or uncertain food supply. Landes's (1938) description of Ojibwa Windigo as a severe anxiety neurosis manifested as obsessive cannibalism has been criticized. However, others argue that the more significant question is, Under what conditions is a person likely to be accused of being a Windigo (Marano 1982)? While Windigo beliefs may structure how anxieties and psychoses are talked about, as reflected in the analysis of Cree "cannibalistic" myths, actual cases of cannibalistic psychotic behaviour are absent or very few in number. More significant questions concern how concepts like the Windigo relate to the mental health of First Nations peoples (Waldram 2004).

- **Evil eye (mal ojo)—Mediterranean and Latin American Hispanic groups:** Fitful sleep, crying without apparent cause, diarrhea, vomiting, and fever in a child or infant may be attributed to a fixed stare from an adult. An adult, usually female, may also be harmed by the evil and envious eye of another. Migliore (1997) looked at evil eye beliefs among Sicilian immigrants in Ontario, arguing that the term may refer to causes of general misfortune or specific illness. Carroll (1984) has linked evil eye beliefs to the weaning conflict and the loss of the maternal breast, setting up an emotional pattern that carries into adult life.

- **Nerves (Nervios, Nevra)—widespread in Euro-American contexts:** "Nerves" is a general term that refers to a culturally acceptable way of describing psychosocial distress to family and health professionals. Symptoms include headaches, dizziness, chest pain, trembling, disorientation, fatigue, lack of appetite, and feelings of melancholy and despair. Dona Davis (1984) reported cases of middle-aged women from the outports of Newfoundland complaining of bad nerves to their doctors and being given prescriptions for tranquilizers. In the local fishing communities, "woman the worrier" is a noble role and carries a wide range of meanings. Similarly, the narratives of first-generation Greek immigrant women in Montreal stressed their experiences of isolation, discrimination, and marital discord expressed through complaints of nevra (Lock and Wakewich-Dunk 1990). In both cases, nerves may be thought of as a form of communication about living with stress, poverty, and deprivation.

A wooden phallus in a household compound in a village in northeastern Thailand is displayed to protect men from a sudden attack or death. ■ (Source: Mary Beth Mills)

men, from the "nightmare deaths" (lai tai) at the hands of malevolent "widow ghosts" (phii mae maai). (249)

As radio and other news coverage of the deaths in Singapore diminished over several weeks, so did concerns about widow ghosts, and villagers quietly removed the protective phalluses.

Ways of Healing

In this section, we consider two approaches to healing, one in southern Africa and the other in Malaysia, Southeast Asia. We also discuss healers and healing substances.

Community Healing Systems

A general distinction can be drawn between private and **community healing.** The former addresses individual bodily ailments in isolation and the latter emphasizes social context as crucial to healing. Compared to Western biomedicine, many non-Western systems make greater use of public healing and community involvement. Many First Nations groups in Canada make use of healing circles to restore balance in their lives. Often the medicine wheel, a symbol for the balance of spirit, heart, mind, and body is used in community healing. An example of public or community healing comes from the Ju/wasi foragers of the Kalahari Desert in southern Africa (review the Ethnographic Profile in Chapter 1 on page 22). Ju/wasi healing emphasizes the mobilization of community "energy" as a key element in the cure:

> The central event in this tradition is the all-night healing dance. Four times a month on the average, night signals the start of a healing dance. The women sit around the fire, singing and rhythmically clapping. The men, sometimes joined by the women, dance around the

A Ju/wasi healer in a trance, in the Kalahari Desert, southern Africa. Most healers are men, but some are women. ■ (Source: © Irven DeVore/AnthroPhoto)

singers. As the dance intensifies, *num* or spiritual energy is activated by the healers, both men and women, but mostly among the dancing men. As *num* is activated in them, they begin to kia or experience an enhancement of their consciousness. While experiencing kia, they heal all those at the dance. . . . (Katz 1982:34)

An important aspect of the Ju/'hoansi healing system is its openness. Everyone has access to it. The role of healer is also open. There is no special class of healers with special privileges. More than half of all adult men and about 10 percent of adult women are healers.

Humoral Healing Systems

Humoral healing systems are approaches to healing based on a philosophy of balance among certain elements within the body and within the person's environment (McElroy and Townsend 1996). In this system, food and drugs have different effects on the body and are classified as either "heating" or "cooling" (the quotation marks indicate that these properties are not the same as thermal measurements). Diseases are the result of bodily imbalances—too much heat or coolness—which must be counteracted through dietary changes or medicines that will restore balance.

Humoral healing systems have been practised for thousands of years in the Middle East, the Mediterranean, and much of Asia, and spread to the New World through Spanish colonization. They have shown substantial resilience in the face of Western biomedicine, often incorporating it into their own framework—for example, in the classification of biomedical treatments as either heating or cooling. Humoral logic persists in Euro-American public culture in advice such as "feed a cold; starve a fever."

In Malaysia, several different humoral traditions coexist, reflecting the region's history of contact with outside cultures. Malaysia has been influenced by trade and contact between its indigenous culture and that of India, China, and the Arab-Islamic world for around 2000 years. Indian, Chinese, and Arabic medical systems are similar in that all define health as the balance of opposing elements within the body, although each has its own variations. Indigenous belief systems may have been especially compatible with these imported models because they also were based on concepts of heat and coolness.

Insights about what the indigenous systems were like comes from ethnographic accounts about the Orang Asli, Aboriginal peoples of the Malaysian interior who are less affected by contact. A conceptual system of hot–cold opposition dominates Orang Asli cosmological, medical, and social theories. The properties and meanings of heat

---

humoral healing systems: approaches to healing based on a philosophy of balance among certain elements within the body and within the person's environment.

shaman: a healer who mediates between humans and the spirit world.

ethnobotany: explores the cultural knowledge of local plants, including the use of plants as medicines.

and coolness differ from those of Islamic, Indian, or Chinese humoralism in several ways. In the Islamic, Indian, and Chinese systems, for example, death is the ultimate result of too much coolness. Among the Orang Asli, excessive heat is the primary cause of mortality. Heat emanates from the sun, and it is associated with excrement, blood, misfortune, disease, and death. Humanity's hot blood makes people mortal, and their consumption of meat speeds the process. Heat causes menstruation, violent emotions, aggression, and drunkenness.

Coolness, in contrast, is vital for health. Health is protected by avoiding the harmful effects of the sun by staying in the forest shade. This belief justifies the rejection of agriculture by some groups because it exposes people to the sun. Treatment of illness is designed to reduce or remove heat. If someone were to fall ill in a clearing, the entire group would relocate to the coolness of the forest. The forest is also a source of cooling leaves and herbs. Healers are cool and retain their coolness by bathing in cold water and sleeping far from the fire.

Extreme cold, however, can be harmful. Dangerous levels of coolness are associated with the time right after birth since the mother is believed to have lost substantial heat: The new mother must avoid drinking or bathing in cold water. She increases her body heat by tying sashes

Steven Benally, Jr., an apprentice medicine man, practises for a ceremony in his hogan on the Navajo Reservation near Window Rock, Arizona. An apprentice often studies for a decade or more.
■ (Source: Kevin Fleming/CORBIS)

containing warm leaves or ashes around her waist, bathing herself and her newborn child in warm water, and lying near a fire.

Healers

In an informal sense, everyone is a "healer" since self-treatment is always the first consideration in dealing with a perceived health problem. Yet in all cultures some people become recognized as having special abilities to diagnose and treat health problems. Specialists include midwife, bonesetter (someone who resets broken bones), **shaman** (a healer who mediates between humans and the spirit world), herbalist, general practitioner, psychiatrist, acupuncturist, chiropractor, dentist, and hospice worker. Cross-cultural evidence indicates some common features of healers: selection (certain individuals may show more ability for entry into healing roles); training (this often involves years of observation and practice, and the training may be arduous); certification (this may be either legal or ritual); professional image (the role is demarcated through behaviour, dress, and markers such as the white coat in the West or the Siberian shaman's tambourine for calling the spirits); and expectation of payment (compensation is expected in kind or cash) (Foster and Anderson 1978:104–115).

Several nonbiomedical healing specializations have declined due to pressures from and competition with Western biomedicine. Midwifery is an important example of a healing role that is endangered in many parts of the world as birth has become increasingly medicalized and brought into the institutional world of the hospital rather than the home. In Costa Rica (see Map 7.2 on page 179), a recent government campaign to promote hospital births with a biomedical doctor in attendance has achieved a rate of 98 percent of all births taking place in hospitals (Jenkins 2003). This achievement means that midwives, especially in rural areas, can no longer support themselves, and they are abandoning their profession. The promotion of hospital births has destroyed the positive elements of community-based midwifery and its provision of social support and techniques such as massage for the mother-to-be.

Healing Substances

Around the world, many different natural or manufactured substances are used as medicines for preventing or curing health problems. Anthropologists have spent more time studying the use of medicines in non-Western cultures than in the West, although a more fully cross-cultural approach is emerging that examines the use of Western pharmaceuticals as well (van der Geest, Whyte, and Hardon 1996). **Ethnobotany** explores the cultural knowledge of local plants, including the use of plants as medicines. Increasing awareness of the range of potentially useful plants worldwide provides a strong incentive for protecting both

Traditional medicines available in a shop in Toronto include dried ingredients and patent medicines from Hong Kong, Taiwan, and mainland China. ■ (Source: Courtesy of Ana Ning)

biodiversity and indigenous cultural knowledge of plant uses. A family physician from Toronto visited Ojibwa elders in a Georgian Bay community, where women healers explained their use of plant products for healing, including catnip, licorice, cedar leaves, peppermint, and red sumac berries (Borins 1995; see also Walker's inventory of edible forest plants of the Northwest Territories, 1984).

Leaves of the coca plant have for centuries been a key part of the medicinal systems of the Andean region of South America (Allen 2002). Coca is important in rituals, in masking hunger pains, and in combatting the cold (Carter, Morales, and Mamani 1981). In terms of health, Andean people use coca to treat gastrointestinal problems, sprains, swellings, and colds. A survey of coca use in Bolivia showed a high prevalence rate. About 85 percent of 3500 people reported that they use coca medicinally. The leaf may be chewed or combined with herbs or roots and water to make a *maté*, a medicinal beverage. Trained herbalists have specialized knowledge about preparing some matés. One maté, for example, is for treating asthma. Made of a certain root and coca leaves, it is taken three to four times a day until the patient is cured.

Minerals are also widely used for prevention and healing. For example, many people worldwide believe that bathing in water that contains high levels of sulphur or other minerals promotes health and cures ailments such as arthritis and rheumatism. Thousands of people every year go to the Dead Sea, which lies beneath sea level between Israel and Jordan, for treating skin diseases

(Lew 1994). The mud from the shore and the nearby sulphur springs relieves skin ailments such as psoriasis. German studies conclude that it is more cost-effective to pay for a trip to the Dead Sea than to hospitalize a psoriasis patient. In Japan, bathing in mineral waters is popular as a health-promotion practice.

Western patent medicines are increasingly popular worldwide. Although these medicines have many benefits, some negative effects include frequent use without prescription and overprescription. Sale of patent medicines is often unregulated, and self-treating individuals can buy them in a local pharmacy. The popularity and overuse of capsules and injections has led to a growing health crisis related to the emergence of drug-resistant disease strains. In addition, multinational pharmaceutical companies aggressively market medicines, and even "dump" out-of-date and recalled products not permitted for sale in North America.

Theoretical Approaches in Medical Anthropology

Here we consider four approaches to understanding health systems. The first emphasizes the importance of the environment in shaping health problems and their spread. The second highlights symbols and meaning as critical in people's expression of suffering and healing practices. The third underlines the need to look at economic and political factors, and the fourth applies anthropological knowledge to improving health care.

The Ecological/Epidemiological Approach

The **ecological/epidemiological approach** examines how aspects of the natural environment interact with culture to cause health problems and to influence their spread throughout populations. According to this approach, research should focus on gathering information about the environmental context and social patterns that affect health, such as food distribution within the family, sexual practices, hygiene, and population contact. Research tends to be quantitative and etic, although this approach is often combined with qualitative and emic methods to provide richer results (as we discussed in Chapter 2).

The ecological/epidemiological approach yields findings relevant to public health programs by revealing causal links between environmental context and health problems. It also helps by providing socially targeted

---

ecological/epidemiological approach: examines how aspects of the natural environment interact with culture to cause

health problems and to influence their spread throughout populations.

Women working in padi fields near Jinghong, China. Agricultural work done in standing water increases the risk of hookworm infection.
■ (Source: Peter Menzel/Stock Boston)

information about groups "at risk" for specific problems. For example, although hookworm is extremely common throughout rural China, researchers learned that rice cultivators have the highest rates of all. This pattern is related to the fact that the disease is spread through night soil (human excrement used as fertilizer) that is applied to the fields where the cultivators work.

Another significant environmental factor that has important effects on health is urbanization. As archaeologists have documented about the past, settled populations living in dense clusters are more likely than mobile populations to experience a range of health problems, including infectious diseases and malnutrition (Cohen 1989). Such problems are apparent among many recently settled pastoralist groups in East and West Africa. One study compared the health status of two groups of Turkana men in northwest Kenya (see Map 6.2 on page 159): those who were still mobile pastoralists and those who lived in a town (Barkey, Campbell, and Leslie 2001). The two groups differ strikingly in diet, physical activities, and health. Pastoralist Turkana eat mainly animal foods (milk, meat, and blood), spend much time in rigorous physical activity, and live in large family groups. Settled Turkana men eat mainly maize and beans. Their sedentary (settled) life means less physical activity and exercise. In terms of health, the settled men had more eye infections, chest infections, backache, and cough/colds. Pastoralist Turkana men were not, however, free of health problems. One-fourth of the pastoralist men had eye infections, but among the settled men, one-half had eye infections. In terms of nutrition, the settled Turkana were shorter and had greater body mass than the taller and slimmer pastoralists.

Cities present many stressors to human health as well as opportunities for improved health through greater access to health care. Often, cities are comprised of diverse social categories, varying by class and ethnicity. These groups have different experiences of health stressors and opportunities. In the United States, the incidence of tuberculosis (TB) has increased in recent years, and this increase has occurred mainly in urban areas (DeFirdinando 1999). Tuberculosis is spread by infected humans, and its rate of spread is increased by crowding, poverty, poor housing, and lack of access to health care. In the United States, rates of tuberculosis are generally higher in southern than in northern states, with the exceptions of New York and Illinois, given their large urban populations. Beginning in the 1990s, outbreaks of multidrug-resistant mycobacterium tuberculosis (MDRTB), a new strain of TB that is resistant to conventional drugs, led to its being recognized by public health authorities as a major "new" infectious disease.

Tuberculosis, and its several new strains, is also a frequent complication of HIV/AIDS. In New York City, far more people have TB and HIV/AIDS than can be accommodated in public hospitals. Homeless shelters are inadequate to care for the number of applicants who are not only homeless but also seriously ill with infectious diseases such as HIV/AIDS

Colonialism and Disease

Anthropologists have applied the ecological/epidemiological approach to the study of the impaired health and survival of indigenous peoples resulting from colonial contact. Findings about the effects of colonial contact are negative, ranging from the quick and outright extermination of indigenous peoples to resilient adjustment, among other groups, to drastically changed conditions.

In the western hemisphere, European colonialism brought a dramatic decline in the indigenous populations they contacted, although disagreements exist about the numbers involved (Joralemon 1982). In coordination with archaeologists and colonial historians, medical anthropologists have tried to estimate the role of disease in depopulation compared with other factors such as warfare, harsh labour practices, and general cultural disruption, and to discover which diseases were most important. Research along these lines indicates that the precontact New World was largely free of the major European infectious diseases such as smallpox, measles, and typhus, and perhaps also syphilis, leprosy, and malaria. The exposure of indigenous peoples to these infectious diseases, therefore, was likely to have a massive impact, given the people's complete lack of resistance. One analyst compared contact to a "biological war":

> Smallpox was the captain of the men of death in that war, typhus fever the first lieutenant, and measles the second lieutenant. More terrible than the conquistadores on horseback, more deadly than sword and gunpowder, they made the conquest by the whites a walkover as compared to what it would have been without their aid. They were the forerunners of civilization, the companions of Christianity, the friends of the invader. (Ashburn 1947:98, quoted in Joralemon 1982:112)

This quotation emphasizes the importance of the three major diseases in Latin American colonial history: smallpox, measles, and malaria. A later arrival, cholera, also had severe effects because its transmission through contaminated water and food thrives in areas of poor sanitation. In Canada, the two greatest epidemics affecting Aboriginal health were smallpox in the sixteenth and seventeenth centuries, and tuberculosis, which continues to be a major problem today (Waldram, Herring, and Young 1995). First Nations groups in Canada today also face the chronic diseases of the twentieth century, such as diabetes and heart disease. Some of these diseases may be linked to disruptions in traditional diets, a key component of maintaining health.

Enduring effects of European colonialism among indigenous peoples worldwide include high rates of depression and suicide, low self-esteem, high rates of child and adolescent drug use, and high rates of alcoholism, obesity, and hypertension. **Historical trauma** refers to the intergenerational transfer of the emotional and psychological effects of colonialism from parents to children (Brave Heart 2004). It is closely associated with substance abuse as a vehicle for attempting to cover the continued pain of historical trauma. Troubled parents create a difficult family situation for children who tend to replicate their parents' negative coping mechanisms. The concept of historical trauma helps to expand the scope of traditional epidemiological studies by drawing on factors from the past to explain the social and spatial distribution of contemporary health problems. Such an approach may prove more effective in devising culturally appropriate ways to alleviate health problems.

The Interpretive Approach

Interpretive approaches to health systems consider how people in different cultures label, describe, and experience illness and how healing offers meaningful responses to individual and communal distress. An important direction in interpretive medical anthropology has been to focus on the explanatory models and illness narratives of individual sufferers in order to understand the cultural realities of individual patients (Kleinman 1988). Illness

A Korean mansin performs the Tale of Princess Pari, a female hero who braves the perils of the underworld in quest of an herb that will restore her dying parents. Twenty years ago, this segment of the *kut* for the dead would have been performed outside the house gate. In urban Korea, it is performed inside to avoid complaints about noise and traffic obstruction. ■ (Source: Laurel Kendall)

historical trauma: the intergenerational transfer of the emotional and psychological effects of colonialism from parents to children.

placebo effect: a healing effect obtained through the positive power of believing that a particular method is efficacious

critical medical anthropology: considers the way economic and political structures shape people's health status, their access to health care, and the prevailing healing systems.

medicalization: the labelling of a particular issue or problem as medical and requiring medical treatment when, in fact, its cause may be economic or political.

and healing as dialectical processes involve the interaction between physical processes and social, cultural, and psychological contexts. Kleinman argued that Western biomedicine fails to recognize this, unlike many non-Western medical systems, which consider sufferers in their sociocultural context.

Interpretive approaches also pay attention to symbolic aspects of healing, such as ritual trance. Claude Lévi-Strauss, in a classic essay called "The Effectiveness of Symbols" (1967), examined how a song sung during childbirth among the Kuna Indians of Panama helps women through the difficulties of childbirth. His main point was that healing systems provide meaning to people who are suffering. The provision of meaning offers psychological support and courage to the afflicted and may enhance healing through what Western science calls the **placebo effect** (a healing effect obtained through the positive power of believing that a particular method is efficacious). Anthropological research suggests that between 10 and 90 percent of the efficacy of medical prescriptions lies in the placebo effect (Moerman 1979, 1983, 1992). Several features may be involved: the power of the person prescribing a particular treatment, the very act of prescription, and concrete details about the medicine, such as its colour, name, and place of origin (van der Geest, Whyte, and Hardon 1996).

Critical Medical Anthropology

Critical medical anthropology considers the way economic and political structures shape people's health status, their access to health care, and the prevailing healing systems. Critical medical anthropologists examine how economic and political systems create and perpetuate social inequality in health status. They have also exposed the power of **medicalization,** or the labelling of a particular issue or problem as medical and requiring medical treatment when, in fact, its cause may be economic or political.

Critical medical anthropologists examine how larger structural forces determine the distribution of illness and people's responses to it. But they are also concerned to see how individuals may, through personal agency, resist such forces. Critical medical anthropology also examines Western biomedicine itself, viewing it as a global power structure, critiquing medical training, and looking at doctor–patient relationships as manifestations of social control rather than social liberation. For example, Canadian medical anthropologist Pamela Downe (1999) analyzed how street prostitutes in Costa Rica medicalize the violence and discrimination in their lives, but resist and cope through their own brand of humour and jokes.

Many Canadian medical anthropologists favour a critical medical anthropology approach, reflecting, perhaps, their experience with national debates about universal health care and the social safety net. Margaret Lock and Gilles Bibeau (1995) link Canadian debates about language, national identity, and multiculturalism to the eclecticism and pluralism of method characteristic of medical anthropology in Canada.

Social Inequality and Poverty

Broad distinctions exist between the most common health problems of rich, industrial countries and those of poor, less industrial countries (United Nations Development Programme 1995). In the former, major causes of death are circulatory diseases, malignant cancers, HIV/AIDS, alcohol consumption, and tobacco consumption. In poor countries, tuberculosis, malaria, and HIV/AIDS are the three leading causes of death. Substantial evidence indicates that poverty is the primary cause of morbidity (sickness) and mortality (death) in both industrialized and developing countries (Farmer 2005). It may be manifested in different ways—for example, though child malnutrition in Chad or Nepal and through street violence among the urban poor of wealthy countries.

Throughout the developing world, rates of childhood malnutrition are inversely related to income. As income increases, calorie intake as a percentage of recommended daily allowances also increases (Zaidi 1988:122). Thus, increasing the income levels of the poor may be the most direct way to influence health and nutrition. Yet, in contrast to this seemingly logical approach, many health and nutrition programs around the world have been focused on treating the outcomes of poverty rather than its causes.

Critical medical anthropologists describe the widespread practice of treating health problems caused by poverty with pills or other medical options. An example is Nancy Scheper-Hughes's research in Bom Jesus, northeastern Brazil, mentioned in Chapters 5 and 6 (1992) (see Map 3.4, page 74). The people of Bom Jesus who experienced symptoms of weakness, insomnia, and anxiety received pills from the local doctor. But the people were, in fact, hungry and needed food. This medicalization of poverty serves the interests of pharmaceutical companies and helps to keep inequitable social systems in place.

Similar critical analyses show how Western psychiatry often treats symptoms and serves to keep people in their places rather than addressing root causes such as powerlessness, unemployment, and thwarted social aspirations. One example of psychiatric medicalization is the high rates of depression among women in North America and their treatment with psychotropic drugs.

Western Medical Training Examined

Since the 1980s, critical medical anthropologists have studied Western biomedicine as a cultural system. They advocate for greater recognition of social factors in diagnosis and treatment, reduction of the spread of biomedical technology, and diversification of medical specialists

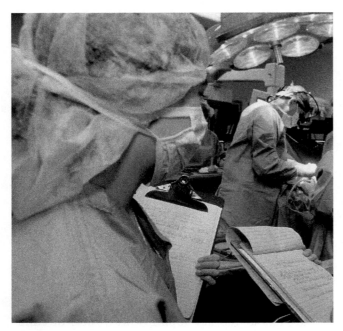

Medical students in training in a Western biomedical setting. These students are observing brain surgery.
■ (Source: © Lara Jo Regan/Getty Images)

to include alternative healing, such as massage, acupuncture, and chiropracty (Scheper-Hughes 1992). Some of their work critiques Western medical school training and its emphasis on technology.

Robbie Davis-Floyd (1987) examined how obstetric students absorbed the technological model of birth as a core value of Western obstetrics. This model treats the body as a machine. One of the residents in the study explained: "We shave 'em, we prep 'em, we hook 'em up to the IV and administer sedation. We deliver the baby, it goes to the nursery and the mother goes to her room. There's no room for niceties around here. We just move 'em right on through. It's not hard to see it like an assembly line" (292). The goal is the "production" of a healthy baby, with little concern for the mother's experience.

This goal involves the use of sophisticated machines such as fetal monitors and ultrasound. Lisa Mitchell (2001) shows how ultrasound allows people to "see" into the interior of pregnant women, creating images formed around competing discourses about the fetus as cultural object.

How does obstetrical training socialize medical students into accepting this technological model? First, medical training involves a lengthy process of "cognitive retrogression" in which the students go through an intellectual hazing process. During the first two years of medical school, most courses are basic sciences; learning tends to be rote, and vast quantities of material must be memorized. The second phase, which could be termed dehumanization, is one in which medical school training succeeds in overriding humanitarian ideals through its emphasis on technology and objectification of the patient (Davis-Floyd 1987:299). Since midwifery was legalized in Ontario in 1994, midwives are using more medical technology to fulfill their professional obligations and to respond to the choices of their clients. However they still resist the medicalization of childbirth in structural, cultural and interpretive ways (MacDonald 2007).

Studies of other biomedical specialists, such as surgeons, make the same point (Cassell 1991) and show how the power of the physician is correlated with the complexity of the technology they use. Other studies reveal the problem of reliance on technology when healing requires human understanding and interaction rather than machines (Fadiman 1997).

Clinical Medical Anthropology

Clinical medical anthropology, or applied medical anthropology, is the application of anthropological knowledge to further the goals of health-care providers. It may involve improving doctor–patient understandings in multicultural settings, making recommendations about culturally appropriate health intervention programs, and providing insights about factors related to disease that medical practitioners do not usually take into account. For example, making use of ethnographic work on Ojibwa concepts of disease categories, a successful treatment program for diabetes was developed for Ojibwa in Toronto. The program was effective because it acknowledged the historical and social context of the disease and emphasized personal control over lifestyle in the rapidly changing urban environment of Toronto (Hagey 1984).

Although critical medical anthropology and clinical medical anthropology may seem diametrically opposed to each other (with the first seeking to critique and even limit the power and range of the medical establishment and the second seeking to make it more effective), some medical anthropologists are building bridges between the two perspectives.

An example of a clinical medical anthropologist who combines the two approaches is Robert Trotter (1987), who conducted research on lead poisoning among children in Mexican American communities. The three most common sources of lead poisoning of children in North America are eating lead-based paint chips, living near a smelter where the dust has high lead content, and eating or drinking from pottery made with an improperly treated lead glaze. The discovery of an unusual case of

clinical medical anthropology: the application of anthropological knowledge to further the goals of health-care providers.

Lessons Applied

PROMOTING VACCINATION PROGRAMS

Vaccination programs, especially as promoted by UNICEF, are often introduced in countries with much fanfare, but they are sometimes met with little enthusiasm by the target population. In India, many people are suspicious that vaccination programs are clandestine family planning programs (Nichter 1996). In other instances, fear of foreign vaccines prompts people to reject inoculations. Overall, acceptance rates of vaccination have been lower than Western public health planners expected. What factors have limited the acceptance of vaccination?

Public health planners have not paid enough attention to the reasons why certain innovations are accepted or rejected. There have been problems in supply (clinics do not always have vaccines on hand). Cultural understandings of illness and the role of inoculations have not been considered. Surveys show that many mothers have a partial or inaccurate understanding of what the vaccines protect against. In some cases, people's perceptions and priorities did not match what the vaccines were supposed to address. In others, people did not see the value of multiple vaccinations; a once-vaccinated and healthy child was not considered to be in need of another inoculation.

To improve the acceptance of vaccinations, applied medical anthropologists might work on promoting trust in the public health program, providing locally sensible understandings of what the vaccinations do and do not do, and making more effective public health communication by working with public health specialists to enhance their understanding of and attention to local cultural practices and beliefs.

FOOD FOR THOUGHT

- Are all vaccines of unquestionable benefit to the recipients? Search the Internet for information on the pros and possible cons of new vaccines.

---

lead poisoning by health-care professionals in Los Angeles in the early 1980s prompted investigations that produced understanding of a fourth cause: the use of a traditional healing remedy, *azarcon,* which contained lead, by people of the Mexican-American community. *Azarcon* is given for the treatment of *empacho,* which is a combination of indigestion and constipation, believed to be caused by food sticking to the abdominal wall. Trotter then investigated the availability and use of *azarcon* in Mexico, and its distribution in the North America. His work resulted in restrictions on *azarcon* to prevent its further use, recommendations about the need to provide a substitute remedy for the treatment of *empacho* that would not have harmful side effects, and ideas about how to advertise this substitute. Throughout his involvement, Trotter combined several roles: researcher, consultant, and program developer, all of which brought anthropological knowledge toward the solution of a health problem.

Much work in clinical medical anthropology involves health communication (Nichter and Nichter 1996: 327–328). Anthropologists can help health educators in the development of more meaningful messages through

- addressing local images of ethnophysiology and acknowledging popular health concerns;
- taking seriously local illness terms and conventions;
- adopting local styles of communication;

- identifying subgroups within the population that may be responsive to different types of messages and incentives;
- monitoring the response of communities to health messages over time and facilitating corrections in communication when needed; and
- exposing and removing possible victim-blaming in health messages.

These principles helped health-care officials understand local response to public vaccination programs in several countries of Asia and Africa (Nichter 1996) (see the Lessons Applied box).

Communication through audio teleconferencing has also provided support to people in more remote or rural areas. In Newfoundland, women with a history of breast cancer found teleconferencing to be invaluable in dealing with the emotional upheaval of the disease. They needed to talk with other women who knew what living with breast cancer was about, particularly long-term survivors. With teleconferencing, one participant explained, the community didn't have "to know my business" (Church, Curran, and Solberg 2000:22).

Cross-cultural communication is also important in multicultural health settings in Canada, an issue addressed in the book *Cross-Cultural Caring: A Handbook for Health Professionals in Western Canada* (Waxler-Morrison, Anderson, and Richardson 2005). The authors provide culturally sensitive advice about

---

the cultural context of disease to help practitioners make sense of their patients' distress. However, cultural sensitivity and even ethnic matching of patients and practitioners does not guarantee good health care.

Globalization and Change

With globalization, health problems move around the world and into remote locations and cultures more rapidly than ever before. The HIV/AIDS pandemic is one tragic example. Other new epidemics include SARS and avian (bird) flu. At the same time, Western culture, including biomedicine, is on the move. Perhaps no other aspect of Western culture, except for the capitalist market system and the English language, has so permeated the rest of the world as Western biomedicine. But the cultural flow is not one-way. Many people in North America and Europe are turning to forms of non-Western and nonbiomedical healing, such as acupuncture and massage therapy. In this section, we consider new and emerging health challenges, changes in healing, and examples of how applied medical anthropology has increasing relevance.

The New Infectious Diseases

The 1950s brought hope that infectious diseases were being controlled through Western scientific advances such as antibiotic drugs, vaccines against childhood diseases, and improved technology for sanitation. In North America, death from infections common in the late nineteenth and early twentieth centuries was no longer a major threat in the 1970s. In tropical countries, pesticides lowered rates of malaria by controlling the mosquito populations. The 1980s, however, were the beginning of an era of shaken confidence with the onset and rapid spread of the HIV/AIDS pandemic. New contexts for exposure and contagion are being created through increased international travel and migration, expansion of populations into previously uninhabited forest areas, changing sexual behaviour, and overcrowding in cities. Several new and re-emerging diseases are related to unsafe technological developments. For example, soft contact lenses can cause eye infections from a virus. In the early 1980s, many women in North America were diagnosed with a new disease, toxic shock syndrome, caused by a bacterial toxin possibly related to dioxins, a by-product of the chlorine bleaching process used to bleach tampons.

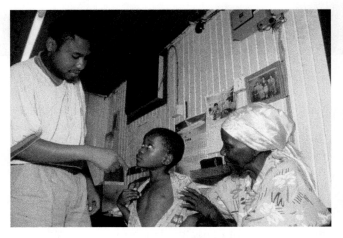

A woman takes her 8-year-old grandson who has HIV/AIDS to a clinic in Dar es Salaam, Tanzania. Throughout the world, increasing numbers of children are infected and are, at the same time, orphaned because their parents have died of the disease.
■ (Source: © Sean Sprague/Stock Boston, LLC)

Many medical anthropologists are contributing their expertise to understanding the causes for and distribution of the new infectious diseases through studying social patterns and cultural practices. Research about HIV/AIDS addresses factors such as intravenous drug use, sexual behaviour, and condom use among different groups and how intervention programs could be better designed and targeted (see the Critical Thinking box on page 192).

Diseases of Development

Diseases of development are health problems (both diseases and illnesses) caused or increased by economic development activities (O'Manique 2004). Examples of diseases in this category are schistosomiasis, river blindness, malaria, and tuberculosis. The construction of dams and irrigation systems throughout the tropical world has brought dramatically increased rates of schistosomiasis (a disease caused by the presence of a parasitic worm in the blood system). Over 200 million people suffer from this debilitating disease, with prevalence rates the highest in sub-Saharan countries in Africa (Michaud, Gordon, and Reich 2004). The larvae hatch from eggs and mature in slow-moving water such as lakes and rivers (see Figure 7.2). When mature, they can penetrate human (or other

---

disease of development: a health problem caused or increased by economic development activities that affect the environment and people's relationship with it.

medical pluralism: the existence of more than one health system in a culture, or a government policy to promote the

integration of local healing systems into biomedical practice.

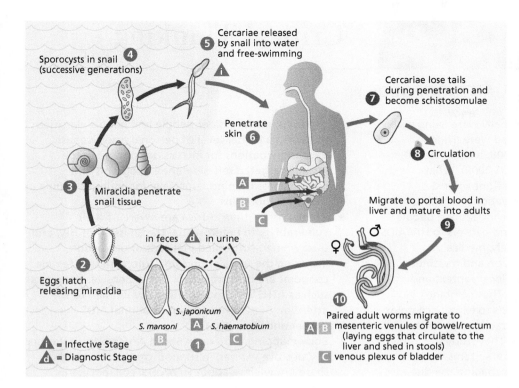

FIGURE 7.2 The Schistomomiasis Cycle. Cultural anthropologists are less interested in the technical details of the cycle of infection and re-infection as they are in the environmental, structural, and social context of the disease, and its social effects. (*Source:* Centers for Disease Control, www.dpd.cdc. gov/dpdx.)

animal) skin with which they come into contact. Once inside the human body, the adult schistosomes breed in the veins around the human bladder and bowel. They send fertilized eggs through urine and feces into the environment. These eggs then contaminate water in which they hatch into larvae.

Anthropologists' research has documented steep increases in the rates of schistosomiasis at high dam sites in developing countries (Scudder 1973). This increased risk is caused by the dams slowing the rate of water flow. Stagnant water systems offer an ideal environment for development of the larvae. Opponents of the construction of large dams have used this information in support of their position.

New diseases of development continue to appear. One of these is Kyasanur forest disease, or KFD (Nichter 1992). This viral disease was first identified in 1957 in southern India:

> Resembling influenza, at onset KFD is marked by sudden chills, fever, frontal headaches, stiffness of the neck, and body pain. Diarrhea and vomiting often follow on the third day. High fever is continuous for five to fifteen days, during which time a variety of additional symptoms may manifest themselves, including gastrointestinal bleeding, persistent cough with blood-tinged sputum, and bleeding gums. In more serious cases, the infection progresses to bronchial pneumonia, meningitis, paralysis, encephalitis, and hemorrhage. (1992:224)

In the early 1980s, an epidemic of KFD swept through over 30 villages near the Kyasanur forest in Karnataka state, southern India (see Map 8.5 on page 215).

Mortality rates in hospitals ranged between 12 and 18 percent of those admitted. Investigation revealed that KFD especially affected agricultural workers and cattle tenders who were most exposed to newly cleared areas near the forest. In the cleared areas, international companies established plantations and initiated cattle raising. Ticks were the vector transmitting the disease from the cattle to the people. Ticks had long existed in the local ecosystem, but their numbers greatly increased in the cleared area, finding many inviting hosts in the cattle and in the workers. Thus, human modification of the ecosystem through deforestation and introduction of large-scale cattle raising caused the epidemic and shaped its social distribution.

Medical Pluralism

Contact between cultures may lead to a situation in which aspects of both cultures coexist: two (or more) different languages, religions, systems of law, or health systems, for example. The term **medical pluralism** refers to the presence of multiple health systems within a society. Medical pluralism provides both options and complications. First, something may be classified as a health problem in some cultures and not in others. For example, spirit possession is welcomed in some cultures but might be labelled schizophrenia by Western psychiatry. Second, the same issue may be classified as having a different cause (such as supernatural versus germ theories) and therefore require different treatments. Third, certain treatments may be rejected as violating cultural rules.

HIV/AIDS AND MEDICAL ANTHROPOLOGY

In 2007, over 33 million people globally were living with HIV, and 68 percent of those infected were living in sub-Saharan Africa. In Canada in 2008, around 58 000 people were living with HIV (UNAIDS 2008). What role do medical anthropologists play in the fight against HIV/AIDS? They bring special observational methods to HIV/AIDS research teams, often living among people with HIV/AIDS in order to understand barriers to HIV/AIDS prevention and treatment. Ultimately, medical anthropologists help make prevention and treatment programs more appropriate to the local context and language, and thus more effective. They combine qualitative and quantitative methods to explore complex and sensitive issues such as the interaction between gender, body image, and sexuality. They study the links between individual practices, cultural systems, and the larger political and economic forces shaping the disease. For example, holistic approaches have been effective in showing how AIDS relates to poverty and food insecurity.

The following examples show the kind of issues medical anthropologists are exploring in HIV/AIDS research, particularly on the topics of local perception of disease and on improving prevention and treatment programs.

- In the late 1980s, when HIV/AIDS was first recognized in Haiti, many Haitians thought it was a "disease of the city," contracted through sexual intercourse, or a "jealousy sickness" brought on one poor person by another through magic (Farmer 1990). The first explanation emphasizes the conventional biomedical definition of HIV/AIDS as an infectious disease; the second speaks to the Haitians' recognition of the social, political, and economic influences that render particular individuals or groups susceptible to illnesses of all kinds.
- San Jose prostitutes also recognize HIV/AIDS as an infectious disease, but locate it as part of a complex of contagion that includes drug abuse, diabetes, and violence (Downe 1997). While they are ready to embrace biomedicine—specifically "germs"—as a way to explain this contagion, they refuse to be defined as the vectors of the disease.
- A study assessing attitudes toward condom use among white, African American, and Hispanic respondents in the United States (Bowen and Trotter 1995) found that whites were more likely to use condoms, followed by Hispanics, with lowest use among African Americans. Across all groups, people with "main partners" compared to "casual partners" were more likely to use condoms, as were older people and people classified as having a higher level of personal assertiveness. Recommendations for increasing condom usage include targeted self-awareness programs and assertiveness training, especially for younger people in casual relationships.
- Women in southern Africa are aware of their vulnerability to heterosexual transmission of HIV, and seek women-controlled methods of protection, including the female condom. Unfortunately, female condoms are in short supply and expensive. Networks such as ATHENA bring the needs of women to the attention of national and international AIDS agencies (Susser and Stein 2004).
- Body mapping projects in South Africa bring together HIV positive women in support groups, where they share knowledge about HIV/AIDS, collaborate in narrative and artistic therapy, advocate for treatment, and celebrate with body-based performances. The traced and decorated outline of their bodies becomes a starting point for discussing life histories and experiences of being HIV positive, and brings together biomedical and local knowledge of the body (Wienand 2006, page 23).
- Even preventive programs that emphasize social conditions can be ineffective in practice if bureaucracies stigmatize and target marginal groups, especially low-caste and ethnic minority sex workers. For example, in Nepal, Pigg (2001) found that groups working on AIDS prevention and treatment do not challenge power relations that perpetuate patterns of ill health. Similarly, lack of informed consent and the need for constant attention to ethical issues in HIV/AIDS research are issues for anthropologists working in bureaucratic settings (de la Gorgendiere 2005).
- Research on HIV infection among intravenous cocaine users in Montreal and Vancouver demonstrated that needle exchange programs alone cannot stem the spread of HIV. By integrating qualitative participant observation methods into the substance abuse and HIV prevention studies, anthropologist Philippe Bourgois and epidemiologist Julie Bruneau (2000) were able to show the broader social and economic context of needle exchange programs for street addicts in Montreal and Vancouver. Bourgois likens the Canadian drug policy to abusive parents who alternatively whip and pamper their children.

All of these issues affect how a particular culture will react to exogenous (outside) medical practices. In some cases, the coexistence of many forms of healing provides clients a range of choices and enhances the quality of health. In other cases, people are confronted by conflicting models of illness and healing, a situation that can result in misunderstandings between healers and clients and in unhappy outcomes.

In some cases, we find the coexistence of alternative forms of healing that offer clients a range of choices. For example, traditional Chinese medicine, particularly acupuncture, is available in most Canadian cities as complementary treatment. In others cases, conflicting explanatory models of illness and healing result in serious misunderstandings between healers and clients.

Selective Pluralism

The Sherpas of Nepal offer an unusual example of a newly capitalizing context in which preference for traditional healing systems remains strong, along with the adoption of certain aspects of biomedicine (V. Adams 1988). Former pastoralist–farmers, the Sherpas are now heavily involved in providing services for international tourism. They work as guides, porters, cooks, and administrators in trekking agencies, and in hotels and restaurants. Thus, many Sherpas are well acquainted with the cosmopolitan cultures of international travellers (506). The wide variety of healing therapies available in the Upper Khumbu region fit into three general categories: (1) orthodox Buddhist practitioners, such as lamas, who are consulted for both prevention and cure through their blessings, and *amchis*, who practise Tibetan medicine, a system largely derived from India's Ayurvedic medicine; (2) unorthodox religious or shamanic practitioners, who perform divination ceremonies for diagnosis; and (3) biomedical practitioners, who initially used their diagnostic techniques and medicines for tourists, and then established a permanent medical facility in 1967.

In Khumbu, traditional healers are thriving and in no way threatened by wider economic changes brought by the tourist trade and influx of wealth. The reason is that high-mountain tourism is a particular form of capitalist development that does not radically change the social relations involved in production. This type of tourism brings in money but does not require large-scale capital investment from outside. Thus the Sherpas maintain control of their productive resources, their family structures remain largely the same, and wider kinship ties remain important in the organization of tourist business.

Canadian medical anthropologist Stacey Pigg (1996) found that shamanic healing is also central to experiences of modernity in Kathmandu, Nepal, where ritual healing thrives alongside biomedical services.

Conflicting Explanatory Models

Compared to the positive aspects of the multiple health-care options in Upper Khumbu, in many other contexts, anthropologists have documented serious disjunctures between Western biomedicine and local health systems. Miscommunication often occurs between biomedical doctors and patients in matters as seemingly simple as a prescription that should be taken with every meal. The Western biomedically trained doctor assumes that this means three times a day. But some people do not eat three meals a day and thus they unwittingly fail to follow the doctor's instructions.

One anthropological study of a case in which death ultimately resulted from cross-cultural differences shows the complexity of communication across medical cultures. The F family are Samoan immigrants living in Honolulu, Hawaii (Krantzler 1987). Neither parent speaks English. Their children are "moderately literate" in English, but speak a mixture of English and Samoan at home. Mr. F was trained as a traditional Samoan healer. Mary, a daughter, was first stricken with diabetes at the age of 16. She was taken to the hospital by ambulance after collapsing, half-conscious, on the sidewalk near her home in a Honolulu housing project. After several months of irregular contact with medical staff, she was again brought to the hospital in an ambulance, unconscious, and she died there. Her father was charged with causing Mary's death through "medical neglect." Nora Krantzler analyzes this case from the perspectives of the Western medical providers and Samoan culture.

Mary was diagnosed with juvenile-onset diabetes mellitus and treated in a hospital. She and her family were taught how to give insulin injections and urine tests. However, Mary did not keep her appointments and returned to the hospital four months later, blind in one eye. Although told of the need for compliance, her father also insisted on preparing a potion to supplement the insulin. The medical experts increasingly judged that "cultural differences" were the basic problem, and that in spite of all their attempts to communicate with the F family, her family was basically incapable of caring for Mary.

The family's perspective, in contrast, was grounded in *fa'a Samoa*, the Samoan way. In the family's opinion, Mary never had a single physician responsible for her care and they were never given adequate explanation of her problem and its treatment. Thus, the family lost trust in the hospital and began to rely on the father's skill as a healer.

While cultural differences may cause problems of communication, they may also marginalize certain groups and deny them adequate health-care services. Dara Culhane Speck's ethnography of the politics of

Ethnographic Profile

The Sherpa of Nepal

The name Sherpa means "person." About 35 000 Sherpa live in Nepal, mainly in the northeastern region. Another 10 000 reside in Bhutan and Sikkim (Fisher 1990), and another 5000 live in cities of Europe and North America.

In Nepal, the Sherpa are most closely associated with the Khumbu region. Khumbu is a valley set high in the Himalayas, completely encircled by mountains and with a clear view of Mount Everest (Karan and Mather 1985). The Sherpa have a mixed economy involving animal herding, trade between Tibet and India, small businesses, and farming, with the main crop being potatoes. Since the 1920s and the coming of Western mountaineers, Sherpa men became increasingly employed as guides and porters for trekkers and climbers. Many Sherpa men and women now run guest houses or work in guest houses as cooks, food servers, and cleaners.

The Sherpa are organized into eighteen separate lineages, or *ru* ("bones"), with marriage taking place outside one's birth lineage. Recently, they have begun marrying into other ethnic groups, thus expanding the definition and meaning of what it is to be Sherpa. Because of increased intermarriage, the number of people who can be considered Sherpa to some degree is 130,000. Status distinctions include "big people," "middle people," and "small people," with the middle group being the largest by far (Ortner 1999:65). The main privilege of those in the top level is not to carry loads. Those in the poorest level are landless and work for others.

The Sherpa practise a localized version of Tibetan Buddhism which contains non-Buddhist elements having to do with nature spiritualism that connects all beings. The place name Khumbu, for example, refers to the guardian deity of the region.

Tourism has been and still is a major change factor for the Sherpa. In Khumbu, the number of international tourists per year exceeds the Sherpa population.

Global warming is also having significant effects. Glaciers are melting, lakes are rising, and massive flooding is frequent. Some of the swollen lakes are in danger of breaking their banks (United Nations Environment Programme 2002). Many community development projects are aimed at reforestation, planting fruit orchards, and protecting and expanding local knowledge of medicinal herbs.

Readings

Vincanne Adams. *Tigers of the Snow and Other Virtual Sherpas: An Ethnography of Himalayan Encounters.* Princeton, NJ: Princeton University Press, 1996.

James Fisher. *Sherpas: Reflections on Change in Himalayan Nepal.* Berkeley: University of California Press, 1990.

Sherry Ortner. *Life and Death on Mt. Everest: Sherpas and Himalayan Mountaineering.* Princeton, NJ: Princeton University Press, 1999.

Video

Trekking on Tradition (Documentary Educational Resources, 1992).

Thanks to Vincanne Adams, University of California at San Francisco, for reviewing this material.

A Nepalese Sherpa porter carries a load up a steep mountain path in the Himalayas. Porters earn relatively good wages, especially when they work for international tourists (left). ■ (Source: Royalty Free/CORBIS) *Among the many forms of medical treatment available to the Sherpa, shamanic healing remains a popular choice (right).* ■ (Source: Vincanne Adams)

MAP 7.3 *Nepal. The Kingdom of Nepal has a population of almost 30 million inhabitants. Most of its territory is in the Himalayas, and Nepal has eight of the world's ten highest mountains.*

health care in a First Nations community on Alert Bay, adjacent to the northeastern end of Vancouver Island, British Columbia, is a powerful indictment of Native–white relations and the consequences of the destruction of an indigenous health-care system. *An Error in Judgement* (1987) documents the death from an undiagnosed ruptured appendix of Renee Smith, an 11-year-old Nimpkish girl. The island's sole medical practitioner was considered responsible for the girl's death through his negligence, alcoholism, and racism; nevertheless, community members were reluctant to lose access to the doctor and the community hospital.

The family and leaders of the Nimpkish band wrote to the attorney general of British Columbia, the provincial minister of health, and the College of Physicians and Surgeons to complain about the quality of health care on the island and to request an inquiry into the deaths of band members. In 1974, the British Columbia Medical Association published a report on *Native Health*, stressing that Natives fail to recognize early symptoms of illness; have a higher tolerance for pain and discomfort and a fatalistic acceptance of things as they are; and present themselves in the acute and often fatal stages of an illness (Culhane Speck 1987:100).

The report perpetuated the idea that Natives were responsible for the quality of health care they received. In 1980, the Government of Canada Inquiry into Indian Health and Health Care in Alert Bay was convened. According to the Nimpkish Band Council, the community wanted to know why their rates of hospitalization and death were so high: ". . . Why is our life expectancy so low? Why is our survival threatened? What is the quality of our health care services?

Why have so many of our people lost confidence in the health care we have been receiving?" (Culhane Speck 1987:234). Answers to these and other questions probably lie in the complex ethnohistory of British Columbia (Kelm 1999).

Working Together: Western Biomedicine and Traditional Healing

Since 1978, the World Health Organization (WHO) has endorsed the incorporation of local healing practices in national health systems. This policy emerged in response to increasing appreciation of local healing traditions, the shortage of trained biomedical personnel, and growing awareness of the deficiencies of WBM in addressing psychosocial factors in healing.

Debates continue about the efficacy of many traditional medical practices compared to biomedicine. For instance, opponents of the promotion of traditional medicine claim that it has no effect on such infectious diseases as cholera, malaria, tuberculosis, schistosomiasis, leprosy, and others. They insist that it makes no sense to allow for or encourage ritual practices against malaria, for example, when a child has not been inoculated against it. Supporters of traditional medicine as one component of a pluralistic health system point out that biomedicine neglects a person's mind, soul, and social setting. Also, indigenous curers are more likely to know clients and their families, thus facilitating therapy. Critical medical anthropologists point out that international health policy-makers still have the power to define what is traditional and therefore worthy of being included in WHO training programs.

Key Questions Revisited

WHAT is ethnomedicine?

Ethnomedicine is the study of health systems of specific cultures. Health systems include categories and perceptions of illness and approaches to prevention and healing. Research in ethnomedicine shows how perceptions of the body differ cross-culturally and reveals both differences and similarities across health systems in perceptions of illness and symptoms. Culture-specific syndromes are found in all cultures, not just non-Western societies, and many are now globalizing.

Ethnomedical studies of healing, healing substances, and healers reveal a wide range of approaches. Community healing systems are more characteristic of small-scale nonindustrial societies. They emphasize group interaction and treating the individual within the social context. Humoral healing systems seek to maintain balance in bodily fluids and substances through diet, activity, and behaviour. In industrial/informatics societies, biomedicine emphasizes the body as a discrete unit, and treatment addresses the individual body or mind and frames out the wider social context. Biomedicine is increasingly reliant on technology and is increasingly specialized.

WHAT are the major theoretical approaches in medical anthropology?

Ecological/epidemiological medical anthropology emphasizes links between the environment and health. It reveals how certain categories of people are at risk of contracting particular diseases within various contexts in historical times and the present. The interpretive approach focuses on studying illness and healing as a set of symbols and meanings. Cross-culturally, definitions of health problems and healing systems for these problems are embedded in meanings. Critical medical anthropologists focus on health problems and healing within a political economic framework. They ask what power relations are involved and who benefits from particular forms of healing. They analyze the role of inequality and poverty in health problems. Clinical medical anthropologists apply anthropological knowledge to improving the delivery of health facilities and interventions.

HOW are disease, illness, and healing changing during globalization?

Health systems everywhere are facing accelerated change in the face of globalization, which includes the spread of Western capitalism as well as new diseases and new medical technologies. The "new infectious diseases" are a challenge to health-care systems in terms of prevention and treatment. Diseases of development are health problems caused by development projects (such as dams) that change the physical and social environments.

The spread of Western biomedicine to many non-Western contexts is a major direction of change. As a consequence, medical pluralism exists in all countries. The availability of Western patent medicines has had substantial positive effects, but widespread overuse and self-medication can result in negative health consequences for individuals and more widely due to the emergence of drug-resistant disease strains.

Medical anthropologists play several roles in improving health systems. They may inform medical-care providers of more appropriate forms of treatment, guide local people about their increasingly complex medical choices, help prevent health problems through changing detrimental practices, or improve public health communication by making it more culturally informed and effective.

KEY CONCEPTS

clinical medical anthropology, p. 188
community healing, p. 181
critical medical anthropology, p. 187
culture-specific syndrome, p. 177
disease, p. 176
disease of development, p. 190

ecological/epidemiological approach, p. 184
ethnobotany, p. 183
ethno-etiologies, p. 178
ethnomedicine, p. 174
historical trauma, p. 186
humoral healing systems, p. 182
illness, p. 176
medical pluralism, p. 191

medicalization, p. 187
placebo effect, p. 187
shaman, p. 183
somatization, p. 177
structural suffering, p. 178

myanthrolab

To reinforce your understanding of this chapter, and to identify topics for further study, visit MyAnthroLab at www.myanthrolab.com for diagnostic tests and a multimedia ebook.

SUGGESTED READINGS

Nancy N. Chen. *Breathing Spaces: Qigong, Psychiatry, and Healing in China.* New York: Columbia University Press, 2003. This ethnography explores *qigong* (pronounced CHEE-GUNG), a charismatic form of healing popular in China that involves meditative breathing exercises. The author links the growing practice of qigong in China with the rise of capitalism and urban development.

Paul Farmer. *Pathologies of Power: Health, Human Rights, and the New War on the Poor.* Berkeley: University of California Press, 2005. Farmer blends interpretive medical anthropology with critical medical anthropology in his study of how poverty kills through diseases such as tuberculosis and HIV/AIDS. He takes an advocacy position.

Bonnie Glass-Coffin. *The Gift of Life: Female Spirituality and Healing in Northern Peru.* Albuquerque: University of New Mexico Press, 1998. The author examines women traditional healers in northern Peru. She provides a descriptive account of their practices and an experiential account about her experiences with two healers who worked to cure her of a spiritual illness.

Stephanie Kane. *AIDS Alibis: Sex, Drugs and Crime in the Americas.* Philadelphia: Temple University Press, 1998. Kane examines the combined forces of sex, drugs, and crimes in Chicago and Belize. An activist anthropologist, she critiques the U.S. war on drugs, the war on crime, and public health programs.

Richard Katz, Megan Biesele, and Verna St. Davis. *Healing Makes Our Hearts Happy: Spirituality and Cultural Transformation among the Kalahari Ju/'hoansi.* Rochester, VT: Inner Traditions, 1997. This book presents the story of how traditional healing dances help the Ju/'hoansi cope with recent and contemporary social upheaval. Their healing dances help them maintain a sense of community and are important for their cultural survival.

Arthur Kleinman and James L. Watson, eds. *SARS in China: Prelude to Pandemic?* Stanford, CA: Stanford University Press, 2006. An introduction and 10 chapters consider such topics as SARS in historical context, the epidemiology of SARS, public health responses, economic and political consequences, social and psychological consequences, and links with globalization.

Luisa Margolies. *My Mother's Hip: Lessons from the World of Eldercare.* Philadelphia: Temple University Press, 2004. After the author's mother broke her hip and entered a long-term care institution in Florida, Margolies began her study of chronic illness and eldercare. She chronicles her mother's case and interweaves a cultural critique of elder health care in the United States, Medicaid, and end-of-life questions such as resuscitation.

Carol Shepherd McClain, ed. *Women as Healers: A Cross-Cultural Perspective.* New Brunswick, NJ: Rutgers University Press, 1989. Case studies discuss women healers in Ecuador, Sri Lanka, Mexico, Jamaica, the United States, Serbia, Korea, Southern Africa, and Benin.

David McKnight. *From Hunting to Drinking: The Devastating Effects of Alcohol on an Australian Aboriginal Community.* New York: Routledge, 2002. Alcohol has had devastating effects over a period of 30 years on Mornington Island, Australia. McKnight discusses the history of drinking in Australia, causes of excessive alcohol consumption, and vested interests of authorities in the sale of alcohol on the island.

Daniel Moerman. *Meaning, Medicine and the "Placebo Effect."* New York: Cambridge University Press, 2002. In this book, Moerman considers medical practices in terms of how their meaning has an influence on their effect. The author reviews many studies, mainly conducted in the United States.

Ethan Nebelkopf and Mary Phillips, eds. *Healing and Mental Health for Native Americans: Speaking in Red.* New York. AltaMira Press, 2004. Various contributors consider mental health and substance abuse among Native North Americans and provide cases of healing that involve Native American culture. Many of the authors are Native Americans who are anthropologists, social workers, or social psychologists.

Kathryn S. Oths and Servando Z. Hinajosa, eds. *Healing by Hand: Manual Medicine and Bonesetting in Global Perspective.* New York: AltaMira Press, 2004. Chapters explore varieties of "manual medicine" such as massage therapy, bonesetting, chiropractics, and osteopathy. Cases include the United States, Denmark, Guatemala, Kenya, and Wales.

Sherry Saggers and Dennis Gray, *Dealing with Alcohol: Indigenous Usage in Australia, New Zealand and Canada.* New York: Cambridge University Press, 1998. This comparative study looks at structural issues such as European colonialism and interests of liquor companies in creating and sustaining high rates of alcohol consumption among many indigenous groups, and people's own understanding of their situation.

Merrill Singer. *Something Dangerous: Emergent and Changing Illicit Drug Use and Community Health.* Long Grove, IL: Waveland Press, 2005. This ethnography combines theory with research and applied anthropology about drug use and public health responses in the United States.

Paul Stoller. *Stranger in the Village of the Sick: A Memoir of Cancer, Sorcery, and Healing.* Boston: Beacon Press, 2004. After being diagnosed with lymphoma, the author enters the "village of the sick" as he goes through diagnostic testing, chemotherapy, and eventual remission. He offers observations about being a cancer patient in the United States and describes how he found strength through his earlier association with a West African healer.

J. Waldram, A. Herring, and K. Young, *Aboriginal Health in Canada: Historical, Cultural, and Epidemiological Perspectives.* Toronto: University of Toronto Press, 1995. This volume offers very comprehensive coverage of First Nations health issues and includes discussions of current health problems, an overview of health and health care from an historical perspective, and ideas on what future changes need to be made.

Johan Wedel. *Santería Healing.* Gainesville: University of Florida Press, 2004. This book discusses Santería healing in Cuba. The author conducted interviews with priests and others knowledgeable about Santería and observed many Santería consultations.

PART III Social Organization

FREDY PECCERELLI, A FORENSIC ANTHROPOLOGIST, risks his personal security working for victims of political violence in his homeland. Peccerelli is founder and executive director of the Guatemalan Forensic Anthropology Foundation (Fundación de Antropología Forense de Guatemala or FAFG), a group that focuses on the recovery and identification of some of the 200 000 people, mostly indigenous Maya of the mountainous regions, that Guatemalan military forces killed or "disappeared" during the brutal civil war that occurred between the mid-1960s and the mid-1990s.

Peccerelli was born in Guatemala. His family immigrated to the United States when his father, a lawyer, was threatened by death squads. He grew up in New York and attended Brooklyn College in the 1990s. But he felt a need to reconnect with his heritage and began to study anthropology as a vehicle that would allow him to serve his country.

The FAFG scientists excavate clandestine mass graves, exhume the bodies, and identify them through several means, such as matching dental and/or medical records. In studying skeletons, they try to determine the person's age, gender, stature, ancestry, and lifestyle. DNA studies are few because of the expense. The scientists also collect information from relatives of the victims and from eye-witnesses of the massacres. Since 1992, the FAFG team has discovered and exhumed approximately 200 mass grave sites in villages, fields, and churches.

Anthropologists at Work

Peccerelli sees the FAFG's purpose as applying scientific principles to basic human concerns. Bodies of identified victims are returned to their families to allow them some sense of closure about what happened to their loved ones. Families can honour their dead with appropriate burial ceremonies.

The scientists also give the Guatemalan government clear evidence on the basis of which to prosecute the perpetrators of these atrocities. However, Guatemala was long structured in terms of a ruling military and a largely disenfranchised indigenous population. Many members of the former millitia are still in positions of power within the government.

Peccerelli, his family, and his colleagues have been harassed and threatened. Eleven of the FAFG scientists have received written death threats. Bullets have been fired into Peccerelli's home, and it has been burglarized. The United Nations and other human rights organizations have made it clear to the government that they support FAFG's investigations, and exhumations continue with heightened security measures.

The American Association for the Advancement of Science, an organization committed to "advance science and serve society," honoured Peccerelli and his colleagues in 2004 for their work in promoting human rights at great personal risk. In 1999, *Time* magazine and CNN chose Peccerelli as one of the 50 "Latin American Leaders for the New Millennium." During the same year, the Guatemalan Youth Commission named him an "icon" for the youth of the country.

Currently, Peccerelli is on sabbatical to work on a master's degree in forensic and biological anthropology at the University of Bournemouth, United Kingdom. He intends to return to Guatemala: "There is enough work for another 25 years."

8

Kinship and Domestic Life

Key Questions

- HOW do cultures create kinship through descent, sharing, and marriage?

- WHAT is a household and what do anthropologists study about household life?

- HOW are kinship and households changing?

A Minangkabau bride in Sumatra, Indonesia, wears an elaborate gold headdress. Women play a central role among the Minangkabau. *(Source: © CORBIS)*

Learning another culture's kinship system is as challenging as learning another language. Robin Fox became aware of this challenge during his research among the Tory Islanders of Ireland (see Map 8.1) (1995 [1978]). Some Tory Island kinship terms are similar to North American English usage; for example, the word *muintir* means "people" in its widest sense, as in English. It can also refer to people of a particular social category, as in "my people," that refers to close relatives. Another similarity is with *gaolta,* the word for "relatives" or "those of my blood." In its adjectival form, *gaolta* refers to "kindness," like the English word *kin.* Tory Islanders have a phrase meaning "children and grandchildren," also like the English term *descendants.* One major difference is that the Tory Island word for "friend" is the same as the word for "kin." This usage reflects the cultural context of Tory Island with its small population, all related through kinship. So, logically, a friend is also kin.

All cultures have ways of defining *kinship,* or a sense of being related to another person or persons. Rules about who comprise kinship can be either informal or formalized in law. From infancy, people begin learning about their particular culture's **kinship system**, the combination of rules about who are kin and the expected behaviour of kin. Like one's language, one's kinship system is so ingrained that it is taken for granted as something natural rather than cultural.

In this chapter, we first consider cross-cultural variations in kinship systems. We then focus on a key unit of domestic life: the household. In the last section, we provide examples of contemporary change in kinship patterns and household organization.

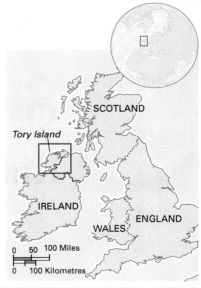

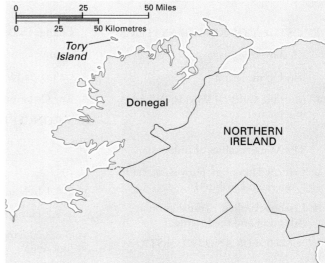

MAP 8.1   Ireland. Ireland's population is roughly 4 million. Its geography is low central plains surrounded by a ring of mountains. Membership in the European Union (EU) and a rising standard of living earned Ireland the nickname of the Celtic Tiger. Its economic opportunities are attracting immigrants from places as diverse as Romania, China, and Nigeria. Most people are Roman Catholics, followed by the Anglican Church of Ireland.

The Study of Kinship Systems

In many cultures, kinship systems are linked with symbols and beliefs about relationships, reproduction and child-rearing. Depending on the cultural context, various kinds of kinship systems shape children's personality development, influence marriage options, and affect the care of the aged. Nineteenth-century anthropologists found that kinship was the most important organizing principle in nonindustrial, nonstate cultures. The kinship group performs the functions of ensuring the continuity of the group through arranging marriages; maintaining social order through setting moral rules and punishing offenders;

and providing for the basic needs of members through regulating production, consumption, and distribution. In large-scale industrial societies, kinship ties exist, but many other forms of social affiliation draw people together.

Nineteenth-century anthropologists also discovered that definitions of who counts as kin differed widely from those of Europe and North America. Western cultures

---

kinship system: the predominant form of kin relationships in a culture and the kinds of behaviour involved.
kinship diagram: a schematic way of presenting data on kinship relationships

of an individual (called "ego") depicting all of ego's relatives, as remembered by ego and reported to the anthropologist.

genealogy: a record of a person's relatives constructed beginning with the earliest ancestors.

emphasize "blood" relations as primary, or relations through birth from a biological mother and biological father (Sault 1994). "Blood" is not a universal basis for kinship, however. Even in some cultures that do have a "blood"-based understanding of kinship, variations exist in defining who is a "blood" relative and who is not. For example, in some cultures, male offspring are considered of one "blood," whereas female offspring are not.

Behaviour is a common non-blood basis for determining kinship. Among the Native groups of northern Alaska, people who act like kin are kin (Bodenhorn 2000). If a person ceases to act like kin, he or she stops being a kinsperson. So, someone might say that a certain person "used to be" his or her cousin. In this system, the kin of anyone considered kin are also one's kin.

In some other cultures, a more important criterion for kinship is breastfeeding: Babies who were nursed by the same woman are considered related and cannot marry each other. The popular Western view of kinship as based on "blood" relationships and its contemporary grounding in a genetic relationship with the birth mother and "procreative father" (the male who provides the semen that fertilizes the female's ovum) is so widely accepted as real and natural that understanding other kinship theories is difficult for westerners.

Kinship Analysis

Early anthropological work on kinship tended to focus on finding out who is related to whom and in what way. Typically, the anthropologist would interview one or two people, asking questions such as, What do you call your brother's daughter? Can you (as a man) marry your father's brother's daughter? What is the term you use to refer to your mother's sister? In another approach, in an interview the anthropologist would ask an individual to name all his or her relatives, explain how they are related

to the interviewee, and provide the terms by which they refer to him or her.

From this information, the anthropologist would construct a **kinship diagram**, a schematic way of presenting data on the kinship relationships of an individual, called "ego" (see Figure 8.1). This diagram depicts all of ego's relatives, as remembered by ego and reported to the anthropologist. Strictly speaking, information gained from the informant for his or her kinship diagram is not supplemented by asking other people to fill in where ego's memory failed (in contrast to a genealogy; see the next paragraph). In cultures where kinship plays a greater role in social relations, it is likely that an informant will be able to provide information on more relatives than in one where kinship ties are less important in comparison to other networks such as friendships and work groups.

In contrast to a kinship diagram, a **genealogy** is a schematic way of presenting a family tree, constructed by beginning with the earliest ancestors that can be traced and working down to the present. A genealogy, thus, does not begin with ego. When Robin Fox attempted to construct kinship diagrams beginning with ego, the Tory Islanders were uncomfortable with the approach. They preferred to proceed genealogically, so he followed their preference. Tracing a family's complete genealogy may involve archival research in the attempt to construct as full a record as possible. Many cultures have trained genealogists whose task is to help families discover or maintain records of their family lines. In Europe and North America, Christians often record their "family tree" in the front of the family Bible.

Decades of anthropological research have produced a mass of information on kinship terminology, or the terms that people use to refer to kin. For example, in Euro-American kinship, children of one's father's sister and brother and one's mother's sister and brother are all referred to by the same kinship term: cousin. Likewise, one's father's

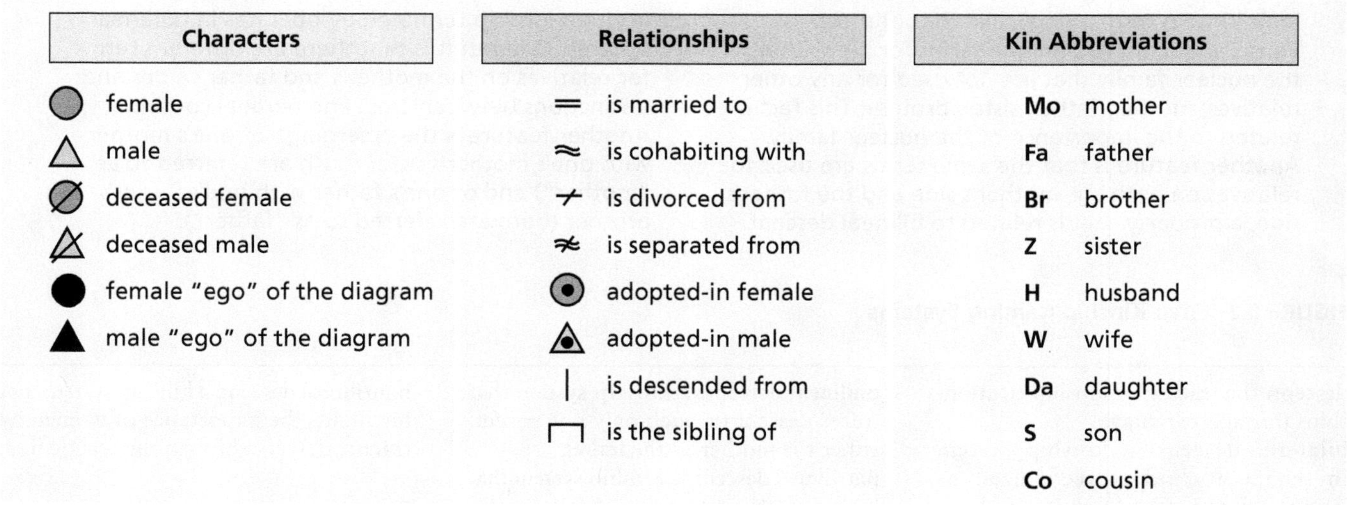

Characters		Relationships		Kin Abbreviations	
◯	female	=	is married to	**Mo**	mother
△	male	≈	is cohabiting with	**Fa**	father
⊘	deceased female	⊬	is divorced from	**Br**	brother
⧄	deceased male	≭	is separated from	**Z**	sister
●	female "ego" of the diagram	⊙	adopted-in female	**H**	husband
▲	male "ego" of the diagram	⧆	adopted-in male	**W**	wife
		│	is descended from	**Da**	daughter
		⊓	is the sibling of	**S**	son
				Co	cousin

FIGURE 8.1   Symbols Used in Kinship Diagrams

sister and one's mother's sister are both referred to as aunt, and one's father's brother and one's mother's brother are both referred to as uncle. And the terms *grandmother* and *grandfather* refer to the ascending generation on either one's father's or mother's side. This merging pattern is not universal. In some cultures, different terms apply to kin on one's mother's and father's sides, so a mother's sister has a different kin term than a father's sister. In yet another type of system solidarity along lines of siblings of the same gender is emphasized. One's mother and mother's sisters all have the same term, which translates as "mother"—a system found among the Navajo, for example.

Anthropologists have classified the cross-cultural variety in kinship terminology into six basic types, named after groups that were first discovered to have that type of system; for example, there is an "Iroquois" type and an "Eskimo" type (see Figure 8.2). Anthropologists would place various cultures with similar kinship terminology, no matter where they lived, into one of the six categories. The Yanomami, an Amazonian tribe who live in the rainforest in Venezuela, would, in this way, be identified as having an Iroquois naming system. Contemporary anthropologists who study kinship have moved beyond these categories, since the six kinship types do not promote understanding of actual kinship dynamics. In this text, therefore, we merely present two examples and avoid going into detail on the six classic types.

Kinship in Action

Today, the formalism of early kinship studies has been replaced by a renewed interest in kinship that considers it in relation to other topics such as power relations, reproductive decision-making, women's changing work roles, and ethnic identity (Carsten 2000).

Anthropologists who study kinship as a living and changing aspect of life use varied methods of data gathering, rather than simply interviewing informants. Participant observation is extremely valuable for learning about who interacts with whom, how they interact with each other, and why their relationship has the content it has. Observations can provide understanding, for example, of the frequency and intensity of people's kinship interactions and the degree to which they have supportive social networks. The life history method (see Chapter 2) reveals changes through an individual's lifetime and the way they are related to other events such as migration, a natural disaster, or political change. Focused life histories are useful in targeting key events related to kinship, such as marriage or cohabitation, divorce, or widowhood/widowerhood. Anthropologists interested in population dynamics, for example, use focused life histories, interviews, and questionnaires to gather information on personal demographics to learn at what age a woman commenced sexual relations, how many pregnancies she had, if and when she

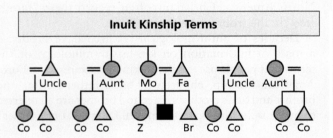

Inuit kinship terminology, like that of most Euro-Canadians, has unique terms for kin within the nuclear family that are not used for any other relatives: mother, father, sister, brother. This fact is related to the importance of the nuclear family. Another feature is that the same terms are used for relatives on both the mother's side and the father's side, a property that is related to bilineal descent.

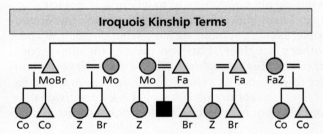

Iroquois kinship terminology operates in unilineal systems. One result is that there are different terms for relatives on the mother's and father's sides and distinctions between cross and parallel cousins. Another feature is the "merging" of one's mother with one's mother's sister (both are referred to as "mother") and of one's father with one's father's brother (both are referred to as "father").

FIGURE 8.2   Two Kinship Naming Systems

descent: the tracing of kinship relationships through parentage.
bilateral descent: a kinship system in which a child is recognized as being related by descent to both parents.

unilineal descent: a kinship system that traces descent through only one parent, either the mother or the father.
patrilineal descent: a kinship system that highlights the importance of men in tracing descent.

matrilineal descent: a kinship system that highlights the importance of women by tracing descent through the female line.

had an abortion or bore a child, whether the child lived or died, and when she stopped having children.

Descent

Descent is the tracing of kinship relationships through parentage. It is based on the assumption that everybody is born from someone else. Descent creates a line of people from whom someone is descended, stretching through history. But not all cultures recognize descent in the same way. Some cultures have a **bilateral descent** system, in which a child is recognized as being related by descent to both parents. Others have a **unilineal descent** system, which recognizes descent through only one parent, either the father or mother. The distribution of bilateral and unilineal systems have been correlated with different modes of production. This correspondence makes sense because economies—production, consumption, and exchange—can be tied to the way people and their labour power are organized and how commodities are used and transferred. We discuss examples of this correlation in the following section. We begin with the descent system that is the most prevalent cross-culturally.

Unilineal Descent

Unilineal descent systems are the basis of kinship in about 60 percent of the world's cultures, making some form of unilineality the most common form of descent. In general, unilineal systems characterize societies with a "fixed" resource base, such as cropland or herds. Thus, unilineal descent is most common among pastoralists,

horticulturalists, and farmers. Inheritance rules that regulate the transmission of property through only one line help maintain cohesiveness of the resource base.

Unilineal descent has two major forms: One is **patrilineal descent**, in which kinship is traced through the male line. The other is **matrilineal descent**, in which kinship is traced through the female line. In a patrilineal system, only male children can carry on the family line, that is, only their children become members of the patrilineage. Female children "marry out" and become members of their husband's lineage. In matrilineal descent systems, only daughters are considered to carry on the family line, and sons "marry out."

Patrilineal descent is found among roughly 45 percent of all cultures. It occurs throughout much of India, East Asia, the Middle East, Papua New Guinea, northern Africa, and some horticultural groups of sub-Saharan Africa. Cultures with patrilineal descent tend to have ideologies that are consistent with that concept. For example, theories of how conception occurs and how the fetus is formed give priority to the male role. Among the Kaliai people of Papua New Guinea, people say that an infant is composed entirely of *aitama aisuru*, the "father's water" or semen, which is channelled to the fetus. The mother is an "incubator" who contributes nothing substantial to the developing fetus. The mother's relationship with the infant develops later, through breastfeeding.

Margery Wolf's book, *The House of Lim* (1968), is a classic ethnography of patrilineal descent. Wolf lived for two years with the Lims, a Taiwanese farming household (see Figure 8.3). In her book, she describes first the village

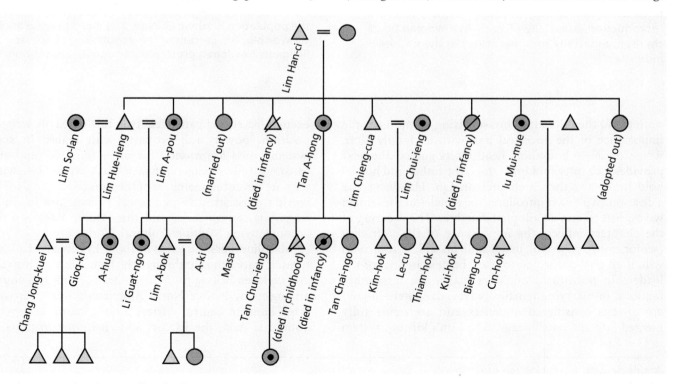

FIGURE 8.3   The Lim Family of Taiwan

Multiple Cultural Worlds

WHAT'S IN A NAME?

Naming children is always significant. Parents may follow cultural rules that a first-born son receives the name of his father's father or a first-born daughter receives the name of her mother's mother. Some parents believe that a newborn should not be formally named for a year or two and is instead referred to by a nickname. Others think that a name must convey some special hoped-for attribute of the child, or that a name should be unique.

The village of Ha Tsuen is located in the northwest corner of a rural area of Hong Kong (Watson 1986). Roughly 2500 people live in the village. All the males belong to the same patrilineage and all have the same surname of Teng. They are descended from a common male ancestor who settled in the region in the twelfth century. Daughters of Ha Tsuen marry into families outside the village, and marital residence is patrilocal.

Women do not own property, and they have no direct control of the means of production. Few married women are employed in wage labour. They depend on their husbands for financial support. Local politics is a male domain, as is all public decision-making. A woman's status as a new bride is low, and the transition from daughter to bride can be difficult psychologically. Women's primary role is in reproduction, especially of sons. As a woman bears children, especially sons, her status in the household rises.

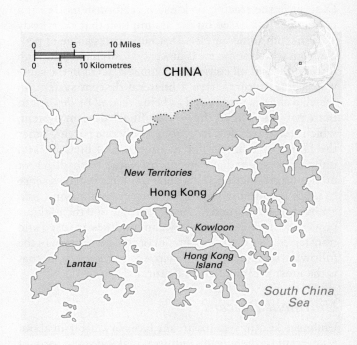

MAP 8.2 Hong Kong. The formal title of Hong Kong is the Hong Kong Special Administrative Region of the People's Republic of China. A world centre of finance and trade, it lacks natural resources and agricultural land, so it imports most of its food and raw materials. With 7 million residents, Hong Kong's population density is high. Most of the population is ethnic Chinese, and many practise ancestor worship. Ten percent of the population is Christian. Religious freedom is protected through its constitution.

---

setting and then the Lims' house, giving attention to the importance of the ancestral hall with its family altar, where the male household head meets guests. She next provides a chapter on Lim Han-ci, the father and household head, and then a chapter on Lim Hue-lieng, the eldest son. Wolf next introduces the females of the family: wives, sisters, and an adopted daughter. The ordering of the chapters reflects the importance of the *patriarch* (senior, most powerful male) and his eldest son, who will, if all goes according to plan, be next in line for the leadership position. Daughters marry out into other families. In-marrying females (wives, daughters-in-law) are always considered outsiders and are never fully merged into the patrilineage. The Lim's kinship system

exemplifies strong patrilineality in that it heavily weights position, power, and property with males. In such systems, girls are raised "for other families" and are, thus, not fully members of their birth family. Likewise, they are never full members of their marriage family. The world's most strongly patrilineal systems are found in East Asia, South Asia, and the Middle East (see the accompanying Multiple Cultural Worlds box).

Matrilineal descent exists in about 15 percent of all cultures. It traces kinship through the female line exclusively, and children belong to their mother's group. It is found among many Native North American groups; across a large band in central Africa; among many groups of Southeast Asia, the Pacific, and Australia; in parts of

---

double descent: a combination of patrilineal and matrilineal descent.

The local naming system reflects the power, importance, and autonomy of males. All children are first given a name referred to as their *ming* when they are a few days old. If the baby is a boy, the 30-day ceremony is as elaborate as the family can afford. It may include a banquet for many neighbours and the village elders and the presentation of red eggs to everyone in the community. For a girl, the 30-day ceremony may involve only a special meal for close family members. Paralleling this public expenditure bias toward sons is the thinking that goes into selecting the ming. A boy's ming is distinctive and flattering. It may have a classical literary connection. A girl's ming often has negative connotations, such as "Last Child," "Too Many," or "Little Mistake." One common ming for a daughter is "Joined to a Brother," which implies the hope that she will be a lucky charm, bringing the birth of a son next. Sometimes, though, people give an uncomplimentary name to a boy such as "Little Slave Girl." The reason is protection, to trick the spirits into thinking the baby is only a worthless girl so that the spirits will do no harm.

Marriage is the next formal naming occasion. When a male marries, he is given or chooses for himself a *tzu,* or marriage name. Gaining a tzu is a key marker of male adulthood. The tzu is not used in everyday address, but appears mainly on formal documents. A man also has a *wai hao,* "outside name," which is his public nickname. As he enters middle age, he may take a *hao,* or courtesy name, which he chooses and which reflects his aspirations and self-perceptions.

In the case of a woman, her ming ceases to exist when she marries. She no longer has a name. Instead, her husband refers to her as *nei jen,* "inner person," since now her life is restricted to the domestic world of household, husband's family, and neighbourhood. People may also refer to her by *teknonyms,* or names for someone based on their relationship to someone else, such as "Wife of So and So" or "Mother of So and So." In old age, she becomes *ah po,* "Old Woman," like every other aged female in the village.

Throughout their lives, men accumulate more and better names than women. They choose many of the names themselves. Over the course of their lives, women have fewer names than men. Women's names are standardized, not personalized, and women never get to choose any of their names.

FOOD FOR THOUGHT

- Go to www.slate.com/id/2116505 (*Trading Up: Where Do Baby Names Come From?* by Steven D. Levitt and Stephen J. Dubner) and read about the status game of child naming. How does your first name fit into this picture?

eastern and southern India; in a small pocket of northern Bangladesh; and in localized areas of the Mediterranean coast of Spain and Portugal. Matrilineal societies vary greatly, from foragers to intensive agricultural societies (Lepowsky 1993:296). Most, however, are horticultural economies in which women dominate the production and distribution of food and other goods.

Often, but not always, matrilineal kinship is associated with recognized public leadership positions for women, as among the Iroquois and Hopi. The Minangkabau (pronounced mee-NAN-ka-bow, the last syllable rhyming with "now") of Indonesia are the largest matrilineal group in the world (see the Ethnographic Profile on page 208).

Double Descent

A minority of cultures have **double descent** systems (also called *double unilineal descent*) that combine patrilineal and matrilineal descent. In these systems, offspring are believed to inherit different personal attributes and property from both their father's line and their mother's line. Many early anthropologists mistook this mixed system for a patrilineal system, demonstrating once again the power of ethnocentrism in interpretation. For example, the Bangangté of Cameroon in West Africa have a double descent system, although it was first described by anthropologists as patrilineal (Feldman-Savelsberg 1995). This misrepresentation was probably the result of interviewing only men and focusing on the inheritance of land property rather than on other traits.

THINKING OUTSIDE THE BOX

IF YOU were going to write an ethnography of your family, like Wolf's book about the Lims, what chapter titles would you choose and what would be their sequence?

Ethnographic Profile

The Minangkabau of Indonesia

The Minangkabau are the world's largest matrilineal culture, numbering between 4 and 5 million people (Sanday 2002). Most live in West Sumatra, Indonesia, and about 500 000 live in Malaysia. The Minangkabau are primarily farmers, producing substantial amounts of surplus rice. Many Minangkabau, both women and men, take up employment in Indonesian cities for a time and then return home.

In this strongly matrilineal kinship system, Minangkabau women hold power through their control of lineage land, its products, and agricultural employment on their land (Sanday 2002). Many have prominent positions in business, especially having to do with rice. Men are more likely to become scholars, merchants, and politicians. Inheritance of property, including farmland and the family house, passes from mothers to daughters.

Members of each submatrilineage, constituting several generations, live together in a lineage house or several nearby houses. Often, men and older boys live in a separate structure, such as the village mosque. In the household, the senior woman controls the power, and she makes decisions in all economic and ceremonial matters. The senior male of the sublineage has the role of representing its interests to other groups, but he is only a representative, not a powerful person in his own right.

Water buffaloes are important in both the Minangkabau rice economy and symbolically. The roofline of a traditional house has upward curves that echo the shape of water buffalo horns. Minangkabau women's festive headdress has the same shape. The Minangkabau are mostly Muslims, but they mix their Muslim faith with elements of earlier traditions and Hinduism. They have long-standing traditions of music, martial arts, weaving, wood carving, and making fine filigree jewellery of silver and gold.

Many of the traditional wooden houses and palaces in Western Sumatra are falling into a state of disrepair (Vellinga 2004). The matrilineal pattern of only women living in the house is changing and men and women are more likely to live together in nuclear households.

Readings

Evelyn Blackwood. *Webs of Power: Women, Kin, and Community in a Sumatran Village.* Lanham, MD: Rowman and Littlefield, 2000.

Kirstin Pauka. *Folk Theater, Dance, and Martial Arts of West Sumatra.* Ann Arbor, MI: University of Michigan Press, 2002 (with CD-ROM).

Peggy Reeves Sanday. *Women at the Center: Life in a Modern Matriarchy.* Ithaca, NY: Cornell University Press, 2002.

Anne Summerfield and John Summerfield. *Walk in Splendor: Ceremonial Dress and the Minangkabau.* Los Angeles: UCLA Fowler Museum of Cultural History. Textile Series No. 4, 1999.

Thanks to Michael G. Peletz, Emory University, for reviewing this material.

A traditional wooden Minangkabau longhouse with its distinctive upward-pointing roof (left). The house interiors are divided into separate "bays" for submatrilineal groups. Many are no longer places of residence but are used as meeting halls or are falling into ruin. ■ (Source: © Wolfgang Kachler/CORBIS) *The symbolic importance of water buffaloes, apparent in the shape of traditional rooftops, is reiterated in the shape of girls' and women's ceremonial headdress (right). The headdress represents women's responsibilities for the growth and strength of Minangkabau culture.*
■ (Source: © Lindsay Hebberd/CORBIS)

MAP 8.3 *Minangkabau Region in Indonesia.* *The shaded area shows the traditional heartland of Minangkabau culture in western Sumatra. Many Minangkabau people live elsewhere in Sumatra and in neighbouring Malaysia.*

Research among married women uncovered double descent. Through the maternal line, one inherits movable property (such as household goods and cattle), personality traits, and a type of witchcraft substance that resides in the intestines. Patrilineal ties determine physical resemblance and rights to land and village residence. Matrilineally related women tend to bond together and visit each other frequently, consulting on marriage partners for their children, advising on child naming choices, and supporting each other in times of trouble.

Bilateral Descent

Bilateral descent traces kinship from both parents equally to the child. Family groups tend to be nuclear, with strong bonds among father, mother, and their children. Marital residence is predominantly **neolocal**, that is, residence for the newly married couple is somewhere away from the residences of both the bride's and the groom's parents. Neolocality offers more flexibility than what is usual in unilineal systems. Inheritance of property from the parental generation is allocated equally among all offspring regardless of their gender. In bilateral descent systems, conception theories can emphasize an equal biological contribution to the child from the mother and father. For example, contemporary Western science states that the sperm contributed by the male and the ovum contributed by the female are equally important in the formation of a new person.

Bilateral descent is found in less than one-third of the world's cultures (Murdock 1965:57). The highest frequency of bilateral descent is found at the opposite ends of the production continuum. For example, the Ju/wasi have bilateral descent, and most people think bilateral descent is the prevalent pattern in North America (see the Critical Thinking box on page 210).

Given that most of the world's people recognize some connection between a baby and both parents, it is puzzling as to why the majority of kinship systems are unilineal and thus emphasize only one parent. Cultural evolutionists of the late nineteenth century thought that people in prehistoric societies did not understand the biological role of the father. Bilateral kinship, in their view, emerged as "higher civilization" and unilineal kinship systems are remnants of earlier times. This argument is weak on two grounds. First, it is ethnocentric to claim that contemporary bilateral cultures, especially Euro-American culture, are the only ones that recognize

the father's role in paternity. Evidence from many unilineal cultures indicates widespread recognition of paternity. Second, foraging peoples tend to have bilateral kinship, suggesting that the world's earliest humans may have also had bilateral kinship, assuming that foraging was the first human mode of production.

In attempting to explain the relative scarcity of bilateral systems, some anthropologists have offered a theory that looks to the mode of production as influencing the type of kinship system. They point out that bilateral kinship systems are associated mainly with two modes of production: foraging and industrialism. Both modes of production rely on a flexible gender division of labour in which both males and females contribute, relatively equally, to production and exchange. Logically, then, a bilateral kinship system recognizes the strengths of both the mother's and father's sides. Bilateral kinship is also an adaptive system for members of foraging and industrial populations because it fits with small family units that are spatially mobile. Bilateral kinship offers the most flexibility in terms of residence, keeping open opportunities related to making a living.

Residence rules, where a newly married couple takes up residence, often match the prevailing "direction" of descent rules. Thus, in most patrilineal societies, marital residence is **patrilocal**, with or near the husband's family. In most matrilineal societies, it is **matrilocal**, with or near the wife's family or **avunculocal**, with or near the husband's mother's brother. Common in Western industrialized society is the practice of neolocality, residence in a place different from either the bride's or groom's family. Residence patterns have political, economic, and social implications. The combination of matrilineal descent and matrilocal residence, for example, is often found among groups that engage in long-distance warfare (Divale 1974). Strong female household structures maintain the domestic scene while the men are absent on military campaigns, as among the pre-colonial Iroquois of upstate New York and the Nayar of southern India. Patrilineal descent and patrilocal residence promote the development of cohesive male-focused lineages that are associated with frequent local warfare, which requires the presence of a force of fighting men on the home front.

Sharing

Many cultures emphasize kinship ties based on acts of sharing and support. These relationships may be informal

---

neolocality: a kinship rule that defines preferred marital residence in a new location not linked to either the bride's or the groom's parents' residence.
patrilocality: a kinship rule that defines preferred marital residence with or near the groom's kin.

matrilocality: a kinship rule that defines preferred marital residence with or near the bride's kin.

avunculocality: a kinship rule that defines preferred marital residence with or near the groom's mother's brother.

HOW BILATERAL IS "AMERICAN KINSHIP"?

"American kinship" refers to a general model based on the bilateral system of Euro-Americans of the 1960s (Schneider 1968). According to this model, children are considered to be descended from both mother and father, and general inheritance rules suggest that property would be divided equally between sons and daughters. Given the rich cultural diversity of Canada and the United States, most would now consider the label "American kinship" and its characterization as bilateral to be overgeneralized.

Even within the so-called American kinship of the 1960s, bilaterality was not strictly followed. Indications of patrilineality include the practice of a wife dropping her surname at marriage and taking her husband's sur-name, and using the husband's surname for offspring. This is called patrimony. Although inheritance is sup-posedly equal among all offspring regardless of gender, often it is not. In many business families, the business is passed from father to sons, while daughters are given a different form of inheritance such as a trust fund. Increasing trends toward matrifocality are caused by high rates of divorce and the trend of more young children living with the mother than with the father.

In order to explore descent patterns, each student in the class should draw his or her own kinship diagram. Students should note their ethnicity at the top of the chart, choosing the label with which they feel most comfortable. Then, each student should draw a circle around the relatives who are "closest" to "ego," including parents, grandparents, aunts, uncles, cousins—whoever fits in this category as defined by ego. As a group, students in the class should then consider the following questions about the kinship diagrams.

CRITICAL THINKING QUESTIONS
- How many students drew equal circles around relatives on both parents' sides?
- How many emphasized the mother's side? How many emphasized the father's side?
- Do ethnic patterns emerge in terms of the circled kin?
- From this exercise, what can be said about "American kinship" in Canada?

---

or formally certified. God-parenthood and blood broth-erhood are examples of sharing-based kinship that is ritually formalized.

Food Sharing Sharing-based kinship is common in Southeast Asia, Papua New Guinea, and Australia (Carsten 1995). Among inhabitants of Langkawi, one of Malaysia's many small islands, sharing-based kinship starts in the womb when the mother's blood feeds the fetus. After birth, the mother's breast milk nourishes the infant. This tie is crucial. A child who is not breastfed will not "recognize" its mother. Breastfeeding is also the basis of the incest rule. People who have been fed from the same breast are kin and may not marry. After the baby is weaned, its most important food is cooked rice. Sharing cooked rice, like breast milk, becomes another way that kinship ties are created and maintained, espe-cially between women and children. Men are often away on fishing trips, in coffee shops, or at the mosque and so are not likely to have rice-sharing kinship bonds with children.

Adoption and Fostering Another form of sharing-based kinship is the transfer of a child or children from the birth parent(s) to the care of someone else. *Adoption* is a formal and permanent form of child transfer. Com-mon motivations for adoption include infertility and the desire to obtain a particular kind of child (often a son). Motivations for the birth parent to transfer a child to someone else include a premarital pregnancy in a disap-proving context, having "too many" children, and having "too many" of a particular gender. Among the Maasai, a woman who has several children might give one to a friend, neighbour, or aged person who has no children to care for her or him.

Currently, roughly 1 of every 10 couples in Canada is infertile, and many of these couples would like to have children. Some use fertility drugs, in vitro fertil-ization (IVF), or surrogate child-bearing. Many people, including those who have biologically recognized children, choose to adopt (see the accompanying Lessons Applied box).

Fostering a child is sometimes similar to a formal adoption in terms of permanence and a sense of kinship. Or it may be temporary placement of a child with some-one else for a specific purpose, with little or no sense of kinship. Child fostering is common throughout sub-Saharan Africa. Parents foster out children to enhance the

Lessons Applied

TRANSNATIONAL ADOPTION AND THE INTERNET

China's population policy (discussed in Chapter 5) has made children—especially girls—available for international adoption. While sons ensure the continuity of the patrilineage, girls are considered better caregivers to the elderly. Ann Anagnost (2004) explored the world of transnational adoption where North American parents adopt infants from China. She noted that many people outside China assume that baby girls there are abandoned because of Chinese cultural attitudes and government policy. However, Anagnost notes that baby girls do find adoptive homes in China. Nevertheless, many children are made available for international adoption every year.

Her research explores how adoptive parents use Internet communication to articulate thoughts they might otherwise never express. Online discussions explore the best adoption agencies, the process of referral when an infant is assigned to waiting parents, the arrival of the child, and later adjustment. These informal parent networks are used to ask practical advice and share information. When they settle into the daily routine of parenting, their Internet participation tapers off.

Adoptive parents express concern about the possibility of "reactive attachment disorder" in their adoptions caused by the lack of nurturing contact in the early weeks and months after birth. Yet, Chinese adoptions are favoured because they are secure, fast, inexpensive, and final—final because there is no danger the birth parent will try to reclaim the child. One popular topic of discussion is how to construct a cultural identity for a Chinese adoptee. For example, parents search out ethnically marked clothes and toys, particularly dolls, and send their children to special summer "culture camps."

FOOD FOR THOUGHT

- If you were conducting an applied project to improve parental and child experiences using an agency specializing in transnational adoptions, what ethical concerns would you have? Would you consider the discussion rooms "off limits" for an applied anthropologist? How would you put your advice on policy changes at the agency into effect?

An orphanage in Shanghai, China. Human-rights activists have claimed that abuse was widespread in Chinese orphanages, especially of children with physical handicaps. Following this allegation, foreign media were invited to visit the Shanghai Children's Welfare Institute. ■ (Source: © Reuters/Will Burgess)

child's chances for formal education or so that the child will learn a skill such as marketing. Most fostered children go from rural to urban areas and from poorer to better-off households. Fieldwork conducted in a neighbourhood in Accra, Ghana (see Map 8.4), sheds light on the lives of fostered children (Sanjek 1990). Child fostering in the neighbourhood is common: About one-fourth of the children were foster children. Twice as many of the fostered children were girls as boys. School attendance is biased toward boys. All of the boys were attending school, but only 4 of the 31 girls were. An important factor affecting the treatment of the child is whether the fostered child is related to his or her sponsor. Although 80 percent of the fostered children as a whole were kin of their sponsors, only 50 percent of the girls were kin. People who sponsor nonkin girls make a cash payment to the girl's parents. These girls cook, do housecleaning, and assist in market work by carrying goods or watching the trading area. Fostered boys, most of whom are kin of their sponsors, do not perform such tasks because they attend school.

Ritually Established Sharing Bonds   Ritually defined "sponsorship" of children descended from other people is common among Christians, especially Catholics, worldwide. Relationships between godparents and godchildren often involve strong emotional ties and financial flows from the former to the latter. In Arembepe, a village in Bahia state in northeastern Brazil, children ask their godparents for a blessing the first time they see them each day (Kottak 1992:61). Godparents give their godchildren cookies, candy, and money, and larger presents on special occasions.

Among the Maya of Oaxaca, Mexico, godparenthood is both a sign of the sponsor's status and the means to increased status (Sault 1985). The request by parents that someone sponsor their child is a public acknowledgment of the sponsor's standing. The godparent gains influence over the godchild and can call on the godchild for labour. A godparent of many children can amass a large labour force when needed and gain further status. Most godparents in Oaxaca are husband–wife couples, but many are women alone, a pattern that reflects the high status of Maya women.

Marriage

The third major basis for forming close interpersonal relationships is through marriage or other forms of "marriage-like" relationships, such as long-term cohabitation. In this section, we focus on marriage.

Toward a Definition   Anthropologists recognize that some form of marriage exists in all cultures, though it may take different forms and serve different functions. What constitutes a cross-culturally valid definition of marriage is open to debate. A standard definition from 1951 is now discredited: "Marriage is a union between a man and a woman such that children born to the woman are the recognized legitimate offspring of both parents" (Barnard and Good 1984, 89). This definition says that the partners must be of different sexes. It implies that a child born outside a marriage is not socially recognized as legitimate. Exceptions exist to

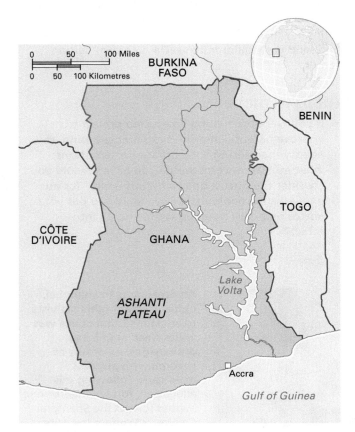

MAP 8.4   Ghana. The Republic of Ghana has over 20 million people. Ghana has rich natural resources and exports gold, timber, and cocoa. Agriculture is the basis of the domestic economy. Several ethnic groups exist, with the Akan people constituting over 40 percent of the population. English is the official language, but another 80 or so languages are also spoken. Over 60 percent of the people are Christian, 20 percent follow traditional religions, and 16 percent are Muslim.

---

marriage: many factions make the definition of marriage a contentious issue; anthropologist Linda Stone defines it as an intimate relation between spouses that creates culturally recognized in-law kin relations.

incest taboo: a rule prohibiting marriage or sexual intercourse between certain kinship relations.

Two young lesbian women in Ontario celebrate their marriage dressed in traditional white wedding dresses. ■ (Source: © CP PHOTO/Ryan Remiorz)

both these features cross-culturally. Same-sex marriages are now legal in Denmark, Norway, the Netherlands, and Canada. The legal status of same-gender marriage is still a matter of debate and disagreement throughout the United States.

In many cultures, no distinction is made between legitimate and illegitimate children on the basis of whether they were born within a marriage. Women in the Caribbean region, for example, typically do not marry until later in life. Before that, a woman has sequential male partners with whom she bears children. None of her children is considered more or less "legitimate" than any other.

Given the range of practices that can come under the heading of marriage, many anthropologists have given up trying to find a working definition that will fit all cases. Others have suggested an open checklist of features, such as reproduction, sexual rights, raising children, or a ritual ceremony. Anthropologist Linda Stone has developed a definition that focuses on the kinship relationships formed upon marriage. This may be the most inclusive definition possible. She defines **marriage** as an intimate relation between spouses that creates culturally recognized in-law kin relations (Stone 1998:183). This definition accounts for all possible combinations of number and sex of spouses and avoids the problem of confounding marriage with more casual relations

Selecting a Spouse All cultures have preferences about whom one should and should not marry or with whom one should or should not have sexual intercourse. Sometimes, these preferences are informal and implicit; other times, they are formal and explicit.

THINKING OUTSIDE THE BOX

DO SOME RESEARCH on www.match.com to learn what cultural preferences people mention in their profiles.

Rules of Exclusion

Some sort of **incest taboo**, or a rule prohibiting marriage or sexual intercourse between certain kinship relations, is one of the most basic and universal rules of exclusion.

In his writings of the 1940s, French anthropologist Claude Lévi-Strauss dealt with the question of why all cultures have kinship systems. In his classic ethnological study, *The Elementary Structures of Kinship* (1949), Lévi-Strauss argues that incest avoidance motivated men to exchange women between families. This exchange, he says, is the foundation for social networks and social solidarity beyond the immediate group. Such networks allow for trade between areas with different resources and the possibility that peaceful relations will exist between bride-exchangers.

Genetic research suggests an alternative theory for universal incest taboos. Larger breeding pools help reduce the frequency of certain genetically transmitted conditions. Like the theory of Levi-Strauss the genetic theory is also functional. Each theory attributes the universal existence of incest taboos to their adaptive contribution, although in two different ways.

The most basic and universal form of incest taboo is against marriage or sexual intercourse between fathers and their children, and mothers and their children. In most cultures, brother–sister marriage has also been forbidden. But there are exceptions. The most well-known example of the allowance of brother–sister marriage comes from Egypt at the time of the Roman Empire (Barnard and Good 1984:92). Census data from that era show that between 15 and 20 percent of marriages were between full brothers and sisters, not just within a few royal families. Incest taboos do not universally rule out marriage with cousins. In fact, some kinship systems promote cousin marriage, as we discuss next. Cousin marriage, like brother–sister marriage, builds tightly localized kin networks. In contrast, among the pastoralist Nuer of southern Sudan, the incest taboo includes all members of the patrilineage, which may be hundreds of people. This kind of incest taboo creates widely dispersed kinship networks.

Preference Rules

Many preference rules exist cross-culturally concerning whom one should marry. Rules of **endogamy**, or marriage within a particular group, stipulate that the spouse must be from a defined social category. In kin endogamy, certain relatives are preferred, often cousins. Two major forms of cousin marriage exist. One is marriage between **parallel cousins**, children of either one's father's brother or one's mother's sister—the term *parallel* indicates that the linking siblings are of the same gender (see Figure 8.4). The second is marriage between **cross-cousins**, children of either one's father's sister or one's mother's brother—the term *cross* indicates the different genders of the linking siblings. Parallel-cousin marriage is favoured by many Muslim groups in the Middle East and northern Africa, especially the subform called *patrilateral parallel-cousin marriage,* which is cousin marriage into the father's line.

Hindus of southern India favour matrilateral cross-cousin marriage, which is cousin marriage into the mother's line for a male ego. Although cousin marriage is preferred, it nonetheless constitutes a minority of all marriages in the region. A survey of 3527 couples in the city of Chennai (formerly called Madras; see Map 8.5) in South India showed that three-fourths of all marriages involved unrelated people, while one-fourth were between first cross-cousins (or between uncle and niece, which is considered the same relationship as cross-cousin) (Ramesh, Srikumari, and Sukumar 1989).

Readers who are unfamiliar with cousin marriage systems may find them objectionable on the basis of the potential genetic disabilities from "close inbreeding." A study of thousands of such marriages in South India, however, revealed only a very small difference in rates of certain "birth defects" compared with cultures in which cousin marriage is not practised (Sundar Rao 1983). Marriage networks in South India are diffuse, extending over a wide area and offering many options for "cousins." This situation contrasts to the much more closed situation of a single village or town.

Endogamy may also be based on location. Village endogamy is a basis of arranging marriages throughout the eastern Mediterranean among both Christians and Muslims. Village endogamy is the preferred pattern among Muslims throughout India and among Hindus of southern India. In contrast, Hindus of northern India forbid village endogamy and consider it a form of incest. Instead, they practise village **exogamy** ("marriage out"). For them, a preferred spouse should live in a far-off village or town. Thus, marriage distance is greater in the north than in the south, and brides are far less likely to maintain regular contact with their natal kin in the north. Many songs and folktales of North Indian women

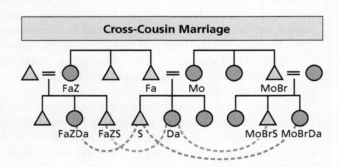

Cross-cousin marriage: A daughter marries either her father's sister's son or her mother's brother's son. A son marries either his father's sister's daughter or his mother's brother's daughter.

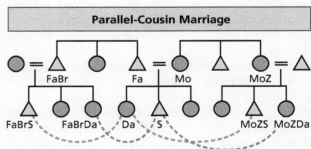

Parallel-cousin marriage: A daughter marries either her father's brother's son or her mother's sister's son. A son marries either his father's brother's daughter or his mother's sister's daughter.

FIGURE 8.4 Two Major Types of Cousin Marriage

---

endogamy: marriage within a particular group or locality.
parallel cousin: offspring of either one's father's brother or one's mother's sister.
cross-cousin: offspring of either one's father's sister or one's mother's brother.

exogamy: marriage outside a particular group or locality.
hypergyny: a marriage in which the groom is of higher status than the bride.

hypogyny: a marriage in which the bride is of higher status than the groom.
isogamy: marriage between status equals.

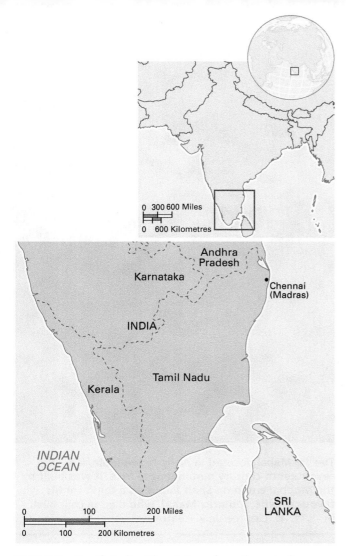

MAP 8.5   South India. The states of southern India, compared to the northern states, have lower population density, lower fertility rates, higher literacy rates, and less severe gender inequality. Agriculture is the mainstay of the region's economy and the population is predominantly rural. Industry, information technology, and business process outsourcing (BPO) are of increasing importance in cities such as Chennai and Bangalore.

convey sadness about being separated from their natal families, a theme that may not make much sense in a situation of village endogamy, where the bride's parents are likely to be close by.

Status considerations often shape spouse selection (see Figure 8.5). The rule of **hypergyny** requires the groom to be of higher status than the bride; in other words, the bride "marries up." Hypergyny is a strong rule in northern India, especially among upper-status groups. It is also implicitly followed among many people in North America where females "at the top" have the hardest time finding an appropriate partner because there are so few options "above them." Women in top professions such as medicine and law have a difficult time finding an appropriate partner because there are few, if any, options for higher-status marriage partners. Women medical students in North America are experiencing an increased marriage squeeze because of status hypergyny. The opposite is **hypogyny**, when the female "marries down." Status hypogyny is rare cross-culturally, as is age hypo-gyny, in which the groom is younger than the bride. Age hypogyny, though rare as a preferred pattern, is increasing in North America because women who would otherwise prefer a husband of equal age or somewhat older are marrying younger men. **Isogamy,** marriage between partners who are status equals, occurs in cultures where male and female roles and status are equal.

Features, such as ability, looks, and appearance, are factors that may be explicitly or implicitly recognized, or both. Features such as facial beauty, skin colour, hair texture and length, height, and weight are variously defined as important, depending on the culture. Invariably, however, "looks" tend to be more important for females. Marriage advertisements placed in newspapers in India (similar to the "personal ads" in Western newspapers) that describe an available bride often mention that her skin colour is "fair" or "wheatish" and may note that she is slender and tall—although she should not be too tall, that is, taller than a potential groom. Preference for having the groom be taller than the bride is more common in male-dominated contexts. Marriages where the spouses are similar in height are common in cultures where gender roles are relatively equal and where sexual *dimorphism* (differences in shape and size of the female body compared to the male body), is not marked, as in much of Southeast Asia.

The role of romantic love in spouse selection is debated by biological determinists and cultural constructionists.

Hypergyny	The bride marries a groom of higher status.	The groom may be wealthier, more educated, older, taller.
Hypogyny	The bride marries a groom of lower status.	The bride may be wealthier, more educated, older, taller.
Isogamy	The bride and groom are status equals.	The bride and groom have similar wealth, education, age, height.

FIGURE 8.5   Status Considerations in Partner Selection (Heterosexual Pairing)

Males and females throughout much of Southeast Asia are approximately the same size, as is the case with this couple from Bali, Indonesia. ■ (Source: © Rick Smolan/Stock Boston, LLC)

The Taj Mahal, located in Agra, North India, is a seventeenth-century monument to love. It was built by the Mughal emperor, Shah Jahan, as a tomb for his favourite wife, Mumtaz Mahal, who died in childbirth in 1631. ■ (Source: Jack Heaton)

Biological determinists argue that feelings of romantic love are universal among all humans because they play an adaptive role in uniting males and females in care of offspring. Cultural constructionists, in contrast, argue that romantic love is far from universal, that it is an unusual, even "aberrant" factor influencing spouse selection (Little 1966, quoted in Barnard and Good 1984:94). The cultural constructionists point to variations in male and female economic roles to explain cross-cultural variations in an emphasis on romantic love. Romantic love is more likely to be an important factor in relationships in cultures where men contribute more to subsistence, and where women are therefore economically dependent on men. Sri Lankan young people in Toronto are reported to see love marriages as occurring between inexperienced or immature individuals. For many couples, an arranged marriage "offers a tangible sense of security, family support and approval" (Morrison, Guruge, and Snarr 1999:151). Whatever the cause of romantic love, it is a common basis for marriage in many cultures (Levine et al. 1995).

The new billionaires of China (multimillionaires in terms of dollars) are men with wealth and interest in marrying a virgin woman (French 2006). They have turned to advertising to seek applications from prospective brides. In Shanghai, an enterprising lawyer began a business by managing the advertising and applicant screening for over 50 billionaires. On average, the process takes three months.

Marriage Gifts Most marriages are accompanied by gift-giving of goods or services between the partners, members of their families, or friends (see Figure 8.6). The major forms of marital exchanges cross-culturally are dowry and bridewealth.

THINKING OUTSIDE THE BOX

WHAT IS your opinion about the relative merits of love marriages versus arranged marriages, and on what do you base your opinion?

Dowry is the transfer of goods, and sometimes money, from the bride's side to the new married couple for their use. The dowry includes household goods such as furniture, cooking utensils and sometimes rights to a house. Dowry is the main form of marriage transfer in farming societies throughout Eurasia, from Western Europe through the northern Mediterranean and into China and India (Goody 1976). In northern India, what is called

---

bride-service: a form of marriage exchange, in which the groom works for his parents-in-law for a certain period of time before returning home with the bride.

monogamy: marriage between two people.

polygamy: marriage involving multiple spouses.

FIGURE 8.6   Major Types of
Marriage Gifts and Exchanges

Dowry	Goods and money given by the bride's family to the married couple	European and Asian cultures; agriculturalists and industrialists
Groomprice	Goods and money given by the bride's family to the married couple and to the parents of the groom	South Asia, especially northern India
Brideprice	Goods and money given by the groom's family to the parents of the bride	Asian, African, and Central and South American cultures; horticulturalists and pastoralists
Brideservice	Labour given by the groom to the parents of the bride	Southeast Asian, Pacific, and Amazonian cultures; horticulturalists

Hausa dowry goods in Accra, Ghana. The most valuable part of a Hausa bride's dowry is the *kayan dak'i* ("things of the room"). It consists of bowls, pots, ornamental glass, and cookware which are conspicuously displayed in the bride's marital house so that the local women can get a sense of her worth. The bride's parents pay for these goods as well as other more utilitarian dowry goods such as everyday cooking utensils. ■ (Source: Deborah Pellow)

"dowry" is more appropriately termed "groomwealth" because the goods and money pass not to the new couple, but instead to the groom's family (Billig 1992). In China during the Mao era, the government considered dowry a sign of women's oppression and made it illegal. The practice of giving dowry in China has returned with increased personal wealth and consumerism, especially among the newly rich urban populations (Whyte 1993).

Bridewealth, is the transfer of goods or money from the groom's side to the bride's parents. It is more common in horticultural and pastoral cultures. **Bride-service**, a subtype of bridewealth, is a transfer of labour from the groom to his parents-in-law for a designated time period. It is still practised in some horticultural societies, especially in the Amazon.

Many marriages involve gifts from both the bride's and groom's sides. For example, a typical pattern in Canada is for the groom's side to be responsible for the rehearsal dinner the night before the wedding, while the bride's side is responsible for everything else.

THINKING OUTSIDE THE BOX

IN YOUR FAMILY, what are the prevailing ideas about wedding expenses and who should pay for them?

Forms of Marriage   Cultural anthropologists distinguish two basic forms of marriage on the basis of the number of partners involved. **Monogamy** is marriage between two people—a male and female if the pair is heterosexual, or two people of the same sex in the case of a gay or lesbian pair. Heterosexual monogamy is the most common form of marriage cross-culturally, and in many countries, it is the only legal form of marriage.

Polygamy is a marriage with multiple spouses, a pattern allowed in many cultures (Murdock 1965:24).

The woman on the lower right is part of a polyandrous marriage, which is still practised among some Tibetan peoples. She is married to several brothers, two of whom stand behind her. The older man with the sash in the front row is her father-in-law. ■ (Source: © Thomas L. Kelly/Woodfin Camp & Associates)

Two forms of polygamous marriage exist. The more common of the two is **polygyny**, marriage of one man with more than one woman. **Polyandry**, or marriage between one woman and more than one man, is extremely rare. The only place where polyandry is prevalent is in the Himalayan region that includes parts of Tibet, India, and Nepal. Non-polyandrous people in the area look down on the people who practise polyandrous marriage as backward (Haddix McCay 2001).

Households and Domestic Life

In casual conversation, North Americans might use the words *family* and *household* interchangeably to refer to people who live together. Social scientists, however, propose a distinction between the two terms. A **family** is a group of people who consider themselves related through kinship. In North American English, the term includes both close or immediate relatives and more distant relatives. All members of a family do not necessarily live together or have strong bonds with one another.

A related term is the **household,** a person or persons who occupy a shared living space and who may or may not be related by kinship. Most households consist of members who are related through kinship, but an increasing number do not. An example of a nonkin household is a group of friends who live in the same apartment. A single person living alone also constitutes a household. In this section of the chapter, we look at household forms and organization cross-culturally, and relationships between and among household members.

The Household: Variations on a Theme

Here, we consider three forms of households and the concept of household headship. The topic of female-headed households receives detailed attention because this pattern of headship is widely misunderstood.

Household Forms

Household organization is divided into types according to how many married adults are involved. The **nuclear household** (which many people call the nuclear family) is a domestic group that contains one adult couple (married or "partners"), with or without children. An **extended household** is a domestic group that contains more than one adult married couple. The couples may be related through the father–son line (making a *patrilineal extended household*) such as the Lims of Taiwan (see Figure 8.3 on page 205), through the mother–daughter line (a *matrilineal extended household*), or through sisters or brothers (a *collateral extended household*). Polygynous (multiple wives) and polyandrous (multiple husbands) households are *complex households,* domestic units in which one spouse lives with or near multiple partners and their children.

The precise cross-cultural distribution of these various types is not known, but some broad generalizations can be offered. Nuclear households are found in all cultures but are the exclusive household type in roughly one-fourth of the world's cultures (Murdock 1965 [1949]:2). Extended households are the most important form in about one-half of all cultures. The distribution of these

---

polygyny: marriage of one husband with more than one wife.
polyandry: marriage of one wife with more than one husband.
family: a group of people who consider themselves related through a form of kinship, such as descent, marriage, or sharing.

household: a group of people, who may or may not be related by kinship, who share living space.
nuclear household: a domestic unit containing one adult couple (married or partners), with or without children.
extended household: a co-residential group that comprises more than one parent–child unit.

stem household: a co-residential group that comprises only two married couples related through males, commonly found in East Asian cultures.
matrifocality: a household system in which a female (or females) is the central, stable figure around whom other members cluster.

two household forms corresponds roughly with the modes of production. The nuclear form is most characteristic of economies at the two extremes of the continuum: in foraging groups and in industrialized societies. This pattern reflects the need for spatial mobility and flexibility in both modes of production. Extended households constitute a substantial proportion of households in horticultural, pastoralist, and farming economies.

In Japan, a subtype of the extended household structure has endured within the context of an industrial/post-industrial and urban economy. The *ie*, or **stem household**, is a variation of an extended household that contains two (and only two) married couples related through the male line. In it, only one son remains in the household, bringing in his wife, who is expected to perform the important role of caregiver to the husband's parents as they age. The stem household is still widely preferred throughout much of East Asia, although it is increasingly difficult to achieve due to changing economic aspirations of children and lowered fertility rates. Aging parents find that none of their children is willing to live with them and take responsibility for their care. Some parents exert considerable pressure on an adult child to come and live with them (Traphagan 2000). A compromise is for an adult child and his or her spouse to live near the parents but not with them.

Household Headship

The question of who heads a household is often difficult to answer. In this section, we review some approaches to this question and provide insights into how cross-cultural perceptions about household headship differ.

The *head* is the primary person, or persons, responsible for supporting the household financially and making major decisions. This concept of household head is based on a Euro-American view that emphasizes the income contribution of the head who was traditionally a man. European colonialism spread the concept of the male, income-earning head of household around the world, along with laws that vested household authority in male headship.

The model of a male household head influences the way official statistics are gathered worldwide. If a household has a co-resident man and woman, there is a tendency to report the household as male headed. In Brazil, for example, the official definition of household head considers only a husband to be head of the household, regardless of whether he contributes to the household budget. Single, separated, or widowed women who are responsible for household support are deprived of the title of household head. If they happen to have a man visiting them on the day the census official arrives, he is considered to be the household head (de Athayde Figueiredo and Prado 1989:41). Similarly, according to official reports, 90 percent of households in the Philippines are headed by males (Illo 1985). Filipina women, however, play a prominent role in income generation and budgetary control, and both partners share decision-making. Thus, co-headship would be a more appropriate label for many households in the Philippines and elsewhere.

Matrifocality refers to a household pattern in which a woman (or women) is the central, stable domestic figure around whom other members cluster (González 1970). In a matrifocal household, the mother is likely to be the primary or only income provider. The concept of matrifocality does not exclude the possibility that men may be part of the household, but they are not the central income providers or decision-makers.

In China, the stem household system is changing because many people have one daughter and no son as a result of lowered fertility and the One-Child-Per-Family-Policy. ■ (Source: © Keren Su/Stock Boston, LLC)

Members of a matrifocal household in rural Jamaica: two sisters and their children. ■ (Source: Barbara Miller)

The number of woman-headed households is increasing worldwide, and these households are more likely to be poorer than other households. Most popular theories do not take into account ethnographic insights about the several possible causes of this form of household headship. A woman-headed household can come about if a partner never existed, if a partner existed at one time, but for some reason—such as separation, divorce, or death—is no longer part of the household, or if a partner exists but is not a co-resident because of migration, imprisonment, or some other form of separation. Most thinking about woman-headed households assumes a heterosexual relationship and thus does not account for woman-headed households formed by a single woman with children either adopted or conceived through artificial insemination, with or without a visiting woman partner. A variety of household forms are to be expected, depending on such factors as men's and women's economic roles, especially access to work, wages, and the distribution of productive resources such as property. It is not simply the gender of the household head that is of importance in the healthy functioning of households. It has more to do with the resources that the head (or co-heads) has, both material and social, such as property ownership, a decent job, and living in a safe neighbourhood.

Domestic Violence

Domestic violence can occur between domestic partners, parents and children, and siblings. In this section, we are concerned with the first of these. Violence between domestic partners, with males dominating as perpetrators

and women as victims, seems to be found in nearly all cultures, although in varying forms and frequencies (J. Brown 1999). A cross-cultural review reveals that wife beating is more common and more severe in contexts where men control the wealth. It is less common and less severe where women's work groups exist (Levinson 1989). The presence of women's work groups is related to a greater importance of women in production and matrifocal residence. These factors provide women with the means to leave an abusive relationship. For example, among the Garifuna, an African-Indian people of Belize, Central America (see Map 7.2 on page 179), incidents of spouse abuse occur, but they are infrequent and not extended (Kerns 1999). Women's solidarity in this matrifocal society limits male violence against women.

Increased domestic violence worldwide throws into question the notion of the house as a refuge or place of security. In North America, there is evidence of high and increasing rates of intrahousehold abuse of children (including sexual abuse), violence between spouses or partners, and abuse of aged family members. Anthropological research will help policy-makers and social workers better understand the factors affecting the safety of individuals within households and to be able to design more effective programs to promote personal safety.

Household Transformations

The composition and sheer existence of a particular household can change as a consequence of several factors, including divorce, death, and possible remarriage.

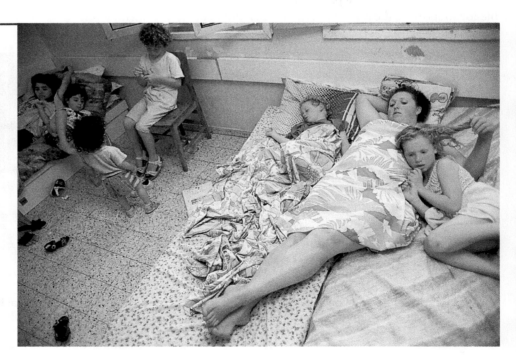

A shared bedroom in a battered woman's shelter, Tel Aviv, Israel. Many people wonder why abused women do not leave their abusers. Part of the answer lies in the unavailability and low quality of shelters throughout much of the world. ■ (Source: © David Wells/The Image Works)

In this section, we review anthropological findings on these topics.

Divorce and Kinship Patterns   Divorce and separation, like marriage and other forms of long-term union, are cultural universals, even though they may be frowned on or forbidden. Marriages may break up for several reasons—the most common are voluntary separation and death of one of the partners. Globally, variations exist in the legality and propriety of divorce. Some religions, such as Roman Catholicism, prohibit divorce. In Muslim societies, divorce by law is easier for a husband to obtain than for a wife. Important research questions about marital dissolution include the causes for it, the reasons why divorce rates appear to be rising worldwide, and the implications for the welfare of children of divorced parents and other dependents.

One hypothesis for why divorce rates vary cross-culturally says that divorce rates will be lower in cultures with unilineal descent. In such cultures, a large descent group has control over and interests in offspring and control over in-marrying spouses due to their dependence (Barnard and Good 1984:119). Royal lineages, with their strong interests in maintaining the family line, are examples of groups especially unlikely to favour divorce, because it generally means losing control of offspring. In bilateral foraging societies, there is more flexibility in both marriage and divorce. The hypothesis, in general, appears to have some merit.

Another question is the effect of multiple spouses on divorce. A study in Nigeria, West Africa, found that two-wife arrangements are the most stable, whereas marriages involving three or more wives have the highest rates of disruption (Gage-Brandon 1992). Similar results come from an analysis of household break-up in a polyandrous group of Tibetan people living in northwestern Nepal (see Map 7.3 on page 194) (Haddix McCay 2001). Wealth of the household is an important factor affecting household stability, but the number of brothers is another strong factor. Polyandrous households comprising two brothers are far less likely to break up than those with four or more brothers. An additional factor, although more difficult to quantify, are the social support and networks that a brother has beyond the polyandrous household. Only with such social support will he be able to build a house and establish a separate household on his own.

Widow(er)hood   The position of a widow or widower carries altered responsibilities and rights. Women's position as widows is often marked symbolically. In Mediterranean cultures, a widow must wear modest, simple, and black-coloured clothing, sometimes for the rest of her life. Her sexuality is supposed to be virtually dead. At the same time, her new "asexual" status allows her greater spatial freedom than before. She can go to

public coffeehouses and taverns, something not done by women whose husbands are living.

Extreme restrictions on widows are recorded for parts of South Asia where social pressures on a widow enforce self-denial and self-deprivation, especially among the propertied class. A widow should wear a plain white sari, shave her head, eat little food, and live a celibate life. Many widows in India are abandoned, especially if they have no son to support them. They are considered polluting and inauspicious. Widows elsewhere experience symbolic and life-quality changes much more than do widowers. For example, in South Africa, a widower's body is not marked in any significant way except to have his head shaved. He is required to wear a black button or armband for roughly six months. A widow's body is marked by shaving her head, smearing a mixture of herbs and ground charcoal on her body, wearing black clothes made from an inexpensive material, and covering her face with a black veil and her shoulders with a black shawl. She may even wear her clothes inside out, wear one shoe, eat with her wrong hand, or dine from a lid instead of a plate (Ramphele 1996:100).

Changing Kinship and Household Dynamics

In this section, we provide examples of how marriage and household patterns are changing. Many of these changes have roots in colonialism whereas others are the result of recent changes effected by globalization.

Change in Descent

Matrilineal descent is declining worldwide as a result of both European colonialism and contemporary Western globalization. European colonial rule in Africa and Asia contributed to the decline in matrilineal kinship by registering land and other property in the names of assumed male heads of household, even where females were the heads (Boserup 1970). This process eroded women's previous rights and powers. Western missionaries contributed to transforming matrilineal cultures into patrilineal systems (Etienne and Leacock 1980). European colonial influences led to the decline of matrilineal kinship among Native North Americans. Before European colonialism, North America had one of the largest distributions of matrilineal descent worldwide, although not all Native North American groups were matrilineal. A comparative study of kinship among three reservation-based Navajo groups in Arizona shows that matrilineality is stronger where conditions most resemble the pre-reservation era (Levy, Henderson, and Andrews 1989). Among the Minangkabau of Indonesia (review the Ethnographic Profile in this chapter), three factors are related to the decline of matrilineal kinship (Blackwood 1995):

- Dutch colonialism promoted the image of male-headed nuclear families as an ideal.
- Islamic teachings idealize women as wives and men as household heads.
- The modernizing Indonesian state has a policy of naming males as household heads

Change in Marriage

Although the institution of marriage in general remains prominent, many of its details are changing. New forms of communication are affecting ways of finding a potential partner and courtship. In a village in western Nepal people's stories of their marriages reveal that arranged marriages have decreased and elopement has increased since the 1990s. Through interviews with dozens of married women, Laura Ahern learned of the growing importance in the 1990s of love letters in establishing marital relationships (2001). Dating is not allowed, so sending love letters is how young people court. One woman offered to share a love letter from her husband and gave permission for it to be copied. Eventually, many

A newly married husband and wife and their relatives in front of a church in Seoul, Republic of Korea. ■ (Source: © Noboro Komine/Photo Researchers, Inc.)

other villagers did the same. Of the 200 letters Ahern collected, 170 were written by men and 30 by women. Typically, the man starts the correspondence. For example, one man's love letter contains the following lines: "I'm helpless and I have to make friends of

THINKING OUTSIDE THE BOX

WHAT FORMS of communication do young people use to "court" someone in your cultural world? How was it different in your parents' time?

a notebook and pen in order to place this helplessness before you. . . . I'll let you know by a 'short cut' what I want to say: Love is the union of two souls. The 'main' meaning of love is 'life success.' I'm offering you an invitation to love" (2001:3). Love letters became possible only in the 1990s because of increased literacy rates in the village. Literacy facilitated self-selected marriages and thus supported an increasing sense of personal agency among the younger people of the village.

Nearly everywhere, the age at first marriage is rising. The later age at marriage is related to increased emphasis on completing a certain number of years of education before marriage and to higher material aspirations such as being able to own a house. Marriages between people of different nations and ethnicities are increasing, partly because of growing rates of international migration. Migrants take with them many of their marriage and family practices. They also adapt to rules and practices in their area of destination. Pluralistic practices evolve, such as conducting two marriage ceremonies—one conforming to the "original" culture and the other to the culture in the place of destination.

Marriage crises are situations in which people who want to marry cannot do so for one reason or another. They appear to be more frequent now than in the past, at least as perceived and reported by young people in the so-called marriage market. Two examples illustrate variations in how a marriage crisis comes about and how it plays out for those caught up in it. In a town of about 38 000 in rural Niger, West Africa, the marriage crisis involves young men's inability to raise the necessary funds for the bridewealth and additional gifts to the bride's family (Masquelier 2005). Among these Muslim, Hausa-speaking people, called Mawri, marriage is the crucial ritual that changes a boy into a man. Typically, a prospective groom receives financial assistance from his kin and friends. In Niger, the economy has been declining for some time, and typical farm or other wages are worth less than they were in earlier times. Marriage costs for the groom have not declined, however—quite the opposite. Wealthy young men can afford to give a car to the bride's parents as a wedding gift. But most young Mawri men cannot afford such gifts and are caught in the marriage crisis. They remain sitting at home in their parents' house, something that only females do. The many young, marriage-age women who remain single gain a reputation of being immoral, as they occupy a new and suspect social space between girl and wife.

Weddings are important, culture-revealing events in themselves. Style changes in weddings worldwide abound. Factors of changes to consider are the ceremony, costs, appropriate clothing, and the possibility of a honeymoon. The globalization of Western-style "white weddings" promotes the adoption of many features familiar in the West: a white wedding gown for the bride, a multilayered wedding cake, and certain kinds of floral arrangements. What the bride and groom wear is an expression of their personal identity as well as the cultural identity of their families and larger social group. Clothing choice may reflect adherence to "traditional" values or may reject those in favour of more "modern" values. Euro-American trends are prominent worldwide. Throughout much of East and Southeast Asia, advertisements and upscale stores display the Western-style white wedding gown (but less so in India, where white clothing for women signifies widowhood and is inauspicious). On the other hand, resurgence of local styles is occurring in some contexts, such as in Morocco, where there is a trend for "modern" brides to wear a Berber costume (long robes and silver jewellery characteristic of the rural, mountain pastoralists) at one stage of the wedding ceremony.

Changing Households

Globalization is creating rapid change in household structure. One assumption is that the frequency of extended households will decline with industrialization and urbanization and the frequency of nuclear households will rise. Given what we mentioned earlier in this chapter about the relationship between nuclear households and industrialism, it is highly possible that with the spread of this mode of production, nuclear households will increase, too.

This projection finds strong confirmation in the changes that have occurred in household structure among the Kelabit people of highland Borneo since the early 1990s (Amster 2000) (see Map 8.6). One Kelabit settlement was founded in 1963 near the Indonesian border. At the time, everyone lived in one longhouse with over 20 family units. It was a "modern" longhouse, thanks to roofing provided by the British army and the innovation of private sleeping areas. Like more traditional longhouses, though, it was an essentially egalitarian living space within which individuals could freely move. Today, that longhouse is no more. Most of the young people have migrated to coastal towns and work in jobs related to the offshore oil industry. Most houses

MAP 8.6   Kelabit Region in Malaysia. The Kelabit people's homeland is the Kelabit Highlands in Sarawak, a plateau ringed by mountain peaks that are forest-covered. One of Malaysia's smallest indigenous tribes, they number around 6000 people, or 0.4 percent of Sarawak's population of 1.5 million, and .03 percent of Malayasia's total population of 22 million. Less than one-third of the Kelabit people live in the highlands.

are now single-unit homes with an emphasis on privacy. The elders complain of a "bad silence" in the village. No one looks after visitors with the old style of hospitality. There is no longer one common longhouse for communal feasts and rituals.

International migration is another major cause of change in household formation and internal relationships (discussed further in Chapter 14). Dramatic reductions in fertility can occur in one generation when members of a farming household in, for example, Taiwan or Egypt, migrate to England, France, Canada, or the United States. Having many children makes economic sense in their homeland, but not in the new destination. Many such migrants decide to have only one or two children. They tend to live in small, isolated nuclear households. International migration creates new challenges for relationships between parents and children. The children often become strongly identified with the new culture and have little connection with their ancestral culture. This rupture creates anxiety for the parents and conflict between children and parents over issues such as dating, dress, and career goals.

A modern-style Kelabit longhouse built in the 1990s (top). It is the home of six families who formerly lived in a 20-family longhouse, seen in the background, which is being dismantled. Since the 1990s, houses built for a nuclear unit have proliferated in the highlands (bottom). These houses stand on the site of a former multi-unit longhouse. ■ (Source: Matthew Amster)

Change in everyday life in households is an understudied topic. Basic outlines of the near future in industrial societies point to the reduced economic dependence of women on men as wage earners and the possible decline of heterosexual marriage (Cherlin 1996: 478–480). These changes, in turn, will lead to increased movement away from nuclear household living and to increased diversity in household forms. During the second half of the twentieth century, household size in Canada shrank from an average of 3.9 in 1961 to 2.4 persons in 2001. The current situation contains several seemingly contradictory patterns first noted in

the early 1980s by two sociologists (Cherlin and Furstenberg 1992 [1983]). They reported that the number of unmarried couples living together has more than tripled since 1970 and that one out of four children does not live with both parents. Other studies show that at current rates, more than one-third of all marriages in Canada will end in divorce (Campbell and Carroll 2007:123).

Early in the twenty-first century, three kinds of households are most common in North America: households composed of couples living in their first marriage, single-parent households, and households formed through remarriage. A new fourth category is the *multigenerational household,* in which an "adult child" (or "boomerang kid") lives with his or her parents. Roughly one in three unmarried adults between the ages of 25 and 55 share a home with their mother or father or both (*Psychology Today* 1995 [28]:16). Another variation of this type of household is the skip-generation household where grandparents care for their grandchildren. In Canada, First Nations families are disproportionably represented in this category with 17 percent of grandparents raising a grandchild without a parent present (Campbell and Carroll: 122).

Currently, adult offspring spend over 2 hours a day doing household chores, with adult daughters contributing roughly 17 hours a week and adult sons putting in 14.4 hours. Daughters spend most of their time doing laundry, cooking, cleaning, and washing dishes. Sons are more involved in yard work and car care. Parents in multigenerational households still do three-quarters of the housework.

Kinship and household formation are certainly not dull or static. Just trying to keep up with changing patterns in North America is a daunting task, to say nothing of the challenge of keeping up with changes worldwide.

Key Questions Revisited

HOW do cultures create kinship ties through descent, sharing, and marriage?

Key differences exist between unilineal and bilateral descent systems. Within unilineal systems, further important variations exist between patrilineal and matrilineal systems in terms of property inheritance, residence rules for married couples, and the relative status of males and females. Worldwide, unilineal systems are more common than bilateral systems. Within unilineal kinship systems, patrilineal kinship is more common than matrilineal kinship.

A second important basis for kinship is sharing. Sharing one's child with someone else through either informal or formal processes is probably a cultural universal. Sharing-based kinship is created through food transfers, including breastfeeding (in some cultures, children breastfed by the same woman are considered kin and cannot marry). Ritualized sharing creates kinship, as in the case of godparenthood.

The third basis for kinship is marriage, another universal factor, even though definitions of marriage may differ substantially. All cultures have rules of exclusion and preference rules for spouses.

WHAT is a household and what do anthropologists study about household life?

A household may consist of a single person living alone or may be a group comprising more than one person who may or may not be related by kinship; these individuals share a living space and, often, financial responsibilities for the household.

Nuclear households consist of a mother and father and their children, but they also can be just a husband and wife without children. Nuclear households are found in all cultures but are most common in foraging and industrial societies. Extended households include more than one nuclear household. They are most commonly found in cultures with a unilineal kinship system. Stem households, which are most common in East Asia, are a variant of an extended household in which only one child, usually the firstborn, retains residence with the parents.

Household headship can be shared between two partners or can be borne by a single person, as in a woman-headed household. Study of intrahousehold dynamics between parents and children and among siblings reveals complex power relationships as well as security, sharing, and sometimes violence. Household breakup comes about through divorce, separation of cohabiting partners, or death of a spouse or partner.

HOW are kinship and households changing?

The increasingly connected world in which we live is having marked effects on kinship formation and household patterns and dynamics. Matrilineal systems have been declining in distribution since European colonialist expansion beginning in the 1500s.

Many aspects of marriage are changing, including a trend toward later age at marriage in many developing countries. Although marriage continues to be an important basis for the formation of nuclear and extended households, other options (such as cohabitation) are increasing in importance in many contexts, including urban areas in developed countries.

Contemporary changes in kinship and in household formation raise several serious questions for the future, perhaps most importantly about the care of dependent members such as children, the aged, and disabled people. As fertility rates decline and average household size shrinks, kinship-based entitlements to basic needs and emotional support disappear.

KEY CONCEPTS

avunculocality, p. 209
bilateral descent, p. 205
bride-service, p. 217
cross-cousin, p. 214
descent, p. 205
double descent, p. 207
endogamy, p. 214
exogamy, p. 214
extended household, p. 218
family, p. 218
genealogy, p. 203

household, p. 218
hypergyny, p. 215
hypogyny, p. 215
incest taboo, p. 213
isogamy, p. 215
kinship diagram, p. 203
kinship system, p. 202
marriage, p. 213
matrifocality, p. 219
matrilineal descent, p. 205
matrilocality, p. 209

monogamy, p. 217
neolocality, p. 209
nuclear household, p. 218
parallel cousin, p. 214
patrilineal descent, p. 205
patrilocality, p. 209
polyandry, p. 218
polygamy, p. 217
polygyny, p. 218
stem household, p. 219
unilineal descent, p. 205

myanthrolab

To reinforce your understanding of this chapter, and to identify topics for further study, visit MyAnthroLab at www.myanthrolab.com for diagnostic tests and a multimedia ebook.

SUGGESTED READINGS

Irwin Altman and Joseph Ginat, eds. *Polygynous Families in Contemporary Society.* Cambridge, UK: Cambridge University Press, 1996. This book provides a detailed account of polygyny as practised in two fundamentalist Mormon communities of Utah, one rural and the other urban.

Dorothy Ayers Counts, Judith K. Brown, and Jacquelyn C. Campbell, eds. *To Have and to Hit: Cultural Perspectives on Wife Beating.* Champaign/Urbana, IL: University of Illinois Press, 1999. Chapters include an introductory overview, and cases from Australia, southern Africa, Papua New Guinea, India, Central America, the Middle East, and the Pacific.

Jamila Bargach. *Orphans of Islam: Family, Abandonment, and Secret Adoption in Morocco.* Lanham, MD: Rowman and Littlefield, 2002. According to Islam, adoption is not legal. Many Muslim childless couples, however, secretly adopt children and cover up their identity. Most adoptees are second-class members of their new families and cannot inherit property.

Amy Borovoy. *The Too-Good Wife: Alcohol, Codependency, and the Politics of Nurturance in Postwar Japan.* Berkeley, CA: University of California Press, 2005. This book explores the experiences of middle-class women in Tokyo who participated in a weekly support meeting for families of substance abusers. The women attempt to cope with their husbands' alcoholism while facing the dilemma that being a good wife may be part of the problem.

Helen Bradley Foster and Donald Clay Johnson, eds. *Wedding Dress across Cultures.* New York: Berg, 2003. Chapters examine the evolution and ritual functions of wedding attire in cultures such as urban Japan, First Peoples of Alaska, Swaziland, Morocco, Greece, and the Andes.

Sara L. Friedman. *Intimate Politics: Marriage, the Market, and State Power in Southeastern China.* Cambridge, MA: Harvard University Press, 2006. Village culture along China's southeastern coast is distinct from mainstream Han culture. Women have much autonomy, are important in production, and have strong networks with other women. This woman-centred culture conflicts with official state reforms.

Irene Glasser and Rae Bridgman, *Braving the Street: The Anthropology of Homelessness. Public Issues in Anthropological Perspective*, vol. 1. New York: Berghahn Books, 1999. Fieldwork with homeless people reveals complexities of the problem that have been overlooked by public officials. The authors propose solutions.

Laurel Kendall, *Getting Married in Korea: Of Gender, Morality, and Modernity.* Berkeley: University of California, 1996. The ethnographic study examines preferences about desirable spouses, matchmaking, marriage ceremonies and their financing, and the effect of women's changing work roles on their marital aspirations.

Judith S. Modell, *A Sealed and Secret Kinship: The Culture of Policies and Practices in American Adoption.* New York, Berghahn Books, 2002. This books focuses on the increasing debate about adoption by reviewing case examples of parents, children, kin, and nonkin adoptive families in the United States. The author addresses topics such as adoption reform, adoptee experiences of searching for their birth parents, current practices of placing children, and changes in welfare policy.

Richard Parkin and Linda Stone, eds. *Kinship and Family: An Anthropological Reader.* Oxford, England: Blackwell Publishing, 2004. This collection traces the history of the anthropological study of kinship from the early 1900s to the present. It includes classical and contemporary works and situates them in the context of major theoretical debates.

Peter H. Stephenson, *The Hutterian People: Ritual and Rebirth in the Evolution of Communal Life.* Lanham, MD: University Press of America, 1991. This ethnography investigates how the Hutterites have maintained a vital and long-lived utopian religious community. Many of them live in Western Canada.

Nancy Tapper, *Bartered Brides: Politics, Gender and Marriage in an Afghan Tribal Society.* New York: Cambridge University Press, 1991. Based on fieldwork before the Soviet invasion, this study examines marriage among the Maduzai, a tribal society of Turkistan. The book looks at how marriage relates to productive and reproductive aspects of society and the role it plays in managing political conflict and competition.

Margaret Trawick, *Notes on Love in a Tamil Family.* Berkeley, CA: University of California Press, 1992. This reflexive ethnography takes a close look at the daily dynamics of kinship in one Tamil (South Indian) family. Special attention is given to sibling relationships, the role of older people, children's lives, and the way love and affection are played out in a particularly Tamil way.

Toby Alice Volkman, ed. *Cultures of Transnational Adoption.* Durham, NC: Duke University Press, 2005. Chapters discuss Korean adoptees as a global family, transational adoption in North America, shared parenthood among low-income people in Brazil, and representations of "waiting children."

9

Social Groups and Social Stratification

Key Questions

- WHAT is the range of cross-cultural variation of social groups?

- WHAT is social stratification, and what are its effects on people?

- WHAT is civil society?

A young woman of the Kabylie people, a Berber group of Algeria, wears a headband that signifies mourning during a public march to protest the government's denial of human rights to the Kabylie people. (*Source:* © *Tiz/CORBIS SYGMA*)

Canada's small population in a gigantic territory with two official languages "requires a greater use of the imagination . . . [demanding] of the citizenry a more open and active imagination, a more acute sensibility. It is not a situation for lazy minds and easy emotions" (Saul 1997:57).

The United States, which the early nineteenth century French political philosopher Alexis de Tocqueville called a "nation of joiners," has been united around powerful and unifying symbols like the "stars and stripes." Some have questioned whether Canada has developed a similar sense of unity and it often seems the nation faces imminent dissolution. Yet, there is no question that, for many Canadians, membership in social groups beyond the family is an important aspect of life. The questions of what motivates people to join groups, what holds people together in groups, and how groups deal with leadership and participation have intrigued many scholars for centuries.

In this chapter, we focus primarily on nonkin groups and relate to the issue of cultural formation. In Chapter 1, several factors related to the formation of local cultures were defined: class, race, ethnicity, gender, age, region, and institutions such as prisons and retirement homes. Thus far, we have looked at how these factors affect fieldwork, and how they vary in different economies and in different reproductive systems. In this chapter, we look again at these key factors of social differentiation in order to see how they affect group formation and the relationships between groups in terms of hierarchy and power. We first examine a variety of social groups and then consider inequalities between certain key social categories.

Social Groups

A **social group** is a cluster of people beyond the domestic unit who are usually related on grounds other than kinship, although kinship relationships may exist between people in the group. Two basic categories exist: the **primary group**, consisting of people who interact with each other and know each other personally, and the **secondary group**, consisting of people who identify with each other on some common ground but who may never meet with one another or interact with each other personally.

Members of all social groups have a sense of rights and responsibilities in relation to the group which, if not maintained, could mean loss of membership. Because of its face-to-face nature, membership in a primary group involves more direct accountability about rights and responsibilities than secondary group membership. When discussing different kinds of groups, social scientists also draw a distinction between *informal groups* and *formal groups* (March and Taqqu 1986:5):

- Informal groups are smaller and less visible.
- Members of informal groups have close, face-to-face relationships with one another, while members of formal groups may or may not know each other.
- Organizational structure is less hierarchical in informal groups.
- Informal groups do not have legal recognition.

Modes of economies seem to affect the proliferation of social groups, the greatest variety being found in agricultural and industrial societies. One theory suggests that mobile populations, such as foragers and pastoralists, are less likely to develop enduring social groups beyond kin relationships. Although foragers and pastoralists have less variety of social groups, they do not completely lack social groupings. A prominent form of social group among foragers and pastoralists is an **age set,** a group of people close in age who go through certain rituals, such as circumcision, at the same time.

A related hypothesis is that settled and densely populated areas have more social groups as a way to organize society. Again, this may be generally true, but important variations and exceptions exist. Both informal and formal groups appear to be more varied and active in Africa and Latin America than in South Asia (Uphoff and Esman 1984). In Bangladesh (see Map 9.1), a densely populated and agrarian country of South Asia, indigenous social groups are rare. The most prominent ties beyond the household are kinship-based (Miller and Khan 1986). In spite of the lack of indigenous social groups, however, Bangladesh has gained world renown for its success in forming local credit groups for grassroots development through an organization called the Grameen Bank, which gives loans to poor people to help them start small businesses.

In Bali, an island province of Indonesia, several formal and focused groups exist for specific purposes, including temple committees to provide for the costs of temple

---

social group: a cluster of people beyond the domestic unit who are usually related on grounds other than kinship.
primary group: a social group in which members meet on a face-to-face basis.

secondary group: people who identify with each other on some basis but may never meet with one another personally.

age set: a group of people close in age who go through certain rituals, such as circumcision, at the same time.

maintenance and collective rites; custom-law wards to cooperate in cremation ceremonies; neighbourhood groups to send food to the temple for the gods; and irrigation groups to provide water for the rice fields (Lansing 1995). Members of all households participate in several of these groups at the same time. The precise reasons that some cultures have strong and enduring social groups and others do not await further exploration.

In the following sections, we describe a wide variety of social groups starting with the most face-to-face, primary groups of two or three people based on friendship. The discussion moves to larger groups and more formal groups with explicit goals, such as countercultural groups and activist groups.

Friendship

Friendship refers to close social ties between at least two people that are informal, are voluntary, and involve personal, face-to-face interaction. Generally, friendship involves people who are nonkin, but in some cases kin are also friends (recall the Tory Islanders discussed in Chapter 8). Friendship fits in the category of a primary social group. One question that cultural anthropologists ask is whether friendship is a cultural universal. Two factors make it difficult to answer this question. First,

insufficient cross-cultural research exists to answer the question definitively. Second, defining friendship cross-culturally is problematic. It is likely, however, that something like "friendship" is a cultural universal, but shaped in different degrees from culture to culture (see the Multiple Cultural Worlds box on page 232).

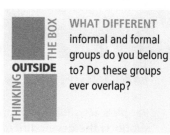

THINKING OUTSIDE THE BOX
WHAT DIFFERENT informal and formal groups do you belong to? Do these groups ever overlap?

Social Characteristics of Friendship

People choose their friends, and friends remain so on a voluntary basis. Even so, the criteria for who qualifies as a friend may be culturally structured. For instance, gender segregation will limit cross-gender friendships and promote same-gender friendships. In Thailand, "friends until death" are usually same-gender friends who can be trusted with intimate knowledge of one's motivations and desires. Another characteristic of friendship is that friends are supportive of each other, psychologically and sometimes materially. Support is mutual, shared back and forth in an expectable way. Friendship generally occurs between social equals.

Anthropologist Thomas Dunk researched how a group of working-class men friends in Thunder Bay, Ontario, informally ensure that everyone contributes their fair share (as in balanced exchange, see Chapter 4). After a game of lob-ball (a form of softball) the men meet at a bar. In the bar after the game, everyone takes turns buying rounds. If someone is short of money one evening, someone else or several other people stand him drinks. This "just happens"; one does not need to ask. True friends, for these men, are people who give to each other without asking, and this extends beyond the walls of the bar after a game (Dunk 1991:92).

Sharing stories is often a basis of friendship groups. In a study of male peer groups focused on interactions in rumshops in Guyana, South America (see Map 9.2), Indo-Guyanese men who have known each other since childhood reaffirm their solidarity through spending time, every day, at the rumshop eating, drinking, and regaling each other with stories (Sidnell 2000). Through shared storytelling about village history and other aspects of local knowledge, men display their equality with each other. The pattern of storytelling, referred to as "turn-at-talk," in which efforts are made to include everyone as a storyteller in turn, also serves to maintain equality and solidarity. These friendship groups are tightly knit, and the members can call on one another for economic, social, political, and ritual help.

Cell phone use among low-income people in Jamaica has wide use for "linking up," or creating extensive

MAP 9.1 Bangladesh. The People's Republic of Bangladesh is located on a deltaic floodplain with rich soil but also serious risk of flooding. One of the world's most densely populated countries, its 150 million people live in an area that is roughly the size of Canada's Maritime provinces. Bangladesh is the third-largest Muslim majority country.

MAKING FRIENDS

People's activities often provide a shared interest that supports the development of friendship ties. In Andalusia, southern Spain, the gender division of labour means that men and women pursue separate kinds of work and thus have differing friendship patterns (Uhl 1991). Men's work takes place outside the house and neighbourhood either in the fields or in manufacturing jobs. Women devote most of their time to unpaid household work within the domestic domain. This dichotomy is somewhat fluid, however, as women's domestic roles sometimes take them to the market or the town hall.

For men, an important category of friend is an *amigo*, a friend with whom one casually interacts. This kind of friendship is acted out and maintained in the context of bars, drinking together night after night. Bars are a man's world. Amigos share common experiences of school, sports and hobbies, and working together. In contrast, women refer to their friends either with kin terms or as *vecina*, "neighbour," reflecting women's primary orientation to family and neighbourhood.

Differences between men and women also emerge in the category of *amigos(as) del verdad*, or "true friends." True friends are those with whom one shares secrets without fear of betrayal. Most men have many more true friends than the women do, a pattern that reflects their wider social networks.

FOOD FOR THOUGHT

- What different categories of friends do you have? Are some kinds of friends "closer" or "truer" than others?

---

networks that include close friends, possible future sexual partners, and members of one's church (Horst and Miller 2005). Phone numbers of kin are also prominent on people's cell phone number lists. Participant observation and interviews with a sample of both rural and urban Jamaicans reveals that cell phone use is frequent, and Jamaicans are keenly aware of their call lists and how often they have kept in touch with the many individuals on their lists. By linking up periodically with people on their lists, low-income Jamaicans maintain friendship and other ties with people who they can call on when they need support. Cell phones allow a more extensive network of friends and other contacts than was previously possible.

MAP 9.2 Caribbean Countries of South America. The ethnically and linguistically diverse countries of the Caribbean region of South America include Guyana, Suriname, and French Guiana. Guyana (pronounced GAI-a-na), or the Co-operative Republic of Guyana, is the only South American country whose official language is English. Other languages are Hindi, Wai Wai, and Arawak. Its population is around 800 000. The Republiek Suriname, or Surinam, was formerly a colony of the Netherlands and is the smallest independent state in South America. Its population is 440 000. Dutch is the official language but most Surinamese also speak Sranang Tongo, or Surinaams, a mixture of Dutch, English, Portuguese, French, and local languages. French Guiana is an overseas department of France and is thus part of the European Union (EU). The smallest political unit in South America, its population is 200 000. Its official language is French but several other languages are spoken, including indigenous Arawak and Carib.

Friendship among the Urban Poor

Carol Stack's study of how friendship networks promote economic survival among low-income African Americans is a landmark contribution (1974). Her research was conducted in the late 1960s in "The Flats," the poorest section of a black community in a Midwestern American city. She found extensive networks of friends "supporting, reinforcing each other—devising schemes for self-help, strategies for survival in a community of severe economic deprivation" (28). Close friends, in fact, are referred to by kin terms.

People in The Flats, especially women, maintain a set of friends through exchange: "swapping" goods (food, clothing) needed by someone at a particular time, sharing "child keeping," and giving or loaning food stamps and money. Such exchanges are part of a clearly understood pattern—gifts and favours go back and forth over time. Friends bound together in such a way are obligated to one another and can call on each other in times of need. In opposition to theories that suggest the breakdown of social relationships among the very poor, this research documents how poor people strategize and cope through social ties.

Clubs and Fraternities

Clubs and fraternities are social groups that define membership on some sense of shared identity and objectives. They may comprise people of the same ethnic heritage (such as the United Empire Loyalists in Canada), occupation or business, religion, or gender. Although many clubs appear to exist primarily to serve functions of sociability and psychological support, deeper analysis often shows that these groups do have economic and political roles as well.

Women's clubs in a lower-class neighbourhood in Paramaribo, Suriname (see Map 9.2), have multiple functions (Brana-Shute 1976). Here, as is common elsewhere in Latin America, clubs raise funds to sponsor special events and support individual celebrations, meet financial needs, and send cards and flowers for funerals. Members attend each other's birthday parties and death rites as a group. The clubs thus offer to the women psychological support, entertainment, and financial supports. A political aspect exists, too. Club members are often members of the same political party, and attend political rallies and events together. These women constitute political interest groups that can influence political outcomes. Politicians and party workers confirmed that real pressure is exerted on them by women individually and in groups.

Men's clubs in which strong male–male bonds are created and reinforced by the objectification and mistreatment of women are common, but not universal. They are especially associated with cultures where male–male competitiveness is an important feature of society (Bird 1996) and in which warfare and group conflict are frequent. In many indigenous Amazonian groups, the men's house is fiercely guarded from being entered by women. If a woman were to trespass on male territory, she would be subject to punishment by gang rape. One interpretation is that males have a high degree of anxiety about their identity as fierce warriors and as sexually potent beings (Gregor 1982). Maintaining their identity as fierce males toward outsiders involves taking an aggressive position in relation to women of their own group.

In a low-income neighbourhood in Rio de Janeiro, Brazil, men play dominoes and drink beer while others observe. ■ (Source: © Stephanie Maze/Woodfin Camp & Associates)

Countercultural Groups

Several kinds of groups are formed by people who, for one reason or another, are outside the mainstream of society and resist conforming to the dominant cultural pattern, as in the hippie movement of the 1960s. In this section, we consider examples of countercultural groups. One similarity among these groups, as with clubs and fraternities, is the importance of bonding through shared initiation and other rituals.

Youth Gangs

The term *gang* can refer to a variety of groups, such as one's friends, as in, "I think I'll invite the gang over for pizza" (Short 1996:325). The more specific term **youth gang** refers to a group of young people, found mainly in urban areas, who are often considered a social problem by adults and law-enforcement officials (Sanders 1994:5–15).

Youth gangs vary in terms of how formally they are organized. Gangs—like clubs and fraternities—often have formalized rituals of initiation for new members, a recognized leader, and symbolic markers of identity such as tattoos or special clothing. An example of an informal youth gang with no formal leadership hierarchy or initiation rituals are the "Masta Liu," found in Honiara, the capital city of the Solomon Islands (Jourdan 1995) (see Map 9.3). The primary unifying feature of the male youth who become Masta Liu is the fact that they are unemployed. Most have migrated to the city from the countryside to escape what they consider an undesirable lifestyle there: working in the fields under control of their elders. Some liu live with extended kin in the city; others organize liu-only households. They spend their time wandering around town (*wakabaot*) in groups of up to 10 people:

> They stop at every shop on their way, eager to look at the merchandise but afraid to be kicked out by the security guards; they check out all the cinemas only to dream in front of the preview posters . . . not even having the $2 bill that will allow them to get in; they gaze for hours on end, and without moving, at the electronic equipment displayed in the Chinese shops, without saying a word: one can read in their gaze the silent dreams they create (1995:210)

Street gangs are a more formal variety of youth gang. They generally have leaders and a hierarchy of membership roles and responsibilities. They are named and their members mark their identity with tattoos or "colours." Much popular thinking associates street gangs with violence, but not all are involved in violence. An anthropologist who did research among nearly 40 street gangs in New York, Los Angeles, and Boston learned much about why individuals join gangs, providing insights that contradict popular thinking (Jankowski 1991). One common perception is that young boys join gangs because they are from homes with no male authority figure with whom they could identify. In the gangs studied, just as many gang members were from intact nuclear households as from families with an absent father. Another common perception is that the gang replaces a missing feeling of "family" as a motive. This study showed that the same number of gang members reported having close family ties as those who did not.

What, then, might be the reasons behind joining a male urban gang? A particular personality type characterized

many gang members, a type that could be called a *defiant individualist*. The defiant individualist type has five traits: intense competitiveness, mistrust or wariness, self-reliance, social isolation, and a strong survival instinct. Urban poverty possibly leads to the development of this kind of

THINKING **OUTSIDE** THE BOX

THINK OF some examples in which socially excluded groups have contributed to changing styles of music, dress, and other forms of expressive culture of so-called mainstream groups.

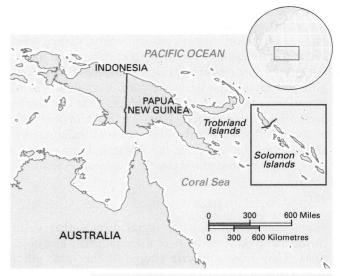

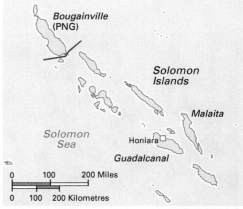

MAP 9.3   The Solomon Islands. This country consists of nearly 1000 islands. Its capital, Honiara, is located on the island of Guadalcanal. The Solomons were the site of some of the bitterest fighting during World War II. Most of the people earn a living through small-scale farming and fishing. Commercial exploitation of local timber has led to severe deforestation. The population is 540 000. Over seventy languages are spoken, and four have recently gone extinct. The majority of the people are Christian, mainly Anglican.

---

youth gang: a group of young people, found mainly in urban areas, who are often considered a social problem by adults and law-enforcement officials.

Members of the gang "18" in San Salvador, El Salvador, passing time on the street. The group's leader prohibits the use of alcohol and drugs except on Saturdays and Sundays. ■ (Source: © Jerome Sessini/In Visu/CORBIS)

Members of the Hells Angels biker gang leave a chapel in Edmonton after the funeral of a brother who was killed in a motor vehicle accident. ■ (Source: Canadian Press EDMS)

personality structure. It becomes a reasonable response to the economic obstacles and uncertainty.

The global spread of urban youth gangs relates to global economic changes in urban employment. In many countries, the declining urban industrial base has created persistent poverty in inner-city communities (Short 1996:326). At the same time, aspirations for a better life have been promoted through schooling and the popular media. Urban gang members, in this view, are the victims of large structural forces beyond their control. Yet research with gangs shows that they are not just passive victims of structural forces. Many of these youths want to be economically successful, but social conditions channel their interests and skills into illegal pursuits rather than into legal pathways to achievement.

Motorcycle Gangs

Another countercultural group similar to the street gangs is the widespread North American (and growing global) phenomenon of outlaw motorcycle gangs. In the late 1940s, young men, who had served in the citizen armies of Canada and the United States, formed clubs of motorcycle riders. Some of these developed into the "one percenters," the one percent of motorcyclists who were troublemakers according to mainstream motorcycle enthusiasts. Such "outlaw" clubs are characterized by wearing colours, or a club insignia, which often include pictures of skulls or weapons meant to intimidate citizens and other gang members alike. The gang member typically "chops" or modifies his "hog" (a Harley-Davidson motorcycle), and exhibits loyalty to his brothers by helping defend a particular territory by physical force, if necessary.

Daniel R. Wolf (1991), an anthropologist who was a member of one such gang in Edmonton, describes how and why young working-class men find identity and satisfaction in the gang. Working-class employment does not provide the sense of self or meaning that may be available to other societal roles in industrial Canada. Wolf argues that the motorcycle club provides these young alienated men with an identity and community they cannot find elsewhere (340). Riding in the wind, partying with brothers, and participating in sexual exploits with their girlfriends ("mamas") balance the constant threat of being hassled by the police and the dangers of physical injury both from citizens in "cages" (cars or trucks) running them off the roads and from fights with other gangs.

Body-Modification Groups

Of the many nonmainstream movements in North America, one includes people who have a sense of community strengthened through forms of body alteration. James Myers (1992) did research in California among people who feel they are a special group because of their interest in permanent body modification, especially genital piercing, branding, and cutting. Myers was involved in six workshops organized especially for the San Francisco SM (sadomasochist) community by Powerhouse, a San Francisco Bay Area SM organization; the Fifth Annual Living in Leather Convention held in Portland, Oregon, in 1990; and time in tattoo and piercing studios as well as talking with students and others in his hometown who were involved in these forms of body modification. The study population included males and females, heterosexuals, gays, lesbians, bisexuals, and SMers. The two largest groups were SM gays and bisexuals, those in the study were mainly white, and most had either attended or graduated from college.

Myers witnessed many modification sessions at workshops: Those seeking modification go up on stage and have their chosen procedure done by a well-known expert. Whatever the procedure, the volunteers evidence little pain (usually a sharp intake of breath at the moment the needle passes through or the brand touches skin). After that critical moment, the audience breathes an audible sigh of relief. The volunteer stands up, adjusts clothing, and members of the audience applaud. Myers interprets this public event as a kind of initiation ritual that binds the expert, the volunteer, and the group together. Pain has long been recognized as an important part of rites of passage, providing an edge to the ritual drama. The audience in this case witnesses and validates the experience and also becomes joined to the initiate through witnessing.

A prominent motivation for seeking permanent body modification was a desire to identify with a specific group of people, and the body marking is thus a sign of affiliation. As one informant said,

> It's not that we're sheep, getting pierced or cut just because everyone else is. I like to think it's because we're a very special group and we like doing something that sets us off from others. . . . Happiness is standing in line at a cafeteria and detecting that the straight-looking babe in front of you has her nipples pierced. I don't really care what her sexual orientation is, I can relate to her. (292)

Left: A Tahitian chief wears traditional tattoos that indicate his high status. ■ (Source: © Charles & Josette Lenars/CORBIS) **Right: A North American woman with tattooed arms and a pierced nose.** ■ (Source: © Royalty-Free/CORBIS)

cooperatives: a form of economic group with two key features: surpluses are shared among the members, and decision-making follows the democratic principle of one person, one vote.

Work Groups

Work groups are organized to perform specific tasks, although they also may have other functions, including sociality and friendship among members. They are found in all modes of production, but they tend to be more prominent in pre-industrialized horticultural and agricultural communities where land preparation, harvesting, or repair of irrigation canals requires large inputs of labour that exceed the capability of a single household unit. In her classic study of the Bemessi people of Cameroon, West Africa, Phyllis Kaberry (1952) describes a labour group system called a *tzo,* translated as "working bee." Among the Bemessi, women were responsible for horticulture. Related to this role, women were also responsible for organizing collective work. For preparing corn beds, ten to twelve women worked on each others' plots. For weeding, smaller groups of three to four women formed. At the end of the workday, the women have a meal of fish provided for them by their husbands.

Youth work groups are common in African regions south of the Sahara, particularly in settled, crop-growing areas. The major responsibility of the youth groups is providing field labour. The group works one or more days in the village chief's fields for no reward or pay. They also maintain public paths and the public meeting area, construct and maintain roads between villages, build and repair canals, combat brush fires, maintain the village mosque, and prevent animals from grazing where they aren't allowed (Leynaud 1961). Girls' groups exist, but in patrilocal contexts they are less durable because their marriage and relocation breaks ties with childhood companions (Hammond 1966:133). As adults, however, women in African cultures have many types of associations, such as mothers' groups, savings groups, and work groups.

Irrigation organizations are formal groups devoted to maintaining irrigation canals and dealing with the tricky issue of distributing the water. These organizations are responsible for a highly valued good, and they tend to develop leadership and membership rules and roles. Because watershed systems are connected across large regions, irrigation organizations often provide a link between local groups.

Allocating the water from the canals also requires careful administration. As is often the case, water is allocated proportionally according to landholdings (Coward 1976, 1979). But farmers who are downstream are more likely to be deprived of their fair share than farmers who are upstream and can divert more water to their fields. In order to deal with conflicts that arise from this built-in inequity in one area of the Philippines, subgroups of farmers formed to meet and discuss distribution problems.

Another administrative issue is corruption such as water theft, in which a farmer taps off water out of turn (D. H. Price 1995). Water theft in Egypt, as elsewhere, is more common as distance from the main canal increased. Farmers further from the source feel they are justified in their actions because they get less water through the distribution system than farmers closer to the source.

Cooperatives

Cooperatives are a form of economic group with two key features: surpluses are shared among the members, and decision-making follows the democratic principle of one person, one vote (Estrin 1996). Agricultural and credit cooperatives are the most common forms of cooperatives worldwide, followed by consumer cooperatives.

Craft Cooperatives in Panama

In Panama's east coastal region, Kuna women have long sewn beautiful *molas,* or cloth with appliquéd designs (see Map 9.4 on page 238). This cloth is made for their own use as clothing (Tice 1995). Since the 1960s, *molas* have been important items for sale both on the world market and to tourists who come to Panama. Revenue

Kuna Indian woman selling *molas,* San Blas Islands, Panama. ■ (Source: © Wolfgang Koehler)

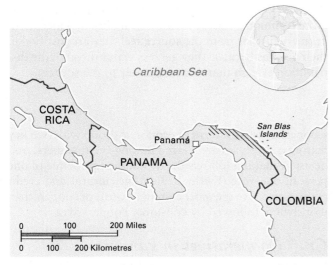

MAP 9.4 Kuna Region in Panama. The Kuna are an indigenous people who live mainly in the eastern coastal region of Panama, including its offshore islands. Some live in cities and a few live in villages in neighbouring Colombia. Each community has its own political organization, and the Kuna as a whole are organized into the Kuna General Congress. The Kuna population is around 150 000. Most speak Kuna, or Dulegaya ("People's Language") and Spanish. They follow traditional religious practices, often with a mixture of Christian elements. Farming, fishing, and tourism are important parts of the economy.

from selling *molas* is now an important part of the household income of the Kuna. Some women continue to operate independently, buying their own cloth and thread and selling their *molas* either to an intermediary who exports them or in the local tourist market. But many other women have joined cooperatives that offer them greater economic security.

The cooperative buys cloth and thread in bulk and distributes it to the women. The women are paid almost the entire sale price for each *mola,* with only a small amount of the eventual sale prices being taken out for cooperative dues and administrative costs. Their earnings are steadier than what the fluctuating tourist season offers.

Beyond the initial economic reasons for joining the cooperative, other benefits include the use of the cooperative as a consumer's cooperative (buying rice and sugar in bulk for members), as a source of mutual strength and support, and as a basis for women's greater leadership skills and opportunities for political participation in the wider society.

Self-Help Groups

Recent years have seen a worldwide proliferation of *self-help groups,* or groups formed to achieve specific personal goals, such as coping with illness or bereavement, or lifestyle change, such as trying to exercise more or lose weight. Self-help groups also increasingly use the Internet to form virtual support communities. Anthropologists who study these groups focus on why members join, on rituals of solidarity, and on leadership and organization patterns.

An ethnography of Alcoholic Anonymous groups in Mexico City reports that most members are low-income, working-class males (Brandes 2002). Most of these men migrated to Mexico City from rural areas several decades earlier to find work and improve their standard of living. Their drinking problems are related both to their poverty and to the close links between alcohol consumption and male gender identity in Mexico (a "real man" consumes a lot of alcohol). Through a dynamic of shared stories and regular meetings, AA members in Mexico City achieve a high rate of sobriety.

The success of AA in Mexico is leading to a rapid proliferation of groups. Membership is growing at about 10 percent a year, a remarkably high rate of growth for a self-help organization. At the end of the twentieth century, Latin America accounted for almost one-third of the world AA membership. Thus, a model of a middle-class self-help organization that originated in the United States has been culturally localized by low-income men throughout Latin America.

Social Stratification

Social stratification consists of hierarchical relationships between different groups—as if they were arranged in layers or "strata." Stratified groups may be unequal on a variety of measures, including material resources, power, human welfare, education, and symbolic attributes. People in groups in higher positions have privileges

---

social stratification: hierarchical relationships between different groups as though they were arranged in layers or "strata."
ascribed position: a person's standing in society, based on qualities gained through birth.

achieved position: a person's standing in society, based on qualities gained through action.
status: a person's position or standing in society.

role: comprises both expected behaviour for someone of a particular status and a "script" for how to behave, look, and talk.

not experienced by those in lower groups, and they are likely to be interested in maintaining their privileged position. Social stratification emerged late in human history, most clearly with the emergence of agriculture. Now some form of social stratification is nearly universal.

Analysis of the categories—such as class, race, gender, and age—that form stratification systems reveals a crucial difference in the degree to which membership in a given category is an **ascribed position**, based on qualities of a person gained through birth, or an **achieved position**, based on qualities of a person gained through action. Ascribed positions include one's race, ethnicity, gender, age, and physical ability. These factors are usually out of the control of the individual, although some scope for flexibility exists in gender through surgery and hormonal treatments and for certain kinds of physical conditions. Also, one can sometimes "pass" for being a member of another race or ethnic group. Age is an interesting ascribed category because an individual will pass through several different status levels associated with age. Achievement as a basis for group membership means that a person belongs on the basis of some valued attainment. Ascribed systems are thus more "closed" and achievement-based systems more "open" in terms of mobility within the system (either upward or downward). Some scholars of social status believe that increasing social complexity and modernization led to an increase in achievement-based positions and a decline in ascription-based positions. In the next section, we look at the way key social categories define group membership and varying relations of inequality among groups.

The Concept of Status Groups

Societies place people into categories—student, husband, child, retired person, political leader, or member of the Order of Canada—which are referred to as a person's **status** (position or standing in society) (C. Wolf 1996). Each status has an accompanying **role** which is expected behaviour for someone of a particular status, and a "script" for how to behave, look, and talk. Some statuses have more prestige attached to them than others (the word *status* can be used to mean prestige, relative value, and worth). Groups, like individuals, have status, or standing in society. German sociologist Max Weber called lower-status groups *disprivileged* groups. These include, in different contexts and in different times, physically disabled people, people with certain illnesses such as leprosy or HIV/AIDS, indigenous peoples, minorities, members of particular religions, women, and others.

Within societies that have marked status positions, different status groups are marked by a particular lifestyle, including goods owned, leisure activities, and linguistic styles. The maintenance of group position by higher-status categories is sometimes accomplished by exclusionary practices in relation to lower-status groups through a tendency toward group in-marriage and by socializing only within the group.

Class

Social class refers to a person's or group's position in society defined primarily in economic terms. In many cultures, class is a key factor determining a person's status, whereas in others it is less important than, for example, birth into a certain family. However, class and status do not always match. A rich person may have become wealthy in disreputable ways and never gain high status. Both status and class groups are secondary groups, because a person is unlikely to know every other member of the group, especially in large-scale societies. In most instances, they are also informal groups since there are no recognized leaders or elected officials of the "urban elite" or the "working class." Subsegments of these large categories do organize themselves into formal groups, such as labour unions or exclusive clubs for the rich and famous. Class can be both ascribed and achieved since a person who is born rich has a greater than average chance of living an upper-class lifestyle.

In "open" capitalist societies, the prevailing ideology is that the system allows for upward mobility and that every individual has the option of moving up. Some anthropologists refer to this ideology as *meritocratic individualism*—the belief that rewards go to those who deserve them (Durrenberger 2001). This ideology would seem to be most valid for people with decent jobs rather than menial workers or the unemployed, but in fact the ideology is widely held outside the middle class. In Canada and the United States, the pervasive popular belief in rewards for equal opportunity and merit is upheld and promoted in schools and universities, even in the face of substantial evidence to the contrary.

Conservative governments and political parties have long sought to weaken labour unions, and they continue to promote the fantasy of a classless society based on meritocratic individualism to support their anti-union policies. Some anthropologists point to the power of economic class position in shaping a person's lifestyle and his or her ability to choose a different one. Obviously, a person born rich can, through individual agency, become poor, and a poor person can become rich. But in spite of exceptions to the rule, a person born rich is more likely to lead a lifestyle typical of that class, just as a person born poor is more likely to lead a lifestyle typical of that class.

The concept of class was central to the theories of Karl Marx. Situated within the context of Europe's industrial revolution and the growth of capitalism, Marx wrote that class differences, exploitation of the working class by the owners of capital, class consciousness among workers, and class conflict are forces of change that would eventually bring the downfall of capitalism.

In contrast to Marx's approach, French sociologist Émile Durkheim viewed social differences (including class) as the basis for social solidarity (1966 [1895]). He distinguished two major forms of societal cohesion: **mechanical solidarity**, which exists when groups that are similar join together, and **organic solidarity**, which prevails when groups with different abilities and resources join. Mechanical solidarity creates less enduring relationships because it involves little mutual need. Organic solidarity builds on need and creates stronger bonds. Durkheim placed these two concepts in an evolutionary framework, saying that in pre-industrial times, the division of labour was only minimally specialized: Everyone did what everyone else did. With increasing social complexity and economic specialization, organic solidarity developed.

Boys in a small town of Brazil exhibit the skin-colour diversity in the Brazilian population. ■ (Source: © David G. Houser/CORBIS)

Race, Ethnicity, and Caste

Three major ascribed systems of social stratification are based on divisions of people into groups on the basis of race, ethnicity, and **caste**. Ranking within the caste system is determined by birth and is often linked to a particular occupation. This system is often associated with South Asian cultures. Like status and class groups, these three categories are secondary social groups, because no one can have a personal relationship with all other members of the entire group. Each system takes on local specificities depending on the context. For example, race and ethnicity are interrelated and overlap with conceptions of culture in much of Latin America, although differences in what they mean in terms of identity and status occur in different countries in the region (de la Cadena 2001). For some the concept of *mestizaje,* or racial mixture, refers to people who are disenfranchised and cut off from their Indian roots, but for others it can refer to literate and successful people who retain indigenous cultural practices. One has to know the local system of categories and meanings attached to them to understand the dynamics of inequality that go with them.

Systems based in difference defined in terms of race, ethnicity, and caste share with each other, and with class-based systems, some important features. First, they relegate large numbers of people to particular levels of entitlement to livelihood, power, security, esteem, and freedom (Berreman

1979:213). This simple fact should not be overlooked. Second, those with greater entitlements dominate those with lesser entitlements. Third, members of the dominant groups tend—consciously or unconsciously—to seek to maintain their position. Fourth, in spite of efforts to maintain systems of dominance, instances of subversion and rebellion do occur, indicating the potential for agency among the oppressed.

Race

Racial stratification is a relatively recent form of social inequality. It results from the unequal meeting of two formerly separate groups through colonization, slavery, and other large-group movements (Sanjek 1994). Europe's "age of discovery," beginning in the 1500s, ushered in a new era of global contact. In contrast, in relatively homogeneous cultures, ethnicity is a more important distinction than race. In contemporary Nigeria, for example, the population is relatively homogeneous, and ethnicity is the more salient term there (Jinadu 1994). A similar situation prevails in Rwanda and other African states.

A key feature of racial thinking is its insistence that behavioural differences among peoples are "natural," inborn, or biologically caused (in this, it resembles sexism, ageism, and casteism). Throughout the history of racial categorizations in the West, such features as head size, head shape, and brain size have been accepted as the

---

mechanical solidarity: social bonding among groups that are similar.

organic solidarity: social bonding among groups with different abilities and resources.

caste: a ranked group, determined by birth, often linked to a particular occupation and to South Asian cultures.

In 2003, the Treatment Action Campaign (TAC) began a program of civil disobedience to prompt the government of South Africa to sign and implement a National Prevention and Treatment Plan for HIV/AIDS. The TAC uses images of Hector Peterson, the first youth killed in the Soweto uprising against apartheid, and slogans such as "The Struggle Continues: Support HIV/AIDS Treatment Now. ■ (Source: © Gideon Mendel/CORBIS)

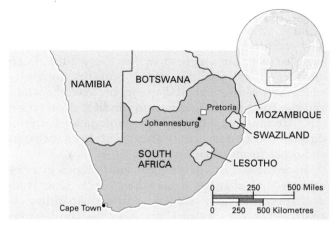

MAP 9.5 South Africa. The Republic of South Africa (which has 11 official names in different languages), had the highest level of colonial immigration of any country of Africa. Its rich mineral wealth attracted interest from global powers through the Cold War era. Of its population of over 47 million people, 80 percent are black South Africans. The rest are of mixed ethnic backgrounds (referred to as "coloureds"), Indian (from India), or white descendants of colonial immigrants. South Africa has 11 official languages, and it recognizes 8 nonofficial languages. Afrikaans and English are the major languages of the administration. Nonofficial languages include those of the San and other indigenous peoples.

reasons for behavioural differences. Writing early in the twentieth century, Franz Boas contributed to de-linking supposed in-born, racial attributes from behaviour. He showed that people with the same head size but from different cultures behaved differently, and people with different head sizes within the same cultures behaved similarly. For Boas, culture, not biology, is the key explanation for behaviour. Following this approach, anthropologists have concluded that race is not a biological reality; there is no way to divide the human population into races on the basis of biological features. Yet, *social race* and racism exist. In other words, the concept of "race" in many contexts has a social reality in terms of people's entitlements, status, and treatment. In spite of some progress in reducing racism in North America in the twentieth century, racial discrimination persists. One way of understanding this persistence is to see racial discrimination as linked to class formation, rather than separate from it (Brodkin 2000). In this view, racial stereotyping and discrimination functions to maintain people in less desirable jobs, or unemployed, as necessary aspects of advanced industrial capitalism, which depends on a certain number of low-paid workers and even a certain amount of unemployment.

Racial classifications in the Caribbean and Latin America are especially complicated systems of status classification. This complexity results from the variety of contact over the centuries between peoples from Europe, Africa, Asia, and indigenous populations. Skin tone is one basis of racial classification, but it is mixed with other physical features and economic status as

well. In Haiti, for example, racial categories take into account physical features such as skin texture, depth of skin tone, hair colour and appearance, and facial features (Trouillot 1994). Racial categories also include a person's income, social origin, level of formal education, personality or behaviour, and kinship ties. Depending on how these variables are combined, a person occupies one category or another—and may even move between categories. Thus a person with certain physical features who is poor will be considered to be a different "colour" than a person with the same physical features who is well off.

An extreme example of racial stratification was the South African policy of apartheid, legally sanctioned segregation between dominant whites and non-whites. White dominance in South Africa (see Map 9.5) began in the early 1800s with white migration and settlement. In the 1830s, slavery was abolished. At the same time, increasingly racist thinking developed among whites (Johnson 1994:25). Racist images, including visions of Africans as lazy, uncontrolled, and libidinous, served as the rationale for colonialist domination in place of outright slavery. In spite of years of African resistance to white domination, the whites succeeded in maintaining and increasing their control for nearly two centuries. In South Africa, blacks constitute 80 percent of the population, a numerical majority dominated through strict apartheid by the white minority until only recently. Every aspect of life for the majority of Africans was far worse than for the whites. Every measure of life quality—infant mortality, longevity, education—showed great disparity between the whites and the Africans. In addition to physical deprivation, the Africans experienced psychological suffering through constant insecurity about raids from the police and other forms of violence.

Since the end of apartheid in South Africa in 1994, many social changes have taken place. One study describes the early stages of the dismantling of apartheid in the city of Umtata, in the southeastern part of the country (Johnson 1994). Before the end of apartheid, Umtata "was like other South African towns: all apartheid laws were in full force; public and private facilities were completely segregated; only whites could vote or serve in the town government; whites owned all the major economic assets" (1994:viii). When the change came, Umtata's dominant whites bitterly resisted at first. They did not want to lose their privileges, and they feared reprisals by the Africans. These things did not happen, however. The initial stages of transition brought "neoapartheid," in which white privilege was not seriously threatened. Then members of the dominant group began to welcome the less tense, "nonracial" atmosphere.

In contrast to the explicitly racist discrimination of South African apartheid, racism exists within contexts where no public discourse about race or racism is found, where instead there is silence about it (Sheriff 2000). In such a context, the silence works to allow racial discrimination to continue in ways that are as effective as a clearly stated policy such as apartheid, or perhaps even more so since it is more difficult to critique and dismantle an institution whose existence is denied. Canadian anthropologist Stanley Barrett argues

> Racism has been endemic in Canada. . . . It has reached from the Pacific to the Atlantic, taking different forms according to the local ethnic composition, targeting Asians in Vancouver, blacks in Nova Scotia, and Jews everywhere. . . . It has appeared both visibly in the form of violent attacks and covertly in the form of variations in wages and employment opportunities based on racial criteria. (Barrett 1987: 307–308)

Ethnicity

Ethnicity is a sense of group membership based on a shared sense of identity (Comaroff 1987). Identity is formed sometimes on the basis of a perception of shared history, territory, language, or religion. Ethnicity can be a basis for claiming entitlements to resources such as land or artifacts, and for defending or regaining those resources.

States are interested in managing ethnicity to the extent that it does not threaten security. China has one of the most formalized systems for monitoring its many ethnic groups, and it has an official policy on ethnic minorities, meaning the non-Han groups (Wu 1990). The government lists a total of 54 groups other than the Han majority, which constitutes about 94 percent of the total. The other 6 percent of the population is made up of the 54 groups, about 67 million people. The non-Han minorities occupy about 60 percent of China's land mass and are located in border or "frontier" areas such as Tibet, Yunnan, Xinjiang, and Inner Mongolia. Basic criteria for defining an ethnic group include language, territory, economy, and "psychological disposition." The Chinese government establishes strict definitions of group membership and group characteristics, including setting standards for ethnic costumes and dances. The Chinese treatment of the Tibetan people is especially severe and can be considered an attempt at ethnocide or annihilation of the culture of an ethnic group by a dominant group. The Tibetans continue to resist the loss of their culture and absorption into the Han mainstream. The government's treatment of Tibetan traditional medicine over the past several decades illustrates how the Han majority uses certain aspects of minority cultures (see the accompanying Critical Thinking box).

People of one ethnic group who move from one place to another are at risk of exclusionary treatment from the local residents at their new location. Roma were formerly called gypsies by outsiders, but it is considered a derogatory term by the Roma. They are a **diaspora population**, a dispersed group living outside their original homeland, and are scattered throughout Europe and North America (see the Ethnographic Profile box on page 245).

A less difficult but still not easy adjustment is being experienced by Indo-Canadians (immigrants from India to Canada). In research among a sample of nearly 300 Indo-Canadians in Vancouver, British Columbia, about half of all the respondents reported experiencing some form of discrimination in the recent past (Nodwell and Guppy 1992). The percentage was

---

diaspora population: dispersed group of people living outside their original homeland.

caste system: a social stratification system linked with Hinduism and based on a person's birth into a particular group.

Critical Thinking

THE CHINESE TAKEOVER OF TIBETAN MEDICINE

In 1951, Tibet became part of China, and the Chinese government undertook measures to bring about the social and economic transformation of what was formerly a decentralized, Buddhist feudal regime. This transformation has brought increasing ethnic conflict between Tibetans and Han Chinese, including demonstrations by Tibetans and crackdowns from the government. Traditional Tibetan medicine has become part of the Chinese–Tibetan conflicts because of its culturally significant and religiously important position in Tibetan society (Janes 1995:7).

Several policy swings of the Chinese state toward Tibetan traditional medicine occurred in the second half of the twentieth century: Between 1951 and 1962, it was tolerated but largely ignored; by 1962, it was officially included as a component of the public health system and given funds for clinical operations and training programs; in 1966, it was delegitimized; in 1978, it was near extinction; and in 1985, it re-emerged as a legitimate sector of the government health bureaucracy, having a major role in providing primary health care in the Tibetan region, with a substantial operating budget and over 1200 physicians.

Linkage with a centralized medical system substantially transformed traditional Tibetan medicine.

The training of physicians is one area of major change. Previously based on a model of apprenticeship training, it is now westernized and involves several years of classroom-based, lecture-oriented learning followed by an internship. At Tibet University, only half of all formal lecture-based instruction is concerned with traditional Tibetan medicine. Curriculum changes have reduced the integrity of Tibetan medicine: It has been separated from its Buddhist content, and parts of it have been merged with a biomedical approach. While one might say that overall, traditional Tibetan medicine has been "revived" in China, stronger evidence supports the argument that the state has co-opted it and transformed it for its own purposes.

CRITICAL THINKING QUESTIONS

- How could the Chinese government justify the suppression of traditional Tibetan medicine?
- Why do you think the Chinese government eventually revived traditional Tibetan medicine?
- Which form of medicine dominates Chinese government health planning and policy—biomedical or traditional medicine? Can you suggest why?

---

higher among men (54 percent) than among women (45 percent). The higher level for men was consistent across the four categories: verbal abuse, property damage, workplace discrimination, and physical harm. Verbal abuse was the most frequent form of discrimination, reported by 40 percent of both men and women. Indo-Canadians of the Sikh faith who were born in India say that they experience the highest levels of discrimination in Canada. Apparently, however, their actual experience of discrimination is not greater than for other Indo-Canadians. The difference is that Sikhs who were born in India are more sensitive to discrimination than others. Sikhism, as taught and practised in India, supports a strong sense of honour, which should be protected and, if wronged, avenged. This study helps explain differences in perception of discrimination among ethnic migrants. It does not explain why such high levels of discriminatory treatment exist in a nation committed to ethnic tolerance.

Caste

The **caste system** is a form of social stratification linked with Hinduism and based on a person's birth into a particular group. It exists in its clearest form in India, among its Hindu population, and in other areas of Hindu culture such as Nepal, Sri Lanka, and Fiji. The caste system is particularly associated with Hindu peoples because ancient Hindu scriptures are taken as the foundational sources for defining the major social categories called *varnas* (a Sanskrit word meaning "colour," or "shade") (see Figure 9.1 on page 244). The four *varnas* are the *brahmans*, who were priests; the *kshatriya*, or warriors; the *vaishya*, or merchants; and the *shudras*, or labourers. Of these, men of the first three *varnas* go through a ritual ceremony of "rebirth" after which they may wear a sacred thread across their chest, indicating their purity and high status as "twice-born." Beneath the four *varna* groups were people considered so low that they were outside the caste system itself, hence, the

English term *outcast.* Another English term for them is *untouchables,* since people of the upper *varnas* avoided any kind of contact with them in order to maintain their purity. Mahatma Gandhi, himself a member of an upper caste, renamed them *harijans* (or "children of god") as part of his attempt to raise their status into that of the shudras. Currently, members of this category have adopted the term ***dalit***, which means "oppressed" or "ground down."

The four traditional varnas and the *dalit* category contain many hundreds of locally named groups called *castes* or, more appropriately, *jatis* (birth group). The term *caste* is a Portuguese word meaning "breed" or "type" and was first used by Portuguese colonialists in the fifteenth century to refer to the closed social groups they encountered (Cohn 1971:125). *Jati* a more emic term, conveys the meaning that a Hindu is born into his or her group. *Jatis* are ascribed status groups. Just as the four *varnas* are ranked with each other, so are all the *jatis* within them. For example, the *jati* of brahmans is divided into priestly and nonpriestly subgroups, the priestly brahmans are separated into household-priests, temple-priests, and funeral-priests; the household-priests are divided into two or more categories; and each of those are split into subgroups based on lineage ties (Parry 1966:77). Within all these categories, well-defined status hierarchies exist.

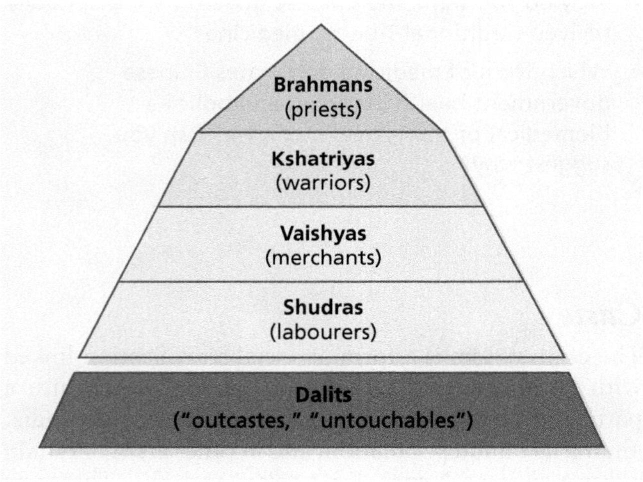
Brahmans
(priests)
Kshatriyas
(warriors)
Vaishyas
(merchants)
Shudras
(labourers)
Dalits
("outcastes," "untouchables")

FIGURE 9.1 Model of the Varna System in India Within each of the major categories presented here, numerous castes and subcastes exist. The shape of the model is intended to suggest that the higher-ranking categories include fewer numbers of people than lower-ranking categories. The name for the priestly varna is variously transliterated into English as brahman or brahmin.

Status levels also exist among *dalits.* In western Nepal, which, like India, has a caste system, *dalit* artisans such as basket-weavers and ironsmiths are the highest tier (M. Cameron 1995). They do not touch any of the people beneath them. The second tier includes leatherworkers and tailors. The bottom tier comprises people who are "untouchable" to all other groups including other *dalits* because their work is extremely polluting according to Hindu rules. This category includes musicians (because some of their instruments are made of leather and they perform in public) and sex workers.

Indian anthropologist M. N. Srinivas (1959) contributed the concept of the *dominant caste* to refer to the tendency for one caste in any particular village to control most of the land and, often, to be numerically preponderant as well. Brahmans are at the top of the social hierarchy in terms of ritual purity; they are often, but not always, the dominant caste. Throughout northern India, it is common for *jatis* of the *kshatriya varna* to be the dominant village group. This is the case in Pahansu village, where a group called the Gujars is dominant (Raheja 1988). The Gujars constitute the numerical majority, and they control most of the land (see Table 9.1 on page 246). Moreover, they dominate in the *jajmani system,* a patron-provider system in which landholding patrons (jajmans) are linked through exchanges of food for services with brahman priests, artisans (blacksmiths, potters), agricultural labourers, and other workers such as sweepers (Kolenda 1978:46–54). In Pahansu, Gujars have power and status as the major patrons, supporting many different service providers who are thus beholden to them.

Some anthropologists have described the *jajmani* service system as one of mutual interdependence (organic solidarity, to use Durkheim's term), which provides security for the less well-off. Others argue that the system benefits those at the top to the detriment of those at the bottom. This perspective, from "the bottom up," views the patron-service system and the entire caste system as one of exploitation by those at the top (Mencher 1974). The benign interpretation is based on research conducted among the upper castes who present this view. From low-caste people's perspective, it is the patrons who have the power. Dissatisfied patrons can dismiss service providers, refuse them

dalit: the preferred name for the socially defined lowest groups in the Indian caste system, meaning "oppressed" or "ground down."

Ethnographic Profile

The Roma of Eastern Europe

The Roma, better known by the derogatory term "gypsies," are Europe's largest minority population. They live in nearly all the countries of Europe and central Asia. In Europe, total Roma population is between 7 and 9 million people (World Bank 2003). They are most concentrated in the countries of Eastern Europe, where they constitute around 10 percent of the population.

Roma history is one of mobility and marginality ever since several waves of migrants left their original homeland in northern India between the ninth and fourteenth centuries CE (Crowe 1996). For many Roma in Europe, their lifestyle continues to involve movement. Temporary camps of their wagons often appear overnight on the outskirts of a town. Settled Roma typically live in marginalized areas that lack decent housing, clean water, and good schools. Most members of mainstream society look down on, and even despise, the Roma.

In Budapest, Hungary, the Roma minority is the most disadvantaged ethnic group (Ladányi 1993). Not all Roma in Budapest, however, are poor. Roughly 1 percent have gained wealth. The other 99 percent live in substandard housing in the slums of inner Pest. Since the fall of state socialism in Hungary, discrimination against the Roma has increased. Hungary's government has a policy that allows the Roma a degree of local minority self-government (Schaft and Brown 2000). Some Roma communities are mobilizing to improve their living conditions.

In Slovakia, one-third of the Roma live in ghetto-like enclaves called *osada* (Scheffel 2004). The heaviest concentration of *osadas* is in the eastern province. These settlements lack clean water, sewage treatment, reliable electricity, access to decent housing, good schools, and passable roads; they exist in close proximity to affluent neighbourhoods of ethnic Slovaks, or "whites." In one village, Svinia (pronounced SVIH-neeyah), roughly 700 Roma are crowded together on a hectare of swampy land while their 670 ethnic Slovak neighbours own over 1400 hectares of land (2004:8).

As more Eastern European countries seek to enter the European Union (EU), they are initiating programs to improve Roma living conditions and enacting laws to prevent discrimination. Field research in Slovakia suggests that the government, in fact, is doing little to improve the lives of the Roma. The situation for the Roma in Hungary, in contrast, is more hopeful. After Hungary's accession to the European Union in 2004, it elected two Roma to the EU Parliament. In Bulgaria, the Roma won a court case in 2005 declaring that segregated schools were unconstitutional.

Readings

David Z. Scheffel. "Slovak Roma on the Threshold of Europe." *Anthropology Today,* 20 (1): 6–12, 2004.
_____. *Svinia in Black and White: Slovak Roma and Their Neighbours.* Peterborough, ON: Broadview Press, 2005.
Carol Silverman. "Persecution and Politicization: The Roma of Eastern Europe." *Cultural Survival Quarterly,* 19 (2): 43–49, 1995.

Video

Suspino: A Cry for Roma. (Bullfrog Films, 2003).

Websites

www.svinia.net
http://news.nationalgeographic.com/news/2007/01/070104-gypsy-roma.html

Thanks to David Z. Scheffel, Thompson Rivers University, for reviewing this material.

The Roma settlement of Svinia in 1993 (left). The standard of living has not improved since then, but the population has increased by nearly 50 percent, resulting in serious overcrowding and high levels of stress. Roma children's access to school facilities is severely restricted (right). A few Romani schoolchildren participate in the school lunch program but in a separate room next to the cafeteria. ■ (Source: David Z. Scheffel)

MAP 9.6 *Roma Population in Eastern Europe. Romania has the highest number of Roma of any country in the world, between 1 and 2 million. Macedonia has the highest percentage of Roma.*

Only a special category of brahman priests can officiate at the Chidambaram temple in South India. Here, members of an age-mixed group of priests sit for a moment's relaxation. ■ (Source: Barbara Miller)

loans, or not pay them. Service providers who are dissatisfied with the treatment they receive from their patrons have little recourse. In addition, male patrons often demand sexual access to females of service-providing households.

Throughout South Asia, the growth of industrial manufacturing and marketing has reduced the need for some service providers, especially craftspersons such as tailors, potters, and weavers. Many of these people have left their villages to work in urban areas. The tie that remains the strongest is between patrons and their brahman priests, whose ritual services cannot be replaced by machines.

The caste system involves several mechanisms that maintain it: marriage rules, spatial segregation, and ritual. Marriage rules strictly enforce *jati* endogamy. Marriage outside one's *jati,* especially in rural areas and particularly between a higher-caste female and lower-caste male, is cause for serious, even lethal, punishment by caste elders and other local power-holders. Among urban educated elites, a trend toward inter-*jati* marriages is emerging.

Spatial segregation functions to maintain the privileged preserve of the upper castes and to continually remind the lower castes of their marginal status. In many rural contexts, the *dalits* live in a completely separate cluster; in other cases, they have their own neighbourhood sections into which no upper-caste

TABLE 9.1   Caste Ranking in Pahansu Village, North India

Caste Name	Traditional Occupation	Number of Households	Occupation in Pahansu
Gujar	agriculturalist	210	owner cultivator
Brahman	priest	8	priest, mailperson
Baniya	merchant	3	shopkeeper
Sunar	goldsmith	2	silversmith, sugar cane press operator
Dhiman (Barhai)	carpenter	1	carpenter
Kumhar	potter	3	potter, tailor
Nai	barber	3	barber, mailperson
Dhobi	washer	2	washer
Gadariya	shepherd	4	agricultural labourer, weaver
Jhivar	water-carrier	20	agricultural labourer, basket-weaver
Luhar	ironsmith	2	blacksmith
Teli	oil-presser	2	beggar, cotton-carder, agricultural labourer
Maniharan	bangle-seller	1	bangle-seller
Camar	leatherworker	100	agricultural labourer
Bhangi	sweeper	17	sweeper, midwife

Source: Adapted from Raheja 1988:19.

civil society: the collection of interest groups that function outside the government to organize economic and other aspects of life.

A village carpenter in front of his house in a north Indian village. The status of carpenters is midlevel, between the landholding elites or brahman priests and those who deal with polluting materials such as animal hides or refuse. ■ (Source: Barbara Miller)

person will venture. Ritual rules and practices also serve to maintain dominance. The rich upper-caste leaders sponsor important annual festivals, thereby regularly restating their claim to public prominence (Mines 1994).

Social mobility within the caste system has traditionally been limited, but instances have been documented of group "up-casting." Several strategies exist, including gaining wealth, affiliation, or merger with a somewhat higher *jati,* education, migration, and political activism (Kolenda 1978). A group that attempts to gain higher *jati* status takes on the behaviour and dress of twice-born *jatis.* These include men's wearing the sacred thread, vegetarianism, non-remarriage of widows, seclusion of women from the public domain, and the giving of larger dowries for the marriage of a daughter. Some *dalits* have opted out of the caste system by converting to Christianity or Buddhism. Others are becoming politically organized through the Dalit Panthers, a social movement seeking greater

power and improved economic status for *dalits* (Omvedt 1995).

The Indian constitution of 1949 declared that discrimination on the basis of caste is illegal. Constitutional decree, however, did not bring an end to these deeply structured inequalities. In the late twentieth century, the government of India instituted policies to promote the social and economic advancement of *dalits,* such as reserving places for them in medical schools, seats in the government, and public sector jobs. This "affirmative action" plan has infuriated many of the upper castes, especially brahmans, who feel most threatened. Is the caste system on the decline? Surely, aspects of it are changing. Especially in large cities, people of different *jatis* can "pass" and participate more equally in public life—if they have the economic means to do so.

Civil Society

Civil society consists of the social domain of diverse interest groups that function outside the government to organize economic, political, and other aspects of life. It has a long history in Western philosophy, with many different definitions proposed by thinkers such as John Locke, Thomas Paine, Adam Smith, and Karl Marx (Kumar 1996:89). According to the German philosopher, G. W. F. Hegel, civil society encompasses the social groups and institutions between the individual and the state. Italian social theorist Antonio Gramsci wrote that there are two basic types of civic institutions: those that support the state, such as the church and schools, and those that oppose state power, such as trade unions, social protest groups, and citizens' rights groups.

Civil Society for the State: The Chinese Women's Movement

In many instances, governments seek to build civil society to further their goals. The women's movement in China is an example of such a state-created organization. Canadian anthropologist Ellen Judd conducted a study of the women's movement in China, within the constraints that the government imposes on anthropological fieldwork by foreigners. Under Mao's leadership, foreign anthropologists were not allowed to do research of any sort in China. The situation began to change in the 1980s, when some field research, within strict limitations, became possible.

Judd has developed a long-term relationship with China over several decades, having lived there as a student from 1974 to 1977, undertaking long-term fieldwork there in 1986, and returning almost every year since for research or some other activity, such as being involved in a development project for women or attending the Beijing Fourth World Conference on Women. According to Judd, "These various ways of being in China all allowed me some interaction with Chinese women and some knowledge of their lives" (2002:14). In her latest project to study the Chinese women's movement, Judd wanted to conduct research as a cultural anthropologist would normally do, through intensive participant observation over a long period of time.

Even now, the Chinese government prohibits such research, keeping foreigners at a distance from everyday life. Judd was not allowed to join the local women's organization or to speak privately with any of the women. Officials accompanied her on all household visits and interviews. She was allowed to attend meetings, however, and she had access to all the public information about the goals of the women's movement, which is called the Women's Federations. A policy goal of the Chinese government is to improve the quality of women's lives, and the Women's Federations were formed to address that goal. The government oversees the operation at all levels, from the national level to the township and village. The primary objective is to mobilize women, especially rural women, to participate in literacy training and market activities.

Judd's fieldwork, constrained as it was by government regulations and oversight, nevertheless yielded some insights. She learned, through interviews with women members, about some women who have benefited from the programs, and she discovered how important education for women is in terms of their ability to enter into market activities. The book she wrote is largely descriptive, focusing on the "public face" of the Women's Federations in one locale. Such a descriptive account is the most that can emerge from research in China at this time. Given that the women's organizations are formed by and for the government, this example stretches the concept of civil society to— and perhaps beyond—its limits.

Activist Groups

Activist groups are groups formed with the goal of changing certain conditions, such as political repression, violence, and human-rights violations. In studying activist groups, cultural anthropologists are interested in learning what motivates the formation of such groups, what their goals and strategies are, and what leadership patterns they exhibit. Sometimes, anthropologists join the efforts of activist groups and use their knowledge to support these groups' goals (see the accompanying Lessons Applied box).

Many, but certainly not all, activist groups are initiated and organized by women. CO-MADRES of El Salvador is an important, women-led social movement in Latin America (Stephen 1995). CO-MADRES is a Spanish abbreviation for an organization called, in English, the Committee of Mothers and Relatives of Political Prisoners, Disappeared and Assassinated of El Salvador. It was founded in 1977 by a group of mothers in denunciation of the atrocities committed by the Salvadoran government and military. During the civil war that lasted from 1979 until 1992, a total of 80 000 people had died and 7000 more had disappeared, or 1 in every 100 Salvadorans.

At its inception, the group comprised 9 mothers. A year later, it had grown to nearly 30 members, including some men. In 1979, they made their first international trip to secure wider recognition. This developed into a full-fledged and successful campaign for international solidarity in the 1980s, with support in other Latin American countries, Europe, Australia, the United States, and Canada. The group's increased visibility earned it repression from the government. Its office was first bombed in 1980 and then four more times after that. In addition, a majority of the most active CO-MADRES have been detained, tortured, and raped. Forty-eight members of the CO-MADRES have been detained since 1977; five have been assassinated. Harassment and disappearances continued even after the signing of the Peace Accords in January 1992: "In February 1993, the son and the nephew of one of the founders of CO-MADRES were assassinated in Usulutan. This woman had already lived through the experience of her own detention, the detention and gang rape of her daughter, and the disappearance and assassination of other family members" (814).

In the 1990s, CO-MADRES focused on holding the state accountable for human-rights violations during the civil war, as well as some new areas, such as providing better protection for political prisoners, seeking assurances of human-rights protection in the future, working against domestic violence, educating women about political participation, and developing some economic projects to help women attain financial autonomy. They are part of a coalition of women's groups that worked on the 1994 political platform to secure better rights and conditions for women. The work of CO-MADRES, throughout its history, has incorporated elements of both the "personal" and the "political," concerns of mothers and family members for lost kin and for exposing and halting abuses of the state and military. The lesson learned from the case of CO-MADRES is that activist groups formed by women can be based on issues related to the domestic domain (murdered sons and other kin), but their activities can extend to the top of the public political hierarchy.

Other activist organizations formed around the problem of the marketing of infant formula in the developing countries and the subsequent decline in breastfeeding rates. In the 1970s, activist groups in North America and Europe mobilized to expose how large multinational corporations were seeking markets

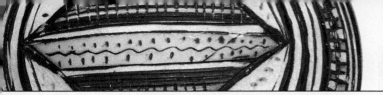

Lessons Applied

ANTHROPOLOGY AND COMMUNITY ACTIVISM IN PAPUA NEW GUINEA

A controversial issue in applied anthropology is whether or not an anthropologist should take on the role of community activist or act as an advocate on behalf of the people among whom he or she has conducted research (Kirsch 2002). Some say that anthropologists should maintain a neutral position in a conflict situation and simply offer information on issues—information that may be used by either side. Others say that it is appropriate and right for anthropologists to take sides and help support less powerful groups against more powerful groups. Those who endorse anthropologists' taking an activist or advocacy role argue that neutrality is never truly neutral: By seemingly taking no position, one indirectly supports the status quo, and information provided to both sides will generally serve the interests of the more powerful side in any case.

Stuart Kirsch took an activist role after conducting field research for over 15 years in a region of Papua New Guinea that has been negatively affected by a large copper and gold mine called the Ok Tedi mine. The mine releases 73 000 tonnes of mining wastes into the local river system daily, causing extensive environmental damage that in turn affects people's food and water sources. Kirsch has joined with the local community in their extended legal and political campaign to limit further pollution and to gain compensation for damages suffered. He explains his involvement with the community as a form of reciprocal exchange. The community members have provided him with information about their culture for over 15 years. He believes that his knowledge is part of the people's cultural property and that they have a rightful claim to its use.

Kirsch's support of the community's goals took several forms. First, his scholarly research provided documentation of the problems of the people living downstream from the mine. Community activists incorporated his findings in their speeches when travelling in Australia, Europe, and the Americas to spread awareness of their case and gather international support. During the 1992 Earth Summit, one leader presented the media with excerpts from an article by Kirsch during a press conference held aboard the Greenpeace ship, *Rainbow Warrior II,* in the Rio de Janeiro harbour. Second, Kirsch worked closely with local leaders, helping them decide how best to convey their views to the public and in the court. Third, he served as a cultural broker in discussions among community members, politicians, mining executives, lawyers, and representatives of NGOs in order to promote solutions for the problems faced by people living downstream from the mine. Fourth,

Yonggam people gather at a meeting in Atkamba village on the Ok Tedi River to discuss legal proceedings in 1996. At the end of the meeting, leaders signed an agreement to an out-of-court settlement, which was presented to the Victorian Supreme Court in Melbourne, Australia. The current lawsuit concerns the Yonggam people's claim that the 1996 settlement agreement has been breached. ■ (Source: Courtesy of Stuart Kirsch)

he convened an international meeting of environmental NGOs in Washington, D.C., in 1999 and secured funding to bring a representative from the community to the meeting.

In spite of official reports recommending that the mine be closed in 2001, its future remains uncertain. No assessment of past damages to the community has been prepared. As the case goes on, Kirsch will continue to support the community's efforts by sharing with them the results of his research, just as they have for so long shared their culture with him. Indigenous people worldwide are increasingly invoking their rights to anthropological knowledge about themselves. According to Kirsch, these claims require anthropologists to rethink their roles and relationships with the people they study. It can no longer be a relationship in which the community provides knowledge and the anthropologist keeps and controls that knowledge for his or her intellectual development alone. Although the details are still being worked out, the overall goal must be one of collaboration and cooperation.

FOOD FOR THOUGHT

• Consider the pros and cons of anthropological advocacy, and decide what position you would take on the Ok Tedi case. Be prepared to defend your position.

A march of the "Mothers of the Disappeared" in Argentina. This organization of women combines activism motivated by personal causes (the loss of one's child or children to political torture and death) and wider political concerns (state repressiveness in general). ■ (Source: © Peter Menzel/Stock Boston, LLC)

for their infant formulas. Protest groups argued that selling breast milk substitutes to mothers who could not afford the cost of an adequate supply and who had limited access to clean water and fuel to sterilize bottles was causing a major health crisis, and they began consumer boycotts of companies such as the Nestlé Company. This attention to unethical marketing practices ultimately forced debates resulting in the World Health Assembly passing the International Code on Marketing of Breast Milk Substitutes in 1981. Because of continuing flagrant violations of this code by several food and pharmaceutical corporations promoting infant formula, groups such as the International Baby Food Action Network (IBFAN) continue to monitor their compliance to the code. An umbrella organization, the World Alliance for Breastfeeding Action (WABA), formed by activists from various countries in 1991, continues to encourage the practice of breastfeeding through worldwide campaigns. For example, the Baby-Friendly Hospital initiative encourages health-care providers to assist mothers to breastfeed immediately after birth, World Breastfeeding Week mobilizes grassroots support for breastfeeding, and

Mother-Friendly Workplaces assists employed women to combine breastfeeding and employment (P. Van Esterik 1995:160).

Another example of activist group formation under difficult conditions comes from urban Egypt (Hopkins and Mehanna 2000). The Egyptian government frowns on overt political action outside the realm of the government. Although Egyptian citizens are deeply concerned about environmental issues such as waste disposal, clean air and water, and noise, group formation for environmental causes is not easily accomplished. People interviewed in Cairo reported that they rarely discuss environmental issues with one another. One example of environmental concern, however, did result in the closing of a highly polluting lead smelter. In this case, the people in the affected neighbourhood banded together around this particular issue and called attention to the situation in the public media, prompting high-level officials to take up their case. They were successful partly because their target was localized— one relatively small industry—and also because the industry was so clearly guilty of polluting the environment. This effort, however, did not lead to the formation of an enduring group.

New Social Movements and Cyberpower

Social scientists have begun to use the term *new social movements* to refer to the many new groups that emerged in the late 1980s and 1990s. These groups are often made up of disprivileged minorities—ethnic groups, women, the poor. Increasingly, they involve networks wider than the immediate social group, and most recently, they have taken advantage of cybertechnology to broaden their membership, exchange ideas, and raise funds (Escobar 2002).

Cyber-enhanced social movements are important new political actors and the source of promising ways to resist, transform, and present alternatives to current political structures. The importance of cybernetworking has, of course, not been lost on formal political leaders, who are paying increased attention to their personal websites and those of their parties.

Key Questions Revisited

WHAT is the range of cross-cultural variation of social groups?

Social groups can be classified in terms of whether all members have face-to-face interaction with one another, whether membership is based on ascription or achievement, and how formal the group's organization and leadership structure is. Thus, groups extend from the most informal, face-to-face groups, such as those based on friendship, to groups that have formal membership requirements and whose members are widely dispersed and never meet each other. All groups have some criteria for membership, often based on a perceived notion of similarity in terms of gender or class criteria, work roles, opposition to mainstream culture, economic goals, or self-improvement.

Many groups require a formal ritual of initiation of new members. In some cases, initiation into the group involves dangerous or frightening activities that serve to bond members to one another through a shared experience of helplessness.

WHAT is social stratification, and what are its effects on people?

Social stratification consists of hierarchical relationships between and among different groups, usually based on some culturally defined concept of status. Depending on the context, categories such as class, race, ethnicity, gender, age, and ability may determine group and individual status.

The degree of social inequality among different status groups is highly marked in agricultural and industrial societies. Marked status inequalities are not characteristic of most foraging societies. Status inequalities are variable in pastoral and horticultural societies with levelling mechanisms typically at play to prevent the formation of severe inequalities.

India's caste-based system is an important example of a rigid structure of social inequality based on a person's birth group. According to ancient Hindu scriptures, the population is divided into mutually exclusive groups with different rights and privileges. Discrimination on the basis of caste is banned by the Indian constitution, yet it still exists, as does racism in other contexts even though formally illegal.

WHAT is civil society?

Civil society consists of groups and organizations that, although they are not part of the formal government, perform functions that are economic or political. Civil society groups can be roughly divided into those that support government policies and initiatives, and, thus, further the interests of government, and those that oppose government policies and actions, such as environmental protest groups.

Some anthropologists who study activist groups decide to take an advocacy role and apply their knowledge to further the goals of the group. This direction in applied anthropology is related to the view that anthropological knowledge is partly the cultural property of the groups who have shared their lives and insights with the anthropologist.

New forms of information and communication technology are helping civil society groups gain visibility and stay in touch with their supporters.

KEY CONCEPTS

achieved position, p. 239
age set, p. 230
ascribed position, p. 239
caste, p. 240
caste system, p. 243
civil society, p. 247
cooperatives, p. 237

dalit, p. 244
diaspora population,
   p. 242
mechanical solidarity,
   p. 240
organic solidarity, p. 240
primary group, p. 230

role, p. 239
secondary group, p. 230
social group, p. 230
social stratification,
   p. 238
status, p. 239
youth gang, p. 234

myanthrolab

To reinforce your understanding of this chapter, and to identify topics for further study, visit MyAnthroLab at www.myanthrolab.com for diagnostic tests and a multimedia ebook.

SUGGESTED READINGS

Sandra Bell and Simon Coleman, eds., *The Anthropology of Friendship.* New York: Berg, 1999. The editors provide an introductory chapter on enduring themes and future issues in the anthropological study of friendship. The nine essays that follow discuss friendship in contemporary Melanesia, historical friendship as portrayed in Icelandic sagas, friendship in the context of a game of dominoes in a London pub, how friendship creates support networks in northeastern Europe, and the globalization of friendship ties revealed through an East African case.

Stanley Brandes, *Staying Sober in Mexico City.* Austin, TX: University of Texas Press, 2002. This ethnography of Alcoholics Anonymous groups in Mexico City focuses on how these groups help low-income men remain sober through social support. Although emphasizing the role of human agency in these men's attempts to remain sober, the author reminds us that the high rate of alcoholism among poor Mexican men must be viewed in the context of structural conditions that make life very difficult.

Liliana Goldin, ed., *Identities on the Move: Transnational Processes in North America and the Caribbean Basin.* Austin: University of Texas Press, 2000. This collection offers essays on identity formation and change in the process of voluntary migration or displacement and on how states label and exclude transnationals, often in racialized ways.

Thomas A. Gregor and Donald Tuzin, eds., *Gender in Amazonia and Melanesia: An Exploration of the Comparative Method.* Berkeley, CA: University of California Press, 2001. Two anthropologists, one a specialist on indigenous peoples of Amazonia and the other on Papua New Guinea, are the editors of this volume, which includes a theoretical overview chapter and then several chapters addressing similarities and differences between cultures of the two regions in domains such as fertility cults, rituals of masculinity, gender politics, and age-based gender roles.

Jerome Rousseau, *Central Borneo: Ethnic Identity and Social Life in a Stratified Society.* Oxford: Clarendon Press, 1990. Based on fieldwork and archival material, this book outlines the social organization, kinship patterns, and interregional links among the peoples of central Borneo.

Cris Shore and Stephen Nugent, eds., *Elite Cultures: Anthropological Perspectives.* New York: Routledge, 2002. This volume contains two introductory chapters and a concluding chapter framing 12 ethnographic cases from around the world. The major issues addressed are how elites in different societies maintain their positions, how elites represent themselves to others, how anthropologists study elites, and the implications of research on elites for the discipline of anthropology.

Karin Tice, *Kuna Crafts, Gender, and the Global Economy.* Austin: University of Texas Press, 1995. This ethnographic study looks at how the tourist market has affected women's production of *molas* in Panama and how women have organized into cooperatives to improve their situation.

Kevin A. Yelvington, *Producing Power: Ethnicity, Gender, and Class in a Caribbean Workplace.* Philadelphia: Temple University Press, 1995. This ethnography examines class, race, and gender inequalities as linked processes of social stratification within the context of a factory in Trinidad and in the wider social sites of households, neighbourhoods, and global interconnections.

10

Politics, Conflict, and Social Order

Key Questions

- WHAT is the scope of political and legal anthropology?

- WHAT are the major cross-cultural forms of political organization and social order?

- WHAT are cross-cultural patterns of social conflict?

A political leader of the Ashanti people, Ghana. British colonialists referred to such leaders with the English term "chief" although the term "king" might have been more appropriate. *(Source: © Henning Cristoph/DAS FOTOARCHIV/Peter Arnold)*

News events during the first decade of the twenty-first century are typified by bloodshed, conflict, and disturbing threats. Canadian troops are fighting in Afghanistan, armed conflict continues in the Middle East, and more nations are seeking nuclear weapons.

Political anthropology, a subfield of cultural anthropology, addresses the area of human behaviour and thought related to power: who has it and who doesn't; degrees of power; the bases of power; abuses of power; relationships between political and religious power; political organization and government; social conflict and social control; and morality and law. The subfield of legal anthropology focuses on the issues of order and conflict.

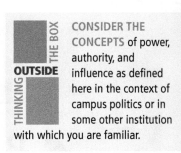

CONSIDER THE CONCEPTS of power, authority, and influence as defined here in the context of campus politics or in some other institution with which you are familiar.

Political Anthropology

Cultural anthropologists take a broader view of *politics* than political scientists do because their cross-cultural data indicate that many kinds of behaviour and thought are political in addition to formal party politics, voting, and government. Cultural anthropologists offer important examples of political systems that might not look like political systems at all to people who have grown up in large states. In this section, we explore basic political concepts from an anthropological perspective and raise the question of whether political systems are universal to all cultures.

British anthropologists, especially Bronislaw Malinowski and A. R. Radcliffe-Brown, long dominated theory-making in political anthropology. Their approach, referred to as *functionalism,* emphasized how institutions such as political organization and law promote social cohesion. Later, the students of these two teachers developed divergent theories. For example, in the late 1960s, some scholars began to look at aspects of political organization that pull societies apart. The new focus on disputes and conflict prompted anthropologists to gather information on dispute "cases" and to analyze the actors involved in a particular conflict through "processual analysis."

The approach has been countered by a swing toward a more macro view (Vincent 1996), which examines politics, no matter how local, within a global context (Asad 1973). This global perspective has prompted many studies of colonialism and neo-colonialism in political anthropology and historical anthropology. Ann Stoler's book, *Capitalism and Confrontation in Sumatra's Plantation Belt,* 1870–1979 (1985), on the history and cultural impact of Dutch colonialism in Indonesia, is a classic study in this genre. In the 1980s, the experiences of *subaltern* peoples (those subordinated by colonialism) and subaltern movements in former colonized regions attracted research attention, particularly from native anthropologists of decolonizing countries.

The history of political anthropology in the twentieth century illustrates the theoretical tensions between the individual-as-agent approach (processual approach) and the structural, political economy perspective that sees people as constrained in their choices by larger forces.

Politics: The Use of Power, Authority, and Influence

In this book, we use the term **politics** to refer to the organized use of public power, as opposed to the more private politics of family and domestic groups. **Power** is the ability to bring about desired results, often through the possession or use of forceful means. Closely related to power are authority and influence. **Authority** implies the right to take certain forms of action. It is based on a person's achieved or ascribed status or moral reputation. Authority differs from power in that power is backed up by the potential use of force, and power can be wielded by individuals without their having the authority in the moral sense.

Influence is the ability to achieve a desired end by exerting social or moral pressure on someone or some group. Unlike authority, influence may be exerted from a low-status and marginal position. All three terms are relational. A person's power, authority, or influence exists in relation to other people. Power implies the greatest likelihood of a coercive and hierarchical relationship, and authority and influence offer the most scope for consensual, cooperative decision-making. Power, authority, and influence are all related to politics, power being the strongest basis for action and decision-making—and potentially the least moral.

Politics: A Cultural Universal?

Is politics a human universal? Some anthropologists would say no. They point to instances of cultures with scarcely any institutions that can be called political, with no durable

---

politics: the organized use of public power, as opposed to the more private politics of family and domestic groups.
power: the capacity to take action in the face of resistance, through force if necessary.

authority: the ability to take action based on a person's achieved or ascribed status or moral reputation.
influence: the ability to achieve a desired end by exerting social or moral pressure on someone or some group.

political organization: the existence of groups for purposes of public decision-making and leadership, maintaining social cohesion and order, protecting group rights, and ensuring safety from external threats.

Multiple Cultural Worlds

SOCIALIZATION OF WOMEN POLITICIANS IN KOREA

Parental attitudes affect children's involvement in public political roles. Chunghee Sarah Soh's (1993) research in the Republic of Korea reveals how variation in paternal roles affects daughters' political leadership roles. Korean women members of the National Assembly can be divided into two categories: elected members (active seekers) and appointed members (passive recipients). Korea is a strongly patrilineal and male-dominated society, so women political leaders represent "a notable deviance from the usual gender-role expectations" (54). This "deviance" is not stigmatized in Korean culture; instead, it is admired within the category of *yŏgŏl*. A *yŏgŏl* is a woman with "manly" accomplishments. Her personality traits include extraordinary bravery, strength, integrity, generosity, and charisma. Physically, a *yŏgŏl* is likely to be taller, larger, and stronger than most women, and to have a stronger voice than other women. Why do some girls grow up to be a *yŏgŏl*?

Analysis of the life histories of elected and appointed women legislators offers clues about differences in their socialization. Elected women legislators were likely to have had atypical paternal experiences of two types: either an absent father or an atypically nurturant father. Both of these experiences facilitated a girl's socialization into *yŏgŏl* qualities, or, in the words of Soh, into developing an androgynous personality combining traits of both masculinity and femininity. In contrast, the presence of a "typical" father results in a girl developing a more "traditional" female personality that is submissive and passive.

Representative Kim Ok-son greets some of her constituents who are members of a local Confucian club in Seoul, Republic of Korea. She is wearing a men's-style suit and has a masculine haircut. ■ (Source: Chunghee Sarah Soh)

One intriguing question that follows from Soh's findings is, What explains the socialization of different types of fathers—those who help daughters develop leadership qualities and those who socialize daughters for passivity?

FOOD FOR THOUGHT

- In your experience, what socialization factors might influence boys or girls to become politicians?

---

ranking systems, and very little aggression. Foraging lifestyles, as a model for early human evolution, suggest that nonhierarchical social systems characterized human life for 90 percent of its existence. Only with the emergence of private property, surpluses, and other changes did ranking systems, government, formal law, and organized group aggression emerge. Also, studies show how dominance-seeking and aggression are learned behaviours, emphasized in some cultures and among some segments of the population, such as the military, and de-emphasized among others, such as religious leaders, healers, and child-care providers. Being a good politician or a major-general is a matter of socialization (see the accompanying Multiple Cultural Worlds box).

Other anthropologists argue that, despite a wide range of variation, politics is a human universal. Every society

is organized to some degree by kinship relationships, and many anthropologists would not draw a clear boundary between how kinship organizes power and how political organization organizes power.

Political Organization and Leadership

Political organization is the existence of groups for purposes such as public decision-making and leadership, maintaining social cohesion and order, protecting group rights, and ensuring safety from external threats. Power relationships situated in private, within the household, for example, may be considered "political" and may be related

---

to wider political realities, but they are not forms of political organization. Political organizations have several features that overlap with the groups and organizations that we discussed in the previous chapter:

- *Recruitment principles:* Criteria for determining admission to the unit.
- *Perpetuity:* Assumption that the group will continue to exist indefinitely.
- *Identity markers:* Particular characteristics that distinguish it from others, such as costume, membership card, or title.
- *Internal organization:* An orderly arrangement of members in relation to each other.

- *Procedures:* Prescribed rules and practices for behaviour of group members.
- *Autonomy:* Ability to regulate its own affairs. (Tiffany 1979:71–72)

Cultural anthropologists cluster the many forms of political organization that occur cross-culturally into four major types (see Figure 10.1). The four types of political organization correspond, generally, to the major economic forms (see Chapter 3). Recall that the categories of economies represent a continuum, suggesting that there is overlap between the different types rather than neatly drawn boundaries; this overlap exists between types of political organization as well.

FIGURE 10.1 Modes of Political Organization

Foraging	Horticulture	Pastoralism	Agriculture	Industrialism/Informatics
Political Organization				**Political Organization**
Band	Tribe	Chiefdom	Confederacy	State
Leadership				**Leadership**
Band leader	Headman/Headwoman	Chief		King/queen/president
	Big-man	Paramount chief		prime minister/emperor
	Big-woman			
Social Conflict				**Social Conflict**
Face-to-face	Armed conflict	War		International war
Small-scale	Revenge killing			Technological weapons
Rarely lethal				Massively lethal
				Ethnic conflict
				Standing armies
Social Control				**Social Control**
Norms				Laws
Social pressure				Formal judiciary
Ostracism				Permanent police
				Imprisonment

Social Control

Increased population density and residential centralization ⟶

More surpluses of resources and wealth ⟶

More social inequality/ranking ⟶

Less reliance on kinship relations as the basis of political structures ⟶

Increased internal and external social conflict ⟶

Increased power and responsibility of leaders ⟶

Increased burdens on the population to support political organization ⟶

band: the political organization of foraging groups, with minimal leadership and flexible membership.
tribe: a political group that comprises several bands or lineage groups, each with similar language and lifestyle and occupying a distinct territory.
clan: a structure in which most people claim descent from a common ancestor, although they may be unable to trace the exact relationship.

segmentary model: type of political organization in which smaller units unite in the face of external threats and then disunite when the external threat is absent.

Bands

A **band**, the form of political organization associated with foraging groups, involves flexible membership and the lack of formal leaders. Because foraging has been the predominant mode of production for almost all of human history, the band has been the most long-standing form of political organization. A band comprises between twenty people and a few hundred people at most, all related through kinship. These units come together at certain times of the year, depending on their foraging patterns and ritual schedule.

Band membership is flexible: If a person has a serious disagreement with another person or a spouse, one option is to leave that band and join another. Leadership is also informal in most cases, with no one person being named as a permanent leader for the whole group at all times. Depending on events, such as organizing the group to relocate or to send people out to hunt, a particular person may come to the fore as a leader for that time. This is usually someone whose advice and knowledge about the task are especially respected.

All members of the group are social equals, and a band leader has no special status. He has a certain degree of authority or influence, as perhaps a respected hunter or storyteller, but he does not have power, nor can he enforce his opinions on others. Social levelling mechanisms prevent anyone from accumulating much authority or influence. Political activity in bands involves mainly decision-making about migration, food distribution, and resolution of interpersonal conflicts. External conflict between groups is rare because territories of different bands are widely separated and the population density is low.

The band level of organization barely qualifies as a form of political organization because groups are flexible, leadership ephemeral, and there are no signs or emblems of political affiliation. Some anthropologists argue that "real" politics did not exist in undisturbed band societies.

Tribes

A tribe is a more formal type of political organization than the band. Typically associated with horticulture and pastoralism, tribal organization developed only with the advent of these modes of production. A **tribe** is a political group that comprises several bands or lineage groups, each with similar language and lifestyle and occupying a distinct territory. These groups may be connected through a **clan** structure in which most people claim descent from a common ancestor, although they may be unable to trace the exact relationship. Kinship is the primary basis of membership. Tribes contain from a hundred to several thousand people. They are found in the Middle East, South Asia, Southeast Asia, the Pacific, Africa, and among First Nations people in North America.

A tribal headman or headwoman (most are male) is a more formal leader than a band leader. Key qualifications for this position are being hardworking and generous and possessing good personal skills. A headman is a political leader on a part-time basis only, yet this role is more demanding than that of a band leader. Depending on the mode of production, a headman will be in charge of determining the times for moving herds, planting and harvesting, and setting the time for seasonal feasts and celebrations. Internal and external conflict resolution is also his responsibility. A headman relies mainly on authority and persuasion rather than power. These strategies are effective because tribal members are all kin and have a loyalty to each other. Furthermore, exerting force on kinspersons is generally avoided.

Ethnohistorical research found that the Ojibwa of northwestern Ontario, who were previously thought to have lived in small, mutually hostile bands, participated in a tribe-wide organization called the Grand Council that involved ranked male leaders, including a grand chief, civil chiefs, war chiefs, and others. Abundant resources, especially wild rice and sturgeon, allowed the Rainy River Ojibwa in the mid-nineteenth century to control access to their territory. Seasonal gatherings in large groupings at maple groves (to tap for maple sugar), fishing stations, berry patches, garden sites (growing potatoes and corn), and rice fields were "the foundation for tribal government and Ojibwa military power" (Lovisek, Holzkamm, and Waisberg 1997:138). Colonial officials had to abide by the Grand Council's rules when moving through the territory, and Ojibwa religious leaders were successful in resisting Christian missionizing for a time.

Among many horticultural groups of the Amazonian rainforest, such as the Kayapo (see Map 10.1 on page 260), tribal organization is the dominant political pattern. Each local tribal unit, which is itself a lineage, has a headman (or perhaps two or three). Each tribal group is autonomous, but recently many have united temporarily into larger groups, in reaction to threats to their environment and lifestyle from outside forces.

Pastoralist tribal formations are often linked into a confederacy, with local units or segments each maintaining substantial autonomy. The local segments meet together rarely, usually at an annual festival. In case of an external threat, the confederacy gathers together. Once the threat is removed, local units resume their autonomy. The overall equality and autonomy of each unit in relation to the others, along with their ability to unite and then disunite, is referred to as a **segmentary model** of political organization (a pattern of smaller units within larger units that can unite and separate depending on external threats).

MAP 10.1   Kayapo Region in Brazil. The Kayapo live in several rainforest villages in the Matto Grosso plains region, south of the Amazon River. Their total population is around 7000. The Kayapo use their traditional political organizing skills to help them deal with outsiders who seek to pursue commercial logging, mining, and hydroelectric development in the area.

Chief Paul Payakan, leader of the Kayapo, a group of indigenous people living in the rainforest of the Brazilian Amazon. Payakan was instrumental in mobilizing widespread political resistance in the region against the construction of a hydroelectric dam.
■ (Source: © Hank Wittemore/CORBIS SYGMA)

Big-Man and Big-Woman Leadership

In between tribal and chiefdom organizations is the **big-man system** or **big-woman system**, in which key individuals devote efforts to developing a political following through a system of redistribution based on personal ties and grand feasts (as mentioned in Chapter 4). Anthropological research in Melanesia, a large region in the South Pacific, established the big-man type of politics, and most references to it are from this region (Sahlins 1963; A. Strathern 1971). Personalistic, favour-based political groupings are, however, also found elsewhere.

The political ties of a successful big-man or big-woman includes people in several villages. A big-man tends to have greater wealth than his followers, although people continue to expect him to be generous. The core supporters of a big-man tend to be kin, with extended networks including nonkin. A big-man has heavy responsibilities. He is responsible for regulating internal affairs, such as the timing of crop planting, and external affairs, such as intergroup feasts, trade, and war. In some instances, a big-man is assisted in carrying out his responsibilities by a group of other respected men. These councils include people from the big-man's different constituencies.

In several tribes in the Mount Hagen area of the Papua New Guinea highlands (see Map 1.4 on page 18), an aspiring big-man develops a leadership position through a process called **moka**, mentioned in Chapter 4 (Strathern 1971). Moka is a strategy for developing political leadership that involves exchanging favours and gifts, such as pigs, and sponsoring large feasts where further gift-giving occurs. A crucial factor in big-manship in the Mount Hagen area is having at least one wife. An aspiring big-man urges his wives to work harder than ordinary women in order to grow more food to feed more pigs. The number of pigs a man has is an important measure

---

big-man or **big-woman system:** a form of political organization midway between tribe and chiefdom involving reliance on the leadership of key individuals who develop a political following through personal ties and redistributive feasts.

moka: a strategy for developing political leadership in highland Papua New Guinea that involves exchanging gifts and favours with individuals and sponsoring large feasts where further gift giving occurs.

chiefdom: a political unit of permanently allied tribes and villages under one recognized leader.

of his status and worth. Given the importance of a wife or wives in maintaining a large collection of pigs, a man whose parents die when he is young is at an extreme disadvantage because he lacks financial support for the bridewealth required for marriage. Without parents, he has no bridewealth, no wife, no one to feed and care for pigs, no resource base for moka, and no chance of becoming a big-man.

A married man will use his wife's (or wives') production as a basis for developing and expanding exchange ties with contacts throughout the region. An aspiring big-man builds moka relationships first with kin and then beyond. By giving goods to people, he gains prestige over them. The recipient will later make a return gift of somewhat greater value. The exchanges go back and forth, over the years. The more he gives, and the more people in his exchange network, the greater prestige the big-man develops.

Although big-manship is an achieved position, analysis of the family patterns of big-manship in the Mt. Hagen area shows that most big-men are the sons of big-men (see Table 10.1). This is especially true of major big-men, of whom over three-quarters were sons of former big-men. It is unclear whether this pattern results from the greater wealth and prestige of big-man families, from socialization into big-manship through paternal example, or from a combination of these aspects.

With few exceptions, the early anthropological literature about Melanesian tribal politics portrays men as dominating public exchange networks and the public political arenas. Women as wives are mentioned as important in providing the material basis for men's political careers. A study of Vanatinai, however, a Pacific island that is gender-egalitarian, reveals the existence of big-women as well as big-men (Lepowsky 1990). In this culture, both men and women can gain power and prestige by sponsoring feasts at which valuables are distributed, especially mortuary feasts (feasts for the dead). Although more Vanatinai men than women are involved in political exchange and leadership-building, some women are extremely active. These women lead sailing expeditions to neighbouring islands to visit their exchange partners, who are both male and female, and they sponsor lavish feasts attended by many people. On Vanatinai, big-women also include powerful sorcerers, famous healers, and successful gardeners.

Throughout much of the South Pacific, big-man politics has long involved the demonstration of generosity on the part of the leaders, who are expected to be able to mobilize resources for impressive feasts such as this one on Tanna Island. ■ (Source: © Kal Muller/Woodfin Camp & Associates)

Contact with European colonial culture gave men a political edge that they had not had before on Vanatinai. The Europeans traded with men for goods and approached women mainly for sexual relations. Formal government councils were established. Thus far, all councillors on Vanatinai have been male. In addition, some Vanatinai men have received training in the English language, the language of government, and thus have another advantage. In other cases, European domination led to more political equality between men and women with the imposition of "pacification," which ended local warfare and thereby eliminated one of the traditional paths to power for men.

Chiefdoms

A **chiefdom** is a political grouping of permanently allied tribes and villages under one recognized leader. Compared to most tribes, chiefdoms have larger populations, often numbering in the thousands, and are more centralized and socially complex. Hereditary systems of social ranking and economic stratification are found in chiefdoms

	Father Was a Big-Man	Father Was Not a Big-Man	Totals
Major Big-Men	27	9	36
Minor Big-Men	31	30	61
Total	58	39	97

TABLE 10.1 Family Background of Big-Men in Mt. Hagen, Papua New Guinea

Source: From *The Rope of Moka: Big-Men and Ceremonial Exchange in Mount Hagen, New Guinea,* p. 209, by Andrew Strathern. Copyright © 1971. Reprinted by permission of Cambridge University Press.

(Earle 1991), with social divisions existing between the chiefly lineage or lineages and nonchiefly groups. Chiefs and their descendants are considered to be superior to commoners, and intermarriage between the two strata is forbidden. Chiefs are expected to be generous, but they may have a more luxurious lifestyle than the rest of the people.

The chiefship is an "office" that must be filled at all times. When a chief dies or retires, he or she must be replaced. In contrast, the death of a band leader or big-man does not require that someone else be chosen as a replacement. A chief has more responsibilities than a band or tribal leader. He or she regulates production and redistribution, solves internal conflicts, and plans and leads raids and warring expeditions. Criteria for becoming a chief are more clearly defined. Besides ascribed criteria (birth in a chiefly lineage, or being the first son or daughter of the chief), achievement is still important. Achievement is measured in terms of personal leadership skills, charisma, and accumulated wealth. Chiefdoms have existed in many places throughout the world.

Anthropologists and archaeologists are interested in how and why chiefdom systems evolved as an intermediary unit between tribes and states, and what the political implications of this evolution are (Earle 1991). Several political strategies support the expansion of power in chiefdoms: controlling more internal and external wealth and distributing feasting and gift exchanges that create debt ties; improving local production systems; applying force internally; forging stronger and wider external ties; and controlling ideological legitimacy. Depending on local conditions, different strategies were employed. Internal control of irrigation systems was the most important factor in the emergence of chiefdoms in prehistoric southeastern Spain, while control of external trade was more important in the prehistoric Aegean region (Gilman 1991).

Gender and Leadership in Chiefdoms

Much evidence about leadership patterns in chiefdoms comes from historical examples. Prominent chiefs—men and women—are documented in colonial archives and missionary records. Many historic examples of women chiefs and women rulers come from West Africa, including the Queen Mother of the Ashanti of Ghana and of the Edo of Nigeria (Awe 1977).

Oral histories and archival records show that Yoruba women had the institution of the *iyalode,* or chief of the women. The *iyalode* was the women's political spokesperson in the "council of kingmakers," the highest level of government. She was a chief in her own right, with chiefly insignia, including a necklace of special beads, a wide-brimmed straw hat, a shawl, personal servants, special drummers, and bell ringers. She had her own council of subordinate chiefs. The position of *iyalode* was based on achievement. The most important qualifications were a woman's proven ability as a leader, economic resources to maintain her new status as chief, and popularity. Tasks included settling disputes via her court and meeting with women to formulate the women's stand on such policy issues as the declaration of war and the opening of new markets. Although she represented all women in the group and had massive support, she was outnumbered at the council of kingmakers because she was the only female and the only representative of all women.

Why do women play greater political roles in some chiefdoms than others? The most successful answers point to women's economic roles as the primary basis for

THINKING OUTSIDE THE BOX

WHAT IMAGES do you have of Pocahontas and what is their source? Do some research to trace her story and perhaps compare it to the depiction of Pocahontas in the Walt Disney movie about her.

Ætatis suæ 21. A°. 1616.

Matoaks als Rebecka daughter to the mighty Prince Powhatan Emperour of Attanoughkomouck als Virginia converted and baptized in the Christian faith and Wife to the wor.t M.r Tho: Rolff

Pocahontas played an important role in First Nations–British relations during the early colonial period. ■ (Source: North Wind Picture Archives)

matriarchy: a society in which women are dominant in terms of economics, politics, and ideology.

state: a centralized political unit encompassing many communities and possessing coercive power.

political power, as among the Iroquois and many African horticultural societies. Some have said that the Iroquois are an example of a **matriarchy**, or a society in which women are dominant in terms of economics, politics, and ideology. But most anthropologists think that the Iroquois are better characterized as an egalitarian society, because women did not control the society to the exclusion of men nor did they oppress men as a group. Men and women participated equally on the councils.

In contrast, the dominant economic role of men in Native American groups of the prairies, following the introduction of the horse by the Spanish and the increased importance of buffalo hunting by men, supported male-dominated political leadership in such groups as the Cheyenne.

A marked change in leadership patterns among chiefdoms in the past few hundred years has been the decline of women's political status in many groups, mainly because of European and North American colonial and missionary influences (Etienne and Leacock 1980). For example, the British colonialists redefined the institution of *iyalode* in Nigeria. Now "she is no longer a member of any of the important councils of government. Even the market, and therefore the market women, have been removed from her jurisdiction, and have been placed under the control of the new local government councils in each town" (146).

Ethnohistorical research on chiefdoms in Hawaii provides a similar view of formerly powerful women chiefs (Linnekan 1990). Following Captain James Cook's arrival in 1778, a Western-model monarchy was established. By the time the United States annexed the islands in 1898, indigenous Hawaiian leaders had been displaced from prominent economic and political roles by Westerners.

Confederacies

An expanded version of the chiefdom occurs when several chiefdoms are joined in a confederacy, headed by a chief of chiefs, "big chief," or paramount chief. Many prominent confederacies have existed: in Hawaii in the late 1700s and in other parts of North America, including the Iroquois league of five nations that stretched across New York state, the Cherokee of Tennessee, the Algonquins who dominated the Chesapeake region in present-day Virginia and Maryland, and the Huron of southern Ontario. The Huron confederacy, called *Wendat*, included five distinct groups living in the region around Lake Simcoe, Georgian Bay, and Lake Huron in southern Ontario. In the Huron confederacy, each village had a chief and there were regional and confederacy councils that brought together chiefs from all the villages. Chiefs of principal villages were the heads of councils. The confederacy council met at least once a year and decided issues of war and peace. Special pools of goods were built up as a public treasury and were administered by chiefs for long-distance trade (Trigger 1969, 1976).

States

A **state** is a centralized political unit encompassing many communities and possessing coercive power. The earliest evidence of the state form of political organization comes from Mesopotamia, China, India, and Egypt, perhaps as early as 4000 BCE. States emerged in these several locations with the development of intensive agriculture, increased surpluses, and increased population density. The state is now the form of political organization in which all people live. Band organizations, tribes, and chiefdoms still exist, but they are incorporated, to a greater or lesser degree, within state structures.

There are many theories proposed for why the state evolved (Trigger 1996). Marxist theory says that the state emerged to maintain ruling-class dominance. Demographic theory posits that population density drove the need for central mechanisms for social control. Economic theory argues that the state emerged in response to the increased surpluses of food production in the Neolithic Era, which produced sufficient wealth to support a permanent ruling class. Political theory says that the state arose as a necessary arbiter as competition increased for arable land and access to food surpluses. Rather than emphasizing a single causal factor, most scholars now incorporate multiple causes in their theories. Another development is that scholars have moved from the "why" question to the "how" question (Trigger 1996). New areas of inquiry include the state's increased bases for central power, such as finances and information management. There is more interest now in how states become and remain states than why they first emerged.

The Power of the State

Cultural anthropologists seek to learn how states operate and relate to their citizens. Their research shows that states have much more power compared to bands, tribes, and chiefdoms (see Figure 10.2 on page 264). Religious beliefs and symbols are often closely tied to the power of state leadership: The ruler may be considered to be a deity or part deity, or may be a high priest of the state religion, or perhaps be closely linked with the high priest, who serves as advisor. Architecture and urban planning remind the populace of the greatness of the state. In pre-Columbian Mexico, the central plaza of city-states, such as Tenochtitlan (founded in 1345), was symbolically equivalent to the centre of the cosmos and was thus the locale of greatest significance (Low 1995). The most important temples and the residence of the head of state were located around the plaza. Other houses and structures, in decreasing order of status, were located on avenues in decreasing proximity to the centre. The grandness and individual character of the leader's residence indicate power, as do monuments—especially tombs to past leaders or heroes or heroines. Egypt's pyramids,

FIGURE 10.2   The Powers of States

- *States define citizenship and its rights and responsibilities.* In complex nations, since early times, not all residents were granted equal rights as citizens.
- *States monopolize the use of force and the maintenance of law and order.* Internally, the state controls the population through laws, courts, and the police. Externally, the state uses force defensively to maintain the nation's borders and offensively to extend its territory.
- *States maintain standing armies and police* (as opposed to part-time forces).
- *States keep track of their citizens in terms of number, age, gender, location, and wealth through census systems that are regularly updated.* A census allows the state to maintain formal taxation systems, military recruitment, and policy planning such as population settlement, immigration quotas, and social benefits such as old-age pensions.
- *States have the power to extract resources from citizens through taxation.* All political organizations are supported by contributions of the members, but variations occur in the rate of contributions expected, the form in which they are paid, and the return that members get in terms of services. Public finance in states is based on formal taxation that takes many forms. **In-kind taxation** is a system of mandatory, noncash contributions to the state. For example, the Inca state used the *corvée*, a labour tax, to finance public works such as roads and monuments and to provide agricultural labour on state lands. Cash taxes, such as the income tax that takes a percentage of wages, emerged only in the past few centuries.
- *States manipulate information.* Control of information to protect the state and its leaders can be done directly (through censorship, restricting public access to certain information, and promoting favourable images via propaganda) and indirectly through pressure on journalists and television networks to present information in certain ways.

China's Great Wall, and India's Taj Mahal are a few of the world's great architectural reminders of state power.

In democratic states where leaders are elected by popular vote and in socialist states where political rhetoric emphasizes social equality, expense and elegance are muted by the adoption of more egalitarian ways of dress (even though in private, these leaders may live relatively opulent lives in terms of housing, food, and entertainment). The earlier practice of all Chinese leaders wearing a "Mao jacket," regardless of their rank, was a symbolic statement of their anti-hierarchical philosophy. A quick glance at a crowd of people, including the prime minister of Canada or Britain or the president of the United States, would not reveal who was the leader because dress differences are avoided. Even members of British royalty wear "street clothes" on public occasions where regalia are not required.

Local Power and Politics in Democratic States

The degree to which states influence the lives of their citizens varies, as does the ability of citizens to influence the political policies and actions of their governments. Some anthropologists, as citizens, use their knowledge of culture at home or abroad to influence politics in their own countries. So-called totalitarian states have the most direct control of local politics. In most other systems, local politics and local government are granted some degree of power. In highly centralized states, the central government controls public finance and legal institutions, leaving little power or autonomy in these matters to local governments. In decentralized systems, local governments are granted some forms of revenue generation (taxation) and the responsibility of providing certain services. Local politics continue to exist within state systems, with their strength and autonomy dependent on how centralized the state apparatus is.

THINKING OUTSIDE THE BOX

WHAT ARE some key symbols of state power in your home country?

In Japan, relatively egalitarian systems of local power structures exist in villages and hamlets. Families subtly vie for status and leadership roles through gift-giving, as is common in local politics worldwide (R. Marshall 1985). Egalitarianism prevails as a community value, but people strive to be "more than equal" by making public donations to the *buraku,* or hamlet. The custom of "giving a gift to

---

in-kind taxation: a system of mandatory noncash contributions to the state.

faction: a politically oriented group with strong lateral ties to a leader.

Afghanistan Prime Minister Hamid Karzai wears a carefully assembled collection of regional political symbols. The striped cape is associated with northern tribes. The Persian-lamb hat is an Uzbek style popular in the capital city, Kabul. He also wears a tunic and loose trousers, which are associated with villagers, and sometimes adds a Western-style jacket as well.
■ (Source: © Reuters NewMedia Inc./CORBIS)

the community" is a way that hamlet families can improve their positions in the local ranking system. In one hamlet, all 35 households recently gave gifts to the community on specified occasions: the forty-second birthday of male family members, the sixty-first birthday of male family members, the seventy-seventh birthday of male family members, the marriage of male family members, the marriage of female family members whose husband will be the household successor, the birth of the household head or successor couple's first child, and the construction of a new house. These occasions for public gift-giving always include an invitation to a meal for members of all hamlet households. Since the 1960s, it has also become common to give an item that is useful for the hamlet, such as a set of fluorescent light fixtures for the hamlet hall, folding tables, space heaters, and vacuum cleaners.

Local politics within a democratic framework reveal another type of gift-giving and exchange in the interest of maintaining or gaining power. Here we see people in elected positions of power giving favours in expectation of political loyalty in return. In these cases, various factions vie with each other. A **faction**, a more formalized aspect of local politics, is a politically oriented conflict group whose members are mobilized and maintained by a leader to whom the main ties of loyalty and affiliation are lateral—from leader to follower—rather than horizontal between members (Brumfiel 1994). Factions tend to be personalistic, transitory, lacking formal rules and meeting times, and lacking formal succession. Factional politics is not redistributive, however. It often leads to conflict and unequal resource distribution.

Gender and Leadership

Most contemporary states are hierarchical and patriarchal, excluding members of lower classes and women from equal participation. Some states are less male-dominated than others, but none are female-dominated. Strongly patriarchal contemporary states preserve male dominance through ideologies that restrict women's political power, such as *purdah* (female seclusion and segregation from the public world), as practised in much of the Muslim Middle East, Pakistan, and North India. In China, scientific beliefs that categorize women as less strong and dependable than men have long been used to rationalize the exclusion of women from politics (Dikötter 1998). Although women account for roughly half of the world's population, they form only, on average, 16 percent of the world's parliamentary members (Lederer 2006). The proportion has risen from 11.3 percent in 1995. Regional differences range from an average of 40 percent female parliamentarians in the Nordic states to 8 percent in Arab states.

A few contemporary states have or have recently had women as prime ministers or presidents. Such powerful women of the twentieth century include Indira Gandhi in India, Golda Meir in Israel, Margaret Thatcher in the United Kingdom, and Benazir Bhutto in Pakistan. Female heads of state are often related by kinship (as wife or daughter) to former heads of state. Indira Gandhi, for example, was the daughter of the popular first prime minister of independent India, Jawaharlal Nehru. But it is unclear whether these women's leadership positions can be explained by their inheriting the role or through the political socialization they may have received, directly or indirectly, as a result of being born into political families. In the early years of the twenty-first century, several women gained positions as heads of state: Michelle Bachelet as president of Chile, Angela Merkel as chancellor of Germany, Ellen Johnson-Sirleaf as president of Liberia, Tarja Halonen as president of Finland, and Cristina Fernandez De Kirchner as president of Argentina.

Change in Political Systems

In the early days of political anthropology, researchers examined the varieties of political organization and leadership and created categories such as bands, tribes, chiefdoms, and states. Contemporary political anthropologists are more interested in political dynamics and change, especially in how the pre-eminent political form, the state, affects local people's lives. In this section, we cover selected topics in the anthropological study of political change.

Emergent Nations and Transnational Nations

Many different definitions exist for a *nation,* and some of them overlap with definitions given for a *state* (Maybury-Lewis 1997:125–132). One definition says that a **nation** is a group of people who share a language, culture, territorial base, political organization, and history (Clay 1990). In this sense, a nation is culturally homogeneous, and, thus, Canada would not be considered a nation but instead a unit composed of many nations. According to this definition, groups that lack a territorial base cannot be termed nations. A related term is the *nation-state,* which some people say refers to a state that comprises only one nation, while others think it refers to a state that comprises many nations. An example is the Iroquois nation.

Depending on their resources and power, nations may constitute a political threat to states. In response to this (real or perceived) threat, states seek to create and maintain a sense of unified identity. Political scientist Benedict Anderson, in his widely read book *Imagined Communities* (1991), writes about the efforts of state-builders to create a sense of belonging and commitment—"imagined community"—among diverse peoples. Strategies for building state identity among the many nations within a state

A political rally of indigenous people in Bolivia.
■ (Source: Roshani Kothari)

President Evo Morales of Bolivia, elected in 2005, is the country's first indigenous head of state. He opposes what he refers to as "savage capitalism" and supports policies to improve the conditions for indigenous people in Bolivia. As the new president, his first international tour was to several Latin American countries, including Cuba, thus breaking with the tradition of the United States as the first international destination of a new president.
■ (Source: David Mercado/Reuters/CORBIS)

nation: a group of people who share a language, culture, territorial base, political organization, and history.

include the imposition of one language as "the" national language; the construction of monuments and museums; and the creation of songs, poetry, and other media-relayed messages about the "motherland." One strategy is to draw on symbols of minority or ancestral groups and bring them into the centre, thus creating a sense of belonging through recognition. Such recognition may also be interpreted as a form of co-optation, depending on the context. When South Africa launched its new coat of arms in 2000, then President Thabo Mbeki pointed out that the inclusion of a rock art drawing and a slogan in an extinct San language were intended to evoke both South Africa's distant past and its emerging identity as a socially complex and peaceful country.

Inspired by Anderson's writings, many anthropologists study state laws, policies, and other practices that seek to create a sense of unity out of diversity. Their work shows that attempts by states to force homogenization of nations and ethnic groups will inevitably prompt resistance of varying degrees from those groups that wish to retain or regain autonomy. Mexico, for example, is promoting a unified identity centred in *mestizaje* (*mestizo,* or people of mixed Spanish and Indian ancestry) culture and heritage (Alonso 2004). Monuments and museums in Mexico City place *mestizaje* symbols at the forefront and draw links to Aztec ancestors. They suppress connections with both highland Indians and the Spanish colonialists in an attempt to forge a new sense of political nationalism and consciousness that values hybridity and mixture. Emphasizing the Aztecs as the cultural roots of Mexican heritage frames out other indigenous groups and further marginalizes their position in the imagined nation-state of Mexico. On the other side of the world, in the Middle East, the Kurds provide an example of an ethnic group spanning several countries whose cultural rights are consistently denied (see the Ethnographic Profile on page 278).

For the past few centuries, leading global powers have promoted the notion of the strong state as the best option for promoting world peace. To that end, minority group movements for autonomy have been suppressed, sometimes brutally, or have led to long-term internal conflicts.

THINKING OUTSIDE THE BOX

WHAT IS your position on states? Are they the best option for a peaceful world and for providing internal security and services for citizens? What are some examples of successful states? Can you name some unsuccessful states?

Globalization and Politics

Since the seventeenth century, the world's nations have been increasingly linked in a hierarchical structure. This structure of power relations is largely regulated through international trade. In the seventeenth century, Holland was the one core nation and it dominated world trade. The Dutch were then surpassed by England and France, which remained the two most powerful nations up to

Supporters of independence for East Timor celebrate on the streets of Dili as Indonesian soldiers leave the capital in September 1999. ■ (Source: © Reuters/Jason Reed)

The coat of arms of South Africa, adopted in 2000, is meant to highlight democratic change and multicultural unity. ■ (Source: Republic of South Africa)

Ethnographic Profile

The Kurds of the Middle East

The Kurds are an ethnic group of between 20 to 30 million people, most of whom speak some dialect of the Kurdish language, which is related to Persian (Major 1996). The majority are Sunni Muslims. Kurdish kinship is strongly patrilineal and Kurdish family and social relations are male dominated.

Their home region, called Kurdistan ("Place of the Kurds"), extends from Turkey into Iran, Iraq, and Syria. This area is grasslands, interspersed with mountains, with no coastline. Before World War I, many Kurds were full-time pastoralists, herding sheep and goats. Following the war and the creation of Iraq, Syria, and Kuwait, many Kurdish herders were unable to follow their traditional grazing because they crossed the new country borders. Herders no longer live in tents year-round, though some do for part of the year. Others are farmers. In towns and cities, Kurds own shops, are professionals, and are employed in many different occupations.

Reliable population data for the Kurds in the Middle East do not exist, and estimates vary widely. About half of all Kurds, numbering between 10 and 15 million, live in Turkey where they constitute 20 percent or perhaps more of the total population. Approximately 6 million live in Iran, 4 to 5 million in Iraq, and 1.5 million in Syria. Others live in Armenia, Germany, France, and the United States.

The Kurds have attempted to establish an independent state for decades, with no success and often facing harsh treatment from government forces. In Turkey, the state used to refer to them as "Mountain Turks," and in many ways still refuses to recognize them as a legitimate minority group. Use of the Kurdish language is restricted in Turkey. The Kurds have faced similar repression in Iraq, especially following their support of Iran during the 1980–1988 Iran–Iraq war. Saddam Hussein razed villages and used chemical weapons against the Kurds. After the Persian Gulf War, 2 million Kurds fled to Iran. Many others have emigrated to Europe and the United States. Iraqi Kurds gained political autonomy from Baghdad in 1991 following a successful uprising aided by Western forces.

Many Kurds feel united by the shared goal of statehood, but several strong internal political factions and a guerrilla movement in Turkey also exist among the Kurds. Kurds in Turkey seek the right to have Kurdish-language schooling and television and radio broadcasts, and they would like to have their folklore recognized as well. The Kurds are fond of music and dancing, and Kurdish villages are known for their distinct performance styles.

Readings

Diane E. King. Asylum Seekers/Patron Seekers: Interpreting Iraqi Kurdish Migration. *Human Organization* 64(4):316–326.

Lokman I. Meho and Kelly Maglaughlin. *Kurdish Culture and Society: An Annotated Bibliography.* Westport, CT: Greenwood Press, 2001.

Martin Van Bruinessen. *Agha, Shaikh, and the State: On the Social and Political Organization of Kurdistan.* Atlantic Highlands, NJ: Zed Press, 1992.

Videos

Jiyan (Jano Rosebiani, dir., 2002).
Long Live the Bride . . . and the Liberation of Kurdistan (Hiner Saleem, dir., 1997).
Turtles Can Fly (Bahman Ghobadi, dir., 2004).

Website

www.kurd.org/kurdlinks.html

Thanks to Diane E. King, Brown University and Washington State University, for reviewing this material.

Kurdish sheep herders (left). Goat and sheep herding is still a major part of the Kurdish economy throughout Kurdistan. ■ (Source: blickwinkel/Alamy) **In Dohuk, Iraq, the Mazi Supermarket and Dream City are a combination shopping and amusement park (right). The goods in the market come mainly from Dubai and Turkey.** ■ (Source: Ed Kashi/CORBIS)

MAP 10.2   Kurdish Region in the Middle East. *Kurdistan includes parts of Iran, Iraq, Syria, Turkey, and Armenia. About half of the Kurds live in Turkey.*

Aung San Suu Kyi is the leader of the Burmese democracy and human rights movement. The daughter of Burma's assassinated national hero, Aung San, she has been under house arrest from 1989 to the present (except for a brief period in the mid-1990s). She was awarded the Nobel Peace Prize, making her the eighth woman to receive the award. ■ (Source: © Daniel Simon/Gamma Images)

around 1900. In the early part of the twentieth century, challenges for world dominance were made by the United States and later by Germany and Japan. The outcome of World War II placed the United States as leader of the "core." Greater complexities in world-systems theory now allow for an additional category of semiperiphery states, intermediary between the core and the periphery.

Cultural anthropology's traditional strength has been the study of small, bounded local groups, so anthropologists have had relatively little to say about international affairs. Now, more anthropologists have enlarged their focus to include the international level, studying both how global changes affect local politics and how local politics affect international affairs. Worldwide communication networks facilitate global politics. Ethnic politics, although locally initiated, increasingly has international repercussions. Migrant populations promote interconnected interests across state boundaries.

Culture exists at all levels of human interaction—local, national, international, and transnational, and even in cyberspace—and power relations are embedded in culture at all these levels. Anthropologists are now contributing to debates about the definition and use of the term *culture* by international organizations such as UNESCO: Happy as we are that organizations pay attention to culture, our wish is that they would not use outdated concepts that portray cultures as nicely bounded entities with a simple list of traits, such as language, dress, and religion (Wright 1998; Eriksen 2001).

Anthropologists are also tackling the study of powerful international organizations such as NATO (Feldman 2003); they must "study up," as Laura Nader urged us to do more than 35 years ago (1972), because people, power, and culture are "up" there. Anthropologists need to examine their own culture, which tends to be power-averse, to feel empathy with the powerless—with "the village people" and not the people who wield power at NATO. As one anthropologist urges, it is high time that anthropologists break their silence about institutions with lethal powers (Feldman 2003).

The Anthropology of Order and Conflict

Socially agreed-upon ways of behaving shape people's everyday life in countless ways. We wait for our turn to get on a bus rather than pushing to the head of the line, and we pay for a sandwich at the deli instead of stealing it. Anthropologists in all four fields have devoted attention to the subjects of social order and social conflict. Historical archaeologists, studying cultures that had writing, have traced the development of written law through time. Other archaeologists have examined artifacts such as weapons, remains of forts, and the waxing and waning of political centres in order to understand group conflict in the past. Many primatologists study nonhuman primate patterns of cooperation, coalitions, and conflict. Linguistic anthropologists have done research on social conflict related to national language policies and on how communication patterns within the courtroom influence legal outcomes. Legal anthropology is the subfield within cultural anthropology that is most directly concerned with the study of social control and social conflict.

Over the course of the twentieth century, the direction of legal anthropology has headed away from its original foundations in functionalism (the way a particular practice or belief contributed to social cohesion) toward a view that focuses on internal divisiveness. Helping to launch the subfield through his classic book *Crime and Custom in Savage Society* (1962 [1926]), functionalist Bronislaw Malinowski wrote that in the Trobriand Islands, social ties themselves promoted mutual social obligation and harmony. No separate legal institutions existed throughout Melanesia; instead, law was embedded in social life. Thus, he made the important contribution that social relationships can perform the same functions as formal laws and courts.

Several new directions have emerged in legal anthropology (Merry 1992):

■ Law in post-colonial settings
■ Legal discourse in courtrooms

- **Critical legal anthropology** (the study of how law and judicial institutions serve to maintain and expand dominant power interests rather than protect marginal and less powerful people)
- Law, human rights, and globalization

Systems of Social Control

Social control is the processes which help produce and maintain orderly social life (Garland 1996:781). Social control systems define agreed-upon rules and ways to ensure conformity to those rules. Because some people may violate the rules (what sociologists refer to as "deviant behaviour"), social control systems include ways to deal with such breaches.

Social control systems include *internalized* social controls that exist through socialization for proper behaviour, education, and peer pressure. They may also include formal systems of codified rules about proper behaviour and punishments for deviation. In the United States and Canada, the Amish and Mennonites rely on internalized social controls far more than most other similar groups. They have no police force or legal system; the way social order is maintained is through religious teaching and group pressure. If a member veers from correct behaviour, punishment such as ostracism ("shunning") may be applied.

Cultural anthropologists distinguish two major instruments of social control: norms and laws. A **norm** is an accepted standard for how people should behave that is usually unwritten and learned unconsciously through socialization. All societies have norms. Norms include, for example, the expectation that children should follow their parents' advice, that people standing in line should be orderly and not try to "jump" the line, and that an individual should accept an offer of a handshake (in cultures where handshakes are the usual greeting) when meeting someone for the first time. In rural Bali, etiquette dictates certain greeting forms between people of different status: "[P]ersons of higher status and power are shown very marked respect: they are greeted submissively and treated obsequiously; if seated, then others moving past them crouch . . . so as not to loom above them" (Barth 1993:114). Enforcement of norms tends to be informal; for example, a violation may simply be considered rude and the violator avoided in the future. In others, punishment may be involved, such as asking someone who is disruptive in a meeting to leave.

A **law** is a binding rule created through custom or official enactment that defines correct behaviour and the punishment for misbehaviour. Systems of law are more common and more elaborate in state-level societies, but many nonstate societies have formalized laws. Religion often provides legitimacy for law. For example, Australian Aborigines believe that law came to humans during the "Dreamtime," a time in the mythological past when the ancestors created the Aboriginal world. Contemporary Islamic states explicitly link law and religion. Secular Western states consider their laws to be religiously neutral, but in fact, much Western legal practice is heavily influenced by Judeo-Christian beliefs.

Social Control in Small-Scale Societies

Anthropologists distinguish small-scale societies and large-scale societies in terms of prevalent forms of conflict resolution, social order, and punishment of offences. Formal laws are rare among foraging groups, although Inuit and Australian Aborigines are notable for their more formalized, although unwritten, law systems. Because bands are small, close-knit groups, disputes tend to be handled at the interpersonal level through discussion or one-on-one fights. The group may act together to punish an offender through shaming and ridicule. Emphasis is on maintaining social order and restoring social equilibrium, not hurtfully punishing an offender. Ostracizing an offending member (forcing the person to leave the group) is a common means of formal punishment. Capital punishment has been documented, but is rare. For example, in some Australian Aboriginal societies, a law restricts access to religious rituals and paraphernalia to men who have gone through a ritual initiation. If an initiated man shared secrets with an uninitiated man, the elders would delegate one of their group to kill the offender. In such instances, the elders act like a court.

In nonstate societies, punishment is often legitimized through belief in supernatural forces and their ability to affect people. Among the highland horticulturalists of the Indonesian island of Sumba, one of the greatest offences is to fail to keep a promise (Kuipers 1990). Breaking a promise will bring on "supernatural assault" by the

---

critical legal anthropology: an approach within the cross-cultural study of law that examines how law and judicial systems serve to maintain and expand dominant power interests rather than protect marginal and less powerful people.
social control: processes that maintain orderly social life, including informal and formal mechanisms.

norm: a generally agreed-upon standard for how people should behave, usually unwritten and learned unconsciously.
law: a binding rule created through enactment or custom that defines right and reasonable behaviour and is enforceable by threat of punishment.
policing: the exercise of social control through processes of surveillance and the

threat of punishment related to maintaining social order.
trial by ordeal: a way of determining innocence or guilt in which the accused person is put to a test that may be painful, stressful, or fatal.

ancestors of those who have been offended by the person's misbehaviour. The punishment may come in the form of damage to crops, illness or death of a relative, destruction of the offender's house, or having clothing catch on fire. When such a disaster occurs, the only choice is to sponsor a ritual that will appease the ancestors.

Conflict resolution among horticulturalists relies on many of the same methods as among foragers, notably public shaming and ridicule. In the Trobriands of the early twentieth century, Malinowski (1961) reports,

> The rare quarrels which occur at times take the form of an exchange of public expostulation (yakala) in which the two parties assisted by friends and relatives meet, harangue one another, hurl and hurl back recriminations. Such litigation allows people to give vent to their feelings and shows the trend of public opinion, and thus it may be of assistance in settling disputes. Sometimes it seems, however, to harden the parties. In no case is there any definite sentence pronounced by a third party, and agreement is but seldom reached then and there. (60)

The overall goal in dealing with conflict in small-scale societies is to return the group to harmony. Village *fission* (breaking up) and ostracism are other common mechanisms for dealing with irresolvable conflict.

Social Control in States

In densely populated societies with more social stratification and more wealth, increased stress occurs in relation to the distribution of surplus, inheritance, and rights to land. In addition, increased social scale means that not everyone knows everyone else. Face-to-face accountability exists only in localized groups. Yet, informal mechanisms also exist. In the Lessons Applied box on page 272, an activist anthropologist provides a cultural critique of one example of informal social control in states.

Specialization

The specialization of tasks related to law and order—police, judges, lawyers—increases with the emergence of state organization. In nonstate societies, society at large determines right from wrong and punishes offenders, or the elders may have special authority and be called on for advice. Full-time professionals, such as judges and lawyers, emerged with the state. These professionals often come from powerful or elite social groups, a fact that perpetuates elite biases in the justice process itself. In North America, the legal profession is committed to opposing discrimination on the basis of gender and race, but it is nonetheless characterized by a lack of representation of women and minorities. Minority women, who face a double bind, are especially under-represented (Chanen 1995:105).

Policing is a form of social control that includes processes of surveillance and the threat of punishment related to maintaining social order (Reiner 1996). Police are the specific organization and personnel who discover, report, and investigate crimes. As a specialized group, police exist mainly in complex state societies.

Trials and Courts

In societies where spirits and ancestors define wrongdoing and punishment, a person's guilt is evidenced simply by the fact that misfortune has befallen him or her. If a person's crops were damaged by lightning, then that person must have done something wrong. In other instances, guilt may be determined through **trial by ordeal**, a form of trial in which the accused person is put through some kind of test that is often painful. An accused person may be required to place his or her hand in boiling oil, for example, or to have a part of his or her body touched by a red-hot knife. Being burned is a sign of guilt, whereas not being burned means the suspect is innocent.

The court system, with lawyers, judge, and jury, is used in many contemporary societies, although there is variation in how cases are presented and juries constituted. The goal of contemporary court trials is to ensure both justice and fairness. Analysis of actual courtroom dynamics and patterns of decision-making in North America and elsewhere, however, reveals serious problems in achieving these goals.

Punishment

Administering punishment involves doing something unpleasant to someone who has committed an offence. Cultural anthropologists have examined forms of punishment cross-culturally, as well as the relationship between types of societies and forms of punishment. In small-scale societies, punishment is socially rather than judicially managed. The most extreme form of punishment is usually ostracism and only rarely death. Another common form of punishment is that in the case of theft or murder, the guilty party must pay compensation to members of the harmed family. The prison, as a place where people are forcibly detained as a form of punishment, has a long history. The dungeons and "keeps" of old forts and castles all over the world are vivid evidence of the power of some people to detain and inflict suffering on others (Millett 1994). In general, however, such prisoners were not detained for long periods—they were tried and punished and their cell emptied.

Long-term detention of prisoners did not become common until the seventeenth century in Europe (Foucault 1977). The first penitentiary in the United States was built in Philadelphia in the late 1700s (Sharff 1995), and the first in Canada in Kingston, Ontario, in 1835. Cross-nationally and through history, percentages of imprisoned people vary widely. The United States and Russia have high percentages compared to other contemporary Western countries: 550 and 470 prisoners per 100 000 inhabitants, respectively. The British Isles rate is about 100; Canada's is 111; the Scandinavian countries have among the lowest rates, at

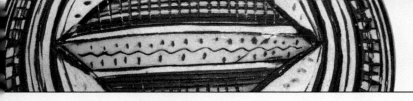

Lessons Applied

LEGAL ANTHROPOLOGIST ADVISES RESISTANCE TO "COERCIVE HARMONY"

Laura Nader is an anthropologist who uses her cross-cultural insights to provide a critique of her own culture, with an eye to producing improved social relations (Nader 2001). Nader had conducted extensive fieldwork in Latin America, as well as in the World Court in Europe. Her main interest lies in cross-cultural aspects of conflict and conflict resolution. In terms of her observations of her home country, the United States, she points out that leading politicians are currently emphasizing the need for unity, consensus, and harmony among citizens. But the United States, Nader points out, was founded by dissenters, and democracy depends on people speaking out. Democracy, in her view, supports the right to be indignant and the idea that "indignation can make Americans more engaged citizens" (B13).

A professor of anthropology at the University of California at Berkeley, Nader fosters the expression of critique, opinion, and even indignation when she teaches. One of her students commented that "Dr. Nader is a pretty good professor, except she has opinions" (B13). She took that as a compliment.

Nader feels that Europeans are generally less concerned about social harmony than North Americans are. In the United States, it's considered bad manners to be contentious, whereas in Europe, debate—even bitterly contentious debate—is valued. She uses the term *coercive harmony* to refer to the informal but strong pressure in the United States to agree, to be nice, to avoid digging beneath the surface, to stifle indignation at the lack of universal health care or the low voter turnout in presidential elections. The unstated, informally enforced policy of coercive harmony labels cultural critique as bad behaviour, as negative rather than positive. Nader finds it alarming that in a country proclaiming freedom as its primary feature, coercive harmony in fact suppresses contrary views and voices through the idiom of politeness, niceness, and friendliness.

How can this insight be used to improve the situation in the United States? Nader suggests one step: Make sure that critique, dissent, and indignation are supported in schools. Teachers should avoid contributing to the informal enforcement of social harmony and consensus and should instead proactively encourage critique.

FOOD FOR THOUGHT

- Would you say Canadians are closer to the style of Americans or Europeans? Do you find that your teachers encourage critique, dissent, and indignation?

---

fewer than 60. In the United States, the prison population has tripled over the past 100 years to nearly 2 million people, in spite of fairly even levels of crime. In Canada, the prison populations in both federal and provincial jurisdictions dropped in the 1990s and have never attained the levels of incarceration observed in the United States.

The death penalty (capital punishment) is rare in pre-state societies because condemning someone to death requires a high degree of power. A comparison of capital punishment in the contemporary United States with human sacrifice among the Aztecs of Mexico of the sixteenth century reveals striking similarities (Purdum and Paredes 1989). Both systems involve the death of mainly able-bodied males who are in one way or another socially marginal. In the United States, most people who are executed are non-white, have killed whites, are poor, and have few social ties. Aztec sacrificial victims were mainly male war captives from neighbouring states, but Aztec children were also

sometimes sacrificed. The deaths in both contexts have a political message: They communicate a message of the state's power and strength to the general populace, which is why they are highly ritualized and well publicized as events.

WHAT IS your position on the death penalty? Where do your views come from?

THINKING OUTSIDE THE BOX

Social Inequality and the Law

Critical legal anthropologists examine the role of law in maintaining power relations through discrimination against indigenous people, women, and minorities in various judicial systems around the world. While one could draw examples from many countries about how racial biases and discrimination affect legal processes, the following statistics come from Canada.

---

legal pluralism: a situation in which more than one way exists of defining acceptable and unacceptable behaviour and ways to deal with the latter.

The interior scene of the Cellular Jail in India's Andaman Islands, which was so named because all prisoners had single cells, arranged in long rows, in order to prevent them from having any social interaction for the purpose of colluding to escape or rebel. ■ (Source: Barbara Miller)

First Nations peoples in Canada make up 3 percent of the total population, but account for 12 percent of federal prison admissions and 20 percent of provincial prison admissions (Ponting and Kiely 1997). Lawyers in Canada spend less time with First Nations clients than with other clients. Accused First Nations peoples are more likely to be denied bail, and First Nations defendants are more than twice as likely to be incarcerated. In Manitoba, typical of Western Canada, more than half of all inmates are First Nations peoples (155).

Change in Legal Systems

Law-and-order systems, like other cultural domains, change over time. European colonialism since the seventeenth century has had major impacts on indigenous systems. Legal systems of contemporary countries have to deal with social complexity that has its roots in colonialism and new patterns of migration.

European Colonialism and Indigenous Systems

Colonial governments, to varying degrees, attempted to learn about and rule their subject populations through what they termed *customary law* (Merry 1992). By seeking to codify customary law, colonial governments created fixed rules where flexibility and local variation had formerly existed. Often, the colonialists overrode customary law and imposed their own laws. Homicide, marriage, land rights, and indigenous religion were frequent areas of European imposition. Colonial governments everywhere banned headhunting and blood feuds. Among the Nuer of Sudan, British legal interventions resulted in substantial confusion among the Nuer about the issue of blood feuds (Hutchinson 1996). Nuer practices involved either the taking of a life in repayment for a previous homicide or negotiated payments in cattle, depending on the relations between the victim and the assailant, what type of weapon was used, and a consideration of current rates of bridewealth as an index of value. In contrast, the British determined a fixed (non-negotiable) amount of indemnity. They imprisoned people for committing a vengeful murder. From the Nuer point of view, these changes were incomprehensible. They interpreted being put in prison as a way of protecting the person from a reprisal attack.

When European administrators and missionaries encountered aspects of marriage systems different from their own, they often tried to impose their own ways. Europeans tried in most cases to stop polygamy as unchristian and uncivilized. In South Africa, however, British and Afrikaaner whites tolerated the continuation of traditional marriage practices of South African peoples (D. L. Chambers 2000). So-called customary law, applying to the many diverse practices of South African black communities, permits a number of marriage forms that, despite their variety, share two basic features. First, marriage is considered a union between two families, not two individuals. Second, bridewealth is paid in nearly all groups, though formerly in cattle and now in cash. These traditions made sense in a largely rural population in which men controlled the major form of movable wealth: cattle. In the latter part of the twentieth century, many people no longer lived in rural areas within extended families, and most of these people worked in the wage economy. In the view of South African blacks of the 1990s, much of customary marriage law appeared inequitable to women, and so the 1994 black-majority parliament that came to power adopted a new marriage law that eliminated a large part of the customary law. This change reflects a split between the views of "modernist" legislators, who favour gender equity in the law as provided for in the new constitution, and the views of especially rural elders, who feel that tradition has been forsaken.

Colonial imposition of European legal systems onto indigenous systems added another layer, and one that had pre-eminent power over others. **Legal pluralism** refers to a situation in which more than one kind of legal process might be applied to identical cases (Rouland 1994:50). For example, should a case of murder in the Sudan be tried according to indigenous Sudanese principles or

European ones? Post-colonial nations are now in the process of attempting to reform their legal systems and develop more unified codes (Merry 1992:363).

Social Conflict and Violence

All systems of social control have to deal with the fact that conflict and violence may occur. In this section, we turn to a consideration of the varieties of social conflict as studied by cultural anthropologists.

Feuding

Feuding is a form of intergroup aggression that involves long-term, retributive violence that may be lethal between families, groups of families, or tribes. A concept of revenge motivates such back-and-forth violence between two groups. It is widely distributed cross-culturally.

Feuding has long had an important role among the horticultural Ilongot people of the Philippine highlands (Rosaldo 1980). From 1883 to 1974, Ilongot feuds were structured around headhunting as the redress for an insult or offence. Manhood was defined by the taking of a first head, and fathers were responsible for transferring the

The Hatfield clan in West Virginia in 1899. The long-standing feud between the Hatfields and the McCoys is legendary in the United States. ■ (Source: © Bettmann/CORBIS)

elaborate knowledge of headhunting to their sons. In 1972, the government banned headhunting and attempted to stop the Ilongot from practising shifting cultivation. The repercussion of these changes has been devastating. The banning of headhunting weakened father–son ties that had been solidified by the handing down of the elaborate techniques of headhunting. The people said they were no longer Ilongots.

Ethnic Conflict

Ethnic pluralism is a characteristic of most states in the world today. Ethnic conflict and grievances may result from an ethnic group's attempt to gain more autonomy or more equitable treatment (Esman 1996). It may also be caused by a dominant group's actions to subordinate, oppress, or eliminate an ethnic group by genocide or ethnocide. In the past few decades, political violence has increasingly been enacted within states rather than between states and constitutes the majority of "the 120-odd shooting wars in the world today" (Clay 1990). Political analysts and journalists often cite ethnicity, language, and religion as the causes of certain conflicts. Ethnic identities give people an ideological sense of commitment to a cause, but one must always look beneath these labels to see if deeper issues exist. Such deeper causes may include claims to land, water, ports, and other material resources.

The vast region of central Asia (see Map 10.3) is populated by many ethnic groups, none of whom has a pristine indigenous claim to the land. Yet, in central Asia, every dispute appears on the surface to have an ethnic basis: "Russians and Ukrainians versus Kazakhs over land rights and jobs in Kazakhstan, Uzbeks versus Tajiks over the status of Samarkhand and Bukhara, conflict between Kirghiz and Uzbeks in Kyrghyzstan, and riots between Caucasian Turks and Uzbeks in the Fergana Valley of Uzbekistan" (Clay 1990:48).

Attributing the causes of all such problems to ethnic differences overlooks resource competition based on regional, not ethnic, differences. Uzbekistan has most of the cities and irrigated farmland, whereas Kyrgyzstan and Tajikistan control most of the water, and Turkmenistan has vast oil and gas riches. Competition among groups in these different regions appears to be "ethnic" while its roots are in the local and global political economy. So-called ethnic conflicts are waged in many different ways, from the cruellest and most gruesome killings and rapes to more subtle forms. Throughout the history of the state, and seemingly at increasing rates in recent decades,

---

feuding: long-term, retributive violence that may be lethal between families, groups of families, or tribes.
revolution: a political crisis prompted by illegal and often violent actions of

subordinate groups that seek to change the political institutions or social structure of a society.

war: organized and purposeful group action directed against another group and involving lethal force.

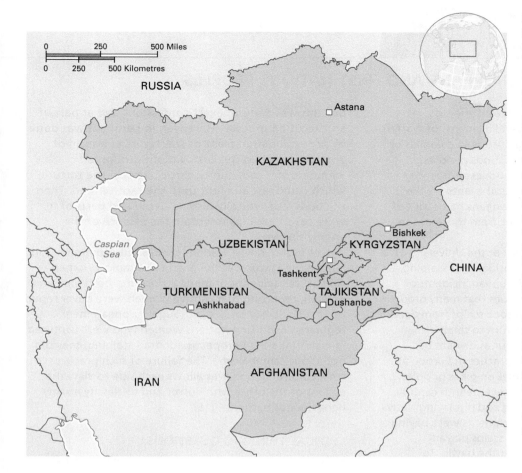

MAP 10.3 Central Asian States. The five states of central Asia are Kazakhstan, Turkmenistan, Uzbekistan, Kyrgyzstan, and Tajikistan. It is a large, landlocked region that is historically linked with pastoralism and the famous Silk Road, a trade route linking the Middle East with China. The region's terrain encompasses desert, plateaus, and mountains. Given its strategic location near several major world powers, it has often been a battleground of other states' interests. The predominant religion is Islam, and most central Asians are Sunnis. Languages are of the Turkic language group. Central Asia has an indigenous form of rap-style music in which lyrical improvisers engage in battles, usually accompanied by a stringed instrument. These musical artists, or *akyns,* are now using their art to campaign for political candidates.

violence linked to ethnicity has led to the breakup of states and the forced displacement of millions of people.

Revolution

A **revolution** is a form of conflict involving illegal and usually violent actions by subordinate groups that seek to change the status quo (Goldstone 1996:740). Revolutions have occurred in a range of societies, including monarchies, post-colonial developing countries, and totalitarian states. Comparison of revolutions in modern times—England, 1640; France, 1789; Mexico, 1910; China, 1911; Russia, 1917; and Iran, 1979—reveal that their causes involve interrelated factors, such as a military crisis, a fiscal crisis, and a weak state. The process of revolution varies in terms of the degree of popular participation, the roles of radicals and moderates, and leadership.

Theorists also argue about the different role of rural versus urban sectors in fomenting revolution. Many revolutions occurred in mainly agrarian countries and were propelled by rural participants, not urban radicalism (Skocpol 1979; E. Wolf 1969). Such agrarian-based revolutions include the French, Russian, and Chinese revolutions. A rural-based movement also characterizes

many national liberation movements against colonial powers, such as French Indochina, Guinea-Bissau, Mozambique, and Angola (Gugler 1988). Algeria was a somewhat more urbanized country, but it was still about two-thirds rural in 1962 when the French finally made peace there. In all of these cases, the colonial power was challenged by a rural-based guerrilla movement that controlled crop production, processing, and transport and thus could strike at the heart of the colonial political economy.

In contrast, some revolutions have been essentially urban in character, including those in Bolivia, Iran, and Nicaragua. The importance of cities in these revolutions is related to the fact that the countries were highly urbanized. Thus, revolutionary potential exists where resources are controlled and where the bulk of the population is located. Given the rapid urban growth and limited resources in developing countries, it is possible that the world may be entering "the age of urban revolutions" (Gugler 1988).

Warfare

Several definitions of **war** exist (Reyna 1994). One view is that war is an open and declared conflict between two political units. This definition would rule out many

WARFARE BETWEEN EUROPEANS AND FIRST NATIONS PEOPLES

In the seventeenth and eighteenth centuries in northeastern North America, several incidents of warfare occurred between the advancing European colonials or frontiersmen and groups of First Nations peoples. Warfare is a cultural phenomenon no less influenced by rules of behaviour than other cultural events. At the time of this particular conflict, Europeans had codes of behaviour during warfare different from those of the First Nations people.

Thomas Abler, an anthropologist at the University of Waterloo, compares First Nations incidents of scalping, torture, and cannibalism to the European incidents of rape during warfare (1992). He argues that many groups of First Nations people in warfare took scalps from dead enemies and displayed them on return to camp. Europeans interpreted this behaviour as deviant or strange, although it was common practice in Europe at the time to display heads of enemies on pikes or poles. Abler notes that by the end of the seventeenth century, European frontiersmen were taking and displaying Native scalps, and European colonial governments were paying for them. For First Nations peoples, scalps played important roles in ritual events after the battle. To participate in colonial payment schemes, they divided a scalp in two, one part for the cash reward, the second for ritual events.

The other feature of warfare that disturbed Europeans was the torture and cannibalism of captives in war performed by First Nations peoples throughout the northeast. Of course, Europeans tortured captives,

but this was done to exact confessions and as part of an execution process. Moreover, in Europe it was done by professionals in front of spectators as a form of entertainment. In the First Nations groups, all members of a community participated in the torture, which could last all night until the captive died. Then the body was typically dismembered and parts of it were eaten perhaps to obtain the essence of the enemy's power.

Not found in First Nations groups but common among Europeans at war was the practice of raping women. Abler gives evidence of many Europeans, both men and women, reporting that captive women were never raped by First Nations warriors, although European men regularly raped First Nations women who were captured in war. While the Europeans adopted scalping, they did not adopt cannibalism. "The failure of such practices to cross cultural boundaries allows each side to view the actions of the other with horror and to classify enemy behaviour as barbaric" (15).

CRITICAL THINKING QUESTIONS

- Looking at warfare from a critical thinking perspective, consider what aspects of it are universal.

- How do societies try to put limits on the excesses of war? How successful do you think these attempts are?

- How would a cultural anthropologist study contemporary warfare?

warlike conflicts, including the American–Vietnam War because it was undeclared. Or, is war simply organized aggression? This definition is too broad because not all organized violence can be considered warfare. Perhaps the best definition is that war is organized conflict involving group action directed against another group and involving lethal force (Ferguson 1994, quoted in Reyna 1994:30). Lethal force during war is legal if it is conducted according to the rules of battle (See the Critical Thinking box).

Cultural variation exists in the frequency and seriousness of wars. Intergroup conflicts among free-ranging foragers that would fit the definition of war do not exist in the ethnographic record. The informal, nonhierarchical political organization among bands is not conducive to waging armed conflict. Bands do not have specialized military forces or leaders.

Archaeological evidence indicates that warfare emerged and intensified during the Neolithic Era. Plant and animal domestication required more extensive land use, and it was accompanied by increased population densities. The combined economic and demographic pressures put more and larger groups in more direct and more intense competition with each other. Tribal leadership patterns facilitate mobilization of warrior groups for raids, but not all tribes have equal levels of warfare.

Many chiefdoms are characterized by relatively high rates of warfare and casualty rates. They have increased capacity for war in terms of personnel and surplus foods to support long-range expeditions. In

OUTSIDE THINKING THE BOX

HOW WOULD you define war? Given your definition, how many wars are currently ongoing and where are they?

Women near Kabul, Afghanistan, look at replicas of land mines during a mining-awareness program sponsored in 2003 by the International Committee of the Red Cross (ICRC). Afghanistan is still heavily mined, and rates of injury and mortality from mines are high. ■ (Source: © Reuters NewMedia Inc./CORBIS)

many chiefdoms, the chief could call on his or her retainers as a specialized fighting force as well as general members of society. Chiefs and paramount chiefs could be organized into more effective command structures (Reyna 1994:44–45).

In states, standing (permanent) armies and complex military hierarchies are supported by the increased material resources under the control of leaders through taxation and other forms of revenue generation. Greater state power allows for more powerful and effective military structures, which in turn increase the state's power; thus, a mutually reinforcing relationship emerges between the military and the state.

Examining the causes of war between states has occupied scholars in many fields for centuries. Some experts point to common, underlying causes, such as attempts to extend boundaries, secure more resources, ensure markets, support political and economic allies, and resist aggression from other states. Others point to humanitarian concerns that prompt participation in "just wars," to defend values such as freedom or to protect human rights as defined in one nation and being violated in another

Causes of wars in Afghanistan have changed over time (Barfield 1994). Since the seventeenth century warfare increasingly became a way for kings to justify their power in terms of the necessity to maintain independence from outside forces such as the British and czarist Russia. The last Afghan king was murdered in a coup in 1978. When the then Soviet Union invaded in 1979, there was no centralized ruling group to meet it. The Soviet Union deposed the ruling faction and replaced it with one of their own and then engaged in a wholesale war against

the population. Three million Afghans fled to Pakistan and Iran, over one million were killed, millions of others were displaced internally" (7). In spite of having no central command, divided by ethnic and sectarian differences, and outmatched in equipment by Soviet forces, a war of resistance eventually wore down the Soviets, who withdrew in 1989. Subsequently, in 2001 and 2002, the United States with its allies deposed another Afghan government, the Taliban, in the aftermath of the 9/11 attacks on the World Trade Center and the Pentagon.

The case of Afghanistan suggests that war was a more effective tool of domination in the pre-modern period when war settled matters more definitively. "The number of troops needed after a conquest were relatively few because they were not expected to have to put down continual internal revolts, but to defend the new conquest from rival outsiders" (7). Success in the Soviet Union's attempt to hold Afghanistan would have required more extensive involvement and commitment, including introduction of a new political ideology or economic structure that would win the population over, population transfer to remove opposition, and immigration of allies into the area. Barfield notes that in contemporary times, "winning battles or wars becomes only the first stage in a much more complicated process with no guarantees of ultimate success" (10).

Current events in both Iraq and Afghanistan show only too clearly that winning a war and taking over a country represent only the first stage in a process much more complicated than the term *regime change* implies. Afghanistan is now attempting to recover and rebuild after 30 years of war in the context of another foreign invasion. Its problems of national integration and security have roots that go much deeper than these intrusions (Shahrani 2002). These roots include powerful local codes of honour that value political autonomy and require vengeance for harm received, the moral system of Islam, the revitalized drug economy, and the effects of intervention from outside powers involving governments and corporations, including Unocal of California, Delta Oil of Saudi Arabia, and Bridas of Argentina. It is very difficult to construct a strong state with loyal citizens in the face of these conflicting internal and external factors.

Nonviolent Conflict

Mahatma K. Gandhi was one of the greatest designers of strategies for bringing about peaceful political change. Born in India, Gandhi studied law in London and then went to South Africa, where he worked as a lawyer serving the Indian community, and evolved his primary method of civil disobedience through nonviolent resistance (Caplan 1987). In 1915, he returned to India, joined the nationalist struggle against British

A child soldier named Alfred walks to a UN disarmament camp in the Liberian city of Tubmanburg in 2004. Many countries have programs in place to help child soldiers adjust to life after war. ■ (Source: © Emmanuel Tobey/Reuters/CORBIS)

Mahatma Gandhi (left), leader of the Indian movement for freedom from British colonial control, on his famous "Salt March" of 1930, in which he led a procession to the sea to collect salt in defiance of British law. He is accompanied by Sarojini Naidu, a noted freedom fighter. ■ (Source: © Bettmann/CORBIS)

colonialism, and put into action his model of civil disobedience through nonviolent resistance, public fasting, and strikes.

Celibacy is another key feature of Gandhian philosophy because avoiding sex helps maintain one's inner strength and purity. Regardless of whether one agrees with Gandhi's approach to food and sex, it is clear that the methods he developed of nonviolent civil disobedience have had a profound impact on the world. Martin Luther King, Jr., and his followers adopted many of Gandhi's tactics during the civil rights movement in the United States, as did members of the 1960s and '70s peace movement and the 1990s environmental movement in North America.

Political scientist James Scott (1985) used the phrase "weapons of the weak" as the title of his book on rural people's resistance to domination by landlords and government through tactics other than outright rebellion or revolution. Most subordinate classes throughout history have not had the "luxury" of open, organized political activity because of its danger. Instead, people have had to resort to ways of living with or "working" the system. Everyday forms of resistance include "foot dragging," desertion, false compliance, feigned ignorance, and slander, as well as more aggressive acts such as theft, arson, and sabotage. Many contemporary anthropologists have followed Scott's lead and contributed groundbreaking studies of everyday resistance.

Maintaining World Order

Computer-operated war missiles, email, faxes, satellite television, and jet flights mean that the world's nations are more closely connected and able to influence each other's fate than ever before. Modern weaponry means that such influences can be even more lethal. In the face of these geopolitical realities, politicians, academics, and the public ponder the possibilities for world peace. Anthropological research on peaceful, local-level societies shows that humans are capable of living together in peace. The question is, Can people living in larger groups that are globally connected also live in peace?

International Legal Disputes

Numerous attempts have been made, over time, to create institutions to promote world peace, of which the United Nations is the most established and respected. One of the United Nations' significant accomplishments was the creation of a world court, the International Court of Justice, which is located at The Hague in Holland (Nader 1995). In 1946, two-thirds of the Court's judges were from the United States or Western Europe. Now, the Court has many judges from developing countries and more sympathy for such nations. Despite this more balanced representation from a wide range of countries, there has been a decline in use of the International Court of Justice and an increased use of international negotiating teams for resolving disputes between nations.

Laura Nader (1995) analyzed this decline and found that it follows a trend in the United States, beginning in the 1970s, to promote *alternate dispute resolution* (ADR). The goal was to move more cases out of the courts and to privatize dispute resolution. On the surface, ADR seems a more peaceful and more dignified option. Deeper analysis of actual cases and their resolution shows, however, that this bilateral process favours the stronger party. *Adjudication* (formal decree by a judge) would have resulted in a better deal for the weaker party than bilateral negotiation did. Thus, less powerful nations are negatively affected by the move away from the World Court.

The United Nations and International Peacekeeping

What role might cultural anthropology play in international peacekeeping? Robert Carneiro (1994) has a pessimistic response. During the long history of human political evolution from bands to states, Carneiro says that warfare has been the major means by which political units enlarged their power and domain. Foreseeing no logical end to this process, he predicts that war will follow war until superstates become ever larger and one

Representatives of 10 NATO countries at the World Court in The Hague. This distinguished body of legal experts exhibits a clear pattern of age, gender, and ethnicity. ■ (Source: © Reuters/Fred Ernst)

megastate is the final result. He also considers the United Nations powerless in overcoming the principal obstacle to world peace: national sovereignty interests. If the belief exists that war is inevitable, that leaves little room for hope that anthropological knowledge might be applied to peacemaking efforts.

Despite Carneiro's views, cultural anthropologists have shown that war is not a cultural universal, and that different cultures have ways of solving disputes without resorting to killing. The cultural anthropological perspective of critical cultural relativism (review this concept in Chapter 1) can provide useful background on issues of conflict and prompt a deeper dialogue between parties.

One positive point emerges with regard to the possibility of world peace. The United Nations does provide an arena for airing disputes. This more optimistic view suggests that international peace organizations play a major role in providing analysis of the interrelationships among world problems and helping others see the causes of violence (Vickers 1993:132). In addition, some people see hope for local and global peacemaking through nongovernmental organizations (NGOs) and local grassroots initiatives that seek to bridge group interests.

Key Questions Revisited

WHAT is the scope of political and legal anthropology?

Political anthropology is the study of power relationships in the public domain and how they vary and change cross-culturally. Political anthropologists study the concept of power, as well as related concepts such as authority and influence. They have discovered differences and similarities between politics and political organization in small-scale societies and large-scale societies as they looked at issues such as leadership roles and responsibilities, the social distribution of power, and the emergence of the state. Legal anthropology encompasses the study of cultural variation in social order and social conflict. Legal anthropologists are increasingly examining how legal systems change. Global colonialism and contemporary globalization have changed indigenous systems of social control and law, often resulting in legal pluralism.

WHAT are the major cross-cultural forms of political organization and social order?

Patterns of political organization and leadership vary according to mode of production and global economic relationships. Foragers have a minimal form of leadership and political organization in the band. Band membership is flexible. If a band member has a serious disagreement with another person, including a spouse, one option is to leave that band and join another. Social control in small-scale societies seeks to restore order more than to punish offenders. Leadership in bands is informal. A tribe is a more formal type of political organization than the band. A tribe comprises several bands or lineage groups, with a headman or headwoman as leader. Big-man political systems are an expanded form of tribe, with leaders having influence over people in several different villages. Chiefdoms may include

several thousand people. Rank is inherited and social divisions exist between the chiefly lineage or lineages and nonchiefly groups. A state is a centralized political unit encompassing many communities and possessing coercive power. A wide variety of types of legal specialists is more frequently associated with the state than with small-scale societies, in which social shaming and shunning are common methods of punishment. States arose in several locations with the emergence of intensive agriculture, increased surpluses, and increased population density. Most states are hierarchical and patriarchal. In states, imprisonment and capital punishment may exist, reflecting the greater power of the state. Strategies for building nationalism include imposition of one language as "the" national language, monuments, museums, songs, poetry, and other media-relayed messages about the "motherland." Ethnic/national politics have emerged within and across states as groups compete for either increased rights within the state or autonomy from it.

WHAT are cross-cultural patterns of social conflict?

Cross-cultural data on levels and forms of conflict and violence indicate that high levels of lethal violence are not universal and are more associated with the state than earlier forms of political organization. Social conflict ranges from face-to-face conflicts, as among neighbours or domestic partners, to larger group conflicts among ethnic groups and states. Solutions that would be effective at the interpersonal level are often not applicable to large-scale, impersonalized conflict. Cultural anthropologists are turning their attention to studying global conflict and peacekeeping solutions. Key issues involve the role of cultural knowledge in dispute resolution and how international or local organizations can help achieve or maintain peace.

KEY CONCEPTS

authority, p. 256
band, p. 259
big-man system/big-woman
    system, p. 260
chiefdom, p. 261
clan, p. 259
critical legal
    anthropology, p. 270
faction, p. 265
feuding, p. 274

influence, p. 256
in-kind taxation, p. 264
law, p. 270
legal pluralism, p. 273
matriarchy, p. 263
moka, p. 260
nation, p. 266
norm, p. 270
policing, p. 271
political organization, p. 257

politics, p. 256
power, p. 256
revolution, p. 275
segmentary model, p. 259
social control, p. 270
state, p. 263
trial by ordeal, p. 271
tribe, p. 259
war, p. 275

myanthrolab

To reinforce your understanding
of this chapter, and to identify
topics for further study,
visit MyAnthroLab at
www.myanthrolab.com for
diagnostic tests and a
multimedia ebook.

SUGGESTED READINGS

Stanley R. Barrett, *Culture Meets Power*. Westport, CT: Praeger, 2002.
The author examines why the concept of power has gained ascendancy in anthropology, seeming to eclipse the concept of culture. Barrett argues that the concept of power is no less ambiguous than that of culture and that the two concepts both need to be considered in understanding contemporary affairs, including events such as the September 11, 2001, attacks on the United States.

Jane K. Cowan, Marie-Bénédicte Dembour, and Richard A. Wilson, eds., *Culture and Rights: Anthropological Perspectives*. New York: Cambridge University Press, 2001. This collection includes three overview/theoretical chapters, seven case studies that address issues such as child prostitution and ethnic and women's rights, and a chapter that critiques the UNESCO concept of culture.

Mona Etienne and Eleanor Leacock, eds., *Women and Colonization: Anthropological Perspectives*. New York: Praeger, 1980. This classic collection examines the impact of Western colonialism and missionary intervention on women of several indigenous groups of North America, South America, Africa, and the Pacific.

Thomas Gregor, ed., *A Natural History of Peace*. Nashville, TN: Vanderbilt University Press, 1996. This book contains essays on the question of what is peace, reconciliation among nonhuman primates, the psychological bases of violent and caring societies, community-level studies on Amazonia and Native America, and issues of peace and violence between states.

Phillip Gulliver, *Disputes and Negotiations: A Cross-Cultural Perspective*. New York: Academic Press, 1979. This classic analysis shows how the issues and behaviour surrounding negotiation are similar in cultures that differ widely in values, rules, and cultural assumptions.

Bruce Miller. *The Problem of Justice: Tradition and Law in the Coast Salish World*. Lincoln, NE: University of Nebraska Press, 2001. The author compares several legal systems operating in the Northwest Coast region from Washington State to British Columbia. The effects of colonialism differ from group to group. Some are strong and independent, whereas others are disintegrating.

Carolyn Nordstrom and Antonius C. G. M. Robben, eds., *Fieldwork under Fire: Contemporary Studies of Violence and Survival*. Berkeley, CA: University of California Press, 1995. After an introductory chapter that discusses general themes, several examples of fieldwork experiences in dangerous situations including Palestine, China, Sri Lanka, United States, Croatia, Guatemala, and Ireland are given.

Dan Rabinowitz, *Overlooking Nazareth: The Politics of Exclusion in Galilee*. New York: Cambridge University Press, 1997. This book presents an ethnographic study of Palestinian citizens in an Israeli new town. It examines specific situations of conflict and cooperation and provides wider theoretical insights about nationalism and ethnicity. Biographical accounts of three Palestinians—a medical doctor, a basketball coach, and a local politician—are included.

Bruce G. Trigger, *The Huron: Farmers of the North*, 2nd ed. Belmont, CA: Wadsworth, 1990. This fascinating monograph combines archaeological, historical, linguistic, and ethnographic evidence on the Huron of southern Ontario.

Joan Vincent, *Anthropology and Politics: Visions, Traditions, and Trends*. Tucson, AZ: The University of Arizona Press, 1990. In this text, Vincent offers a definitive history of the emergence of political anthropology, with a detailed presentation of theories and findings through the late 1980s.

Symbolic Systems

GRANT McCRACKEN, born in Vancouver and educated at the University of British Columbia and University of Chicago, is an anthropologist, a writer, and a consultant on marketing and consumer research. Over the last decade, McCracken has done ethnographic research for many international companies, including Campbell Soup, Coca-Cola, IBM, McDonald's, and Molson Breweries. He uses ethnographic methods to help his clients identify consumer preferences, predict cultural trends and analyze changing tastes. As an anthropologist, he helps his clients take a broad view of the marketplace, and the cultural forces that shape it. His anthropological background lets him pose and tackle problems that his clients may not have thought about. His graduate training and expertise in material culture gives him a different "take" on subjects like fashion, style, creativity, tourism, celebrity endorsements and business trends.

Grant McCracken is also a serious blogger. Like many other anthropologists, he uses blogging and other forms of accessible social media to create an intellectual space where people discover worlds by creating them. With more than 100 million blogs online, blogging is a serious business for those who know how to use social media effectively. According to McCracken, this creative media tests the blogger to sustain a discourse that is recognizable but that cannot be anticipated—a way of thinking that draws from but does not duplicate other players in the idea space.

Anthropologists at Work

Blogging attunes anthropologists to matters of immediate, everyday worlds. Grant McCracken's work shows why business students interested in marketing and consumer behaviour have an affinity for anthropology—for what we buy is less a matter of rational choice than cultural meaning. His blog (www.cultureby.com) "sits at the intersection of anthropology and economics" and has logged over 5400 comments and 1 350 000 views. He argues that our approach to brands has changed; we now build our own identity through choosing and mixing our own brands. Consumers then become co-creators of brand meaning; people build portfolios of selves from their consumer choices, much like the multiple selves of gaming environments. McCracken's most recent book, *Transformations: Identity Construction in Contemporary Culture* (2008), explores this process of self-transformation in popular culture today.

Not all of McCracken's clients are corporations; he researched the real costs and benefits of smoking for Health Canada, using ethnographic techniques. As if he were studying in a foreign land, McCracken uncovered the cultural logic of smoking among Canadian teens, revealing the complex ways that smoking becomes a social accessory, and an important part of teen self-definition. With the knowledge of what smoking means to teenagers in hand, policy-makers have a better understanding of why it is so difficult for teens to quit smoking. The addiction is not simply to the nicotine, but to the social identities and relationships created by smoking. Health-promotion messages that stress the risk and danger of smoking simply make smoking more attractive to risk-taking teens.

11
Religion

Key Questions

- WHAT is religion and what are the basic features of religions?

- HOW do world religions illustrate globalization and localization?

- WHAT are some important aspects of religious change in contemporary times?

A Catholic procession during Easter week in Guatemala. (*Source: Robert Frerck/Woodfin Camp*)

When studying the religious life of people of rural northern Greece, anthropologist Loring Danforth observed rituals in which participants walk across several metres of burning coals (1989). They do not get burned, they say, because their faith and a saint protect them. Experimentation has shown that anyone can walk on burning coals if they keep moving; a layer of sweat on the bottom of the feet keeps the heat from damaging the skin as long as the fire is not an open flame.

Upon his return to the United States, Danforth met a countryman who regularly walks on fire as part of his New Age faith and also organizes training workshops for people who want to learn how to fire-walk. Danforth himself fire-walked in a ceremony in rural Maine.

While not every anthropologist who studies religion undertakes such challenges during fieldwork, they all share an interest in enduring questions about humanity's understanding of the supernatural realm and relationships with it: Why do some religions have many gods and others just one? Why do some religions advocate animal sacrifice? Why do some religions give greater room for women's participation? How do different religions respond to changing conditions in the political economy?

Religion has been a cornerstone topic in cultural anthropology since the beginnings of the discipline. Over many decades, a rich collection of material has accumulated. The early focus was on religions of indigenous and tribal peoples. More recently, anthropologists have been studying the major religions of state-level societies and the effects of globalization on religious change.

Christian fire-walkers in northern Greece express their faith by walking on hot coals and reaffirm divine protection by not getting burned. ■ (Source: © Loring Danforth)

Religion in Comparative Perspective

In this section, we set the stage for the chapter by reviewing basic areas in the anthropology of religion, including how to define religion and a discussion of theories about the origin of religion. We also cover types of religious beliefs, rituals, and religious specialists.

What Is Religion?

Since the earliest days of anthropology, scholars have proposed various definitions of religion. In the late 1800s, British anthropologist Sir Edward Tylor defined religion as the belief in spirits. A more comprehensive, current definition says that **religion** is beliefs and actions related to supernatural beings and forces. This definition includes both beliefs and behaviour, parallel to our definition of culture. This definition specifically avoids linking religion with belief in a supreme deity since no concept of a supreme deity exists in some religions, whereas others have multiple deities.

Religion is related to, but not the same as, a people's *worldview*, or way of understanding how the world came to be, its design, and their place in it. Worldview is a broader concept and does not necessarily include the criterion of concern with a supernatural realm. An atheist has a worldview, but not a religious one.

Magic versus Religion

Sir Edward Tylor wrote that magic, religion, and science are alike in that they are different ways people have tried to explain the physical world and events in it. He considered science to be the superior, most rational of the three. Sir James Frazer, writing at about the same time as Tylor, defined **magic** as people's attempt to compel supernatural forces and beings to act in certain ways (1978 [1890]). He contrasted magic with religion, which he said is the attempt to please supernatural forces or beings. Frazer differentiated two general principles of magic:

■ *The law of similarity*, which is the basis of *imitative magic*. It is founded on the assumption that if person or item *X* is like person or item *Y*, then actions done to person or item *X* will affect person or item *Y*. A familiar example is a voodoo doll. If someone sticks

---

religion: beliefs and actions related to supernatural beings and forces.
magic: the attempt to compel supernatural forces and beings to act in certain ways.

animism: the belief in souls or "doubles."
polytheism: the belief in many deities.

monotheism: the belief in one supreme deity.

pins into a doll *X* that represents person *Y*, then person *Y* will experience pain or suffering.

- *The law of contagion,* which is the basis of *contagious magic.* It says that persons or things once in contact with a person can still have an effect on that person. Common items for working contagious magic include a person's hair trimmings, nail clippings, teeth, spit, blood, fecal matter, and the placenta of a baby. In cultures where contagious magic is practised, people are careful about disposing of their bodily wastes so that no one else can get hold of them.

Tylor and Frazer, and other early anthropologists supported an evolutionary model, with magic preceding religion. They evaluated magic as less spiritual and ethical than religion and therefore more "primitive." They assumed that, in time, magic would be completely replaced by the "higher" system of religion, and then ultimately by science as the most rational way of thinking. They would be surprised to see the widespread presence of magical religions in the modern world such as so-called Wicca, or neopagan, religion that centres on respect for the planet, nature, and the seasonal cycle. An anthropologist who studied Wicca in the San Francisco Bay area learned about beliefs, rituals, and magical practices through participant observation (Magliocco 2004). One of the prominent Wicca symbols is the pentacle (see Figure 11.1).

FIGURE 11.1 A Pentacle. Sometimes called a pentagram, it is a five-pointed star surrounded by a circle. An important symbol in neopagan and Wiccan religions, the pentacle is also a magical tool used for summoning energies and commanding spirits.

Many people turn to magical behaviour at certain times in their everyday lives, especially in situations of uncertainty. Magic, for example, is prominent in sports (Gmelch 1997). Some professional baseball players repeat actions or use charms, including a special shirt or cap, to help them win. This practice is based on the assumption that if it worked before, it may work again following the law of contagion. In baseball, pitching and hitting involve more uncertainty than fielding and baserunning, so pitchers and hitters are more likely to use magic. Magical practices are also common in farming, fishing, the military, and love.

OUTSIDE **THINKING THE BOX** **TAKE CAREFUL** note of your daily thoughts and activities for a week in terms of how magic, religion, and science are involved. What did you learn?

Theories of the Origin of Religion

Many theorists adopt a functionalist approach in explaining why religion is such a pervasive aspect of human culture. According to this view, religion provides ways of explaining and coping with universal human problems such as life and death, illness, and misfortune.

Tylor's theory, as proposed in his book, *Primitive Culture* (1871), was based on his assumption that early human ancestors needed to explain the difference between the living and the dead. They therefore developed the concept of a soul that exists in all living things and departs from the body after death. Tylor named this way of thinking **animism**, the belief in souls or "doubles." Tylor speculated that the concept of the soul eventually became personified and human-like deities were conceived. For Tylor, religion evolved from animism to **polytheism** (the belief in many deities) to **monotheism** (the belief in one supreme deity). Once again, this evolutionary model is proved wrong. Animistic beliefs exist in many religions, including, for example, Christian beliefs about visitations of the dead (Stringer 1999), and many contemporary religions are polytheistic.

French scholar Émile Durkheim presented a different functional theory in his book, *The Elementary Forms of the Religious Life* (1965 [1915]). He speculated that early humans understood the benefits of social contact, so they developed symbols to represent the group and rituals to maintain continuity. Bronislaw Malinowski's functional theory says that rituals help reduce anxiety and uncertainty. Karl Marx took a class conflict approach to understanding how religion functions, emphasizing religion's role as an "opiate of the masses." Marx thought that religion provides a superficial form of comfort to the poor, masking the harsh realities of class inequality and thereby preventing uprisings against the rich.

Religion provides an important source of social cohesion and psychological support for many immigrant groups, whose places of worship attract both worshippers and cultural anthropologists interested in learning how religion fits into migrants' adaptation. This is a scene at a North American Lao Buddhist temple. ■ (Source: Ruth Krulfeld)

Another functional theory comes from symbolic analysis, as informed by Sigmund Freud's emphasis on the role of the unconscious. For Freud, religion is a "projective system" that expresses people's unconscious thoughts, wishes, and worries. Clifford Geertz provides a theoretical approach combining Durkheimian functionalism with symbolic analysis (1966). In his view, religions are primarily systems of meaning that provide for people a *model of life* (how to understand the world) and a *model for life* (how to behave in the world).

Varieties of Religious Beliefs

Religions comprise beliefs and behaviour. Scholars of religion generally address belief systems first since they appear to inform patterns of religious behaviour. Religious beliefs tend to be shared by a group, sometimes by millions of people, and are passed on through the generations. Elders teach children the group's songs and tales, artists paint the stories on rocks and walls, and sculptors create images in wood and stone that depict aspects of religious belief.

How Beliefs Are Expressed

Beliefs are expressed and transferred over the generations in two main formats:

- **Myth,** narrative stories about supernatural forces or beings
- **Doctrine,** direct and formalized statements about religious beliefs

San rock paintings in the Tsodillo Hills (left), southwestern Botswana. Some of the paintings date back to 800 CE. The site is sacred to the San people. ■ (Source: © Galen Rowell/CORBIS) A stone sculpture at Mamallapuram, South India (right), dating from the eighth or ninth century, depicts the triumph of the goddess Durga (riding the lion, left of centre) over the bull-headed demon Mahishasura. ■ (Source: Simon Hiltebeitel)

myth: a narrative with a plot that involves the supernaturals.

doctrine: direct and formalized statements about religious beliefs.

A myth is a narrative that has a plot with a beginning, middle, and end. The plot may involve recurrent motifs, the smallest units of narrative. Myths convey messages about the supernaturals indirectly, through the story itself, rather than by using logic or formal argument. Greek and Roman myths, such as the stories of Zeus, Athena, Orpheus, and Persephone, are world-famous. Some people would say that the Bible is a collection of mythology; others would object to that categorization, as it suggests that the stories are not "real" or "sacred." Myths have long been part of people's oral tradition, and many are still unwritten.

Anthropologists have asked why myths exist. Malinowski says that a myth is a *charter* for society in that it expresses core beliefs and teaches morality. French anthropologist Claude Lévi-Strauss, the most famous mythologist, saw myths as functional but in a philosophical and psychological way. In his view, myths help people deal with the deep conceptual contradictions between, for example, life and death and good and evil, by providing stories in which these dualities find a solution in a mediating third factor. These mythological solutions are buried within a variety of surface details in the myth. For example, many myths of the Pueblo Indians of the American Southwest juxtapose grass-eating animals (herbivores) with predators (carnivores). The mediating third character is the raven, who is a carnivore but, unlike other creatures, does not have to kill to eat meat because it is a scavenger.

A cultural materialist perspective, also functionalist, says that myths store and transmit information related to making a living and managing economic crises (Sobel and Bettles 2000). Analysis of 28 myths of the Klamath and Modoc Indians (see Map 11.1) reveals that subsistence risk is a consistent theme. The myths also describe ways to cope with hunger, such as skill in hunting and fishing, food storage, resource diversification, resource conservation, spatial mobility, reciprocity, and the role of supernatural forces. Thus, myths are repositories of knowledge related to economic survival, crisis management, and environmental management and conservation.

Doctrine, the other major form in which beliefs are expressed, explicitly defines the supernaturals, the world and how it came to be, and people's roles in relation to the supernaturals and to other humans. Doctrine is written and formal. It is close to law because it links incorrect beliefs and behaviours with punishments. Doctrine is associated with institutionalized, large-scale religions rather with than small-scale "folk" religions.

Doctrine can and does change (Bowen 1998:38–40). Over the centuries, various popes have pronounced new doctrine for the Catholic Church. A papal declaration of 1854, made with the intent of reinvigorating European

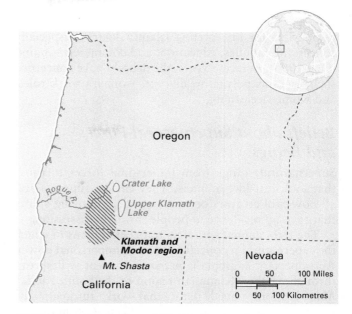

MAP 11.1   Klamath and Modoc Region in Oregon and Washington.

Catholicism, bestowed authenticity on the concept of the Immaculate Conception, an idea with substantial popular support.

Muslim doctrine is expressed in the Qur'an, the basic holy text of the Islamic faith that consists of revelations made to the prophet Muhammad in the seventh century, and the *hadith*, collections of Muhammad's statements and deeds (J. Bowen 1998:38). In Kuala Lumpur, Malaysia, a small group of highly educated women called the Sisters in Islam regularly debate with members of the local *ulama* (male religious authorities who are

Celebration of Holi, a spring festival popular among Hindus worldwide. In this scene in New Delhi, a young woman sprays coloured water on a young man as part of the joyous event. ■ (Source: © AFP/CORBIS)

responsible for interpreting Islamic doctrine especially concerning families, education, and commercial affairs) (Ong 1995). In recent years, the debates have concerned such issues as polygamy, divorce, women's work roles, and women's clothing.

Beliefs about Supernatural Forces and Beings

Supernaturals range from impersonal forces to those that look just like humans. They can be supreme and all-powerful creators or smaller-scale, annoying spirits that take up residence in people through possession.

The term **animatism** refers to belief systems in which the supernatural is conceived of as an impersonal power. An important example is *mana*, a concept widespread throughout the Melanesian region of the South Pacific. *Mana* is a force outside nature that works automatically; it is neither spirit nor deity. It manifests itself in objects and people and is associated with personal status and power since some people accumulate more of it than others.

Some supernaturals are **zoomorphic**, deities that appear in the shape, or partial shape, of animals. No satisfactory theory has appeared to explain why some religions develop zoomorphic deities, and for what purposes, and why others do not. Religions of classical Greece and Rome, and ancient and contemporary Hinduism are especially rich in zoomorphic supernaturals. **Anthropomorphic** supernaturals, deities in the form of humans, are common, but not universal. The human tendency to perceive of supernaturals in their own form was noted 2500 years ago by the Greek philosopher Xenophanes (circa 570–470 BCE). He said, "If cattle and horses, or lions, had hands, or were able to draw with their feet and produce the worlds which men do, horses would draw the forms of gods like horses, and cattle like cattle, and they would make the gods' bodies the same shape as their own" (Fragment 15). The question, though, of why some religions do and others do not have anthropomorphic deities is impossible to answer.

Anthropomorphic supernaturals, like humans, can be moved by praise, flattery, and gifts. They have emotions: They get annoyed if neglected, they can be loving and caring, or they can be distant and unresponsive. Most anthropomorphic supernaturals are adults. Few are very old or very young. Supernaturals tend to have similar marital and sexual relationships as the humans who worship them do and, in polygynous societies, male gods have multiple wives. Although many supernaturals have children, grandchildren are not prominent. In *pantheons* (collectivities of deities), a division of labour reflects specializations in human society. There may be deities of forests, rivers, the sky, wind and rain, agriculture, childbirth, disease, warfare, and marital happiness. The supernaturals have political roles and hierarchies. High gods, such as Jupiter and Juno of classical Roman religion, are all powerful with a range of less powerful deities and spirits below them.

Deceased ancestors can also be supernaturals. In some religions, spirits of the dead can be prayed to for help, and in turn they may require respect and honour from the living (J. Smith 1995:46). Many African, Asian, and First Nations religions have a cult of the ancestors, as did religions of ancient Mesopotamia, Greece, and Rome. In contemporary Japan, ancestor veneration is the principal religious activity of many families. Three national holidays recognize the importance of the ancestors: the annual summer visit of the dead to their home and the visits by the living to graves during the two equinoxes. Important ancestors sometimes evolved into deities with wide popularity. Similarly, humans other than ancestors may also, after their death, be transformed into deities. Although not seen as deities, the Roman Catholic tradition has established a group of deceased humans who can become saints (see the Multiple Cultural Worlds box).

Beliefs about Sacred Space

Beliefs about the sacredness of certain spaces are probably found in all religions, but such beliefs are more prominent in some religions than others. Sacred spaces may or may not be marked in a permanent way. Unmarked spaces include rock formations or rapids in a river (Bradley 2000). The fact that unmarked spaces in prehistory may have been religious sites poses a major challenge to archaeologists interested in reconstructing early religion. Sometimes, though, archaeologists can find evidence of sacrifices at such sites to attest to their ritual importance.

Among the indigenous Saami people of northern Norway, Sweden, and Finland, religious beliefs were, before Christian missionary efforts, strongly associated with sacred natural sites, which were often unmarked (Mulk 1994). These sites included rock formations resembling humans, animals, or birds. The Saami sacrificed animals and fish at these sites until strong pressures from

---

animatism: a belief system in which the supernatural is conceived of as an impersonal power.

zoomorphic: deities that appear in the shape, or partial shape, of animals.
anthropomorphic: deities that appear in the form of humans.

ritual: a patterned form of behaviour that has to do with the supernatural realm.

Multiple Cultural Worlds

THE BLESSED KATERI TEKAKWITHA: A "SAINT" FOR ALL FIRST NATIONS PEOPLES

Kateri Tekakwitha was a Mohawk First Nations woman born in upstate New York in 1656. She was converted to Christianity by the French Jesuit missionaries in 1676 at the age of 20 and moved to the Jesuit mission at Kahnawake near Montreal. Under the influence of the Jesuits, Kateri took a vow of virginity and practised extreme austerities such as flagellations, branding, exposure, and fasting (Holmes 2001:89). She died after only two years at the mission, but her piety was celebrated by the Jesuits, who reported she died calling out "Jesus! Mary! I love you!" Pope John Paul II beatified her in 1980. Many First Nations people hoped the Pope would canonize her on his visit to Toronto in 2002, but this did not happen.

Her devotees are found among many First Nations converts to Roman Catholicism all over North America. Paula Holmes reports that knowledge about her reached the Navajo and Pueblo of the American Southwest in the 1930s. For these people, Kateri represents hope for unity among all First Nations people in North America. One Pueblo person reported that Kateri's deathbed words were, "You must gather people from all different places and start having conferences." Another claimed she said, "The Catholic way and the Native American way can just build [together]" (96). Kateri has come to represent unity between the "Indian" way and the "Catholic" way and, moreover, unity among "her" people, that is, all the First Nations people of North America (94). For many of her people, she is already a saint.

FOOD FOR THOUGHT

- Can you think of another important religious figure that unites a particular group of people?

Christian missionaries forced them to repress their practices and beliefs. Although many Saami today still know where the sacred sites are, they will not reveal them to others.

Another important form of sacred space that has no permanent mark occurs in an important domestic ritual conducted by Muslim women throughout the world called the *khatam quran*, the "sealing" or reading of the holy book, the Qu'ran (Werbner 1988). A study of Pakistani migrants living in the city of Manchester, England (see Map 11.2 on page 292), reveals that this ritual involves a gathering of mostly women who read the Qu'ran and then share a ritual meal. The reason for gathering can be to give thanks or to seek divine blessing. During the ritual, the otherwise nonsacred space of the house becomes sacred. A "portable" ritual such as this one is especially helpful in migrant adaptation, because it can be conducted without a formally consecrated ritual space. All that is required is a supportive group of kin and friends and the Qu'ran.

In another example the sacred space was clearly defined. A piece of land was a summer meeting ground for the Dunne-Za/Cree of the North River region of British Columbia. These hunting and gathering peoples spent part of the summer round of activities, including important religious ceremonies, on what they called "the land where happiness dwells." This land was sold in 1945 to the Department of Indian Affairs at the instigation of the Indian agent. Many years later, in 1987, a suit to take back the land was initiated by the band, which argued that the land could not be alienated from the Dunne-Za/Cree because of responsibilities accepted by the government in an 1899 treaty with the band (Riddington 1990:186ff). Anthropologist Hugh Brody testified on behalf of the Dunne-Za/Cree as an expert witness. He tried to convey to the court how decisions were made in hunting and gathering groups where there is no leader, and how important a summer gathering place is for people who travel in smaller groups hunting and trapping elsewhere in the other seasons. Unfortunately, the judge never accepted this picture of the band life and decided against the Dunne-Za/Cree. The land was now valuable due to the discovery of oil and gas deposits. He did not see that the band had suffered a significant cultural and religious loss (see the Lessons Applied box on page 293 for a similar case in Australia).

THINKING OUTSIDE THE BOX

THINK OF some examples of sacred space, unmarked or marked, in your experience. What patterns emerge?

Ritual Practices

A **ritual** is a patterned form of behaviour that has to do with the supernatural realm. Many rituals are the

---

MAP 11.2   England. England is the largest of the constituent countries of the United Kingdom, and its population of 50 million accounts for 84 percent of the total. DNA analysis reveals that a majority of the English are of Germanic descent, as is their language. The terrain is mainly rolling hills, with some mountains in the north and east. London is by far the largest city, with Manchester and Birmingham competing for second place. English is the dominant language, with its diverse regional accents. Many different languages brought into the country by immigrant communities are spoken as first languages, including several South Asian languages, Polish, Greek, and Cantonese. An estimated 250 000 people speak British Sign Language. Although the Church of England is the state religion, everyone in England has the right to religious freedom.

enactment of beliefs expressed in myth and doctrine, such as the Christian ritual of communion. There are also *secular rituals* such as a sorority or fraternity initiation or a common-law wedding, all patterned forms of behaviour with no connection to the supernatural realm. It is not always easy to distinguish a religious ritual from a secular ritual. Consider the holiday of Thanksgiving, which originated as a sacred meal, with its primary purpose to give thanks to God for the first fruits of the harvest. Today, its original Christian meaning is not maintained by everyone who celebrates this holiday with a special meal of a roasted turkey.

Anthropologists of religion have categorized rituals in many ways. One division is based on how regularly the ritual is performed. Regularly performed rituals are called *periodic rituals*. Many periodic rituals are performed annually to mark a seasonal event like planting or harvesting, or to commemorate some important event. For example, an important periodic ritual in Buddhism, *Visakha Puja*, or Buddha's Day, commemorates the birth, enlightenment, and death of the Buddha (all on one day). On this day, Buddhists gather at monasteries, hear sermons about the Buddha, and perform rituals such as pouring water over images of the Buddha. Calendrical events such as the shortest or longest day of the year, or the new moon or full moon, often shape ritual cycles. *Nonperiodic rituals*, in contrast, occur irregularly, at unpredictable times, in response to unscheduled events such as a drought or flood, or to events in a person's life, such as illness, infertility, birth, marriage, or death.

Life-Cycle Rituals

Belgian anthropologist Arnold van Gennep (1960 [1908]) first proposed the category of life-cycle rituals in

A gathering of modern-day Druids at Stonehenge, England. They are one of the several groups that have interests in the preservation of and access to this UNESCO World Heritage Site. Debates concern possible changes in the location of nearby roads and planting or removing trees. The Druids claim that the site is important to their religion. ■ (Source: © Adam Wolfitt/CORBIS)

Lessons Applied

ABORIGINAL WOMEN'S CULTURE, SACRED SITE PROTECTION, AND THE ANTHROPOLOGIST AS EXPERT WITNESS

A group of Ngarrindjeri (prounounced NAR-en-jeery) women and their lawyer hired Diane Bell to serve as a consultant to them in supporting their claims to a sacred site in southern Australia (Bell 1998). The area was threatened by the proposed construction of a bridge that would cross sacred waters between Goolwa and Hindmarsh Island. The women claimed protection for the area and sought prevention of the bridge building on the basis of their secret knowledge of its sacredness—knowledge that had been passed down from mother to daughter over generations. The High Commission formed by the government to investigate their claim considered it to be a hoax perpetrated to block a project important to the country. Helping the women prove their case to a white, male-dominated court system was a challenging task for Diane Bell, an anthropologist teaching in the United States but also a white Australian by birth, with extensive fieldwork experience among Aboriginal women.

Bell conducted research over many months to marshal evidence for the validity of the women's claims—including newspaper archives, early recordings of ritual songs, and oral histories of Ngarrindjeri women. She prepared reports for the courtroom about women's sacred knowledge that were general enough to avoid violating the rule of women-only knowledge but detailed enough to convince the High Court judge that the women's sacred knowledge was authentic. In the end, the judge was convinced, and the bridge project was cancelled in 1999.

FOOD FOR THOUGHT

- On the Internet, learn more about this case and other disputes in Australia or elsewhere about sacred sites.

MAP 11.3 Hindmarsh Island in Southeast Australia. The Ngarrindjeri name for Hindmarsh Island is Kumarangk.

1908. A **life-cycle ritual,** or rite of passage, marks a change in status from one life stage to another of an individual or group. Victor Turner's (1969) fieldwork among the Ndembu, horticulturalists of Zambia, provided insights about the phases of life-cycle rituals. Among the Ndembu, and cross-culturally, life-cycle rituals have three phases: separation, transition, and reintegration.

In the first phase, the initiate (the person undergoing the ritual) is separated physically, socially, or symbolically from normal life. Special dress may mark the separation; for example, a long white gown for a baby that is to be baptized in a church. In many cultures of the Amazon and in East and West Africa, adolescents are secluded for several years in separate huts or areas away

---

life-cycle ritual: a ritual performed to mark a change in status from one life stage to another of an individual or group; also called *rite of passage.*

An Apache girl's puberty ceremony. Cross-cultural research indicates that the celebration of girls' puberty is more likely to occur in cultures in which adult women have valued productive and reproductive roles.
■ (Source: © CORBIS)

A woman praying at a Buddhist pagoda in Ho Chi Minh City, Vietnam, is dwarfed by spiralled hanging incense. The temple is dedicated to Me Sanh, a fertility goddess. Both men and women, but especially women, come here to pray for children. ■ (Source: John Annerino/Liaison

from the village. The transition phase, or the "liminal phase," is the time when the person is no longer in their previous status, but is not yet a member of the next stage. Liminality often involves the learning of specialized skills that will equip the person for the new status. Reintegration, the last stage, occurs when the initiate emerges and is welcomed by the community in the new status.

Differences in the distribution of puberty rituals for boys and girls have been interpreted as reflecting the value and status of males and females within society. Most societies have some form of puberty ceremony for boys, but puberty ceremonies for girls are less common. A cross-cultural analysis found that this difference is related to the mode of production and gender division of labour (J. K. Brown 1978). In societies where female labour is important and valued, girls have elaborate (and sometimes painful) puberty rites. Where their labour is not important, menarche is unmarked and there is no puberty ceremony. Female puberty rites function to socialize the female labour force. Girls going through initiations often receive training related to their expected adult economic roles. For example, among the Bembe of southern Africa, a girl learns to distinguish 30 or 40 different kinds of mushrooms and to know which ones are edible and which are poisonous.

Pilgrimage

Pilgrimage is round-trip travel to a sacred place or places for purposes of religious devotion or ritual. Prominent pilgrimage places are Varanasi in India (formerly called Banaras) for Hindus; Mecca in Saudi Arabia for Muslims; Bodh Gaya in India for Buddhists; Jerusalem in Israel for Jews, Christians, and Muslims; and Lourdes in France for Christians. Pilgrimage often involves hardship, with the implication that the more suffering that is involved, the more merit the pilgrim accumulates. Compared to a weekly trip to church or synagogue, pilgrimage removes a person further from everyday life, is more demanding, and is therefore potentially more transformative.

ritual of inversion: a ritual in which normal social roles and order are temporarily reversed.

Millions of Muslim pilgrims every year do the Hajj to Mecca, in Saudi Arabia. The Hajj is one of the Five Pillars of Sunni Islam and is also important in Shi'a Islam. A person who has done the Hajj is referred to as a *hajji,* a term of honour. ■ (Source: © Reuters/CORBIS)

Victor Turner applied his three sequences of life-cycle rituals to pilgrimage as well: the pilgrim first separates from everyday life, then enters the liminal stage during the actual pilgrimage, and finally returns to be reintegrated into society in a transformed state. A person who has done certain pilgrimages often gains enhanced public status.

Rituals of Inversion

In some rituals, normal social roles and order are temporarily inverted. A functionalist perspective says that these rituals allow for social pressure to be released. They also provide a reminder about the propriety of normal, everyday roles and practices to which people must return once the ritual is over.

Carnival (or *carnaval* in Brazil) is a **ritual of inversion** with roots in the northern Mediterranean region. It is celebrated widely throughout southern Europe and the western hemisphere. Carnival is a period of riotous celebration before the Christian fast of Lent. It begins at different times in different places, but always ends on Mardi Gras (or Shrove Tuesday), the day before the fasting period of Lent begins. The word *carnival* is derived from Latin and means "flesh farewell," referring to Lent.

In Bosa, a town in Sardinia, Italy, (see Map 11.4 on page 296) carnival involves several aspects of social role reversal and relaxing of usual social norms: The discotheques extend their hours, mothers allow their daughters to stay out late, and men and women flirt with each other and fondle each other in the discotheques and during masquerades in ways that are forbidden during the rest of the year (Counihan 1985). Carnival in Bosa has three major phases. The first is impromptu street theatre and masquerades that take place over several weeks, usually on Sundays. The theatrical skits are social critiques of current events and local happenings. The masquerades mainly involve men dressing up as exaggerated women:

> Young boys thrust their padded breasts forward with their hands while brassily hiking up their skirts to reveal their thighs. . . . A youth stuffs his shirt front with melons and holds them proudly out. . . . The high school gym teacher dresses as a nun and lifts up his habit to reveal suggestive red underwear. Two men wearing nothing but bikinis, wigs, and high heels feign a stripper's dance on a table top. (1985:15)

The second phase occurs during the morning of Mardi Gras, when hundreds of Bosans, mostly men, dress in black like widows and flood the streets. They accost passersby, shaking in their faces dolls and other objects that are maimed in some way or bloodied. They shriek at the top of their lungs as if mourning, and they say, "Give us milk, milk for our babies. . . . They are dying, they are neglected, their mothers have been gallivanting since St. Anthony's Day and have abandoned their poor children" (1985:16). The third phase, called *Giolzi,* takes place during the evening. Men and women dress in white, wearing sheets for cloaks and pillow cases for hoods. They blacken their faces. Rushing into the street, they hold hands and chant the word "Giolzi." They storm at people, pretending to search their bodies for *Giolzi,* and then say "Got it!" It is not clear what *Giolzi* is, but whatever it is, it represents something that makes everyone happy.

Elements of class inequality and global capitalism emerge as important in the celebration of carnival in the historic city centre of Puebla, Mexico (Churchill 2006). This area was declared a UNESCO World Heritage Site in 1987. Since then, entrepreneurs have made several proposals to improve the area, which is mainly inhabited by working-class people living in crowded, low-rent housing. One project would convert much housing into hotels, restaurants, and tourist shops. The plan would have gone forward on the basis that no "traditional culture" existed in the barrios, or neighbourhoods. Anthropological research, however, revealed much "traditional culture," especially the working-class celebration of carnival. Armed with the concept of *intangible cultural heritage,* residents campaigned to

MAP 11.4 Italy. Officially the Italian Republic, the country includes the mainland and two large islands. In 2006, Italy had the seventh-highest GDP in the world and is home to the largest number of UNESCO World Heritage Sites. A mountain system forms the backbone of the peninsula, and the climate varies according to altitude. Its population of nearly 60 million makes it one of the most densely populated countries in Europe. Roman Catholicism is the dominant religion. Recent waves of immigration, especially from northern Africa, have increased the number of Muslims to perhaps 1 million. The official language is standard Italian, descended from the Tuscan dialect centred in Florence. Cherished dialects exist throughout the country, and people in some northern border provinces speak dialects of German and French.

protect their neighbourhoods from demolition and "development." In Puebla, the principal figure of carnival is the *huehue*, a working-class man who masquerades as a rich landowner. He wears a mask to disguise his identity, and prances through the streets, head thrown back, and kicking up his heels. The men who take time off from work to perform in carnival are sometimes in danger of losing their jobs. City administrators have attempted to take over the celebration and replace the huehue with floats and "dignified" events that they believe will be more acceptable to tourists. This story, as so many others, is still in flux, as is carnival itself in Puebla and elsewhere.

Sacrifice

Many rituals involve **sacrifice**, or offering of something for transference to the supernaturals. Sacrifice has a long history throughout the world and may be one of the oldest forms of ritual. It may involve the killing and offering of animals, or humans (offerings may be of a whole person, parts of a person's body, or blood), and the offering of vegetables, fruits, grains, flowers, or other products. Flowers may be symbolic replacements for former animal sacrifices (Goody 1993).

Spanish documents from the sixteenth century describe the Aztec practice of public sacrifice of humans and other animals to please the gods. The details are gory and involve cutting the heart from living beings so that the blood spurts forth (see the accompanying Critical Thinking box).

Religious Specialists

Not all rituals require the presence of a religious specialist, or someone with special and detailed training, but all require some level of knowledge on the part of the performer(s) about how to do them correctly. Even the daily, household veneration of an ancestor requires some knowledge gained through informal learning. At the other extreme, many rituals cannot be done without a highly trained specialist.

Shamans and Priests

General features of the categories of shaman and priest illustrate some key differences between these two types of specialists (as with all types, many specialists fit somewhere in between). A *shaman*, or *shamanka* (the female form with the *–ka* ending derives from the original Siberian usage), is a part-time religious specialist who gains status through direct relationship with the supernaturals, often by being "called." A potential shaman may be recognized by special signs, such as the ability to go into a trance. Anyone who demonstrates shamanic abilities can become a shaman; in other words, this is an openly available role.

Shamans are more often associated with nonstate societies, yet faith healers and evangelists in North America could be considered to fit in this category. One of the most important functions of shamanic religious specialists is in healing, usually upon request from an afflicted individual (review Chapter 7).

In states, the more complex occupational specialization in religion means that there is a wider variety of types of specialists, especially what anthropologists

---

sacrifice: a ritual in which something is offered to the supernaturals.

priest/priestess: male or female full-time religious specialist whose position is based

mainly on abilities gained through formal training.

Critical Thinking

WHY DID THE AZTECS PRACTISE HUMAN SACRIFICE AND CANNIBALISM?

Evidence of state-sponsored human sacrifice among the Aztecs of Mexico comes from accounts written by the Spanish conquistadors (Harris 1977, 1989; Sanday 1986). The Aztec gods required human sacrifice. They "ate" human hearts and "drank" human blood. Most of the victims were prisoners of war, but many others were slaves, and sometimes young men and women, and even children. There is more to the ritual than sheer death of the sacrificial victims. The archives report that the dead were also eaten.

The victims were marched up the steep steps of the pyramid, held lying on their backs over a stone altar, and slit open in the chest by a priest, who wrenched out the heart, still beating, which was then burned in offering to the gods. The gods were satisfied.

The body was rolled down the other side of the temple, where it was retrieved by butchers and prepared for cooking. The skull was returned to the temple area to be displayed. No one knows for sure how many victims were sacrificed, but estimates are in the hundreds of thousands. At a single site, one chronicler reported that the display racks contained more than 100 000 skulls (Harris 1977:106). At one especially grand event, victims to be sacrificed were arranged in four lines, each two miles long. Priests worked for four days to complete the sacrifices.

Human sacrifice and cannibalism of any scale invite the question, Why? Here, we compare two theoretical perspectives: an etic view and an emic view. First, Michael Harner (1977) and Marvin Harris (1977, 1989) propose an etic, cultural materialist explanation based on factors in the regional ecology and the politics of Aztec expansionism. They say that the Aztec empire lacked sufficient amounts of animal sources of protein to satisfy its growing population. The ruling classes managed to maintain their supply of delicacies, such as dog, turkey, duck, deer, rabbit, and fish, but little was available for the poor.

Yet, the rulers needed to support and retain the loyalty of their army in order to protect and expand the empire's boundaries, and they needed to keep the masses happy. Providing the gods with human hearts and blood was a powerful statement of the empire's strength. It had the additional benefit of yielding huge amounts of meat for soldiers and commoners. Such "cannibal redistribution" could be manipulated by the state to reward particular groups and to compensate for periodic shortages in the agricultural cycle.

Peggy Sanday (1986) rejects the cultural materialist perspective of Harris and Harner. She provides an emic, interpretive view based on texts describing the Aztec people's rationale and motives. Sacrifice and cannibalism, she says, followed religious logic and symbolism. They were practised to satisfy the gods' hunger, not human hunger. According to Aztec religion, the gods require blood sacrifices in order for the universe to continue to operate. Human flesh was consumed not as an "ordinary meal" but as part of a religious identification with the gods, just as people would wear the skins of sacrificed victims in order to participate in their sacredness. Sanday says that the etic explanation, in focusing on the "business" aspects of Aztec sacrifice and cannibalism, has overlooked the tradition's religious meaning for the Aztecs.

CRITICAL THINKING QUESTIONS

- How do the two explanations differ in the data they use?
- Which do you find more convincing, and why?
- What other explanations might apply to Aztec human sacrifice and cannibalism?

refer to as *priests* (not the same as the specific modern role of the Catholic priest), and the development of religious hierarchies and power structures. The terms **priest** and **priestess** refer to a category of full-time religious specialists whose positions are based mainly on abilities gained through formal training. A priest may receive a divine call, but more often the role is hereditary, passed on through priestly lineages. In terms of ritual performance, shamans are more involved with nonperiodic rituals. Priests perform a wider range of rituals, including periodic state rituals. In contrast to shamans, who rarely have much secular power, priests and priestly lineages often do play a large secular role.

Other Specialists

Many other specialized religious roles exist cross-culturally. *Diviners* are specialists who are able to discover the will and wishes of the supernaturals through techniques such as reading animal entrails. Palm readers and tarot card readers fit into the category of diviners. *Prophets* are specialists who convey divine revelations usually gained through visions or dreams. They often possess charisma (a specially attractive and powerful personality) and may be able to perform miracles. Prophets have founded new religions, some long-lasting and others short-lived. *Witches* use psychic powers and affect people through emotion and thought. Mainstream society often condemns witchcraft as negative. Some scholars of ancient and contemporary witchcraft differentiate between positive forms that involve healing and negative forms that seek to harm people.

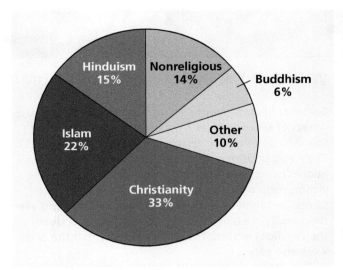

FIGURE 11.2 Population Distribution of Major World Religions

World Religions and Local Variations

The term **world religions** was coined in the nineteenth century to refer to religions with many followers that crossed national borders and had a few other specific features, such as a concern with salvation (the belief that human beings require deliverance from an imperfect world). At first, the term referred only to Christianity, Islam, and Buddhism. It was later expanded to include Judaism, Hinduism, Confucianism, Taoism, and Shintoism. Because of the global importance of the African diaspora that began with the European colonial slave trade, a sixth category of world religions is included here that describes key elements shared among the diversity of traditional African belief systems.

Cultural anthropologists emphasize that no world religion exists as a single, homogeneous entity. Each comprises many local variants, raising a "predicament" for centrally organized religions in terms of how to maintain a balance between standardization based on core beliefs and the local variations (Hefner 1998).

In this section, we first discuss the five traditional world religions in terms of their history, distribution, and basic teachings (see Figure 11.2). It then provides examples of variations in local cultural contexts. When a world religion moves into a new cultural region, it encounters indigenous religious traditions. In many cases, the incoming religion and local religions coexist as separate traditions, either as complements or competitors, in what is called **religious pluralism**. In religious

syncretism, elements of two or more religions blend together. It is most likely to occur when aspects of two religions form a close match with each other. For example, if a local myth involves a hero who has something to do with snakes, there may be a syncretistic link with the Catholic belief in St. Patrick, who is believed to have driven snakes out of Ireland.

For many centuries, the world religions have travelled outside their original borders through intentional attempts to expand and gain converts or through migration of believers to new locales. European colonialism was a major force that led to the expansion of Christianity through the missionary work of Protestant sects. Now, the increased rate of population migration and the expansion of television and the Internet give even greater impetus to religious movement and change. The designation of only five world religions is increasingly inappropriate, because many religions cross state boundaries and have a farther reach.

Many situations of nonfit can also be provided. Christian missionaries have had difficulty translating the Bible into indigenous languages because of lack of matching words or concepts, and because of differing kinship and social structures. Some Amazonian groups, such as the Pirahã, have no word that fits the Christian concept of "heaven" (Everett 1995, personal communication).

---

world religions: a term coined in the nineteenth century to refer to religions that had many followers, that crossed state borders, and that exhibited other features such as a concern with salvation.

religious pluralism: when one or more religions co-exist as either complementary to each other or as competitive systems.

syncretism: the blending of features of two or more cultures, especially used in discussion of religious change.

An early nineteenth-century painting of the Virgin of Guadalupe by Isidro Escamilla, a Mexican artist. The Virgin of Guadalupe, or Our Lady of Guadalupe, is Mexico's most popular image. Her depiction may involve syncretism with the indigenous Aztec goddess Tonantzin, part of a conscious strategy of Christian clergy to convert the Indians. Today, the Virgin of Guadalupe conveys messages of sacrifice and nurturance as well as strength and hope. She appeals to Mexican mothers, nationalists, and feminists alike.
■ (Source: © Brooklyn Museum of Art/CORBIS)

In other cases, matrilineal peoples have found it difficult to understand the significance of the Christian construct of "god the father."

The two world religions that emphasize proselytizing, or seeking converts, are Christianity and Islam. Their encounters with indigenous religions have sometimes been violent, involving physical destruction of sacred places and objects (Corbey 2003). Common methods include burning, overturning, dismantling, or cutting up sacred objects, dumping them into rivers, and hiding them in caves. European Christian missionaries in the 1800s often confiscated sacred goods and shipped them to Europe for sale to private owners or museums. Both Christian and Islamic conversion efforts frequently involved the construction of their own places of worship on top of the original sacred site.

Hinduism

Around 900 million people in the world are Hindus.* The majority live in India, where Hinduism accounts for about 80 percent of the population. The other 20 percent live in the United States, Britain, Canada, Malaysia, Fiji, Trinidad, Guyana, and Hong Kong. A Hindu is typically born a Hindu, and Hinduism does not actively seek converts. The four Vedas, composed in Sanskrit in northern India between 1200 and 900 BCE, are the core texts of Hinduism. Many other scholarly texts and popular myths and epics, especially the *Mahabharata* (the story of a war between two lineages, the Pandavas and the Kauravas) and the *Ramayana* (the story of king Rama and his wife Sita), also serve as unifying scriptures. Throughout India, a multiplicity of local traditions exist, some of which carry forward elements from pre-Vedic times. Thus, Hinduism incorporates a diversity of ways to be a Hindu. It offers a rich polytheism and at the same time a philosophical tradition that reduces the multiplicity of deities into oneness.

Deities range from simple stones placed at the foot of a tree to elegantly carved and painted icons of gods such as Shiva, Vishnu, and the goddess Durga. Everyday worship of a deity involves lighting a lamp in front of the god, chanting hymns and mantras (sacred phrases), and taking *darshan* (sight of) the deity (Eck 1985). These acts bring blessings to the worshipper.

Local variations of worship often involve deities and rituals unknown elsewhere. For example, firewalking is an important part of goddess worship in southern and eastern India (Freeman 1981; Hiltebeitel 1988) and among some Hindu groups living outside India, notably Fiji (C. Brown 1984).

Caste differences in beliefs and practices are also marked, even within the same village. Lower-caste deities prefer offerings of meat sacrifices and alcohol, whereas upper-caste deities prefer offerings of flowers, rice, and fruit. Yet the "unity in diversity" of Hinduism has long been recognized as real, mainly because of the shared acceptance of elements of at least some elements of Vedic thought.

---

*The population statistics for the world religions are rough averages derived from several Internet sources.

Hindu Women and Karma in Britain

One of Hinduism's key concepts is that of *karma*, translated as "destiny" or "fate." A person's karma is determined at birth on the basis of his or her previous life and how it was conducted. The karma concept has prompted many outsiders to judge Hindus as fatalistic, that is, lacking a sense of agency. But anthropological research on how people actually think about karma in their everyday lives reveals much individual variation from fatalism to a strong sense of being in charge of one's destiny. One study looked at women's perceptions of karma among Hindus living in Britain (Knott 1996). Some Hindu women are fatalistic in their attitudes and behaviour, while others are not. One woman who had a strongly fatalistic view of karma said,

> [W]hen a baby's born . . . we have a ritual on the sixth day. That's when you name the baby, you know. And on that day, we believe the goddess comes and writes your future . . . we leave a blank white paper and a pen and we just leave it [overnight], and a pair of brand new clothes. . . . So I believe that my future—whatever happens—is what she has written for me. That tells me [that] I have to do what I can do, and if I have a mishap in between I have to accept that. (24)

Another woman said that her sufferings were caused by the irresponsibility of her father and the "bad husband" to whom she had been married. She challenged her karma and left her husband: "I could not accept the karma of being with Nirmal [her husband]. If I had done so, what would have become of my children?" (25). Since Hindu women's karma dictates being married and having children, leaving one's husband is a major act of resistance.

Options for women seeking support for their struggle to sort out their roles can be either religious (praying more and fasting) or secular (seeking the advice of a psychological counsellor or social worker). Some Hindu women in Britain have themselves become counsellors and help support other women's independence and self-confidence. They illustrate how human agency can work against traditional religious rules.

Buddhism

Buddhism originated in a founding figure, Siddhartha Gautama (circa 566–486 BCE), revered as the Buddha or Awakened One (Eckel 1995:135). It began in northern India, where the Buddha grew up. From there, it spread throughout the subcontinent, into Inner Asia and China, to Sri Lanka and on to Southeast Asia. In the past 200 years, Buddhism has spread to Europe and North America. Its popularity subsequently faded in India, and Buddhists now constitute less than 1 percent of India's population. Buddhism's global spread is matched by a great diversity of doctrine and practice, to the extent that it is difficult to point to a single essential feature (for example, no single text is accepted as authoritative for all forms of Buddhism) other than the importance of Gautama Buddha. Many Buddhists worship the Buddha as a deity, while others do not—they honour his teachings and follow the pathway he suggested for reaching nirvana, or release from worldly life.

Buddhism first arose as a protest against certain features of Hinduism, especially caste inequality, yet it retained and revised several Hindu concepts, such as karma. In Buddhism, everyone has the potential for achieving nirvana (enlightenment and the overcoming of human suffering in this life), the goal of Buddhism. Good deeds are one way to achieve a better rebirth with each incarnation until, finally, release from *samsara* (the cycle of birth, reincarnation, death, and so on) is achieved. Compassion toward others, including animals, is a key virtue. Branches of Buddhism have different texts that they consider their canon. The major division is between the Theravada Buddhism practised in Southeast Asia and the Mahayana Buddhism of Tibet, China, Taiwan, Korea, and Japan. Buddhism is associated with a strong tradition of monasticism through which monks and nuns renounce the everyday world and spend their lives meditating and doing good works. Buddhists have many and varied annual festivals and rituals. Some events bring pilgrims from around the world to India—to Sarnath, where the Buddha gave his first teaching, and Gaya, where he gained enlightenment.

Buddhism and Indigenous Spirits in Burma

One theory says that wherever Buddhism exists outside India, it is never the exclusive religion of the devotees because it arrived to find established religions already in place (Spiro 1967). In any particular context, Buddhism and the local traditions may have blended (such blending is called *religious syncretism*), both may coexist in a pluralistic fashion, or Buddhism may have taken a major role and incorporated the indigenous traditions. The situation in Burma (also called Myanmar) fits in the second category. Indigenous Burmese beliefs remained strong because they offer a more satisfying way of explaining and dealing with everyday problems.

Buddhism gained an established footing in Japan in the eighth century. The city of Nara was an important early centre of Buddhism. Here, the emperor sponsored the casting of a huge bronze statue of the Buddha, housed in the Todaiji, the "Great Eastern Temple."
■ (Source: Jack Heaton)

According to Burmese Buddhism, a person's karma is a result of action in previous lives and determines his or her present condition. If something bad happens, it's because of karma and the person can do little but suffer through it. Burmese supernaturalism, on the other hand, says that the bad thing happened because of the actions of capricious spirits called *nats*. Ritual actions can combat the influence of *nats*. In other words, *nats* can be dealt with, karma cannot.

Buddhism, however, became an important cultural force and the key basis for social integration in Burma. One village, for example, had three Buddhist monasteries, with four resident Buddhist monks and several temporary monks. Every male child was ordained as a temporary member of the monastic order. Almost every villager observed Buddhist holy days. While Buddhism is held to be the supreme truth, spirits are called upon when it comes to dealing with everyday problems such as a toothache or a monetary loss.

Buddhism and Religious Roles for Women

In Theravada Buddhism, there are limited religious roles for women. However, women in many parts of Southeast Asia have created roles for the pursuit of a religious path. One possible route in Thailand is to begin wearing white robes, following the eight precepts or Buddhist commandments (which forbid taking life, stealing, lying, and taking intoxicants, among others), and living in a

monastic establishment. In urban Thailand there are several such centres for "women in white." A growing trend is for young women who are dissatisfied with the demands of village life to go to the city and take up the white robe, spending their days in meditation and religious study (P. Van Esterik 2000). Another possibility for women is to intensify religious activity, especially meditation, while continuing their normal everyday activities. A very few of these women become meditation teachers educating their followers, both lay and monastic, in the intricacies of Buddhist thought and the techniques of meditation that can eventually lead to nirvana (J. Van Esterik 1996).

Judaism

The first and basic Judaic religious system was defined around 500 BCE, following the destruction of the Temple in Jerusalem by Babylonians in 586 BCE (Neusner 1995). The early writings, called the Pentateuch, established the theme of exile and return as a paradigm for Judaism that endures today. The Pentateuch is also called the Five Books of Moses, or the Torah.

Followers of Judaism share in the belief in the Torah as the revelation of God's truth through Israel, a term for the "holy people." The Torah explains the relationship between the supernatural and human realms and guides people in how to carry out the worldview through appropriate actions. A key feature of all forms of Judaism is the identification of what is wrong with the present and how to escape, overcome, or survive that situation. Jewish life is symbolically interpreted as a tension between exile and return, given its foundational myth in the exile of the Jews from Israel and their period of slavery in Egypt.

Judaism is monotheistic, teaching that God is one, unique, and all-powerful. Humans have a moral duty to follow Jewish law, to protect and preserve life and health, and to follow certain duties such as observing the Sabbath. The high regard for human life is reflected in the general opposition to abortion within Jewish law and in opposition to the death penalty. Words, both spoken and written, have unique importance in Judaism: There is an emphasis on truth-telling in life and on the use of established literary formulas at precise times during worship. These formulas are encoded in a *siddur*, or prayer book. Dietary patterns also distinguish Judaism from other religions; for example, rules of kosher eating forbid the mixing of milk or milk products with meat.

Contemporary varieties of Judaism range from conservative Hasidism to Reform Judaism, which emerged in the early 1800s. One difference between these two perspectives concerns the question of who is Jewish. Jewish law traditionally defined a Jewish person as someone born of a Jewish mother. In contrast, reform Judaism recognizes as Jewish the offspring of a Jewish father and a non-Jewish mother. Currently, the Jewish population numbers roughly 15 million worldwide, with about half living in North America, a quarter in Israel, and another 20 percent in Europe and Russia. Smaller populations are scattered across the globe.

Who's Who at the Kotel

The most sacred place to all Jews is the *Kotel,* or Western Wall in Jerusalem (see Map 11.5). Since the 1967 war, which brought Jerusalem under Israeli rule, the *Kotel* can be considered the most important religious shrine and pilgrimage site of Israel. The *Kotel* is located at one edge of the Temple Mount (or Haram Sharif), an area sacred to Jews, Muslims, and Christians. According to Jewish scriptures, God asked Abraham to sacrifice his son Isaac on this hill. Later, King Solomon built the First Temple here in the middle of the tenth century BCE. It was destroyed by Nebuchadnezzar in 587 BCE, when the Jews were led into captivity in Babylon. Around 500 BCE, King Herod built the Second Temple on the same site. The *Kotel* is a remnant of the Second Temple. Jews of all varieties and non-Jews come to the *Kotel* in vast numbers from around the world. The *Kotel* plaza is open to everyone, pilgrims and tourists. The wall is made of massive rectangular stones weighing between two and eight tonnes each. At its base is a synagogue area, partitioned into men's and women's sections.

The *Kotel* (or Western Wall) in Jerusalem is a sacred place of pilgrimage especially for Jews. Males pray at a section marked off on the left while women keep to the area on the right. Both men and women should cover their heads, and women should take care when leaving the wall area to keep their faces toward it and avoid turning their backs to it. ■ (Source: Barbara Miller)

An ethnographic study of what goes on at the *Kotel* reveals how this single site brings together a variety of Jewish worshippers and more secular visitors. There is great diversity among the visitors, evident in the various styles of dress and gesture:

> The Hasid . . . with a fur shtreimel on his head may enter the synagogue area alongside a man in shorts who utilizes

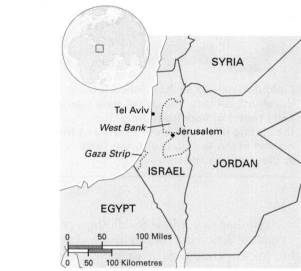

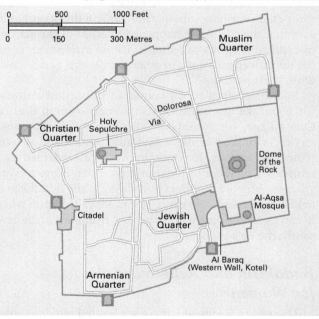

MAP 11.5 Sacred Sites in the Old City of Jerusalem, Israel. Jerusalem is the holiest city of Judaism, the third holiest city of Islam, and holy to some Christian denominations. The section called the Old City is surrounded by walls that have been built, razed, relocated, and rebuilt over several hundred years. The Old City contains four quarters: Armenian, Christian, Jewish, and Muslim, and many sacred sites such as the *Kotel* and the Via Dolorosa.

a cardboard skullcap available for "secular" visitors. American youngsters in jeans may ponder Israeli soldiers of their own age, dressed in uniform, and wonder what their lot might have been if they were born in another country. Women from Yemen, wearing embroidered trousers under their dresses, edge close to the Wall as do women accoutred in contemporary styles whose religiosity may have been filtered through a modern education. . . . The North African-born Israeli, uttering a personal prayer with his forehead against the Wall becomes an object of comment for a European tourist. Pious women, with their heads covered for modesty, instruct their children in the decorum appropriate to the prayer situation. People from many parts of the country, nay the world, meet unexpectedly. (Storper-Perez and Goldberg 1994:321)

In spite of plaques that state the prohibition against begging, there are beggars who offer to "sell a blessing" to visitors. They may remind visitors that it was the poor who built the wall in the first place. Another category of people is young Jewish men in search of prospective "born again" Jews who "hang around" looking for a "hit" (in their words). Most of the hits are young North Americans who are urged to take their Jewishness more seriously and, if male, to be sure to marry a Jewish woman. Other regulars are Hebrew-speaking men who are available to organize a prayer service. One of the most frequent forms of religious expression at the *Kotel* is the insertion of written prayers into the crevices of the wall.

The social heterogeneity of the Jewish people is, thus, brought together in a single space, creating some sense of what Victor Turner (1969) called *communitas*, a sense of collective unity out of individual diversity.

Passover in Kerala

The Jews of the Kochi area (formerly called Cochin) of Kerala, South India, have lived there for about 1000 years (Katz and Goldberg 1989). The Maharaja of Kochi had good relations with and respect for the Jewish people, who were mainly merchants. He relied on them for external trade and contacts. In recognition of this, he allowed a synagogue, which is still standing, to be built next to his palace. Syncretism is apparent in Kochi Jewish lifestyle, social structure, and rituals. Crucial aspects of Judaism are retained, along with adoption of many aspects of Hindu practices.

Three aspects of syncretism with Hinduism are apparent in Passover, one of the most important annual rituals of the Jewish faith. First, compared to the typically joyous Western/European Passover celebration, the Kochi version has adopted a tone of austerity and is called "the fasting feast." Kochi Passover, second, allows no roles for children who, at a traditional *Seder* (ritual meal) usually ask four questions as a starting-point of the narrative. The Kochi Jews chant the

A celebration of the Christian holy day of Palm Sunday in Port-au-Prince, Haiti. European colonialism brought thousands of Africans as slaves to the "New World," and it also exported Christianity through missionary efforts. Many forms of Christianity are now firmly entrenched in the Caribbean region as well as in Central and South America. ■ (Source: Edward Keller III)

questions in unison. This change relates to the fact that in Hinduism, children do not have solo roles in rituals. Third, a Kochi Seder stresses purity even more than standard Jewish requirements. Standard rules about maintaining the purity of kosher wine usually mean that no gentile (non-Jew) should touch it. But Kochi Jews say that if the shelf or table on which the wine sits is touched by a gentile, the wine is impure. This extra level of "contagion" is influenced by Hindu concepts of pollution.

Christianity

Christianity has many ties with Judaism, from which it sprang, especially in terms of the Biblical teachings of a coming saviour, or *messiah* (anointed one). It began in the eastern Mediterranean in the second quarter of the first century (Cunningham 1995:240–253). Most of the early believers were Jews, who took up the belief in Jesus Christ as the messiah who came to earth in fulfillment of prophesies contained in the Hebrew Scriptures. Today, Christianity is the largest of the world's religions with about 2 billion adherents, or nearly one-third of the world's population. It is the majority religion of Australia, New Zealand, the Philippines, Papua New Guinea, most countries of Europe, and North and South America, and about a dozen southern African countries. Christianity is a minority religion throughout Asia, but Asian Christians constitute 16 percent of the world's total Christians and are thus a significant population.

Christians accept the Bible (Old and New Testaments) as containing the basic teachings, the belief that a supreme God sent his son to earth as a sacrifice for the welfare of humanity, and the importance of Jesus as the model to follow for moral guidance. The three largest branches of Christianity are Roman Catholic, Protestant, and Eastern Orthodox. Within each of these branches, various denominations exist. Christianity has existed the longest in the Middle East and Mediterranean regions. In contemporary times, the greatest growth in Christianity is occurring in sub-Saharan Africa, parts of India, and Indonesia. It is currently experiencing a resurgence in Eastern Europe.

Protestantism among White Appalachians

Studies of Protestantism in Appalachia describe local traditions that outsiders who are accustomed to standard, urban versions may view as "deviant." For example, churches in rural West Virginia and North Carolina, called Old Regulars, emphasize in their worship three obligatory rituals: foot washing, communion (a ritual commemorating the "Last Supper" that Jesus had with his disciples), and baptism (Dorgan 1989). The foot-washing ceremony occurs once a year in conjunction with communion, usually as an extension of the Sunday service. An elder is called to the front of the church, and he preaches for about 10 to 20 minutes. A round of handshaking and embracing follows. Two deaconesses then come forward to "prepare the table" by uncovering the sacramental

elements placed there earlier under a white tablecloth. The elements are unleavened bread, serving plates for the bread, cups for the wine, and a decanter or quart jar or two of wine. The deacons break the bread into pieces and the moderator pours the wine into the cups. Men and women form separate groups as the deacons serve the bread and wine. The deacons serve each other, and then it is time for the foot washing.

The moderator begins by quoting from the New Testament (the book of John, Chapter 13, Verse 4): "He riseth from supper, and laid aside his garments; and he took a towel and girded himself." While speaking these lines, he removes his coat and then ties a long towel around his waist. He takes a basin from the piles of basins by the communion table and puts water in it, selects a senior elder and removes his shoes and socks, then washes his feet slowly and attentively. Other members come forward and take towels and basins. Soon, "the church is filled with crying, shouting, and praising as these highly poignant exchanges unleash a flood of emotions. A fellowship that may have remained very solemn during the communion will now participate in a myriad of intense expressions of religious enthusiasm and literally scores of high-pathos scenes will be played out" (106). Participants take turns washing and being washed. A functional interpretation of the ritual of foot washing is that it helps maintain interpersonal harmony in small religious communities.

Another feature of worship in some small Protestant churches in remote, rural areas of West Virginia involves the handling of poisonous snakes. This practice finds legitimation in the New Testament (Daugherty 1997),

The Vatican in Rome (left). The Vatican attracts more pilgrims/visitors each year than any religious site in the world. In the nearby neighbourhood (right), shops cater to pilgrims/visitors by offering a variety of religious and secular goods. ■ (Source: Barbara Miller)

according to a passage in Mark (16:15–18): "In my name shall they cast out devils; they shall speak with new tongues; they shall take up serpents; and if they drink any deadly thing, it shall not hurt them; they shall lay hands on the sick, and they shall recover." Members of "Holiness-type" churches believe that the handling of poisonous snakes is the supreme act of devotion to God. They are Biblical literalists and have chosen serpent handling as their way of celebrating life, death, and resurrection, and proving that only Jesus has the power to deliver them from death. During their services, the Holy Ghost (not the Holy Spirit) enables them to pick up serpents, speak in tongues, testify to the Lord's greatness, and drink strychnine or lye. Most serpent handlers have been bitten many times, but few have died.

The Last Supper in Fiji

Among Christians in Fiji, the image of the "Last Supper" is a dominant motif (Toren 1988). This scene, depicted on tapestry hangings, adorns most churches and many houses. People say, "Christ is the head of this household, he eats with us and overhears us" (697). The image's popularity is the result of its fit with Fijian notions of communal eating and kava drinking. Seating rules at such events place the people of highest status, such as the chief and others close to him, at the "above" side of the room, away from the entrance. Others sit at the "lower" end, facing the highly ranked people. Intermediate positions are located on either side of the person of honour, in ranked order. Leonardo da Vinci's rendition of the Last Supper places Jesus Christ in the position of a chief, with the disciples in an ordered arrangement around him. "The image of an ordered and stratified society exemplified in people's positions relative to one another around the kava bowl is encountered virtually every day in the village" (706). The disciples and the viewers "face" the chief and eat and drink together, as is appropriate in Fijian society.

Islam

Islam is based on the teachings of the prophet Muhammad (570–632) and is thus the youngest of the world religions (Martin 1995:498–513). The Arabic word *Islam* means "submission" to the will of the one god, Allah, through which peace will be achieved. Followers of Islam, known as Muslims, believe that Muhammad was God's final prophet. Islam has several denominations with essentially similar beliefs but also distinct theological and legal approaches. The two major schools of thought are Sunni and Shi'a. Sunnis make up about 85 percent of the total Muslim population worldwide, with Shi'as roughly 15 percent. Sufism is a more mystical variant, with

much smaller numbers of adherents. Many other subgroups exist.

The Five Pillars of Islam are profession of faith in Allah, daily prayer, fasting, contributing alms for the poor, and pilgrimage to Mecca (the *Hajj*). They are central to Sunni Islam but less so to the Shi'a and Sufi branches.

The total number of Muslims worldwide is about 1.4 billion, making it the second largest religion. Muslim-majority nations are located in northern Africa; the Middle East, including Afghanistan, Pakistan, and

THINKING OUTSIDE THE BOX

VISIT THE Vatican website (www.vatican.va) and explore the Vatican's position on the "Da Vinci code" phenomenon.

The Hassan II Mosque was built for the sixtieth birthday of Morocco's previous king, Hassan II. It is the largest religious monument in the world, after Mecca, with space for 25 000 worshippers inside and another 80 000 outside. The minaret, 210 metres in height, is the tallest in the world. ■ (Source: Jack Heaton)

Ethnographic Profile

Hui Muslims of Xi'an, China

The Hui, one of China's largest designated minorities, number around 10 million people. Most live in the northwestern part of the country. The state classifies the Hui as "backward" and "feudal" in comparison to China's majority Han population. Hui residents of Xi'an, however, reject the official characterization of them as less civilized and less modern than the Han majority (Gillette 2000).

Roughly 60 000 Hui live in Xi'an, mainly in the so-called Old Muslim Area, which is dominated by small shops, restaurants, and mosques. The quality of housing and public services is inferior to that found elsewhere in the city. Parents worry that their children are not getting the best education and feel that the state is not providing adequate schooling in their neighbourhood. Many Hui have taken steps to improve their houses themselves and to send their children to schools outside the district.

The Hui of Xi'an construct what they consider to be a modern and civilized lifestyle by choosing aspects of Muslim culture and Western culture. Their form of "progress" is visible in many aspects of their daily life, such as eating habits, dress styles, housing, religious practices, education, and family organization.

Being Muslim in China poses several challenges in relation to the dominant Han culture. Diet is one prominent example. The Qu'ran forbids four types of food to Muslims: animal flesh that has not been consecrated to God and properly slaughtered, blood, pork, and alcohol (Gillette 2000:116). Three of the four rules apply to meat, and meat is the central part of a proper meal for Muslims. The Hui say that pork is especially impure. This belief differentiates the Hui clearly from other Chinese people for whom pork is a major food item. Given the Hui belief that the kinds of food one eats affect a person's essence and behaviour, they view pork eaters with disdain.

Hui residents consider alcohol even more impure than pork (Gillette 2000:167). Hui of Xi'an do not drink alcohol. They avoid using utensils that have touched alcohol and people who are drinking it. Many Hui of Xi'an, however, make a living in the restaurant business, which caters to Chinese Han and foreign tourists. While selling alcohol boosts business, many Hui object to it. Several Hui formed the Anti-alcohol Committee to advocate for banning the sale of alcohol in restaurants in the Hui quarter and preventing customers from bringing their own alcohol. Some areas of the market section are alcohol-free zones. Committee members say that restricting alcohol has improved the quality of life by making the neighbourhood more peaceful and orderly.

In 2003, an urban development project in the Old Muslim Quarter was launched with financial support from the Norwegian government (*People's Daily* 2003). The project will widen the main street, replace "shabby" housing and infrastructure, and restore crumbling buildings of historic interest. A commercial area will be dedicated to restaurants serving Hui food in recognition of the touristic appeal of traditional Hui specialties such as baked beef and mutton, buns with beef, mutton pancake, and mutton soup. It is unclear where alcohol consumption will fit into this plan.

Reading

Maris Boyd Gillette. *Between Mecca and Beijing: Modernization and Consumption among Urban Chinese Families.* Stanford, CA: Stanford University Press, 2000.

Thanks to Maris Boyd Gillette, Haverford College, for reviewing this material.

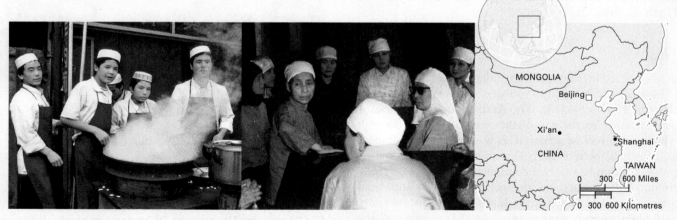

At a street stand in Xi'an (left), Hui men prepare and sell a noodle dish. Like Muslim men in many parts of the world, they wear a white cap. ■ (Source: Eddie Gerald/Alamy) Hui women in Xi'an (right) participate in a ritual that commemorates Hui people who died in a massive conflict that spread across northwestern China from 1862 to 1874. ■ (Source: Maris Boyd Gillette)

MAP 11.6 *The City of Xi'an in China. Xi'an, the capital of Shaanxi province, is one of the most economically developed cities in the northwestern part of China.*

Bangladesh in South Asia; and several nations in central Asia and Southeast Asia. Most of the world's Muslims (60 percent) live in South Asia or Southeast Asia. Muslims live as minorities in many other countries, including China, where they seek to maintain their religious practices (see the accompanying Ethnographic Profile). Although Islam originally flourished among pastoralists, only 2 percent of its adherents now are in that category.

A common and inaccurate stereotype of Islam among many non-Muslims is that wherever it exists, it is the same. This erroneously monolithic model tends to be based on an image of conservative Wahhabist Islam as practised in Saudi Arabia. It is only one of many "Islams." A comparison of Islam in highland Sumatra, Indonesia, and Morocco, North Africa, reveals differences that are the result of local cultural adaptations (Bowen 1992). Eid-ul-Adha, or the Feast of Sacrifice, is celebrated annually by Muslims around the world. It commemorates Ibrahim's willingness to sacrifice his son Ishmael (Isaac in Christian and Jewish traditions) to Allah. It occurs on the tenth of the last month of the year, called Pilgrimage Month and marks the end of the Hajj. The ritual reminds Muslims of their global unity within the Islamic faith.

An important aspect of this ritual in Morocco involves the king publicly plunging a dagger into a ram's throat, a re-enactment of Muhammad's performance of the sacrifice on the same day in the seventh century. Each male head of household follows the pattern and sacrifices a ram. Size and virility of the ram are a measure of the man's power and virility. Other men of the household stand to witness the sacrifice, while women and children are absent or in the background. After the ram is killed, the men come forward and dab its blood on their faces. In some villages, women play a more prominent role before the sacrifice by daubing the ram with henna (red dye), thus sanctifying it, and using its blood afterward in rituals to protect the household. These state and household rituals are symbolic of male power in the public and private domains—the power of the monarchy and the power of patriarchy.

In Isak, Sumatra, the cultural context is less patriarchal and the political structure does not emphasize monarchy. Isak is a traditionalist Muslim village where people have been Muslims since the seventeenth century. They sacrifice many kinds of animals: chickens, ducks, sheep, goats, and water buffalo. The people believe that so long as the animal's throat is cut and the meat is eaten, the sacrifice satisfies God. Most sacrifices are family affairs and receive little public notice. They are done in the back of the house. Both women and men of the household refer to it as "their" sacrifice, and there are no signs of male dominance. Women may sponsor a sacrifice, as did one wealthy woman trader who sacrificed a buffalo (the cutting was done by a man).

The Moroccan ritual emphasizes fathers and sons, whereas the Isak ritual includes attention to a wider range of kin on both the husband's and wife's sides, daughters as well as sons, and even dead relatives. In Isak, the ritual carries no centralized political meanings. The differences are not due to the fact that Moroccans know the scriptures better than Sumatrans do. The Isak area has many Islamic scholars who are familiar with the scriptures and regularly discuss them with each other. Rather, the two cultural contexts, including kinship and politics, shape the ritual to local realities.

African Religions

Many African religions are global. In earlier centuries, they spread outside Africa through the coerced movement of people as slaves. African diaspora religions are especially prominent in the United States, the Caribbean region, and Central and South America. This section summarizes some key features of African religions and then offers two examples of African religions in the western hemisphere.

Features of African Religions

With its diverse geography, cultural variation, and history, Africa encompasses a wide range of religious affiliations, including many Muslims, Christians, Jews, Hindus, practitioners of indigenous religions, and people who follow some combination of these.

Indigenous African religions are difficult to typify, but some of their shared features are

- myths about a rupture that once occurred between the creator deity and humans
- a pantheon that includes a high god and many secondary supernaturals ranging from powerful gods to lesser spirits
- elaborate initiation rituals
- rituals involving animal sacrifices and other offerings, meals, and dances
- altars within shrines as focal places where humans and deities meet
- close links between healing and divination

Although these features are fairly constant, African religions are rethought and reshaped locally and over time with complex and variable results (Gable 1995). In

A sacred altar in a local African religion in Togo, West Africa. ■ (Source: © Gerd Ludwig/Woodfin Camp & Associates)

their home locations, they have been influenced by foreign religions, notably Islam and various types of Christianity. The outmigration of African peoples has brought African religions to new locations where they have been localized in their new contexts and also revitalized (Clarke 2004). Kamari Clarke's research on the Yorùbá revivalist religion in the United States took her from New York City to South Carolina and Nigeria. The focal point of her fieldwork was in Ọ̀yọ̀túnjí Village near Beaufort, South Carolina. African American Yorùbá revivalists have created a place that reconstructs royal Yorùbá spiritual leadership and worship that helps some African Americans reconnect with their lost identity. In the words of Kamari Clarke, "Ritual initiations and rhythmic drumming echo in the endless hours of the night as residents remake their ancestral homeland outside the territory of Africa" (2004:51). The place, the rituals, and the music tie the people to Africa. Many Yorùbá-descent Americans, like other African Americans, go even further in their attempt to reconnect with their heritage. "Roots tourism" is a growing industry that provides culturally informed travel for African Americans to their places of ancestral origin in Africa.

Many religious syncretisms in North and South America combine African traditions with aspects of Christianity, indigenous Indian religions, and other traditions. Widely popular in Brazil are Afro-Brazilian religions such as *umbanda, santería*, and *condomblé*—they appeal to people of all social classes, urban and rural, especially for providing social support and alleviation of stress (Burdick 2004).

THINKING OUTSIDE THE BOX

LEARN ABOUT Ọ̀yọ̀túnjí Village from the Web. What goes on there? Do people live there? If you went to visit, where would you stay, what would you eat, and what would you do?

Ras Tafari

Also called Rastafarianism, Ras Tafari is a relatively new religion—it was first enunciated in the 1930s—of the Caribbean, North America, and Europe. Numbers of Rastafarians are unknown because they refuse to be counted (J. Smith 1995:23). Ras Tafari is an unorthodox, protest religion that shares few of the features of African religions mentioned above. Ras Tafari traces its history to several preachers of the early twentieth century who taught that Ras ("Prince") Tafari, then the Ethiopian Emperor Haile Selassie I, was the "Lion of Judah" who would lead blacks to the African Promised Land. Rastafarianism does not have an organized set of doctrines, and there are no written texts or enforced orthodoxy. However, Yawney and Homiak report that a Ras Tafari assembly in 1983 declared that one group in the movement, the House of Nyahbinghi, be accepted as the foundational Ras Tafari orthodoxy (2001:256). This orthodoxy includes such shared beliefs of the many diffuse groups that Ethiopia is Zion, or heaven on earth, and Emperor Haile Selassie I of Ethiopia is a living god, and that all African people are one and have the right of return to Africa. Since the death of Haile Selassie in 1975, a greater emphasis has been placed on pan-African unity and black power, and less on Ethiopia. Rastafarianism is particularly strong in Jamaica, where it first emerged. It is associated with reggae music, dreadlocks, and *ganja* (marijuana) smoking. Variations within the Rastafarian movement in Jamaica range from beliefs that one must fight oppression to the position that living a peaceful life brings victory against evil.

Directions of Religious Change

All religions have established mythologies and doctrines that provide for continuity in beliefs and practices. Yet, nowhere are religions frozen and unchanging. Cultural anthropologists have traced the resurgence of religions that seemed to have been headed toward extinction

revitalization movement: a religious movement, usually organized by a prophetic leader, that seeks to construct a more satisfying situation by reviving all or parts of a religion that has been threatened by outside forces or by adopting new practices and beliefs.

cargo cult: a form of revitalization movement that emerged in Melanesia and New Zealand, in response to Western and Japanese influences.

through colonial forces, and they have documented the emergence of seemingly new religions. Likewise, they are observing the contemporary struggle of once-suppressed religions in socialist states to find a new position in the post-socialist world. Religious icons, once a prominent part of Russian Orthodox churches, were removed and placed in museums. Now, the churches want them back.

Indigenous people's beliefs about the sacredness of their land are an important part of their attempts to protect their territory from encroachment and development by outside commercial interests. The world of religious change offers these examples, and far more, as windows into wider cultural change.

Revitalization Movements

Revitalization movements are social movements that seek to bring about positive change, either through re-establishing all or parts of a religion that has been threatened by outside forces or by adopting new practices and beliefs. Such movements often arise in the context of rapid cultural change and appear to represent a way for people to try to make sense of their changing world and their place in it. One such movement that emerged as a response of First Nations to the invasion of their land by Europeans and Euro-Americans was the Ghost Dance movement (J. Smith 1995:385). In the early 1870s, a shaman of the Paiute tribe in California named Wodziwob declared that the world would soon be destroyed and then renewed: First Nations peoples, plants, and animals would come back to life. He instructed people to perform a circle dance, known as the Ghost Dance, at night.

This movement spread to other tribes in California, Oregon, and Idaho, but ended when the prophet died and his prophecy was unfulfilled. A similar movement emerged in 1890, led by another Paiute prophet, Wovoka, who had a vision during a total eclipse. His message was the same: destruction, renewal, and the need to perform circle dances in anticipation of the impending event. The dance spread widely and with differing effects. Among the Pawnee, it provided the basis for a cultural revival of old ceremonies that had fallen into disuse. The Sioux altered Wovoka's message and adopted a more overtly hostile stance toward the United States government and white people. Newspapers began to carry stories about the "messiah craze," referring to Wovoka. Ultimately, the government took action against the Sioux, killing Chief Sitting Bull and Chief Big Foot and about 300 Sioux at Wounded Knee. In the 1970s, the Ghost Dance was revived by the American Indian Movement, an activist organization seeking to improve First Nations rights.

A Ghost Dance shirt of the Arapaho Indians of the Plains Region, with painted designs of birds, turtle, and stars. These specially decorated garments were believed to protect the wearer from the white man's bullets. ■ (Source: © Visual Arts Library [London]/Alamy)

Cargo cults are a variety of revitalization movements that emerged in much of Melanesia (including Papua New Guinea and Fiji) and in New Zealand among the indigenous Maori peoples, in response to Western and Japanese influences. Most prominent in the first half of the nineteenth century, they are characterized by their emphasis on the acquisition of Western trade goods, or *cargo* in local terms. It was difficult for many island people to understand why Western people in their midst sat around in an office all day doing very little work but receiving large deliveries of goods by ship from abroad. The islander worked hard every day in his or her yam garden but never received these wonderful goods from afar. As a consequence, prophetic leaders emerged with a vision of how the cargo would arrive for the islander. In one instance, the leader predicted that a ship would come, bringing not only cargo, but also islanders' dead ancestors. Followers set up tables for the expected guests, complete with flower arrangements.

Later, after World War II and the islanders' experiences of aircraft cargo deliveries, the mode of arrival changed to planes. Once again, people would wait expectantly for the arrival of the plane. The cargo cults emerged as a response to the disrupting effects of new goods being suddenly introduced into indigenous settings. The outsiders imposed a new form of exchange system that emphasized the importance of Western goods and denied the importance of indigenous valuables, such as shells and pigs. This transformation undermined traditional patterns of status-gaining through the exchange of indigenous goods. Cargo cult leaders sought help, in the only way they knew, in obtaining Western goods so they could gain social status in the new system.

Contested Sacred Sites

Religious conflict often becomes focused on sacred sites. One place of recurrent conflict is Jerusalem, where many religions and sects within religions compete for control of sacred terrain. Three major religions claim they have primary rights: Islam, Judaism, and Christianity. Among the Christians, several different sects vie for control of the Church of the Holy Sepulchre. In India, frequent conflicts occur between Hindus and Muslims over sacred sites. Hindus claim that Muslim mosques have been built on sites sacred to Hindus. On some occasions, the Hindus have proceeded to tear down the mosques. Many conflicts that involve secular issues surrounding sacred sites also exist worldwide. In Israel, some Jewish leaders object to archaeological research because the ancient Jewish burial places should remain undisturbed.

The same situation exists for First Nations peoples, whose burial grounds have often been destroyed for the sake of urban development in North America. Around the world, large-scale development projects such as dams and mines have destroyed indigenous sacred areas.

Religious Freedom as a Human Right

According to a United Nations Declaration, freedom from religious persecution is supposed to be a universal human right. Yet, violations of this right by nations and by competing religions are common. Sometimes, people who are being persecuted on religious grounds can seek and obtain sanctuary in other places or nations. Thousands of Tibetan Buddhist refugees, including their leader the Dalai Lama, fled Tibet after it was taken over by the Chinese. Several Tibetan communities have been established in exile in India, the United States, and Canada, where the Tibetan people attempt to keep their religion, language, and heritage alive.

The post-9/11 policy enactments, particularly in the United States, Canada, and Britain related to the so-called war on terror, are seen by many as dangerous

Supporters of the John Frum Movement, a cargo cult, stand guard around one of the cult's flag poles at Sulphur Bay village (Tanna, Vanuatu). ■ (Source: Lamont Lindstrom)

After the Chinese takeover of Tibet, many Tibetans became refugees, including the revered head of Tibetan Buddhism, the Dalai Lama. Buddhism, founded in India as a protest against Hinduism, is a minority religion in its homeland. It has millions of followers elsewhere, from Scotland to San Francisco.
■ (Source: AP/Wide World Photos)

steps against constitutional principles of personal liberty—specifically, as infringements on the religious rights of practising Muslims. The prevalent mentality in these governments, and in much of the general populace, links the whole of Islam with terrorism and thereby stigmatizes all Muslims as potential terrorists. Physical attacks against people assumed to be Muslim were another aspect of such extreme thinking. Many anthropologists (for example, Mamdani 2002) have spoken out against the wrong-headedness and indecency of labelling an entire religion dangerous and putting all its members under the shadow of suspicion.

Religions—like economies, reproduction, health systems, kinship and social organization, politics, and other areas of culture discussed in this book—are often the focal point of conflict and dissension and the source of conflict resolution. As an integral part of the heritage of humanity, they can be better understood from a cross-cultural and contextualized perspective, and such understanding can contribute to a more peaceful future.

Key Questions Revisited

WHAT is religion and what are the basic features of religions?

Early cultural anthropologists defined religion in contrast to magic and suggested that religion was a more evolved form of thinking about the supernatural realm. They collected information on religions of non-Western cultures and constructed theories about the origin and functions of religion. Since then, ethnographers have described many religious systems and documented a rich variety of beliefs, forms of ritual behaviour, and types of religious specialists. Beliefs are expressed in either myth or doctrine and often are concerned with defining the roles and characteristics of supernatural beings and how humans should relate to them.

Religious beliefs are enacted in rituals. They are periodic (regular) or nonperiodic (irregular). Some common rituals worldwide are life-cycle rites, pilgrimage, rituals of inversion, and sacrifice. Rituals are meant to be transformative for the participants. Many rituals require the involvement of a trained religious specialist such as a shaman/shamanka or priest/priestess. Compared to states, in nonstate societies, religious specialist roles are fewer, less formalized, and carry less secular power. In states, religious specialists are often organized into hierarchies, and many specialists gain substantial secular power.

HOW do world religions illustrate globalization and localization?

The five traditionally named world religions of long standing are based on texts and generally agreed-on teachings. In order of historic age, they are Hinduism, Buddhism, Judaism, Christianity, and Islam. Christianity has the largest number of adherents, with Islam second and Hinduism third. As members of the world religions have moved around the world, religious beliefs and practices have become contextualized into localized variants. When a new religion moves into a culture, it may be blended with indigenous systems (syncretism), may coexist with indigenous religions in a pluralistic fashion, or may take over and obliterate the original beliefs.

Due to accelerated global population migration in the past few centuries, many formerly local religions now have a worldwide membership. African diaspora religions are particularly prominent in the western hemisphere, with a variety of syncretistic religions attracting many adherents.

WHAT are some important aspects of religious change in contemporary times?

Cultural anthropologists have documented and sought to explain why and how religious change occurs. Religious movements of the past two centuries have often been prompted by colonialism and other forms of social contact. In some instances, indigenous religious leaders and cults arise in the attempt to resist unwanted outside forces of change; in other instances, they arise as ways of incorporating new ideas and values from the outside.

KEY CONCEPTS

animatism, p. 290
animism, p. 287
anthropomorphic, p. 290
cargo cult, p. 309
doctrine, p. 288
life-cycle ritual, p. 293
magic, p. 286
monotheism, p. 287

myth, p. 288
polytheism, p. 287
priest/priestess, p. 297
religion, p. 286
religious pluralism, p. 298
revitalization movement,
   p. 309
ritual, p. 291

ritual of inversion,
   p. 295
sacrifice, p. 296
syncretism, p. 298
world religions, p. 298
zoomorphic, p. 290

myanthrolab

To reinforce your understanding of this chapter, and to identify topics for further study, visit MyAnthroLab at www.myanthrolab.com for diagnostic tests and a multimedia ebook.

SUGGESTED READINGS

Paulo Apolito. *The Internet and the Madonna: Religious Visionary Experience on the Web*. Antony Shugaar, trans. Chicago: University of Chicago Press, 2003. In this book, Apolito traces the Christian cult of Mary as it has developed and grown through the medium of the World Wide Web. Apparitions, or sightings of Mary, are an important theme.

Diane Bell, *Ngarrindjeri Wurruwarrin: A World That Is, Was, and Will Be*. North Melbourne, Australia: Spinifex Press, 1998. This is an ethnography about Australian Aboriginal struggles to protect their sacred land from encroachment by developers, with attention to the people's own voices, the perspective of the Australian government, the media, and even disputes among anthropologists about what constitutes truth and validity.

Karen McCarthy Brown, *Mama Lola: A Vodou Priestess in Brooklyn*. Berkeley, CA: University of California Press, 1991. The life story of Mama Lola, a Vodou practitioner, is set within an ethnographic study of a Haitian community in New York.

Gregory Forth, *Beneath the Volcano: Religion, Cosmology and Spirit Classification among the Nage of Eastern Indonesia*. Leiden, Netherlands: KITLV Press, 1998. This ethnography focuses on Nage ideas about spirits and how these influence ritual practice and relations with humans. This book is an important addition to scholarship; it examines the religion of a people not previously investigated in the anthropological literature.

Susan Greenwood, *Magic, Witchcraft and the Otherworld: An Anthropology*. New York: Berg, 2000. In this book, Greenwood examines modern magic as practised by pagans in Britain, focusing on the pagan view of the essence of magic as communication with an otherworldly reality. Chapters address witchcraft, healing, goddess worship, and the relationship between magic and morality.

Klara Bonsack Kelley and Harris Francis, *Navajo Sacred Places*. Bloomington: Indiana University Press, 1994. The authors report on the results of a research project to learn about Navajo cultural resources, especially sacred sites, and the stories associated with them in order to help protect these places.

Melvin Konner. *Unsettled: An Anthropology of the Jews*. New York: Penguin Compass, 2003. A biological anthropologist is the author of this cultural history of the Jewish people and their religion. It extends from the origins of Judaism among pastoralists in the Middle East during the Bronze Age through enslavement in the Roman Empire, to the Holocaust and the creation of modern Israel.

Michael Lambek, *Knowledge and Practice in Mayotte: Local Discourses of Islam, Sorcery, and Spirit Possession*. Toronto: University of Toronto Press, 1993. This reflexive study of religious practice among an Islamic people on an island off the east coast of Africa probes the meanings of sorcery and spirit possession.

Anna S. Meigs, *Food, Sex, and Pollution: A New Guinea Religion*. New Brunswick, NJ: Rutgers University Press, 1984. Here, Meigs provides an analysis of taboos surrounding food, sex, and vital bodily essences among the Hua people of Papua New Guinea.

Fatima Mernissi, *Beyond the Veil: Male–Female Dynamics in Modern Muslim Society*. Bloomington, IN: Indiana University Press, revised edition, 1987. The author considers how Islam perceives female sexuality and seeks to regulate it on behalf of the social order. This edition contains a new chapter on Muslim women and fundamentalism.

Katharine L. Wiegele. *Investing in Miracles: El Shaddai and the Transformation of Popular Catholicism in the Philippines*. Honolulu: University of Hawai'i Press, 2005. In this book, the author examines the widespread popularity in the Philippines of a charismatic businessman who became a preacher, Brother Mike. Brother Mike appears at huge outdoor rallies and uses mass media to spread his message of economic prosperity within a Catholic framework.

12
Communication

Key Questions

- HOW do humans communicate?

- WHAT are the links between communication, cultural diversity, and inequality?

- HOW does language change?

Indigenous language dictionaries and usage guides are available on the Web and may help indigenous people preserve their culture (check out The Internet Guide to Australian Languages). *(Source: Robert Essel NYC/CORBIS)*

Most people are in almost constant communication—with other people, with supernaturals, or with pets. We communicate in face-to-face situations or indirectly through mail or email. **Communication** is the process of sending and receiving messages. Among humans, it involves some form of **language**, a systematic set of symbols and signs with learned and shared meanings. Language may be spoken, hand-signed, written, or conveyed through body movements, body markings and modifications, hairstyle, dress, and accessories.

This chapter is about human communication and language, drawing on work in both linguistic anthropology and cultural anthropology. We look at communication with a wide-angle lens to include topics from word choice to language extinction. First, we discuss how humans communicate and what distinguishes human communication from that of other animals. Next, we offer examples of local language use and inequality. In the third section, we discuss language change from its origins in the distant past to contemporary concerns about language loss.

The Varieties of Human Communication

Humans can communicate with words, either spoken or signed, with gestures and other forms of body language such as clothing and hairstyle, and through methods such as telephone calls, "snail" mail, and email.

Language and Verbal Communication

Specialists can get quite engaged in arguing about what a *language* is, how many languages there are in the world, and whether animals other than humans have language. Most agree that language and its subvarieties are systems of symbols and signs, and rules for their meaningful combination and use. The term **dialect** usually refers to a subvariety of language associated with a region, social class, or ethnic group. A speaker of the main language should be able to understand local dialects, though perhaps with difficulty.

Two Features of Human Language

Scholars of language, over many years, have proposed two characteristics of human language that distinguish it from communication among other living beings. First, human language has **productivity**, or the ability to create an infinite range of understandable expressions from a finite set of rules. This characteristic is a result of the rich variety of symbols and signs that humans use in their communication. In contrast, nonhuman primates have a more limited set of communicative resources. They rely on a **call system**, or a form of oral communication among nonhuman primates with a set repertoire of meaningful sounds generated in response to environmental factors. Nonhuman primates do not have the physiological capacity for speech that humans do. In captivity, however, some bonobos and chimpanzees have learned to communicate effectively with humans through sign language and by pointing to symbols on a chart. The world's most famous bonobo is Kanzi, who lives at the Great Ape Trust in Des Moines, Iowa (www.greatapetrust.org/bonobo/meet/kanzi.php). He can understand what humans are saying, and can respond by combining symbols on a printed board. Kanzi is also able to play simple video games, such as Ms. Pac-Man.

Second, human language emphasizes the feature of **displacement**, the ability to refer to events and issues beyond the immediate present. The past and the future, in this view, are considered to be *displaced domains*. They include reference to people and events that may never exist at all, as in fantasy and fiction. Some bonobos who have been raised by and live in a close relationship with humans do exhibit the ability for displacement (www.smithsonianmag.com/science-nature/speakingbonobo.html). Thus, they have the capacity for displacement but, especially in the wild, are likely to use it far less than humans do.

In respect to productivity and displacement in human language, the case of language among the Pirahã of Brazil is challenging (Everett 2005) (see Map 12.1). Their language does not appear to emphasize either productivity or displacement, though both exist to some degree. The Pirahã are a group of 300 to 350 foragers living on a reservation in the Amazonian rainforest near the Maici River. Their language contains only three pronouns, few words associated with time, no past-tense verbs, no colour terms, and no numbers other than a word that translates into English roughly as "about one." Grammar is simple, with no subordinate clauses. Kinship terms are

---

communication: the conveying of meaningful messages from one person, animal, or insect to another.

language: a form of communication that is a systematic set of learned and shared symbols and signs shared among a group and passed on from generation to generation.

dialect: a way of speaking in a particular place or a variety of a language arising from local circumstances.

productivity: a feature of human language that offers the ability to communicate many messages efficiently.

call system: a form of oral communication among nonhuman primates with a

set repertoire of meaningful sounds generated in response to environmental factors.

displacement: a feature of human language that allows people to talk about events in the past and future.

phoneme: a sound in a language that makes a difference in meaning.

Primatologist Sue Savage-Rumbaugh, working with Kanzi, an adult male bonobo. Kanzi has been involved in a long-term project about ape language. He has learned to communicate with researchers using a variety of symbols. Some chimpanzees, bonobos, orangutans, and gorillas have learned to communicate using American Sign Language and symbols on computer keyboards. ■ (Source: © Frans Lanting/Minden Pictures)

simple and few. The Pirahã have no myths or stories and no art other than necklaces and a few rudimentary stick figures. In spite of over 200 years of regular contact with Brazilians and neighbouring Indians who speak a different language, the Pirahã remain monolingual.

Since 1977, linguist Daniel Everett has lived with the Pirahã and learned their language, so it is unlikely that he has overlooked major aspects of it. He insists that Pirahã language is in no way "primitive." It has extremely complex verbs and rich and varied uses of stress and intonation, referred to in linguistics as *prosody*. The Pirahã especially enjoy verbal joking and teasing, both among themselves and with researchers.

Formal Properties of Verbal Language

Human language can be analyzed in terms of its formal properties: sounds, vocabulary, and syntax or grammar, the formal building blocks of all languages. But languages differ widely in which sounds are important, what words are important in the vocabulary, and how people put words together to form meaningful sentences.

Learning a new language usually involves learning different sets of sounds. The sounds that make a difference for meaning in a language are called **phonemes**. Anthropologist Diamond Jenness, who learned several First Nations languages, considered the Algonquian languages the most musical because of their richness of vowel sounds, avoidance of harsh consonants, and use of whispered syllables. He found the Salish languages very harsh because of consonant clusters that English speakers find hard to pronounce, and found the Athabascan languages the most difficult to learn (J. Price 1979:23). Similarly, Sharon Hutchinson (1996) was attracted to the rich, melodic qualities of the Nuer language, but found it difficult to hear and control the heavy aspiration (audible release of breath). These subjective judgments about other languages reflect our experience using different phonemes.

A native English-speaker learning to speak Hindi, the major language of North India, must learn to produce and recognize several new sounds. Four different "d" sounds exist. None is the same as an English "d," which is usually pronounced with the tongue placed on the ridge behind the upper front teeth (try it). One "d" in Hindi, which linguists refer to as a "dental" sound, is

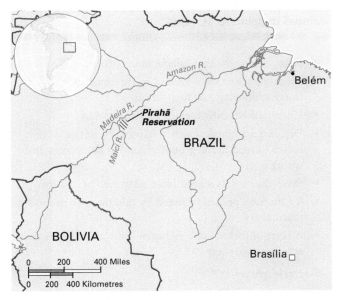

MAP 12.1   Pirahã Reservation in Brazil. Linguistic anthropologist Daniel Everett helped to define the boundaries of the Pirahã reservation in the 1980s. With support from Cultural Survival and other sources, the demarcation was legally declared in 1994.

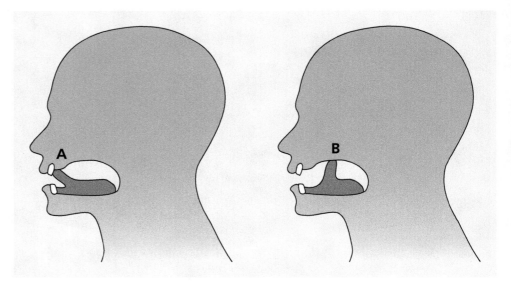

FIGURE 12.1 Dental and retroflex tongue positions. When making a dental sound, the speaker places the tongue against the upper front teeth (position A on the diagram). When making a retroflex sound, the speaker places the tongue up against the roof of the mouth (position B on the diagram).

pronounced with the tongue pressed firmly behind the upper front teeth (try it) (see Figure 12.1). Next is a dental "d" that is also aspirated (pronounced "with air"); making this sound involves the tongue being in the same position and a puff of air expelled during pronunciation (try it, and try the regular dental "d" again with no puff of air at all). Next is what is referred to as a "retroflex" sound, made by flipping the tongue back to the central dome of the roof of the mouth (try it, with no puff of air). Finally, there is the aspirated retroflex "d" with the tongue in the centre of the roof of the mouth and a puff of air. Once you can do this, try the whole series again with a "t," because Hindi follows the same pattern with this letter as with the "d." Several other sounds in Hindi require careful use of aspiration and placement of the tongue for communicating the right word. A puff of air at the wrong time can produce a serious error, such as saying the word for "breast" when you want to say the word for "letter."

All languages have a *lexicon*, or vocabulary, which consists of all its meaningful words. Words are combined in phrases and sentences to create meaning. *Semantics* refers to the study of the meaning of words, phrases, and sentences. Anthropologists add the concept of **ethnosemantics**, the study of the meaning of words, phrases, and sentences in particular cultural contexts. They find that different languages classify the world in different ways, and categorize even such seemingly natural things as colour and disease in different ways (recall the discussion of Subanun disease categories in Chapter 7). By doing ethnosemantic research, one can learn much about how people define the world and their place in it, how they organize their social lives, and what is of value to them. *Focal vocabularies* are

clusters of words that refer to important features of a particular culture (see Figure 12.2). For example, many circumpolar languages, including Inuktitut, have rich focal vocabularies related to snow, as do English speakers who are avid skiers; Arabic has many words for camels, and a horse breeder has an elaborate focal vocabulary for kinds of horses.

Syntax, or grammar, consists of the patterns and rules for organizing word sequences that carry meaning. All languages have rules for syntax, although they vary in form. Even within the languages of contemporary Europe syntactical variation exists. German,

FIGURE 12.2 Kinds of "Snow" the Saami Recognize Related to Reindeer Herding

- Firm, even snow that falls in mild weather
- Thickly packed snow caused by intermittent freezing/thawing and high winds
- Hard-packed snow formed by strong wind
- Dry, large-grained, water-holding snow at the deepest layers, closest to the ground, found in late winter and spring
- Snow that forms a hard layer after rain
- Ice sheet on pastures formed by rain on open ground that freezes
- A layer of frozen snow between other snow layers that acts as an ice sheet

Source: Jernsletten 1997.

---

ethnosemantics: the study of the meaning of words, phrases, and sentences in particular cultural contexts.

sign language: a form of communication that uses mainly hand movements to convey messages.

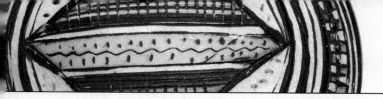

Lessons Applied

ANTHROPOLOGY AND PUBLIC UNDERSTANDING OF THE LANGUAGE AND CULTURE OF PEOPLE WHO ARE DEAF

Ethnographic studies of the communication practices and wider culture of people who are deaf have great importance and practical application (Senghas and Monaghan 2002). This research demonstrates the limitations and

In Uganda, James Mwadha, a deaf attendee at a meeting for Action on Disability and Development (ADD), signs to others in the group. The ADD group seeks to promote the rights of disabled people.
■ (Source: © Penny Tweedie/CORBIS)

inaccuracy of the "medical model" that construes deafness as a pathology or deficit and sees the goal as curing it. Instead, anthropologists propose the "cultural model," which views deafness simply as one possibility in the wide spectrum of cultural variation. (In the context of using this cultural model, a capital *D* is often used: Deaf culture.)

Deafness leaves plenty of room for human agency. The strongest evidence of agency among people who are deaf is sign language itself, which exhibits adaptability, creativity, and change. This new view helps to promote a nonvictim, nonpathological identity for people who are deaf and to reduce social stigma related to deafness.

Anthropologists working in the area of Deaf culture studies are examining how people who are deaf become bilingual—for example, fluent in both English and Japanese sign languages. Their findings are being incorporated in markedly improved ways of teaching sign language.

FOOD FOR THOUGHT

- Learn the signs for five words in English sign language, and then learn the signs for the same words in another sign language. Are they the same or different, and how might one explain the similarity or difference?

for example, places verbs at the end of the sentence (try to compose an English sentence with its main verb at the end).

Nonverbal Language and Embodied Communication

In this section, we review forms of language and communication that do not rely on verbal speech. Like verbal language, though, they are based on symbols and signs and have rules for their proper combination and meaning.

Sign Language

Sign language is a form of communication that uses mainly hand movements to convey messages. A sign language provides a fully competent communicative system for its users just as spoken language does (Baker 1999). Around the world, many varieties of sign language exist, including American Sign Language, British Sign Language, Japanese Sign Language, Russian Sign Language, and many varieties of indigenous Australian sign languages. Most sign

languages are used by hearing-impaired people as their main form of communication. Indigenous Australian sign languages, in contrast, are used by people who have the capacity for verbal communication. They switch to sign language in situations in which verbal speech is forbidden or undesirable (Kendon 1988). Verbal speech is forbidden in some sacred contexts and for widows during mourning. It is also undesirable when hunting.

Although sign languages are complete and complex languages in their own right, they are often treated as second-class versions of "real" languages. A breakthrough in recognition of the validity and communicative competence of sign languages came in 1983 when the government of Sweden recognized Swedish Sign Language as a native language. Such recognition is especially important in contexts where a person's sense of identity, and even citizenship itself, is based on the ability to speak an officially accepted language. Anthropologists collaborate with people who are deaf to help promote public understanding of the legitimacy of their language and to advocate for improved teaching of sign language (see the accompanying Lessons Applied box).

Gestures are movements, usually of the hands, that convey meanings. Some gestures may be universally meaningful, but most are culturally specific and often completely arbitrary. Some cultures have more highly developed gesture systems than others. Black urban youths in the province of Gauteng, South Africa, in which the cities of Pretoria and Johannesburg are located, use a rich repertoire of gestures (Brookes 2004) (see Map 9.5 on page 241). Although some of the gestures are widely used and recognized, many vary by age, gender, and situation (see Figure 12.3). Men use more gestures than women do; the reason for this difference is not clear.

Greetings, an important part of communication in every known culture, often involve gestures (Duranti 1997b). They are typically among the first communicative routines that children master, as well as tourists and anyone trying to learn a foreign language. Greetings establish a social encounter. They typically involve both verbal and nonverbal language. Depending on the context and the social relationship, many variations exist for both the verbal and the nonverbal component. Contextual factors include the degree of formality or informality. Social factors include gender, ethnicity, class, and age.

Silence

Silence is another form of nonverbal communication. Its use is often related to social status, but in unpredictable ways. In rural Siberia, an in-marrying daughter-in-law has the lowest status in the household, and she rarely speaks (Humphrey 1978). In other contexts, silence is associated with power. In North American courts, lawyers speak the most, the judge speaks rarely but has more power than a lawyer, while the silent jury holds the most power (Lakoff 1990). While some First Nations groups value oratory, others value silence. For example, the Kaska of northern British Columbia and Yukon did not value verbal fluency or use baby talk, and they used silence as a response to pain or frustration. Knowing how and when to keep silent was highly valued (Darnell 1970).

Silence is an important part of communication in many First Nations cultures. Anglo outsiders, including social workers, have sometimes misinterpreted this silence as either a reflection of a sense of dignity, or, more insultingly, a lack of emotion or intelligence. How wrong and ethnocentric such judgments are is revealed by a study of silence among the Western Apache of Arizona (Basso 1972) (see Map 12.2). The Western Apache use silence in four contexts. First, when meeting a stranger (someone who cannot be identified), especially at fairs, rodeos, or other public events, it is considered bad manners to speak right away. That would indicate interest in something like money, or work, or transportation, which are possible reasons for

OUTSIDE THE BOX **THINKING**

SPEND A WEEK observing how people greet each other, both verbally and nonverbally. What are your major findings?

child
Fingers of one hand are brought together at the tips pointing upwards.

father/male elder/boyfriend
Side of knuckle of forefinger, with thumb under chin, strokes chin downwards once or twice.

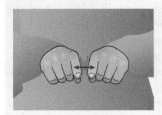

friendship
Sides of first fingers of each hand are tapped together several times.

girl/girlfriend
Thumb touches each breast starting with the breast opposite to the hand being used and then touches the first breast again.

secret lover
One hand placed under opposite armpit.

drunk (she/he is drunk)
Side of curved first finger is drawn across the forehead.

FIGURE 12.3 Some South African Gestures Used by a Man. (*Source:* Adapted from Heather Brookes, "A Repertoire of South African Quotable Gestures," *Journal of Linguistic Anthropology* 14[2001]: 186–224).

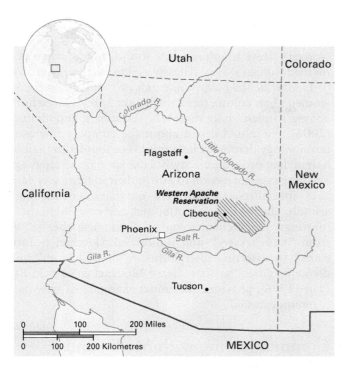

MAP 12.2   Western Apache Reservation in Arizona.

Different cultures emphasize different body language channels more than others. Some are more touch oriented than others, and some use facial expressions more. Eye contact is valued during Euro-American conversations, but in many Asian contexts, direct eye contact is considered rude or perhaps a sexual invitation.

Modification of and marks on the body, clothing, and hairstyles convey messages about age, gender, sexual interest or availability, profession, wealth, and emotions. Colour of clothing can send messages about a person's identity, class, gender, and more. In North America, gender differentiation begins in the hospital nursery with the colour coding of blue for boys and pink for girls. In some parts of the Middle East, public dress is black for women and white for men.

Covering or not covering various parts of the body with clothing is also culturally coded. Consider the different meaning of veiling/head covering in Egypt and Kuwait (MacLeod 1992). Kuwaiti women's head covering distinguishes them as relatively wealthy, leisured, and honourable, in contrast to the immigrant women workers from Asia who do not cover their heads. In contrast, the head covering in Egypt is done mainly by women from the lower and middle economic levels. For them, it is a way to accommodate conservative Islamic values while preserving their right to work outside the home. In Egypt, the head covering says, "I am a good Muslim and

THINKING OUTSIDE THE BOX

DO YOU wear different-coloured clothing in your everyday life compared to when you are "going out" or attending a special occasion such as a wedding or funeral? If yes, what are the differences and how do you explain them? If not, how do you explain that? Is there a "culture colour code" at work?

exhibiting such bad manners. Second, silence is important in the early stages of courting. Sitting in silence and holding hands for several hours is appropriate. Speaking "too soon" would indicate sexual willingness or interest. That would be immodest. Third, when children come home after a long absence at boarding school, parents and children should meet each other with silence for about 15 minutes rather than rushing into a flurry of greetings. It may be two or three days before sustained conversations are initiated. Last, a person should be silent when "getting cussed out," especially at drinking parties. An underlying similarity of all these contexts is the uncertainty, ambiguity, and unpredictability of the social relationships.

Body Language

Human communication, in one way or another, inevitably involves the body in sending and receiving messages. Beyond the mechanics of speaking, hearing, gesturing, and seeing, the body itself can function as a "text" that conveys messages. The full range of *body language* includes eye movements, posture, walking style, the way of standing and sitting, cultural *inscriptions* on the body such as tattoos and hairstyles, and accessories such as dress, shoes, and jewellery. Body language follows patterns and rules just as verbal language does. Like verbal language, the rules and meanings are learned, often unconsciously. Without learning the rules and meanings, one will commit communication errors, which are sometimes funny and sometimes serious.

Japanese businessmen meet each other, bow, and exchange business cards. Bowing is an important part of nonverbal communication in Japan. ■ (Source: © Olympia/PhotoEdit)

Tuareg men in Niger, West Africa, greeting each other. Tuareg men's greetings involve lengthy handshaking and close bodily contact. ■ (Source: Charles O. Cecil)

one's status, the shorter the sleeve of one's kimono. Men's kimono sleeve comes in one length: short. Unmarried women's sleeve length is nearly to the ground, whereas a married woman's sleeve is nearly as short as that of a man's.

Lanita Jacobs-Huey's research on African American women's hair culture (review Chapter 2) reveals the links among women's hair, their talk about hair, and identity (2006). She also learned about the complex linguistic terminology that black hairstylists use to refer to various hair styling procedures. Stylists use specialized language and language correction to affirm their identities as hair-care specialists. In hair-care seminars, cosmetology schools, client–stylist negotiations, and even Bible study meetings, black cosmetologists distinguish themselves from "hairdressers" and unlicensed "kitchen beauticians" by asserting their status as "hair doctors" and divinely "gifted" stylists. Grant McCracken's book, *Big Hair* (1996), provides additional examples of how hair communicates.

Communicating with Media and Information Technology

Media anthropology is the cross-cultural study of communication through electronic media such as radio, television, film, recorded music, the Internet, and print media, including newspapers, magazines, and popular literature (Spitulnik 1993). In the 1950s and 1960s, long before media anthropology became popular, Marshall McLuhan, the University of Toronto English professor who became the chief theorist and prophet of mass communication, examined how new technologies created new environments for communication (1964).

a good wife/daughter." In Kuwait, the head scarf says, "I am a wealthy Kuwaiti citizen."

In Japan, the kimono provides an elaborate coding system for gender and life-cycle stage (Dalby 2001). The higher

A horse race at Ascot, England, attended by members of the elite. ■ (Source: © 2004 Getty Images)

critical media anthropology: an approach that examines the degree to which access to media messages is liberating or controlling, and whose interests the media serves.

The *furisode* kimono is distinguished by its fine silk material, long sleeves, elaborate colours and designs. A girl's twentieth birthday gift is typically a furisode, marking her transition to young adulthood. Only unmarried women wear furisode, so wearing one is a statement of marital availability. Fluttering the long, wide sleeves at a man is a way to express love for him. ■ (Source: © Around the World in a Viewfinder/Alamy Images)

Two girls watch powwow dancing in eastern Pennsylvania. Hairstyles may communicate gender, ethnic identity, and age, among other things.
■ (Source: Barbara Miller)

He predicted the importance of the media using phrases such as "global village" and "the medium is the message/massage." Contemporary media anthropologists study the media process and content, the audience response, and the social effects of media presentations. **Critical media anthropology** asks to what degree access to its messages is liberating or controlling, and whose interests the media serve. It is widely used in examining journalism, television, advertising, and new information technology, as the following examples illustrate.

The Politics of Journalism

Mark Pedelty studied war correspondents in El Salvador to learn about journalists and journalistic practices during war (1995). He found that the lives and identities of war correspondents are highly charged with violence and terror: "War correspondents have a unique relationship to terror . . . that combines voyeurism and direct participation. . . . They need terror to . . . maintain their cultural identity as 'war correspondents'" (1995:2). The primary job of journalists, including war correspondents, is communication, of a specific sort. They gather information that is time sensitive and often brutal. Their job is to provide brief stories for the public. A critical media anthropology perspective reveals the important role of the news agency that pays their salary or, if they are freelancers or "stringers," that buys their story. War correspondents in El Salvador, Pedelty found, would write a story about the same event differently, depending on whether they were sending it to a U.S. newspaper or a European newspaper. Canadian newspapers take stories from both European and U.S. wire services such as Reuters and AP, as well as Canadian freelance stringers. How "accurate," then, is "the news"?

Nationalist media bias is clear in reports of sporting events. Canadian Donovan Bailey from Oakville, Ontario, won the 100-metre final at the 1996 Summer Olympics in Atlanta. In the history of the modern Olympics, whoever won the 100-metre race was considered the

Critical Thinking

BIAS IN NEWS REPORTING

Frances Henry and Carol Tator (2002) researched how mainstream Canadian media construct a view of Canadian society that silences, erases, or marginalizes a significant proportion of this country's population (226). They argue that mainstream media representations define dominant discourses (ways of talking about a topic). The way the media interpret events influences the way readers think about events, creating an ideological climate that seems natural, but in fact contains unchallenged assumptions about the world (26). As this study shows, images disseminated by the mainstream media of ethno-racial groups (African Canadians or Asian Canadians, for example), immigrants, and First Nations peoples are not the images these groups would present of themselves, and these images often reinforce negative stereotypes.

The authors document how the mainstream media select news stories that raise the public's anxiety about crime, heighten sensationalism in the news, over-report crimes allegedly committed by people of colour—especially young black males—and describe such crimes with emotional hyperbole. They analyzed the news reports about the murder in Toronto of a young white woman by several black Jamaican men in the Just Desserts Café in Toronto in 1994 to reveal how the use of phrases such as "urban terrorism," "slaughter," "drug-crazed," and "gun-toting barbarians" helped create a moral panic about the need for law and order (202). By selection of stories, editorials, and specific rhetorical strategies, the mainstream media produce discourse that constructs immigrants as prone to criminality. News reports about Jamaicans and Vietnamese, for example, emphasized crime, immigration, and social problems. In an analysis of news stories from 1994 to 1997 on Jamaicans in Canada, 45 percent of the stories fell into

the categories of sports or entertainment (Henry and Tator 2002:167). Coverage of First Nations peoples in several newspapers represented them stereotypically as pathetic victims, angry warriors, or noble environmentalists.

The problem, according to Henry and Tator, is lack of reflexivity and critical self-awareness among journalists who work for mainstream media outlets, few of whom are visible minorities, with the result that few oppositional and counter-discourses are widely articulated. But resistance to media stereotyping is growing. The Canadian Tamil community launched a lawsuit against the *National Post* for targeting its community and for labelling Tamils as "terrorists" and "criminals." The Canadian Islamic Congress continuously monitors the media for bias in the coverage of Islam and the representation of Muslim Canadians—a particularly important task following the events of September 11, 2001. Ethnic news outlets also have a critical role to play by challenging familiar stereotypes and providing the social, cultural, historical, and political context missing from the mainstream press (239).

CRITICAL THINKING QUESTIONS

- Can you identify any differences in content or approach in two versions of the same story presented in different daily newspapers published on the same day?
- Do the stories reveal any bias on the basis of culture, gender, or race?
- Is there any difference in the way the same story is covered in the ethnic press and alternative press?
- Can you identify any other dominant discourses that might influence the selection of articles and the content of editorials in the mainstream press?

"world's fastest man." However, the U.S. media claimed that the title should go to homegrown sprinter Michael Johnson on the basis of his record-breaking performance in the 200-metre race. Bailey complained that he did not get the respect he deserved from the U.S. media because he was Canadian. *Sports Illustrated* responded by calling Bailey a "whiner." To determine who was the "world's fastest man," Bailey and Johnson ran a

150-metre race at the SkyDome in Toronto on June 1, 1997. Johnson quit midway through the race, complaining of a strained quadriceps muscle, with Bailey well out in front. Not surprisingly, the event was reported very differently in the respective U.S. and Canadian media outlets. In addition to nationalist bias, racial bias is also evident in news reporting (see the accompanying Critical Thinking box).

digital divide: social inequality in access to new and emerging information technology, notably access to up-to-date computers, the Internet, and training related to their use.

Gender and Television Programming

Most television programming in Japan presents women as housewives, performing traditional domestic roles (Painter 1996). Many Japanese women are now rejecting such shows. In response, producers are experimenting with new sorts of dramas in which women are shown as active workers and aggressive lovers. One such show is a 10-part serial that first aired in the 1990s called *Selfish Women*. The story concerns three women: an aggressive, single businesswoman who faces discrimination at work, a young mother who is raising her daughter alone while her photographer husband lives with another woman, and an ex-housewife who divorced her husband because she found home life empty and unrewarding. There are several male characters, but except for one, they are depicted as less interesting than the women.

The show's title is ironic. In Japan, men often label women who assert themselves as "selfish." The lead women in the drama use the term in a positive way to encourage each other: "Let's become even more selfish!" Although dramas like *Selfish Women* may not be revolutionary, they indicate that telerepresentations of gender in Japan are changing, largely through the agency of Japanese women.

Canada's Public Broadcaster: The CBC

The Canadian Broadcasting Corporation (CBC), a Crown corporation, was created in 1936 to enhance Canadians' sense of national identity through its emphasis on homegrown content, and to give citizens an alternative to U.S. programming. As the most substantial and broadly based broadcast journalism organization in Canada, the CBC is funded directly through Parliament, and, thus, by the people of Canada. Its mandate is to reflect the multicultural nature of the country. Because all three of its radio, television, and Internet branches are publicly funded, there is often much debate in Canada about how the CBC would best serve citizens.

Crossing the Digital Divide in Rural Hungary

The term **digital divide** refers to social inequality in access to new and emerging information technology, especially access to up-to-date computers, the Internet, and training related to their use. Local attempts to overcome the digital divide between Hungary and countries in the European Union involve the development of the Hungarian Telecottage Association (HTA) (Wormald 2005) (see Map 12.3). The idea of the telecottage, which started in Sweden and Scotland, involves dedicating some space such as an unused workshop or part of a house, for public use in which a computer with Internet access is provided.

The HTA, centred in Budapest, promotes village-based Internet access in order to improve the lives of rural people through enhanced communication. Most telecottages in Hungary are located in rural communities of fewer than 5000 people. The HTA website provides announcements about funding opportunities and relevant news. While all this sounds highly populist and positive, some emerging interpersonal problems exist related to who gets access first to information for posting on the website and information hoarding by some managers.

Like the Hungarian villagers, many marginalized people around the world, including indigenous people, women, and youth, realize the importance of having access to the Internet and other information and communication technologies (ICT). These technologies can help people preserve and learn their ancestral languages, record traditional agricultural and medical knowledge, and otherwise protect their culture and improve their lives (Lutz 2005; Turner 2002).

MAP 12.3 **Hungary.** The Republic of Hungary has a population of around 10 million people. Its landscape is mainly plains with hills and low mountains to the north. One of the newest members of the European Union, Hungary has a growing economy. The main religion is Christianity, with Catholicism accounting for about half of the total; about 30 percent, however, are atheists. The Roma population, variously estimated at between 450 000, and 600 000, has increased rapidly in recent years. Magyar, the Hungarian language, is one of the few European languages that does not belong to the Indo-European language family but belongs instead to the Finno-Ugric family.

Communication, Cultural Diversity, and Inequality

In this section, we present material about the links among language, local cultures, and social inequality. We begin with a brief discussion of research methods in the study of language. Two major models of the relationship between language and culture are presented next. After a look at the issue of bilingualism, we focus on critical discourse analysis. Examples follow about class, gender and sexuality, and race and ethnicity.

Fieldwork Challenges

Research about human communication shares the basic methods of cultural anthropology: fieldwork and participant observation. Some topics require more specialized data gathering and analysis. The study of language relies heavily on tape recordings or video recordings of people and events (Kuipers 2004; Brookes 2004). The tapes are then analyzed qualitatively or quantitatively. Video recordings, for example, may be subjected to a detailed *frame analysis* that can pinpoint when communication breaks down or misunderstandings occur.

Analysis of recorded linguistic data must be informed by knowledge of the cultural context. Bronislaw Malinowski, early in the twentieth century, pointed out that communication is always embedded in its cultural context. An example of a contextualized approach is a study in Western Samoa that included tape-recordings of many hours of speech and also involved extensive participant observation in the community (Duranti 1994) (see Map 1.6 on page 28). Analysis of the transcriptions of the recorded talk revealed two major findings about how speech in village council meetings is related to social status: (1) turn-taking patterns and (2) particular words and grammatical forms to indirectly praise or blame others. Nonlinguistic data that helped inform these interpretations included observation of seating arrangements and the order of the distribution of *kava* (a ritually shared and mildly intoxicating beverage made from a local plant). Seating, kava drinking, and speech patterns all reflected and restated people's relative status.

Anthropologists who study language in everyday use face the problem of the **observer's paradox**, the fact

A satellite dish now dominates the view of a village in Niger, West Africa. Throughout the world, the spread of electronic forms of communication have many and diverse social effects. ■ (Source: © Charles O. Cecil)

that the research process alters people's normal behaviour (McMahon 1994:234). The mere presence of an anthropologist with a tape or video recorder affects how people speak and behave. Being studied often makes people speak and behave more "correctly" and more formally. The ways of dealing with the observer's paradox are

- Observe and record speech outside an interview situation.
- Record speech in a group situation.

---

observer's paradox: the logical impossibility of doing research on natural communication events without affecting the naturalness sought.

Sapir-Whorf hypothesis: a theory in linguistic anthropology that says language determines thought.

sociolinguistics: a theory in linguistic anthropology that says that culture and society and a person's social position determine language.

indexicality: a characteristic of language that "indexes," or points to, the identities, actions, or feelings of the speaker and conveys important social information.

A Samoan kava drinking ceremony begins. Kava is made from the roots of a plant in the black pepper family. The roots are dried, pounded, and mixed with water. A social beverage, kava is a relaxant also used for healing.
■ (Source: © Don Smetzer)

- Initiate role-plays in which participants act out a particular scene, such as arguing about something. The drama involved helps create a "natural" situation.
- Conduct structured interviews in which the participant is asked to perform speech tasks at varying levels of formality, starting with the most formal and moving to informal, open-ended conversation.

Language and Culture: Two Theories

During the twentieth century, two major theoretical perspectives were influential in defining how language, thought, and society are related. The first argues that language determines culture; the second reverses the causality, arguing that culture determines language. They are presented here as alternative models, but they actually overlap in real life and anthropologists tend to draw on both of them (Hill and Mannheim 1992).

The first was formulated by two early founding figures in linguistic anthropology, Edward Sapir and Benjamin Whorf. In the mid-twentieth century, they formulated an influential model called the **Sapir-Whorf hypothesis,** which says that people's language affects how they think. If a language has many words for different kinds of snow, for example, then someone who speaks that language can "think" about snow in more ways than someone can whose language has fewer "snow" terms. Among the Saami, whose traditional occupation was reindeer herding (see the Ethnographic Profile on page 338), a rich set of terms exists for "snow" (review Figure 12.2 on page 318). If a language has no word for "snow," then someone who speaks that language cannot think of "snow." Thus, a language constitutes a *thought world* and people who speak different languages inhabit different thought worlds. This catchy phrase became the basis for *linguistic determinism,* a theory stating that language determines consciousness of the world and behaviour. Extreme linguistic determinism implies that the frames and definitions of a person's primary language are so strong that it is impossible to learn another language fully or, therefore, to understand another culture fully. Most anthropologists see value in the Sapir-Whorf hypothesis, but not in its extreme form.

A second model for understanding the relationship between language and culture is proposed by scholars working in the area of **sociolinguistics,** the study of how cultural and social context shapes language. These theorists support a *cultural constructionist* argument that a person's context and social position shape the content, form, and meaning of their language. Most anthropologists see value in this model and agree that language and culture are interactive: Language shapes culture and culture shapes language.

Lisa Valentine (1995) conducted a sociolinguistic study of the discourse or language-in-use of the Severn Ojibwe people of northern Ontario, demonstrating how new speech forms are shaped by the liturgy and music of the Anglican Church, and the newspapers, radio, and television services provided by the Native Communications Society in the small, isolated community where everyone speaks Severn Ojibwe.

Language is also an important part of socializing children into a culture. Research shows again that culture shapes the content and process of such socialization. Language has the characteristic of **indexicality;** that is,

Multiple Cultural Worlds

CODE-SWITCHING IN MARTINIQUE

Martinique is an overseas department of France located in the eastern Caribbean. Martinicans are officially French citizens. As part of his ethnographic fieldwork in Martinique, David Murray (2002) had to learn to code-switch between Creole and French; learning to code-switch also socialized him into how the ambiguities of gender, race, and class are performed linguistically.

In Martinique, Creole and French have coexisted for centuries. French is generally the language of authority, prestige, legitimacy, and official discourse, and it is used for media and schooling. Creole is the language of subversion, marginality, and emotion. Locals know how to code-switch between French and Creole to reinforce gender distinctions, disrupt normative conduct, and mark outsiders from insiders. For example, while men switch freely between Creole and French, women are not encouraged to speak Creole, as it is considered vulgar. However, some men speak French exclusively, and women vendors usually speak

Creole to each other in the female-dominated space of the market (39).

Murray's ethnography explores the local complexities of identity formation made visible through language use. While French is considered necessary for economic reasons in the global economy, it reflects Martinique's colonial past. But Creole has not emerged as a symbol of Martinique separatism or identity. Both languages are central in public life.

As Martinique explores the politics of separation from and unity with a colonizing nation-state, Quebec has emerged as a utopian destination of possible escape from the confines of the island. It is idealized as a French-speaking zone of racial and sexual freedom where people are friendlier and more tolerant than the French, a place like Martinique that has a shared colonial history with France. Thus, as Murray learned, the effects of colonialism are implicated in code-switching and language use in interesting and unpredictable ways (150).

---

certain linguistic features "index," or point to, the identities, actions, or feelings of the speaker and convey important social information.

Within a single language, particular subcultures are likely to have distinctive **codes**, or ways of speaking, that may include marked vocabulary, grammar, and intonation depending on age, gender, occupation, class, region, and family role of the speaker and listener. Most people know more than one code and are able to **code-switch**, or move from one code to another as needed. For example, consider how you talk to your school acquaintances when you are in a group, compared to how you might speak to a physician or potential employer. Code-switching can be an intentional strategy used to further the interests of the speaker. Generally, code-switching follows status lines, with a dominant language or code being used to make a statement of power or authority (see the accompanying Multiple Cultural Worlds box).

Bilingualism

One characteristic of contemporary language use is the proliferation of people who speak more than one language. Much of this change is the result of colonialism and, now, increased migration related to economic globalization. **Bilingualism** is the capacity to speak two languages. A true bilingual has "native" speaking abilities in two languages. Bilingualism is often the result of migration from one language area to another.

Many world populations are bilingual because their country was colonized and a second language was introduced. As a result of the close proximity and high exposure to many languages, Europeans often grow up learning more than one language. The emergence of large populations speaking multiple languages has led to debates about the value and cost of **linguistic pluralism** (the presence of linguistic diversity within a particular context). This is an important policy issue in Canada.

---

code: way of speaking, that may include marked vocabulary, grammar, and intonation depending on age, gender, occupation, class, region, and family role of the speaker and listener.
code-switch: the move from one code to another as needed.

bilingualism: the capacity to speak two languages.
linguistic pluralism: the presence of linguistic diversity within a particular context.

critical discourse analysis (CDA): the study of the relations of power and inequality in language.
tag question: a question seeking affirmation, placed at the end of a sentence.

Bilingualism in Canada requires signs in both official languages. ■ (Source: Michael Ponomareff/PONO-PRESSE)

The British North America Act of 1867, the Canadian Constitution, and the Official Languages Act of 1969 guarantee the equality of English and French as part of the national identity of Canada. Efforts of the federal government to promote bilingualism and of the Quebec provincial government to promote a unilingual French society are complicated by political opposition to Quebec separation, and the cost of maintaining bilingual policies and programs across Canada.

Bilingualism confers substantial advantages to people, giving them access to an alternative way of viewing the world and in some cases economic advantages. However, in a study conducted in the 1960s, monolingual French speakers in Quebec were found to have the lowest income, monolingual English speakers the highest income, and bilingual speakers intermediate incomes (Dorais 1979:165). Studies of the effects of differing degrees of bilingualism on the problem-solving abilities of children in grade 3 suggested that bilingual children had higher levels of control of attention when solving linguistic problems than monolingual children, and used the higher levels of control in more generalized situations (Bialystok and Majumder 1998).

Critical Discourse Analysis

Critical discourse analysis (CDA) is an emerging area that focuses on the relations of power and inequality in language (Blommaert and Bulcaen 2000). In this part of the chapter, we look at distinctive communication styles, or *registers,* that include variation in vocabulary, grammar, and intonation. Critical discourse analysis reveals links among language and social inequality, power, and stigma as well as agency and resistance through language.

Class and Language

William Labov launched the subfield of sociolinguistics with his classic study of accents among mainly Euro-American people of different socioeconomic classes in New York City (1966). His research revealed that pronunciation of the consonant "r" in words such as *car, card, floor,* and *fourth* tends to be associated with upper-class people, whereas its absence ("caw," "cawd," "flaw," "fawth") is associated with lower-class people. Class difference is not the only social factor affecting language use. For instance, researchers who study Montreal French (e.g., Sankoff and Laberge 1978) found that people's language use correlates with the linguistic demands of their job: People employed as lawyers, teachers, and receptionists tend to use more standard or prestigious speech variants than do those whose jobs require less public use of language, such as laboratory technicians, mechanics, and computer programmers. This variation cuts across class; for example a receptionist, whose job ranks lower than that of a laboratory technician, feels more pressure to use standard language.

THINKING OUTSIDE THE BOX

THESE BROAD generalizations about Euro-American conversational styles do not apply to all situations. What are your cultural rules about interruptions and taking turns?

Gender in Euro-American Conversation

Gender codes, or socially prescribed ways of speaking like a female or like a male, exist in most languages. Early studies of language and gender among white Euro-Americans revealed three general characteristics of female speech, including politeness, rising intonation at the end of sentences, and frequent use of **tag questions** (questions seeking affirmation placed at the end of sentences, such as, "It's a nice day, *isn't it?*") (Lakoff 1973).

In North America, women are widely regarded as being cooperative speakers, men as competitive speakers; women as indirect speakers, and men as direct speakers (Tannen 1990). However, such generalizations are suspect. Linguistic research shows that women and men vary their speech according to the particular context of the interaction and the degree of formality of the situation. Uniform use of stereotypically male or female speech probably exists only in parody, such as in situation comedies or in drag performances.

Gender and Politeness in Japanese, and Those Naughty Teenage Girls

Gender registers in spoken Japanese reflect gender differences (Shibamoto 1987). Certain words and sentence structures convey femininity, humbleness, and politeness. One important contrast between male and female speech is the attachment, by female speakers, of the honorific prefix "o-" to nouns (see Table 12.1). This addition gives women's speech a more refined and polite tone.

A contrasting pattern of gendered language comes from the *Kogals*, young Japanese women roughly between 14 and 22 years of age, known for their "female-centered coolness" (Miller 2004). The term *Kogal* is a label created by the media. Kogals' self-reference term is *gyaru* ("girl"). The Kogals have distinctive language, clothing, hairstyles, makeup, attitude, and activities, all of which challenge prescriptive norms for young women. Their overall style is flashy and exuberant, combining global and local elements. Heavy users of cell phones, Kogals have created an extensive set of emoticons, or "face characters," far more complex than the North American smiley face. Read vertically, they include icons for "wow," "ouch," "applause," and "I can't hear you." They have also invented a unique text-message code for their cell

phones that uses mixed scripts such as mathematical symbols and Cyrillic letters.

The spoken language of Kogals is a rich and quickly changing mixture of slang, some classic but much newly created. They create new words through compounds and by adding the Japanese suffix *-ru*, which turns a noun into a verb such as *maku-ru* ("go to McDonald's). They intentionally use strongly masculine language forms, openly talk about sex, and rework taboo sexual terms into new meanings. Reactions from mainstream society to Kogals are mixed, ranging from horror to fascination. No matter what, in the words of Laura Miller, they have cultural influence and are shaking up the gender order.

"Fat Talk" among Euro-American Adolescent Girls

Euro-American adolescent girls' conversations exhibit a high level of concern with their body weight and image (Nichter 2000). A study of 253 girls in the eighth and ninth grades in two urban high schools in the American Southwest reveals the contexts and meanings of *fat talk*. Fat talk usually starts with a girl commenting, "I'm so fat." The immediate response from her friends is, "No, you're not." Girls who use fat talk are typically not overweight and are not dieting. The weight of the girls in the study was within "normal" range, and none suffered from a serious eating disorder. Fat talk occurs frequently throughout a day. Sometimes it appears to function as a call for reinforcement from friends that the initiator is an accepted group member. In other cases, it occurs at the beginning of a meal. In this context, fat talk may function to absolve the girl from guilty feelings and to give her a sense of agency.

A Kogal in Tokyo's trendy Shibuyu district displays her cell phone that is covered with stickers. Her facial makeup and dress are characteristic of some, but not all, Kogals. Various Kogal makeup and dress styles, like their language, exist and keep changing. ■ (Source: Eriko Sugita/Reuters/CORBIS)

TABLE 12.1 Male-Unmarked and Female-Marked Nouns in Japanese

	Male	Female
Box lunch	bentoo	obentoo
Money	kane	okane
Chopsticks	hasi	ohasi
Book	hon	ohon

Source: From "The Womanly Woman: Manipulation of Stereotypical and Nonstereotypical Features in Japanese Female Speech," pg. 28, by Janet Shibamoto in *Language, Gender, and Sex in Comparative Perspective*, ed. by S. U. Philips, S. Steel, and C. Tanz. Copyright © 1987. Reprinted by permission of Cambridge University Press.

Gay Language and Belonging in Indonesia

Many gay men in Indonesia speak *bahasa gay*, or "gay language," based on *bahasa Indonesia*, the national language (Boellstorff 2004). Indonesia is the world's fourth-largest country in terms of population, with nearly 250 million citizens living in over 6000 islands and speaking nearly 700 local languages. In spite of this diversity, bahasa gay is remarkably standardized. Bahasa gay has a distinctive vocabulary that plays humorously on mainstream language and provides a political commentary on mainstream life.

Some of the vocabulary changes involve sound-alikes; others add a suffix to a standard word. In terms of state power and the state's heterosexual image, Indonesian gays would seem to be a clearly excluded group. Nonetheless, bahasa gay is moving into mainstream culture where it conveys agency and freedom from official control.

Cueing among the Akwesasne Mohawks

Linguistic cues are words or phrases that preface a remark to indicate the speaker's attitude toward what is being said. Standard English cues include *maybe* and *in my opinion* (Woolfson et al. 1995). Three functions of cueing exist in Mohawk English, a version of English spoken by the Akwesasne people of the St. Lawrence River area (see Map 12.4). They are

- The speaker's unwillingness or inability to verify the certainty of a statement
- Respect for the listener
- The inability to make statements that have to do with matters that are in the domain of religion

Frequent miscommunication occurs between the Akwesasne people and English-speaking medical professionals. Analysis of doctor–patient conversations reveals the role that Akwesasne cueing plays, and how it is misinterpreted by the professionals. Here is a response to a question posed by an anthropologist about the kinds of diseases Akwesasne people had in the past, with the cues italicized:

> Hmm . . . That [tuberculosis] . . . was mostly, it well . . . they always said cirrhosis. . . . *It seems* like no matter what anybody died from . . . if they drank, it was cirrhosis. *I don't know* if anybody *really* knew a long time ago what anybody really died from. Even if the doctor requested an autopsy, the people would just say no . . . you know . . . it won't be done. So *I don't think* it was . . . you know . . . it was just what the doctor thought that would go down on the death certificate. (1995:506)

The medical practitioners misinterpret such clues as indications of indecisiveness or noncooperation. The Akwesasne speakers are following linguistic rules about truthfulness, humility, and the sacred.

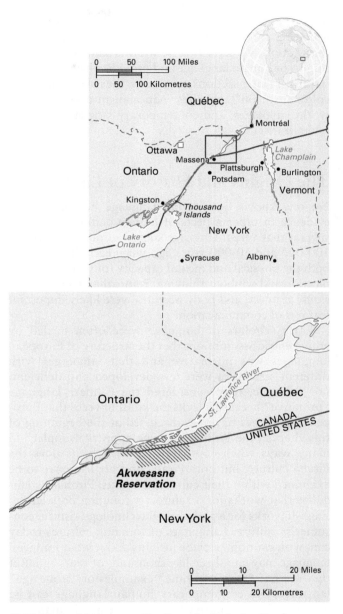

MAP 12.4 Akwesasne Territory in Ontario, Quebec, and New York. The Akwesasne Territory has an international border running through it with Ontario and Quebec on one side and New York on the other. The Mohawk Council of Akwesasne comprises 12 district chiefs and a grand chief. Since the 1960s, the Akwesasne Territory has been affected by environmental pollution of the water, soil, and food supply from industries along the St. Lawrence River. In 1987, the Akwesasne formed a task force to restore and protect the environment and the survival of their culture.

Language Change

Languages, like the cultures in which they are embedded, experience both continuity and change, and for similar reasons. Human creativity and contact lead to linguistic innovation and linguistic borrowing. War, imperialism, genocide, and other disasters may destroy languages. In this section, we look first at what is known about the origins of human language and provide a brief history of writing. In later sections, we discuss the role of European colonialism on languages, nationalism and language, world languages, and contemporary language loss and revitalization.

The Origins and History of Language

No one knows how verbal language began. Current evidence of other aspects of human cultural evolution suggest that verbal language started to develop between 100 000 and 50 000 years ago when early humans had both the physical and mental capacity for verbal communication and symbolic thinking. Before that, facial expressions, gestures, and body postures were likely important features of communication.

Early scholars of language were often misled by ethnocentric assumptions that the structure of European languages was normative and that languages with different structures were less developed and deficient. For example, they considered the Chinese language "primitive" because it lacks the kinds of verbs that European languages have. As discussed at the beginning of this chapter, the Pirahã language appears "simpler" in many ways when compared to English, as does the Pirahã culture, but both Pirahã and English have to be examined within their cultural contexts. Pirahã is a language that works for a rainforest foraging population. English works for a globalizing, technology-driven, consumerist culture. Languages of foraging cultures today can, with caution, provide insights about what foragers' language may have been like thousands of years ago. But they are not "frozen in time" examples of "stone age" language. No contemporary human language can be considered a "primitive" model of early human language. That would defy the principle of **linguistic relativism**, which says that all languages have passed through thousands of years of change, and all are equally successful forms of communication.

An African bonobo male waves branches in a display of power (top). ■ (Source: © Gallo Images/CORBIS) **In North America, women lacrosse players (bottom) use sticks in a competitive sport invented by First Nations peoples. In the top photograph, communication is clearly involved in the use of the branches.** ■ (Source: Ed Bock/CORBIS)

---

linguistic relativism: a scholarly approach that says that all languages have passed through thousands of years of change, and all are equally successful forms of communication.

historical linguistics: the study of language change using formal methods that compare shifts over time and across space in aspects of language such as speech sounds, syntax, and semantics.

language family: languages descended from a parent language.

Historical Linguistics

Historical linguistics is the study of language change through history. It relies on many specialized methods that compare shifts over time and across space in aspects of language such as speech sounds, syntax, and meaning. It originated in the eighteenth century with a discovery made by Sir William Jones, a British colonial administrator working in India. During his spare time, Jones studied Sanskrit, a classical language of India. He noticed strong similarities among Sanskrit, Greek, and Latin in vocabulary and syntax. For example, the Sanskrit word for "father" is *pitr*, in Greek it is *patér*, and in Latin it is *pater*. This was an astounding discovery for the time, given the prevailing European mentality that placed its cultural heritage firmly in the classical Graeco-Roman world and depicted the "Orient" as completely separate from "Europe" (Bernal 1987).

Following Jones's discovery, other scholars began comparing lists of words and grammatical forms in different languages: the French *père*, the German *Vater*, the Italian *padre*, the Old English *faeder*, the Old Norse *fadhir*, the Swedish *far*. These lists allowed scholars to determine degrees of closeness and distance in their relationships. Later scholars contributed the concept of **language families**, or languages descended from a parent language (see Figure 12.4). Descendant languages that are part of the same language are referred to as *sister languages*, such as French and Spanish.

Using comparative evidence from historical and contemporary Eurasian languages, historical linguists developed a hypothetical model of the original parent language, or *proto-language*, of most Eurasian languages. It is called *Proto-Indo-European* (PIE). Linguistic evidence suggests that PIE was located in Eurasia, either north or south of the Black Sea (see Map 12.5). From its area of origin, between 6000 and 8000 years ago, PIE spread

MAP 12.5 Two Sites of Proto-Indo-European Origins. Two major theories about the location of PIE exist, with the site south of the Black Sea considered to be earlier.

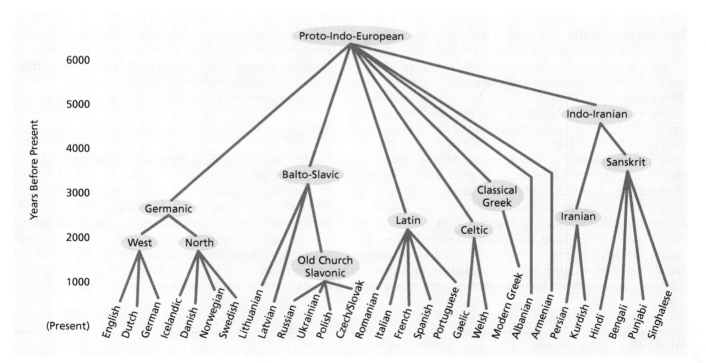

FIGURE 12.4 The Indo-European Language Family

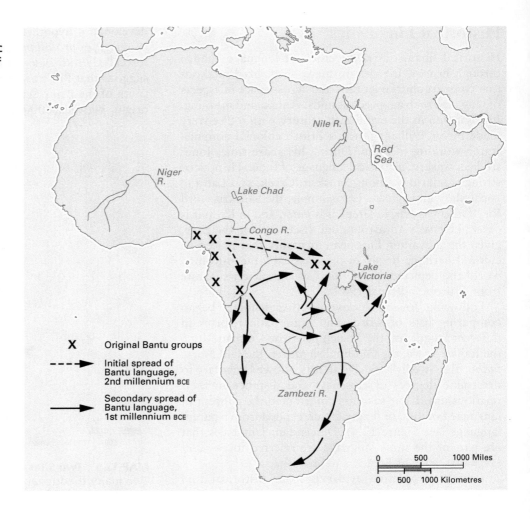

MAP 12.6 The Bantu Migrations in Africa. Linguistic evidence for the migrations of Bantu-speaking people relies on similarities between languages in parts of eastern, central, and southern Africa and languages of the original Bantu homeland in West Africa. Around 450 Bantu languages are now spoken in sub-Saharan Africa.

Map labels: Nile R.; Red Sea; Niger R.; Lake Chad; Congo R.; Lake Victoria; Zambezi R.

Legend:
X Original Bantu groups
- - - → Initial spread of Bantu language, 2nd millennium BCE
——→ Secondary spread of Bantu language, 1st millennium BCE

0   500   1000 Miles
0   500   1000 Kilometres

into Europe, central and eastern Asia, and South Asia, where local variants developed over the centuries.

Similar linguistic methods reveal the existence of the original parent form of the Bantu language family, *Proto-Bantu* (Afolayan 2000). Scholars can trace the so-called *Bantu expansion* in Africa starting around 5000 years ago (see Map 12.6). Today, some form of Bantu language is spoken by over 100 million people in Africa, not to mention the number of people in the African diaspora worldwide. Over 600 African languages are derived from Proto-Bantu. According to linguistic analysis, the homeland of Proto-Bantu can be found in the present-day countries of Cameroon and Nigeria, West Africa. It is likely that Proto-Bantu spread through population migration as the farming population expanded and moved, over hundreds of years, into areas occupied by indigenous foragers. Bantu cultural imperialism may have wiped out

some local languages, although it is impossible to document possible extinctions. Substantial linguistic evidence, however, suggests some interactions between the farmers and the foragers through which standard Bantu absorbed elements from local languages.

Writing Systems

Evidence of the earliest written languages comes from Mesopotamia, Egypt, and China. The oldest writing system was in use in the fourth millennium BCE in Mesopotamia (Postgate, Wang, and Wilkinson 1995). All early writing systems used **logographs**, signs that indicate a word, syllable, or sound. Over time, some logographs retained their original meaning, others were kept but given more abstract meaning, and nonlogographic symbols were added (see Figure 12.5).

---

logograph: a symbol that conveys meaning through a form or picture resembling that to which it refers.

khipu: cords of knotted strings used during the Inca empire for keeping accounts and recording events.

Old Style   New Style

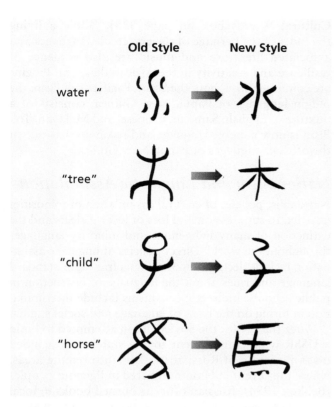

water "

"tree"

"child"

"horse"

FIGURE 12.5 Logographic and Current Writing Styles in China (*Source:* Courtesy of Molly Spitzer Frost).

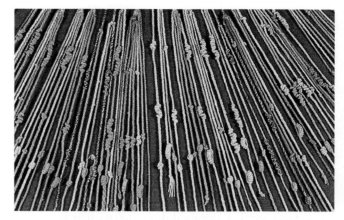

Khipu, or knotted strings, were the basis of state-level accounting in the Inca empire. The knots convey substantial information for those who could interpret their meaning. ■ (Source: © M. Vautier, Anthropological & Archaeological Museum, Lima, Peru/Woodfin Camp & Associates)

The emergence of writing is associated with the development of the state. Some scholars take writing as a key diagnostic feature that distinguishes the state from nonstate political forms because record-keeping was such an essential task of the state. The Inca empire, centred in the Peruvian Andes, is a notable exception to this generalization. It used **khipu**, or cords of knotted strings of different colours, for keeping accounts and recording events. Scholars are not quite sure how khipu worked in the past because their coding system is so complicated. Debates are ongoing as to whether khipu served as an actual language or more simply as an accounting system. Whatever is the answer, the world's largest empire in the fourteenth century relied on khipu.

Two interpretations of the function of early writing systems exist. The first is that early writing was mainly for ceremonial purposes because of its prevalence on tombs, bone inscriptions, or temple carvings. The second is that early writing was mainly for secular use in government record-keeping and trade. The archaeological record is biased toward durable substances such as stone. Since ceremonial writing was intended to last, it was more likely to be inscribed on stone. Utilitarian writing, in contrast, was more likely to have been done on perishable materials because people would be less concerned with permanence (consider the way you treat shopping lists). Compared to what has been preserved,

more utilitarian writing, and other forms of nonceremonial writing must have existed.

The scripts of much of South and Southeast Asia originated in the Aramaic system of the Middle East (Kuipers and McDermott 1996). It spread eastward to India, where it took on new forms, and continued to move into much of Southeast Asia, including Thailand and Cambodia but excluding Vietnam. The functions of the scripts vary from context to context. Writing for record-keeping and taxation exists but is subordinate to, and carries less status than, writing for communication with the spirits, to record medical knowledge, and for love poetry. Writing love poetry is exalted and esteemed, and sometimes done in secret. Some love songs in the Philippine highlands have strict rules regulating such matters as how many syllables may be used per line. All adolescents seek to learn the rules of writing love poetry and to be able to write it well.

Colonialism, Nationalism, and Globalization

Languages change constantly, sometimes slowly and in small ways, other times rapidly and dramatically. European colonialism was a major force of change. Not only did colonial powers declare their own language as the language of government, business, and higher education, but they often took direct steps to suppress indigenous languages and literatures. Globalization is also having substantial and complex effects on language.

European Colonialism and Contact Languages

Beginning in the fifteenth century, European colonialism had dramatic effects on the people with whom it came into contact. Language change is an important part of the story of colonialism and indigenous cultures. Depending on the type and duration of contact, it resulted in the development of new languages, the decline of others, and the extinction of many, along with the people who spoke them (Silverstein 1997). Two forms of new languages prompted by European colonialism are pidgins and creoles.

A **pidgin** is a language that blends elements of at least two parent languages and that emerges when two different cultures with different languages come in contact and need to communicate (Baptista 2005). All speakers have their own native language(s) but learn to speak pidgin as a second, rudimentary language. Pidgins are typically limited to specific functional domains, such as trade and basic social interactions. Many pidgins of the western hemisphere developed as a result of the Atlantic slave trade and plantation slavery. Owners needed to communicate with their slaves, and slaves from various parts of Africa needed to communicate with each other.

A pidgin often evolves into a **creole**, which is a language descended from a pidgin with its own native speakers, richer vocabularies, and more developed grammar. Throughout the western hemisphere, many localized creoles have developed in areas such as Louisiana, Haiti, Ecuador, Suriname, and Martinique (see the Multiple

French colonialism added another cultural layer to Arabic influences in Morocco, resulting in many bilingual and trilingual shop signs. ■ (Source: Barbara Miller)

Cultural Worlds box on page 328). While a living reminder of the heritage of slavery, creole languages and associated literature and music are also evidence of resilience and creativity in the African diaspora. Pidgins are common throughout the South Pacific. Tok Pisin, the pidgin language of Papua New Guinea, consists of a mixture of English, Samoan, Chinese, and Malayan. Tok Pisin is now a creole language and recognized as one of the official languages of Papua New Guinea.

Nationalism and Linguistic Assimilation

Nationalist policies of cultural assimilation of minorities have led to suppression and loss of local dialects and the extinction of many indigenous and minority languages throughout the world. Direct policies of linguistic assimilation include declaration of a lingua franca, or standard language and rules about the language of instruction in public schools. Indirect mechanisms include discrimination in hiring on the basis of language and social stigma.

After the 1930s, the Soviet Union attempted to build a USSR-wide commitment to the state; this included mass migration of Russian speakers into remote areas, where they eventually outnumbered indigenous peoples (Belikov 1994). Russian officials burned books in local languages. Many children were forcibly sent away to boarding schools, where they were taught in Russian. The indigenous Komi traditionally formed the majority population in an area around the Pechora River (see Map 12.7). Russian immigration brought in so many outsiders that the Komi were outnumbered. The Soviets initiated the use of the Russian language in schools, and the Komi people became bilingual. Eventually, the Komi language was so heavily influenced by Russian that it may now be extinct.

This story can be repeated for many indigenous languages. Enforced attendance at boarding schools was also a strategy of the United States, Canada, and Australia in their attempts to assimilate indigenous peoples. For example, residential schools for First Nations children in British Columbia lasted from 1880 into the 1960s. Conditions were harsh; punishment was most severe for using Aboriginal languages (Tennant 1990:78). Often, Christian groups ran the schools and worked to suppress indigenous languages as part of their attempts to "civilize" "pagan" peoples (see the Ethnographic Profile on page 338). In June, 2008, Canada's federal government

---

pidgin: a contact language that blends elements of at least two languages and that emerges when people with different languages need to communicate.

creole: a language directly descended from a pidgin but possessing its own native speakers and involving linguistic expansion and elaboration.

global language or **world language:** a language spoken widely throughout the world and in diverse cultural contexts often replacing indigenous languages.

language decay or **language shift:** condition of a language in which speakers adopt a new language for most situations, begin to use their native language only in certain contexts, and may be only semi-fluent and have limited vocabulary in their native language.

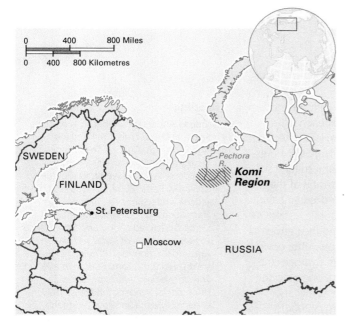

MAP 12.7 **Komi Region in Russia.** The Komi were traditionally reindeer hunters. The Komi language belongs to the Finno-Ugric language family and is closer to Finnish and Estonian than to Russian.

issued a public apology to First Nations, Métis, and Inuit for the abuses that took place in residential schools.

Global Languages

Ninety-six percent of the world's population speaks 4 percent of the world's languages (Crystal 2000:14). The eight most-spoken languages are Mandarin, Spanish, English, Bengali, Hindi, Portuguese, Russian, and Japanese. Languages that are gaining widespread currency are called **global languages,** or **world languages.** Global languages are spoken worldwide in diverse cultural contexts. As they spread to areas and cultures beyond their home area and culture, they take on new, localized identities. At the same time, the "mother language" picks up words and phrases from local languages (see Figure 12.6).

English is the most globalized language in history (Bhatt 2001; Crystal 2003). British English was first transplanted through colonial expansion to present-day Canada, the United States, Australia, New Zealand, South Asia, Africa, Hong Kong, and the Caribbean. English was the dominant language in the colonies, used in government and commerce and taught in schools. Over time, regional and subregional varieties of English have developed, often leading to a "New English" that a native speaker from England cannot understand at all. So many varieties of English now exist that scholars are beginning to talk of the *English language family* that comprises varieties such as Spanglish, Japlish, and Tex-Mex.

Global languages may act as both a form of linguistic and economic opportunity and a form of linguistic imperialism.

FIGURE 12.6 Loan Words in North American English

Alcohol	Arabic, Middle East
Avocado	Nahuatl, Mexico/Central America
Banana	Mandingo, West Africa
Bogus	Hausa, West Africa
Candy	Arabic, Middle East
Caucus	Algonquin, Virginia/Delaware, North America
Chimpanzee	Bantu, West and central Africa
Chocolate	Aztec Nahuatl, Mexico/Central America
Dungaree	Hindi, North India, South Asia
Gong	Malaysia, Southeast Asia
Hammock	Arawakan, South America
Hip/hep	Wolof, West Africa
Hurricane	Taino, Caribbean
Lime	Inca Quechua, South America
Moose	Algonquin, Virginia/Delaware, North America
Panda	Nepali, South Asia
Savannah	Taino, Caribbean
Shampoo	Hindi, North India, South Asia
Sugar	Sanskrit, South Asia
Teepee	Sioux, Dakotas, North America
Thug	Hindi, North India, South Asia
Tobacco	Arawak, South America
Tomato	Nahuatl, Mexico/Central America
Tundra	Saami, Lapland, Northern Europe
Tycoon	Japanese
Typhoon	Mandarin Chinese, East Asia
Zombie	Congo and Angola, central and West Africa

Endangered Languages and Language Revitalization

The field of linguistic anthropology, as mentioned in Chapter 1, was prompted by the need to document disappearing indigenous languages in North America. Today, anthropologists and other scholars, as well as descendant language communities themselves, are still concerned about the rapid loss of languages (Fishman 1991; Maffi 2005). The task of documenting declining languages is urgent. It is often accompanied by applied work to preserve and revive endangered and dying languages.

Scholars have proposed ways to assess degrees of language loss or decline (Walsh 2005). The general stages proceed from "shift" to extinction. **Language decay,** or **language shift,** is a category of

THINKING OUTSIDE THE BOX

VISIT THE WEBSITE of Terralingua (www.terralin-gua.org), a nonprofit research organization devoted to the environment and to linguistic and cultural survival. Be prepared to give a three-minute briefing to the class on its mission, projects, and achievements.

Ethnographic Profile

The Saami of Lapland, or Sapmi

The Saami are indigenous, "fourth world" people who live in the northernmost stretches of Norway, Sweden, Finland, and western Russia (Gaski 1993). The area is called Lapland or Sapmi, the land of the Saami. The total Saami population is around 100 000 people, with the majority in Norway (Magga and Skutnabb-Kangas 2001).

At the time of the earliest written records of 1000 years ago, all Saami hunted wild reindeer, among other land and sea species, and may have kept some tamed reindeer for transport (Paine 2004). Over time, herding domesticated reindeer developed and became the economic mainstay. In the past few hundred years, though, reindeer pastoralism declined to the point where it is now a specialization of about 10 percent of the population. Settled Saami are farmers or work in trade, small-scale industry, handicrafts, services, and the professions.

Traditional Saami reindeer herding has been a family-based system. Men and women cared for the herd, and sons and daughters inherited equally the rights to the herd (Paine 2004). The value of social equality was strong, entailing both rights and privileges.

In their relationships with the modern state, the Saami have experienced discrimination, exclusion, loss of territorial rights, and cultural and linguistic repression. Specific risks to Saami cultural survival include being downwind of the 1986 Chernobyl nuclear disaster, being near the earlier Soviet atomic testing grounds in Siberia, having their ancestral territory and sacred spaces suffer environmental degradation from hydroelectric dam construction, and having grazing lands taken over for use as military training grounds (Anderson 2004).

State policies of cultural assimilation and forced Christianization in the twentieth century marginalized the Saami language and led to serious language loss (Magga and Skutnabb-Kangas 2001). Several Saami languages and dialects still exist, with spatially distant versions being mutually unintelligible (Gaski 1993:116). Language is of central cultural value to the Saami, and efforts to maintain it have been under way since the 1960s.

Besides the Saami language, a traditional song form, the *yoik,* is of particular importance (Anderson 2005). Yoik lyrics allow a subtle system of double meanings that can camouflage political content (Gaski 1997).

Readings

Myrdene Anderson. "Reflections on the Saami at Loose Ends." In Myrdene Anderson, ed., *Cultural Shaping of Violence: Victimization, Escalation, Response.* West Lafayette, IN: Purdue University Press, 2004, pp. 285–291.

Myrdene Anderson. "The Saami Yoik: Translating Hum, Chant, or/and Song." In Dinda Gorlée, ed., *Song and Significance: Virtues and Vices of Vocal Translation.* Amsterdam: Rodopi, 2005, pp. 213–233.

Harald Gaski (Ed.), *Sami Culture in a New Era: The Norwegian Sami Experience.* Seattle: University of Washington Press, 1997.

Ole Henrik Magga and Tove Skutnabb-Kangas. "The Saami Languages: The Present and the Future." *Cultural Survival Quarterly, 25* (2), 26–31, 2001.

Robert Paine. "Dam a River, Damn a People? Saami (Lapp) Livelihood and the Alta-Kautokeino Hydro-Electric Project and the Norwegian Parliament." *IWGIIA Document 45,* 1992.

Video

Even If a Hundred Ogres. (Introduced and narrated by Joanne Woodward. 1996. www.nativevideos.com.)

Website

Saami Council, www.saamicouncil.net.

Thanks to Myrdene Anderson, Purdue University, for reviewing this material.

The well-known Saami singer-songwriter Marie Boine performs at the Easter Festival in Kautokeino, Sapmi, north Norway (left). ■ (Source: © Anders Ryman/Alamy) *A Saami herder, named Aslak, with his reindeer herd in Kautokeino (right).* ■ (Source: © Bryan and Cherry Alexander Photography/Alamy)

MAP 12.8 *Saami Region in Lapland, or Sapmi. Sapmi spreads across Norway, Sweden, Finland, and Russia's Kola Peninsula.*

language decline when speakers have limited vocabulary in their native language and more often use a new language in which they may be semifluent or fluent (Hill 2001). An intermediary stage, **language endangerment**, is judged to exist when a language has fewer than 10 000 speakers. Near-extinction is a situation in which only a few elderly speakers are still living. **Language extinction**, or language death, occurs when the language no longer has any competent users (Crystal 2000:11). Dialects follow a similar pattern of decline from decay to near-extinction to extinction. In 1777, Dolly Penreath, the last speaker of the Cornish dialect of British English died and Cornish became officially extinct (Lightfoot 2006:2).

Keeping track of endangered and dying languages is difficult because no one is sure how many languages have existed in the recent past and even now (Crystal 2000). Estimates of living languages today range between 5000 and 7000. Part of the explanation for the fuzzy numbers is the problem in separating languages from dialects. The largest number of languages of any world region is in New Guinea, an area comprising Papua New Guinea, Irian Jaya, and several neighbouring, smaller islands but not including Australia (Foley 2000). In this area alone are some 1000 languages, many from completely separate language families.

Language extinction is a serious problem worldwide. It is perhaps especially acute in the Australia/Pacific region, where 99.5 percent of the indigenous languages have fewer than 100 000 speakers (Nettle and Romaine 2000:40). The situation of indigenous languages in the Americas, Siberia, Africa, and South and Southeast Asia is increasingly serious. Over half of the world's languages have fewer than 10 000 speakers; a quarter of them have less than 1000 speakers.

In Canada, Aboriginal languages were not totally obliterated. Of those who identify an Aboriginal language as their first language, 43 percent speak Cree, 14 percent speak Inuktitut, 13 percent speak Ojibwe, 3 percent speak Athabascan, and 1 percent speak Sioux; but the average age of the speakers is over 40 (Frideres 1998:136). There are policies in place to revive and maintain these languages. While Inuit residential schooling used to be English- or French-based, grades 1 to 3 are now taught in Inuktitut, even for non-Inuit children (Frideres 1998:400). Native-as-a-second-language (NSL) programs in Ontario aim to develop literacy and encourage the functional use of Aboriginal languages such as Cree, Delaware, Ojibwe, Cayuga, Oneida, and Mohawk. The 2001 Aboriginal Peoples Survey reported that 63 percent of Inuit children and 80 percent of those over the age of 15 could speak Inuktitut relatively well, but only 15 percent of off-reserve Aboriginal people indicated they could speak their language well or relatively well.

Linguistic diversity is closely tied to cultural survival and diversity. It is also closely tied to biological diversity. The greatest linguistic diversity is found in the same regions as the greatest biodiversity (Maffi 2005). These are areas where indigenous people live, the "keepers" of much of the world's cultural and biological heritage, including the knowledge of how to live a culturally and biologically sustainable life. Yet, they are also the people, languages, and biological species most in danger of extinction in the near future.

Efforts to revive or maintain local languages face many challenges (Fishman 2001). Political opposition may come from governments that fear local identity movements. Governments are often averse to devoting financial resources to supporting minority language programs. Deciding which version of an endangered language to preserve may have political consequences at the local level (Nevins 2004). Notable achievements have been made, however, with perhaps one of the most robust examples of language maintenance occurring in French-speaking Quebec. Many of the language policies of Quebec, such as Bill 101, reflect the fear that without protection, the French language in Quebec will be contaminated by English, become corrupted and degenerate, with a resulting loss in cultural identity. Others argue that only in a bilingual Canada will French be protected, and that separation would result in a loss of French language in anglophone North America, particularly in the era of the North American Free Trade Agreement (NAFTA).

Approaches to language maintenance and revitalization must respond to local circumstances and factors such as how serious the degree of loss is, how many living speakers there are, what version of the language should be maintained or revived, and what resources for maintenance and revitalization programs are available. Major strategies include formal classroom instruction, a master-apprentice system in which an elder teaches a nonspeaker in a one-on-one situation, and the use of web-based tools and services to support language learning (Walsh 2005). Each method has both promise and pitfalls. One thing is key: It takes living communities to activate and keep alive the knowledge of a language (Maffi 2003).

---

language endangerment: a stage in language decline when a language has fewer than 10 000 speakers.

language extinction: a situation, either gradual or sudden, in which language speakers abandon their native language in favour of a new language to the extent that the native language loses functions and no longer has competent users.

Key Questions Revisited

HOW do humans communicate?

Human communication is the sending of meaningful messages through language. Language is a systematic set of symbols and signs with learned and shared meanings. It may be spoken, hand-signed, written, or conveyed through body movements, marking, or accessories. Languages include subvarieties such as dialects.

Human language has two characteristics that distinguish it from communicative systems of other living beings. It has productivity, or the ability to create an infinite number of novel and understandable messages, and displacement, the ability to communicate about the past, the future, and imaginary things.

Language consists of basic sounds, vocabulary, and syntax. Cross-culturally, however, languages vary substantially in the details of all three features.

Humans use many forms of nonverbal language to communicate with each other. Sign language is a form of communication that uses mainly hand movements to communicate. Silence is a form of nonverbal communication with its own cultural values and meaning. Body language includes body movements and placement in relation to other people, body modifications such as tattoos and piercing, dress, hairstyles, and odours.

Media anthropology sheds light on how culture shapes media messages and the social dynamics in media institutions. Critical media anthropology examines the power relations involved in the media.

WHAT are the links between communication, cultural diversity, and inequality?

In order to study language in society, anthropologists have to deal with the observer's paradox, or the difficulty of collecting data on language without affecting the object of study in the process. Translation is another challenge.

The Sapir-Whorf hypothesis places emphasis on how language shapes culture. Another model, called sociolinguistics, emphasizes how culture, and one's position in it, shape language. Many anthropologists draw on both models.

Critical discourse analysis studies the relations of power and inequality in language. Language can reveal social difference and reinforce exclusion. It can also empower oppressed people, depending on the context. In mainstream North America, women's speech is generally more polite and accommodating than that of men. In Japan, gender codes emphasize politeness in women's speech, but many young Japanese women, such as Kogals, are creating a linguistic style of resistance. Gay language in Indonesia is entering the mainstream as an expression of freedom from official control. Linguistic cueing among the Akwesasne Mohawks has been frequently misinterpreted by Anglo medical practitioners as a sign of indecisiveness or non-cooperation.

HOW does language change?

The exact heritage of human verbal language will never be known. The discovery of language families provides insights about human history and settlement patterns. The emergence of writing can be traced to around 6000 years ago, with the emergence of the state in Mesopotamia. Scripts have spread widely throughout the world, with the Aramaic system the basis of scripts in South and Southeast Asia. The functions of writing vary from context to context. In some situations, official record-keeping predominates, whereas in others, writing is important for courtship.

The recent history of language change has been influenced by the colonialism of past centuries and by Western globalization of the current era. Nationalist policies of cultural integration often involve the repression of minority languages and promotion of a lingua franca. Colonial contact created the context for the emergence of pidgin languages, many of which evolved into creoles. Western globalization supports the spread of English and the development of localized variants.

In the past 500 years, colonialism and globalization have resulted in the extinction of many indigenous and minority languages. Many others are in danger of dying. Applied anthropologists seek to preserve the world's linguistic diversity. They document languages and participate in designing programs for teaching dead and dying languages. Efforts to maintain or revive languages at risk face many challenges. One of the basic elements for success is to have living communities use the language.

KEY CONCEPTS

bilingualism, p. 328
call system, p. 316
code, p. 328
code-switch, p. 328
communication, p. 316
creole, p. 336
critical discourse
    analysis (CDA), p. 329
critical media anthropology,
    p. 323
dialect, p. 316
digital divide, p. 325
displacement, p. 316

ethnosemantics, p. 318
global language/world
    language, p. 337
historical linguistics, p. 333
indexicality, p. 327
khipu, p. 335
language, p. 316
language decay/language
    shift, p. 337
language endangerment,
    p. 339
language extinction, p. 339
language family, p. 333

linguistic pluralism, p. 328
linguistic relativism, p. 332
logograph, p. 334
observer's paradox,
    p. 326
phoneme, p. 317
pidgin, p. 336
productivity, p. 316
Sapir-Whorf
    hypothesis, p. 327
sign language, p. 319
sociolinguistics, p. 327
tag question, p. 329

SUGGESTED READINGS

Keith H. Basso, *Wisdom Sits in Places: Landscape and Language among the Western Apache*. Albuquerque, NM: University of New Mexico Press, 1996. Fieldwork on the Fort Apache Indian Reservation, Arizona, reveals the importance of natural places in people's everyday life, thought, and language.

David Crystal, *English as a Global Language*, 2nd ed. New York: Cambridge University Press, 2003. In this book, Crystal discusses the history, current status, and future of English as a world language. He covers the role of English in international relations, the media, world travel, education, and "New Englishes."

John Edwards, *Language in Canada*. Cambridge: Cambridge University Press, 1998. This book examines bilingualism, multiculturalism, Aboriginal languages, and language issues in every province of Canada.

Joshua A. Fishman, ed. *Can Threatened Languages Be Saved?* Buffalo, NY: Multilingual Matters Ltd., 2001. Seventeen case studies examine language shift and language loss and the attempts to reverse such changes.

Marjorie H. Goodwin. *He-Said-She-Said: Talk as Social Organization among Black Children*. Bloomington, IN: Indiana University Press, 1990. A study of everyday talk among children of an urban African American community in the United States, this book shows how children construct social relationships among themselves through verbal interactions, including disputes, pretend play, and stories.

Jack Goody, *The Power of the Written Tradition*. Washington, DC: The Smithsonian Institution, 2000. This book focuses on how writing confers power on societies that have it, compared to those that rely on oral communication. Goody's analysis encompasses the changing power of books in the age of the Internet.

Niloofar Haeri, *Sacred Language, Ordinary People: Dilemmas of Culture and Politics in Egypt*. New York: Palgrave Macmillan, 2003. Classical Arabic is the official language of all Arab states and the language of the Qur'an, but no Arabs speak it as their mother tongue. This book uses ethnographic research in Cairo to demonstrate the role that classical Arabic plays in how the state maintains its identity and in people's everyday lives.

Jennifer Hasty. *The Press and Political Culture in Ghana*. Bloomington, IN: Indiana University Press, 2005. The author worked as a journalist in Accra, Ghana, while doing research on the practices of journalism at privately owned and state-operated daily newspapers. She discusses differences in ways of gathering the news, assigning beats, using sources, and writing articles. Underlying these contrasts is a generally unified sense of Ghanaian national identity as expressed in the printed news.

Lanita Jacobs-Huey. *From the Kitchen to the Parlor: Language and Becoming in African-American Women's Hair Care*. New York: Oxford University Press, 2006. Jacobs-Huey combines childhood experiences as the daughter of a cosmetologist with multisited fieldwork in the United States and England. She finds a rich and complex world centred on hair that relates to race, gender, religion, body aesthetics, health, and verbal language.

William L. Leap. *Word's Out: Gay Men's English*. Minneapolis: University of Minnesota Press, 1996. Fieldwork among gay men in the Washington, D.C., area produced this ethnography. It addresses gay men's speech as a cooperative mode of discourse, bathroom graffiti, and discourse about HIV/AIDS.

Daniel Miller and Don Slater, *The Internet: An Ethnographic Approach*. New York: Berg, 2000. This is the first ethnography of Internet culture. Based on fieldwork in Trinidad, it offers an account of the political and social contexts of Internet use, individual experiences of being online, and the impact of the Internet on Trinidadian people and their culture.

Donna Patrick, *Language, Politics, and Social Interaction in an Inuit Community*. New York: Mouton De Gruyter, 2003. This book examines indigenous language maintenance among the Inuit of Arctic Quebec. The promotion and maintenance of Inuktitut has taken place through changes in language policy and Inuit control over institutions in a place where Inuktitut, Cree, French, and English are spoken.

Frank Salomon, *The Cord Keepers: Khipus and Cultural Life in a Peruvian Village*. Durham, NC: Duke University Press, 2004. The pre-Columbian Incas of the Andes used khipus, or knotted cords, to manage their empire. This ethnography describes the use of khipus in a contemporary Peruvian village where village leaders wear them on ceremonial occasions in order to signal their political identity and ancestry.

Lisa Philips Valentine. *Making It Their Own: Ojibwe Communicative Practices*. Toronto: University of Toronto Press, 1995. This ethnography examines speech events in a small Ojibwe community in northern Ontario. It considers speech variations among speakers, code switching, multilingualism, and church music.

Peter Wogan. *Magical Writing in Salasaca: Literacy and Power in Highland Ecuador*. Boulder, CO: Westview Press, 2004. This ethnography about highland people in Ecuador focuses on the importance and power of different forms of writing. The author describes writing in relation to ethnicity, the role of the state, social conflict, and religious beliefs and practices.

13

Expressive Culture

Key Questions

- HOW is culture expressed through art?

- WHAT do play and leisure activities reveal about culture?

- HOW is expressive culture changing in contemporary times?

The decorated facade of a domestic dwelling in Kano, northern Nigeria (*Source: Robert Frerck/Odyssey Productions, Inc.*)

In 2006, the Louvre in Paris, one of the most famous art museums in the world, opened a new museum, the Musée du Quai Branly, in the shadow of the Eiffel Tower to display so-called tribal art of Africa, Asia, the South Pacific, and the Americas. This project reflected the interest of France's then president, Jacques Chirac, in non-Western art. The museum is also an example of the growing role of cultural anthropologists in helping museums provide contextual information for objects that are displayed, because Maurice Godelier, a specialist on Papua New Guinea, was closely involved in planning the exhibits in the new museum (Corbey 2000). The Musée du Quai Branly elevates "tribal" objects to the level of art, rather than placing them in a museum of natural history as is the practice in the United States. It does, however, segregate "tribal" art in a museum physically separate from the Louvre with all its "classic" treasures. This long-standing conceptual division, beginning in the European Enlightenment, links the West with "civilization" and non-Western peoples with that which is "uncivilized."

In this chapter, we consider a vast area of human behaviour and thought called **expressive culture**, behaviour and beliefs related to learned and patterned ways of creative art, leisure, and play (definitions of these terms are provided below). We start with some theoretical perspectives on cross-cultural art. In the next section, we review findings from the field of museum studies, in which scholars seek appropriate ways of representing culture in a museum context. We then take a cross-cultural look at play and leisure activities, and, lastly, we consider directions of change in expressive culture.

Art and Culture

Compared to questions raised in art history classes you may have taken, you will find that cultural anthropologists have a rather different view of art and how to study it. Their findings, here as in other cultural domains, stretch and subvert the Western concepts and categories and prompt us to look at art within its context. Thus anthropologists consider many products, practices, and processes to be art. They also study the artist and the artist's place in society. In addition, they ask questions about how art, and expressive culture more generally, is related to cultural variation, inequality, and power.

What Is Art?

Are ancient rock carvings art? Is subway graffiti art? An embroidered robe? A painting of a can of Campbell's soup? Philosophers, art critics, anthropologists, and art lovers have all struggled with the question of what art is. The question of how to define art involves more than mere word games. The way art is defined affects the manner in which a person values and treats artistic creations and those who create art. Anthropologists propose broad definitions of art to take into account emic definitions cross-culturally. One definition says that **art** is the application of imagination, skill, and style to matter, movement, and sound that goes beyond the purely practical (Nanda 1994:383). The anthropological study of art considers the products of such human skill as well as the process of making art, variations in art and its preferred forms cross-culturally, and the way culture constructs and changes artistic traditions.

Such culturally judged skill can be applied to any number of substances and activities and can be considered art: for example, a beautifully presented meal, a well-told story, or a perfectly formed basket. In this sense, art is a human universal, and no culture can be said to lack artistic activity.

Within the general category of art, subcategories exist, sometimes denoting certain eras such as paleolithic or modern art. Other subcategories are based on the medium of expression—for example, graphic or plastic arts (painting, drawing, sculpture, weaving, basketry, and architecture); the decorative arts (interior design, landscaping, gardens, costume design, and body adornment such as hairstyles, tattooing, and painting); performance arts (music, dance, and theatre); and verbal arts (poetry, writing, rhetoric, and telling stories and jokes). All these are Western, English-language categories.

A long-standing distinction in the Western view exists between "fine art" and "folk art." This distinction is based on a Western-centric judgment that defines fine art as rare, expensive art produced by artists usually trained in the Western classical tradition. This is the kind of art that is included in university and college fine arts departments. The implication is that all other art is less than fine and is more appropriately called folk art, ethnic art, primitive art, or crafts. Characteristics of Western fine art are as follows: The product is created by a formally schooled artist, it is made for sale on the market, it is clearly associated with a particular artist,

---

expressive culture: behaviour and beliefs related to art, leisure, and play.

art: the application of imagination, skill, and style to matter, movement, and sound that goes beyond what is purely practical.

ethno-aesthetics: cultural definitions of what art is.

Rock paintings in Arnhemland, Australia, an important site for the Kunwinjku people. Arnhemland stretches across the northern part of the country and is the largest Aboriginal reserve in Australia. ■ (Source: Penny Tweedy/Panos Pictures)

its uniqueness is valued, and it is not primarily utilitarian but is rather "art for art's sake." In contrast, all the rest of the world's art that is non-Western and non-classical is supposedly characterized by the opposite features:

■ It is created by an artist who has not received formal training.

■ It is not produced for the market.

■ The artist is anonymous and does not sign or individually claim the product.

■ It is made primarily for everyday use, such as food procurement, processing, or storage; in ritual; or in war.

Closer examination of these two categories is in order. All cultures have art, and all cultures have a sense of what makes something art versus "non-art."

The term *aesthetics* refers to agreed-upon notions of quality (R. Thompson 1971:374). Before anthropologists proved otherwise, Western art experts considered that aesthetics either did not exist or were poorly developed in non-Western cultures. We now know that aesthetic principles, or established criteria for artistic quality, exist everywhere regardless of whether they are

written down and formalized. Franz Boas, from his wide review of many forms of art including Northwest Coast and Inuit art, deduced principles that he claimed were universal for these cultures, especially symmetry, rhythmic repetition, and naturalism (Jonaitis 1995:37). These principles do apply in many cases, but they are not as universal as Boas thought.

Ethno-aesthetics considers local variations in aesthetic criteria. The set of standards concerning wood carving in West Africa illustrates the importance of considering cultural variation (R. Thompson 1971). Among the Yoruba of Nigeria, aesthetic guidelines include the following:

■ Figures should be depicted midway between complete abstraction and complete realism so that they resemble "somebody," but no one in particular (portraiture in the Western sense is considered dangerous).

■ Humans should be depicted at their optimal physical peak, not in infancy or old age.

A carver of the Asmat culture in northern Papua New Guinea, with a shield he carved. ■ (Source: Roger Dashow/AnthroPhoto)

Yoruba wood carving is done according to aesthetic principles that require clarity of line and form, a polished surface that creates a play of light and shadows, symmetry, and the depiction of human figures that are neither completely abstract nor completely realistic and that are shown as adults and never very young or very old. ■ (Source: Courtesy of the Peabody Museum, Harvard University)

- There should be clarity of line and form.
- The sculpture should have the quality of luminosity achieved through a polished surface, the play of incisions, and shadows.
- The piece should exhibit symmetry.

Some anthropological studies have a documented intracultural differences in aesthetic standards as well as cross-cultural variation. For example, one anthropologist showed computer-generated graphics to the Shipibo Indians of the Peruvian Amazon and learned that the men liked the abstract designs, whereas the women thought they were ugly (Roe in Anderson and Field 1993:257). If you are wondering why this difference would exist, consider the interpretation of the anthropologist: Shipibo men are the shamans and take hallucinogenic drugs that may give them familiarity with more "psychedelic" images.

Studying Art in Society

The anthropological study of art seeks to understand not only the products of art, but also who makes it and why, its role in society, and its wider social meanings. Franz Boas was the first anthropologist to emphasize the importance of studying the artist in society. A significant thread in anthropology's theoretical history—functionalism—also dominated work of the early twentieth century on art. Anthropologists wrote about how paintings, dance, theatre, and songs serve to socialize children into the culture, provide a sense of social identity and group boundaries, and promote healing. Art may legitimize political leaders and enhance efforts in war through magical decorations on shields and weapons. Art may serve as a form of social control, as in African masks worn by dancers who represent deities visiting humans to remind them of the moral order. Art, like language, can be a catalyst for political resistance or rallying point for ethnic solidarity in the face of state oppression.

The anthropology of art relies on a range of methods in data gathering and analysis. For some research projects, participant observation provides most of the necessary data. In others, participant observation is complemented by collecting and analyzing oral or written material such as video and audio recordings. Thus, strong ties often exist between cultural and linguistic anthropologists in the study of art.

Many anthropologists have become apprentices in an artistic tradition. For example, in undertaking one of the earliest studies of Native American potters of the Southwest, Ruth Bunzel (1929) learned how to make pottery and thereby gained important data on what the potters thought constituted good designs. Kathy M'Closkey's experience as a weaver facilitated her research on Navajo rugs (see the accompanying Critical Thinking box).

In contrast, anthropologists who study past traditions, such as paleolithic art, cannot do participant observation or talk to the artists. They have to rely on indirect interpretation of silent symbols, shapes, colours, and contexts. Ethno-archaeology helps in this endeavour by providing clues about the past from the present. One example of this is a recent interpretation of the "Venus" figurines, the first human images from the European Upper Paleolithic period between 27 000 and 21 000 BCE (McDermott 1996). Little is known about why these palm-sized statuettes were made or who made them. Stylistically, each figurine has large breasts, abdomen, and buttocks, and small head, arms, and legs. Past interpretations of this characteristic shape

Critical Thinking

NAVAJO TEXTILES: BACK TO THE REZ

The blankets and rugs woven by thousands of Navajo women living in the American Southwest are highly desired by art collectors. Pre-1940 textiles typically sell for thousands of dollars at international auctions and galleries. Anthropologist/weaver Kathy M'Closkey of the University of Windsor spoke at a conference about the difficulties faced by contemporary Navajo weavers unable to receive adequate compensation for their rugs. The investment potential of historic weaving diminished the demand for contemporary textiles. However, the recent popularity of the Southwest look in fashion and home furnishings created a demand for Navajo-like patterns. Entrepreneurs appropriated the designs using illustrations of historic textiles as models for copyweaving, or knockoffs, made in Mexico and other countries. Navajo patterns remain unprotected by copyright, as the designs have been part of the public domain for decades.

After hearing M'Closkey's presentation, a conference participant donated the century-old Navajo blanket pictured here to the Navajo Nation Museum and Cultural Center in Window Rock, Arizona. He found it in his mother's cedar chest, where she had carefully stored it away after purchasing it in Arizona during the 1920s. Navajo weavers were thrilled with the gift, as they seldom see the old textiles. Their ancestors had to exchange textiles for groceries at reservation trading posts in order to survive. Averaging two cents per hour in credit, Navajo women's weaving was treated as raw wool by the traders, ignoring the hours of work Navajo women put into creating the rugs.

Well-known abstract artists in the United States collected historic Navajo textiles for more than 50 years. Several artists were greatly influenced by Navajo blanket weavers' use of colour and design. The first international

Anthropologist/weaver Kathy M'Closkey displays a century-old Navajo blanket. ■ (Source: Courtesy of Judy Chapman)

touring exhibition of historic Navajo blankets (1972–1974) featured many examples from the collections of famous artists. Almost immediately, the demand for the rare textiles escalated, culminating in a $522 000 sale of a historic Navajo blanket at Sotheby's in 1989. Formerly referred to as "craft," these old blankets are now revered as "art" (M'Closkey 1994). The blanket shown could have been sold as art on the auction block; instead, it went back home.

CRITICAL THINKING QUESTIONS

- Since many languages lack a term that translates as "art," how can art be defined cross-culturally?
- Why are textiles and weavings more likely to be exhibited in museums rather than art galleries?

have seen it as an intentional distortion to emphasize sexuality and fertility. A new theory proposes that women, especially pregnant women, sculpted these figurines as self-representations. A woman who used herself as a model would have a view of her body very much like that of the figurines (McCoid and McDermott 1996).

Focus on the Artist

In the early twentieth century, Boas urged his students to go beyond the study of the products of artistic endeavour and study the artists. The special role of the anthropologist is to add to the understanding of art by studying the process of creating art both within its social context and

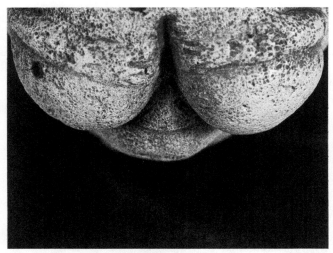

A top-down view of the "Venus" figurine, one of the first human images known. These small statues have often been interpreted as fertility goddesses on the basis of the large breasts, abdomen, and buttocks, and small head, arms, and legs. These features are said to be intentional distortions of the artist done to emphasize fertility. ■ (Source: Courtesy of Catherine H. McCoid and LeRoy D. McDermott. Reproduced by permission of the American Anthropological Association from *American Anthropologist* 98:2, June 1996.)

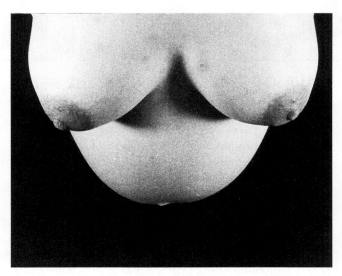

A new theory about the Venus figurines claims that they were self-portraits, crafted by women. A photograph of a pregnant woman looking down at herself presents a shape very much like that of the Venus figurines—but the shape is actual, not a distortion. ■ (Source: Courtesy of Catherine H. McCoid and LeRoy D. McDermott. Reproduced by permission of the American Anthropological Association from *American Anthropologist* 98:2, June 1996.

from the artist's perspective. Ruth Bunzel's (1972 [1929]) study of Pueblo potters is an example of this tradition. She paid attention to the variety of pot shapes and motifs employed and also interviewed individual potters about their personal design choices. One Zuni potter commented, "I always know the whole design before I start to paint" (49). A Laguna potter said, "I made up all my designs and never copy. I learned this design from my mother. I learned most of my designs from my mother" (1972:52). Brunzel discovered the importance of both past traditions and individual agency.

The social status of artists varies widely. Artists, individually or as a group, may be revered and wealthy, or stigmatized and economically marginal. In ancient Mexico, gold workers were a highly respected group. In First Nations groups of the Pacific Northwest, male carvers and painters had to be initiated into a secret society, and they had higher status than other men. Often, a gender division of artistic involvement exists. Among the Navajo, men do silversmithing, while women weave. In the Caribbean, women of African descent are noted for their carvings of calabashes (large gourds). Artists and performers often live outside the boundaries of mainstream society or challenge social boundaries.

In Morocco (see Map 5.3 on page 128), a *shikha* is a female performer who sings and dances at festivities, including rites-of-passage ceremonies such as birth, circumcision, and marriage (Kapchan 1994). They usually appear in a group of three or four with accompanying musicians. Their performance involves suggestive songs and body movements, including reaching a state of near-possession when they loosen their hair buns. With their long hair waving, they "lift the belt," a special technique accomplished through an undulating movement that rolls the abdomen up to the waist. Their performances at these mixed-gender events create a lively atmosphere. "Through the provocative movements and loud singing of the shikhat, the audience is drawn up and into a collective state of celebration, their bodies literally pulled into the dance" (93).

In their private lives, *shikhat* are on the social fringes, leading lives as single women who transgress limits applied to proper females. They own property, drink alcohol, smoke cigarettes, and may have several lovers. Most of the *shikhat* have been rejected by their families and by the wider society. Middle- and upper-class women consider them vulgar and generally distance themselves from them. Yet, *shikhat* who become successful, widening their performance spheres to larger towns and

ethnomusicology: the cross-cultural study of music.

cities, manage to save money and become landowners and gain economic status. Furthermore, the modern mass media is contributing to an increased status of *shikhat* as performers. Recordings of *shikha* music are popular in Morocco. State-produced television broadcasts carry performances of regional *shikha* groups as a way of presenting the diverse cultures of the country.

As with other occupations, artists are more specialized in state-level societies. Generally, among foragers, little specialization exists. Artistic activity is open to all, and artistic products are shared equally. With increasing social complexity and a market for art, specialized training is required to produce certain kinds of art and the products are sought after by those who can afford them. Class differences in artistic styles and preferences emerge along with the increasingly complex division of labour.

Art, Identity, and Power

Art forms and styles, like languages, are often associated with particular ethnic groups' identity and sense of pride. For example, the Berbers of the highlands in Morocco are associated with carpets, the Navajo with woven blankets, and the Inuit with stone carvings of figurines.

Cultural anthropologists provide many examples of linkages between various dimensions such as ethnicity and gender and power issues. In some instances, more powerful groups appropriate the art forms of less powerful groups. In others, forms of art are said to be expressive of resistance.

Gender relations are also played out in expressive culture. A study of a form of popular performance art in a Florida town, male strip dancing, shows how societal power relations between men and women are reinforced in this form of leisure activity (Margolis and Arnold 1993). Advertisements in the media tell women that seeing a male strip dancer is "their chance," "their night out." Going to a male strip show is marketed as a time of reversal of the traditional gender roles where men are dominant and women submissive. Are gender roles actually reversed in a male strip club? The short answer is no. Women customers are treated like juveniles. As they stand in line waiting for the show to open, the manager instructs them on how to tip. They are symbolically dominated by the dancers, who take on various roles such as lion-tamers. The *dive-bomb* is further evidence of women's subordinate position. The dive-bomb is a form of tipping the dancer in which the woman customer gets on her hands and knees and tucks a bill held between her teeth into the dancer's g-string. The interpretation of all this behaviour is that, rather than reversing the gender hierarchy, it is reinforced.

Not all forms of popular art and performance are mechanisms of social control and hierarchy maintenance. In North America, for example, urban black youths' musical performance through rap music can be seen as a form of protest. Some hip-hop artists, including Toronto based artist, k-os, protest economic oppression, the danger of drugs, and other social justice issues in their lyrics. The spread of hip-hop culture is another example of social resistance through song and performance.

Performance Arts

The performance arts include music, dance, theatre, rhetoric (public speech-making) and narrative (such as storytelling). **Ethnomusicology**, an established subfield, examines musical traditions cross-culturally. Ethnomusicologists study a range of topics including the form of the music itself, the social position of musicians, how music interacts with other domains of culture, and change in musical traditions. In this section, we provide a case study of the parallels between musical patterns and the gender division of labour in a foraging group in Malaysia. Here, we provide examples about music and gender in Malaysia, music and globalization in Brazil, and theatre and society in India.

Music and Gender among the Temiar of Malaysia

An important topic for ethnomusicologists is gender differences in access to performance roles in music (for readers interested in doing research on this topic, see Figure 13.1 on page 350). Ethnomusicologists would predict that in cultures where gender roles are relatively egalitarian, access to and meanings in music will tend to be egalitarian. This is the case among the Temiar, a group of foragers of highland Malaysia (see Map 8.3 on page 208). Their musical traditions emphasize balance and complementarity between males and females (Roseman 1987).

Among the Temiar, kinship and marriage rules are flexible and open. Marriages are based on the mutual desires of the partners. Descent is bilateral (review Chapter 8), and marital residence follows no particular rule after a period of bride service. Marriages often end in separation, and serial monogamy is common. Men have a certain edge over women in political and ritual spheres. They are typically the village leaders, and they are the spirit mediums who sing the songs that energize the spirits. Historical records, however, indicate that women were spirit mediums in the past.

Although men singers are the nodes through which the songs of the spirits enter the community, women's performance role is significant and the male spirit-medium role is not of greater importance or status. The distinction between male leader and female chorus is blurred through overlap between phrases and repetition. The performance is one of general community participation with integrated male and female roles, just as in Temiar society in general.

FIGURE 13.1   Five Ethnographic Questions about Gender and Music

■ ■ ■

If you were doing an ethnographic study of gender roles in musical performance, the following questions would be useful in starting the inquiry. But they would not exhaust the topic. Can you think of questions that should be added to the list?

1. Are men and women equally encouraged to use certain instruments and repertoires?

2. Is musical training available to all?

3. Do male and female repertoires overlap? If so, how, when, and for what reasons?

4. Are the performances of men and women public, private, or both? Are women and men allowed to perform together? In what circumstances?

5. Do members of the culture give equal value to the performances of men and women? On what criteria are these evaluations based, and are they the same for men and women performers?

Source: From "Power and Gender in the Musical Experiences of Women," pp. 224–225, by Carol E. Robertson in *Women and Music in Cross-Cultural Perspective,* ed. by Ellen Koskoff. Copyright © 1987. Reprinted by permission of Greenwood Publishing Group, Inc., Westport, CT.

Country Music and Globalization in Brazil

Linguistic anthropologist Alexander Dent studies the growing popularity of *música sertaneja,* Brazilian country music (2005). Although drawing on U.S. country music, *música sertaneja* is significantly localized within Brazilian social contexts. Brazilian performers creatively use North American country music songs, such as "Achy Breaky Heart" to convey messages that make sense in the Brazilian context about gender relationships, intimacy, the family, the past, and the importance of the countryside. In their performances and recordings, therefore, they may use an American genre to critique certain U.S.-led processes such as rampant capitalism and globalization and to critique the Brazilian adoption of such Western ways.

A prominent feature of Brazilian country music is performance by a *dupla,* a duo of brothers. They emphasize their similarity in terms of physical looks by cutting their hair the same way and wearing similar clothes.

Musically, they blend their voices without one voice dominating the other. When performing, they may sing part of a song with their arms over each other's shoulders and gazing at each other affectionately. In these ways, the *dupla* and their music emphasize kinship and caring as important aspects of Brazilian tradition that should be preserved.

Theatre and Myth: Ritual Dance-Drama in India and Canada

Theatre is a type of enactment that seeks to entertain through movement, and words related to dance, music, parades, competitive games and sports, and verbal art (Beeman 1993). Cross-culturally, strong connections exist among myth, ritual, and performance.

One theatrical tradition that offers an exuberant blend of mythology, acting, and music is Kathakali ritual dance-drama of southern India (Zarrilli 1990). Stylized hand gestures, elaborate makeup, and costumes contribute to the attraction of these dramas, which dramatize India's great Hindu epics, especially the *Ramayana* and the *Mahabharata.*

Costumes and makeup transform the actor into one of several well-known characters from Indian mythology. The audience can easily recognize the basic character types at their first entrance by "reading" the costuming and makeup. Six basic makeup types exist to depict characters, ranging from the most refined to the most vulgar, going along a continuum. Characters such as kings and heroes have green facial makeup, reflecting their high degree of refinement and moral uprightness. The most vulgar characters are associated with black facial makeup and occasionally black beards.

The teaching and performance of Hindu dance-dramas in Canadian cities offer opportunities to observe processes of cultural change and adaptation. First-generation South Asian immigrants to Canada introduced Kathakali and other classical forms to immigrant and non-immigrant audiences, creating an appreciation for Indian dance-drama. Second-generation Indo-Canadian dancers recognize the need to preserve the integrity of the classical repertoire, but also use dance as a means of personal expression and seek opportunities for collaborative multicultural dance exchanges. "The Rebel Goddess," an experimental work performed in Toronto in 1999, draws attention to the crisis of the creative spirit of the dancer trapped within the elaborate rules of the classical Indian dance.

theatre: a form of enactment, related to other forms such as dance, music, parades, competitive games and sports, and verbal art, that seeks to entertain through acting, movement, and sound.

Dance ethnologist Sarala Dandekar in Odissi costume represents the dancer/goddess of classical Indian dance. ■ (Source: © Sarala Dandekar/ photographer Arbindam Basu)

Yurts in Pamir, Afghanistan. The yurt form of domestic architecture is widespread across Asia among pastoralists. ■ (Source: R. & S. Michaud/Woodfin Camp)

Architecture and Decorative Arts

Like all art forms, architecture is interwoven with other aspects of culture. Architecture may reflect and protect social rank and class differences as well as gender, age, and ethnic differences (Guidoni 1987). Decorative arts—including interior decoration of homes and buildings, and external design features such as gardens—reflect people's social position and taste. Local cultures have long defined preferred standards in these areas of expression, but global influences from the West as well as from Japan and other non-Western cultures, have been adopted and adapted by other traditions.

Architecture and Interior Decoration

Foragers, being highly mobile, build dwellings as needed, and then abandon them. Having few personal possessions and no supply of goods they need no permanent storage structures. The construction of dwellings does not require the efforts of groups larger than the family unit.

Foragers' dwellings are an image of the family and not of the wider society. The dwellings' positioning in relation to each other reflects the relations among families. More elaborate shelters and greater social cohesiveness in planning occur as foraging is combined with horticulture, as in the semi-permanent settlements in the Amazon rainforest. People live in the settlement for part of the year, but break up into smaller groups that spread out into a larger area for foraging. Important decisions concern location of the site in terms of weather, availability of drinking water, and defensibility. The central plaza must be elevated for drainage, and drainage channels must be dug around the hearths. The overall plan is circular. In some groups, separate shelters are built for extended family groups; in others, they are joined into a continuous circle with connected roofs. In some cases, the headman has a separate and larger shelter.

Pastoralists have designed ingenious portable structures such as the teepee and yurt. The teepee is a conical tent made with a framework of four wooden poles tied at the top with thongs, to which are joined other poles to complete the cone; this frame is then covered with buffalo hide. A yurt is also a circular, portable dwelling, but its roof is flatter than that of a teepee. The covering is made of cloth. This extremely lightweight structure is easy to set up, take down, and transport, and is highly adaptable to all weather conditions. Encampments often involved the arrangement of the teepees or yurts in several concentric circles, with social status as the structuring principle, placing the council of chiefs and the head chief in the centre.

In settled agricultural communities where permanent housing is the norm, decoration is more likely to be found in homes. Wall paintings, sculptures, and other features may distinguish the homes of more wealthy individuals. The great wooden houses with their painted facades and carved totem poles made by First Nations communities on the Northwest Coast of North America reflected the stability of their resource base and the high value placed on displaying rank.

With the development of the state, urban areas grew and showed the effects of centralized planning and power, for example, in grid-style street planning rather than haphazard street placement. The symbolic demonstration of the power, grandeur, and identity of states was—and still is—expressed architecturally through the construction of impressive monuments: temples, administrative buildings, memorials, and museums.

Universities also exhibit their own unique use of space, from the ivy-covered walls of Canada's oldest universities to the modern suburban high-rise campuses. In Toronto, York University's Anthropology Department is housed in Vari Hall, a new building whose open rotunda space has become a focal point for a university lacking ivy-covered walls. The space has been used for official functions and has become a symbol of the university. However, the round, light, three-storey space is also used by students for studying, sleeping, talking, cuddling, and watching others from the higher floors. It has become a contested space, as it has also been appropriated for student and faculty protests (Rodman, Hawkins, and Teramura 1998).

Studying the way people design and decorate the interior of buildings and homes links cultural anthropologists with people working in other professions and disciplines, including interior design, advertising, and consumer studies. One study of interior decoration in Japan used as data the contents of home decorating magazines and observations within homes to see what decorative choices people made (Rosenberger 1992). Findings reveal how people incorporate and localize selected aspects of Western decorating styles. Home decorating magazines target middle- and upper-class housewives who seek to identify their status through new consumption styles. A trend was the abandonment of three features of traditional Japanese design: *tatami, shoji,* and *fusuma. Tatami* are 5-centimetre-thick mats, about 1 metre by 2 metres. *Shoji* are the sliding screen

Worldwide, Hilton hotels look much like each other and do not reflect local cultural architectural styles.
■ (Source: Paul Konklin/PhotoEdit)

doors of *tatami* rooms, one covered with glass and the other with translucent rice paper often printed with a design of leaves or waves. *Fusuma* are sliding wall panels made of thick paper; they are removable so that rooms can be enlarged for gatherings. The *tatami* room usually contains a low table with pillows for seating on the floor. A special alcove may contain a flower arrangement, ancestors' pictures, and a Buddhist altar. Futons are stored in closets around the edges and brought out at night for sleeping.

In seeking to distance themselves from the old style, the Japanese have made several changes, including giving the kitchen a more central location and displaying objects such as furniture, DVD players, and stereos. These design changes accompany deeper social changes involving new aspirations about marriage and family relationships. The home decorating magazines promote

heterotopia: the creation of an internally varied place by collecting things from diverse cultures and locations.

the idea that the new style brings with it happier children with better grades, and closer husband–wife ties. Tensions exist, however, between these ideals and the realities of middle- and upper-class life in Japan. Women feel compelled to work either part-time or full-time to be able to contribute to satisfying their new consumer needs. Simultaneously, Japanese women are discouraged from pursuing careers and are urged to devote more time to domestic pursuits, including home decorating and child care, in order to provide the kind of life portrayed in the magazines. Furthermore, the Western-style happy nuclear family image contains no plan for the aged. The wealthiest Japanese families manage to satisfy both individualistic desires and filial duties because they can afford a large house, in which they devote a separate floor to the husband's parents, complete with traditional *tatami* mats. Less wealthy people have a more difficult time dealing with this complex and conflicting set of values.

Gardens and Flowers

Gardens for use, especially for food production, are differentiated from gardens dedicated to decoration and beauty. Not all cultures have developed the concept of the decorative garden. Inuit peoples cannot construct gardens in the snow, and mobile pastoralists have no gardens since they are on the move. The decorative garden seems to be a product of state-level societies, especially in the Middle East, Europe, and Asia (Goody 1993). Variation exists in what is considered to be the appropriate contents, design, and purpose of a garden. A Japanese garden may contain no blooming flowers, focusing instead on the shape and placement of trees, shrubs, stones, and bodies of water (Moynihan 1979). Elite Muslim culture, with its core in the Middle East, has long been associated with formal decorative gardens. A garden, enclosed with four walls, is symbolically equivalent to the concept of "paradise." The Islamic garden pattern involves a square design with symmetrical layout, fountains, waterways, and straight pathways, all enclosed within walls through which symmetrically placed entrances allow access. Islamic gardens were often used to surround the tombs of prominent people, with the usual plan placing the tomb in the centre of the garden. India's Taj Mahal, built by Muslim Emperor Shah Jahan, follows this pattern, with one modification in the landscaping: The tomb was placed at one edge of the garden rather than in the centre. The result is a dramatic stretch of fountains and flowers leading up to the monument from the main gate.

The contents of a garden, like a fancy dinner menu with all its special ingredients or a personal collection of

Women practising the art of flower arrangement in Japan.
■ (Source: Catherine Karnow/Woodfin Camp)

souvenirs from around the world with all their memories and meanings, makes a statement about its owner's identity and status. For example, in Europe during the height of colonialism, imperial gardens contained specimens from remote corners of the globe, collected through scientific expeditions. Such gardens are created through the intentional collection and placement of plants from many parts of the world. The practice of cultural displacement of diverse objects into a single collection with a new identity is called **heterotopia** (Foucault 1970). These gardens expressed the owner's worldliness and intellectual status.

THINKING **OUTSIDE** THE BOX

WHAT ROLE do flowers play in your cultural world?

Cut flowers are now important economic products; they provide income for gardeners throughout the world. They are also exchange items. In France, women receive flowers from men more than any other kind of gift (Goody 1993:316). In much of the world, "special occasions" require gifts of flowers. In the West, as well as in East Asia, funerals are times for special displays of flowers. Ritual offerings to the deities in Hinduism are often flowers such as marigolds woven into a chain or necklace.

Individual flowers also acquire local meanings, as in Canada, where poppies are associated with Remembrance Day (commemorating the world wars), and daffodils with the Canadian Cancer Society.

Flowers are prominent motifs in Western and Asian secular and sacred art, although less so in African art. Some possible reasons for this variation include ecological and economic factors. Eurasia's more temperate environment possesses a greater variety of blooming plants than Africa's does. In wealthy African kingdoms, prominent luxury goods include fabrics, gold ornaments, and wooden carvings rather than flowers. This pattern of production is changing with globalization, however. Many African countries now grow flowers for export to the world market.

Museums and Culture

In this section, we consider the concept of the museum and the debates about the role of museums in exhibiting and representing culture. Museum studies in anthropology developed in the 1980s. It includes both anthropologists who work in museums helping to prepare exhibits and anthropologists who study museums—what they choose to display and how they display it—as important sites of culture itself (M. Ames 1992; A. Jones 1993; Stocking 1985).

What Is a Museum?

A **museum** is an institution that collects, preserves, interprets, and displays objects on a regular basis (Kahn 1995:324). Its purpose may be aesthetic or educational. Museums have played and continue to play a key role in Canadian anthropology. The term comes originally from a Greek word referring to a place for the muses to congregate, where one would have philosophical discussions or see artistic performances. In Europe, the concept of the museum developed into a place where art objects were housed and displayed. Ethnographic and science museums came later, inspired by Europe's emerging interests in exploration in the 1500s and the accompanying scientific urge to gather specimens from around the world and classify them into an evolutionary history.

The concept of the museum and its several forms has now diffused to most parts of the world. Contemporary versions include children's museums, heritage parks, and local museums. The Saputik ("The Weir") Museum in Puvirnituq, Quebec, is an example of a community museum created by an Inuit elder. Aptly named, The Weir is a place to catch and hold personal objects before they pass out to sea to be lost forever (Graburn 1998). The Canadian Museum of Civilization and many other museums have shifted from an exclusively object-oriented approach to one that stresses cultural performances and interactive media experiences using new information and communication technologies (McDonald and Alsford 1989).

The Politics of Exhibits

REVIEW INTERNET research on the repatriation of potlatch goods in Canada.

Within anthropology, the subfield of *museum anthropology* is concerned with studying how and why museums choose to collect and display particular objects (Ames 1992; A. Jones 1993). Museum anthropologists are at the forefront of serious debates about who gets to represent whom, the ownership of particular objects, and the public service role of museums versus their possible elitism. The political aspects of museums have always existed, but now they are part of explicit discussion (see the accompanying Multiple Cultural Worlds box). A major area of debate is whether objects from non-Western cultures should be exhibited, like Western art objects, with little or no ethnographic context (Clifford 1988; Watson 1997). Most anthropologists would support the need for context, not just for non-Western objects but for all objects on display. For example, a museum label of Andy Warhol's hyperrealistic painting of a can of Campbell's soup should include information on the social context in which such art was produced and some background on the artist. The anthropological view that all forms of expressive culture are context bound and are better understood and appreciated within their social context is, however, still rare among Western art historians and critics (Best 1986).

Debates also exist about who should have control of objects in museums that may have been claimed through colonial and neo-colonial domination. The issue of **repatriation**, or returning objects to their original homes, is a matter of international and national concern. The complexity of this process can be seen in the repatriation of objects confiscated by the Canadian government in 1922 following a large "illegal" potlatch held in Alert Bay, British Columbia. The local Indian Agent alerted the RCMP about the potlatch, and authorities confiscated over 450 ritual items such as coppers, masks, rattles, headdresses, blankets, and boxes, paying their owners a small price for them. The regalia ended up in major Canadian and U.S. museums. The Canadian Museum of Civilization and the Royal Ontario Museum (ROM) agreed to return their collections not to individual families, but to two local museums that would be built to preserve and display the items. The Kwagiulth Museum and Cultural Centre on Quadra Island (opened in 1979) and the U'mista Cultural Centre in Alert Bay, Cormorant Island (opened

---

museum: an institution that collects, preserves, interprets, and displays objects on a regular basis.

repatriation: returning art or other objects from museums to the people with whom they originated.

Multiple Cultural Worlds

EXHIBITING RACISM

"Into the Heart of Africa" was the Royal Ontario Museum's (ROM) most controversial exhibit. From November 1989 until its premature closing in August 1990, the temporary exhibition displayed photographs and objects such as masks, jewellery, and sculptures collected between 1870 and 1925 by Canadian missionaries to Africa, soldiers serving in the British Army, and explorers. These artifacts were not presented to the public as a traditional museum exhibit. Canadian anthropologist Jeanne Cannizzo designed the exhibit to encourage audiences to actively engage with and interpret the displays rather than passively observe them. As an example of reflexive museology, viewers were expected to critique British colonial ideology and the complicity of Canadians in sustaining it. For example, Cannizzo highlighted racist colonial language by using such phrases as the "unknown continent" and "barbarous customs" in the explanatory panels of the exhibits. She placed these terms in quotation marks to encourage museum users to challenge and critique their use.

Unfortunately, many visitors to the ROM did not recognize the reflexive and ironic nature of the exhibits. Instead, they thought Into the Heart of Africa glorified imperialism and was racist in its portrayal of Africans. In March 1990, a group called the Coalition for the Truth about Africa (CFTA) began weekly protests outside the ROM. The CFTA and others challenged the authority of the ROM to represent Africa, and criticized the museum's failure to consult black community members about the exhibit.

While the media portrayed the controversy as a conflict between the ROM and the CFTA, Shelley Butler's ethnographic analysis of the exhibit (1999) reveals the many differing views and understandings of both the exhibit and the controversy. The ROM was accused by the CFTA of being elitist and representing the interests of only a small portion of Toronto's population. Nevertheless, Into the Heart of Africa provided a forum for highlighting contemporary issues of racism in Canada and the authority of the museum to represent the "truth" about other peoples, cultures, and objects (Butler 2008).

FOOD FOR THOUGHT

- Is an "ironic stance" appropriate for exhibits in a public institution? Where would such a stance be acceptable and even expected?

---

in 1980), stress the family ownership of the items, and the local histories of the objects. The U'mista Cultural Centre displays large white cards with texts and quotations about the confiscation of the regalia that was repatriated. In contrast, the University of British Columbia Museum of Anthropology provides brief labels with a small drawing of the object in its original setting (Clifford 1997; D. Cole 1985).

In 1999, museum officials returned four intricate 500-year-old wampum belts to an assembly of Iroquois chiefs at a ceremony at the Six Nations Grand River Territory near Brantford, Ontario. The belts had been stored in the ROM since 1922, when they were given to the museum by a Mohawk woman for safekeeping. They were repatriated after the Six Nations reserve approached the museum to return the wampum records. They received similar ones from other museums around North America. Wampum served as a record of laws, treaties, and promises, and it helps the Iroquois remember their oral history. One member of the reserve commented, "The last person we had who could recite the entire Great Law passed away. . . . Getting the wampum back may help stop the erosion" (*Toronto Star*, November 12, 1999).

In Canada and the United States, many Aboriginal groups have lobbied successfully for the return of ancestral bones, grave goods, and potlatch goods. In 1990, the United States passed the Native American Graves Protection and Repatriation Act (NAGPRA), after two decades of lobbying by Native American groups (Bray 1996; Rose, Green, and Green 1996), opting for legislation requiring inventories of archaeological and ethnographic holdings. Tensions between museums and First Nations peoples in Canada came to a head over an exhibit entitled "The Spirit Sings," developed by the Glenbow Museum to celebrate the

1988 Calgary Winter Olympics. The Lubicon Cree of northern Alberta called for an international boycott of the exhibit because they were engaged in a land-claim dispute with the provincial and federal governments. The exhibit was sponsored by Shell Oil, the company drilling on the land they claimed. The confrontation resulted in the formation of the Task Force on Museums and First Peoples in 1989, under the joint sponsorship of the Assembly of First Nations and the Canadian Museums Association. The task force, which included Native and non-Native members, opted to develop a cooperative model of equal partnerships guided by moral, ethical, and professional responsibilities, rather than by legislation such as NAGPRA. The task force developed principles to serve as a basis for recommendations, including acknowledging that both museums and First Nations peoples share a mutual interest in the cultures and histories of Aboriginal peoples; that museums should recognize the authority of First Nations peoples to speak for themselves and that First Nations peoples should recognize the professional knowledge of museum academics; and that both should work together as equal partners to meet their differing needs and interests (Nicks 1992).

Other parts of the world face different repatriation problems. The breakup of the Soviet Union prompted claims from several independent states seeking to retrieve artistic property that originated in their locale but was taken to Soviet national museums in Moscow and St. Petersburg. For example, Ukraine (see Map 13.1) is demanding the return of about 2 million art objects that are currently housed in Russian museums (Akinsha 1992b).

Another dimension of disputes about art in Russia concerns the state and the church. In the Soviet era, authorities put many icons and other religious objects in museums and also turned churches into museums. The Russian Orthodox Church has been campaigning for the return of church property. Churches are demanding that all sacred objects of the church, all church buildings, and masterpieces of church art that were confiscated by the state after 1917 be returned to the ownership of the Russian Orthodox Church (Akinsha 1992a:102). Art historians and museum officials protest that the churches lack the resources and the experience to care for these treasures. Another complication comes from occasional threats of theft and violence from those who wish to return the icons to churches and monasteries. In response, some museums have removed certain pieces from display.

MAP 13.1   Ukraine. Ukraine became independent after the collapse of the Soviet Union in 1991. It is mostly fertile plains, or steppes, crossed by rivers. Since independence and privatization, the economy has been unstable with high inflation rates. Related to the economic crisis, sex trafficking of women became a serious problem, infant mortality rates rose, and the birth rate fell. The total population is around 50 million and declining. Ukrainian is the official language, though many people speak Russian, especially in the south and east. In reality, many people speak a mixture of both languages. Government policy is to promote "Ukrainization," especially the increased use of the Ukrainian language. The dominant religion is Eastern Orthodox Christianity. The tradition of colouring Easter eggs began in Ukraine in pre-Christian times.

wa: Japanese word meaning discipline and self-sacrifice for the good of the whole.

Play, Leisure, and Culture

In this section, we turn to the area of expressive culture related to what people do for fun and relaxation. It is impossible to draw clear lines between the concepts of play, leisure, art, and performance since they often overlap. For example, a person could paint watercolours in her leisure time, yet simultaneously be creating a work of art. In most cases, though, play and leisure can be distinguished from other activities by the fact that they have no direct, utilitarian purpose for the participant.

In the 1930s, Dutch historian Johan Huizinga offered some features of play: It is unnecessary and, thus, free action; it is outside of ordinary life; it is closed and limited in terms of time; and it has rules and it contains elements of tension and chance (as summarized in Hutter 1996).

Leisure activities often overlap with play, but many leisure activities, such as reading or lying on a beach, would not be considered play because they lack rules, tension, and chance. Within the broad category of play and leisure activities, several subcategories exist, including varieties of games, hobbies, and recreational travel. Although play and leisure, and their subcategories, may be pursued from a nonutilitarian perspective, they are often situated in a wider context of commercial and political interests. The Olympic Games are a good example of such complexities.

Cultural anthropologists study play and leisure within their cultural contexts as part of social systems. They ask, for example, why some activities involve teams rather than individuals; what are the social roles and status of people involved in particular activities; what the goals of the activities are and how they are achieved; how much danger or violence is involved; how certain activities are related to group identity; and how such activities link or separate different groups within or between societies or nations.

Games and Sports

Games and sports, like religious rituals and festivals, can be interpreted as reflections of broader social relationships and cultural ideals. In Clifford Geertz's terms (1966), they are both *models of a culture*, depicting in miniature, key ideals, and *models for a culture* socializing people into certain values and ideals. American football can be seen as a model for corporate culture in that it relies on a clear hierarchy with leadership vested in one key person (the quarterback), and its goal of territorial expansion by taking over areas from the competition.

Contrast the expansionist/corporate ethos and huge paydays for mercenary players in U.S. football and other major North American professional sports with the approach in Japan of that country's baseball players. In the Japanese league, players are influenced by a primary national value: *wa,* meaning discipline and self-sacrifice for the good of the whole. In Japanese baseball, players must seek to achieve and maintain team harmony; they have a negative view of flamboyant showmanship and extremely individualistic, egotistical plays and strategies.

Canadian football, unlike the U.S. version of the sport, carries less mythic value as a symbol of national identity, as it is more of a historical compromise between British rugby and U.S.-style football. In spite of the historic importance of the Grey Cup, it is hockey that inspires a shared national identity.

Hockey in Canada, both casual street hockey and professional sport spectacle, has deeply rooted meanings linked to images of national character and identity (Gruneau and Whitson 1993). Hockey is part of the collective memory of many English and French Canadian men who grew up in towns with community hockey leagues. The organized, rule-governed professional game emerged in Montreal in the 1870s, as an event with spectators. In 1892, Governor General Lord Stanley donated a trophy cup to recognize the Dominion of Canada's best hockey team. In 1917, the National Hockey League (NHL) formed and in the next few years added franchises in the United States. Canada's national winter pastime became a continental business, and the movement stateside fuelled fears that the NHL would no longer be Canadian, that it would be taken over by U.S. business interests. By the 1930s, radio broadcasts of *Hockey Night in Canada* could be heard across the country and became a national symbol in spite of American money, influence, and teams in the NHL. Later, television provided the same unifying national entertainment.

Hockey continues to be part of a collective representation of what it means to be Canadian—a representation that ignores differences of race, ethnicity, class, and gender in participation, as if hockey emerged as a natural adaptation to ice and cold winters. Yet, the game has deep roots in both rural and urban communities. Over the years, showdowns between the Toronto Maple Leafs and the Montreal Canadiens dramatized the rivalry between the two solitudes (anglophones and francophones); other NHL match-ups (such as when two Sunbelt teams are vying for Lord Stanley's Cup) have brought out fears that the league is selling out to U.S. interests and losing its "Canadianness." Many fans view the game of hockey as a piece of distinctive national culture. Canada's win over the Soviet hockey team in the landmark 1972 Summit Series is still celebrated as a reflection of national identity and national character (Gruneau and Whitson 1993).

Sports and Spirituality: Male Wrestling in India

In many non-Western contexts, sports are closely tied with aspects of religion and spirituality. Asian martial arts, for example, require forms of concentration much like meditation, leading to spiritual self-control. Male wrestling in India, a popular form of entertainment at rural fairs and other public events is strongly linked with spiritual development and asceticism (Alter 1992). A wrestler's daily routine is one of self-discipline. Every act—defecation, bathing, comportment, devotion—is integrated into a daily regimen of discipline. Wrestlers come to the *akhara* (equivalent to a gymnasium) early in the morning for practice under the supervision of a guru or other senior *akhara* member. They practise moves with different partners for two to three hours. In the early evening, they return for more exercise. In all, a strong young wrestler will do around 2000 push-ups and 1000 deep knee bends a day in sets of 50 to 100.

The wrestler's diet is prescribed by the wrestling way of life. Most wrestlers are vegetarian and avoid alcohol and tobacco, although they do consume *bhang,* a beverage made of blended milk, spices, almonds, and concentrated marijuana. In addition to regular meals, wrestlers consume large quantities of milk, *ghee* (clarified butter), and almonds. These substances are considered sources of strength as they help to build up the body's semen, according to traditional dietary principles.

Several features about the wrestler's life are similar to those of a Hindu *sannyasi,* or holy man who renounces life in the normal world. The aspiring *sannyasi* studies under a guru and learns to follow a strict routine of discipline and meditation called *yoga,* and has a restricted diet to achieve control of the body and its life force. Both wrestler and *sannyasi* roles focus on discipline to achieve a controlled self. In Indian wrestling does not involve the stereotype of the "dumb jock" that it sometimes does in

Wrestlers in the village of Sonepur, India. These wrestlers follow a rigorous regimen of dietary restrictions and exercise in order to keep their bodies and minds under control. Like Hindu ascetics, they seek to build up and maintain their inner strength through such practices.
■ (Source: © CORBIS. All Rights Reserved.)

North America; instead, the image is of perfected physical and moral health.

Play, Pleasure, and Pain

Many leisure activities combine pleasure and pain. Serious injuries can result from mountain climbing, horseback riding, or playing touch football in the backyard. Hockey, both recreational and professional, has increasingly incorporated violence in what is undeniably a forceful, physical game. A more intentionally dangerous category of athletic competition is **blood sports**, competition that explicitly seeks to bring about a flow of blood, with death even being a possible outcome. Blood sports may involve human contestants, humans contesting against animal competitors, or animal–animal contestants (Donlon 1990). Professional boxing is a highly popular blood sport in many parts of the world. Loic Wacquant has critiqued the sport while documenting its allure (2004). Cultural anthropologists have looked more at the use of animals in blood sports such as cockfights and bullfights. Interpretations of these sports range from seeing them as forms of sadistic pleasure or vicarious self-validation (usually of males) through the triumph of their representative pit bull or fighting cock, or as the triumph of culture over nature in the symbolism of bullfighting.

Even the seemingly pleasurable experience of a Turkish bath can involve discomfort and pain. One phase involves scrubbing the skin roughly several times with a rough natural sponge, a pumice stone, or a piece of cork wood wrapped in cloth (Staats 1994). The scrubbing removes layers of dead skin and "opens the pores" so that the skin will be beautiful. In Turkey, an option for men is a massage that can be quite violent, involving deep probes of leg muscles, cracking of the back, and being walked on by the (often hefty) masseur. In Ukraine, being struck repeatedly on one's bare skin with birch branches is the final stage of the bath. However, violent scrubbing, scraping, and even beating of the skin, combined with radical temperature changes in the water, are combined with valued social interaction as well.

Leisure Travel

Anthropologists who study leisure travel, or tourism, have often commented that their work is taken less seriously than it should be because of the perspective that they are

THINKING OUTSIDE THE BOX

IN YOUR CULTURAL world, what are some examples of leisure activities that combine pleasure and pain? Conduct some informal interviews with participants to learn why they are attracted to such activities.

blood sport: a form of competition that explicitly seeks to bring about a flow of blood, with death being a possible outcome; it can involve human–human contestants, human–animal contestants, or animal–animal contestants.

just "hanging out" at the beach or at five-star hotels. Anthropological research on tourism and its impact is an important subject and involves the same amount of effort as any other fieldwork. Tourism is now one of the major economic forces in the world and has dramatic effects on people and places in tourist destination areas. A large percentage of worldwide tourism involves individuals from Europe, North America, and Japan travelling to less industrialized nations. Ethnic tourism, cultural tourism, and ecotourism are attracting increasing numbers of travellers. They are often marketed as providing a view of "authentic" cultures. Images of indigenous people figure prominently in travel brochures and advertisements.

Tourist promotional literature often presents a "myth" of other peoples and places (Silver 1993:304) and offers travel as a form of escape to a mythical land of wonder. For example, tourist promotional literature presents the Kenyan safari as a particular kind of imaginative representation of the wild (Little 1991). Western travel literature shows that from the time of the earliest explorers to the present, it has been full of "primitivist" images about indigenous peoples. They are portrayed as having static or "stone age" traditions remaining largely unchanged by the forces of Western colonialism, nationalism, economic development, and tourism itself (Bruner 2005). Tourists often seek the culture that the tourist industry defines rather than gaining a more complicated, and perhaps less photogenic version of the culture. For the traveller, obtaining these desired cultural images through mass tourism involves packaging the "primitive" with the "modern" because most tourists want comfort and convenience along with their "authentic experience." Thus, advertisements may minimize the foreignness of the host country, noting, for example, that English is spoken and that the destination is remote yet accessible, while simultaneously promoting primitivist and sometimes racist imagery. Julia Harrison's interviews with Canadian tourists revealed more details about how they interpret their experiences of travel (2003).

Not all tourism requires overseas travel. The century-old Ontario pattern of spending the summer in cottage country reflects the search for pristine paradise in Muskoka or on other northern lakes. The joy of escaping urban constraints for the waterfront cottage still motivates many to communicate with nature by "roughing it" in the woods (Satsuka 1997).

The anthropology of tourism has focused on the impact of global and local tourism on indigenous peoples and places. Such studies are important in exposing the degree to which tourism helps or harms local people and local ecosystems. For example, the formation of Amboseli National Park in Kenya negatively affected the access of the Maasai to strategic water resources for their herds (Honadle 1985, as summarized in Drake 1991). The project staff promised certain benefits to the Maasai if they stayed off the reserve, but many of those benefits (including shares of the revenues from the park) never

MAP 13.2 **Costa Rica.** The Republic of Costa Rica was the first country in the world to constitutionally abolish its army, and it has largely escaped the violence that its neighbours have endured. Agriculture is the basis of the economy with tourism, especially ecotourism, playing an increasing role. Most of the 4 million inhabitants of Costa Rica are descended from Spanish colonialists. Less than 3 percent are Afro-Costa Ricans, and less than 2 percent, or around 50 000, are indigenous people. Seventy-five percent of the people are Roman Catholic and 14 percent Protestant. The official language is Spanish.

materialized. In contrast, local people in Costa Rica were included in the early planning stages of the Guanacaste National Park and have played a greater role in the park-management system there (see Map 13.2)

Many studies show how local residents are exercising agency and playing an active role in transforming the effects of tourism to their advantage and designing and managing tourist projects (Stronza 2001; Natcher, Davis, and Hickey 2005; Miller 2005). The Gullah people of South Carolina are one such example (see the Ethnographic Profile on page 362); other examples are described in the last section of this chapter.

Change in Expressive Culture

Nowhere are forms and patterns of art, play, and leisure frozen in time. Much change is influenced by Western culture through globalization, but influence does not occur in only one direction. African musical styles have transformed the American musical scene since the days of slavery. Japan has exerted a strong influence on upper-class garden styles in North America. Cultures in which tradition and conformity have been valued in pottery-making, dress, or theatre find themselves having to make choices about whether to innovate, and if so, how. Many contemporary artists (including musicians and playwrights) from Latin America to China are fusing ancient and "traditional" motifs and styles with more contemporary themes and messages.

Changes occur through the use of new materials and technology and through the incorporation of new ideas, tastes, and meanings. These changes often accompany other aspects of social change, such as colonialism, global tourism, or political transitions. For example, Nelson Graburn (2004) has analyzed the range of indigenous art made by the Inuit and found a range from traditional activities and products made for internal consumption to those invented for external markets.

Colonialism and Syncretism

Western colonialists had dramatic effects on the expressive culture of indigenous peoples with whom they came into contact. In some instances, colonial disapproval of particular art forms and activities resulted in their extinction. For example, when colonialists banned headhunting in various cultures, this change also meant that body decoration, weapon decoration, and other related expressive activities

were abandoned. In this section, we provide an example of how colonial repression of indigenous forms succeeded— but only temporarily.

In the Trobriand Islands of Papua New Guinea (see Map 2.1 on page 40), British administrators and missionaries sought to eradicate the frequent tribal warfare as part of its pacification process. One strategy was to replace it with intertribal competitive sports (Leach 1975). In 1903, a British missionary introduced the British game of cricket in the Trobriands as a way of promoting a new morality, separate from the former warring traditions. As played in England, cricket involves particular rules of play and a proper look of pure-white uniforms. In the early stages of the adoption of cricket in the Trobriands, the game followed the British pattern closely. As time passed and the game spread into more regions, it developed local versions.

Throughout the Trobriands, cricket was merged into indigenous political competition between big-men (Foster 2006). Big-men leaders would urge their followers to increase production in anticipation of a cricket match since the matches were followed by a redistributive feast. The British missionaries had discouraged traditional magic in favour of Christianity, but the Trobriand Islanders brought war-related magic into cricket. For example, spells were used to help one's team win, and the bats were ritually treated in the way that war weapons were. Weather

Classical dancers perform in Thailand. The intricate hand motions, with their impact augmented by the wearing of metal finger extenders, have meanings that accompany the narrative being acted out. International tourism is a major support for such performance arts in Thailand.
■ (Source: © Dallas and John Heaton/CORBIS)

material cultural heritage: sites, monuments, buildings, and movable objects considered to have outstanding value to humanity. Also called *cultural heritage.*

intangible cultural heritage: UNESCO's view of culture as manifested in oral traditions, languages, performing arts, rituals and festive events, knowledge and practices about nature and the universe, and craft making. Also called *living heritage.*

magic was also important. If things were not going well for one's team, a spell to bring rain and force cancellation of the game would perhaps be invoked.

Other changes occurred. The Trobrianders stopped wearing the crisp white uniforms and instead donned paint, feathers, and shells. They announced their entry into the host village with songs and dances, praising their team in contrast to the opposition. Many of the teams, and their songs and dances, draw on Western elements such as the famous entry song of the "P-K" team. (P-K is the name of a chewing gum. This team chose the name because the stickiness of gum is likened to the ability of their bat to hit the ball.) Other teams incorporated sounds and motions of airplanes, objects that they first saw during World War II. The songs and dances are explicitly sexual and enjoyed by all, in spite of missionaries' attempts to suppress the "immoral" aspects of Trobriand culture. The Trobrianders have changed some of the rules of play as well. The home team should always win, but not by too many runs. In this way, guests show respect to the hosts. Winning is not the major goal. The feast after the match is the climax.

In Bermuda, as elsewhere in the West Indies, cricket is "played with elegant skill, studied with scholarly intensity, argued with passionate conviction, and revered with patriotic pride" (F. Manning 1981:617). Participation in cricket festivals is marked by indulgence and festive sociability. These are cultural performances where blacks dress in "whites" to play a white game they have transformed into a celebration of black culture. But in Bermuda, where economic power is very much in white hands, the cricket games and related festivals reveal tensions between celebrations of black culture and economic dependency.

Tourism's Complex Effects

Global tourism has had varied effects on indigenous arts. In many cases, tourist demand for ethnic arts and souvenirs has led to mass production of sculpture or weaving or jewellery of a lesser quality than was created before the demand. Tourists' interests in seeing an abbreviated form of a traditionally long dance or theatre performance has led to the presentation of "cuts" rather than an entire piece. As a result, some scholars say that tourism leads to the decline in quality and authenticity of indigenous arts.

Often, tourist support for indigenous arts is the sole force maintaining them, since local people in a particular culture may be more interested in foreign music, art, or sports. Vietnamese water puppetry is an ancient performance art, dating back at least to the Ly Dynasty of 1121 CE (Contreras 1995). Traditionally, water puppet shows took place in the spring during a lull in the farm work, or at special festival times. The stage for this performance art is either a small natural pond or an artificial water tank, with a backdrop that hides the puppeteers from the audience. They operate wooden puppets with bamboo poles, wires, and strings to make the puppets glide over the water as if on their own. Since the 1980s, water puppetry has grown in popularity among Vietnamese people and international tourists (Foley 2001). It has spread from its core area in the Red River Delta in the northern part of the country to being nationwide, and from being a seasonal performance to being year-round.

One positive result of global tourism is the growing support for preservation of **material cultural heritage**, which includes sites, monuments, and buildings, and movable objects considered of outstanding value in terms of history, art, and science (Cernea 2001). UNESCO proposed the basic definition of material cultural heritage in 1972. Since then, many locations worldwide have been placed on its World Heritage List for preservation. In the Middle East and North Africa alone, 60 places are on UNESCO's list. Many invaluable sites and other aspects of material cultural heritage are lost to public knowledge through destructive engineering projects, war, looting, and private collecting.

Applied anthropologists are involved in promoting better stewardship of material cultural heritage. Some are motivated by a desire to preserve the record of humanity for future generations, or for science. Others see that material cultural heritage, especially in poorer countries, can serve to promote improvements in human welfare, and they endorse forging a link between material cultural heritage and sustainable development (see the Lessons Applied box on page 364).

In 2003, UNESCO ratified a new policy aimed at protecting **intangible cultural heritage**, or living heritage manifested in oral traditions, languages, performing arts, rituals and festive events, knowledge and practices about nature and the universe, and craft making (http://portal.unesco.org/culture). Support for this policy is based on

A water puppet performance in Hanoi, Vietnam. Water puppet shows are far more popular among international tourists than among the Vietnamese. ■ (Source: © John Elk III/Stock Boston)

Ethnographic Profile

The Gullah of South Carolina

The Gullah culture in South Carolina stretches along the coast, going inland roughly 48 kilometres (National Park Service 2005:10–11). The Gullah are descended from western- and central-Africa slaves. In the early eighteenth century, Charleston, South Carolina, was the location of the largest transatlantic slave market on the coast of British North America (National Park Service 2005:18).

The enslaved people brought with them many forms of knowledge and practice. Rice was a central part of their African heritage and identity. They knew how to plant it in swamps, harvest it, and prepare it. Gullah ancestors in colonial South Carolina were influential in developing *tidal irrigation methods* of rice growing, using irrigation and management of the tides to increase yields compared to yields from rainfall-dependent plantings.

Experts at net fishing, the Gullah made hand-woven nets that are masterpieces of folk art. Their textile arts include a form of quilting, or sewing strips of cloth together into a larger piece. Gullah women combined their African quilting styles with those of Europeans to form new styles and patterns. Many quilts tell a story in their several panels.

Gullah cuisine combines African elements such as rice, yams, peas, okra, hot peppers, peanuts, watermelon, and sesame seeds with European ingredients, and Indian foods such as corn, squash, tomatoes, and berries (National Park Service 2005:62). Popular dishes are stews of seafood and vegetables served over rice. Rice is the cornerstone of the meal, and the family rice pot is a treasured possession passed down over the generations.

Gullah culture in South Carolina has become a major tourist attraction, including music, crafts, and cuisine. If there is a single item that tourists identify with the Gullah, it is sweetgrass baskets. Although basket-making was once common among all Gullah people in South Carolina, it is thriving in the Charleston area largely due to a combination of tourist demand and the creativity of local artists. Both men and women "sew" the baskets. They sell them in shops in Charleston's historic centre and along nearby Highway 17.

As the success of the basket-makers has grown and the popularity of the baskets has increased, so too has the need for sweetgrass. Sweetgrass baskets, thus, are a focal point of conflict between Gullah cultural producers and local economic developers who are destroying the land on which the sweetgrass grows. Since tourism in low country South Carolina is increasingly dependent on cultural tourism, some planners are trying to find ways to devote land to growing sweetgrass.

The story of the Gullah of South Carolina begins with their rich African cultural heritage, through their suffering as slaves, to racism and social exclusion, and to their current situation in which their expressive culture is a key factor in the state economy.

Readings

Josephine Beoku-Betts. "We Got Our Way of Cooking Things." *Gender and Society*, 9, 535–555, 1995.

Virginia M. Geraty, *Gullah fuh Oonum: A Gullah English Dictionary.* Orangeburg, SC: Sandlapper Publishing, 1997.

National Park Service. *Low Country Gullah Culture: Special Resource Study and Final Environmental Impact Statement.* Atlanta: NPS Southeast Regional Office, 2005. www.nps.gov.

Dale Rosengarten. *Row upon Row: Sea Grass Baskets of the South Carolina Lowcountry.* Columbia, SC: University of South Carolina Press, 1994.

Drummers at the Gullah Festival in Beaufort (pronounced BYOO-FORT) (left). The Festival celebrates the cultures and accomplishments of the Gullah people. ■ (Source: © Bob Krist/CORBIS) *The hands of Mary Jackson (right) are shown making a sweetgrass basket.* ■ (Source: © Karen Kasmauski/CORBIS)

MAP 13.3 *The Gullah Region of South Carolina. The heartland of Gullah culture is in the low country area of South Carolina, Georgia, and Florida, and on the Sea Islands.*

the understanding that intangible culture provides people with a sense of identity and continuity, promotes respect for cultural diversity and human creativity, is compatible with human-rights promotion, and supports sustainable development. Through this initiative, member countries of the United Nations are to make lists of valuable forms of intangible culture and take steps to preserve them. This policy has stimulated discussion and debate among cultural anthropologists who see culture as more than a list of traits, highly contextualized, always changing, and not amenable to being managed or preserved through policy mandates (Handler 2003).

The preservation of indigenous forms of expressive culture can also occur as a form of resistance to outside development forces. One example of this phenomenon is the resurgence of the hula, or Hawaiian dance (Stillman 1996). Beginning in the early 1970s, the "Hawaiian Renaissance" grew out of political protest, mainly against U.S. colonialism. Hawaiian youth began speaking out against encroaching development from the outside that was displacing the indigenous people from their land and destroying their resources. They promoted a concerted effort to revive the Hawaiian language, the hula, and canoe paddling, among other things. Since then, hula schools have proliferated, and hula competitions among the islands are widely attended by local people and international tourists. The 1990s saw the inauguration of the International Hula Festival in Honolulu, which has attracted competitors from around the world. The hula competitions have helped ensure the continued survival of this ancient art form, although some Hawaiians have voiced concerns: First, they feel that allowing non-Hawaiians to compete is compromising the quality of the dancing. Second, the format of the competition violates traditional rules of style and presentation, which require more time than is allowed, so important dances have to be cut. Third, for Hawaiians, hula has close ties to religious beliefs and stories about the deities (Silva 2004). Performing hula in a mainly secular format is offensive to the gods and violates the true Hawaiian way.

Another approach to cultural heritage preservation that is not top-down is "people-first" cultural heritage projects (Miller 2005). These are projects designed by the people whose culture is to be preserved, designed for their benefit, and managed by them. A growing number of examples worldwide demonstrate the value of *people-first cultural heritage preservation* as having strong, positive, measurable effects. One major area of impact is on the very survival of a culture through territorial entitlements, community security, poverty reduction, improved mental health, and educating youth in traditional knowledge. Other important domains where people-first cultural heritage preservation has demonstrable positive effects include minority rights, conflict prevention and resolution, and environmental conservation and sustainability.

An example of people-first heritage preservation with implications for territorial entitlements and cultural survival is the Waanyi Women's History Project, Northern Queensland, Australia (Smith, Morgan, and van der Veer 2003) (see Map 4.3 on page 107). This is a case of a community-driven project devoted to archiving cultural heritage and to establishing local community management. The "community" is a group of Waanyi women who value their family history as heritage. The traditional way of maintaining this heritage has been to pass it on verbally from mother to daughter. The women were interested in having a written record of their history and wanted to record sites and places of significance to women. They hired an anthropologist consultant to collect and record their narratives. An interesting feature of this case, which contrasts with traditional academic research, is that the knowledge generated cannot be published. The role of the researcher is limited to supporting the aspirations of the Waanyi women.

The project had positive effects in providing a new source of income and, thus, reducing material deprivation and entitlement insecurity through the formal recognition of Waanyi custodial rights and the establishment of a National Park. It generated new sources of cash income for some Waanyi women through employment in the National Park as "cultural rangers" responsible for conservation of women's sites. This project is a clear case of a community-initiated and community-controlled heritage project. It involved concern for, and recognition of, community interests and goals. It produced benefits to the local people in terms of firmer entitlement to the land, new sources of income, skill acquisition, and pride.

Post-Communist Transitions

Major changes have occurred in the arts in states of the former USSR-led Eastern Bloc for two reasons: loss of state financial support and removal of state controls over subject matter and creativity. A generation of talented young artists has appeared in the last 15 or 20 years (Akinsha 1992c:109). They are looking for something new and different. Art for art's sake, independent from the socialist project, is possible in the post-communist era. Many of the newer artists find inspiration in and nostalgia for popular culture items of the 1950s and 1960s, such as a pack of Yugoslav chewing gum, or the cover of a once-taboo Western magazine. Commercial galleries have been springing up everywhere, and a museum of modern art in Moscow opened in 1999.

Theatre in China is passing through a transition period with the recent development of some features of capitalism. Since the beginning of the People's Republic in 1949, the arts have gone through different phases, from being suppressed as part of the old feudal tradition to being revived under state control. In the mid-1990s, nearly all

A STRATEGY FOR THE WORLD BANK ON CULTURAL HERITAGE

With headquarters in Washington, D.C., and offices throughout the world, the World Bank is an international organization funded by member nations that works to promote and finance economic development in poor countries. Even though most of its permanent professional staffers are economists, the World Bank has begun to pay more attention to noneconomic factors that affect development projects. One of the major moves in that direction occurred in 1972, when the Bank hired its first anthropologist, Michael Cernea. For more than three decades, Cernea has drawn attention to the cultural dimensions of development, especially in terms of the importance of local participation in development projects and people-centred approaches to project-forced resettlement (when, for example, large dams are being planned). His most recent campaign has been to convince top officials at the Bank that the institution should become involved in supporting cultural heritage projects as potential pathways to development.

The World Bank already has in place a "do no harm" rule when it approves and financially supports construction projects. Cernea agrees that a "do no harm" rule is basic to preventing outright destruction, but it is a passive rule and does nothing to provide resources to preserve sites. He wants the Bank to move beyond its "do no harm" rule and has written a strategy for it that is active, not passive. The strategy has two major objectives:

- The World Bank should support cultural heritage projects that promote poverty reduction and cultural heritage preservation by creating employment and generating capital from tourism.
- The projects should emphasize the educational value to local people and international visitors on the grounds that cultural understanding promotes value for goodwill and relations at all levels—local, state, and international.

Cernea also offers two suggestions for better management of cultural heritage projects: (1) selectivity in site selection on the basis of the impact in reducing poverty and (2) building partnerships for project planning and implementation among local, national, and international institutions.

FOOD FOR THOUGHT

- Find on the Internet the UNESCO World Heritage Site that most interests you. What does the site contain, and what can you learn about its possible or potential role in generating income for the local people?

---

of China's theatre companies were in financial crisis (Jiang 1994:72). Steep inflation means that actors can no longer live on their pay. Theatre companies are urging their workers to find jobs elsewhere, such as making movies or videos, but this is not an option for provincial troupes. Local audience preferences have changed: "People are fed up with shows that 'educate,' have too strong a political flavor, or convey 'artistic values.' They no longer seem to enjoy love stories, old Chinese legends, or Euro-American theater. Most of the young people prefer nightclubs, discos, or karaokes. Others stay at home watching TV" (1994:73). The new materialism in China means that young people want to spend their leisure time having fun. For the theatre, too, money now comes first. One trend is toward the production of Western plays.

For example, acclaimed British playwright Harold Pinter's *The Lover* was an immediate success when it was performed in Shanghai in 1992. In explaining its success, observers said that sex was a big part of the reason. The topic of sex was taboo in China for a long time and censored in theatre and films. The producers of the play warned parents not to bring children with them, fuelling speculation about a possible sex scene. Although *The Lover* contains only hints of sexuality, it was bold by Chinese standards. The female lead's alluring dress had seldom, if ever, been seen by Chinese theatregoers in the early 1990s. There was also bold language—talk about female breasts, for example. Another feature was the play's focus on private life, interiority, and individual thoughts and feelings. This emphasis corresponds with a new emphasis on, and cultivation of, private lives in China. Change in the performing arts in China, thus, is being shaped both by changes in the local political economy and by globalization.

Key Questions Revisited

HOW is culture expressed through art?

Cultural anthropologists choose a broad definition of art that takes into account cross-cultural variations. In the anthropological perspective, all cultures have some form of art and a concept of what is good art. Ethnographers document the ways in which art is related to many aspects of culture: economics, politics, human development and psychology, healing, social control, and entertainment. Art may serve to reinforce social patterns, and it may also be a vehicle of protest and resistance.

In state societies, especially in Europe, people began collecting art worldwide and placing it in museums a few hundred years ago. Later, ethnographic museums were established in Europe as the result of scientific and colonialist interest in learning about other cultures. Anthropologists study museum displays as a reflection of cultural values as well as sites where perceptions and values are formed. Many indigenous and formerly colonized people are reclaiming objects from museums as part of their cultural heritage.

WHAT do play and leisure activities reveal about culture?

Anthropological studies of play and leisure examine such activities within their cultural context. Cultural anthropologists view games as cultural microcosms, both reflecting and reinforcing dominant social values. Sports and leisure activities, although engaged in for nonutilitarian purposes, are often tied to economic and political interests. In some contexts, sports are related to religion and spirituality.

Tourism is a fast-growing part of the world economy with vast implications for culture. Anthropologists who study tourism examine the impact of tourism on local cultures and questions of authenticity in the tourist's experience. Tourism companies often market "other" cultures to appeal to the consumers, a phenomenon that perpetuates stereotypes and denigrates the "host" culture. Cultural anthropologists are working with the tourism industry to find better ways of representing culture that are more accurate, less stigmatizing to the host culture, and more informative for tourists.

HOW is expressive culture changing in contemporary times?

Major forces of change in expressive culture include Western colonialism, contemporary tourism, and globalization in general. As with other kinds of cultural change through contact, expressive culture may reject, adopt, and adapt new elements. Syncretism is a frequent occurrence, as exemplified in the Trobriand Islanders' co-optation and re-creation of cricket as a performative event leading up to a traditional feast.

In some cases, outside forces have led to the extinction of local forms of expressive culture. In others, outside forces have promoted continuity or the recovery of practices that had been lost. Resistance to colonialism and neo-colonialism has inspired cultural revitalization, as in the Hawaiian Renaissance. Post-communist states, in the past two decades, have reacted to freedom of expression and the privatization of art in various ways. Artists find new subject matter and audiences have more options.

KEY CONCEPTS

art, p. 344
blood sport, p. 358
ethno-aesthetics, p. 345
ethnomusicology, p. 349
expressive culture, p. 344

heterotopia, p. 353
intangible cultural heritage,
　　p. 361
material cultural heritage,
　　p. 361

museum, p. 354
repatriation, p. 354
theatre, p. 350
wa, p. 357

SUGGESTED READINGS

Michael Ames, *Cannibal Tours and Glass Boxes: The Anthropology of Museums.* Vancouver: University of British Columbia Press, 1992. Written by the director of the Museum of Anthropology at UBC, this book wrestles with the role of anthropology in creating concepts of Natives, Native art, and the use of museums in these constructions.

G. Whitney Azoy. *Buzkashi: Game and Power in Afghanistan,* 2nd ed. Long Grove, IL: Waveland, 2003. The first full-length ethnography of a sport, this study has been updated with a chapter on buzkashi as played through 2002. This game, which involves tribal groups of men on horseback competing for a goat or calf carcass, is probably ancestral to polo.

Tara Browner. *Heartbeat of the People: Music and Dance of the Northern Pow-Wow.* Urbana, IL: University of Illinois Press, 2002. An ethnomusicologist of Choctaw heritage uses archival research on the powwow and participant observation to show how elements of the powwow in North America have changed.

Shirley F. Campbell. *The Art of Kula.* New York: Berg, 2002. The author focuses on designs painted on kula canoes and finds that kula art and its associated male ideology linked to the sea competes with female ideology and symbolism linked to the earth.

Rebecca Cassidy. *The Sport of Kings: Kinship, Class, and Thoroughbred Breeding in Newmarket.* New York: Cambridge University Press, 2002. This study of British thoroughbred racing is based on fieldwork conducted in Newmarket, England. How people discuss the horses, their breeding, and their capabilities relate to the British class system.

Michael M. Cernea. *Cultural Heritage and Development: A Framework for Action in the Middle East and North Africa.* Washington, DC: The World Bank, 2001. Following an overview of cultural heritage projects and possibilities in the Middle East and North Africa, Cernea presents a strategy to reduce poverty with high-impact cultural heritage projects.

Michael Chibnik. *Carving Tradition: The Making and Marketing of Oaxcan Wood Carvings.* Austin: University of Texas Press, 2003. Chibnik examines the production of and international trade in Oaxacan wood carvings. Wood carving is not an indigenous art form in Oaxaca but was developed to appeal to tourists.

Timothy J. Cooley. *Making Music in the Polish Tatras: Tourists, Ethnographers, and Mountain Musicians.* CD included.

Bloomington, IN: Indiana University Press, 2005. This ethnographic study describes the musicians and music of the Tatra Mountains of southern Poland.

Robert Davis and Garry R. Marvin. *Venice: The Tourist Maze: A Cultural Critique of the World's Most Touristed City.* Berkeley, CA: University of California Press, 2004. The authors include material on the beginnings of Venetian tourism in the late Middle Ages to its current form of mass entertainment through which Venetian residents are a minority in their hometown.

Noel Dyck and Eduardo Archetti, eds. *Sport, Dance, and Embodied Identities.* Oxford: Berg Press, 2003. This edited volume provides ethnographic examples of how social life is reshaped through sport and dance.

Patricia Fogelman Lange. *Pueblo Pottery Figurines: The Expression of Cultural Perceptions in Clay.* Tucson, AZ: University of Arizona Press, 2002. This book offers insights into Pueblo aesthetics by focusing on the figurines made in the late nineteenth century. Their style departed from earlier ones as the artists responded to the presence of Anglo-Americans.

Alaina Lemon. *Between Two Fires: Gypsy Performance and Romani Memory from Pushkin to Post-Socialism.* Durham, NC: Duke University press, 2000. This book examines how theatre in Moscow both liberates Roma in Russia and reinforces their status as stigmatized outsiders.

Beverly B. Mack. *Muslim Women Sing: Hausa Popular Song.* CD included. Bloomington, IN: Indiana University Press, 2004. This ethnography provides an intimate portrait of the life and art of Hausa women singers in northern Nigeria. It shows how Hausa women exercise agency and creativity through music and dance.

Jay R. Mandle and Joan D. Mandle. *Caribbean Hoops: The Development of West Indian Basketball.* Amsterdam: Gordon and Breach Publishers, 1994. In this book, the Mandles describe and analyze the emergence of basketball (mainly men's basketball) as a popular sport in several Caribbean nations. They explore regional differences within the Caribbean.

Kathy M'Closkey. *Swept under the Rug: A Hidden History of Navajo Weaving.* Albuquerque, NM: University of New Mexico, 2002. Based on archival sources and fieldwork with Navajo weavers, this rich historical ethnography explores the complex cultural history of Navajo weaving, with

particular attention to the exploitative relation between traders and weavers.

Louise Meintjes. *Sound of Africa! Making Music Zulu in a South African Studio*. Durham, NC: Duke University Press, 2003. A South African anthropologist reveals the connections among music, culture, and state building. Focused on one studio in Johannesburg, this ethnography describes the roles of artists, sound engineers, emcees, and producers.

Laura Miller. *Beauty Up: Selling and Consuming Body Aesthetics in Japan*. Berkeley, CA: University of California Press, 2006. The author, a linguistic anthropologist, examines the diversity of Japanese personal beauty practices for both males and females. She links eyelid surgery, body-hair removal, and beauty products to a wider context of aesthetics.

Timothy Mitchell. *Blood Sport: A Social History of Spanish Bullfighting*. Philadelphia: University of Pennsylvania Press, 1991. Based on fieldwork and archival study, this book views bullfighting within the context of annual Spanish village and national fiestas, considers the role of the matador in society, and offers a psychosexual interpretation of the bullfight.

Stacy B. Schaefer. *To Think with a Good Heart: Wixárike Women, Weavers, and Shamans*. Salt Lake City: University of Utah Press, 2002. Weaving woollen textiles is a woman-centred activity among the Wixárike of western Mexico. Women generate income from weaving, and master weavers gain status.

R. Anderson Sutton. *Calling Back the Spirit: Music, Dance and Cultural Politics in Lowland South Sulawesi*. New York: Oxford University Press, 2002. The author describes many performance modes in South Sulawesi, Indonesia, from village ceremonies to studio-produced popular music. Accompanying the book is a CD.

PART V Contemporary Cultural Change

14 People on the Move

15 People Defining Development

MAMPHELA RAMPHELE'S life story moves from her being subjected to racial apartheid and gender discrimination as a girl born in 1947 in rural Northern Transvaal, South Africa, to professional and personal achievement as a political activist, medical doctor, anthropologist, teacher, university administrator, mother, and (currently) one of the four managing directors of the World Bank.

As a child, Ramphele saw the injustices of apartheid inflicted on her family when the government retaliated against her relatives who worked for social equality. This experience spurred her on to political activism while she was still pursuing her education. Speaking of her school years, Ramphele says she felt confidence in her intelligence but had a difficult time overcoming the sense of inferiority that apartheid instilled in black people.

In the early 1970s, Ramphele completed her medical studies at the University of Natal. She became a founder of South Africa's Black Consciousness movement to abolish segregation and injustice at a time when the nation's white government was engaged in some of the most brutally repressive activities in its history.

Anthropologists at Work

The consequence of her activism was federal censure under the Terrorism Act. Exiled for six years to Northern Transvaal, Ramphele worked with the rural poor, setting up community health programs. In the 1980s, she became a research fellow with the South African Development Research Unit at the University of Cape Town and earned a doctorate in anthropology. Her dissertation, *A Bed Called Home: Life in the Migrant Labour Hostels of Cape Town*, was later published as a book.

Ramphele also earned a B.Com. degree in administration and diplomas in tropical health and hygiene and public health. She served as senior research officer in the University of Cape Town's Department of Social Anthropology and, in 1996, became the first black person and the first woman to be elected as vice-chancellor of the University of Cape Town.

Since 2000, Ramphele has been with the World Bank, the first South African to become a managing director for the institution. In her position, she oversees the Bank's human-development activities in education; health, nutrition, and population; and social protection. She also monitors and guides the Bank's relationships with client governments in strengthening socioeconomic support programs. In this capacity, she has worked to reduce child mortality, eradicate polio, and reduce the prevalence of HIV/AIDS, tuberculosis, and malaria.

Describing her work as "advocating with all my passion," Ramphele consults globally with several human-rights initiatives. She was also an advisor to Nelson Mandela's government. Ramphele has received many awards and honours and has published books and articles on education, health, and social development.

In 2001, the South African Women for Women organization awarded Ramphele a Woman of Distinction Award that recognizes her "energetic leadership, her commitment to excellence, and her continuing dedication to transforming the lives of those around her."

14
People on the Move

Key Questions

- WHAT are the major categories of migration?

- WHO are examples of the new immigrants in Canada and the United States?

- HOW do anthropologists contribute to migration policies and programs?

The so-called Marsh Arab people, under the rule of Saddam Hussein, suffered from government projects that drained their region as well as from political repression. Many who fled the country as refugees are now returning. *(Source: © Nik Wheeler/CORBIS)*

The current generation of North American youths will experience more moves during their lives than previous generations. University graduates are likely to change jobs an average of eight times during their careers, and these changes may require relocation.

Ecological, economic, familial, and political factors are causing population movements at seemingly all-time high levels. Research in anthropology has shown, however, that frequent moves during a person's life and mass movements of peoples are nothing new; they have occurred throughout human evolution. Foragers and pastoralists relocate frequently as a normal part of their lives.

Migration is the movement of a person or people from one place to another (Kearney 1986:331). It is related to other aspects of life such as job and family status, and it may also affect mental health and social relationships. Thus, many academic subjects and professions are relevant here. Historians, economists, political scientists, sociologists, and scholars of religion, literature, art, and music have studied migration. Migration is one of three core areas of demography, along with fertility and mortality. The professions of law, medicine, education, business, architecture, urban planning, public administration, and social work have specialties that focus on the process of migration and the period of adaptation following a move. Experts working in these areas share with anthropologists an interest in such issues as people who migrate, causes of migration, processes of migration, psychosocial adaptations to new locations, and implications for planning and policy.

Cultural anthropologists have addressed a wide range of issues surrounding migration. They have studied how migration is related to economic and reproductive systems, health and human development over the life cycle, marriage and household formation, politics and social order, and religion and expressive culture. There is no domain of human life that is not affected by migration; hence, this topic pulls together much of the earlier material in this book. Given the breadth of migration studies, cultural anthropologists have used the full range of methods available, from individual life histories to large-scale surveys. Three differences distinguish migration studies in cultural anthropology:

■ Anthropologists studying migration are more likely to have fieldwork experience in more than one location in order to understand the places of origin and destination.

Chinese Canadians mainly live in urban areas such as Vancouver and Toronto. In Vancouver, they constitute about 16 percent of the population. Vancouver's Chinatown is a vibrant tourist site as well as a place where Chinese Canadians reaffirm their cultural heritage, as in the celebration shown here of Chinese New Year. ■ (Source: © Annie Griffiths Belt/CORBIS)

Maxine Margolis (1994), for example, first did fieldwork in Brazil, and then later studied Brazilian immigrants in New York City.

■ Studying migration has challenged traditional cultural anthropology's focus on one village or neighbourhood and created the need to take into account national and global economic, political, and social forces (Basch, Glick Schiller, and Szanton Blanc 1994; Lamphere 1992).

---

migration: the movement of a person or people from one place to another.
internal migration: population movement within state boundaries.
transnational migration: a form of population movement in which a person

regularly moves between two or more countries and forms a new cultural identity transcending a single geopolitical unit.
push-pull theory: an explanation for rural-to-urban migration that emphasizes

people's incentives to move based on a lack of opportunity in rural areas (the "push") compared to urban areas (the "pull").

- Anthropologists who do research on migrants tend to be involved in assisting them, often in resettlement work. Doreen Indra became the director of a large agency for Southeast Asian refugees because of her interest in refugee resettlement; as a professor of anthropology at the University of Lethbridge, she also published extensively on refugee research (Indra 1988).

In this chapter, we first present information on the most important categories of migrants and the opportunities and challenges they face. In the second section, we provide descriptions of several examples of immigrants to Canada and the United States. In the last section, we consider urgent issues related to migration, such as human rights and risk assessment and prevention programs.

Categories of Migration

Migration encompasses many categories depending on the distance of the move, its purpose, duration, degree of voluntarism (was the move forced or more a matter of choice?), and the migrant's status in the new destination. Major differences exist in both causes and consequences between **internal migration**, movement within state boundaries, and *international migration,* moving to a different country. Moving to a new country, in general, involves more challenges in the process of relocation and in adjustment after arrival.

Categories Based on Spatial Boundaries

In this section, we review the basic features of three categories of population movement defined in terms of the spatial boundaries crossed: internal migration, international migration, and the new category of transnational migration. **Transnational migration** is a form of population movement in which a person regularly moves back and forth between two or more countries and forms a new cultural identity transcending a single geopolitical unit

Internal Migration

Rural-to-urban migration was the dominant stream of internal population in most countries during the twentieth century. A major reason for people migrating to urban areas is the availability of work. According to the **push–pull theory** of labour migration, rural areas are increasingly unable to support population growth and

rising expectations about the quality of life (*the push factor*). Cities (*the pull factor*) attract people, especially youth, for employment and lifestyle reasons. The push–pull model makes urban migration sound like a simple function of the rational decision-making of freely choosing human agents who have information on the costs and the benefits of rural versus urban life, weigh that information, and then opt for going or staying (recall the approach to understanding culture that emphasizes human agency, which we described in Chapter 1). But many instances of urban migration are more the result of structural forces (economic need or political factors such as war) that are beyond the control of the individual (see the Critical Thinking box on page 374).

The anonymity and rapid pace of city life and the likelihood of various degrees of stress caused by relocation pose special challenges for migrants from rural areas. Urban life, for example, increases the risk of hypertension (elevated blood pressure through stress or tension), which is related to coronary heart disease. In the Philippines, hypertension is more common among urban migrants, both men and women, than among people living in their rural places of origin (Hackenberg et al. 1983). The relationship between elevated health risks resulting from psychosocial adjustment problems in rural-to-urban migration exists among international immigrants as well—for example, among Samoans who migrate to cities in California (Janes 1990).

International Migration

International migration has grown in volume and significance since 1945 and especially since the mid-1980s (Castles and Miller 1993). It is estimated that nearly 2 percent of the world's population lives outside of their home countries, or around 100 million people, including legal and undocumented immigrants. Migrants who move for work-related reasons constitute the majority of people in this category. Over 35 million people from developing countries have migrated to the industrialized countries in the past three decades. The driving forces behind this trend are economic and political changes that affect labour demands and human welfare.

The major destination countries of early international immigration are Canada, the United States, Australia, New Zealand, and Argentina. The immigration policies of these nations in the early twentieth century have been labelled "white immigration" because they explicitly limited non-white immigration (Ongley 1995). In the 1960s in Canada, for instance, changes made immigration policies less racially discriminatory and more focused on skills and experience. Through the 1980s, further liberalization occurred and family reunification provisions were widened. In Canada,

Critical Thinking

HAITIAN CANE CUTTERS IN THE DOMINICAN REPUBLIC: A CASE OF STRUCTURE OR HUMAN AGENCY?

The circulation of male labour from villages in Haiti to work on sugar estates in the neighbouring Dominican Republic is the oldest and perhaps largest continuing population movement within the Caribbean region (Martínez 1996). Beginning in the early twentieth century, Dominican sugar cane growers began to recruit Haitian workers called *braceros*. Between 1952 and 1986, an agreement between the two countries' governments regulated and organized the labour recruitment. Since then, recruitment has become a private matter, with men crossing the border on their own or with recruiters working in Haiti without official approval. Many studies and reports have addressed this system of labour migration. Two competing perspectives exist:

- View 1, the structural position, says that the bracero system is neoslavery and a clear violation of human rights.
- View 2, the human agency position, says that braceros are not slaves because they migrate voluntarily.

View 1

Supporters of this position point to interviews with Haitian braceros in the Dominican Republic that indicate, they say, a consistent pattern of labour-rights abuses. Haitian recruiters approach poor men, and boys as young as 7 years old, and promise them easy, well-paid employment in the Dominican Republic. Those who agree to go are taken to the frontier on foot and then either transported directly to a sugar estate in the Dominican Republic or turned over to Dominican soldiers for a fee for each recruit and then passed on to the sugar estate. Once there, the workers are given only one option for survival: cutting sugar cane, for which even the most experienced workers can earn only about US$2 a day. Working and living conditions on the estates are bad. The cane cutters are coerced into working even if they are ill; as well, working hours start before dawn and extend into the night. Estate owners frequently prevent Haitian labourers from leaving by having armed guards patrol the estate grounds at night. Many of the workers say that they cannot save enough from their meagre wages to return home.

View 2

According to this view, reports of coercion are greatly exaggerated and miss the point that most Haitian labour migrants cross the border of their own volition. On the basis of his fieldwork in Haiti, cultural anthropologist Samuel Martínez comments that "recruitment by force in Haiti seems virtually unheard of. On the contrary, if this is a system of slavery, it may be the first in history to turn away potential recruits" (1996:20). Some recruits have even paid bribes to recruiters in order to be hired. Most people, even young people, are aware of the terrible working conditions in the Dominican Republic, so they are exercising informed choice when they decide to

---

a combination of changing labour needs and interest in improving its international image prompted these reforms. During the 1980s, increased refugee flows inspired greater attention to humanitarian concerns.

Long-time areas of outmigration of northern, western, and southern Europe are now receiving many immigrants, often refugees from Asia. Hungary, Poland, and the Czech Republic are now popular destinations for many migrants. International population flows in the Middle East are complex, with some countries, such as Turkey, experiencing substantial movements in both directions. Millions of Turkish people have immigrated to Germany in recent decades. Turkey, in turn, has received many Iraqi and Iranian Kurdish refugees. Several million Palestinian refugees live in Jordan and Lebanon. Israel has attracted Jewish immigrants from Europe, northern Africa, the United States, and Russia.

Transnational Migration

Transnational migration is increasing along with other aspects of globalization. It is important to recall, however, that rising rates of transnational migration are related to the creation of state boundaries in recent centuries. Pastoralists with extensive seasonal herding routes were "transnational" migrants long before state boundaries cut across their pathways.

Much contemporary transnational migration is motivated by economic factors. The spread of the global

---

A Haitian migrant labourer. It is a matter of debate how much choice such a labourer has in terms of whether he will migrate to the neighbouring Dominican Republic for short-term work, cutting cane, given the fact that he cannot find paid work in Haiti. ■ (Source: Edward Keller III)

migrate. Repeat migration is common and is further evidence of free choice. The major means of maintaining labour discipline and productivity on the sugar estates is not force but wage incentives, especially piecework. The life histories of braceros show that many of them move from one estate to another, thus discrediting the view that the estates are "concentration camps."

Martínez does, however, raise the issue of how free the "choice" to migrate to the Dominican Republic really is, given the extreme poverty in which many Haitians live. In Haiti, few work opportunities exist, and the prevailing wage for rural workers is US$1 a day. Thus, the poor are not truly free to choose to work in their home country: Labour migration to the Dominican Republic becomes a necessity. What looks like a free choice to participate in the bracero system is actually "illusory" or structured choice. It is based on the unavailability of the option to work for a decent wage in Haiti and on the forced, or structured, choice to work in the Dominican Republic.

CRITICAL THINKING QUESTIONS

- What are the comparative strengths of View 1 and View 2?
- What does each perspective support in terms of policy recommendations?
- How does the concept of structured choice change those policy recommendations?

corporate economy is the basis for the growth of one category of transnational migrants nicknamed "astronauts," business people who spend most of their time flying among different cities as investment bankers or corporate executives. At the lower end of the income scale are transnational migrant labourers who spend substantial amounts of time working in different places and whose movements depend on the demand for their labour.

An important feature of transnational migration is how it affects the migrant's identity and sense of citizenship. Constant movement among different places weakens the sense of having one home and promotes instead a sense of belonging to a diffused community of similar transnational migrants whose lives "in between" locations take on a new transnational cultural reality.

As a response to the increased rate of transnational migration, many of the "sending" countries (those that are the source of emigrants) are making explicit efforts to redefine themselves as transnational nations (Glick Schiller and Fouron 1999). These countries that have high proportions of emigrants include Haiti, Colombia, Mexico, Brazil, the Dominican Republic, Portugal, Greece, and the Philippines. They confer continuing citizenship on emigrants and their descendants in order to foster a sense of belonging and willingness to continue to provide financial support in the form of

Turkish people migrated to Germany in substantial numbers in the 1960s and 1970s as "guest workers" to fill jobs in German factories. German leaders expected them to work, save money, and return to Turkey. Most stayed, and their children are now growing up in Germany, speaking German and having only a distant relationship with Turkey. Many incidents of violence between so-called neo-Nazis and Turkish people have occurred, including the murder of five youths of Turkish ehtnicity in Solingen in 1993. ■ (Source: © David Turnley/CORBIS)

remittances, or economic transfers of money or goods from migrants to their family back home. Remittances are an increasingly large, though difficult to quantify, proportion of the global economy and often a large part of a country's economy. For example, at least 60 percent of the gross domestic product (GDP) of the small Pacific island country of Tonga comes from remittances from members of the Tongan diaspora (Lee 2003:32) (see Map 14.1).

A debate that crosses the social sciences is about the effects of remittances on the welfare of the people and the development of the countries to which they are sent (Binford 2003). The major issue is whether remittances go into long-term investments that raise people's quality of life or are used for short-term consumption purposes. The term *investment* can absorb substantial scholarly thinking in terms of how to define it. Is taking a child to a clinic for a vaccination a short-term expenditure or an investment? Semantic quibbles aside, most experts agree that remittances are important in helping families maintain their health and welfare and in promoting local development through donations to build schools, roads, and clinics.

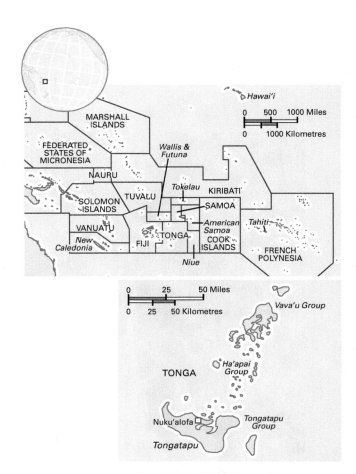

MAP 14.1　Tonga. The Kingdom of Tonga is an archipelago of 169 islands, nicknamed by Captain James Cook as the Friendly Islands on the basis of his reception there. A constitutional monarchy, Tonga has great reverence for its king, stemming from a tradition of the sacred paramount chief. The current king, Taufa'ahau Tupou V, recently replaced his father Taufa'ahau Tupou IV, who reigned from 1965 to 2006. The monarch before him, Queen Salote Tupou II, reigned from 1918 to 1965. Rural Tongans are small-scale farmers. The manufacturing sector is minor while remittances are a major part of the economy. The population is around 113 000, with two-thirds living on the main island, Tongatapu. Many Tongans have emigrated. Most citizens are ethnically Polynesian, and Christianity is by far the dominant religion. Languages are Tongan and English.

---

remittance: transfer of money or goods by a migrant to his or her family back home.
wage labour migration: the movement of people who work for a specific period of time in a location where they have no intent of establishing a permanent residence, or may perhaps even be barred from doing so.
circular migration: a regular pattern of population movement between two or more places, either within or between countries.

displaced person: someone who is forced to leave his or her home and community or country.
refugee: someone who is forced to leave his or her home, community, or country.

Categories Based on Reason for Moving

In this section, we review categories of migrants based on the reason for relocating. The spatial categories just discussed overlap with these categories. An international migrant, for example, may also be a person who moved for employment reasons. Migrants experience different kinds of spatial change and, at the same time, have various reasons for moving.

Labour Migrants

Thousands of people migrate to work for a specific period of time. They do not intend to establish permanent residence and are often explicitly barred from doing so. This form of migration, when legally contracted, is called **wage labour migration**. The period of work may be brief or it may last several years, as among rural Egyptian men who go to other Middle Eastern countries to work for an average period of four years (Brink 1991).

Tourists define Hakka women of rural southern China by their "lamp shade" hats. Here, a Hakka woman who has migrated to Hong Kong for work wears a traditional Hakka woman's hat as she pursues an urban lifestyle.
■ (Source: Hans Blossey/Das Fotoarchiv/Peter Arnold)

Asian women are the fastest-growing category among the world's 35 million migrant workers (International Labour Office 1996:16–17). About 1.5 million Asian women are working outside of their home countries; most are in domestic service jobs, and some work as nurses and teachers. Major sending countries are Indonesia, the Philippines, Sri Lanka, and Thailand. Main receiving countries are Saudi Arabia and Kuwait, and to a lesser degree, Hong Kong, Japan, Taiwan, Singapore, Malaysia, and Brunei. Such women are usually alone and are not allowed to marry or have a child in the country where they are temporary workers. International migrant workers are sometimes illegally recruited and thus have no protection in their working conditions.

Circular migration is a regular pattern of population movement between two or more places. It may occur within or between countries. Internal circular migrants include, for example, female domestic workers throughout Latin America and the Caribbean. These women have their permanent residence in the rural areas, but they work for long periods of time in the city for better-off people. They may leave their children in the care of grandparents in the country, sending remittances for the children's support.

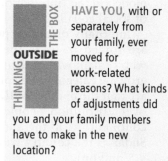

THINKING OUTSIDE THE BOX

HAVE YOU, with or separately from your family, ever moved for work-related reasons? What kinds of adjustments did you and your family members have to make in the new location?

Displaced Persons

Displaced persons are people who are evicted from their homes, communities, or countries and forced to move elsewhere (Guggenheim and Cernea 1993). Colonialism, slavery, war, persecution, natural disasters, and large-scale mining and dam building are major causes of population displacement.

Refugees are internationally displaced persons. Many refugees are forced to relocate because they are victims or potential victims of persecution on the basis of their race, religion, nationality, ethnicity, gender, or political views (Camino and Krulfeld 1994). Refugees constitute a large and growing category of displaced persons. An accurate count of all categories of refugees globally is unavailable, but it probably exceeds 10 million people. About 1 of every 500 people is a refugee (Lubkemann 2002). A quarter of the world's refugees are Palestinians.

Women and children make up the bulk of refugees and are vulnerable to abuse in refugee camps, including rape and children trading sex for food (Martin 2005). Some case studies shed some more positive light (Burton 2004). Refugee women from El Salvador, for example, learned to read and write in the camps and found positive role models in the "internationalist" workers and their vision of social equality.

Internally displaced persons (IDPs) are people who are forced to leave their home and community but who remain within their country. They are the fastest-growing category of displaced people. Current estimates are that the number of IDPs is double that of refugees—over 20 million people (Cohen 2002). Africa is the continent with the most IDPs, and within Africa, Sudan is the country with the highest number (around 4.5 million).

Because IDPs do not cross national boundaries, they do not come under the purview of the United Nations or any other international body. These institutions deal with international problems and have limited authority over problems within countries. Dr. Francis Deng, former Sudanese ambassador, has taken up the cause of IDPs and is working to raise international awareness of the immensity of the problem. His efforts led to the formal definition of IDPs and to legal recognition of their status. In his role as UN secretary-general for internally displaced persons, Deng coordinates a global coalition of institutions (including the UN, governments, and nongovernmental organizations) to provide more timely and effective assistance for IDPs. Many IDPs, like refugees, live for extended periods in camps under miserable conditions with no access to basic supports such as health care and schools.

Development projects are often the reason why people become IDPs. Large dam construction, mining, and other projects have displaced millions in the past several decades. Dam construction alone is estimated to have displaced perhaps 80 million people in the past 50 years (Worldwatch Institute 2003). Forced migration due to development projects is termed **development-induced displacement (DID)**.

Mega-dam projects are now attracting the attention of concerned people worldwide who support local resistance to massive relocation. One of the most notorious cases is India's construction of a series of high dams in its Narmada River Valley, which cuts across the middle of the country from the west coast. This massive project involves relocating hundreds of thousands of people—no one has a reliable estimate of the numbers. The relocation is against the residents' wishes, and government compensation to the "oustees" for the loss of the homes, land, and livelihood is completely inadequate. Thousands of people in the Narmada Valley have organized protests over the many years of construction, and international environmental organizations have lent their support. The celebrated Indian novelist, Arundhati Roy, joined the cause by learning everything she could about the 20 years of government planning for the Narmada dam projects, interviewing people who have been relocated, and writing a passionate statement, called *The Cost of Living* (1999), against this massive project. A man now living in a barren resettlement area told how he used to pick fruit in the forest, 48 kinds. In the resettlement area, he and his family have to purchase all their food, and they cannot afford any fruit at all (54–55).

Governments promote mega-dam projects as important to the state's interest. The uncalculated costs, however, are high for the local people who are displaced. The benefits are skewed toward corporate profits, energy for industrial plants, and water for urban consumers who can pay for it.

In China, the Three Gorges Dam project will, when completed, have displaced perhaps 2 million people (McCully 2003). The Chinese government, however, has consulted with cultural anthropologists, notably Michael Cernea of the World Bank, to learn how to lessen the

Dr. Francis Deng (right), who earned a doctor of law degree from Yale University, is the United Nations secretary-general for internally displaced persons and directs a program on displaced persons at the Brookings Institution in Washington, D.C. He has been instrumental in gaining international recognition of the plight of internally displaced persons. ■ (Source: AP/Wide World Photos)

internally displaced person (IDP): someone who is forced to leave his or her home and community but who remains in the same country.

development-induced displacement (DID): forced migration due to development projects, such as dam building.

institutional migrant: a person who moves into a social institution (such as a school or prison), voluntarily or involuntarily.

damage caused to the displaced people by improving the relocation process.

The manner in which displaced persons are relocated affects how well they will adjust to their new lives. Displaced persons, in general, have little choice about when and where they move, and refugees typically have the least choice of all. The Maya people of Guatemala suffered horribly during years of state violence and genocide. Many became refugees, relocating to Mexico, the United States, and some to Canada. Others fit in the category of internally displaced persons (see the Ethnographic Profile on page 380).

Canada became a signatory to the United Nations Convention on Refugees in 1969, some 18 years after it was drawn up. The Immigration Act of 1976 incorporated into law Canada's responsibility toward the humane treatment of refugee claimants. Since that time, thousands of refugees resettle in Canada each year. Some arrive at the border claiming refugee status and are given a hearing to determine whether they meet the criteria as refugee claimants. Some are resettled directly from refugee camps, as UNHCR (United Nations High Commissioner for Refugees)-defined convention refugees or members of a designated class identified on humanitarian grounds. Some are government sponsored; others are sponsored by groups. Privately sponsored refugee resettlement is organized by sponsorship agreements between a consortium of interested groups, often including religious institutions. Both government and private sponsorships offer advantages and disadvantages to the newcomer. Canada's record of upholding its international obligations to refugees was recognized in 1986, when the United Nations awarded the Nansen medal for efforts on behalf of refugees to Canada, an honour that previously had been given only to individuals (Beiser 1999:41).

Cultural anthropologists have done substantial research with refugee populations, especially those related to war and other forms of violence and terror (Camino and Krulfeld 1994; Hirschon 1989; Manz 2004). They have helped discover the key factors that ease or increase relocation stresses. One basic factor is the extent to which the new location resembles or differs from the home place in features such as climate, language, and food (Muecke 1987). Generally, the more different the places of origin and destination are, the greater the adaptational demands and stress. Other key factors are the refugee's ability to get a job commensurate with his or her training and experience, the presence of family members, and whether people in the new location are welcoming or hostile to the refugees.

Institutional Migrants

Institutional migrants are people who move into a social institution, either voluntarily or involuntarily. They include monks and nuns, the elderly, prisoners, and boarding school or university students. In this section, we consider examples of students and soldiers within the category of institutional migrants.

Student adjustment is similar to many other forms of migration, especially in terms of risks for mental stress (see the Multiple Cultural Worlds box on page 387). International students face serious challenges of spatial and cultural relocation. They are at greater risk of adjustment stress than are local students. Many international students report mental health problems, depending on

As construction of the massive Three Gorges Dam project proceeds in China, residents of Wanzhuo, Chongqing, collect the belongings from their homes as the bulldozers arrive.
■ (Source: © Gilles Sabrié/CORBIS)

Ethnographic Profile

The Maya of Guatemala

The term *Maya* refers to a diverse range of indigenous people who share elements of a common culture and speak varieties of the Mayan language. (*Note:* The spelling of the adjective includes a final *n* only when referring to the language.) Most Maya people live in Mexico and Guatemala, with smaller populations in Belize and the western parts of Honduras and El Salvador. Their total population in Mexico and Central America is about 6 million people.

In Guatemala, the Maya live mainly in the western highlands. The Spanish treated the Maya as subservient, exploited their labour, and took their land. Descendants of a formerly rich and powerful civilization, most Maya now live in poverty and lack basic human rights.

The Maya in Guatemala suffered years of genocide during the 36-year civil war. During the war, roughly 200 000 Maya "disappeared" and were brutally murdered by government military forces (Manz 2004:3). Many more were forcibly displaced from their homeland, with around 250 000 Maya today living as IDPs (Fitigu 2005). Thousands left the country as refugees, fleeing to Mexico and the United States.

Beatriz Manz tells a chilling story of one group of K'iche' Maya and their struggle to survive during the war (2004). Manz began her fieldwork in 1973 among the Maya living in the rural areas near the highland town of Santa Cruz del Quiché in the province of El Quiché. The Maya farmed small plots, growing maize and other food items, but found it increasingly difficult to grow enough food for their families. A U.S. Catholic priest came to them with an idea for a new settlement, over the mountains to the east, in Santa María Tzejá. The new location was hard to get to, requiring days of hiking through dense jungle.

Several Maya from the highlands decided to establish a new village. They divided land into equal-size plots so that everyone had enough to support their families. Settlers established a democratic form of community organization. Over time, more settlers came from the highland village. They cleared land for houses, farms, workshops, and a school.

In the late 1970s, their lives were increasingly under surveillance by the Guatemalan military who suspected the village of harbouring insurgents. In the early 1980s, the military began taking village men away. These men were never seen alive again. In 1982, a brutal attack left the village in flames and survivors fleeing into the jungle. Some went to Mexico, where they lived in exile for years, and others migrated as refugees to the United States. The peace accords of 1996 officially ended the bloodshed (2004:211). Many of the villagers returned and began to rebuild.

Readings

Laurel Bossen. *The Redivision of Labor: Women and Economic Choice in Four Guatemalan Communities.* Albany, NY: State University of New York Press, 1984.

Beatriz Manz. *Paradise in Ashes: A Guatemalan Journey of Courage, Terror, and Hope.* Berkeley, CA: University of California Press, 2004.

Rigoberta Menchú. *I, Rigoberta Menchú: An Indian Woman in Guatemala.* Ann Wright, trans. New York: Verso, 1984.

Websites

Amnesty International Annual Report, http://web.amnesty.org/report

NISGUA, Network in Solidarity with the People of Guatemala, www.nisgua.org

Thanks to Beatriz Manz, University of California at Berkeley, for reviewing this material.

Maya women pray in a church 88 kilometres southeast of Guatemala City in 2003 (left). The coffins contain the remains of the victims of a 1982 massacre inside the church. ■ (Source: © Reuters/CORBIS) *Maya women are active in market trade, as shown in this scene (right) at the Chichicastenango market.* ■ (Source: © Tibor Bogár/CORBIS)

MAP 14.2   *Guatemala. Within the Republic of Guatemala, Maya Indians constitute about 40 percent of the country's population of 14.6 million.*

Multiple Cultural Worlds

SCHOOLGIRLS AND STRESS

Ethnographic research conducted among adolescent boarding school children in Ambanja, a town in Madagascar, showed that girls experience more adjustment strains than boys (Sharp 1990). Ambanja is a booming migrant town characterized by rootlessness and anomie. Boarding-school children in this town constitute a vulnerable group because they have left their families and come alone to the school.

Many of the boarding-school girls, between the ages of 13 and 17, have experienced bouts of "spirit possession." Local people say that the prettiest girls are the ones who become possessed. Research data patterns show that possession is correlated with a girl's being unmarried and pregnant. Many of these schoolgirls become the mistresses of older men, who shower them with expensive gifts such as perfume and gold jewellery. Such girls attract the envy of both other girls and schoolboys, who are being passed over in favour of adult men. Thus, the girls have little peer support among their schoolmates. If a girl becomes pregnant, school policy requires that she be expelled. If the baby's father refuses to help her, she faces severe hardship. Her return home will be a great disappointment to her parents.

Within this context, a girl's spirit possession may be understood as an expression of distress. Through the spirits, girls act out their difficult position between country and city and between girlhood and womanhood.

MAP 14.3   Madagascar. The Republic of Madagascar includes the main island of Madagascar and several much smaller islands off its coast. It is the home of 5 percent of the world's plant and animal species, of which 80 percent are unique to Madagascar. The terrain varies from highlands to lowlands, rainforests, and deserts. The economy is reliant on tourism, especially ecotourism, and mining is increasing. The total population is 18 million. DNA analysis reveals that the population is a mixture of Malay and East African heritage. The primary language is Malagasy, which shares about 90 percent of its vocabulary with a language in southern Borneo. Roughly half the people practise traditional religions related to ancestors, and most others are Catholics or Protestants.

FOOD FOR THOUGHT

- Consider the patterns of psychological stress among university and college students and their possible gender dimensions. How do these patterns of stress differ from or resemble the situation described here?

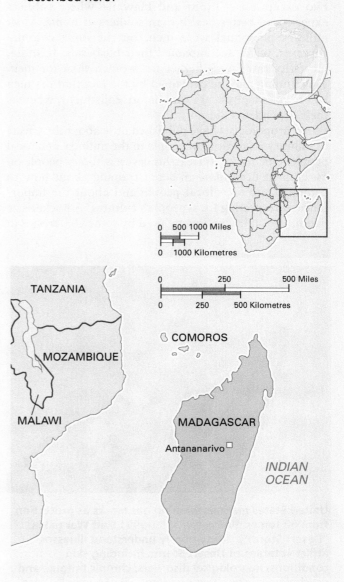

age, marital status, and other factors. Spouses who accompany international students also suffer the strains of dislocation.

Soldiers are often sent on long-distance assignments for lengthy periods of time. Their destination may have negative physical and mental health effects on them, in addition to the fact that they may face combat. During the British and French colonial expansion, thousands of soldiers were assigned to tropical countries (Curtin 1989). Colonial soldiers faced new diseases in their destination areas. Their death rates from disease were twice as high as those of soldiers who stayed home, with two exceptions—Tahiti and Hawaii—where soldiers experienced better health than soldiers at home. Most military personnel were men, but in some colonial contexts, wives accompanied their husbands. In India, mortality rates were higher for women than for men. This finding may be explained by the fact that the men had to pass a physical exam before enlistment, whereas their dependents did not.

Anthropologists have published little about the effects of military migration on people in the military and local people. One matter is clear, however: Military people on assignment need more in-depth training about how to communicate with local people and about the importance of respecting local people's cultures. A pocket-size handbook on Iraqi etiquette used by some U.S. troops in

United States marines wearing gas masks as protection from oil fumes during the 1990–1991 Gulf War (a.k.a. "Desert Storm"). Many poorly understood illnesses afflict veterans of Desert Storm, including skin conditions, neurological disorders, chronic fatigue, and psychological-cognitive problems. ■ (Source: © David Leeson/The Image Works)

Iraq provides extremely basic guidelines (Lorch 2003). It says, for example, that one should avoid arguments and should not take more than three cups of coffee or tea if one is a guest. Also, the "thumbs up" gesture should be avoided since its meaning is obscene, and it's better not to sit with one's feet on a desk. Such basics are helpful, but they do little to provide the cultural understanding that is of critical importance in both conflict and post-conflict situations.

The New Immigrants to Canada and the United States

The term **new immigrant** refers to a person who moved internationally since the 1960s. The category of new immigrants worldwide includes rapidly increasing proportions of refugees, many of whom are destitute and desperate for asylum. Three trends are apparent in the new international migration that began in the 1990s:

- *Globalization:* More countries are involved in international migration, leading to increased cultural diversity in sending and receiving countries.
- *Acceleration:* Growth in numbers of migrants has occurred worldwide.
- *Feminization:* Women are a growing percentage of international migrants to and from all regions and in all types of migration; some forms exhibit a majority of women.

These three trends merit scholarly attention and raise new issues for policy-makers and international organizations as the cultural practices of immigrant groups and the areas of destination increasingly come in contact and, sometimes, in conflict, with each other.

In Canada, the category of "new immigrants" refers to people who arrived following the development of the Immigration Regulations of 1967. These regulations made it possible for far more people from developing countries to enter Canada, especially if they were professionals or trained in some desired skill. Later, the "family reunification" provision allowed permanent residents and naturalized citizens to bring in close family members. Most of the new immigrants to Canada are from Asia, Latin America, and the Caribbean, although increasing numbers are from Eastern Europe, especially Russia.

Canada provides temporary employment visas to allow migrant labourers to work in Canada for up to

new immigrant: international migrant who has moved since the 1960s.

Every year, the Taste of the Danforth celebrates Greek culture and cuisine in multicultural Toronto.
■ (Source: Canadian Press STRGBS)

12 months. Visas are also required by international students studying in Canada, who may stay for the period of their studies. Visa students may work in some limited contexts associated with their studies. Persons immigrating to Canada apply for landed-immigrant status or permanent residence leading to citizenship after three years in the country. Canada's immigration policy tries to balance humanitarian concerns for refugee claimants, family reunification, and the perceived need to attract highly skilled and educated persons.

The New Immigrants from Latin America and the Caribbean

Since the 1960s, substantial numbers of people from Mexico, Central and South America, and the Caribbean have come to Canada. Major flows come from the Caribbean islands of Jamaica, Barbados, and Haiti, among others. This is partly a result of the change in Canada's immigration policy in the 1960s, which had previously excluded people from areas outside Europe (Avery 1995:197). In addition to immigrant and refugee flows, many people came from Mexico and the Caribbean as seasonal farm labourers working in deplorable conditions for little pay. Some of these people work in the tobacco and fruit orchards of southern Ontario.

Chain Migration of Dominicans

The Dominican Republic has ranked among the top 10 source countries of immigrants to the United States since the 1960s (Pessar 1995). Dominicans are one of

the fastest-growing immigrant groups in the United States. They are found in clusters in a few states, with their highest concentration in New York State. Within New York City, Washington Heights is the heart of the Dominican community. Unlike many other new-immigrant streams, the Dominicans are mainly middle and upper class. Most have left their homeland "in search of a better life." Many hope to return to the Dominican Republic, saying that in New York, "there is work but there is no life."

A Dominican Day parade in New York City. ■ (Source: © Stephen Ferry/Getty Images)

Patricia Pessar conducted fieldwork in the Dominican Republic and in New York City, and, thus, she has a transnational view. She studied the dynamics of departure (such as getting a visa), the process of arrival, and adaptation in New York. Like most anthropologists who work with immigrant groups, she became involved in helping many of her informants: "Along the way I also endeavored to repay people's help by brokering for them with institutions such as the Immigration and Naturalization Service, social service agencies, schools, and hospitals" (xv).

For Dominican immigrants, as for most other immigrant groups, the *cadena*, or chain, links one immigrant to another. **Chain migration** is a form of population movement in which a first wave of migrants comes; these migrants then attract relatives and friends to join them in the destination place. Most Dominicans who are legal immigrants have sponsored other family members, so most legal Dominicans have entered through the family unification provision. The U.S. policy defines a family as a nuclear unit, and thus, it excludes important members of Dominican extended family networks such as cousins and ritual kin (*compadres*). To overcome this barrier, some Dominicans use the technique of the "business marriage." In a business marriage, an individual pays a legal immigrant or citizen a fee of perhaps US$2000 to enter into a "marriage." He or she then acquires a visa through the family unification provision. Such a "marriage" does not involve cohabitation or sexual relations; it is meant to be broken.

Dominicans have found employment in New York's manufacturing industries, including the garment industry. They are more heavily employed in these industries than any other ethnic group. Recent declines in the numbers of New York City's manufacturing jobs and the redefining of better positions into less desirable ones through restructuring have disproportionately affected them. Dominicans also work in retail and wholesale trade, another sector that has declined since the late 1960s. Others have established their own retail businesses, or *bodegas*. A problem with this line of work is that many bodegas are located in unsafe areas and some owners have been assaulted or killed. Declining economic opportunities for Dominicans have also been aggravated by arrivals of newer immigrants, especially from Mexico and Central America, who are willing to accept even lower wages and worse working conditions.

Although many families of middle and high status in the Dominican Republic initially secured fairly solid employment in the United States, they have declined economically since then. Dominicans now have the highest poverty rate in New York City, 37 percent, compared with an overall city average of 17 percent. Poverty is concentrated among women-headed households with young children.

The gender gap in wages is high, and women are more likely than men to be on public assistance. On the other hand, Dominican women in the United States are more often regularly employed than they would be in the Dominican Republic. This pattern upsets a patriarchal norm in which the nuclear family depends on male earnings and female domestic responsibilities. A woman's earning power means that husband–wife decision-making is more egalitarian. A working Dominican woman is likely to obtain more assistance from the man in doing household chores. All of these changes help explain why Dominican men are more interested in returning to the Dominican Republic than women are. As one man said, "Your country is a country for women; mine is for men" (81).

THINKING OUTSIDE THE BOX

FIND A detailed map that shows the geography of the Caribbean. Identify the islands, Jamaica, Trinidad, and St. Lucia. Do you know anyone from one of these places?

Caribbean Women: Strategies for Survival

A large portion of recent immigration to Canada was from the Caribbean in the 1980s. Yvonne Bobb Smith (1999) describes how many Caribbean women never lose the sense that "home" is in the islands, whether Jamaica, St. Lucia, or Trinidad. Smith posits three strategies for their survival in a society where racist insults are a constant part of the social environment for people from the Caribbean (Henry 1987). They see education as the first strategy in opening the door to better employment and a more satisfying role in the community. The second strategy is networking, building links with other men and women of the diaspora—the movement of black Caribbean people to industrial nations like Canada, the United States, and Britain. The links may be established though casual meetings that eventually develop into strong, warm friendships. The third strategy is community activism. Caribbean women in Canada have founded or are involved in several community organizations that support and promote causes important to Caribbean immigrant groups and other minorities, including the National Congress of Black Women of Canada, Black Theatre Canada, and the Coalition of Visible Minority Women of Ontario (Y. Smith 1999:163).

---

chain migration: population movement in which a first wave of migrants comes; these migrants then attract relatives and friends to join them in the destination.

The New Immigrants from East Asia

Changing Patterns of Consumption among Hong Kong Chinese

Studies of how international migrants change their behaviour in the new destination have addressed, among other things, the question of whether consumption patterns change and, if so, how, why, and what effects such changes have on other aspects of their culture.

A study in Canada focused on the topic of consumption patterns among four groups: Anglo-Canadians, new Hong Kong immigrants (who had arrived within the previous seven years), long-time Hong Kong immigrants, and Hong Kong residents (W. Lee and Tse 1994). Since 1987, Hong Kong has been the single largest source of migrants to Canada. The new immigrant settlement pattern in Canada is one of urban clustering. The Hong Kong Chinese have developed their own shopping centres, television and radio stations, newspapers, and country clubs. Because of generally high incomes, the Hong Kong immigrants have greatly boosted Canadian buying power.

For most migrants, however, the move brought a lowered economic situation, reflected in consumption patterns. New immigrants may have to reduce spending on entertainment and expensive items. Primary needs of the new immigrants include items that only about half of all households owned: car, DVD player, carpets,

Among the Chinese ethnic population in Canada, the majority come from Hong Kong, with much smaller proportions from Taiwan and China. The Hong Kong Chinese immigrants tend to be well-off in economic terms. Many of the male heads of household are "astronauts," leaving their families in Canada while they fly back and forth from Hong Kong to Canada. ■ (Source: Annie Griffiths Belt/CORBIS)

microwave oven, family house, and multiple TVs. Items in the second-needs category were dining room set, barbecue stove, deep freezer, and dehumidifier. Long-time immigrants tend to own more secondary products, suggesting that, with time and increased economic standing, expanded consumption of Anglo-Canadian products occurs.

At the same time, businesses in Canada have responded to immigrant tastes by providing Hong Kong style restaurants, Chinese branch banks, and travel agencies. Supermarkets have specialized Asian sections. Thus, traditional patterns and ties are maintained to some extent. Two characteristics of Hong Kong immigrants distinguish them from other groups discussed in this section: their relatively secure economic status and their high level of education. Still, in Canada, they often have a difficult time finding suitable employment. Some have named Canada "Kan Lan Tai," meaning a difficult place to prosper, a fact that leads many to become "astronauts," or transnational migrants. Many Hong Kong emigrants saw Canada as a safe haven, not as a place to make great economic progress (J. Smart 1994).

The New Immigrants from Southeast Asia

Three Patterns of Adaptation among the Vietnamese

Over one and a quarter million refugees have left Vietnam since the 1970s. Although most were relocated to the United States, many went to Canada, Australia, France, Germany, and Britain (S. Gold 1992). For example, in the period between 1979 and 1981, Canada accepted 60 000 Southeast Asian refugees. Vietnamese immigrants in Canada constitute a significant Asian minority. Three distinct subgroups are the 1975-era elite, the boat people, and the ethnic Chinese. While they interact frequently, they have retained distinct patterns of adaptation.

The first group avoided many of the traumatic elements of flight. They were U.S. employees and members of the South Vietnamese government and military. They left before having to live under the Communist Party regime, and they spent little time in refugee camps. A few of these came to Canada, especially to Quebec.

The boat people began to enter Canada after the outbreak of the Vietnam–China conflict of 1978. Mainly of rural origin, they lived for three years or more under communism, working in re-education camps or "new economic zones." Their exit, either by overcrowded and leaky boats or on foot through Cambodia, was dangerous and difficult. Over 50 percent died on the way. Those who survived faced many months in refugee camps in Thailand, Malaysia, the Philippines, or Hong Kong before being admitted to

Canada. Many more males than females escaped as boat people; thus, they are less likely to have arrived with intact families. They were less well educated than the earlier wave, half had no competence in English or French, and they faced a depressed economy. They have had a much more difficult time adjusting to life in Canada than the 1975-era elite.

The Sino-Vietnamese, traditionally a distinct and socially marginalized class of entrepreneurs in Vietnam, arrived mainly as boat people. Many of these immigrants have successfully used contacts in the overseas Chinese community and have been able to re-establish their roles as entrepreneurs.

No Vietnamese had lived in the prairie city of Lethbridge, Alberta, before 1979 (Indra 1988). The adaptation of Vietnamese and Sino-Vietnamese to this environment has been relatively successful. The Sino-Vietnamese are able to connect with other Chinese in the community and therefore maintain their cultural identity. In addition, the Sino-Vietnamese have been better able to reconstitute their core families. The Vietnamese in Lethbridge have been less able to adjust, finding it more difficult to re-establish families and feeling a strong attachment to Vietnam as it once was. Despite their being marginally employed, all Vietnamese in Lethbridge had a positive self-concept and even after 10 years, people had kept contact with their sponsors in the community.

Khmer Refugees' Interpretation of Their Suffering

Since the late 1970s, approximately 20 000 people from Cambodia have come to Canada as refugees from the brutal Pol Pot regime. These people survived years of political repression, a difficult escape, and time in a refugee camp before arriving in Canada. One question anthropologists ask is how people who have been through such terror and loss reconstruct their understanding of how the world works and their place in it. In Canada, many Cambodians, or Khmer, are from rural backgrounds and have beliefs in spirits called *neak ta*. Physical complaints are often blamed on these spirits. Some women refugees were possessed by the spirits of those who were murdered or not given proper burial rites, a common occurrence during the Pol Pot years. One cure for this state is giving food to Buddhist monks on behalf of the distressed spirit. Or consultation may be sought with a traditional healer, known as a *Khmer kru*. In this way, the possession can be resolved; but if monks or a traditional healer are not available, the suffering may be expressed in "physical ailments, social withdrawal and mental illness" (McLellan 1996:246). In Ontario, where most Khmer live in Canada, no

programs have focused on the particular problems suffered by this population, despite widespread knowledge about the nature of the Pol Pot regime and the stresses this population has endured.

The New Immigrants from South Asia

The Sikhs in British Columbia: Maintaining Their Religious Identity

Sikhs began coming to British Columbia in the early twentieth century, but they did not arrive in large numbers until the 1960s and 1970s, when Canada's immigration laws were relaxed. Annamma Joy studied the Sikhs in the Okanagan Valley in the interior of British Columbia, an area famous for apple growing (1989). Many of the Sikhs had come to the valley on the recommendation of friends and relatives, an example of chain migration. Most had been successful farmers in India and hoped to be able to live well in Canada, purchasing houses and cars. Many worked in the sawmills of the northern Okanagan. Male Sikhs suffered severe criticism from non-Sikh co-workers because of the visible symbols of their religion—beards and turbans. Even when Sikhs gave in to pressure, by shaving their beards and no longer wearing the turban, they were still subject to prejudice. The Sikhs were recognized as good workers by management, but were seen as a threat by other community members.

The male practices of wearing the turban, having unshorn hair, and carrying the *kirpan* (sword) are important features of the Sikh religion. The bangle, the breeches, and the comb symbolize maintaining a balance between the uncontrollable nature of power and sexual virility and discipline and restraint. The unshorn hair is a symbol of power and virility, which is restrained by the

Immigrants learning English at an adult school.
■ (Source: © David H. Wells/CORBIS)

comb, while the *kirpan* is restrained by the bangle. The *kirpan* is also important in the baptism of Sikhs. It is usually kept in the home, but some Sikhs feel they have the right to carry it, a practice which sometimes causes difficulties with various jurisdictions. Since 1976, Canadian law has allowed Sikhs to carry the *kirpan*, provided it is for religious purposes.

The New Immigrants from Eastern Europe

The breakup of the Soviet Union into 15 separate countries spurred the movement of over 9 million people throughout Eastern Europe and central Asia. Many of these immigrants are people of Slavic descent who had lived in central Asia during the time of the former Soviet Union and are seeking to return to their homelands. Another large category includes people who were forcibly relocated to Siberia or central Asia. Many Soviet Germans have migrated from Siberia to Germany, and Crimean Tatars are shifting from Uzbekistan back to Crimea. Since 1988, people from the former Soviet Union have been the largest refugee nationality to enter the United States (Littman 1993, cited in S. Gold 1995).

Soviet Jews Flee Persecution

Many of the refugees from the former Soviet Union are Jews. Although, the largest number of Soviet Jews live in Israel, since the mid-1960s, about 325 000 have settled in the United States and over 60 000 in Canada.

Steven Gold (1995) has studied different refugee groups in California for many years and speaks from a comparative perspective when he points out unique features of the experience of Soviet Jewish refugees. First, their origins in the Soviet Union accustomed them to the fact that the government controlled almost every aspect of life, "from the production of butter and the administration of summer camps to the shaping of ideology" (xi). These émigrés are used to a wide range of government services, including jobs, housing, daycare, and other basic needs. They have had to find new ways of meeting these needs in a market economy. Second, Soviet Jews, as white Europeans, are members of the dominant racial majority group in the United States. While Soviet Jews have suffered centuries of discrimination in Eastern Europe, they are much closer to the racial mainstream in the United States. Third, they have access to established and prosperous communities of American Jews. They have well-connected sponsors when they arrive. Most other new immigrant groups do not have these advantages.

The economic downturn of the 1990s, however, prompted a wave of anti-immigrant sentiment, of which Soviet Jewish immigrants are "keenly aware" (xiii). They immigrants face other challenges as well. Depending on their area of relocation, many have a difficult time finding a job commensurate with their education and previous work in the Soviet Union. In Canada, many Soviet Jewish immigrants who were highly skilled professionals, such as doctors and dentists, are unable to pass their licensing exams and are forced to accept menial labour jobs far beneath their qualifications.

In January 2004, more than 50 000 Russian immigrants to Israel returned to Russia. Motivations for the move back include the difficult living conditions for many Russian immigrants in Israel, violence, and the improving economic situation in Russia. Nonetheless, people from Russia continue to migrate to Israel, and they now number over 1 million people, roughly 13 percent of the population. ■ (Source: © David H. Wells/CORBIS)

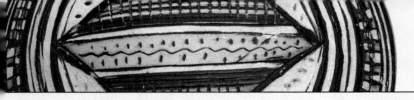

STUDYING PASTORALISTS' MOVEMENTS FOR RISK ASSESSMENT AND SERVICE DELIVERY

Pastoralists are often vulnerable to malnutrition as a consequence of climate changes, fluctuations in food supply, and war and political upheaval. Because of their spatial mobility, they are difficult to reach with relief aid during a crisis. Cultural anthropologists are devising ways to gather and manage basic information about pastoralists' movements and nutritional needs in order to provide improved service delivery (Watkins and Fleisher 2002). The data required for such proactive planning include the following:

- Information on the number of migrants and the size of their herds in a particular location and at a particular time. Such data can inform planners about the level of services required for public health programs, educational programs, and veterinary services. This information can be used to assess the demand on particular grazing areas and water sources and is therefore important in predicting possible future crises.
- Information on patterns of migratory movements. This information can enable planners to move services to where the people are and, thus, avoid the expectation that people will move to the services. Some NGOs, for example, are providing mobile banking services and mobile veterinary services.

Information about pastoralist movements can be used as an early warning to prevent social conflicts that might result if several groups arrived in the same place at the same time. And conflict resolution mechanisms can be put in place more effectively if conflict does occur.

The data collection involves interviews with pastoralists, often with one or two key participants, whom the anthropologists select for their specialized knowledge. Interviews cover topics such as the migratory paths followed (both typical and atypical), population levels, herd sizes, and the nutritional and water requirements of people and animals. Given the complex social systems of pastoralists, the data gathering must also include group leadership, decision-making practices, and concepts about land and water rights.

The anthropologists organize this information into a computerized database, linking the ethnographical data with geographic information systems (GIS) data on the environment and climate information from satellites. The anthropologists can then construct various scenarios and assess the relative risks that they pose to the people's health. Impending crises can be foreseen, and warning can be provided to governments and international aid agencies.

This is especially true for women émigrés who were employed, often as professionals, in the Soviet Union, but who can find no work other than housecleaning or babysitting. Another major challenge relates to marriage options. Cultural norms promote interethnic marriage; however, the number of Soviet Jews in the marriage pool is small.

Migration Policies and Politics in a Globalizing World

Globalization and the increase in migration have attracted more attention to this issue on the part of anthropologists and other social scientists. The major questions raised concern national and international policies of inclusion and exclusion of particular categories of people. The human rights of various categories

of migrants vary dramatically. Migrants of all sorts, including long-standing migratory groups such as pastoralists and horticulturalists, seek to find ways of protecting their lifestyles, maintaining their health, and building a sense of the future.

Protecting Migrants' Health

The health risks to migrants are many and varied because of the wide variety of migrant types and situations. Migrants whose livelihood depends on long-standing migratory economic systems, such as foraging, horticulture, and pastoralism, constitute one area of concern. Given the frequency in recent decades of drought and food shortages in the Sahel region of Africa, anthropologists are conducting studies to see how such conditions can be prevented, monitored, and more effectively coped with through humanitarian aid (see the accompanying Lessons Applied box).

In 2006, after three years of drought, two women of eastern Kenya search out pasture for their few remaining goats. As they walk through a dust storm, rain clouds and a rainbow in the distance are signs that rain is coming. Heavy rains did come in the next few days, but most of the pastoralists in the region, like these women, had lost nearly all of their animals during the drought. They are now dependent on food aid and other forms of humanitarian assistance for their survival. Global climate change is linked to increasingly severe swings in climatic conditions in this region. ■ (Source: Gideon Mendel/CORBIS)

FOOD FOR THOUGHT

- The tracking system described here remains outside the control of the pastoralists themselves. How might it be managed so that they participate more meaningfully and gain greater autonomy?

Inclusion and Exclusion

National immigration policies that set quotas on the quantity and types of immigrants welcomed and determine how they are treated are largely dictated by political and economic interests. Even in the cases of seemingly humanitarian quotas, governments undertake a cost–benefit analysis of how much will be gained and how much will be lost. Politically, governments show either their support or disapproval of other governments through their immigration policies. One of the most obvious economic factors affecting policy is labour flow. Cheap, even illegal, immigrant labour is used around the world to maintain profits for businesses and services for the better-off. Flows of such labour undermine labour unions and the status of established workers.

In Canada, immigration law determines who will be allowed entry and what benefits the government will allow them. The focus on cheap labour was dominant at the beginning of the twentieth century in Canada. The large extraction industries of lumbering and mining, along with the railroads, demanded a large supply of cheap labourers. Business in Canada overrode government concerns about foreign labour even when many residents of Canada complained about the influx of foreigners, mainly southern and eastern Europeans (Avery 1995). Government regulations on immigrants from Asia were more restrictive. For example, the Chinese were subject to an entry tax in 1885, and in 1923, were specifically forbidden to enter the country. The federal government still continues some restrictive policies. In 1995, the government introduced a $975 landing fee for every adult immigrant and refugee applying for permanent residence (in 2002, the fee for refugees was discontinued). Officially, this policy was put in place to offset the costs to the government of settlement programs. But many immigrant and refugee advocates perceive it as an unfair burden on new arrivals who are struggling to become established in Canada.

National immigration policies are played out in local communities. In some instances, local resentments are associated with a so-called **lifeboat mentality**, which seeks to limit enlarging a particular group because of perceived resource constraints. Influxes of immigrants who compete for jobs have led to hostility in many parts of Europe and North America. Some observers have labelled this *working-class racism* because it emerges out of competition with immigrants for jobs and other benefits (J. Cole 1996).

The number of immigrants has grown substantially in southern Italy since the early 1980s. In the city of Palermo, Sicily, with a total population of 800 000, there are now between 15 000 and 30 000 immigrants from Africa, Asia, and elsewhere. Does the theory of working-class racism apply in Palermo? Two conditions seem to say that it would: large numbers of immigrants and a high rate of unemployment.

However, instead of expressing racist condemnation of the immigrants, working-class residents of Palermo accept the immigrants as fellow poor people. One critical factor may be the lack of competition for jobs, which derives from the fact that working Palermitans and immigrants occupy different niches. Immigrant jobs are less desirable, more stigmatized, and less well-paying. African immigrant men work in bars and restaurants, as building cleaners, or as itinerant street vendors. African and Asian women work as domestic servants in the better-off neighbourhoods. Sicilians do refer to immigrants by certain racial/ethnic names, but they seem to be used interchangeably and imprecisely. For example, a common term for all immigrants, Asian or African, is *turchi*, which means *Turks*. The word can be applied teasingly to a Sicilian as well and in conversation may connote alarm as in, "Mom, the Turks!" Other loosely applied terms are the Italian words for Moroccans, blacks, and Tunisians. In a questionnaire given to schoolchildren, the great majority agreed with the statement that "a person's race is not important." The tolerance among Palermo's working class may be only temporary. Nonetheless, it suggests that researchers take a closer look at cases elsewhere that assume working-class racism against immigrants.

Recent politically conservative trends in the United States have succeeded in rolling back more progressive policies about immigration and minorities. Police raids in areas known to have many undocumented migrants have brought mass expulsion. Reversals of affirmative action in university and college admissions, initiated in California in the late 1990s, have gained widespread support among "nativist" Americans. This lifeboat mentality of exclusiveness and privilege is held mainly by the dominant white majority and others who have "made it."

However, political and economic considerations about immigration exist within broad frameworks, such as "melting pot ideology" or "multiculturalism." While the United States refers to the melting pot that assimilates newcomers, Canada's official multiculturalism policy, incorporated into law by the Multiculturalism Act of 1988, encourages individuals and communities to maintain linguistic and cultural diversity.

Migration and Human Rights

Several questions arise in the context of anthropological inquiry about migration and human rights. One important question is whether migration is forced or voluntary (see the Critical Thinking box on page 374). Forced migration itself may be considered a violation of a person's human rights.

Another question concerns whether members of a displaced group have a guaranteed **right of return,** or a person's ability to return to and live in his or her homeland. The right of return, which has been considered a basic human right in the West since the time of the Magna Carta, is included in the United Nations General Assembly Resolution 194 passed in 1948. It was elevated by the UN in 1974 to an "inalienable right."

The right of return is an enduring issue for Palestinian refugees, of whom hundreds of thousands fled or were driven from their homes during the 1948 war (Zureik 1994). They went mainly to Jordan, the West Bank/East Jerusalem, Gaza, Lebanon, Syria, and other Arab states. Jordan and Syria have granted Palestinian refugees rights equal to those of their citizens. In Lebanon, where estimates of the number of Palestinian refugees range between 200 000 and 600 000, the government refuses them such rights (Salam 1994). The lower number is favoured by Israel because it makes the

---

lifeboat mentality: local resentment of an immigrant group because of perceived resource constraints.

right of return: United Nations guaranteed right of refugees to repatriation.

problem seem less severe; the higher number is favoured by the Palestinians to highlight the seriousness of their plight and by the Lebanese government to emphasize its inability to absorb so many. Palestinians know that they are not welcome in Lebanon, but they cannot return to Israel because Israel denies them the right of return. Israel responds to the Palestinians' claims by saying that their acceptance of Jewish immigrants from Arab countries constitutes an equal exchange.

The right of return can be considered, just as validly, within states even though most have no policy close to that of the United Nations. Indigenous people's rights to their ancestral lands are a prominent case in point. Another stark instance of internal displacement and loss of rights to home comes from the 2005 hurricanes in New Orleans and the coastal counties of Mississippi and Louisiana. The racial lines of displacement are nowhere clearer than in the statistics for the city of New Orleans (Lyman 2006). Before Hurricane Katrina, the population of New Orleans was 54 percent white and 36 percent black, with the other 6 percent Latino. In 2006, the population was 68 percent white and 21 percent black, with no change in the Latino percentage. The causes for the differential displacement of the black population are one problem. The fact that many black people became a "New Orleans diaspora" with little chance of returning to their home city and rebuilding their lives is another.

Key Questions Revisited

WHAT are the major categories of migration?

Migrants are classified as internal, international, or transnational. Another category is based on the migrants' reason for moving. On this dimension, migrants are classified as labour migrants, institutional migrants, or displaced persons. People's adjustment to their new situations depends on the degree of voluntarism involved in the move, the degree of cultural and environmental difference between the place of origin and the destination, and how closely expectations about the new location are met, especially in terms of making a living and establishing social ties.

Displaced persons are one of the fastest-growing categories of migrants. Refugees fleeing from political persecution or warfare face serious adjustment challenges because they often leave their home countries with few material resources and frequently have experienced much psychological suffering. The number of internally displaced persons is growing even faster than the number of refugees. Dams and other large-scale development projects result in thousands of people becoming IDPs. Internally displaced persons do not fall under the purview of international organizations such as the United Nations, but their situation is attracting the attention of a global consortium of governments and NGOs.

WHO are examples of the new immigrants in Canada and the United States?

Worldwide, the "new immigrants" are contributing to growing transnational connections and to the formation of increasingly multicultural populations within states. In the United States, the new immigrants from Latin America, especially Mexico and the Dominican Republic, are the fastest-growing category. In both Canada and the United States, members of most refugee immigrant groups tend to have jobs at the lower end of the economic scale. Jewish refugees from the Soviet Union experience a major gap in what their employment was like in Russia versus their limited options in North America. Immigrants from East and South Asia, who are more likely than others to have immigrated voluntarily, have achieved greater levels of economic success than most other new immigrant groups.

Immigrant groups throughout the world may face discrimination in their new destinations, although the degree to which it occurs varies with the level of perceived resource competition from residents. Immigrants from India in Canada experience a range of discriminatory practices that differ on the basis of their gender. In Canada, the three largest non-European immigrant groups in the 1990s were from Hong Kong, India, and the Philippines. In 2004, 20 percent of Canada's population was made up of visible minorities, most of them making up half the population of Canada's three largest cities, Toronto, Montreal, and Vancouver. Immigrant groups throughout the world are likely to face certain forms of discrimination in their new destinations, although the degree to which it occurs varies depending on perceived resource competition from already settled residents.

HOW do anthropologists contribute to migration policies and programs?

Anthropologists have studied national and international migration policies and practices in terms of social inclusion and exclusion. Fieldwork in particular contexts reveals a range of patterns between local residents and immigrants. Working-class resentment among local people against immigrants is not universal and varies with the overall amount and type of employment available.

Anthropologists examine possible infringements of human rights on migrants, especially in terms of the degree of voluntarism in their move and the conditions they face in the destination area. Another human-rights issue related to migration is the right of return. The United Nations proclaimed the right of return for internationally displaced populations. Most countries, however, have no such policy. Internally displaced persons, including the evacuees from the 2005 hurricanes in the southern United States, have no guarantee that they can return to their home area.

Cultural anthropologists find many roles in applied work related to migration. Gathering data on migratory movements of traditionally mobile people, such as pastoralists, can help make humanitarian aid programs more timely and effective.

KEY CONCEPTS

chain migration, p. 384
circular migration, p. 377
development-induced
    displacement (DID),
    p. 378
displaced person, p. 377
institutional migrant,
    p. 378

internal migration, p. 373
internally displaced person
    (IDP), p. 378
lifeboat mentality,
    p. 390
migration, p. 372
new immigrant, p. 382
push–pull theory, p. 373

refugee, p. 377
remittance, p. 376
right of return, p. 390
transnational migration,
    p. 373
wage labour migration,
    p. 377

myanthrolab

To reinforce your understanding of this chapter, and to identify topics for further study, visit MyAnthroLab at www.myanthrolab.com for diagnostic tests and a multimedia ebook.

SUGGESTED READINGS

Rogaia Mustafa Abusharaf, *Wanderings: Sudanese Migrants and Exiles in North America*. Ithaca, NY: Cornell University Press, 2002. In this book, the author explores the topic of Sudanese migration to the United States and Canada. Abusharaf provides historical background on the first wave, information on various Sudanese groups who have migrated, and an interpretation of Sudanese identity in North America as more unified than it is in the homeland.

Linda Basch, Nina Glick Schiller, and Christina Szanton Blanc, *Nations Unbound: Transnational Projects, Postcolonial Predicaments, and Deterritorialized Nation-States*. Langhorne, PA: Gordon and Breach Science Publishers, 1994. In eight chapters, the authors explore theoretical issues in transnational migration and present detailed analysis of cases of migration from the Caribbean, including St. Vincent, Grenada, and Haiti.

Morton Beiser, *Strangers at the Gate: The "Boat People's" First Ten Years in Canada*. Toronto: University of Toronto Press, 1999. Beiser aims to inform the Canadian public about the impact of refugees on Canada, and shows how these newcomers have struggled, without making extensive use of health and social services.

Colin Clarke, Ceri Peach, and Steven Vertovec, eds., *South Asians Overseas: Migration and Ethnicity*. New York: Cambridge University Press, 1990. The text includes 15 chapters plus introductory essays that place the case studies in a broader context. Chapters are divided into two sections: i) South Asians in colonial and post-colonial contexts and ii) South Asians in contemporary Western countries and the Middle East.

W. Giles, H. Moussa, and P. Van Esterik, eds., *Development and Diaspora: Gender and the Refugee Experience*. Dundas, ON: Artemis Enterprises, 1996. Various contributions in this edited volume explore the relation among gender, development, and the movements of refugees, and include an examination of the resettlement process.

Sherri Grasmuck and Patricia R. Pessar, *Between Two Islands: Dominican International Migration*. Berkeley, CA: University of California Press, 1991. Based on fieldwork in the Dominican Republic and New York City, this volume focuses on social ties and networks facilitating migration from rural areas in the Dominican Republic to its largest city, Santo Domingo, and from the Dominican Republic to the United States, and how employment opportunities shape the migration experience.

Julianne Hammer. *Palestinians Born in Exile: Diaspora and the Search for a Homeland*. Austin: University of Texas Press, 2004. In the decade following the 1993 Oslo Peace Accords, 100 000 diasporic Palestinians moved to the West Bank and Gaza. This ethnography documents the experiences of young adults between the ages of 16 and 35 and their adjustment to the move.

Paul R. Magocsi, ed., *Encyclopedia of Canada's Peoples*. Toronto: University of Toronto Press, 1999. Edited by the director of the Multicultural History Society of Ontario, this massive book gathers complex information on about 130 peoples that make up Canadian society, including details about their origins, settlement, and intergroup dynamics.

Beatriz Manz, *Refugees of a Hidden War: The Aftermath of Counterinsurgency in Guatemala*. Albany, NY: State University of New York Press, 1988. This study was conducted to assess whether conditions would allow the return to Guatemala of 46 000 Indian peasant refugees living in camps in Mexico. It gives attention to aspects of family and community life in the camps and in resettled villages in Guatemala, where the Indians face discrimination and harassment from the military.

Jennifer Robertson, *Native and Newcomer: Making and Remaking a Japanese City*. Berkeley, CA: University of California Press, 1991. In this text, Robertson studies the social and symbolic adjustments of native residents of Kodaira, Japan, and the many residents who moved to Kodaira beginning in the 1950s. Detailed attention is given to the role of a community festival in expressing links between the natives and newcomers, while also stating and maintaining group boundaries.

Archana B. Verma, *The Making of Little Punjab in Canada: Patterns of Immigration*. Thousand Oaks, CA; Sage Publications, 2002. Verma traces the historical connections between Hindu migrants from Paldi village, in India's northern state of Punjab, to Vancouver Island, British Columbia. Strong family and kinship ties continue to link the migrants to their home area. Caste group solidarity among the migrants provides support in the face of discrimination on the part of the wider Canadian society.

15

People Defining Development

Key Questions

- WHAT is development and the approaches to achieving it?
- HOW is development related to women and indigenous people?
- WHAT are urgent issues in development?

A traditional custodian from the Ngarrindjeri nation in South Australia holds a box containing four skulls of Australian Aborigines at a ceremony at Manchester University, England, 2003. The skulls were returned, after 100 years in England, to a sacred keeping place. This repatriation is one result of a worldwide campaign by indigenous peoples to retrieve body parts and artifacts taken from graves during the nineteenth and twentieth centuries. *(Source: © Reuters/CORBIS)*

We have had many visitors to Walpole Island since the French "discovered us" in the seventeenth century in our territory, Bkejwanong. In many cases, these visitors failed to recognize who we were and to appreciate our traditions. They tried to place us in their European framework of knowledge, denying that we possessed our indigenous knowledge. They attempted to steal our lands, water, and knowledge. We resisted. They left and never came back. We continued to share our knowledge with the next visitors to our place. . . . It was a long-term strategy that has lasted more than three hundred years. (Dr. Dean Jacobs, Executive Director of Walpole Island First Nation, from his Foreword in Van Wynsberghe 2002:ix)

These are the words of a leader of the Walpole Island First Nation, located in southern Ontario, Canada (see Map 15.1). They, along with many other indigenous groups worldwide, have begun to take strong action in recent decades to protect their culture and its natural environment. The Walpole Island First Nation organized itself and successfully fought to control industrial waste that was polluting its water and land. In the process, the people have regained their pride and cultural integrity.

All cultures go through change, but the causes, processes, and outcomes are varied. Cultural change can be intentional or accidental, forward-looking or backward-looking, rapid or gradual, obvious or subtle, beneficial or harmful.

Biological anthropologists have the longest view. They look back many thousands—even millions—of years to learn how humanity originated and evolved biologically. Archaeologists examine human cultural remains, from prehistory and history, to discover how and when people migrated throughout the world and how social complexity developed. Linguistic anthropologists study the evolution of communication patterns and capabilities in prehistoric times, the spread and change in verbal and written languages with the emergence of settled life and of the state, and change in contemporary patterns of communication, including the effects of mass media.

In contrast to these three fields, cultural anthropology's roots lie in the **synchronic** study of culture, or a "one-time" snapshot view of culture with little attention to the past. This early approach led to a static view of culture as unchanging. Cultural anthropologists are now moving toward a **diachronic** approach that includes attention to time and change in studying culture.

In this chapter, we focus on the topic of contemporary cultural change as shaped by **development** or directed change to achieve improved human welfare, usually through poverty reduction. The subfield within cultural anthropology of *development anthropology* is the study of how culture and development interact. It also has a strong applied component. In the chapter's first section, we consider concepts related to change

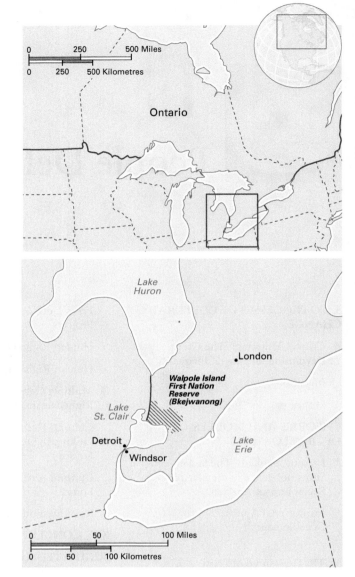

MAP 15.1   Walpole Island Reservation in Southern Ontario, Canada.

and development and approaches to development. In the second section, we focus on development in relation to women and indigenous peoples. In the third section, we look at several emerging and urgent issues in development and what cultural anthropology can contribute to them.

Two Processes of Cultural Change

Two basic processes drive all cultural change. The first is invention, the discovery of something new. The second is diffusion, the spread of cultural innovations through contact.

---

synchronic: a "one-time" view of a culture that devotes little or no attention to its past.

diachronic: the analysis of culture across time.

development: directed change to achieve improved human welfare.

Critical Thinking

THE GREEN REVOLUTION AND SOCIAL INEQUALITY

Agricultural scientists of the 1950s, inspired by the laudable goal of eliminating world hunger, developed genetic variations of wheat, rice, and corn. These *high-yielding varieties* (HYV) of seeds were promoted to farmers throughout the developing world as part of the *Green Revolution* that would feed the planet by boosting production per hectare. In most places where Green Revolution agricultural practices were adopted, grain production did increase. Was world hunger conquered? The answer is no, because world hunger is not merely a problem of production; it also involves distribution.

Analyses of the social impact of the Green Revolution in India reveal that one of its results was to increase disparities between the rich and the poor (Frankel 1971). How did this happen? Green Revolution agriculture requires several expensive inputs:

- Purchase of seeds each year, since HYV seeds are hybridized and cannot be harvested from the crop and used the next year
- Heavy application of commercial fertilizers
- Dependable irrigation sources

Farmers who had success with HYV seeds were those who were already better off than others. First, they were selected for the innovation because they could afford the costly inputs. Small farmers who tried planting HYV seeds but could not provide the inputs experienced crop failure, went deeper into debt, and had to sell their land.

Larger, better-off farmers took advantage of these new openings in the market to buy land and expand their holdings. With the acquisition of tractors and other mechanized equipment, they became even more productive. Small farmers, unable to compete, continued to be squeezed out financially. They became hired day labourers, dependent on seasonal employment by large farmers, or they migrated to cities and joined the urban underclass.

Looking at the Green Revolution from a critical-thinking perspective reveals a larger framework of interests and benefits, regardless of the original intentions of the HYV seed inventors or the program promoters. The big winners are

- Companies that manufacture and sell HYV seeds
- Companies that manufacture and sell chemical fertilizers (largely petroleum-based)
- Companies that manufacture and sell mechanized farm equipment
- Wealthier farmers who could afford the inputs and the risks and were able to increase their land holdings by buying land from small farmers who failed

To a lesser extent, other winners include the scientists who gained funding for their research and world fame for their discoveries.

The big losers are the small farmers who lost their land and were forced to move to cities and take up low-pay wage work. Did malnutrition in India decline? Was the problem of world hunger solved? The simple answer is no, but of course one has to wonder what would have happened if HYV grains had not been discovered. These questions are complicated and extremely timely, given contemporary conflict about the potential of genetically modified foods to solve world hunger.

CRITICAL THINKING QUESTIONS

- Is it likely that the original innovators of HYV grains considered what social transformations might occur in developing countries' agriculture as a result of their invention?
- Would they have been likely to stop their research if they had realized that it would lead to the "rich getting richer and the poor getting poorer"? Should they have done so?
- How does this example inform current debates about genetically modified food?

Invention

Invention often prompts cultural change. Inventions usually evolve gradually, through experimentation and accumulation of knowledge, but some appear suddenly. Examples of technological inventions that have created cultural change include the printing press, gunpowder, the polio vaccine, and satellite communication. Conceptual innovations, such as parliamentary democracy, are also inventions. Not all inventions have positive social outcomes. Even innovations inspired by a socially positive goal may have mixed or even negative social effects (see the Critical Thinking box).

Diffusion

Diffusion is logically related to invention because useful new discoveries are likely to spread. Diffusion can occur in several ways. First, in mutual borrowing, two roughly equal societies exchange elements of their culture with each other. For example, the United States exported rock and roll music to Britain and Britain exported The Beatles to North America. Second, diffusion may involve a transfer from a dominant culture to a less powerful culture. This process may occur through force or more subtly through education or marketing processes that promote adoption of new practices and beliefs. For example, through volunteer groups such as CUSO or WUSC (World University Service of Canada), many North American products, practices, and beliefs are spread to developing countries. Third, a more powerful culture may appropriate aspects of a less powerful culture through *cultural imperialism.* For example, Britain's Tower of London is full of priceless jewels from India. Last, a less powerful and even oppressed cultural group often provides sources of cultural change in a dominant culture.

Changes in a minority culture that make it more like the dominant culture are referred to as **acculturation.** In extreme cases, a culture becomes so thoroughly acculturated that it is **assimilated,** or "decultured"—that is, it is no longer distinguishable as having a separate identity. In the most extreme cases, the impact on the minority culture is that it becomes extinct. These processes parallel degrees of language change resulting from contact with dominating cultures and languages (review Chapter 12). Such changes have occurred among many indigenous people as the result of globalization and the introduction of new technology (see the accompanying Lessons Applied box). Other responses to acculturative influences include partial acceptance of something new with localization and syncretism, as in the case of the game of cricket in the Trobriands (see Chapter 14), or rejection and resistance.

Theories and Models of Development

In this section, we review theories and models of development and the various kinds of institutions involved in development. We then examine development projects. In the last section, we offer insights about special research methods cultural anthropologists use in development work.

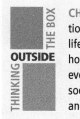

THINKING OUTSIDE THE BOX

CHOOSE TWO inventions made in your lifetime and assess how they affect your everyday activities, social interactions, and ways of thinking.

No single view of development or how to achieve it exists. Debates about these issues are heated and involve experts from many disciplines, governments, and local people worldwide. Five theories or models of development are presented here. They differ in terms of

- The definition of development
- The goal of development
- Measures of development
- Attention to environmental and financial sustainability

Modernization

Modernization is a form of change marked by industrialization, consolidation of the nation-state, bureaucratization, market economy, technological innovation, literacy, and options for social mobility. It derives from a period in Western European history beginning in the seventeenth century, which emphasized the importance of secular rationality and the inevitable advance of scientific thinking (Norgaard 1994). Modernization theory assumes an inevitable process that will, given the insights of science and rationality, spread throughout the world and lead to improvement in people's lives everywhere. The goals of modernization are material progress and individual betterment.

Supporters and critics of modernization are found in both rich and poor countries. Supporters claim that the benefits of modernization (improved transportation; electricity; domestic comforts such as air conditioning and washing machines, biomedical health care, and telecommunications) are worth the costs to the environment and society. Others regard modernization as problematic. Many cultural anthropologists are critics of modernization as a general process of social change because it leads to increased social inequality, the destruction of indigenous cultures, ecological ruin, and the overall decline in global cultural diversity. Selected aspects of modernity, however, such as electricity and antibiotics,

---

diffusion: the spread of cultural innovations through contact.

acculturation: a form of cultural change in which a minority culture becomes more like the dominant culture.

assimilation: a form of cultural change in which a culture is thoroughly acculturated, or decultured, and is no longer distinguishable as having a separate identity.

modernization: a model of change based on belief in the inevitable advance of science and Western secularism and processes including industrial growth, consolidation of the state, bureaucratization, market economy, technological innovation, literacy, and options for social mobility.

social impact assessment: a study conducted to gauge the potential social costs and benefits of particular innovations before change is undertaken.

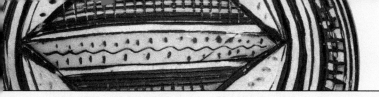

THE SAAMI, SNOWMOBILES, AND THE NEED FOR SOCIAL IMPACT ANALYSIS

How might adoption of a new belief or practice benefit or harm a particular culture and its various members? Although often difficult to answer, this question must always be asked. A classic study of the *snowmobile disaster* among a Saami group in Finland offers a careful response to this question in a context of rapid technological diffusion (Pelto 1973). In the 1950s, the Saami of Finland (review the Ethnographic Profile in Chapter 12 on page 338) had an economy based on fishing and reindeer herding, which provided most of their diet.

Besides supplying meat, reindeer had other important economic and social functions. They were used as draft animals, especially hauling wood for fuel. Their hides were made into clothing and their sinews used for sewing. Reindeer were key items of exchange, both in external trade and internal gift-giving. Parents gave a child a reindeer to mark the appearance of the child's first tooth. When a couple became engaged, they exchanged a reindeer with each other to mark the commitment. Reindeer were the most important wedding gift. Each summer, the herds were let free, and then they were rounded up in the fall, a time of communal festivity.

By the 1960s, all this had changed because of the introduction of the snowmobile. Previously, people herded reindeer on skis. The use of snowmobiles for herd management had several results. The herds were no longer kept domesticated for part of the year, during which they became tame. Instead, they were allowed to roam freely all year and thus became wilder.

Snowmobiles allowed herders to cover larger amounts of territory at round-up time, and sometimes several round-ups occurred instead of one. Herd size declined dramatically. The reasons for the decline included the stress inflicted on the reindeer by the extra distance travelled during round-ups, the multiple round-ups instead of a single one, and the fear aroused by the noisy snowmobiles. Round-ups were held at a time when the females were near the end of their pregnancy, another factor inducing reproductive stress. As the number of snowmobiles increased, the number of reindeer decreased.

Introduction of snowmobiles for herding also increased young men's dominance in herding (Larsson 2005). Before the snowmobiles, reindeer herding was a family operation. Although men did more of the long-distance herding, women also worked closely with the herd. Since snowmobiles were adopted, parents have steered their sons toward herding and their daughters toward education and a professional career. Two rationales for such gender tracking are that driving a snowmobile is difficult due to its heaviness, and the driver may get stuck

Saami herders follow their reindeer led by a man on a snowmobile Sapmi, Norway. ■ (Source: © Bryan and Cherry Alexander Photography/Alamy)

somewhere. The use of snowmobiles also changed the age pattern of reindeer herding in favour of youth over age; thus, older herders were squeezed out.

Another change involved a new dependence on the outside through the cash economy. Cash is needed in order to purchase a snowmobile, to buy gasoline, and to pay for parts and repairs. This delocalization of the economy created social inequality, which had not existed before. Other social and economic repercussions include

- The cash cost of effective participation in herding exceeded the resources of some families, who had to drop out of participation in herding.
- The snowmobile pushed many Saami into debt.
- Dependence on cash and indebtedness forced many Saami to migrate to cities for work.

Pertti Pelto, the anthropologist who first documented this case, calls these transformations a disaster for Saami culture. He offers a recommendation that might be helpful for the future: Communities that are confronting the adoption of new technology should have a chance to weigh evidence on the pros and cons and make an informed judgment. Pelto's work is one of the early warnings from anthropology about the need for **social impact assessments**, studies that gauge the potential social costs and benefits of particular innovations before change is undertaken.

FOOD FOR THOUGHT

- Speculate about what the Saami might have done if they had been able to consider a social impact assessment of the effects of snowmobiles on their culture.

may be accepted as positive. In spite of strong cautionary critiques from anthropologists and environmentalists about the negative impacts of modernization, nations around the world have not slowed their attempts to achieve it. Some governments and citizen groups, however, are promoting lifestyles that rely less on nonrenewable resources and include concern for protecting the environment.

Growth-Oriented Development

International development emerged as a prominent theory about change after World War II. By the middle of the twentieth century, most countries had obtained political independence, but many were in a state of economic dependence. One can think of development as the attempt, through conscious planning and intervention, to increase economic productivity in the developing world. Indeed, **international development**, as conceived by major development institutions such as the World Bank, is similar to modernization in terms of its ultimate goals. The process emphasizes economic growth as the most crucial element in development. According to growth-oriented development theory, investments in economic growth will, through the *trickle-down effect,* lead to improved human welfare among the less well-off. Strategies to promote economic growth in developing countries include increasing economic productivity and trade through modernized agriculture and manufacturing and participation in world markets.

In addition, countries are encouraged to reduce government expenditures on public services such as schools and health in order to reduce debt and reallocate resources to increase productivity. This strategy, called **structural adjustment**, has been promoted by the World Bank since the 1980s. Measures to assess the achievement of development through this model include the rate of growth of the economy, especially the *gross domestic product* (GDP).

Distributional Development

Distributional development contrasts with growth-oriented development in its emphasis on social equity in benefits, especially in terms of increased income, literacy, and health. It rejects the trickle-down process as ineffective in reaching less well-off people. Its position is based on evidence that growth-oriented strategies, applied without concern for distribution, actually increase social inequality. In this view, the growth model ensures that "the rich get richer and the poor get poorer."

The distributional approach opposes structural adjustment policies because they further undermine the welfare of the poor by removing the few entitlements they had in the form of services. Advocates of the distributional model see the need for benevolent governments to ensure equitable access to crucial resources in order to enhance the ability of the poor to provide for their own needs (Gardner and Lewis 1996).

Conservative ("neo-liberal") economists argue that redistribution is not a realistic or a feasible strategy. Supporters of the distributive approach, including many anthropologists, point to cases in the model that have worked. As one example, anthropological research in Nadur village, central Kerala (see Map 15.2 on page 401), considered whether redistribution was an effective development strategy (Franke 1993). The findings showed the answer to be positive. Even though Kerala's per capita income is the lowest of any state in India, it has some of the highest social indicators in the country, including health status and literacy.

Government attention to distribution in Kerala came about through democratic channels, including demonstrations and pressure on the government by popular movements and labour unions. These groups forced the state to reallocate land ownership, which alleviated social inequality somewhat. In other instances, people pressured government leaders to improve village conditions by providing school lunches for poor children, increasing school attendance by *dalit* children (review Chapter 9's definition of *dalit*) and investing in school facilities. Through public action, Nadur village became a better place to live for many people.

Human Development

Another alternative to the "growth-first" strategy is called **human development**, the strategy that emphasizes investing in human welfare. The United Nations adopted the phrase *human development* in order to emphasize the need for improvements in human welfare in terms of health, education, and personal security and safety. According to this approach, improvements in human welfare will lead to economic development. The reverse is not invariably true: The level of economic growth of a

---

international development: as conceived by major development institutions, a process that emphasizes economic growth as the most crucial element in development.
structural adjustment: promoted by the World Bank since the 1980s, a strategy by which countries are encouraged to reduce

government expenditures on public services such as schools and health in order to reduce debt and reallocate resources to increase productivity.
human development: an alternative to the "growth-first" developmental strategy, it emphasizes investing in human welfare.

sustainable development: forms of improvement made to an economy that do not destroy nonrenewable resources and that are financially supportable over time.

Schoolgirls in Bhutan. The government of Bhutan rejects the Western concept of the gross domestic product (GDP) as the best measure of a country's success and instead uses a measure called *gross domestic happiness* (GDH). ■ (Source: Rob Howard/CORBIS)

In 1992, the United Nations Conference on the Environment and Development, better known as the Rio Earth Summit, established goals for global actions to ensure the well-being of the planet and its people. Since then, several follow-up international meetings have occurred, producing more agreements and updated plans. Countries vary in terms of how much they support Earth Summit goals, and they differ in the degree to which they implement policies to which they have agreed. As of November, 2008, 183 parties have signed and ratified the Kyoto Protocol to the UN Convention on Climate Change, including Canada. Although the United States does not intend to sign, more than 200 city mayors have have signed on to the Mayors Climate Protection Agreement, adopting their own targets to reduce global warming (Vidal 2006).

THINKING OUTSIDE THE BOX WHAT DO YOU consider to be the most useful development model? Apply it to one society that you have learned about in this book.

country (or region within a country) is not necessarily correlated with its level of human development, as is clear from the case of Kerala. Thus, in this view, economic growth is neither an end in itself nor even a necessary component of development as measured in human welfare. Economic resources, combined with distributive policies, are a strong basis for attaining high levels of human development.

Sustainable Development

Sustainable development refers to forms of improvement that do not destroy nonrenewable resources and are financially supportable over time. Advocates of sustainable development argue that the economic growth of wealthy countries has been and still is costly in terms of the natural environment and people whose lives depend on fragile ecosystems. This approach emphasizes meeting the needs of the present without compromising the ability of future generations to meet their needs. The Canadian International Development Agency (CIDA) sustainable development program stresses preserving biodiversity, avoiding environmental degradation, and promoting equity and social justice issues.

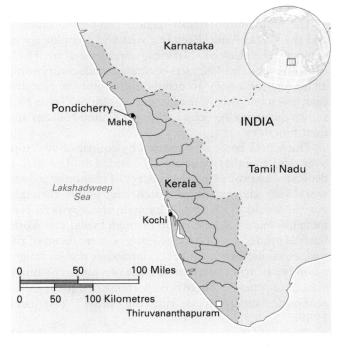

MAP 15.2   Kerala, South India. With a population of 30 million, Kerala's living standard, literacy, and health are high compared to the rest of India. It comprises 14 districts and 3 historical regions: Travancore in the south, Kochi in the central part, and Malabar in the north. Long a socialist democracy, Kerala now allows the free market and foreign direct investment to play larger roles. A major tourist destination due to its tropical ecology and cultural features such as dramatic martial arts and theatre, Kerala also hosts a growing Ayurvedic health tourism industry along its coast.

Institutional Approaches to Development

Cultural anthropologists are increasingly aware of the importance of examining the institutions and organizations involved in international development. This knowledge helps cultural anthropologists have a greater impact on how development is done. They have studied the management systems of large-scale institutions, such as the United Nations agencies and the World Bank, as well as local management systems found in diverse settings. They have examined internal hierarchies and inequalities, social interactions, symbols of power, and development discourse within the institutions themselves. This section first describes some of the major development institutions and then discusses smaller grassroots organizations.

Large-Scale Institutions

Large-scale development institutions can be separated into the *multilaterals* (those that include several nations as donors) and the *bilaterals* (those that involve a relationship between a donor and a recipient).

The major multilaterals include the United Nations and the World Bank. Each is a vast and complex social system. The United Nations, established in 1945, currently includes 192 member states, each contributing an amount of money according to its ability to pay, and each given one vote in the General Assembly. Table 15.1 shows the major agencies within the United Nations and their functions.

The World Bank is supported by contributions from over 150 member countries. Founded in 1944, it is dedicated to promoting the concept of economic growth worldwide and expanded purchasing power throughout the world (Rich 1994). Its main strategy is to promote international investment through loans. The World Bank is guided by a board of governors made up of the finance ministers of member countries; its system assigns a number of votes based on the size of a country's financial commitment: "There is no pretense of equality—the economic superpowers run the show" (Hancock 1989:51).

The World Bank system includes the International Bank for Reconstruction and Development (IBRD) and the International Development Association (IDA). Both are administered at the World Bank headquarters in Washington, D.C. They both lend for similar types of projects and often in the same country, but their conditions differ. The IBRD provides loans to the poorest nations that are generally regarded as "bad risks" on the world commercial market. Thus, the IBRD is a source of interest-bearing loans to countries that otherwise would not be able to borrow. The IBRD has recorded a profit every year of its existence. Most of its loans support large infrastructure projects such as roads and dams. The IDA is the "soft-loan" side of the World Bank because it provides interest-free loans (although there is a 0.75 percent annual "service charge") and a flexible repayment schedule averaging between 35 and 40 years (Rich 1994:77). These concessional loans are granted to the poorest countries for projects of high development priority. The International Monetary Fund (IMF), also created in 1944, monitors the monetary policies of member nations, and provides credit for member countries experiencing temporary balance of payments deficits.

THINKING OUTSIDE THE BOX

VISIT THE WEBSITE of one of the multilateral development organizations and one bilateral organization to learn about their goals, programs, and internship opportunities.

Critics of the World Bank and the IMF come from many directions, including politicians, scholars, and people whose lives have been affected negatively by their projects. Politicians in the United States who oppose foreign aid to developing countries in any form point to the overlapping and wasteful organization of some United Nations institutions. Critics point especially to the biased lending and aid policies that are shaped more by political factors than by economic need.

Prominent bilateral institutions include CIDA, the Japan International Cooperation Agency (JICA), the United States Agency for International Development (USAID), Britain's Department for International Development (DfID), the Swedish Agency for International Development (SIDA), and the Danish Organization for International Development (DANIDA). These agencies vary in terms of the proportion of aid disbursed as loans that have to be repaid or as grants that do not require repayment. Another variation is whether the loans or grants are "tied" to supporting specific projects that also provide for substantial donor country involvement in providing goods, services, and expertise versus being "untied," or allowing the recipient country the freedom to decide how to use the funds. The USAID generally offers more aid in the form of loans than grants, and more in tied than untied aid, whereas Sweden, the Netherlands, Canada, and Norway tend to give untied aid.

Another difference among the bilaterals is the proportion of their total assistance that goes to the poorest of countries. Britain's DfID sends more than 80 percent of its aid to the poorest countries, while the largest chunk of U.S. foreign aid goes to Egypt and Israel. Canada's Official Development Assistance (ODA) used to be motivated by a moral obligation to help those who are oppressed or live in poverty. However, around 1994, priorities shifted to projects that support trade rather than targeting the poorest countries. Nevertheless, Canada seldom uses ODA to secure support for foreign-policy

TABLE 15.1   Major Agencies within the United Nations Related to Development

Agency	Headquarters	Mission
The United Nations Development Program, UNDP	New York City, United States	Supports countries in planning and managing development, including groundwater and mineral exploration, computer and satellite technology, seed production and agricultural extension, and research. UNDP does not implement projects. Implementation is done through UN "executing agencies," some of which are listed here.
The Food and Agricultural Organization (FAO)	Rome, Italy	Implements agricultural projects that receive funding from the UNDP and host governments. Monitors global food stocks and factors affecting food prices.
The World Health Organization (WHO)	Geneva, Switzerland	Disease prevention and control, eradication of major infectious diseases, immunization of all children against major childhood diseases, establishment of primary health-care services.
The United Nations Children's Emergency Fund (UNICEF)	Joint headquarters in New York City and Geneva, Switzerland	Complementary to WHO; promotes children's health and survival, provides support for basic health care and social services for children. Receives most of its funding from UN member states, and the rest from the general public.
The United Nations Educational, Scientific, and Cultural Organization (UNESCO)	Paris, France	Enhances world peace and security through education, science, and culture, and promotes respect for human rights, the rule of law, and fundamental freedoms.
The United Nations High Commission for Refugees (UNHCR)	New York City, United States	Promotes the rights and safety of refugees.
The United Nations International Development Fund for Women (UNIFEM)	New York City, United States	Promotes projects directed toward raising the status of women. Supports gender-equality initiatives that promote the economic, political, and social empowerment of women. Co-ordinates women's issues within the UN.
The United Nations Fund for Population Activities (UNFPA)	New York City, United States	Supports family-planning projects that improve reproductive health.

Source: Adapted from Hancock 1989.

objectives (Morrison 2000:22). Figure 15.1 on page 404 lists CIDA's ODA priorities.

Emphasis on certain types of aid also varies from bilateral institution to bilateral institution. Cuba has long played a unique role in bilateral aid, although this fact is not well known. Rather than offering assistance for a wide range of development projects, Cuba has concentrated on aid for training health care providers and promoting preventive health care (Feinsilver 1993). Most of Cuba's development assistance goes to socialist countries, including many in Africa, and some newly socialist states in Latin America such as Venezuela and Bolivia.

FIGURE 15.1 CIDA and the Millennium Development Goals

Canada's Official Development Assistance (ODA) program aims to reduce poverty, promote human rights, and support sustainable development. It works as part of the global community to achieve the following Millennium Development Goals (MDG):

- Eradicate extreme poverty and hunger
- Achieve universal primary education
- Promote gender equality and empower women
- Reduce child mortality
- Improve maternal health
- Combat HIV/AIDS, malaria, and other diseases
- Ensure environmental sustainability
- Develop a global partnership for development by 2015

CIDA's project with a Montreal-based NGO investigates a 1982 massacre in Guatemala. This project reflects CIDA's development priorities concerning human rights, democracy, and good governance. ■ (Source: William Rodman/ CIDA)

Grassroots Approaches

Many countries have experimented with grassroots approaches to development, or locally initiated small-scale projects. This alternative to top-down development pursued by the large-scale agencies described in the previous section is more likely to be culturally appropriate, locally supported through participation, and successful.

During the 1970s, for example, Kenya sponsored a national program whereby the government committed itself to providing teachers if local communities would build schools (Winans and Haugerud 1977). This program was part of Kenya's promotion of *harambee,* or self-help, in improving health, housing, and schooling. Local people's response to the schooling program, especially, was overwhelmingly positive. They turned out in large numbers to build schools, fulfilling their part of the bargain. They built so many schools that the government found it difficult to hold up its end of the bargain: paying the teachers' salaries. This program shows that self-help movements can be highly successful in mobilizing local participation, if the target is valued.

The term **social capital** refers to the intangible resources of social ties, trust, and cooperation. Many local grassroots organizations around the world have existed for several decades, using social capital to provide basic social needs even in the most desperately poor situations (see the Ethnographic Profile).

Religious organizations sponsor a wide variety of grassroots development projects. In the Philippines, the Basic Ecclesiastical Community (BEC) movement is based on Christian teachings and follows the model of Jesus as a supporter of the poor and oppressed (Nadeau 2002) (see Map 7.1 on page 177). The BECs seek to follow the general principles of liberation theology, which blends Christian principles of compassion and social justice, political consciousness-raising among the oppressed, and communal activism. In the rural areas, several BECs have successfully built trust among group members and leaders and developed people's awareness of the excesses of global capitalism and the dangers of private greed and accumulation. Part of their success is due to the fact that members were able to pursue new economic strategies outside the constraints of capitalism, such as organic farming, that require little capital input.

A BEC in Cebu City, on the Island of Cebu, the Philippines, however, was unsuccessful. It faced the challenge of organizing people who make a living scavenging in a nearby city dump. Both adults and children scavenge for materials that are then sorted and sold for recycling, such as plastic. They work for fourteen hours a day, seven days a week. It is an organized operation, with district officials monitoring the dump. Customary arrangements among the scavengers regulate their work areas. Scavenging requires no formal education and few tools, just a basket and a steel hook, and a kerosene lantern for nighttime work. Scavengers earn

social capital: the intangible resources existing in social ties, trust, and cooperation.

Ethnographic Profile

The Peyizan yo of Haiti

Haiti and the Dominican Republic share the island of Hispaniola. Following the island's discovery by Columbus in 1492, Spanish colonialists exterminated the island's indigenous Arawak Indians. In 1697, the French took control of what is now Haiti and instituted an exceptionally cruel system of African plantation slavery. In the late 1700s, the half million slaves revolted. In what is the only successful slave revolution in history, they ousted the French and established the first black republic in the western hemisphere.

Haiti's population of over 8 million people occupies a territory somewhat smaller than the state of Maryland in the United States (www.unfpa.org). The land is rugged, hilly, or mountainous. More than 90 percent of the forests have been cleared. Haiti is the poorest country in the western hemisphere. Severe inequality exists between the urban elite, who live in the capital city of Port-au-Prince, and everyone else.

The people in the countryside are *peyizan yo* (the plural form of *peyizan*), a Creole term for small farmers who produce for their own use and for the market (Smith 2001). Many also participate in small-scale marketing. Most peyizan yo in Haiti possess their own land. They grow vegetables, fruits (especially mangoes), sugar cane, rice, and corn.

Accurate health statistics are not available, but even rough estimates show that Haiti has the highest prevalence level of HIV/AIDS of any country in the region. Medical anthropologist Paul Farmer emphasizes the role of colonialism in the past and global structural inequalities now in causing these high rates (1992).

Colonial plantation owners grew fabulously rich from this island. It produced more wealth for France than all of France's other colonies combined and more than the 13 colonies in North America produced for Britain. Why is Haiti so poor now? Colonialism launched environmental degradation by clearing forests. After the revolution, the new citizens carried with them the traumatic history of slavery. Now, neo-colonialism and globalization are leaving new scars. For decades, the United States has played, and still plays, a powerful role in supporting conservative political regimes.

In contrast to these structural explanations, some people point to problems with the Haitian people: They cannot work together and they lack a vision of the future. In contrast to these views, Jennie Smith's ethnographic research in southwestern Haiti sheds light on life and perspectives on development of the peyizan yo (2001). She found many active social organizations with functions such as labour sharing to help each member get his or her field planted on time and cost sharing to help pay for health care or funerals. The peyizan yo had clear opinions about their vision for the future, including relative economic equality, political leaders with a sense of social service, *respe* (respect), and access of citizens to basic social services.

Readings

Paul Farmer. *AIDS and Accusation: Haiti and the Geography of Blame.* Berkeley, CA: University of California Press, 1992.

Jennie M. Smith. *When the Hands Are Many: Community Organization and Social Change in Rural Haiti.* Ithaca, NY: Cornell University Press, 2001.

Michel-Rolph Trouillot. *Haiti: State against Nation: The Origins and Legacy of Duvalierism.* New York: Monthly Review Press, 1990.

Video

Désounen: Dialogue with Death (Bullfrog Films).

Thanks to Jeannie Smith-Pariola, Berry College, for reviewing this material.

A woman repays her loan at a small-scale savings and loan business in rural Haiti (left). ■ (Source: © Gideon Mendel/CORBIS) *Many of the credit union members use their loans to set up small businesses. At a school in Port-au-Prince, (right), a teacher instructs a class with minimal equipment.*
■ (Source: © Philip Gould/CORBIS)

MAP 15.3 *Haiti. The Republic of Haiti occupies one-third of the Caribbean island of Hispaniola.*

more than other nonskilled labourers in the city. In the BEC meetings, the scavengers found little on which to build solidarity. Instead, they bickered with each other and complained about each other to the leaders. Kathleen Nadeau's interpretation is that the sheer poverty of the people was so great that communal values could not compete against their daily economic struggle. In such cases of extreme poverty with highly constrained options for alternative forms of income generation, Nadeau suggests that improving the people's lives may require government programs and support in addition to faith-based, grassroots initiatives.

With the push toward privatization in the 1980s in North America and Britain, an emphasis on supporting development efforts through nongovernmental organizations (NGOs) emerged. This trend prompted the formation of many NGOs in developing countries that often became partners with bilateral agencies to develop and support local projects on particular issues, such as girls' education, HIV/AIDS prevention, human rights, or refugee relief. For example, the Canada Fund in Thailand supports Thai NGOs that give small seed grants to grassroots organizations in rural Thailand. In India, CIDA collaborated with government agencies and NGOs to support a Tree Grower's Cooperative in three states undergoing rapid deforestation.

The Development Project

Development organizations, whether they are large multilaterals or local NGOs, implement their goals through the **development project**, a set of activities designed to put development policies into action. For example, suppose a government sets a policy of increased agricultural production by a certain percentage within a certain period. Development projects put in place to achieve the policy goal might include the construction of irrigation canals that would supply water to a specified number of farmers.

Anthropologists and the Development Project Cycle

Although details vary among organizations, all development projects have a **project cycle**, or the full process of a project from initial planning to completion (Cernea 1985). These steps include

- *Project identification:* Selecting a project to fit a particular purpose.

- *Project design:* Preparing the details of the project.
- *Project appraisal:* Assessing the project's budget.
- *Project implementation:* Putting the project into place.
- *Project evaluation:* Assessing whether the project goals were fulfilled.

Since the 1970s, applied anthropologists have been involved in development projects. First, they were hired primarily to do project evaluations, to determine whether the project had achieved its goals. Their research often showed that projects were dismal failures (Cochrane 1979). Three of their most frequent findings are

- The project was inappropriate for the cultural and environmental context.
- The target group, such as the poor or women, had not been reached, but instead project benefits had gone to some other group.
- The intended beneficiaries were actually worse off after the project than before it.

Jim Freedman, a Canadian anthropologist who worked as a consultant for bilateral (CIDA) and multilateral (United Nations) organizations, conducted a study of an irrigation and salinity control project in northern Pakistan. The project cycle provides part of the story about the results, but he goes beyond the project cycle to analyze the impact on the people most affected by the project—the freedom-loving Pathans, people whose ancestral roots lie in stateless, semi-nomadic life. Freedman summarizes the steps of the project cycle:

- *Project identification:* Renovate a water delivery system and reduce soil salination.
- *Project design:* An underground drainage system would be provided to control salination, which would increase food production and result in higher incomes for local farmers.
- *Project appraisal:* The budget was negotiated between CIDA, the World Bank, and Pakistan's government.
- *Project implementation:* The drains were built, and food production (wheat, sugar cane, and maize) increased modestly (around 5 percent over 10 years), but during the process of building the system, some small farmers were displaced.

---

development project: a set of activities designed to put development policies into action.
project cycle: the steps of a development project from initial planning to completion: project identification, project design, project appraisal, project implementation, and project evaluation.

sociocultural fit: a characteristic of informed and effective project design in which planners take local culture into account; opposite of one-size-fits-all project design.
traditional development anthropology (TDA): a scenario in which the anthropologist accepts the role of helping to make development work better, a kind

of "add an anthropologist and stir" approach to development.
critical development anthropology (CDA): an approach to international development in which the anthropologist takes on a critical-thinking role and asks why and to whose benefit particular development policies and programs are pursued.

- *Project evaluation:* The project assumed that the cost to small farmers was a small price to pay for the value of the improved technology to the more productive farmers (200–208).

Freedman drew broad conclusions about the interconnections between prosperity and democracy from the experience of working with this project. He observed that economic growth undermined social equity, and social and economic inequities undermined economic growth, a condition for democracy. What was missing from the project was a consideration of the effect of widening income disparities in the project villages and resultant shifts in power relations. The improved irrigation allowed landlords to increase their power over land and over their tenants, who became even more dependent on the protection of their patrons. The resulting factions intensified the conflict between rival landlords. Although the landlords increased their personal wealth, this did not translate into increased well-being for the villages, where disparities in wealth doubled or tripled (Freedman 2000).

One reason development initiatives often failed was that projects were typically identified and designed by Western economists located in cities far from the intended project site. These experts applied a universal formula, with little or no attention to the local cultural context (J. Scott 1998). In other words, projects were designed by "people-distant" and culturally uninformed economists and planners, but were evaluated by "people-close" and culturally informed anthropologists. By demonstrating the weaknesses in project planning that led to failed projects, and the need to take local cultural context into account in projects, cultural anthropologists gained a reputation in development circles as troublemakers and naysayers. Their role as watchdogs and critics should not be discounted because it draws attention to important problems, but gaining a role earlier in the project cycle, at the stages of project identification and design, would make anthropologists even more useful.

Sociocultural Fit

Review of many development projects over the past few decades reveals the importance of **sociocultural fit**, or taking the local culture into account in project design (Kottak 1985). For example, a project intended to improve nutrition and health in some South Pacific islands involved the transfer of large quantities of powdered milk to an island community. The local people, however, were lactose intolerant (unable to digest raw milk), and they all soon had diarrhea. They stopped drinking the milk and used the powder to whitewash their houses. Beyond wasting resources, inappropriately designed projects result in the exclusion of the intended beneficiaries. Two examples are when a person's signature is required but the people do not know how to write, and when photo identification cards are requested from Muslim women, whose faces may not be shown in public.

The Anthropological Critique of Development Projects

The early decades of development anthropology were dominated by **traditional development anthropology (TDA)**. In TDA, the anthropologist accepts the role of helping to make development work better, a kind of "add an anthropologist and stir" approach to development. Economists and others realize that anthropologists can help make projects more effective. For example, an anthropologist familiar with a local culture can provide information about what kinds of consumer goods would be desired by the people, or what might induce them to relocate with less resistance. The anthropologist may act as a cultural broker using knowledge of both the donor culture and recipient culture to devise a plan.

Anthropologists have expressed concern that helping make large-scale development projects work can be disastrous for local people and their environments (Bodley 1990; Horowitz and Salem-Murdock 1993). For example, a study of the welfare of local inhabitants of the middle Senegal valley (in the country of Senegal, West Africa) before and after the construction of a large dam shows that people's level of food insecurity increased (Horowitz and Salem-Murdock 1993) (see Map 15.4). Before the dam, periodic flooding of the plain supported a dense population supporting itself with agriculture, fishing, forestry, and herding. After the dam was constructed, water was released less often. The people downstream lacked sufficient water for their crops, and fishing was no longer a dependable source of food. At other times, dam managers released a large flood of water, damaging farmers' crops. Many downstream residents have had to leave the area due to the effects of the dam; they are victims of development-induced displacement (review Chapter 14). Downstream people now have high rates of schistosomaisis as a result of the dam construction because the disease spreads in the slow-moving water below the dam.

Other "dam stories" document the negative effects of dam construction on local people, including the destruction of their economy, social organization, sacred space, sense of home, and the environment (Loker 2003). Such megaprojects force thousands, even millions, of people in the affected area to cope with the changes in one way or another. Many leave; others stay and try to replace what they have lost by clearing new land and rebuilding. Most end up in situations far worse than where they lived originally

The growing awareness of the negative impact of many supposedly positive development projects has led to the emergence of **critical development anthropology (CDA)**. In this approach, the anthropologist does not simply accept a supportive role, but instead takes on a critical-thinking role. The question is not, "What can we do to make this project successful?" Instead, the anthropologist asks, "Is this a good project from the perspective of the local people and their environment?" After long and careful thinking, if the answer is yes, then the anthropologist can take a supportive role. If the answer is no, then the anthropologist can intervene with this information, taking on the role of either a whistle-blower to stop the project, or as an advocate promoting ideas about how to change the project in order to mitigate harm. In the case of the Senegal River dam project, applied anthropologists worked in collaboration with engineers and local people to devise an alternative management plan for the water flow in which regular and controlled amounts of water were released. In many other cases, the process is less positive with planners ignoring the anthropologist's advice (Loker 2000).

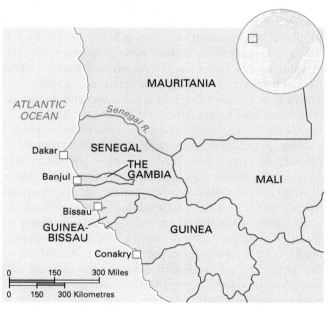

MAP 15.4   Senegal. The Republic of Senegal is mainly rolling sandy plains of the western Sahel. Senegal's economy has been struggling. Social inequality is extreme, and urban unemployment is high. Its population is around 11.7 million, of which 70 percent live in rural areas. Of the many ethnic groups, the Wolof are the largest. Islam is the major religion, practised by 94 percent of the population, with Christians 4 percent. Sufi brotherhoods are the organizing principle of Islam in Senegal.

Methods in Development Anthropology

Research about change and development relies on long-term fieldwork and standard research methods as described in Chapter 2. Often a development agency needs input from an anthropologist faster than what long-term fieldwork would allow. Specialized methods have emerged to respond to shorter time frames in order to provide useful answers to specific questions. Compared to standard long-term fieldwork, the methods used in development anthropology are more narrowly focused with a less holistic research agenda, make more use of multidisciplinary research teams, and rely on rapid research methods and participatory approaches.

Rapid Research Methods

Rapid research methods (RRMs) are research methods designed to provide focused information in a short time period (Chambers 1983). They include strategies such as going to the field with a prepared checklist of questions, conducting focus group interviews (talking to several people at the same time rather than one by one), and conducting "transect" observations (walking through a specific area with key informants and asking for explanations along the way) (Bernard 1995:139–140). When used effectively, RRMs can provide useful data for assessing the problems and opportunities related to development, particularly when several methods are used together.

An effective mix of RRMs was used for development project planning in rural Bali (Mitchell 1994). The research sought to identify environmental and social stresses that might be caused by economic development and then make recommendations to the government in preparing its next five-year development plan. The University of Windsor and an Indonesian university designed an eight-village study to provide data on ecological, economic, and social features. Each village was studied by a four-member team. Teams consisted of Indonesian and Canadian researchers, both men and women. All team members could speak Bahasa Indonesian (the national language) and at least one could also speak Bahasa Bali (the local language).

Researchers lived in the village for four weeks. The teams used several methods for data collection: background data from provincial documents and village records. They conducted household interviews with 15 men and 15 women from different neighbourhoods in

---

rapid research methods (RRMs): research methods designed to provide focused information in a short time period.

participatory research (PR): a method in development anthropology that involves

the local people in gathering data relevant to local development projects.

the village and with a sample of primary schoolchildren. They made observations of the village condition and villagers' daily activities. For each village, they generated a profile of biophysical features, production and marketing, local government, health and welfare, and expressive culture.

After the data collection, researchers gathered to collate their findings and generate a set of recommendations. Their report presented a range of issues for the government's consideration, including a discussion of the environmental and social stresses caused by increasing urbanization and international tourism.

Participatory Research Methods

Building on the RRM approach, another specialized technique is called **participatory research (PR)**, a way of collecting data that includes the involvement of and collaboration with the local people. Participatory research rests heavily on the anthropological assumption that local knowledge should not be bypassed but, rather, should be the foundation of development work. It proceeds by involving key community members at all stages of the research, from data collection to data analysis. This technique responds to the growing awareness that when the target population is involved in a development project, the project is more likely to be successful in the short run and sustainable over the long run (Kabutha, Thomas-Slaytor, and Ford 1993).

Local people, through PR, learn how to collect and analyze data themselves. They gain skills in how to prepare maps and charts and to collect and analyze other forms of local data. Once trained, they can continue data collection and analysis on their own. Participatory research increases the likelihood that projects will be maintained over time and will respond to changing local conditions in terms of design and management.

Development, Gender, and Indigeneity

In this section, we consider two major categories of people who have been affected by international development in various ways and are increasingly taking an active role in redefining development: women and indigenous people. Although they are overlapping categories, we present material about them separately for purposes of illustration.

Women and Development

Women constitute about half of every population, yet many live as subordinates in household configurations with more dominant group members. In the mid-1970s, gender inequity was recognized as a serious constraint to development. Emphasis on women and development— and later gender and development (Rathgeber 1990)—in multilateral and bilateral assistance programs, national governments, and NGOs—encouraged policies that made gender equity a goal of development, a goal that should transform the concept of development itself. Development has also resulted in women losing power in their communities, as well as former rights to property. One reason is that matrilineal kinship, a system that keeps property in the female line, is in decline throughout the world, often as a result of Westernization and modernization. Another is that Western experts have chosen to deal with men in the context of development projects.

In this section, we present examples of the male bias in international development. We then turn to examples in which some women's groups are taking development into their own hands and making it work for both themselves and their families.

The Male Bias in Development

Women have been affected by development differently from men within the same community and even the same household, because development has been pursued in an androcentric (male-centred) way. In the 1970s, researchers began to write about the fact that development projects were male-biased (Boserup 1970; Tinker 1976). Many projects completely bypassed women as beneficiaries or targeted men for such new initiatives as growing cash crops and learning about new technologies (Boserup 1970; Tinker 1976). This male bias in development contributed to increased gender inequality and hierarchy by giving men greater access to new sources of income and depriving women of their traditional economic roles. The development experts' image of a farmer, for example, was male, not female.

Women's projects were focused on the domestic domain. Thus, women's projects were typically concerned with infant feeding patterns, child care, and family planning, and, over time, this has led to what has been labelled the "domestication" of women worldwide (Rogers 1979). For example, University of Windsor anthropologist Lynne Phillips found in her research on rural Ecuadorian women (1998) that development discourses may inadvertently homogenize women's own interpretations of their situations. Terms such as the "feminization of agriculture" may flatten the complexity of women's lives. Her research is a reminder that women in societies exposed to development programs may not necessarily experience development in ways envisioned by policy-makers or by development critics.

The male bias in development also contributed to project failure. In the West African nation of Burkina Faso, a reforestation project targeted men as the sole participants, whose tasks would include planting and caring for the trees. Cultural patterns there dictate that men do not water plants; women do. The men planted the seedlings and left them. Since the women were not included as project participants, the new young trees that were planted died.

Exclusion of women from development continues to be a problem, in spite of many years of work attempting to place and keep women's issues on the development agenda. One such issue is gender-based violence. The problem is gaining attention even among the large multilaterals, where experts now realize that women cannot participate in a development program if they fear their husbands will beat them for leaving the house. The United Nations Commission on the Status of Women drafted a declaration opposing violence against women (Heise, Pitanguy, and Germain 1994). The declaration was adopted by the General Assembly in 1993. Article 1 of the declaration states that violence against women includes "any act of gender-based violence that results in, or is likely to result in, physical, sexual or psychological harm or suffering to women, including threats of such acts, coercion or arbitrary deprivations of liberty, whether occurring in public or private life" (Economic and Social Council 1992). This definition cites women as the focus of concern, but it includes girls (see Figure 15.2).

Programs that target violence against girls and women tend to deal with their effects, not the causes, often with disastrous results. For example, they may seek to increase personal security of women and girls in refugee camps by augmenting the number of guards at the camp when, in fact, it is often the guards who abuse refugee females (Martin 2005).

Women Organizing for Change

In many countries, women have made substantial gains in improving their status and welfare through forming organizations. These organizations range from "mothers' clubs" that provide communal child care to lending and credit organizations that provide women with the opportunity to start their own businesses. Some are local and small-scale; others are global in reach, such as Women's World Banking, an international organization that grew out of credit programs for poor working women in India.

In the 1990s, micro-finance became the leading development strategy adopted by governments and NGOs for alleviating poverty and empowering the poor, especially women. Because of women's higher repayment rates and preference for spending on family welfare, many of these programs target women specifically to increase program efficiency and to achieve more poverty alleviation.

Lynne Milgram's ethnographic research in the upland provinces of northern Luzon, Philippines (1999), documents how Ifugao women meet their households' needs by combining different forms of wage work, such as agriculture, crafts, and trading. In 1997, a new micro-finance initiative developed a local system of village savings-and-loan groups and connected them to local banking cooperatives. Milgram's work analyzes how women use the opportunities and constraints offered by this new project. In the first year of operation, the micro-finance program was very popular, particularly among farmers and craftspeople who do not have access to the formal banking sector because of their lack of collateral. They welcome the opportunity to obtain loans at interest rates of 15 percent per year—well below rates offered by local moneylenders (120 percent per year) and those available through the formal banking sector (21 to 26 percent per year). Realizing the limitations of a credit-only approach that simply gives loans to raise household income, this program also encourages members to contribute to pooled group savings from which they can make small personal loans. Milgram cautions, however, that many women still hesitate to take loans from the banking cooperative, fearing they might fall behind in their repayments.

Another community-based credit system in Mozambique, southern Africa helps farm women buy seeds, fertilizers, and supplies on loan (Clark 1992:24). When the loan program was first started, 32 farm families in the village of Machel formed themselves into 7 solidarity groups, each with an elected leader. The woman-headed farmer groups managed irrigation more efficiently and conferred on how to minimize use of pesticides and chemical fertilizers. Through their efforts, the women

FIGURE 15.2 Gender-Based Violence against Girls and Women throughout the Life Cycle

Prebirth	Sex-selective abortion, battering during pregnancy, coerced pregnancy
Infancy	Infanticide, emotional and physical abuse, deprivation of food and medical care
Girlhood	Child marriage, genital mutilation, sexual abuse by family members and strangers, rape, deprivation of food and medical care, child prostitution
Adolescence	Dating and courtship violence, forced prostitution, rape, sexual abuse in the workplace, sexual harassment
Adulthood	Partner abuse and rape, partner homicide, sexual abuse in the workplace, sexual harassment, rape
Old Age	Abuse and neglect of widows, elder abuse

Source: Adapted from Heise, Pitanguy, and Germain 1994:5.

Grameen Bank, a development project that began in Bangladesh to provide small loans to poor people, is one of the most successful examples of improving human welfare through "micro-credit." Professor Muhammad Yunnus (centre) founded Grameen Bank and continues to be a source of charismatic leadership for it. ■ (Source: © Robert Nickelsberg/Getty Images)

In another case, an informal system of social networks has emerged to help support poor women vendors in San Cristobal, Mexico (Sullivan 1992). Many of the vendors who work in the city square have fled from the highlands because of long-term political conflict there. They manufacture and sell goods to tourists, earning an important portion of household income. In the city, they find support in an expanded social network that compensates for the loss of support from the extensive god-parenthood system of the highlands. The vendors' new networks include relatives, neighbours, church members, and other vendors, regardless of their religious, political, economic, or social background.

These networks first developed in response to a series of rapes and robberies that began in 1987. Because the perpetrators were persons of power and influence, the women never pressed charges. Mostly single mothers and widows, they adopted a strategy of self-protection: They began to group together during the slow period each afternoon. They travel in groups and carry sharpened corset bones and prongs: "If a man insults one of them, the group surrounds him and jabs him in the groin" (39–40). If a woman is robbed, the other women surround her, comfort her, and help contribute something toward her loss. The mid-afternoon gatherings developed into support groups that provide financial assistance, child care, medical advice, and job skills. They have also publicly, and successfully, demonstrated against city officials' attempts to prevent them from continuing their vending. Through their efforts, these women refugees from highland Chiapas have brought greater security into their lives.

A final example of women's empowerment and personal risk reduction through organized efforts comes from Kazakhstan, central Asia. In response to widespread

quadrupled their harvests and were able to pay off their loans. Machel women then turned their attention to getting additional loans to improve their herds and to buy a maize mill. In spite of poverty, military conflict, the lack of government resources, and a drought, the project and the organization it fostered allowed many women farmers to improve their lives.

In the town of San Cristobal de las Casas, the capital city of Chiapas state in Mexico, a Maya vendor sells her goods. The city is located near the Tzotzil Maya communities of Chamula and Zinacantan. ■ (Source: © Philippe Giraud/Goodlook/CORBIS)

domestic violence of husbands against wives, an NGO called the Society of Muslim Women (SMW) defines domestic violence as a problem that the Islamic faith should address at the grassroots level (Snajdr 2005). The organization declines to work with the police and civic activists who provide secular responses that involve criminalization of the offence, arrest of offenders, and other public procedures. Instead, SMW views domestic violence as a private matter that should be dealt with privately, using Islamic and Kazakhi values to deal with the problem. The SMW thus works completely outside the criminal justice system. Its goal is to provide aid to survivors of domestic abuse. Their three approaches are counselling, shelter, and mediation. Members of SMW are available to and supportive of both abusers and their victims. Their support ranges from simply talking with people to helping move an abused woman into a safe living situation. The organization's guiding principle is to find a way, if possible, to rebuild the family. This goal may sound conservative, and even dangerous, in a situation where abuse is reported to occur in four out of five marriages. Yet, without funding or professional training, SMW members have provided support for countless women. They help the women overcome isolation. They shift blame away from the victims by using Islamic rhetoric of familial commitment and gender equality and nationalist rhetoric that links men's alcoholism with occupation by the Russians. Sheltering abused women is defined as a Kazakhi custom of hospitality and as conforming with the Muslim virtue of patience, giving the spouses time to think about their relationship.

Indigenous Peoples and Development

In this section, we describe how indigenous peoples have been victimized by many aspects of growth-oriented development, as they were by colonialism before it. We then look at examples of how many indigenous groups are redefining development and taking it into their own hands.

The term **indigenous peoples** refers to groups of people who are the original inhabitants of a particular territory. Often, indigenous peoples now take the name of First Peoples, or in Canada, First Nations peoples, as a way of self-definition as original claimants to a place. Indigenous peoples are usually a numerical minority in the states that control their territory. The United Nations distinguishes between indigenous peoples and minority groups such as the Roma, the Tamils of Sri Lanka, or Sikhs in Canada, for example. Although this distinction is useful in some ways, it should not be taken as a hard-and-fast

difference (Maybury-Lewis 1997; Plant 1994). It is most useful to think of all these groups as forming a continuum from more clearly indigenous groups, such as the Inuit, to minority/ethnic groups that may not be geographically original to a place but share many problems with indigenous peoples as a result of living within a more powerful majority culture.

Indigenous peoples differ from most national minorities by the fact that they often occupy remote areas and were, until the era of colonial expansion, less affected by outside influences. Now, governments and international businesses have recognized that their lands often contain valuable natural resources, such as natural gas and timber in Canada and gold in Papua New Guinea and the Amazon, sapphires in Madagascar, hydroelectric potential in large rivers throughout the world, and cultural attractions. In different contexts, governments have paid varying degrees of attention to integrating indigenous peoples into mainstream culture in the interests of fostering state unity.

Accurate demographic statistics on indigenous peoples are difficult to obtain (Kennedy and Perz 2000). There are often questions about who should be counted as indigenous, and in some cases, there are political implications to the collecting of statistics. Governments may not bother to conduct a census of indigenous peoples, or if they do, they may underreport counts of indigenous peoples in order to downplay recognition of their very existence as a group (Baer 1982:12). A few island populations in India's Andaman Islands in the Bay of Bengal remain uncounted because Indian officials cannot gain access to them (Singh 1994) (see Map 3.2 on page 71).

Estimates of the total population of indigenous people worldwide range between 300 million and 500 million people (Hughes 2003). The greatest numbers live in Asia, including central Asia, South Asia, East Asia, and Southeast Asia. Canada's First Nations population is under 2 million, whereas that in the United States is around 1 million. Worldwide, indigenous people make up roughly 5 percent of the global population of 6.5 billion people.

Marginalization of Indigenous Peoples

Many indigenous peoples and their cultures have been exterminated as a result of contact with outsiders. Besides death and decline through contagious disease, slavery, warfare, and other forms of violence have threatened their survival. With colonialism, indigenous people experienced wholesale attacks as outsiders sought to take over their land by force, prevented them from practising their traditional lifestyle, and integrated them into the

---

indigenous peoples: groups of people who are the original inhabitants of a particular territory.

colonial state as marginalized subjects. The loss of economic, political, and expressive autonomy have had devastating effects on indigenous peoples.

Like colonialism, contemporary global and state political and economic interests often involve takeover and control of indigenous people's territory. Reduction in the biodiversity of their natural environment is directly linked to impoverishment, despair, and overall cultural decline (Maffi 2005; Arambiza and Painter 2006). These processes are common worldwide, creating new risks for indigenous people's welfare. In Southeast Asia, states use policies of "planned resettlement" in order to displace indigenous people, or "hill tribes," in the name of progress (Evrard and Goudineau 2004).

Anthropological analysis of government policies in Thailand for development of the highlands reveals the complex interplay between outside interests and the welfare of the *chao khao,* or "hill people" (Kesmanee 1994). The hill people include the Karen, Hmong, Mien, Lahu, Lisu, Akha, and others, totalling roughly half a million people or 1 percent of the entire Thai population. There is international pressure for the hill people to replace opium cultivation with other cash crops. The Thai government is concern with political stability and national security in this area, which borders on Burma and Laos. It therefore has promoted development projects to establish more connections between the highlands and the lowlands through transportation and marketing.

Efforts to find viable substitute crops especially among the Hmong, who have traditionally been most dependent on opium as a cash crop, have been unsuccessful. Alternative crops require heavy use of fertilizers and pesticides, which are costly to the farmers and greatly increase environmental pollution. These crops are less lucrative for the farmers. Logging companies have gained access to the hills and have done far more damage to the forests than the highlanders' horticultural practices. Increased penetration of the hill areas by lowlanders and international tourists have promoted the increase in the highlands of HIV/AIDS rates, illegal trafficking of girls and boys for sex work, and opium addiction.

The Thai government, like neighbouring Laos, has attempted to relocate highland horticulturalists to the plains through various resettlement schemes. Highlanders who opt for relocation find the lowland plots to be unproductive due to poor soil quality. Their economic status declined compared to what it had been in the hills. A new risk has emerged for those resettled in Thailand and Laos. They are now heavy consumers of methamphetamines, or amphetamine-type stimulants (Lyttleton 2004). Overall, the effects of 40 years of "development" have been disastrous for the hill peoples of Southeast Asia.

Throughout their recent history of contact with the outside world, indigenous peoples have actively sought to resist the negative effects of "civilization." Since the 1980s, more effective and highly organized forms of protest have become prominent. Indigenous groups hire lawyers and other experts as consultants in order to reclaim and defend their territorial rights, to gain self-determination, and to secure protection from outside risks. Many indigenous people have themselves become trained as lawyers, researchers, and advocates.

Indigenous People and Territorial Entitlements

The many land and resource claims being made by indigenous peoples are a direct response to their earlier losses. Depending on how these disputes are resolved, they can be a basis for conflicts, ranging from fairly benign litigation to attempts at secession (Jensen 2994, Plant 1994). In this section, we provide brief notes on the status of indigenous people's territorial rights, especially to land. Within each large world region, country by country variation exists in legal codes and adherence to such codes that may exist.

Few Latin American countries provide legal protection against encroachment on the land of indigenous groups. Nicaragua, Peru, Colombia, Ecuador, Bolivia, and Brazil have taken the lead in enacting policies that legitimize indigenous rights to land and demarcating and titling indigenous territories (Plant 1998; Stocks 2005). A wide gap often exists, however, between policy and actual protection. Despite the efforts, increasing numbers of Indians throughout the entire region of Latin America have been forced off their land in the past few decades, through poverty, violence, and environmental degradation due to encroachment by logging companies, mining operations, ranch developers, and others. In response, many migrate to cities and seek wage labour. Those who remain face extreme poverty, malnutrition, and personal and group insecurity.

A surge of political activism by indigenous people has occurred since the 1990s, sometimes involving physical resistance. Violence continues to erupt between indigenous groups and state-supported power structures, especially in the southern Mexican state of Chiapas (see Map 5.4 on page 129). In November 2005, participants at the First Symposium on Isolated Indigenous Peoples of the Amazon created a group called the International Alliance for the Protection of Isolated Indigenous Peoples (2005). The group seeks to make the relevant state governments aware of the current endangered situation of many indigenous peoples in Amazonia and in the Gran Chaco region to its south. They demand their right to isolation, if that is their choice, and to protection from unwelcome outside contact and encroachment.

In Canada, the law distinguishes between two different types of Aboriginal land claims (Plant 1994). "Specific claims" concern problems arising from previous agreements or treaties, and are moving through the courts. "Comprehensive claims" are those made by

Hunting remains an important part of Cree subsistence activities. Here, meat dries over a slow fire at a hunting camp. ■ (Source: Naomi Adelson)

several thousand Cree and Inuit were to be affected by a large hydroelectric project. It was agreed that the indigenous peoples would receive $225 million in partial compensation for their original title. A reserve was set aside for hunting, fishing, and trapping, but the agreement said that the government of Quebec and several corporations had the right to develop resources on those lands. In 1989, the Quebec government renewed its interest in hydroelectric development. The Great Whale River project would have threatened the livelihood and environment of the Cree in the area, and they successfully opposed the project on the grounds of global concerns about pollution and the protection of natural environments (Adelson 1998).

THINKING OUTSIDE THE BOX

FOR CURRENT information on territorial rights of indigenous peoples, consult the websites of Cultural Survival (www.cs.org) and Survival International (www.survival-international.org).

In Asia, most countries have been reluctant to recognize the concept of special land rights of indigenous peoples (Plant 1994). In Bangladesh, for example, settlers from the crowded plains have encroached on the formerly protected area of the Chittagong Hill Tracts (see Map 9.1 on page 231). Non-indigenous settlers now occupy the most fertile land. A large hydroelectric dam built in 1963 displaced 100 000 hill dwellers because they could no longer practise horticulture in the flooded areas. A minority received financial aid, but most did not. Tribal opposition groups began emerging, and conflict, although suppressed in the world news, has been ongoing for decades. Other sites of contestation with the state over land and resources in the Asia-Pacific region include the Moros of the southern Philippines (see Map 7.1 on page 177), and the people of Irian Jaya in western Papua New Guinea. In these cases, the indigenous people's fight for succession from the state that controls them is costing many lives.

In Africa, political interests of state governments in establishing and enforcing territorial boundaries have created difficulties for indigenous peoples, especially foragers and pastoralists who are, for example, accustomed to moving their herds freely. Pastoralists in the Sahel region of Africa have been particularly affected by this process. Many formerly autonomous pastoralists of the Sahel region (see Map 15.6 on page 416) have been transformed into refugees living in terrible conditions. The Tuareg, for example, have traditionally lived and herded in a territory crossing what are now five different countries: Mali, Niger, Algeria, Burkina Faso, and Libya (Childs and Chelala 1994). Because of political conflict in the region, thousands of Tuareg people live in exile in Mauritania, and their prospects are grim. Resistance movements spring up, but states move quickly to suppress them. The people of southern Sudan have been living in violence since 1983 (Salih 1999)

Native peoples who have not been displaced and have made no treaties or agreements. Most of the former claims have led to monetary compensation. In the latter category, interest in oil and mineral exploration has prompted governments to negotiate with indigenous peoples in an effort to have their Native claims either relinquished or redefined. In some provinces, especially British Columbia, current claims affect most of the province (Woolford 2005). One recent land claim case has been settled after 112 years of bargaining. A historic land-claim treaty gives the Nisga'a of British Columbia $235 million in cash, 2000 square kilometres of land, and self-government powers (Jensen 2004). The Nunavut land claim was settled, granting about 25 000 Inuit access to a vast tract of land, including subsurface rights (Jensen 2004) (see Map 15.5).

Anthropologists played a role in the 1975 James Bay and Northern Quebec Agreement. The James Bay Cree Project provided the Cree and the Quebec government with information that helped settle the land claim (Salisbury 1986). Traditional hunting and fishing lands of

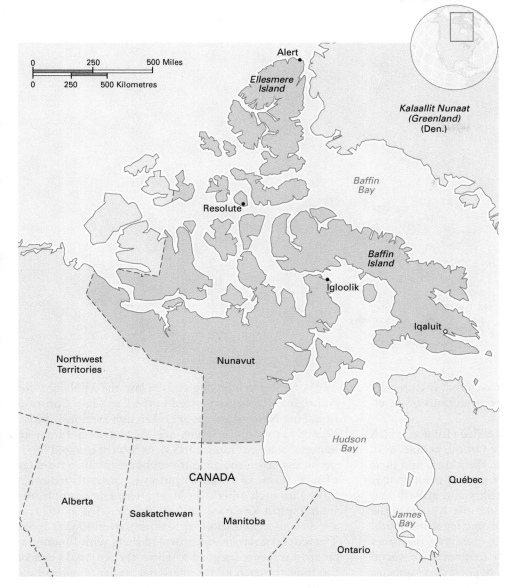

MAP 15.5 Nunavut, Canada. Created in 1999, Nunavut is the newest and largest of Canada's territories and provinces. It is also the least populated, with 30 000 people. About 85 percent of the people are Aboriginal peoples, mainly Inuit. Official languages are Inuktitut, Inuinnagtun, English, and French. The landscape is mainly Arctic tundra. The award-winning movie, *Atanarjuat* (*The Fast Runner*), was produced by Inuit filmmakers and filmed in Nunavut.

(see Map 15.7 on page 417). They have been subject to genocide and violent displacement for global and local political and economic reasons, not the least of which involves the rich deposits of oil in the southern part of the country (Warren 2001) As mentioned in the Ethnographic Profile in Chapter 1 on page 22, South Africa has established more protective legislation for San peoples than have Namibia or Botswana.

The picture is mixed in Australia and New Zealand, with more progress in Australia in terms of legal recognition of Aboriginal territorial rights. Urban development, expansion of the non-Aboriginal population, road building, mineral extraction, and international tourism are some of the major threats to both livelihood and protection of sacred space. Aboriginal activism has seen some notable successes in achieving what is referred to as *native title* (Colley 2002). A key turning point in Australia occurred through the efforts of Eddie Koiko Mabo, from the Torres Strait Islands (see Map 4.3 on page 107). He and his group, the Miriam people, took their claim of rights to their traditional land and water to the High Court, contesting the principle of *terra nullius,* or "empty land." Colonialists and neo-colonialist developers use *terra nullius* to justify territorial takeovers. Mabo convinced the High Court of the legitimacy of the Miriams' claim in 1992.

Organizing for Change

Many indigenous peoples have formed their own organizations for change in order to promote development from within. In Ethiopia, for example, many NGOs organized by local people have sprung up since the 1990s (Kassam 2002). One organization in the southern region is especially noteworthy, because it seeks to provide a model of development based on the oral traditions of the Oromo people. This new model thus combines elements of Western-defined "development" with Oromo values

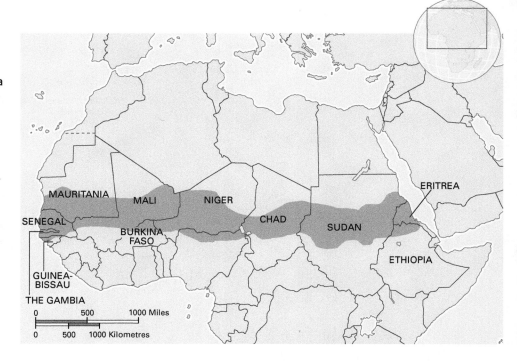

MAP 15.6 Sahel Region. The word *sahel* comes from the Arabic for shore or border, referring in this case to the area between the Sahara desert and the more fertile regions to the south. Primarily savannah, the region has been the home to many rich kingdoms that controlled Saharan trade routes. Most people make their living from pastoralism and semi-sedentary cattle-raising. The region has recently experienced several major droughts, leading to widespread death of herd animals, widespread human starvation and malnutrition, and forced population displacement.

and laws and provides a new approach that is culturally appropriate and goes beyond external notions of development and usual Oromo lifeways.

The indigenous Oromo NGO is called Hundee, which refers to roots, or the origins of the Oromo people, and, by extension, to all Oromo people, their land, and their culture. Hundee uses a theory of development that is based in Oromo metaphors of fertility and growth and involves gradual transformation like the spirals in the horn of a ram. Hundee relies on Oromo legal and moral principles about the communal use of natural resources and the redistribution of wealth to provide a social welfare system. These are elements of good development, as distinguished from the "bad development" that has inflicted hunger and dependency on the Oromo people.

Hundee's long-term goal is to empower Oromo communities to be self-sufficient. It takes the view the Oromo culture is a positive force for social and economic change, rather than a barrier. Hundee members use a participatory approach in all their endeavours. They consult with traditional legal assemblies to identify needs and then to shape projects to address those needs. Specific activities include the establishment of a credit association and a grain bank to help combat price fluctuations and food shortages.

The Assembly of First Nations (AFN), formed in Canada in 1982, has become the unofficial mouthpiece for many First Nations groups, presenting a united front on constitutional and self-government issues (Frideres

1998). Skilled in lobbying and the law, the AFN fights for Aboriginal rights guaranteed in the Canadian Constitution. First Nations groups are taken more seriously today because Aboriginal issues are viewed as a threat to national security (Tanner 1983). In this era of rapid Internet access, many indigenous groups are taking advantage of new forms of communication in order to maintain links with each other over large areas. For example, the Inuit Tapiriit Kanatami of Canada, founded in 1971, is a national organization representing over 40 000 Inuit. The federal government provided them with funding to create a website designed to allow the national voice of the Inuit to reach an international audience, encourage understanding and learning about the Inuit, and provide a virtual community linking Inuit groups and organizations across the Arctic. The Grand Council of the Cree has collaborated with the Inuit Tapiriit Kanatami and other organizations over land issues.

In many cases, indigenous peoples' development organizations have been formed that link formerly separate groups (Perry 1996:245–246) as a response to external threats. In Australia, many indigenous groups have formed pan-Australian organizations and regional coalitions, such as the Pitjantjatjara Land Council, that have had success in land claim cases. In southern Africa, many formerly separate San groups joined together to claim a share in the profits of commercial marketing of hoodia as a diet pill (review the Ethnographic profile in Chapter 1 on

---

development aggression: the imposition of development projects and policies without the free, prior, and informed consent of the affected people.

life project: local people's definition of the direction they want to take in life, informed by their knowledge, history, and context.

MAP 15.7 Sudan. The Republic of Sudan gained its independence from Britain in 1956 but, unlike other former British colonies, did not join the Commonwealth. The year before independence, a civil war began between the north and south. In 2005, a treaty granted southern Sudan the status of an autonomous region for six years to be followed by a referendum. In 2003, conflict erupted in the Darfur region. Sudan and neighbouring Chad are also having conflicts. Most of the economy depends on agriculture, although oil production and trade have increased. The population of 39 million includes two ethnic groups: Arabs with Nubian roots and non-Arab black Africans. Arabic is the dominant language of the north. Most Sudanese also speak local tribal languages. Sunni Islam is the dominant religion (70 percent) in the north, with indigenous religions also important (25 percent). Christianity (5 percent) is practised mainly in the south.

page 22). Many indigenous groups are taking advantage of new forms of communication in order to build and maintain links with each other over large areas.

Although it is tempting to see hope in the newly emerging forms of resistance, self-determination, and organizing among indigenous peoples, such hope cannot be generalized to all indigenous peoples. Many are making progress and their economic status is improving; others are suffering extreme political and economic repression.

Urgent Issues in Development

In this section, we focus on some of the most urgent issues and new directions in development as informed by findings of cultural anthropologists and the views and voices of people themselves. The three topics are the redefinition of development projects as more people-centred, the relationship between human rights and development, and the role of cultural heritage in development.

From Development Projects to Life Projects

As we discussed earlier in this chapter, development projects are the main mechanism through which development institutions implement their goals. They are typically designed by outsiders, often with little local knowledge, and they follow a universal, one-size-fits-all pattern. They range from megaprojects such as massive dams to small projects, with the former being much more damaging to local people than the latter. The so-called beneficiaries or target population are often not consulted at all about projects that will affect their community. Critics of such externally imposed and often damaging initiatives refer to such actions as **development aggression**, the imposition of development projects and policies without the free, prior, and informed consent of the affected people (Tauli-Corpuz 2005).

Moving beyond critique, indigenous people, women, and others who are victimized by external and megadevelopment are redefining what should be done to improve their lives or protect them from further decline.

They propose the concept of the life project rather than the development project. A **life project** is local people's vision of the direction they want to take in life, informed by their knowledge, history, and context, and how to achieve that vision.

Human Rights: Global and Local

Life projects, or people-defined and people-centred development, can be considered a human right and thus in accord with the UN's Declaration of Human Rights that was ratified in 1948. Local people around the world are claiming a right to their culture, most basically, under the rubric of cultural rights (Albro and Bauer 2005). Cultural rights protect cultural difference as a basic factor of human identity, dignity, and survival. Cultural rights seek a universal recognition of the right to be different.

As we discussed earlier, people in developing countries and indigenous people throughout the world have added their voices to discussions of human rights and cultural rights, insisting on group rights to self-determination, locally defined paths of change, and attention to issues such as freedom from hunger. Local groups are engaging with global definitions of human rights and adapting them to their own interests and

In Colombia, a 5-year-old boy, Ever Hernando Salce, has blisters on his face caused by the herbicide sprayed on coca farms from planes working for Plan Colombia, financed by the U.S. war on cocaine *(left)*. ■ (Source: © Reuters/CORBIS) Bolivian security forces confront coca farmers during a protest march to the capital city of La Paz, and they scatter to avoid arrest *(right)*. They were protesting the U.S.-backed coca eradication plan that affects their livelihoods. This photograph was taken before President Evo Morales was elected. His policy allows coca farmers to grow a small amount of coca for traditional consumption. ■ (Source: © George Philipas/Alamy)

needs (Merry 2006). As culturally diverse groups seek to define and claim their rights in an increasingly globalized world, we are all faced with the challenge of considering contending positions (see the Multiple Cultural Worlds box).

Human Rights and Development

In this section, we provide two illustrations of how development and human rights are linked. In the first, we find ties between large-scale development institutions and military control in the Philippines. The second case addresses the question of environmental destruction as a violation of human and cultural rights.

Among the Ifugao, indigenous peoples of the highland region of northern Luzon, the Philippines (see Map 7.1 on page 177), the militarization of everyday life has had serious negative consequences

(Kwiatkowski 1998). The military presence is everywhere—in schools, clinics, and, especially, at sites of large development projects such as dams. The military is there to ensure that people do not participate in what it considers subversive activities. Military force has been used to suppress local resistance to dams funded by the World Bank, resulting in numerous human-rights violations, including torture, killings, imprisonment, and harassment of people for suspected subversive activities (Drucker 1987). Members of a local NGO that support more appropriate, small-scale forms of development that would benefit more people in the area have been harassed by the military. The case of the Ifugao illustrates how the powerful interests of state governments, international development agencies, and corporate interests often promote their plans and projects and violate human rights along the way.

Multiple Cultural Worlds

HUMAN RIGHTS VERSUS ANIMAL RIGHTS

Human rights are often understood to include the right of people, as members of a cultural group, to practise their cultural traditions. This provision extends the notion of human rights from including mainly the right to fulfilling basic physical needs such as health and personal security to including practices such as animal sacrifice, female genital cutting, hunting certain animals, and girls wearing head scarves in school—all issues that have received recent attention from European and North American governments and media because they differ from cultural practices in those countries. In many countries, a debate about some cultural practices is carried out between human-rights activists who support cultural rights and those who support animal rights.

In spring 1999, members of the Makah Nation, a Native American group living in Washington state, undertook a revival of their traditional practice of hunting grey whales (Winthrop 2000). Like many other Native people of the Pacific Northwest, the Makah's traditional economy depended on fish, shellfish, and marine mammals. A treaty of 1855 provides the Makah with the right to hunt whales and seals. The practice died out, however, in the twentieth century due to dwindling supplies as a result of commercial over-hunting. In 1982, the International Whaling Commission (IWC) imposed a ban on all commercial whaling, but allowed continued whale hunting for subsistence purposes. In 1994, the grey whale population had recovered and it was taken off the endangered list. The IWC allocated the Makah the right to harvest 20 whales during the period from 1998 to 2002.

When, under this new plan, the Makah killed a 30 tonne, 10 metre whale in May 1999, the Makah watching the event cheered. The animal-rights activists at the scene, in contrast, protested and said this occasion should have been one of mourning and not celebration.

The Nuu-chah-nulth of Vancouver Island saw the whaling as a potential treaty issue, but voiced concern that it would pit Aboriginal rights against environmental rights. While the Makah see the revival of whale hunting as a sign of cultural revival, some animal-rights activists say that the way the hunt is being carried out is not culturally authentic (the Makah first harpoon the whale and then use a rifle to kill it, for example) and, thus, the claim of whale hunting as a traditional cultural right is not legitimate. Environmental groups argued that cultural rights to whaling could be the "thin edge of the wedge" that opens up commercial whaling in countries such as Japan and Norway that also claim cultural rights to whaling. Other protests are motivated by ecological concerns for preservation of the species against extinction, supporting a concept of animal, especially mammalian, rights to life. The First Nations Environmental Network, based in Tofino, Vancouver Island, is opposed to whale hunting, arguing that the act of killing whales cannot be justified spiritually or morally (Lamirande 1999).

FOOD FOR THOUGHT

• What other examples in the media illustrate the tension between human rights and cultural rights? Compare this case with other examples of human versus animal rights. Where do you stand in these debates and what is the basis for your position?

Development that leads to environmental degradation, such as pollution, deforestation, and erosion, can also be considered a form of human-rights violation. Slain Ogoni leader Ken Saro-Wiwa made this point eloquently in a 1992 speech to the United Nations Working Group on Indigenous Populations:

Environmental degradation has been a lethal weapon in the war against the indigenous Ogoni people. . . . Oil exploration has turned Ogoni into a wasteland: lands, streams, and creeks are totally and continually polluted; the atmosphere has been poisoned, charged as it is with hydrocarbon vapors, methane, carbon monoxide, carbon dioxide, and soot emitted by gas which has been flared 24 hours a day for 33 years in close proximity to human habitation. . . . The rainforest has fallen to the axe of the multinational companies . . . the Ogoni countryside is no longer a source of fresh air and green vegetation. All one sees and feels around is death. (quoted in Sachs 1996:13–16)

Many social scientists now argue, along with Saro-Wiwa, that such forms of development violate human rights

A farmer walks through an oil-soaked field *(left)*. **About 500 000 Ogoni people live in Ogoniland, a deltaic region in southern Nigeria. The fertility of the Niger delta has supported farming and fishing populations at high density for many years. Since Shell discovered oil there in 1958, 100 oil wells were constructed in Ogoniland and countless oil spills have occurred.** ■ (Source: © CORBIS. All Rights Reserved.) **Ogoni author and Nobel prizewinner Ken Saro-Wiwa founded the Movement for Survival of Ogoni People (MOSOP) in 1992 to protest Shell's actions in Ogoniland and the Nigerian government's indifference** *(right)*. **In 1995, he was arrested, tried for murder under suspicious circumstances, and executed by hanging. His execution brought about an international outcry while Shell's response was largely denial of any problem.** ■ (Source: © CORBIS)

since they undermine a people's way of life and threaten their continued existence (Johnston 1994).

Cultural Heritage and Development: Linking the Past and Present to the Future

In Chapter 13, we began the discussion of cultural heritage and its potential for preserving people's heritage, both tangible and nontangible, and creating employment opportunities for local people through cultural tourism. In this section, we go more deeply into the complicated connections between cultural heritage and improving people's welfare from a life-project perspective.

The connection of cultural heritage to development is clearly a double-edged sword (Bauer 2006). In other words, promoting cultural heritage, especially through tourism and expansion of supportive infrastructure such as roads and hotels, can preserve and protect cultural heritage as well as damage and destroy it. An emerging

arena for legal involvement with culture is the area of intellectual property rights law, or cultural property rights law. Legal definitions and protections of rights to various forms of knowledge and behaviour are another double-edged sword. On the one hand, they help people, such as the San of southern Africa, to gain a share of the profits from the hoodia plant (review the Ethnographic Profile in Chapter 1 on page 22). On the other hand, they transform much of everyday life into a legal battle. International and country government laws are one step in seeking to prevent or at least reduce damage and destruction. UNESCO has adopted several guidelines which are just that—they are not binding and have no sanctions in case of violations.

Both the preservation of culture and its protection from damage and destruction connect with the reality that culture is always in process, always changing, and thus policies and laws interact with culture awkwardly. Over the next several years, culture—however defined and understood around the world—will be a major factor in international, regional, and local development and change.

At the Shan-Dany museum in Oaxaca, Mexico, indigenous people established a museum to house artifacts from their culture and to promote economic development for the village and the region by strengthening the local weaving industry. The museum provides outreach to schoolchildren and encourages them to learn more about their culture. ■ (Source: Jeffrey Cohen)

Cultural Anthropology and the Future

During the past few decades, cultural anthropologists have played an important role in defining and exposing a wide range of human-rights abuses. Although this whistle-blowing can promote positive change, cultural anthropologists need to work harder to collaborate with local people to further their goals and to participate more actively in advocacy work directed toward the protection of human/cultural rights. Another important activity is continued dialogue about culture, cultural diversity, and cultural survival across groups in order to promote greater understanding and tolerance.

Determining how cultural anthropologists can contribute more effectively to a better future for humanity is a challenge for a field with its intellectual roots in studying *what is* rather than *what might be*. One path is toward promoting continued dialogue on human rights and cultural diversity, which should help promote greater understanding and tolerance.

But just as local people everywhere are reclaiming their culture, so also are they helping to redefine the theory, practice, and application of anthropology. Although we live in a time of war, it is also a time of hope, in which insights and strength often come from those with the least in terms of material wealth but with cultural wealth beyond measure. As the only discipline concerned with the totality of individual and collective rights and responsibilities, human interaction with the natural environment, people's patterns of production and consumption, family structures and political organizations, language, expressive culture, and religious beliefs, anthropology is a field of study that can speak to and advocate for increased respect for this cultural wealth.

Key Questions Revisited

WHAT is development and the approaches to achieving it?

Several theories or models of development exist, including modernization, growth-oriented development, distributional development, human development, and sustainable development. They differ in terms of how they define development and how to achieve it.

Institutional approaches to development, whether pursued by large-scale or grassroots organizations, tend to rely on the development project as a vehicle of local change. Cultural anthropologists have been hired as consultants on development projects, typically at the end of the project cycle to provide evaluations. Anthropologists have pushed for involvement earlier in the project so that their cultural knowledge can be used in project planning to avoid common errors. A one-size-fits-all project design often results in failed projects because of a lack of sociocultural fit. In traditional development anthropology, anthropological knowledge contributes to development projects by adding insights that will make a project work. In critical development anthropology, anthropological knowledge may suggest that the most socially beneficial path is either to stop the project or to redesign it.

Applied anthropologists involved in development work use several specialized methods for data collection. Rapid research methods (RRMs) provide data in a short time period. Participatory research (PR) is collaborative and involves training local people in how to do applied research such as social mapping and local censuses.

HOW is development related to women and indigenous people?

Indigenous people and women have been affected by international development in various ways, often negatively. They are taking an increasingly active role in redefining development to better suit their vision of the future.

Western development planning and projects have long suffered from a male bias in project design. Excluding women from projects often results in failed projects. Women are stating their needs and visions for the future, and thus redefining development in ways that are helpful

to them. They have added the issue of violence against women and girls to the policy agenda of development institutions worldwide, including the large multilaterals.

Colonialism, neo-colonialism, and globalization have had serious negative effects on indigenous peoples and women worldwide in terms of declines in their entitlements and standard of living. Often, such losses are tied to environmental degradation and violence. Indigenous peoples throughout the world suffer from lack of secure claim to their ancestral territories. They are seeking legal recognition of territorial claims from state governments and protection from encroachment. Some governments are responding to their claims; others are not. Establishing organizations has been a major source of strength for promoting indigenous people's rights.

WHAT are urgent issues in development?

Three urgent issues, as informed by cultural anthropology and the views and voices of people themselves, are (1) the redefinition of development projects as life projects or people-centred projects, (2) the relationship between human rights and development, and (3) the role of cultural heritage in development. Indigenous people, women, and others adversely affected by certain forms of development are promoting a new kind of development that is people-centred and that enhances the life projects that people define for themselves. The concept of the life project is a human right, and a right to live in one's cultural world without encroachment, threat, and discrimination.

Cultural anthropologists contribute insights from different cultures about perceptions of basic human and cultural rights, and this knowledge, linked to advocacy, may be able to help prevent human/cultural rights abuses in the future. People's cultural heritage can be a path toward improved welfare, but it is a double-edged sword. Promoting cultural tourism can protect culture but also lead to damage and destruction. An emerging area is the legalization of cultural heritage through intellectual property rights law, another double-edged sword.

Culture is a central issue of our time, and local people are working with cultural anthropologists to address the challenges of an increasingly globalized, insecure, but exciting world.

KEY CONCEPTS

myanthrolab

To reinforce your understanding of this chapter, and to identify topics for further study, visit MyAnthroLab at www.myanthrolab.com for diagnostic tests and a multimedia ebook.

SUGGESTED READINGS

Robert Albro and Joanne Bauer, eds. Cultural Rights: What They Are, Why They Matter, How They Can Be Realized. Special issue of *Human Rights Dialogue: An International Forum for Debating Human Rights,* Series 2(12), Spring 2005. Articles in this issue address rights to forest resources, languages, marriage practices, and legal issues related to genocide.

Mario Blaser, Harvey A. Feit, and Glenn McRae, eds. *In the Way of Development: Indigenous Peoples, Life Projects and Globalization.* New York: Zed Books, 2004. The authors are indigenous leaders, social activists, and anthropologists. Topics include the environment, women's status, social justice, participation, and dealing with mega-development projects.

Thomas W. Collins and John D. Wingard, eds., *Communities and Capital: Local Struggles against Corporate Power and Privatization.* Athens, GA: University of Georgia Press, 2000. Nine case studies of local resistance against large capitalist forces follow an introductory chapter that sets the stage. Cases include clam farmers of North Carolina, a fishing community in Malaysia, and banana growers in Belize.

H. Dagenais and D. Piché eds., *Women, Feminism and Development/Femmes, Féminisme et Développement.* Montreal and Kingston: McGill-Queen's University Press, 1994. This book contains French- and English-language chapters on development issues in Canada and internationally. The papers were first presented at a conference for the Canadian Research Institute for the Advancement of Women (CRIAW), and highlight feminist contributions to the theory and practice of development.

Ann Frechette. *Tibetans in Nepal: The Dynamics of International Assistance among a Community in Exile.* New York: Bergahn Books, 2002. In this book, Frechette explores how a long history of international assistance to refugees has affected individual and community identity and values. Focusing on Tibetans in Nepal, Frechette shows how aid complicates exiled Tibetans' attempts to define and maintain a sense of community.

Jim Freedman, ed., *Transforming Development: Foreign Aid for a Changing World.* Toronto: University of Toronto Press, 2000. Fourteen essays look at the changing context of Canadian aid arranged around seven themes. Most authors favour the redefinition of development assistance and criticize Canada's reduction in humanitarian-motivated aid to the poorest countries.

Gil Harper and Asha Moodley, eds. *Gender, Culture, and Rights: Empowering Women for Gender Equity. Agenda Special Focus,*

2005. Articles explore current approaches to gender, rights and culture in South Africa. Authors address law, religion, masculinity, violence, and health. For more information, www.agenda. org.za/index.

Dorothy L. Hodgson. *Once Intrepid Warriors: Gender, Ethnicity, and the Cultural Politics of Maasai Development.* Bloomington, IA: Indiana University Press, 2004. This ethnography shows how Maasai identity and gender connect with development and globalization to shape Maasai life today.

Dolores Koenig, Tieman Diarra, Moussa Sow, and Ousmane Diarra, *Innovation and Individuality in African Development: Changing Production Strategies in Rural Mali.* Ann Arbor, MI: University of Michigan Press, 1998. This ethnography of change looks at the history of Malian rural production, agricultural resources, and crop production, and how lessons learned contribute to an improved anthropology of development.

Gideon M. Kressel. *Let Shepherding Endure: Applied Anthropology and the Preservation of a Cultural Tradition in Israel and the Middle East.* Albany, NY: SUNY Press, 2003. This book presents a case study of the Bedu of the Negev, southern Israel. It discusses how globalization is encroaching on herders to their great detriment. The author lays out an applied anthropology program for reconstituting and promoting pastoralism.

David H. Lempert, Kim McCarthy, and Craig Mitchell, *A Model Development Plan: New Strategies and Perspectives.* Westport, CT: Praeger, 1995. A group of university students from different disciplines (including one anthropologist, Lempert) spent six weeks in Ecuador, visiting nearly every province and studying development issues there as the basis for their development plan for Ecuador. A preface explains the background of the project. The rest of the volume consists of a detailed presentation of the plan.

David Mosse. *Cultivating Development: An Ethnography of Aid Policy and Practice.* Ann Arbor, MI: Pluto Press, 2005. Mosse uses his experience as a development worker in India to analyze and critique how the structure of aid shapes the actions of development workers. The subject matter is policy making and projects viewed from a critical ethnographic perspective.

Richard J. Perry, *From Time Immemorial: Indigenous Peoples and State Systems.* Austin: University of Texas Press, 1996. This book provides a comparative examination of the history and status of indigenous peoples of Mexico, the United States, Canada, and

Australia. The conclusion offers findings about state policies, state violence, resistance of the indigenous peoples, and efforts at self-determination.

Joan Ryan, *Doing Things the Right Way.* Calgary: University of Calgary Press, 1995. Using participatory action research, the research team documented Dogrib systems of traditional justice. The work has implications for Native self-government, constitutional rights, and First Nations legal systems.

John Sherry. *Land, Wind and Hard Words: A Story of Navajo Activism.* Albuquerque: University of New Mexico Press, 2002. This book presents the story of the community-based activists of a Navajo environmental organization called Diné CARE that seeks to protect Navajo forests from logging.

Jennie M. Smith. *When the Hands Are Many: Community Organization and Social Change in Rural Haiti.* Ithaca, NY: Cornell University Press, 2001. Fieldwork in southwest Haiti reveals how poor rural people use social organizing and expressive culture to unite in resistance to the larger forces that impoverish them.

Andrew Woolford, *Between Justice and Certainty: Treaty-Making in British Columbia.* Vancouver: UBC Press, 2004. Woolford explores the treaty process for resolving land claims of First Nations in British Columbia, with particular attention to the interplay between the Aboriginal and non-Aboriginal visions of justice.

References

Abler, Thomas S. 1992. Scalping, Torture, Cannibalism, and Rape: An Ethnohistorical Analysis of Conflicting Cultural Values in War. *Anthropologica* 34:3–20.

Abu-Lughod, Lila. 1993. *Writing Women's Worlds: Bedouin Stories*. Berkeley, CA: University of California Press.

Adams, Kathleen M. 1984. Come to Tana Toraja, "Land of the Heavenly Kings": Travel Agents as Brokers in Ethnicity. *Annals of Tourism Research* 11:469–485.

Adams, Vincanne. 1988. Modes of Production and Medicine: An Examination of the Theory in Light of Sherpa Traditional Medicine. *Social Science and Medicine* 27:505–513.

Adelson, Naomi. 1998 Health Beliefs and the Politics of Cree Well-Being. *Health* 2(1):5–22.

———. 2000 *"Being Alive Well": Health and the Politics of Cree Well-Being*. Toronto: University of Toronto Press.

Adlam, Robert. 2000. Fish Talk. *Anthropologica* 44(1):99–111.

Afolayan, E. 2000. Bantu Expansion and Its Consequences. In *African History before 1885*. T. Falola, ed. Pp. 113–136. Durham, NC: Carolina Academic Press.

Agar, Michael. 1994 *Language Shock: Understanding the Culture of Conversation*. New York: William Morrow.

Ahern, Laura. 2001. *Invitations to Love: Literacy, Love Letters, and Social Change in Nepal*. Ann Arbor, MI: University of Michigan Press.

Ahmadu, Fuambai. 2000. Rites and Wrongs: An Insider/Outsider Reflects on Power and Excision. In *Female "Circumcision" in Africa: Culture, Controversy, and Change*. Bettina Shell-Duncan and Ylva Hernlund, eds. Pp. 283–312. Boulder, CO: Lynne Reiner Publishers.

Akinsha, Konstantin. 1992a. Russia: Whose Art Is It? *ARTNews* 91(5):100–105.

———. 1992b. Whose Gold? *ARTNews* 91(3):39–40.

———. 1992c. After the Coup: Art for Art's Sake? *ARTNews* 91(1):108–113.

Albro, Robert, and Joanne Bauer. 2005. Introduction. Human Rights Dialogue: An International Forum for Debating Human Rights. Special issue on Cultural Rights: What They Are, Why They Matter, How They Can Be Realized. *Carnegie Journal* 2(12):2–3.

Allen, Catherine J. 2002. *The Hold Life Has: Coca and Cultural Identity in an Andean Community*. Washington, DC: Smithsonian Institution Press.

Allison, Anne. 1994. *Nightwork: Sexuality, Pleasure, and Corporate Masculinity in a Tokyo Hostess Club*. Chicago: University of Chicago Press.

Alonso, Ana Maria. 2004. Conforming Disconformity: "Mestizaje," Hybridity, and the Aesthetics of Mexican Nationalism. *Cultural Anthropology* 19:459–490.

Alter, Joseph S. 1992. The Sannyasi and the Indian Wrestler: Anatomy of a Relationship. *American Ethnologist* 19(2):317–336.

Ames, David. 1959. Wolof Co-operative Work Groups. In *Continuity and Change in African Cultures*. William R. Bascom and Melville J. Herskovits, eds. Pp. 224–237. Chicago: University of Chicago Press.

Ames, Michael. 1992. *Cannibal Tours and Glass Boxes: The Anthropology of Museums*. Vancouver: University of British Columbia Press.

Amster, Matthew H. 2000. It Takes a Village to Dismantle a Longhouse. *Thresholds* 20:65–71.

Anagnost, Ann. 2004. Maternal Labor in a Transnational Circuit. In *Consuming Motherhood*. Janelle S. Taylor, Linda L. Layne, Danielle F. Wozniak, eds. Pp.139–167. New Brunswick, NJ: Rutgers University Press.

Ancrenaz, Marc, Olivier Gimenez, Laurentius Ambu, Karine Ancrenaz, Patrick Andau, Benoît Goossens, John Payne, Azri Sawang, Augustine Tuuga, and Isabelle Lackman-Ancrenaz. 2005. Aerial Surveys Give New Estimates for Orangutans in Sabah, Malaysia. *PloS Biology* 3(1): e3. www.plosbiology.org.

Anderson, Benedict. 1991[1983]. *Imagined Communities: Reflections on the Origin and Spread of Nationalism*. New York: Verso.

Anderson, Myrdene. 2004. Reflections on the Saami at Loose Ends. In *Cultural Shaping of Violence: Victimization, Escalation, Response*. Myrdene Anderson, ed. Pp. 285–291. West Lafayette, IN: Purdue University Press.

———. 2005. The Saami Yoik: Translating Hum, Chant and/or Song. In *Song and Significance: Virtues and Vices of Vocal Translation*. Dinda Gorlée, ed. Pp. 213–233. Amsterdam: Rodopi.

Anderson, Richard L., and Karen L. Field. 1993. Chapter introduction. In *Art in Small-Scale Societies: Contemporary Readings*. Richard L. Anderson and Karen L. Fields, eds. P. 247. Englewood Cliffs, NJ: Prentice Hall.

Andriolo, Karin. 2002. Murder by Suicide: Episodes from Muslim History. *American Anthropologist* 104:736–742.

Antze, Paul, and Michael Lambek, eds. 1996. *Tense Past: Cultural Essays in Trauma and Memory*. New York: Routledge.

Appadurai, Arjun. 1986. Introduction: Commodities and the Politics of Value. In *The Social Life of Things: Commodities in Cultural Perspective*. Arjun Appadurai, ed. Pp. 3–63. New York: Cambridge University Press.

Arambiza, Evelio, and Michael Painter. 2006. Biodiversity Conservation and the Quality of Life of Indigenous People in the Bolivian Chaco. *Human Organization* 65:20–34.

Arnup, Katherine. 2000. Living in the Margins: Lesbian Families and the Law. In *Open Boundaries: A Canadian Women's Studies Reader*. Barbara A. Crow and Lise Gotell, eds. Pp. 205–214. Toronto: Prentice Hall.

Asad, Talal, ed. 1973. *Anthropology and the Colonial Encounter*. London, UK: Ithaca Press.

Asch, Michael. 1997. *Aboriginal Treaty Rights in Canada: Essays on Law, Equality and Responsibility for Difference*. Vancouver: University of British Columbia Press.

Attwood, Donald W. 1992. *Raising Cane: The Political Economy of Sugar in Western India*. Boulder, CO: Westview Press.

Avery, Donald H. 1995. *Reluctant Host: Canada's Response to Immigrant Workers, 1896–1994*. Toronto: McClelland & Stewart.

Awe, Bolanle. 1977. The Iyalode in the Traditional Yoruba Political System. In *Sexual Stratification: A Cross-Cultural View*. Alice Schlegel, ed. Pp. 144–160. New York: Columbia University Press.

Baer, Lars-Anders. 1982. The Sami: An Indigenous People in Their Own Land. In *The Sami National Minority in Sweden*. Birgitta Jahreskog, ed. Pp. 11–22. Stockholm: Almqvist & Wiksell International.

Baker, Colin. 1999. Sign Language and the Deaf Community. In *Handbook of Language and Ethnic Identity*. Joshua A. Fishman, ed. Pp. 122–139. New York: Oxford University Press.

Barfield, Thomas J. 1993. *The Nomadic Alternative*. Englewood Cliffs, NJ: Prentice Hall.

———. 1994. Prospects for Plural Societies in Central Asia. *Cultural Survival Quarterly* 18(2&3):48–51.

———. 2001. Pastoral Nomads or Nomadic Pastoralists. In *The Dictionary of Anthropology*. Thomas Barfield, ed. Pp. 348–350. Malden, MA: Blackwell Publishers.

Barker, J. 1987. T. F. McIlwraith and Anthropology at the University of Toronto, 1925–1963. *Canadian Review of Sociology and Anthropology* 24:252–268.

Barkey, Nanette, Benjamin C. Campbell, and Paul W. Leslie. 2001. A Comparison of Health Complaints of Settled and Nomadic Turkana Men. *Medical Anthropology Quarterly* 15:391–408.

Barlett, Peggy F. 1980. Reciprocity and the San Juan Fiesta. *Journal of Anthropological Research* 36:116–130.

———. 1989. Industrial Agriculture. In *Economic Anthropology*. Stuart Plattner, ed. Pp. 253–292. Stanford, CA: Stanford University Press.

Barnard, Alan. 2000. *History and Theory in Anthropology*. New York: Cambridge University Press.

Barnard, Alan, and Anthony Good. 1984. *Research Practices in the Study of Kinship*. New York: Academic Press.

Barndt, Deborah, ed. 1999. *Women Working the NAFTA Food Chain: Women, Food and Globalization*. Toronto: Second Story Press.

Barrett, Stanley R. 1987. *Is God a Racist?* Toronto: University of Toronto Press.

Barth, Frederik. 1993. *Balinese Worlds*. Chicago: University of Chicago Press.

Basch, Linda, Nina Glick Schiller, and Christina Szanton Blanc. 1994. *Nations Unbound: Transnational Projects, Postcolonial Predicaments, and Deterritorialized Nation-States*. Langhorne, PA: Gordon and Breach Science Publishers.

Basso, Keith. H. 1972[1970]. "To Give Up on Words": Silence in Apache Culture. In *Language and Social Context*. Pier Paolo Giglioni, ed. Pp. 67–86. Baltimore: Penguin Books.

Bauer, Alexander A. 2006. Heritage Preservation in Law and Policy: Handling the Double-Edged Sword of Development. Paper presented at the International Conference on Cultural Heritage and Development, Bibliotheca Alexandrina, Alexandria, Egypt, January.

Beals, Alan R. 1980. *Gopalpur: A South Indian Village*. Fieldwork edition. New York: Holt, Rinehart and Winston.

Beatty, Andrew. 1992. *Society and Exchange in Nias*. New York: Oxford University Press.

Beck, Lois. 1986. *The Qashqa'i of Iran*. New Haven, CT: Yale University Press.

Beeman, William O. 1993. The Anthropology of Theater and Spectacle. *Annual Review of Anthropology* 22:363–393.

Beiser, Morton. 1999. *Strangers at the Gate: The "Boat People's" First Ten Years in Canada*. Toronto: University of Toronto Press.

Belikov, Vladimir. 1994. Language Death in Siberia. *UNESCO Courier* 1994(2):32–36.

Benedict, Ruth. 1959[1934]. *Patterns of Culture*. Boston: Houghton Mifflin Company.

———. 1969[1946]. *The Chrysanthemum and the Sword: Patterns of Japanese Culture*. Rutland, VT: Charles E. Tuttle Company.

Berg, Karen. 1997. Female Genital Mutilation: Implications for Social Work. *The Social Worker* 65:16–25.

Berlin, Elois Ann, and Brent Berlin. 1996. *Medical Ethnobiology of the Highland Maya of Chiapas, Mexico: The Gastrointestinal Diseases*. Princeton, NJ: Princeton University Press.

Bernal, Martin. 1987. *Black Athena: The Afroasiatic Roots of Classical Civilization*. New Brunswick, NJ: Rutgers University Press.

Bernard, H. Russell. 1995. *Research Methods in Cultural Anthropology: Qualitative and Quantitative Approaches*. 2nd edition. Newbury Park, CA: Sage Publications.

Berreman, Gerald D. 1963. *Hindus of the Himalayas*. Berkeley, CA: University of California Press.

———. 1979[1975]. Race, Caste, and Other Invidious Distinctions in Social Stratification. In *Caste and Other Inequities: Essays on Inequality*. Gerald D. Berreman, ed. Pp. 178–222. New Delhi: Manohar.

Best, David. 1986. Culture Consciousness: Understanding the Arts of Other Cultures. *Journal of Art & Design Education* 5(1&2):124–135.

Beyene, Yewoubdar. 1989. *From Menarche to Menopause: Reproductive Lives of Peasant Women in Two Cultures*. Albany, NY: State University of New York Press.

Bhardwaj, Surinder M. 1973. *Hindu Places of Pilgrimage in India: A Study in Cultural Geography*. Berkeley, CA: University of California Press.

Bhatt, Rakesh M. 2001. World Englishes. *Annual Review of Anthropology* 30:527–550.

Bialystok, Ellen, and Shilpi Majumder. 1998. The Relationship between Bilingualism and the Development of Cognitive Processes in Problem Solving. *Applied Psycholinguistics* 19(1):69–85.

Bigenho, Michelle. 1999. Sensing Locality in Yura: Rituals of Carnival and of the Bolivian State. *American Ethnologist* 26:957–980.

Billig, Michael S. 1992. The Marriage Squeeze and the Rise of Groomprice in India's Kerala State. *Journal of Comparative Family Studies* 23:197–216.

Binford, Leigh. 2003. Migrant Remittances and (Under)Development in Mexico. *Critique of Anthropology* 23:305–336.

Bird, Sharon R. 1996. Welcome to the Men's Club: Homosociality and the Maintenance of Hegemonic Masculinity. *Gender & Society* 10(2): 120–132.

Blackwood, Evelyn. 1995. Senior Women, Model Mothers, and Dutiful Wives: Managing Gender Contradictions in a Minangkabau Village. In *Bewitching Women: Pious Men: Gender and Body Politics in Southeast Asia*. Aihwa Ong and Michael Peletz, eds. Pp. 124–158. Berkeley, CA: University of California Press.

Blaikie, Piers. 1985. *The Political Economy of Soil Erosion in Developing Countries*. New York: Longman.

Blau, Peter M. 1964. *Exchange and Power in Social Life*. New York: John Wiley & Sons.

Bledsoe, Caroline H. 1983. Stealing Food as a Problem in Demography and Nutrition. Paper presented at the annual meeting of the American Anthropological Association.

Bledsoe, Caroline H., and Helen K. Hirschman. 1989. Case Studies of Mortality: Anthropological Contributions. Proceedings of the International Union for the Scientific Study of Population, XXIst International Population Conference, 331–348. Liége: International Union for the Scientific Study of Population.

Blim, Michael. 2000. Capitalisms in Late Modernity. *Annual Review of Anthropology* 29:25–38.

Blommaert, Jan, and Chris Bulcaen. 2000. Critical Discourse Analysis. *Annual Review of Anthropology* 29:447–466.

Boddy, Janice. 2007. *Civilizing Women: British Crusades in Colonial Sudan*. Princeton, NJ: Princeton University Press.

Bodenhorn, Barbara. 2000. "He used to be my relative," Exploring the Bases of Relatedness among the Inupiat of Northern Alaska. In *Cultures of Relatedness: New Approaches to the Study of Kinship*. Janet Carsten, ed. Pp. 128–148. New York: Cambridge University Press.

Bodley, John H. 1988. *Tribal Peoples and Development Issues: A Global Overview*. Mountain View, CA: Mayfield Publishing Company.

———. 1990. *Victims of Progress*. 3rd edition. Mountain View, CA: Mayfield Publishing Company.

Boellstorff, Tom. 2004. Gay Language and Indonesia: Registering Belonging. *Journal of Linguistic Anthropology* 14:248–268.

Bogin, Barry. 1988. *Patterns of Human Growth*. New York: Cambridge University Press.

Borins, M. 1995. Native Healing Traditions Must Be Protected and Preserved for Future Generations. *Canadian Medial Association Journal* 7.153(9):1356–1357.

Borovoy, Amy. 2005. *The Too-Good Wife: Alcohol, Codependency, and the Politics of Nurturance in Postwar Japan*. Berkeley, CA: University of California Press.

Boserup, Ester. 1970. *Woman's Role in Economic Development*. New York: St. Martin's Press.

Bourdieu, Pierre. 1984. *Distinction: A Social Critique of the Judgement of Taste*. Richard Nice, trans. Cambridge, MA: Harvard University Press.

Bourgois, Philippe I. 1995. *In Search of Respect: Selling Crack in El Barrio*. New York: Cambridge University Press.

Bourgois, P., and J. Bruneau. 2000. Needle Exchange, HIV Infection and the Politics of Science: Confronting Canada's Cocaine Infection Epidemic with Participant Observation. *Medical Anthropology* 18(4): 325–350.

Bowen, Anne M., and Robert Trotter II. 1995. HIV Risk in Intravenous Drug Users and Crack Cocaine Smokers: Predicting Stage of Change for Condom Use. *Journal of Consulting and Clinical Psychology* 63:238–248.

Bowen, John R. 1992. On Scriptural Essentialism and Ritual Variation: Muslim Sacrifice in Sumatra. *American Ethnologist* 19(4):656–671.

———. 1998. *Religions in Practice: An Approach to the Anthropology of Religion*. Boston: Allyn and Bacon.

Bradley, Richard. 2000. *An Archaeology of Natural Places*. New York: Routledge.

Brana-Shute, Rosemary. 1976. Women, Clubs, and Politics: The Case of a Lower-Class Neighborhood in Paramaribo, Suriname. *Urban Anthropology* 5(2):157–185.

Brandes, Stanley H. 2002. *Staying Sober in Mexico City*. Austin, TX: University of Texas Press.

Brave Heart, Maria Yellow Horse. 2004. The Historical Trauma Response among Natives and Its Relationship to Substance Abuse: A Lakota Illustration. In *Healing and Mental Health for Native Americans: Speaking in Red*. Ethan Nebelkopf and Mary Phillips, eds. Pp. 7–18. Walnut Creek, CA: AltaMira Press.

Brenneis, Donald, and Laura Lein. 1977. "You Fruithead": A Sociolinguistic Approach to Children's Dispute Settlement. In *Child Discourse*. Susan Ervin-Tripp and Claudia Methcell-Kernan, eds. Pp. 49–65. New York: Academic Press.

Briggs, Jean L. 1970. *Never in Anger*. Cambridge, MA: Harvard University Press.

Brink, Judy H. 1991. The Effect of Emigration of Husbands on the Status of Their Wives: An Egyptian Case. *International Journal of Middle East Studies* 23:201–211.

Brison, Karen J., and Stephen C. Leavitt. 1995. Coping with Bereavement: Long-Term Perspectives on Grief and Mourning. *Ethos* 23:395–400.

Brodkin, Karen. 2000. Global Capitalism: What's Race Got to Do with It? *American Ethnologist* 27:237–256.

Brooks, Alison S., and Patricia Draper. 1998. Anthropological Perspectives on Aging. In *Anthropology Explored: The Best of Smithsonian AnthroNotes*. Ruth Osterweis Selig and Marilyn R. London, eds. Pp. 286–297. Washington, DC: Smithsonian Institution Press.

Brookes, Heather. 2004. A Repertoire of South African Quotable Gestures. *Journal of Linguistic Anthropology* 14:186–224.

Broude, Gwen J. 1988. Rethinking the Couvade: Cross-Cultural Evidence. *American Anthropologist* 90(4):902–911.

Brown, Carolyn Henning. 1984. Tourism and Ethnic Competition in a Ritual Form: The Firewalkers of Fiji. *Oceania* 54:223–244.

Brown, Judith K. 1970. A Note on the Division of Labor by Sex. *American Anthropologist* 72(5):1073–1078.

———. 1975. Iroquois Women: An Ethnohistoric Note. In *Toward an Anthropology of Women*. Rayna R. Reiter, ed. Pp. 235–251. New York: Monthly Review Press.

———. 1978. The Recruitment of a Female Labor Force. *Anthropos* 73(1/2):41–48.

———. 1982. Cross-Cultural Perspectives on Middle-Aged Women. *Current Anthropology* 23(2):143–156.

———. 1992. Introduction: Definitions, Assumptions, Themes, and Issues. In *Sanctions and Sanctuary: Cultural Perspectives on the Beating of Wives*. Dorothy Ayers Counts, Judith K. Brown, and Jacquelyn C. Campbell, eds. Pp. 1–18. Boulder, CO: Westview Press.

Brown, Peter J., Marcia C. Inhorn, and Daniel J. Smith. 1996. Disease, Ecology, and Human Behavior. In *Medical Anthropology: Contemporary Theory and Method*. Carolyn F. Sargent and Thomas M. Johnson, eds. Pp. 183–218. Westport, CT: Praeger Publishers.

Browner, Carole H. 1986. The Politics of Reproduction in a Mexican Village. *Signs: Journal of Women in Culture and Society* 11(4):710–724.

Browner, Carole H., and Nancy Ann Press. 1995. The Normalization of Prenatal Diagnostic Screening. In *Conceiving the New World Order: The Global Politics of Reproduction*. Faye D. Ginsberg and Rayna Rapp, eds. Pp. 307–322. Berkeley, CA: University of California Press.

———. 1996. The Production of Authoritative Knowledge in American Prenatal Care. *Medical Anthropology Quarterly* 10(2):141–156.

Brownmiller, Susan. 1994. *Seeing Vietnam: Encounters of the Road and Heart*. New York: HarperCollins.

Brumfiel, Elizabeth M. 1994. Introduction. In *Factional Competition and Political Development in the New World*. Elizabeth M. Brumfiel and John W. Fox, eds. Pp. 3–14. New York: Cambridge University Press.

Bruner, Edward M. 1991. The Transformation of Self in Tourism. *Annals of Tourism Research* 18:238–250.

———. 2005. *Culture on Tour: Ethnographies of Travel*. Chicago: University of Chicago Press.

Bunzel, Ruth. 1972[1929]. *The Pueblo Potter: A Study of Creative Imagination in Primitive Art*. New York: Dover Publications.

Burdick, John. 2004. *Legacies of Liberation: The Progressive Catholic Church in Brazil at the Turn of a New Century*. Burlington, VT: Ashgate Publishers.

Burton, Barbara. 2004. The Transmigration of Rights: Women, Movement and the Grassroots in Latin American and Caribbean Communities. *Development and Change* 35:773–798.

Butler, Shelley Ruth. 2008. *Contested Representations: Revisiting Into the Heart of Africa*. Peterborough, ON: Broadview Press.

Buvinic, Mayra, and Andrew R. Morrison. 2000. Living in a More Violent World. *Foreign Policy* 118:58–72.

Calhoun, Craig, Donald Light, and Suzanne Keller. 1994. *Sociology*. 6th edition. New York: McGraw-Hill Ryerson.

Cameron, Deborah. 1997. Performing Gender Identity: Young Men's Talk and the Construction of Heterosexual Masculinity. In *Language and Masculinity*. Sally Johnson and Ulrike Hanna Meinhof, eds. Oxford, UK: Blackwell Publishing.

Cameron, Mary M. 1995. Transformations of Gender and Caste Divisions of Labor in Rural Nepal: Land, Hierarchy, and the Case of Women. *Journal of Anthropological Research* 51:215–246.

Camino, Linda A., and Ruth M. Krulfeld, eds. 1994. *Reconstructing Lives, Recapturing Meaning: Refugee Identity, Gender and Culture Change*. Basel, UK: Gordon and Breach Publishers.

Campbell, Lori D., and Michael Carroll. 2007. Aging in Canadian Families Today. In *Canadian Families Today: New Perspectives*. David Cheal, ed. Don Mills, ON: Oxford University Press.

Cancian, Frank. 1989. Economic Behavior in Peasant Communities. In *Economic Anthropology*. Stuart Plattner, ed. Pp. 127–170. Stanford, CA: Stanford University Press.

Caplan, Pat. 1987. Celibacy as a Solution? Mahatma Gandhi and Brahmacharya. In *The Cultural Construction of Sexuality*. Pat Caplan, ed. Pp. 271–295. New York: Tavistock Publications.

Caputo, Virginia. 2001. Telling Stories from the Field: Children and the Politics of Ethnographic Representation. *Anthropologica* 43(2):179–189.

Carneiro, Robert L. 1994. War and Peace: Alternating Realities in Human History. In *Studying War: Anthropological Perspectives*. S. P. Reyna and R. E. Downs, eds. Pp. 3–27. Langhorne, PA: Gordon and Breach Science Publishers.

Carroll, M. 1984. On the Psychological Origins of the Evil Eye: A Kleinian View. *Journal of Psychoanalytic Anthropology* 8(4):360–382.

Carstairs, G. Morris. 1967. *The Twice Born*. Bloomington, IN: Indiana University Press.

Carsten, Janet. 1995. Children in Between: Fostering and the Process of Kinship on Pulau Langkawi, Malaysia. *Man* (N.S.) 26:425–443.

Carsten, Janet, ed. 2000. *Cultures of Relatedness: New Approaches to the Study of Kinship*. New York: Cambridge University Press.

Carter, William E., Mauricio Mamani P., and José V. Morales. 1981. Medicinal Uses of Coca in Bolivia. In *Health in the Andes*. Joseph W. Bastien and John M. Donahue, eds. Pp. 119–149. Washington, DC: American Anthropological Association.

Cassell, Joan. 1991. *Expected Miracles: Surgeons at Work*. Philadelphia: Temple University Press.

Castles, Stephen, and Mark J. Miller. 1993. *The Age of Migration: International Population Movements in the Modern World*. New York: The Guilford Press.

Cátedra, María. 1992. *This World, Other Worlds: Sickness, Suicide, Death and the Afterlife among the Vaqueiros de Alzada of Spain*. Chicago: University of Chicago Press.

Caudill, W., and David W. Plath. 1966. Who Sleeps by Whom? Parent–Child Involvement in Urban Japanese Families. *Psychiatry* 29:344–366.

Cernea, Michael M. 1985. Sociological Knowledge for Development Projects. In *Putting People First: Sociological Variables and Rural Development*. Michael M. Cernea, ed. Pp. 3–22. New York: Oxford University Press.

———. 2001. *Cultural Heritage and Development: A Framework for Action in the Middle East and North Africa*. Washington, DC: The World Bank.

Chagnon, Napoleon A. 1992. *Yanomamö*. 4th edition. New York: Harcourt Brace Jovanovich.

Chambers, David L. 2000. Civilizing the Natives: Marriage in Post-Apartheid South Africa. *Daedalus* 129:101–124.

Chambers, Robert. 1983. *Rural Development: Putting the Last First*. Essex, UK: Longman.

Chanen, Jill Schachner. 1995. Reaching Out to Women of Color. *ABA Journal* 81 (May):105.

Chavez, Leo R. 1992. *Shadowed Lives: Undocumented Immigrants in American Society*. New York: Harcourt Brace Jovanovich.

Cherlin, Andrew J. 1996. *Public and Private Families: An Introduction*. New York: McGraw-Hill Ryerson.

Cherlin, Andrew, and Frank F. Furstenberg, Jr. 1992. The American Family in the Year 2000. In *One World, Many Cultures*. Stuart Hirschberg, ed. Pp. 2–9. New York: Macmillan Publishing Company.

Cheung, Sidney C. H. 1998. Being Here, Searching "There": *Hon Para* as a Virtual Community. In *On the South China Track: Perspectives on Anthropological Research and Teaching*. Sidney C. H. Cheung, ed. Pp. 131–148. Hong Kong: Hong Kong Institute of Asia-Pacific Studies, The Chinese University of Hong Kong.

Childs, Larry, and Celina Chelala. 1994. Drought, Rebellion and Social Change in Northern Mali: The Challenges Facing Tamacheq Herders. *Cultural Survival Quarterly* 18(4):16–19.

Chiñas, Beverly Newbold. 1992. *The Isthmus Zapotecs: A Matrifocal Culture of Mexico*. New York: Harcourt Brace Jovanovich.

Church, Jon, Vernon Curran, and Shirley Solberg. 2000. "Voices and Faces": A Qualitative Study of Rural Women and a Breast Cancer Self-Help Group via Audio Teleconferencing Network. *Centers of Excellence for Women's Health Research Bulletin* 1(1):22–23.

Churchill, Nancy. 2006. Dignifying Carnival: The Politics of Heritage Recognition in Puebla, Mexico. *International Journal of Cultural Property* 13:1–24.

Clark, Gracia. 1992. Flexibility Equals Survival. *Cultural Survival Quarterly* 16:21–24.

Clarke, Maxine Kumari. 2004. *Mapping Yorùbá Networks: Power and Agency in the Making of Transnational Communities*. Durham, NC: Duke University Press.

Clay, Jason W. 1990. What's a Nation: Latest Thinking. *Mother Jones* 15(7):28–30.

Cleveland, David A. 2000. Globalization and Anthropology: Expanding the Options. *Human Organization* 59:370–374.

Clifford, James. 1988. *The Predicament of Culture: Twentieth-Century Ethnography, Literature and Art*. Cambridge, MA: Harvard University Press.

———. 1997. Routes: *Travel and Translation in the Late Twentieth Century*. Cambridge, MA: Cambridge University Press.

Cohen, Mark Nathan. 1989. *Health and the Rise of Civilization*. New Haven, CT: Yale University Press.

Cohen, Mark Nathan, and George J. Armelagos, eds. 1984. *Palaeopathology at the Origins of Agriculture*. New York: Academic Press.

Cohen, Mark Nathan, and Sharon Bennett. 1993. Skeletal Evidence for Sex Roles and Gender Hierarchies in Prehistory. In *Sex and Gender Hierarchies*. Barbara Diane Miller, ed. Pp. 273–296. New York: Cambridge University Press.

Cohen, Roberta. 2002. Nowhere to Run, No Place to Hide. *Bulletin of the Atomic Scientists* November/December:36–45.

Cohn, Bernard S. 1971. *India: The Social Anthropology of a Civilization*. New York: Prentice Hall.

Cole, Douglas. 1985 *The Scramble for Northwest Coast Artifacts*. Seattle: University of Washington Press.

———. 1991. *Chiefly Feasts: The Enduring Kwakiutl Potlatch*. Aldona Jonaitis, ed. Seattle: University of Washington Press / New York: American Museum of Natural History.

Cole, Jeffrey. 1996. Working-Class Reactions to the New Immigration in Palermo (Italy). *Critique of Anthropology* 16(2):199–220.

Colley, Sarah. 2002. *Uncovering Australia: Archaeology, Indigenous People and the Public*. Washington, DC: Smithsonian Institution Press.

Comaroff, John L. 1987. Of Totemism and Ethnicity: Consciousness, Practice and Signs of Inequality. *Ethnos* 52(3–4):301–323.

Contreras, Gloria. 1995. Teaching about Vietnamese Culture: Water Puppetry as the Soul of the Rice Fields. *The Social Studies* 86(1):25–28.

Corbey, Raymond. 2000. *Arts premiers* in the Louvre. *Anthropology Today* 16:3–6.

———. 2003. Destroying the Graven Image: Religious Iconoclasm on the Christian Frontier. *Anthropology Today* 19:10–14.

Cornell, Laurel L. 1989. Gender Differences in Remarriage after Divorce in Japan and the United States. *Journal of Marriage and the Family* 51:45–463.

Cornia, Giovanni Andrea. 1994. Poverty, Food Consumption, and Nutrition during the Transition to the Market Economy in Eastern Europe. *American Economic Review* 84(2):297–302.

Counihan, Carole M. 1985. Transvestism and Gender in a Sardinian Carnival. *Anthropology* 9(1 & 2):11–24.

Coward, E. Walter, Jr. 1976. Indigenous Organisation, Bureaucracy and Development: The Case of Irrigation. *The Journal of Development Studies* 13(1):92–105.

———. 1979. Principles of Social Organization in an Indigenous Irrigation System. *Human Organization* 38(1):28–36.

Craik, Brian. 2004. The Importance of Working Together: Exclusions, Conflicts and Participation in James Bay, Quebec. In *In the Way of Development: Indigenous Peoples, Life Projects and Globalization*. Mario Blaser, Harvey A. Feit, and Glenn McRae, eds. Pp. 166–186. London and New York: Zed Books in Association with the International Development Research Centre.

Crapanzano, Vincent. 1980. *Tuhami: Portrait of a Moroccan*. Chicago: University of Chicago Press.

Crawford, C. Joanne. 1994. Parenting Practices in the Basque Country: Implications of Infant and Childhood Sleeping Location for Personality Development. *Ethos* 22(1):42–82.

Creighton, Millie R. 1992. The Depāto: Merchandising the West While Selling Japanese Sameness. In *Re-Made in Japan: Everyday Life and Consumer Taste in a Changing Society*. Joseph J. Tobin, ed. Pp. 42–57. New Haven, CT: Yale University Press.

Crowe, D. 1996. *A History of the Gypsies of Eastern Europe and Russia*. New York: St. Martin's Press.

Cruickshank, Julia. 1990. *Life Lived Like a Story: Life Stories of Three Yukon elders*. Vancouver: University of British Columbia Press.

Crystal, David. 2000. *Language Death*. New York: Cambridge University Press.

———. 2003. *English as a Global Language*, 2nd ed. New York: Cambridge University Press.

Culhane Speck, Dara. 1987. *An Error in Judgement*. Vancouver: Talon Books.

Cunningham, Lawrence S. 1995. Christianity. In *The HarperCollins Dictionary of Religion*. Jonathan Z. Smith, ed. Pp. 240–253. New York: HarperCollins.

Curtin, Philip D. 1989. *Death by Migration: Europe's Encounter with the Tropical World in the Nineteenth Century*. New York: Cambridge University Press.

Dalby, Liza Crihfield. 1983. *Geisha*. New York: Vintage Books.

———. 2001. *Kimono: Fashioning Culture*. Seattle: University of Washington Press.

Daly, Martin, and Margo Wilson. 1984. A Sociological Analysis of Human Infanticide. In *Infanticide: Comparative and Evolutionary Perspectives*. Glenn Hausfater and Sarah Blaffer Hrdy, eds. Pp. 487–502. New York: Aldine Publishing Company.

Danforth, Loring M. 1989. *Firewalking and Religious Healing: The Anestenaria of Greece and the American Firewalking Movement*. Princeton, NJ: Princeton University Press.

Dannhaeuser, Norbert. 1989. Marketing in Developing Urban Areas. In *Economic Anthropology*. Stuart Plattner, ed. Pp. 222–252. Stanford, CA: Stanford University Press.

Darnell, Regna. 1970. The Kaska Aesthetic of Speech Use. *Western Canadian Journal of Anthropology* 1(1).

———. 1998 Toward a History of Canadian Departments of Anthropology: Retrospect, Prospect and Common Cause. *Anthropologica* XL(2):153–168.

Daugherty, Mary Lee. 1997. Serpent-Handling as Sacrament. In *Magic, Witchcraft, and Religion*. Arthur C. Lehmann and James E. Myers, eds. Pp. 347–352. Mountain View, CA: Mayfield Publishing Company.

Davis, Dona. 1984. Medical Misinformation: Communication between Outport Newfoundland Women and Their Physicians. *Social Science and Medicine* 18(3):273–278.

———. 1989. The Variable Character of Nerves in a Newfoundland Fishing Village. *Medical Anthropology* 11:63–78.

Davis, Susan Schaefer, and Douglas A. Davis. 1987. *Adolescence in a Moroccan Town: Making Social Sense*. New Brunswick, NJ: Rutgers University Press.

Davis-Floyd, Robbie E. 1987. Obstetric Training as a Rite of Passage. *Medical Anthropology Quarterly* 1:288–318.

———. 1992. *Birth as an American Rite of Passage*. Berkeley, CA: University of California Press.

de Athayde Figueiredo, Mariza, and Dando Prado. 1989. The Women of Arembepe. *UNESCO Courier* 7:38–41.

Deitrick, Lynn. 2002. Commentary: Cultural Brokerage in the Newborn Nursery. *Practicing Anthropology* 24:53–54.

De Koninck, Rodolphe. 1992. *Malay Peasants Coping with the World: Breaking the Community Circle?* Singapore: Institute of Southeast Asian Studies.

de la Cadena, Marisol. 2001. Reconstructing Race: Racism, Culture and Mestizaje in Latin America. *NACLA Report on the Americas* 34:16–23.

Delaney, Carol. 1988. Mortal Flow: Menstruation in Turkish Village Society. In *Blood Magic: The Anthropology of Menstruation*. Timothy Buckley and Alma Gottlieb, eds. Pp. 75–93. Berkeley, CA: University of California Press.

de la Gorgendiere, Louise. 2005. Rights and Wrongs: HIV/AIDS Research in Africa. *Human Organization* 64(2): 166–178.

Dent, Alexander Sebastian. 2005. Cross-Culture "Countries": Covers, Conjuncture, and the Whiff of Nashville in *Música Sertaneja* (Brazilian Commercial Country Music). *Popular Music and Society* 28:207–227.

Devereaux, George. 1976. *A Typological Study of Abortion in Primitive Societies: A Typological, Distributional, and Dynamic Analysis of the Prevention of Birth in 400 Preindustrial Societies*. New York: International Universities Press.

Diamond, Jared. 1994. The Worst Mistake in the History of the Human Race. In *Applying Cultural Anthropology: A Reader*. Aaron Podolefsky and Peter J. Brown, eds. Pp. 105–108. Mountain View, CA: Mayfield Publishing Company.

DiFerdinando, George. 1999. Emerging Infectious Diseases: Biology and Behavior in the Inner City. In *Urbanism, Health, and Human Biology in Industrialised Countries*. Lawrence M. Schell and Stanley J. Ulijaszek, eds. Pp. 87–110. New York: Cambridge University Press.

Dikötter, Frank. 1998. Hairy Barbarians, Furry Primates and Wild Men: Medical Science and Cultural Representations of Hair in China. In *Hair: Its Power and Meaning in Asian Cultures*. Alf Hiltebeitel and Barbara D. Miller, eds. Pp. 1–74. Albany, NY: State University of New York Press.

Divale, William T. 1974. Migration, External Warfare, and Matrilocal Residence. *Behavior Science Research* 9:75–133.

Divale, William T., and Marvin Harris. 1976. Population, Warfare and the Male Supremacist Complex. *American Anthropologist* 78:521–538.

Doi, Yaruko, and Masami Minowa. 2003. Gender Differences in Excessive Daytime Sleepiness among Japanese Workers. *Social Science and Medicine* 56:883–894.

Donlon, Jon. 1990. Fighting Cocks, Feathered Warriors, and Little Heroes. *Play & Culture* 3:273–285.

Dorais, Louis-Jacques. 1979. Language and Society. In *Challenging Anthropology*. D. Turner and G. Smith, eds. Toronto: McGraw-Hill Ryerson.

Dorgan, Howard. 1989. *The Old Regular Baptists of Central Appalachia: Brothers and Sisters in Hope*. Knoxville, TN: The University of Tennessee Press.

Douglas, Mary. 1966. *Purity and Danger: An Analysis of Concepts of Pollution and Taboo*. New York: Penguin Books.

Douglas, Mary, and Baron Isherwood. 1979. *The World of Goods: Towards an Anthropology of Consumption*. New York: W. W. Norton and Company.

Downe, Pamela. 1997. Constructing a Complex of Contagion: The Perceptions of AIDS among Working Prostitutes in Costa Rica. *Social Science and Medicine* 44(10):1575–1583.

———. 1999. Laughing When it Hurts: Humor and Violence in the Lives of Costa Rican Prostitutes. *Women's Studies International Forum* 22(1):63–78.

———. 2001. Playing with Names: How Children Create Identities of Self in Anthropological Research. *Anthropologica* 43(2):165–177.

Drake, Susan P. 1991. Local Participation in Ecotourism Projects. In *Nature Tourism: Managing for the Environment*. Tensie Whelan, ed. Pp. 132–155. Washington, DC: Island Press.

Dreifus, Claudia. 2000. Saving the Orangutan, Preserving Paradise. *The New York Times*, March 21:D3.

Drucker, Charles. 1987. Dam the Chico: Hydropower, Development and Tribal Resistance. In *Tribal Peoples and Development Issues: A Global Overview*. John H. Bodley, ed. Pp. 151–165. Mountain View, CA: Mayfield Publishing Company.

Dube, S. C. 1967. *Indian Village*. New York: Harper & Row.

Dunk, Thomas W. 1991. *It's a Working Man's Town: Male Working Class Culture*. Montreal and Kingston: McGill-Queen's University Press.

Duranti, Alessandro. 1994. *From Grammar to Politics: Linguistic Anthropology in a Western Samoan Village*. Berkeley, CA: University of California Press.

———. 1997a. *Linguistic Anthropology*. New York: Cambridge University Press.

———. 1997b. Universal and Culture-Specific Properties of Greetings. *Journal of Linguistic Anthropology* 7:63–97.

Durkheim, Émile. 1965[1895]. *On the Division of Labor in Society*. G. Simpson, trans. New York: Free Press.

———. 1966[1895]. *The Elementary Forms of the Religious Life*. New York: Free Press.

Durning, Alan Thein. 1993. Are We Happy Yet? How the Pursuit of Happiness Is Failing. *The Futurist* 27(1):20–24.

Durrenberger, E. Paul. 2001. Explorations of Class and Class Consciousness in the U.S. *Journal of Anthropological Research* 57:41–60.

du Toit, Brian M. 1990. People on the Move: Rural–Urban Migration with Special Reference to the Third World: Theoretical and Empirical Perspectives. *Human Organization* 49(4):305–320.

Earle, Timothy. 1991. The Evolution of Chiefdoms. In *Chiefdoms, Power, Economy, and Ideology*. Timothy Earle, ed. Pp. 1–15. New York: Cambridge University Press.

Eck, Diana L. 1985. *Darson: Seeing the Divine Image in India*. 2nd edition. Chambersburg, PA: Anima Books.

Eckel, Malcolm David. 1995. Buddhism. In *The HarperCollins Dictionary of Religion*. Jonathan Z. Smith, ed. Pp. 135–150. New York: HarperCollins.

EcoHawk, M. 1997. Suicide: The Scourge of Native American People. *Suicide and Life-Threatening Behavior* 27(1):60–67.

Economic and Social Council. 1992. *Report of the Working Group on Violence against Women*. Vienna: United Nations. E/CN.6/WG.2/1992/L.3.

Edwards, Elizabeth, ed. 1992. *Anthropology and Photography, 1860–1920*. New Haven, CT: Yale University Press.

Edwards, John. 1998. *Language in Canada*. Cambridge, UK: Cambridge University Press.

Ember, Carol R. 1983. The Relative Decline in Women's Contribution to Agriculture with Intensification. *American Anthropologist* 85(2):285–304.

Ennis-McMillan, Michael C. 2001. Suffering from Water: Social Origins of Bodily Distress in a Mexican Community. *Medical Anthropology Quarterly* 15(3):368–390.

Eriksen, Thomas Hylland. 2001. Between Universalism and Relativism: A Critique of the UNESCO Concept of Culture. In *Culture and Rights: Anthropological Perspectives*. Jane K. Cowan, Marie Bénédicte Dembour, and Richard A. Wilson, eds. Pp. 127–148. New York: Cambridge University Press.

Ervin, Alexander M., Antonet T. Kaye, Giselle M. Marcotte, and Randy D. Belon. 1991. *Community Needs, Saskatoon—The 1990s: The Saskatoon Needs Assessment Project*. Saskatoon, SK: University of Saskatchewan, Department of Anthropology.

Escobar, Arturo. 2002. Gender, Place, and Networks: A Political Ecology of Cyberculture. In *Development: A Cultural Studies Reader*. Susan Schech and Jane Haggis, eds. Pp. 239–256. Malden, MA: Blackwell Publishers.

Esman, Milton. 1996. Ethnic Politics. In *The Social Science Encyclopedia*. Adam Kuper and Jessica Kuper, eds. Pp. 259–260. New York: Routledge.

Estioko-Griffin, Agnes. 1986. Daughters of the Forest. *Natural History* 95:36–43.

Estrin, Saul. 1996. Co-operatives. In *The Social Science Encyclopedia*. Adam Kuper and Jessica Kuper, eds. Pp. 138–139. New York: Routledge.

Etienne, Mona, and Eleanor Leacock, eds. 1980. *Women and Colonization: Anthropological Perspectives*. New York: Praeger.

Evans, William, and Julie Topoleski. 2002. *The Social and Economic Impact of Native American Casinos*. Cambridge, MA: NBER Working Papers, No. 9198.

Evans-Pritchard, E. E. 1951. *Kinship and Marriage among the Nuer*. Oxford, UK: Clarendon.

———. 1965[1947]. *The Nuer: A Description of the Modes of Livelihood and Political Institutions of a Nilotic People*. New York: Oxford University Press.

Everett, Daniel L. 1995. Personal communication.

———. 2005. Cultural Constraints on Grammar and Cognition in Pirahã: Another Look at Design Features in Human Language. *Current Anthropology* 46:621–634, 641–646.

Evrard, Olivier, and Yves Goudineau. 2004. Planned Resettlement, Unexpected Migrations and Cultural Trauma in Laos. *Development and Change* 35:937–962.

Ewing, Katherine Pratt. 2000. Legislating Religious Freedom: Muslim Challenges to the Relationship between "Church" and "State" in Germany and France. *Daedalus* 29:31–53.

Fabian, Johannes. 1995. Ethnographic Misunderstanding and the Perils of Context. *American Anthropologist* 97(1):41–50.

Fabrega, Horacio, and Barbara D. Miller. 1995. Adolescent Psychiatry as a Product of Contemporary Anglo-American Society. *Social Science and Medicine* 40(7):881–894.

Fadiman, Anne. 1997. *The Spirit Catches You and You Fall Down: A Hmong Child, Her American Doctors, and the Collusion of Two Cultures*. New York: Farrar, Straus and Giroux.

Farmer, Paul. 1990. Sending Sickness: Sorcery, Politics, and Changing Concepts of AIDS in Rural Haiti. *Medical Anthropology Quarterly* 4:6–27.

———. 2005. *Pathologies of Power: Health, Human Rights and the New War on the Poor*. Berkeley, CA: University of California Press.

Fedigan, L. 1992. *Primate Paradigms: Sex Roles and Social Bonds*. Chicago: University of Chicago Press.

Feinsilver, Julie M. 1993. *Healing the Masses: Cuban Health Politics at Home and Abroad*. Berkeley, CA: University of California Press.

Feldman, Gregory. 2003. Breaking Our Silence on NATO. *Anthropology Today* 19:1–2.

Feldman-Savelsberg, Pamela. 1995. Cooking Inside: Kinship and Gender in Bangangté Idioms of Marriage and Procreation. *American Ethnologist* 22(3):483–501.

Ferguson, James. 1994. *The Anti-Politics Machine: "Development," Depoliticization, and Bureaucratic Power in Lesotho*. Minneapolis, MN: University of Minnesota Press.

Ferguson, R. Brian. 1990. Blood of the Leviathan: Western Contact and Amazonian Warfare. *American Ethnologist* 17(1):237–257.

Firestone, M. 1985. The "Old Hag": Sleep Paralysis in Newfoundland. *Journal of Psychoanalytic Anthropology* 8(1):47–66.

Fischer, Edward F. 2001. *Cultural Logics and Global Economies: Maya Identity in Thought and Practice*. Austin, TX: University of Texas Press.

Fishman, Joshua A., ed. 2001. *Can Threatened Languages Be Saved? Reversing Language Shift, Revisited: A 21st Century Perspective*. Buffalo, NY: Multilingual Matters Ltd.

Fiske, John. 1994. Radical Shopping in Los Angeles: Race, Media and the Sphere of Consumption. *Media, Culture & Society* 16:469–486.

Fitigu, Yodit. 2005. Forgotten People: Internally Displaced Persons in Guatemala. www.refugeesinternational.org/content/article/detail/6344.

Fluehr-Lobban, Carolyn. 1994. Informed Consent in Anthropological Research: We Are Not Exempt. *Human Organization* 53(1):1–10.

Fonseca, Isabel. 1995. *Bury Me Standing: The Gypsies and Their Journey*. New York: Alfred A. Knopf.

Fortune, Reo F. 1959[1932]. *Sorcerers of Dobu: The Social Anthropology of the Dobu Islanders of the Western Pacific*. New York: E. P. Dutton & Co.

Foley, Kathy. 2001. The Metonymy of Art: Vietnamese Water Puppetry as Representation of Modern Vietnam. *The Drama Review* 45(4):129–141.

Foley, William A. 2000. The Languages of New Guinea. *Annual Review of Anthropology* 29:357–404.

Foster, George. 1965. Peasant Society and the Image of the Limited Good. *American Anthropologist* 67:293–315.

Foster, Robert J. 2002. *Materializing the Nation: Commodities, Consumption, and Media in Papua New Guinea*. Bloomington, IN: Indiana University Press.

———. 2006. From Trobriand Cricket to Rugby Nation: The Mission of Sport in Papua New Guinea. *The International Journal of the History of Sport* 23(5):739–758.

Foster, George M., and Barbara Gallatin Anderson. 1978. *Medical Anthropology*. New York: Alfred A. Knopf.

Foster, Helen Bradley, and Donald Clay Johnson, eds. 2003. *Wedding Dress across Cultures*. New York: Berg.

Foucault, Michel. 1970. *The Order of Things: An Archaeology of the Human Sciences*. New York: Random House.

———. 1977. *Discipline and Punish: The Birth of the Prison*. New York: Pantheon Books.

Fox, Richard G., and Andre Gingrich. 2002. Comparison and Anthropology's Public Responsibility. In *Anthropology, By Comparison*. Andre Gingrich and Richard G. Fox, eds. Pp. 1–24. New York: Routledge.

Fox, Robin. 1995[1978]. *The Tory Islanders: A People of the Celtic Fringe*. Notre Dame, IN: University of Notre Dame Press.

Frake, Charles O. 1961. The Diagnosis of Disease among the Subanun of Mindanao. *American Anthropologist* 63:113–132.

Franke, Richard W. 1993. *Life is a Little Better: Redistribution as a Development Strategy in Nadur Village, Kerala*. Boulder, CO: Westview Press.

Frankel, Francine R. 1971. *India's Green Revolution: Economic Gains and Political Costs*. Princeton, NJ: Princeton University Press.

Fratkin, Elliot. 1998. *Ariaal Pastoralists of Kenya: Surviving Drought and Development in Africa's Arid Lands*. Boston: Allyn and Bacon.

Fratkin, Elliot, Kathleen Galvin, and Eric A. Roth, eds. 1994. *African Pastoralist Systems: An Integrated Approach*. Boulder, CO: Westview Press.

Frazer, Sir James. 1978[1890]. *The Golden Bough: A Study in Magic and Religion*. New York: Macmillan.

Freed, Stanley A., and Ruth S. Freed. 1969. Urbanization and Family Types in a North Indian Village. *Southwestern Journal of Anthropology* 25:342–359.

Freedman, Jim. 2000. A Case for Equity. In *Transforming Development: Foreign Aid for a Changing World*. Jim Freedman, ed. Pp. 192–208. Toronto: University of Toronto Press.

Freeman, Derek. 1983. *Margaret Mead and Samoa: The Making and Unmaking of an Anthropological Myth*. Cambridge, MA: Harvard University Press.

Freeman, James A. 1981. A Firewalking Ceremony That Failed. In *Social and Cultural Context of Medicine in India*. Giri Raj Gupta, ed. Pp. 308–336. New Delhi: Vikas Publishing House.

———. 1989. *Hearts of Sorrow: Vietnamese-American Lives*. Stanford, CA: Stanford University Press.

French, Howard. 2006. In a Richer China, Billionaires Put Money on Marriage. *The New York Times*, January 24:A4.

Frideres, James S. 1998. *Aboriginal Peoples in Canada: Contemporary Conflicts*. 5th edition. Scarborough, ON: Prentice Hall Allyn and Bacon.

Friedl, Ernestine. 1986. Fieldwork in a Greek Village. In *Women in the Field: Anthropological Experiences*. Peggy Golde, ed. Pp. 195–220. Berkeley, CA: University of California Press.

Frisch, Rose. 1978. Population, Food Intake, and Fertility. *Science* 199:22–30.

Furst, Peter T. 1989. The Water of Life: Symbolism and Natural History on the Northwest Coast. *Dialectical Anthropology* 14:95–115.

Gable, Eric. 1995. The Decolonization of Consciousness: Local Skeptics and the "Will to Be Modern" in a West African Village. *American Ethnologist* 22(2):242–257.

Gage-Brandon, Anastasia J. 1992. The Polygyny–Divorce Relationship: A Case Study of Nigeria. *Journal of Marriage and the Family* 54:282–292.

Galdikas, Biruté. 1995. *Reflections of Eden: My Years with the Orangutans of Borneo*. Boston: Little, Brown.

Gardiner, Margaret. 1984. *Footprints on Malekula: A Memoir of Bernard Deacon*. Edinburgh, UK: The Salamander Press.

Gardner, Katy, and David Lewis. 1996. *Anthropology, Development and the Post-Modern Challenge*. Chicago: Pluto Press.

Garland, David. 1996. Social Control. In *The Social Science Encyclopedia*. Adam Kuper and Jessica Kuper, eds. Pp. 780–783. Routledge: New York.

Gaski, Harald. 1993. The Sami People: The "White Indians" of Scandinavia. *American Indian Culture and Research Journal* 17:115–164.

———. 1997. Introduction: Sami Culture in a New Era. In *Sami Culture in a New Era: The Norwegian Sami Experience*. Harald Gaski, ed. Pp. 9–28. Seattle: University of Washington Press.

Geertz, Clifford. 1966. Religion as a Cultural System. In *Anthropological Approaches to the Study of Religion*. Michael Banton, ed. Pp. 1–46. London: Tavistock.

Gibb, Camilla. 2002. Deterritorialized People in Hyperspace: Creating and Debating Harari Identity over the Internet. *Anthropologica* 44(1):55–67.

Gifford-Gonzalez, Diane. 1993. You Can Hide, But You Can't Run: Representation of Women's Work in Illustrations of Palaeolithic Life. *Visual Anthropology Review* 9(1):23–41.

Gilman, Antonio. 1991. Trajectories towards Social Complexity in the Later Prehistory of the Mediterranean. In *Chiefdoms: Power, Economy and Ideology*. Timothy Earle, ed. Pp. 146–168. New York: Cambridge University Press.

Gillette, Maris Boyd. 2000. *Between Mecca and Beijing: Modernization and Consumption among Urban Chinese Families*. Stanford, CA: Stanford University Press.

Ginsberg, Faye D., and Rayna Rapp. 1991. The Politics of Reproduction. *Annual Review of Anthropology* 20: 311–343.

Glasser, Irene, and Rae Bridgeman. 1999. *Braving the Street: The Anthropology of Homelessness*. New York: Berghahn Books.

Glick Schiller, Nina, and Georges E. Fouron. 1999. Terrains of Blood and Nation: Haitian Transnational Social Fields. *Ethnic and Racial Studies* 22:340–365.

Glínski, Piotr. 1994. Environmentalism among Polish Youth: A Maturing Social Movement? *Communist and Post-Communist Studies* 27(2):145–159.

Gliotto, Tom. 1995. Paradise Lost. *People Weekly* 43(17):70–76.

Gluckman, Max. 1955. *The Judicial Process among the Barotse of Northern Rhodesia*. Manchester, UK: Manchester University Press.

———. 1963. *Politics, Law and Ritual in Tribal Africa*. London: Cohen and West.

Gmelch, George. 1997[1971]. Baseball Magic. In *Magic, Witchcraft, and Religion*. Arthur C. Lehmann and James E. Myers, eds. Pp. 276–282. Mountain View, CA: Mayfield Publishing.

Godelier, Maurice. 1971. "Salt Currency" and the Circulation of Commodities among the Baruya of New Guinea. In *Studies in Economic Anthropology*. George Dalton, ed. Pp. 52–73. Anthropological Studies No. 7. Washington, DC: American Anthropological Association.

Godoy, Ricardo, Victoria Reyes-Garcia, Tomas Huanca, William R. Leonard, Vincent Valdez, Cynthia Valdes-Galicia, and Dukun Zhao. 2005. Why Do Subsistence-Level People Join the Market Economy? Testing Hypotheses of Push and Pull Determinants in Bolivian Amazonia. *Journal of Anthropological Research* 61:157–178.

Gold, Ann Grodzins. 1988. *Fruitful Journeys: The Ways of Rajasthani Pilgrims*. Berkeley, CA: University of California Press.

Gold, Stevan J. 1992. *Refugee Communities: A Comparative Field Study*. Newbury Park, CA: Sage Publications.

———. 1995. *From the Workers' State to the Golden State: Jews from the Former Soviet Union in California*. Boston: Allyn and Bacon.

Golde, Peggy, ed. 1986. *Women in the Field: Anthropological Experiences*. 2nd edition. Berkeley, CA: University of California Press.

Goldstein, Melvin C., and Cynthia M. Beall. 1994. *The Changing World of Mongolia's Nomads*. Berkeley, CA: University of California Press.

Goldstein-Gidoni, Ofra. 2003. Producers of "Japan" in Israel: Cultural Appropriation in a Non-Colonial Context. *Ethnos* 68(3):365–390.

Goldstone, Jack. 1996. Revolutions. In *The Social Science Encyclopedia*. Adam Kuper and Jessica Kuper, eds. Pp. 740–743. New York: Routledge.

González, Nancie L. 1970. Toward a Definition of Matrifocality. In *Afro-American Anthropology: Contemporary Perspectives*. Norman E. Whitten, Jr. and John F. Szwed, eds. Pp. 231–244. New York: Free Press.

Goodall, Jane. 1971. *In the Shadow of Man*. Boston: Houghton-Mifflin.

———. 1986. *The Chimpanzees of Gombe: Patterns of Behavior*. Cambridge, MA: Harvard University Press.

Goody, Jack. 1976. *Production and Reproduction: A Comparative Study of the Domestic Domain*. New York: Cambridge University Press.

———. 1977. *Cooking, Cuisine and Class: A Study of Comparative Sociology*. New York: Cambridge University Press.

———. 1993. *The Culture of Flowers*. New York: Cambridge University Press.

———. 1996 Comparing Family Systems in Europe and Asia: Are There Different Sets of Rules? *Population and Development Review* 22:1–20.

Goody, Jack, and Stanley J. Tambiah. 1973. *Bridewealth and Dowry*. New York: Cambridge University Press.

Goossens, Benoît, Lounés Chikhi, Marc Ancrenaz, Isabelle Lackman-Ancrenaz, Patrick Andau, and Michael W. Bruford. 2006. Genetic Signature of Anthropogenic Population Collapse in Orangutans. *PloS Biology* 4(2):e25. www.plosbiology.org.

Graburn, Nelson. 1976. Ethnic Arts of the Fourth World: The View from Canada. In *Imagery and Creativity: Ethnoaesthetics and Art Worlds in the Americas*. D. Whitten and N. Whitten, eds. Tucson, AZ: University of Arizona Press.

———. 1998. Weirs in the River of Time: The Development of Historical Consciousness among Canadian Inuit. *Museum Anthropology* 22(1):18–32.

———. 2004. Authentic Inuit Art: Creation and Exclusion in the Canadian North. *Journal of Material Culture* 9(2): 141–159.

Graham, Elizabeth. 1998. Mission Archaeology. *Annual Review of Anthropology* 27:25–62.

Greenhalgh, Susan. 2003. Science, Modernity, and the Making of China's One-Child Policy. *Population and Development Review* 29:163–196.

Gregg, Jessica L. 2003. *Virtually Virgins: Sexual Strategies and Cervical Cancer in Recife, Brazil*. Stanford, CA: Stanford University Press.

Gregor, Thomas. 1981. A Content Analysis of Mehinaku Dreams. *Ethos* 9:353–390.

———. 1982. No Girls Allowed. *Science* 82.

Gremillion, Helen. 1992. Psychiatry as Social Ordering: Anorexia Nervosa, a Paradigm. *Social Science and Medicine* 35(1):57–71.

Grenier, Guillermo J., Alex Stepick, Debbie Draznin, Aileen LaBorwit, and Steve Morris. 1992. On Machines and Bureaucracy: Controlling Ethnic Interaction in Miami's Apparel and Construction Industries. In *Structuring Diversity: Ethnographic Perspectives on the New Immigration*. Louise Lamphere, ed. Pp. 65–94. Chicago: University of Chicago Press.

Grinker, Roy Richard. 1994. *Houses in the Rainforest: Ethnicity and Inequality among Farmers and Foragers in Central Africa*. Berkeley, CA: University of California Press.

Gross, Daniel R. 1984. Time Allocation: A Tool for the Study of Cultural Behavior. *Annual Review of Anthropology* 13:519–558.

Gross, Daniel R., George Eiten, Nancy M. Flowers, Francisca M. Leoi, Madeleine Lattman Ritter, and Dennis W. Werner. 1979. Ecology and Acculturation among Native Peoples of Central Brazil. *Science* 206(30):1043–1050.

Gross, Daniel R., and Barbara A. Underwood. 1971. Technological Change and Caloric Costs. *American Anthropologist* 73:725–740.

Gruenbaum, Ellen. 2001. *The Female Circumcision Controversy: An Anthropological Perspective*. Philadelphia: University of Pennsylvania Press.

Gruneau, Richard S., and David Whitson. 1993. *Hockey Night in Canada: Sport, Identities, and Cultural Politics*. Toronto: Garamond Press.

Guggenheim, Scott E., and Michael M. Cernea. 1993. Anthropological Approaches to Involuntary Resettlement: Policy, Practice, and Theory. In *Anthropological Approaches to Resettlement: Policy, Practice, and Theory*. Michael M. Cernea and Scott E. Guggenheim, eds. Pp. 1–12. Boulder, CO: Westview Press.

Gugler, Josef. 1988. The Urban Character of Contemporary Revolutions. In *The Urbanization of the Third World*. Josef Gugler, ed. Pp. 399–412. New York: Oxford University Press.

Guidoni, Enrico. 1987. *Primitive Architecture*. Robert Erich Wolf, trans. New York: Rizzoli.

Gulliver, P. H., and M. Silverman. 1995. *Merchants and Shopkeepers: A Historical Anthropology of an Irish Market Town, 1200–1991*. Toronto: University of Toronto Press.

Gupta, Akhil, and James Ferguson, eds. 1997. *Anthropological Locations: Boundaries and Grounds of Field Science*. Berkeley, CA: University of California Press.

Hackenberg, Robert A. 2000. Advancing Applied Anthropology: Joe Hill in Cyberspace-Steps Toward Creating "One Big Union." *Human Organization* 59:365–369.

Hackenberg, Robert A., et al. 1983. Migration, Modernization and Hypertension: Blood Pressure Levels in Four Philippine Communities. *Medical Anthropology* 7(1):45–71.

Hacker, Andrew. 1992. *Two Nations: Black and White, Separate, Hostile, Unequal*. New York: Ballantine Books.

Haddix McCay, Kimber. 2001. Leaving Your Wife and Your Brothers: When Polyandrous Marriages Fall Apart. *Evolution and Human Behavior* 22:47–60.

Hagey, Rebecca. 1984. The Phenomenon, the Explanations and the Responses: Metaphors Surrounding Diabetes in Urban Canadian Indians. *Social Science and Medicine* 18:265–272.

Hahn, Robert. 1995. *Sickness and Healing: An Anthropological Perspective*. New Haven, CT: Yale University Press.

Hakamies-Blomqvist, Liisa. 1994. Aging and Fatal Accidents in Male and Female Drivers. *Journal of Gerontology [Social Sciences]* 49(6):S286–5290.

Hale, Horatio. 1883. *Iroquois Book of Rites*. Philadelphia: D.G. Brinton.

Hammerlsey, Martyn. 1992. *What's Wrong with Ethnography: Methodological Explorations*. London: Routledge.

Hammond, Peter B. 1966. *Yatenga: Technology in the Culture of a West African Kingdom*. New York: Free Press.

Hancock, Graham. 1989. *Lords of Poverty: The Power, Prestige, and Corruption of the International Aid Business*. New York: The Atlantic Monthly Press.

Handler, Richard. 2003. Cultural Property and Cultural Theory. *Journal of Social Archaeology* 3:353–365.

Hardman, Charlotte E. 2000. *Other Worlds: Notions of Self and Emotion among the Lohorung Rai*. New York: Berg.

Harner, Michael. 1977. The Ecological Basis of Aztec Sacrifice. *American Ethnologist* 4:117–135.

Harragan, Simon. 2004. Relief and Understanding of Local Knowledge: The Case of Southern Sudan. In *Culture and Public Action*. Vijayendra Rao and Michael Walton, eds. Pp. 307–327. Stanford, CA: Stanford University Press.

Harris, Marvin. 1974. *Cows, Pigs, Wars, and Witches: The Riddles of Culture*. New York: Random House.

———. 1975. *Culture, People, Nature: An Introduction to General Anthropology*. 2nd edition. New York: Thomas Y. Crowell Company.

———. 1977. *Cannibals and Kings: The Origins of Culture*. New York: Random House.

———. 1989. *Our Kind: Who We Are, Where We Came From and Where We Are Going*. New York: HarperCollins.

Harris, Marvin, and Eric B. Ross. 1987. *Death, Sex and Fertility*. New York: Columbia University Press.

Harrison, Julia. 2003. *Being a Tourist: Finding Meaning in Pleasure Travel*. Vancouver: University of British Columbia Press.

Harrison, Simon. 1993. The Commerce of Cultures in Melanesia. *Man* 28:139–158.

Hart, C. W. M., Arnold R. Pilling, and Jane C. Goodale. 1988. *The Tiwi of North Australia*. New York: Holt, Rinehart and Winston.

Hart, Gillian. 2002. *Disabling Globalization: Places of Power in Post-Apartheid South Africa*. Berkeley, CA: University of California Press.

Hartmann, Betsy. 1987. *Reproductive Rights and Wrongs: The Global Politics of Population Control and Reproductive Choice*. New York: Harper & Row.

Hastrup, Kirsten. 1992. Anthropological Visions: Some Notes on Visual and Textual Authority. In *Film as Ethnography*. Peter Ian Crawford and David Turton, eds. Pp. 8–25. Manchester, UK: University of Manchester Press.

Hawn, Carleen. 2002. Please Feedback the Animals. *Forbes* 170(9):168–169.

Hefner, Robert W. 1998. Multiple Modernities: Christianity, Islam, and Hinduism in a Globalizing Age. *Annual Review of Anthropology* 27:83–104.

Heise, Lori L., Jacqueline Pitanguy, and Adrienne Germain. 1994. *Violence against Women: The Hidden Health Burden*. World Bank Discussion Paper No. 255. Washington, DC: The World Bank.

Helleiner, Jane. 2001. "The Right Kind of Children": Childhood, Gender and Race in Canadian Postwar Political Discourse. *Anthropologica* 43(2):143–152.

Henry, Francis. 1984. *Victims and Neighbors: A Small Town in Nazi Germany Remembered*. South Hadley, MA: Bergin and Garvey.

———. 1987. Caribbean Migration to Canada: Prejudice and Opportunity. In *The Caribbean Exodus*. Barry Levine, ed. New York: Greenwood Publishing Group.

Henry, Francis, and Carol Tator. 2002. *Discourses of Domination: Racial Bias in the Canadian English-Language Press*. Toronto: University of Toronto Press.

Herdt, Gilbert. 1987. *The Sambia: Ritual and Gender in New Guinea*. New York: Holt, Rinehart and Winston.

Herrnstein, Richard J., and Charles A. Murray. 1994. *The Bell Curve: Intelligence and Class Structure in American Life*. New York: Free Press.

Hewlett, Barry S. 1991. *Intimate Fathers: The Nature and Context of Aka Pygmy Paternal Care*. Ann Arbor, MI: University of Michigan Press.

Hiatt, Betty. 1970. Woman the Gatherer. In *Woman's Role in Aboriginal Society*. Fay Gale, ed. Pp. 2–28. Canberra, AU: Australian Institute of Aboriginal Studies.

Higginbotham, N., D. Willms, and N. Sewankambo. 2001. Transdisciplinary Work in the Community. In *Health Social Science: A Transdisciplinary and Complexity Perspective*. N. Higginbotham, G Albrecht, and L. O'Connor, eds. South Melbourne, AU: Oxford University Press.

Hill, Jane H. 2001. Dimensions of Attrition in Language Death. In *On Biocultural Diversity: Linking Language, Knowledge, and the Environment*. Luisa Maffi, ed. Pp. 175–189. Washington, DC: Smithsonian Institution Press.

Hill, Jane H., and Bruce Mannheim. 1992. Language and World View. *Annual Review of Anthropology* 21:381–406.

Hiltebeitel, Alf. 1988. *The Cult of Draupadi: Mythologies from Gingee to Kuruksetra*. Chicago: The University of Chicago Press.

———. 1995. Hinduism. In *The HarperCollins Dictionary of Religion*. Jonathan Z. Smith, ed. Pp. 424–440. New York: HarperCollins Publishers.

Hirschfelder, Arlene, ed. 1995. *Native Heritage: Personal Accounts by American Indians 1790 to the Present*. New York: Macmillan.

Hirschon, Renee. 1989. *Heirs of the Catastrophe: The Social Life of Asia Minor Refugees in Piraeus*. New York: Oxford University Press.

Hodge, Robert W., and Naohiro Ogawa. 1991. *Fertility Change in Contemporary Japan*. Chicago: University of Chicago Press.

Hoffman, Danny. 2003. Frontline Anthropology: Research in a Time of War. *Anthropology Today* 19:9–12.

Hoffman, Danny, and Stephen Lubkemann. 2005. Warscape Ethnography in West Africa and the Anthropology of "Events." *Anthropological Quarterly* 78:315–327.

Hollan, Douglas. 2001. Developments in Person-Centered Ethnography. In *The Psychology of Cultural Experience*. Carmella C. Moore and Holly F. Mathews, eds. Pp. 48–67. New York: Cambridge University Press.

Holmes, Paula Elizabeth. 2001. The Narrative Repatriation of Blessed Kateri Tekakwitha. *Anthropologica* 43(1):87–103.

Hopkins, Nicholas S., and Sohair R. Mehanna. 2000. Social Action against Everyday Pollution in Egypt. *Human Organization* 59:245–254.

Horowitz, Irving L. 1967. *The Rise and Fall of Project Camelot: Studies in the Relationship between Social Science and Practical Politics*. Boston: MIT Press.

Horowitz, Michael M., and Muneera Salem-Murdock. 1993. Development-Induced Food Insecurity in the Middle Senegal Valley. *GeoJournal* 30(2):179–184.

Horst, Heather, and Daniel Miller. 2005. From Kinship to Link-up: Cell Phones and Social Networking in Jamaica. *Current Anthropology* 46:755–764, 773–778.

Howell, Nancy. 1979. *Demography of the Dobe !Kung*. New York: Academic Press.

———. 1986. Feedbacks and Buffers in Relation to Scarcity and Abundance: Studies of Hunter–Gatherer Populations. In *The State of Population Theory: Forward from Malthus*. David Coleman and Roger Schofield, eds. Pp. 156–187. New York: Basil Blackwell.

———. 1990. *Surviving Fieldwork: A Report of the Advisory Panel on Health and Safety in Fieldwork*. Washington, DC: American Anthropological Association.

Hughes, Lotte. 2003. *The No-Nonsense Guide to Indigenous Peoples*. London: Verso.

Humphrey, Caroline. 1978. Women, Taboo and the Suppression of Attention. In *Defining Females: The Nature of Women in Society*. Shirley Ardener, ed. Pp. 89–108. New York: John Wiley & Sons.

Hunte, Pamela A. 1985. Indigenous Methods of Fertility Regulation in Afghanistan. In *Women's Medicine: A Cross-Cultural Study of Indigenous Fertility Regulation*. Lucile F. Newman, ed. Pp. 44–75. New Brunswick, NJ: Rutgers University Press.

Hutchinson, Sharon E. 1996. *Nuer Dilemmas: Coping with Money, War, and the State*. Berkeley, CA: University of California Press.

Hutter, Michael. 1996. The Value of Play. In *The Value of Culture: On the Relationship between Economics and the Arts*. Arjo Klamer, ed. Pp. 122–137. Amsterdam: Amsterdam University Press.

Illo, Jeanne Frances I. 1985. Who Heads the Household? Women in Households in the Philippines. Paper presented at the Women and Household Regional Conference for Asia, New Delhi.

Indra, Doreen M. 1988. Self-Concept and Resettlement: Vietnamese and Sino-Vietnamese in a Small Prairie City. In *Ten Years Later: Indochinese Communities in Canada*. Louis-Jacques Dorais, Kwok B. Chan, and Doreen M. Indra, eds. Montreal: Canadian Asian Studies Association.

Inhorn, Marcia C. 2003. Global Infertility and the Globalization of New Reproductive Technologies: Illustrations from Egypt. *Social Science and Medicine* 56:1837–1851.

———. 2004. Middle Eastern Masculinities in the Age of New Reproductive Technologies: Male Infertility and Stigma in Egypt and Lebanon. *Medical Anthropology Quarterly* 18(2):162–182.

International Alliance for the Protection of Isolated Indigenous Peoples. 2005. *Belém Declaration on Isolated Indigenous Peoples*. Adopted at the First International Symposium on Isolated Indigenous Peoples of the Amazon, Belém, Brazil, November.

International Labour Office. 1996. Female Asian Migrants: A Growing But Vulnerable Workforce. *World of Work* 15:16–17.

Jacobs-Huey, Lanita. 2002. The Natives Are Gazing and Talking Back: Reviewing the Problematics of Positionality, Voice, and Accountability among "Native" Anthropologists. *American Anthropologist* 104:791–804.

———. 2006. *From the Kitchen to the Parlor: Language and Becoming in African American Women's Hair Care*. New York: Oxford University Press.

Janes, Craig R. 1990. *Migration, Social Change, and Health: A Samoan Community in Urban California*. Stanford, CA: Stanford University Press.

———. 1995. The Transformations of Tibetan Medicine. *Medical Anthropology Quarterly* 9(1):6–39.

Janes, Craig R., and Oyuntsetseg Chuluundorj. 2004. Free Markets and Dead Mothers: The Social Ecology of Maternal Mortality in Post-Socialist Mongolia. *Medical Anthropology Quarterly* 18(2):230–257.

Jankowski, Martín Sánchez. 1991. *Islands in the Street: Gangs and American Urban Society*. Berkeley, CA: University of California Press.

Jenkins, Gwynne L. 2003. Burning Bridges: Policy, Practice, and the Destruction of Midwifery in Rural Costa Rica. *Social Science and Medicine* 56:1893–1909.

Jenkins, Gwynne L., and Marcia C. Inhorn. 2003. Reproduction Gone Awry: Medical Anthropology Perspectives. *Social Science and Medicine* 56:1831–1836.

Jensen, Marianne Wiben, ed. 2004. Land Rights: A Key Issue. Elaine Bolton, trans. *Indigenous Affairs* 4.

Jentoft, Sven, and Anthony Davis. 1993. Self and Sacrifice: An Investigation of Small Boat Fisher Individualism and Its Implication for Producer Cooperatives. *Human Organization* 52(4):356–367.

Jeter, Jon. 2004. Young Brazilians Find Suicide Only Way Out. *The Washington Post*, April 13:A22.

Jiang, David W. 1994. Shanghai Revisited: Chinese Theatre and the Forces of the Market. *The Drama Review* 38(2):72–80.

Jinadu, L. Adele. 1994. The Dialectics of Theory and Research on Race and Ethnicity in Nigeria. In *"Race," Ethnicity and Nation: International Perspectives on Social Conflict*. Peter Ratcliffe, ed. Pp. 163–178. London: University of College London Press.

Johnson, Walter R. 1994. *Dismantling Apartheid: A South African Town in Transition*. Ithaca, NY: Cornell University Press.

Johnson-Hanks, Jennifer. 2002. On the Limits of Life Stages in Ethnography: Toward a Theory of Vital Conjectures. *American Anthropologist* 104:865–880.

Johnston, Barbara Rose. 1994. Environmental Degradation and Human Rights Abuse. In *Who Pays the Price?: The Sociocultural Context of Environmental Crisis*. Barbara Rose Johnston, ed. Pp. 7–16. Washington, DC: Island Press.

Jonaitis, Aldona. 1995. *A Wealth of Thought: Franz Boas on Native American Art*. Seattle: University of Washington Press.

Jones, Anna Laura. 1993. Exploding Canons: The Anthropology of Museums. *Annual Review of Anthropology* 22: 201–220.

Joralemon, Donald. 1982. New World Depopulation and the Case of Disease. *Journal of Anthropological Research* 38:108–127.

Jordan, Brigitte. 1983. *Birth in Four Cultures*. 3rd edition. Montreal: Eden Press.

Jordan, Mark. 1998. Japan Takes Dim View of Fertility Treatments. *The New York Times*, July 5:A13.

Jourdan, Christine. 1995. Masta Liu. In *Youth Cultures: A Cross-Cultural Perspective*. Vered Amit-Talai and Helena Wulff, eds. Pp. 202–222. New York: Routledge.

Joy, Annamma. 1989. *Ethnicity in Canada*. New York: AMS Press.

Judd, Ellen. 2002. *The Chinese Women's Movement: Between State and Market*. Stanford, CA: Stanford University Press.

Kaberry, Phyllis. 1952. *Women of the Grassfields: A Study of the Economic Position of Women in Bamenda, British Cameroons*. London: Her Majesty's Stationery Office (HMSO).

Kabutha, Charity, Barbara P. Thomas-Slaytor, and Richard Ford. 1993. Participatory Rural Appraisal: A Case Study from Kenya. In *Rapid Appraisal Methods*. Krishna Kumar, ed. Pp. 176–211. Washington, DC: The World Bank.

Kahn, Miriam. 1995. Heterotopic Dissonance in the Museum Representation of Pacific Island Cultures. *American Anthropologist* 97(2):324–338.

Kapchan, Deborah A. 1994. Moroccan Female Performers Defining the Social Body. *Journal of American Folklore* 107(423):82–105.

Kassam, Aneesa. 2002. Ethnodevelopment in the Oromia Regional State of Ethiopia. In *Participating in Development: Approaches to Indigenous Knowledge*. Paul Sillitoe, Alan Bicker, and Johan Pottier, eds. Pp. 65–81. ASA Monographs No. 39. New York: Routledge.

Katz, Nathan, and Ellen S. Goldberg. 1989. Asceticism and Caste in the Passover Observances of the Cochin Jews. *Journal of the American Academy of Religion* 57(1):53–81.

Katz, Richard. 1982. *Boiling Energy: Community Healing among the Kalahari Kung*. Cambridge, UK: Harvard University Press.

Katz, Richard, Megan Biesele, and Verna St. Denis. 1997. *Healing Makes Our Hearts Happy: Spirituality and Cultural Transformation among the Kalahari Jul'hoansi*. Rochester, VT: Inner Traditions.

Kaufert, Patricia. 1986. The Menopausal Transition; the Use of Estrogen. *Canadian Journal of Public Health* 77(1):86–91.

Kaufert, P., and J. O'Neil. 1990. Cooptation and Control: The Reconstruction of Inuit Birth. *Medical Anthropology Quarterly* 4(4):427–442.

Kearney, Michael. 1986. From the Invisible Hand to Visible Feet: Anthropological Studies of Migration and Development. *Annual Review of Anthropology* 15:331–361.

Kearney, Robert N., and Barbara D. Miller. 1985. The Spiral of Suicide and Social Change in Sri Lanka. *Journal of Asian Studies* 48:81–101.

Kelm, Mary-Ellen. 1999. *Colonizing Bodies: Aboriginal Health and Healing in British Columbia*. Vancouver: University of British Columbia Press.

Kennedy, David P., and Stephen G. Perz. 2000. Who Are Brazil's Indígenas? Contributions of Census Data Analysis to Anthropological Demography of Indigenous Populations. *Human Organization* 59:311–324.

Kerns, Virginia. 1992. Preventing Violence against Women: A Central American Case. In *Sanctions and Sanctuary: Cultural Perspectives on the Beating of Wives*. Dorothy Ayers Counts, Judith K. Brown, and Jacquelyn C. Campbell, eds. Pp. 125–138. Boulder, CO: Westview Press.

Kesmanee, Chupinit. 1994. Dubious Development Concepts in the Thai Highlands: The Chao Khao in Transition. *Law & Society Review* 28:673–683.

Kideckel, David A. 1993. *The Solitude of Collectivism: Romanian Villagers to the Revolution and Beyond*. Ithaca, NY: Cornell University Press.

Kirsch, Stuart. 2002. Anthropology and Advocacy: A Case Study of the Campaign against the Ok Tedi Mine. *Critique of Anthropology* 22:175–200.

Kleinman, Arthur. 1988. *Illness Narratives*. New York: Basic Books.

———. 1995. *Writing at the Margin: Discourse between Anthropology and Medicine*. Berkeley, CA: University of California Press.

Kneen, B. 1999. *Farmageddon: Food and the Culture of Biotechnology*. Gabriola Island: New Society Publishers.

Knott, Kim. 1996. Hindu Women, Destiny and Stridharma. *Religion* 26:15–35.

Kolenda, Pauline M. 1968. Region, Caste, and Family Structure: A Comparative Study of the Indian "Joint" Family. In *Structure and Change in Indian Society*. Milton Singer and Bernard S. Cohn, eds. Pp. 339–396. New York: Aldine.

———. 1978. *Caste in Contemporary India: Beyond Organic Solidarity*. Prospect Heights, IL: Waveland Press.

Kondo, Dorinne. 1997. *About Face: Performing Race in Fashion and Theatre*. New York: Routledge.

Konner, Melvin. 1987. *Becoming a Doctor: The Journey of Initiation in Medical School*. New York: Penguin Books.

———. 1989. Homosexuality: Who and Why? *The New York Times Magazine*, April 2:60–61.

Kottak, Conrad Phillip. 1985. When People Don't Come First: Some Sociological Lessons from Completed Projects. In *Putting People First: Sociological Variables and Rural Development*. Michael M. Cernea, ed. Pp. 325–356. New York: Oxford University Press.

———. 1992. *Assault on Paradise: Social Change in a Brazilian Village*. New York: McGraw-Hill Ryerson.

Kovats-Bernat, J. Christopher. 2002. Negotiating Dangerous Fields: Pragmatic Strategies for Fieldwork amid Violence and Terror. *American Anthropologist* 104:1–15.

Krantzler, Nora J. 1987. Traditional Medicine as "Medical Neglect": Dilemmas in the Case Management of a Samoan Teenager with Diabetes. In *Child Survival: Cultural Perspectives on the Treatment and Maltreatment of Children*. Nancy Scheper-Hughes, ed. Pp. 325–337. Boston: D. Reidel.

Kroeber, A. L., and Clyde Kluckhohn. 1952. *Culture: A Critical Review of Concepts and Definitions*. New York: Vintage Books.

Kuipers, Joel C. 1990. *Power in Performance: The Creation of Textual Authority in Weyéwa Ritual Speech*. Philadelphia: University of Pennsylvania Press.

———. 1991. Matters of Taste in Weyéwa. In *The Varieties of Sensory Experience: A Sourcebook in the Anthropology of the Senses*. David Howes, ed. Pp. 111–127. Toronto: University of Toronto Press.

———. 2004. Ethnography of Language in the Age of Video: "Voices" in Context of Religious and Clinical Authority. In *Discourse and Technology: Multimodal Discourse Analysis*. Philip LeVine and Ron Scollon, eds. Pp. 167–183. Washington, DC: Georgetown University Press.

Kumar, Sanjay. 1996. Largest-Ever World Bank Loan Mistrusted in India. *The Lancet* 347(April 20):1109.

Kurin, Richard. 1980. Doctor, Lawyer, Indian Chief. *Natural History* 89(11):6–24.

Kwiatkowski, Lynn M. 1998. *Struggling with Development: The Politics of Hunger and Gender in the Philippines*. Boulder, CO: Westview Press.

Labov, William. 1966. *The Social Stratification of English in New York City*. Washington, DC: Center for Applied Linguistics.

Ladányi, János. 1993. Patterns of Residential Segregation and the Gypsy Minority in Budapest. *International Journal of Urbana and Regional Research* 17(1):30–41.

LaFleur, William. 1992. *Liquid Life: Abortion and Buddhism in Japan*. Princeton, NJ: Princeton University Press.

Lake, Amy, and Steven Deller. 1996. *The Socioeconomic Impacts of a Native American Casino*. Madison, WI: Department of Agricultural and Applied Economics, University of Wisconsin.

Lakoff, Robin. 1973. Language and Woman's Place. *Language in Society* 2:45–79.

———. 1990. *Talking Power: The Politics of Language in Our Lives*. New York: Basic Books.

Lambek, Michael. 1993. *Knowledge and Practice in Mayotte: Local Discourses of Islam, Sorcery, and Spirit Possession*. Toronto: University of Toronto Press.

Lamirande, T. 1999. Whale for the Killing: Controversy Erupts after Washington Natives Pursue a Tradition. *First Perspectives* 8(6).

Lamphere, Louise. 1992. Introduction: The Shaping of Diversity. In *Structuring Diversity: Ethnographic Perspectives on the New Immigration*. Louise Lamphere, ed. Chicago: University of Chicago Press.

Landes, Ruth. 1938. The Abnormal among the Ojibwa Indians. *Journal of Abnormal and Social Psychology* 33:14–33.

Landy, David. 1985. Pibloktoq (Hysteria) and Inuit Nutrition: Possible Implication of Hypervitaminosis A. *Social Science and Medicine* 21(2):173–185.

Lansing, J. Stephen. 1995. *The Balinese*. Toronto: Harcourt Brace College Publishers.

Larsen, Ulla, and Marida Hollos. 2003. Women's Empowerment and Fertility Decline among the Pare of Kilimanjaro region, Northern Tanzania. *Social Science and Medicine* 57:1099–1115.

Larsen, Ulla, and Sharon Yan. 2000. Does Female Circumcision Affect Infertility and Fertility? A Study of the Central African Republic, Côte d'Ivoire, and Tanzania. *Demography* 37:313–321.

Larsson, Sara. 2005. Legislating Gender Equality: In Saami Land, Women Are Encouraged to Become Lawyers—But Many Would Rather Be Reindeer Herders. *Cultural Survival Quarterly* 28(4):28–29.

Lassiter, Luke Eric, Hurley Goodall, Elizabeth Campbell, and Michelle Natasya Johnson. 2004. *The Other Side of Middletown: Exploring Muncie's African American Community*. Walnut Creek, CA: AltaMira Press.

Leach, Jerry W. 1975. *Trobriand Cricket: An Ingenious Response to Colonialism*. Video. Berkeley, CA: University of California Extension Media.

Leacock, Eleanor. 1993. Women in Samoan History: A Further Critique of Derek Freeman. In *Sex and Gender Hierarchies*. Barbara D. Miller, ed., Pp. 351–365. New York: Cambridge University Press.

Lebra, Takie. 1976. *Japanese Patterns of Behavior*. Honolulu: University of Hawaii Press.

Lederer, Edith. 2006. Record Number of Women in Politics. *Guardian Weekly*, March 10, 15:9.

Lee, Gary R., and Mindy Kezis. 1979. Family Structure and the Status of the Elderly. *Journal of Comparative Family Studies* 10:429–443.

Lee, Helen Morton. 2003. *Tongans Overseas: Between Two Shores*. Honolulu: University of Hawaii Press.

Lee, Raymond M., and Claire M. Renzetti. 1993. *Researching Sensitive Topics*. Newbury Park, CA: Sage Publications.

Lee, Richard Borshay. 1969. Eating Christmas in the Kalahari. *Natural History* December.

———. 1979 *The !Kung San: Men, Women, and Work in a Foraging Society*. New York: Cambridge University Press.

Lee, Richard, and Richard Daly, eds. 1999. *The Cambridge Encyclopaedia of Hunters and Gatherers*. Cambridge, UK: Cambridge University Press.

Lee, Wai-Na, and David K. Tse. 1994. Becoming Canadian: Understanding How Hong Kong Immigrants Change Their Consumption. *Pacific Affairs* 67(1):70–95.

Lein, Laura, and Donald Brenneis. 1978. Children's Dispute in Three Speech Communities. *Language in Society* 7:299–323.

Lempert, David. 1996. *Daily Life in a Crumbling Empire*. 2 volumes. New York: Columbia University Press.

Lepowsky, Maria. 1993. *Fruit of the Motherland: Gender in an Egalitarian Society*. New York: Columbia University Press.

Levine, Robert, Suguru Sato, Tsukasa Hashimoto, and Jyoti Verma. 1995. Love and Marriage in Eleven Cultures. *Journal of Cross-Cultural Psychology* 26:554–571.

Levinson, David. 1989. *Family Violence in Cross-Cultural Perspective*. Newbury Park, CA: Sage Publications.

Lévi-Strauss, Claude. 1967. *Structural Anthropology*. New York: Anchor Books.

———. 1968. *Tristes Tropiques: An Anthropological Study of Primitive Societies in Brazil*. New York: Atheneum.

———. 1969[1949]. *The Elementary Structures of Kinship*. Boston: Beacon Press.

Levy, Jerrold E., Eric B. Henderson, and Tracy J. Andrews. 1989. The Effects of Regional Variation and Temporal Change in Matrilineal Elements of Navajo Social Organization. *Journal of Anthropological Research* 45(4):351–377.

Lew, Irvina. 1994. Bathing as Science: Ancient Sea Cures Gain Support from New Research. *Condé Nast Traveler* 29(12):86–90.

Lewin, Ellen. 1993. *Lesbian Mothers: Accounts of Gender in American Culture*. Ithaca, NY: Cornell University Press.

Lewis, Oscar. 1966. The Culture of Poverty. *Scientific American*. 215:19–25.

Leynaud, Emile. 1961. Fraternités d'âge et sociétés de culture dans la Haute-Vallée du Niger. *Cahiers d'Etudes Africaines* 6:41–68.

Leyton, Elliot. 1996. *Men of Blood: Murder in Everyday Life*. Toronto: McClelland & Stewart.

Lightfoot, David. 2006. *How New Languages Emerge*. New York: Cambridge University Press.

Lindenbaum, Shirley. 1979. *Kuru Sorcery: Disease and Danger in the New Guinea Highlands*. Mountain View, CA: Mayfield Publishing Company.

Linnekan, Jocelyn. 1990. *Sacred Queens and Women of Consequence: Rank, Gender, and Colonialism in the Hawaiian Islands*. Ann Arbor, MI: University of Michigan Press.

Lipka, Jerry, Maureen P. Hogan, Joan Parker Webster, Evelyn Yanez, Barbara Adams, Stacy Clark, and Doreen Lacy. 2005. Math in a Cultural Context: Two Case Studies of a Successful Culturally Based Math Project. *Anthropology and Education Quarterly* 36(4):367–385.

Little, Kenneth. 1991. On Safari; The Visual Politics of a Tourist Representation. In *The Varieties of Sensory Experience*. D. Howes, ed. Toronto: University of Toronto Press.

Lloyd, Cynthia B. 1995. *Household Structure and Poverty: What Are the Connections?* Working Papers, No. 74. New York: The Population Council.

Lock, Margaret. 1993. *Encounters with Aging: Mythologies of Menopause in Japan and North America*. Berkeley, CA: University of California Press.

———. 1996. Deadly Disputes: Ideologies and Brain Death in Japan. In *Organ Transplantation: Meanings and Realities*. S. Youngner, R. Fox and L. O'Connell, eds. Madison, WI: University of Wisconsin Press.

———. 2002. *Twice Dead: Organ Transplants and the Reinvention of Death*. Berkeley, CA: University of California Press.

Lock, M., and G. Bibeau. 1995. Healthy Disputes: Some Reflections on the Practice of Medical Anthropology in Canada. *Health and Canadian Society/Santé et Société Canadienne* 1(1):147–175.

Lock, Margaret, and Pamela Wakewich-Dunk. 1990. Nostalgia: Expression of Loss among Greek Immigrants in Montreal. *Canadian Family Physician* 36:253–258.

Lockwood, Victoria S. 1993. *Tahitian Transformation: Gender and Capitalist Development in a Rural Society*. Boulder, CO: Lynne Reiner Publishers.

Loker, William. 1993 Human Ecology of Cattle-Raising in the Peruvian Amazon: The View from the Farm. *Human Organization* 52(1):14–24.

———. 2000. Sowing Discord, Planting Doubts: Rhetoric and Reality in an Environment and Development Project in Honduras. *Human Organization* 59:300–310.

———. 2003. Dam Impacts in a Time of Globalization: Using Multiple Methods to Document Social and Environmental Change in Rural Honduras. *Current Anthropology* 44(supplement):S112–S121.

Long, Susan Orpett. 2005. *Final Days: Japanese Culture and Choice at the End of Life*. Honolulu: University of Hawaii Press.

Lorch, Donatella. 2003. Do Read This for War. *Newsweek* 141(11):13.

Louie, Andrea. 2000. Re-territorializing Transnationalism: Chinese Americans and the Chinese Motherland. *American Ethnologist* 27:645–669.

Lovell, N., and P. Lai. 1994. Lifestyle and Health of Voyageurs in the Canadian Fur Trade. In *Strength in Diversity: A Reader in Physical Anthropology*. A. Herring and L. Chan, eds. Toronto: Canadian Scholars Press.

Lovisek, J., T. Holzkamm, and L. Waisberg. 1997. Fatal Errors: Ruth Landes and the Creation of the "Atomistic Ojibwa." *Anthropologica* 39(1–2):133–145.

Low, Setha M. 1995. Indigenous Architecture and the Spanish American Plaza in Mesoamerica and the Caribbean. *American Anthropologist* 97(4):748–762.

Lozada, Eriberto P. 1998. A Hakka Community in Cyberspace: Diasporic Ethnicity and the Internet. In *On the South China Track: Perspectives on Anthropological Research and Teaching.* Sidney C. H. Cheung, ed. Pp. 149–182. Hong Kong: Hong Kong Institute of Asia-Pacific Studies, The Chinese University of Hong Kong.

Lu, Hanchao. 1995. Away from Nanking Road: Small Stores and Neighborhood Life in Modern Shanghai. *Journal of Asian Studies* 54(1):93–123.

Lubkemann, Stephen C. 2002. Refugees. In *World at Risk: A Global Issues Sourcebook.* Pp. 522–544. Washington, DC: CQ Press.

———. 2005. Migratory Coping in Wartime Mozambique: An Anthropology of Violence and Displacement in "Fragmented Wars." *Journal of Peace Research* 42:493–508.

Luhrmann, Tanya M. 1989. *Persuasions of the Witch's Craft: Ritual Magic in Contemporary England.* Cambridge, MA: Harvard University Press.

Lutz, Ellen L. 2005. The Many Meanings of Technology: A Message from Our Executive Editor. *Cultural Survival Quarterly* 29(2):5.

Lyttleton, Chris. 2004. Relative Pleasures: Drugs, Development and Modern Dependencies in Asia's Golden Triangle. *Development and Change* 35:909–935.

MacDonald, M. 2001. Postmodern Negotiations with Medical Technology: The Role of Midwifery Clients in the New Midwifery in Canada. *Medical Anthropology* 20:245–276.

———. 2007. *At Work in the Field of Birth: Midwifery Narratives of Nature, Tradition, and Home.* Nashville, TN: Vanderbilt University Press.

Maclachlan, Morgan. 1983. *Why They Did Not Starve: Biocultural Adaptation in a South Indian Village.* Philadelphia: Institute for the Study of Human Issues.

MacLeod, Arlene Elowe. 1992. Hegemonic Relations and Gender Resistance: The New Veiling as Accommodating Protest in Cairo. *Signs: The Journal of Women in Culture and Society* 17(3):533–557.

Maffi, Luisa. 2003. The "Business" of Language Endangerment: Saving Language or Helping People Keep Them Alive? In *Language in the Twenty-First Century: Selected Papers of the Millenial Conference of the Center for Research and Documentation on World Language Problems.* H. Tonkin and T. Reagan, eds. Pp. 67–86. Amsterdam: John Benjamins.

———. 2005. Linguistic, Cultural, and Biological Diversity. *Annual Review of Anthropology* 34:599–617.

Magga, Ole Henrik, and Tove Skutnabb-Kangas. 2001. The Saami Languages: The Present and the Future. *Cultural Survival Quarterly* 25(2):26–31.

Magliocco, Sabina. 2004. *Witching Culture: Folklore and Neo-Paganism in America.* Philadelphia: University of Pennsylvania Press.

Malinowski, Bronislaw. 1929. *The Sexual Life of Savages.* New York: Harcourt, Brace & World.

———. 1961[1922]. *Argonauts of the Western Pacific.* New York: E. P. Dutton & Co.

———. 1962[1926]. *Crime and Custom in Savage Society.* Paterson, NJ: Littlefield, Adams & Co.

Mamdani, Mahmoud. 1972. *The Myth of Population Control: Family, Caste, and Class in an Indian Village.* New York: Monthly Review Press.

———. 2002. Good Muslim, Bad Muslim: A Political Perspective on Culture and Terrorism. *American Anthropologist* 104:766–775.

Manning, Frank. 1981. Celebrating Cricket: The Symbolic Construction of Caribbean Politics. *American Ethnologist* 8:616–632.

———, ed. 1983. *Consciousness and Inquiry: Ethnology and Canadian Realities.* Canadian Ethnology Service, Paper No. 89e, Ottawa: National Museum of Man.

Manz, Beatriz. 1988. *Refugees of a Hidden War: The Aftermath of Counterinsurgency in Guatemala.* Albany, NY: State University of New York Press.

———. 2004. *Paradise in Ashes: A Guatemalan Journey of Courage, Terror, and Hope.* Berkeley, CA: University of California Press.

Marano, L. 1982. Windigo Psychosis: The Anatomy of an Emic–Etic Confusion. *Current Anthropology* 23(4):385–397.

March, Kathryn S., and Rachelle L. Taqqu. 1986. *Women's Informal Associations in Developing Countries: Catalysts for Change?* Boulder, CO: Westview Press.

Margolis, Maxine. 1994. *Little Brazil: An Ethnography of Brazilian Immigrants in New York City.* Princeton, NJ: Princeton University Press.

Margolis, Maxine L., and Marigene Arnold. 1993. Turning the Tables? Male Strippers and the Gender Hierarchy in America. In *Sex and Gender Hierarchies.* Barbara D. Miller, ed. Pp. 334–350. New York: Cambridge University Press.

Marshall, Ingeborg. 1996. *A History and Ethnography of the Beothuk.* Montreal and Kingston: McGill-Queen's University Press.

Marshall, Robert C. 1985. Giving a Gift to the Hamlet: Rank, Solidarity and Productive Exchange in Rural Japan. *Ethnology* 24:167–182.

Martin, Richard C. 1995. Islam. In *The HarperCollins Dictionary of Religion.* Jonathan Z. Smith, ed. Pp. 498–513. New York: HarperCollins.

Martin, Sarah. 2005. *Must Boys Be Boys?: Ending Sexual Exploitation and Abuse in UN Peacekeeping Missions.* Washington, DC: Refugees International.

Martínez, Samuel. 1996. Indifference with Indignation: Anthropology, Human Rights, and the Haitian Bracero. *American Anthropologist* 98(1):17–25.

Marx, Karl, and Friedrich Engels. 1964[1848]. *The Communist Manifesto.* Samuel Moore, trans. New York: Monthly Review Press.

Masquelier, Adeline. 2005. The Scorpion's Sting: Youth, Marriage and the Struggle for Social Maturity in Niger. *Journal of the Royal Anthropological Institute* 11:59–83.

Maybury-Lewis, David. 1997a. Museums and Indigenous Cultures. *Cultural Survival Quarterly* 21(1):3.

———. 1997b. *Indigenous Peoples, Ethnic Groups, and the State.* Boston: Allyn and Bacon.

———. 2002. Genocide against Indigenous Peoples. In *Annihilating Difference: The Anthropology of Genocide.* Alexander Laban Hinton, ed. Pp. 43–53. Berkeley, CA: University of California Press.

Mayer, Adrian. 1960. *Caste and Kinship in Central India: A Village and Its Region.* Berkeley, CA: University of California Press.

McCallum, Cecilia. 2005. Explaining Caesarean Section in Salvador da Bahia, Brazil. *Sociology of Health and Illness* 27(2):215–242.

McCallum, Cecilia, and Ana Paula dos Reis. 2005. Childbirth as Ritual in Brazil: Young Mothers' Experiences. *Ethnos* 70(3):335–360.

McCoid, Catherine Hodge, and LeRoy D. McDermott. 1996. Toward Decolonizing Gender: Female Vision in the Upper Paleolithic. *American Anthropologist* 98(2):319–326.

McCracken, Grant. 1996. *Big Hair: A Journey into the Transformation of Self.* Woodstock, NY: The Overlook Press.

McCully, Patrick. 2003. Big Dams, Big Trouble. *New Internationalist* 354:14–15.

McDermott, LeRoy D. 1996. Self-Representation in Upper Paleolithic Female Figurines. *Current Anthropology* 37:227–275.

McDonald, G., and S. Alford. 1989. *Museum for the Global Village.* Hull, Quebec: Canadian Museum of Civilization.

McElroy, Ann, and Patricia K. Townsend. 1996. *Medical Anthropology in Ecological Perspective.* 3rd edition. Boulder, CO: Westview Press.

McIlwraith, T. F. 1948[1992]. *The Bella Coola Indians.* 2 Volumes. Toronto: University of Toronto Press.

McKenna, James. 1993. Rethinking Healthy Infant Sleep. *Breastfeeding Abstracts* 12(3):27.

M'Closkey, Kathy. 1994. Marketing Multiple Myths: The Hidden History of Navajo Weaving. *Journal of the Southwest* 36(3):185–220.

———. 1996. Art or Craft?: The Paradox of the Pangnirtung Weave Shop. In *Women of the First Nations: Power, Wisdom and Strength.* Christine Miller and Patricia Chuchryk, eds. Pp. 113–126. Winnipeg: University of Manitoba Press.

———. 2002. *Swept under the Rug: A Hidden History of Navajo Weaving.* Albuquerque, NM: University of New Mexico Press.

McLellan, Janet. 1996. Silent Screams and Hidden Pain: Barriers to the Adaptation and Integration of Cambodian Women Refugees in Ontario. In *Development and Diaspora: Gender and the Refugee Experience.* Wenona Giles, Helene Moussa, and Penny Van Esterik, eds. Dundas, ON: Artemis Enterprises.

McLuhan, Marshall. 1964. *Understanding Media: The Extensions of Man.* New York: McGraw-Hill Ryerson.

McMahon, April M. S. 1994. *Understanding Language Change.* New York: Cambridge University Press.

Mead, Margaret. 1961[1928]. *Coming of Age in Samoa: A Psychological Study of Primitive Youth for Western Civilization.* New York: Dell Publishing Company.

———. 1963[1935]. *Sex and Temperament in Three Primitive Societies.* New York: William Morrow.

———. 1986. Field Work in the Pacific Islands, 1925–1967. In *Women in the Field: Anthropological Experiences.* Peggy Golde, ed. Pp. 293–331. Berkeley, CA: University of California Press.

Meigs, Anna S. 1984. *Food, Sex, and Pollution: A New Guinea Religion.* New Brunswick, NJ: Rutgers University Press.

Mencher, Joan P. 1974. The Caste System Upside Down, or The Not-So-Mysterious East. *Current Anthropology* 15(4):469–49.

Meneley, Anne, and Donna J. Young, eds. 2005. *Auto-ethnographies: The Anthropology of Academic Practices.* Peterborough, ON: Broadview Press.

Mernissi, Fatima. 1987. *Beyond the Veil: Male–Female Dynamics in Modern Muslim Society.* Revised edition. Bloomington, IN: Indiana University Press.

———. 1995. *Dreams of Trespass: Tales of a Harem Girlhood.* New York: Addison-Wesley.

Merry, Sally Engle. 1992. Anthropology, Law, and Transnational Processes. *Annual Review of Anthropology* 21:357–379.

———. 2006. *Human Rights and Gender Violence: Translating International Law into Local Justice.* Chicago: University of Chicago Press.

Messer, Ellen. 1993. Anthropology and Human Rights. *Annual Review of Anthropology* 22:221–249.

Meyerhoff, Miriam. 1999. *Sorry* in the Pacific: Defining Communities, Defining Practice. *Language in Society* 28:225–238.

Michaelson, Evalyn Jacobson, and Walter Goldschmidt. 1971. Female Roles and Male Dominance among Peasants. *Southwestern Journal of Anthropology* 27:330–352.

Michaud, Catherine M., W. Scott Gordon, and Michael R. Reich. 2005. *The Global Burden of Disease Due to Schistosomiasis.* Cambridge, MA: Harvard School of Public Health, Harvard Center for Population and Development Studies, Schistosomiasis Research Program Working Paper Series. Volume 14, Number 1.

Migliore, Sam. 1983. Evil Eye or Delusions: On the "Consistency" of Folk Models. *Medical Anthropology Quarterly* 14(2):4–9.

Milgram, B. Lynne. 1999. Crafts, Cultivation and Household Economies: Women's Work and Positions in Ifugao, Upland Philippines. In *Research in Economic Anthropology.* Barry Issac, ed. Greenwich, CT: JAI Press.

Miller, Barbara D. 1997[1981]. *The Endangered Sex: Neglect of Female Children in Rural North India.* Ithaca, NY: Cornell University Press.

———. 1987a. Social Patterns of Food Expenditure among Low-Income Jamaicans. In *Papers and Recommendations of the Workshop on Food and Nutrition Security in Jamaica in the 1980s and Beyond.* Kenneth A. Leslie and Lloyd B. Rankine, eds. Pp. 13–33. Kingston, Jamaica: Caribbean Food and Nutrition Institute.

———. 1987b. Female Infanticide and Child Neglect in Rural North India. In *Child Survival: Anthropological Perspectives on the Treatment and Maltreatment of Children.* Nancy Scheper-Hughes, ed. Pp. 95–113. Boston: D. Reidel Publishing Company.

———. 1993. Surveying the Anthropology of Sex and Gender Hierarchies. In *Sex and Gender Hierarchies.* Barbara D. Miller, ed. Pp. 3–31. New York: Cambridge University Press.

———. 2005. Putting People First to Strengthen Cultural Heritage Advocacy: Rationale, Results, and an Advocacy Tool. Paper presented at the Workshop on Preserving the World's Heritage, Cumberland, SC, October.

Miller, Barbara D., and Showkat Hayat Khan. 1986. Incorporating Voluntarism into Rural Development in Bangladesh. *Third World Planning Review* 8(2):139–152.

Miller, Barbara D., and Carl Stone. 1983. The Low-Income Household Expenditure Survey: Description and Analysis. Jamaica Tax Structure Examination Project, Staff Paper No. 25. Syracuse, NY: Metropolitan Studies Program, Syracuse University.

Miller, Daniel, ed. 2001. *Car Cultures.* New York: Berg.

Miller, Laura. 2004. Those Naughty Teenage Girls: Japanese Kogals, Slang, and Media Assessments. *Journal of Linguistic Anthropology* 14:225–247.

Millett, Kate. 1994. *The Politics of Cruelty: An Essay on the Literature of Political Imprisonment.* New York: Norton.

Mills, Mary Beth. 1995. Attack of the Widow Ghosts: Gender, Death, and Modernity in Northeast Thailand. In *Bewitching Women, Pious Men: Gender and Body Politics in Southeast Asia.* Aihwa Ong and Michael G. Peletz, eds. Pp. 244–273. Berkeley, CA: University of California Press.

Millward, Hugh. 1996. Greater Halifax: Public Policy Issues in the Post-1960 Period. *Canadian Journal of Urban Research* 5(1):1–17.

Milton, Katharine. 1992. Civilization and Its Discontents. *Natural History* 3/92:37–92.

Miner, Horace. 1965[1956]. Body Ritual among the Nacirema. In *Reader in Comparative Religion: An Anthropological Approach.* William A. Lessa and Evon Z. Vogt, eds. Pp. 414–418. New York: Harper & Row.

Mines, Mattison. 1994. *Public Faces, Private Voices: Community and Individuality in South India.* Berkeley, CA: University of California Press.

Mir-Hosseini, Ziba. 1993. *Marriage on Trial: A Study of Islamic Family Law: Iran and Morocco Compared.* New York: I. B. Tauris & Co.

Mitchell, Bruce. 1994. Sustainable Development at the Village Level in Bali, Indonesia. *Human Ecology* 22(2):189–211.

Mitchell, Lisa. 2001. *Baby's First Picture: Ultrasound and the Politics of Fetal Subjects.* Toronto: University of Toronto Press.

Mitter, Partha. 1977. *Much Maligned Monsters: A History of European Reactions to Indian Art.* Chicago: University of Chicago Press.

Moerman, Daniel E. 1979. Anthropology of Symbolic Healing. *Current Anthropology* 20:59–80.

———. 1983. General Medical Effectiveness and Human Biology: Placebo Effects in the Treatment of Ulcer Disease. *Medical Anthropology Quarterly* 14:13–16.

———. 1992 Minding the Body: The Placebo Effect Unmasked. In *Given the Body Its Due.* M. Sheets-Johnstone, ed. Pp. 69–84. Albany, NY: State University of New York Press.

Montesquieu. 1949[1748]. *The Spirit of the Laws.* T. Nugent, trans. New York: Hafner.

Montgomery, Heather. 2001. *Modern Babylon: Prostituting Children in Thailand.* New York: Bergahn Books.

Moore, Carmella C., and Holly F. Mathews, 2001. Introduction: The Psychology of Cultural Experience. In *The Psychology of Cultural Experience.* Carmella C. Moore and Holly F. Mathews, eds. Pp. 1–18. New York: Cambridge University Press.

Morgan, Lewis Henry. 1851. *The League of the [Ho-de-ne-sau, or] Iroquois.* New York: Russell Sage.

Morris, Brian. 1998. *The Power of Animals: An Ethnography.* New York: Berg.

Morris, Rosalind. 1994a. *New Worlds from Fragments: Film, Ethnography and the Representation of Northwest Coast Culture.* Boulder, CO: Westview Press.

———. 1994b. Three Sexes and Four Sexualities: Redressing the Discourses on Gender and Sexuality in Contemporary Thailand. *Positions* 2:15–43.

Morrison, David. 2000. Canadian Aid: A Mixed Record and an Uncertain Future. In *Transforming Development: Foreign Aid for a Changing World.* Jim Freedman, ed. Toronto: University of Toronto Press.

Morrison, L., S. Guruge, and K. Snarr. 1999. Sri Lankan Tamil Immigrants in Toronto: Gender, Marriage Patterns, and Sexuality. In *Gender and Immigration.* Gregory A. Kelson and Debra L. Delaet, eds. Pp. 144–162. London: Macmillan Press.

Moynihan, Elizabeth B. 1979. *Paradise As a Garden in Persia and Mughal India.* New York: George Braziller.

Muecke, Marjorie A. 1987. Resettled Refugees: Reconstruction of Identity of Lao in Seattle. *Urban Anthropology* 16(3–4):273–289.

Mulk, Inga-Maria. 1994. Sacrificial Places and Their Meaning in Saami Society. In *Sacred Sites, Sacred Places.* David L. Carmichael, Jane Hubert, Brian Reeves, and Audhild Schanche, eds. Pp. 121–131. New York: Routledge.

Mull, Dorothy S., and J. Dennis Mull. 1987. Infanticide among the Tarahumara of the Mexican Sierra Madre. In *Child Survival: Anthropological Perspectives on the Treatment and Maltreatment of Children.* Nancy Scheper-Hughes, ed. Pp. 113–132. Boston: D. Reidel Publishing.

Murcott, Anne. 1993[1983]. "It's a Pleasure to Cook for Him": Food, Mealtimes and Gender in Some South Wales Households. In *Gender in Cross-Cultural Perspective.* Caroline B. Brettell and Carolyn F. Sargent, eds. Pp. 77–87. Englewood Cliffs, NJ: Prentice Hall.

Murdock, George Peter. 1965[1949]. *Social Structure.* New York: Free Press.

Murphy, Yolanda, and Robert F. Murphy. 1985. *Women of the Forest.* New York: Columbia University Press.

Murray, David. 2002. *Opacity: Gender, Sexuality, Race and the Problem of "Identity" in Martinique.* New York: Peter Lang Publishing.

Myerhoff, Barbara. 1978. *Number Our Days.* New York: Simon and Schuster.

Myers, James. 1992. Nonmainstream Body Modification: Genital Piercing, Branding, Burning, and Cutting. *Journal of Contemporary Ethnography* 21(3):267–306.

Myers, Norman. 2000. Sustainable Consumption. *Science* 287 (March 31):2419.

Myers-Scotton, Carol. 1993. *Social Motivations for Code-Switching.* New York: Oxford University Press.

Nadeau, Kathleen M. 2002. *Liberation Theology in the Philippines: Faith in a Revolution.* Westport, CT: Praeger.

Nader, Laura. 1972. Up the Anthropologist—Perspectives Gained from Studying Up. In *Reinventing Anthropology.* Dell Hymes, ed. Pp. 284–311. New York: Vintage Books.

———. 1995. Civilization and Its Negotiations. In *Understanding Disputes: The Politics of Argument.* Pat Caplan, ed. Pp. 39–64. Providence, RI: Berg.

———. 2001. Harmony Coerced Is Freedom Denied. *The Chronicle of Higher Education,* July 13:B1.

Nag, Moni. 1972. Sex, Culture and Human Fertility: India and the United States. *Current Anthropology* 13:231–238.

———. 1983. Modernization Affects Fertility. *Populi* 10:56–77.

Nag, Moni, Benjamin N. F. White, and R. Creighton Peet. 1978. An Anthropological Approach to the Study of the Economic Value of Children in Java and Nepal. *Current Anthropology* 19(2):293–301.

Nagata, Judith. 1984. *The Reflowering of Malaysian Islam: Modern Religious Radicals and Their Roots.* Vancouver: University of British Columbia Press.

Nanda, Serena. 1990. *Neither Man Nor Woman: The Hijras of India.* Belmont, CA: Wadsworth Publishing Company.

———. 1994. *Cultural Anthropology.* Belmont, CA: Wadsworth Publishing Company.

Nasser, M., M. Katzman, and R. Gordon. 2001. *Eating Disorders and Cultures in Transition.* New York: Taylor & Francis.

Natcher, David C., Susan Davis, and Clifford G. Hickey. 2005. Co-Management: Managing Relationships, Not Resources. *Human Organization* 64:240–250.

Neale, Walter C. 1976. *Monies in Societies.* San Francisco: Chandler & Sharp Publishers.

National Park Service. 2005. *Low Country Gullah Culture: Special Resource Study and Final Environmental Impact Statement.* Atlanta: NPS Southeast Regional Office. www.nps.gov.

Neff, Deborah L. 1994. The Social Construction of Infertility: The Case of the Matrilineal Nayars in South India. *Social Science and Medicine* 39(4):475–485.

Neier, Aryeh. 1996. Language and Minorities. *Dissent* (Summer):31–35.

Nelson, Sarah. 1993. Gender Hierarchies and the Queens of Silla. In *Sex and Gender Hierarchies.* Barbara D. Miller, ed. Pp. 297–315. New York: Cambridge University Press.

Nettle, Daniel, and Suzanne Romaine. 2000. *Vanishing Voices: The Extinction of the World's Languages.* New York: Oxford University Press.

Neusner, Jacob. 1995. Judaism. In *The HarperCollins Dictionary of Religion.* Jonathan Z. Smith, ed. Pp. 598–607. New York: Harper-Collins.

Nevins, M. Eleanor. 2004. Learning to Listen: Confronting Two Meanings of Language Loss in the Contemporary White Mountain Apache Speech Community. *Journal of Linguistic Anthropology* 14:269–288.

Ngokwey, Ndolamb. 1988. Pluralistic Etiological Systems in Their Social Context: A Brazilian Case Study. *Social Science and Medicine* 26:793–802.

Nichter, Mark. 1992. Of Ticks, Kings, Spirits and the Promise of Vaccines. In *Paths to Asian Medical Knowledge.* Leslie Charles and Allan Young, eds. Pp. 224–253. Berkeley, CA: University of California Press.

———. 1996. Vaccinations in the Third World: A Consideration of Community Demand. In *Anthropology and International Health: Asian Case Studies.* Mark Nichter and Mimi Nichter, eds. Pp. 329–365. Amsterdam: Gordon and Breach Publishers.

Nichter, Mark, and Mimi Nichter, eds. 1996. *Anthropology and International Health: Asian Case Studies.* Amsterdam: Gordon and Breach Publishers.

Nichter, Mimi, and Nancy Vuckovic. 1994. Fat Talk: Body Image among Adolescent Girls. In *Many Mirrors: Body Image and Social Relations.* Nicole Sault, ed. Pp. 109–131. New Brunswick, NJ: Rutgers University Press.

Nichter, Mimi. 2000. *Fat Talk: What Girls and Their Parents Say about Dieting.* Cambridge, MA: Harvard University Press.

Nicks, Trudy. 1992. Partnerships in Developing Cultural Resources: Lessons from the Task Force on Museums and First Peoples. *Culture* 12(1):87–94.

Nodwell, Evelyn, and Neil Guppy. 1992. The Effects of Publicly Displayed Ethnicity on Interpersonal Discrimination: Indo-Canadians in Vancouver. *The Canadian Review of Sociology and Anthropology* 29(1):87–99.

Norgaard, Richard B. 1994. *Development Betrayed: The End of Progress and the Coevolutionary Revisioning of the Future.* New York: Routledge.

Nyambedha, Erick Otieno, Simiyu Wandibba, and Jens Aagaard-Hansen. 2003. Changing Patterns of Orphan Care Due to the HIV Epidemic in Western Kenya. *Social Science and Medicine* 57:301–311.

Obeyesekere, Gananath. 1981. *Medusa's Hair: An Essay on Personal Symbols and Religious Experience.* Chicago: University of Chicago Press.

Ochs, Elinor. 1990. Indexicality and Socialization. In *Cultural Psychology: Essays on Comparative Human Development.* James W. Stigler, Richard A. Shweder, and Gilbert Herdt, eds. Pp. 287–308. New York: Cambridge University Press.

Ohnuki-Tierney, Emiko. 1994. Brain Death and Organ Transplantation: Cultural Bases of Medical Technology. *Current Anthropology* 35(3):233–242.

Oinas, Felix J. 1993. Couvade in Estonia. *Slavic & East European Journal* 37(3):339–345.

Oliver-Smith, Anthony. 2002. Theorizing Disasters: Nature, Power, and Culture. In *Catastrophe and Culture: The Anthropology of Disaster.* Anthony Oliver-Smith and Susannah Hoffman, eds. Pp. 23–47. Sante Fe, NM: School of American Research Press.

Oloi-Dapash, Meitamei. 2002. Mau Forest Destruction: Human and Ecological Disaster in the Making. *Cultural Survival Voices* 1(3):1, 9.

Okely, Judith. 1993[1984]. Fieldwork in the Home Counties. In *Talking about People: Readings in Contemporary Cultural Anthropology.* William A. Haviland and Robert J. Gordon, eds. Pp. 4–6. Mountain View, CA: Mayfield Publishing Company.

Omvedt, Gail. 1995. *Dalit Visions: The Anti-Caste Movement and the Construction of an Indian Identity.* New Delhi: Orient Longman/Tracts for the Times/8.

Ong, Aihwa. 1987. *Spirits of Resistance and Capitalist Discipline: Factory Women in Malaysia.* Albany, NY: State University of New York Press.

———. 1995. State versus Islam: Malay Families, Women's Bodies, and the Body Politic in Malaysia. In *Bewitching Women, Pious Men: Gender and Body Politics in Southeast Asia.* Aihwa Ong and Michael G. Peletz, eds. Pp. 159–194. Berkeley, CA: University of California Press.

Ongley, Patrick. 1995. Post-1945 International Migration: New Zealand, Australia and Canada Compared. *International Migration Review* 29(3):765–793.

Oxfeld, Ellen. 1993. *Blood, Sweat and Mahjong: Family and Enterprise in an Overseas Chinese Community.* Ithaca, NY: Cornell University Press.

Paine, Robert. 2004. Saami Reindeer Pastoralism: Quo Vadis? *Ethnos* 69:23–42.

Painter, Andrew A. 1996. The Telerepresentation of Gender. In *Re-Imaging Japanese Women.* Anne E. Imamura, ed. Pp. 46–72. Berkeley, CA: University of California Press.

Panter-Brick, Catherine, and Malcolm T. Smith, eds. 2000. *Abandoned Children.* New York: Cambridge University Press.

Pappas, Gregory. 1989. *The Magic City: Unemployment in a Working-Class Community.* Ithaca, NY: Cornell University Press.

Parker, Richard G. 1991. *Bodies, Pleasures, and Passions: Sexual Culture in Contemporary Brazil.* Boston: Beacon Press.

Parry, Jonathan P. 1966. Caste. In *The Social Science Encyclopedia.* Adam Kuper and Jessica Kuper, eds. Pp. 76–77. New York: Routledge.

Patterson, Thomas C. 2001. *A Social History of Anthropology in the United States.* New York: Berg.

Paxson, Heather. 2003. With or Against Nature: IVF, Gender and Reproductive Agency in Athens, Greece. *Social Science and Medicine* 56:1853–1866.

Peacock, James L., and Dorothy C. Holland. 1993. The Narrated Self: Life Stories in Process. *Ethos* 21(4):367–383.

Pedelty, Mark. 1995. *War Stories: The Culture of Foreign Correspondents.* New York: Routledge.

Peletz, Michael. 1987. The Exchange of Men in 19th-Century Negeri Sembilan (Malaya). *American Ethnologist* 14(3):449–469.

Pelto, Pertti. 1973. *The Snowmobile Revolution: Technology and Social Change in the Arctic.* Menlo Park, CA: Cummings.

Pendergast, David M, Grant D. Jones, and Elizabeth Graham. 1993. Locating Spanish Colonial Towns in the Maya Lowlands: A Case Study from Belize. *Latin American Antiquity* 4(1):59–73.

People's Daily. 2003. Xi'an Protects Oldest Residential Area. April 9.

Perry, Richard J. 1996. *. . . From Time Immemorial: Indigenous Peoples and State Systems.* Austin, TX: University of Texas Press.

Pessar, Patricia R. 1995. *A Visa for a Dream: Dominicans in the United States.* Boston: Allyn and Bacon.

Phillips, Lynne. 1998. Dissecting Globalization: Women's Space–Time in the Other America. In *Transgressing Borders: Critical Perspectives on Gender, Household, and Culture.* Susan Ilcan and Lynne Phillips, eds. Westport, CT: Bergin & Garvey.

Pieterse, Jan Nederveen. 2004. *Globalization and Culture.* Global Mélange. New York: Rowman and Littlefield.

Pigg, Stacey. 1996. The Credible and the Credulous: The Question of Villagers' Beliefs in Nepal. *Cultural Anthropology* 11:160–201.

———. 2001. The Politics of Development and the Politics of Health: Contradictions of AIDS Prevention in Nepal. *Anthropologie-et-Societies* 25(1):43–62.

Pillsbury, Barbara. 1990. The Politics of Family Planning: Sterilization and Human Rights in Bangladesh. In *Births and Power: Social Change and the Politics of Reproduction.* W. Penn Handwerker, ed. Pp. 165–196. Boulder, CO: Westview Press.

Plant, Roger. 1994. *Land Rights and Minorities.* London: Minority Rights Group.

———. 1998. *Issues in Indigenous Poverty.* Washington, DC: Interamerican Development Bank. No. IND-105.

Plattner, Stuart. 1989. Markets and Marketplaces. In *Economic Anthropology.* Stuart Plattner, ed. Pp. 171–208. Stanford, CA: Stanford University Press.

Poirier, Sylvie. 1992. "Nomadic" Rituals: Networks of Ritual Exchange between Women of the Australian Western Desert. *Man* 27:757–776.

Ponting, J. Rick, and Jerilynn Kiely. 1997. Disempowerment: "Justice," Racism, and Public Opinion. In *First Nations in Canada: Perspectives on Opportunity, Empowerment, and Self-Determination.* J. Rick Ponting, ed. Toronto: McGraw-Hill Ryerson.

Population Reference Bureau. 2005. *2005 World Population Data Sheet.* Washington, DC: Population Reference Bureau.

Postgate, Nicholas, Tao Wang, and Toby Wilkinson. 1995. The Evidence for Early Writing: Utilitarian or Ceremonial? *Antiquity* 69:459–480.

Pratt, Mary Louise. 1992. *Imperial Eyes: Travel Writing and Transculturation.* London: Routledge.

Preston, Richard. 1983. The Social Structure of an Unorganized Society: Beyond Intentions and Peripheral Boasians. In *Consciousness and Inquiry: Ethnology and Canadian Realities.* Frank Manning, ed. Pp. 286–305. Canadian Ethnology Service Paper 89E. Ottawa: National Museums of Canada.

Price, David H. 1995. Water Theft in Egypt's Fayoum Oasis: Emics, Etics, and the Illegal. In *Science, Materialism, and the Study of Culture.* Martin F. Murphy and Maxine L. Margolis, eds. Pp. 96–110. Gainesville, FL: University of Florida Press.

Price, John A. 1979. *Indians of Canada: Cultural Dynamics.* Scarborough, ON: Prentice Hall.

Purdum, Elizabeth D., and J. Anthony Paredes. 1989. *Facing the Death Penalty: Essays on Cruel and Unusual Punishment.* Philadelphia: Temple University Press.

Radcliffe-Brown, A. R. 1964[1922]. *The Andaman Islanders*. New York: Free Press.

Radin, Paul. 1963[1920]. *The Autobiography of a Winnebago Indian: Life, Ways, Acculturation, and the Peyote Cult*. New York: Dover Publications.

Raheja, Gloria Goodwin. 1988. *The Poison in the Gift: Ritual, Prestation, and the Dominant Caste in a North Indian Village*. Chicago: University of Chicago Press.

Rahnema, Majid. 1992. Poverty. In *The Development Dictionary: A Guide to Knowledge and Power*. Wolfgang Sachs, ed. Pp. 159–176. Atlantic Highlands, NJ: Zed Press.

Ramesh, A., C. R. Srikumari, and S. Sukumar. 1989. Parallel Cousin Marriages in Madras, Tamil Nadu: New Trends in Dravidian Kinship. *Social Biology* 36(3–4):248–254.

Ramphele, Mamphela. 1996. Political Widowhood in South Africa: The Embodiment of Ambiguity. *Daedalus* 125(1):99–17.

Rapoport, Tamar, Yoni Garb, and Anat Penso. 1995. Religious Socialization and Female Subjectivity: Religious-Zionist Adolescent Girls in Israel. *Sociology of Education* 68:48–61.

Rapp, Rayna. 1993. Reproduction and Gender Hierarchy: Amniocentesis in America. In *Sex and Gender Hierarchies*. Barbara D. Miller, ed. Pp. 108–126. New York: Cambridge University Press.

Rathgeber, Eva M. 1990. WID, WAD, GAD: Trends in Research and Practice. *Journal of Developing Areas* 24:489–502.

Rathje, William, and Cullen Murphy. 1992. *Rubbish! The Archaeology of Garbage*. New York: Harper & Row.

Ravaillon, Martin. 2003. The Debate on Globalization, Poverty and Inequality: Why Income Measurement Matters. *International Affairs* 79:739–753.

Reiner, R. 1996. Police. In *The Social Science Encyclopedia*. Adam Kuper and Jessica Kuper, eds. Pp. 619–621. New York: Routledge.

Rende Taylor, Lisa. 2005. Dangerous Trade-Offs: The Behavioral Ecology of Child Labor and Prostitution in rural Northern Thailand. *Current Anthropology* 46:411–423, 428–431.

Reyna, Stephen P. 1994. A Mode of Domination Approach to Organized Violence. In *Studying War: Anthropological Perspectives*. S. P. Reyna and R. E. Downs, eds. Pp. 29–65. Langhorne, PA: Gordon and Breach Science Publishers.

Rich, Adrienne. 1980. Compulsory Heterosexuality and Lesbian Existence. *Signs* 5:631–660.

Rich, Bruce. 1994. *Mortgaging the Earth: The World Bank, Environmental Impoverishment, and the Crisis of Development*. Boston: Beacon Press.

Riddington, Robin. 1990. *Little Bit Know Something: Stories in a Language of Anthropology*. Iowa City: University of Iowa Press.

Robertson, Carol E. 1987. Power and Gender in the Musical Experiences of Women. In *Women and Music in Cross-Cultural Perspective*. Ellen Koskoff, ed. Pp. 225–244. New York: Greenwood Press.

Robertson, Jennifer. 1991. *Native and Newcomer: Making and Remaking a Japanese City*. Berkeley, CA: University of California Press.

Robins, Kevin. 1996. Globalization. In *The Social Science Encyclopedia*. 2nd edition. Adam Kuper and Jessica Kuper, eds. Pp. 345–346. New York: Routledge.

Robson, Colin. 1993. *Real World Research: A Resource for Social Scientists and Practitioner-Researchers*. Cambridge, MA: Blackwell Publishers.

Rodman, Margaret. 1992. Empowering Place: Multilocality and Multivocality. *American Anthropologist* 94(3):640–56.

Rodman, Margaret, Patti Hall Hawkins, and Daniel Teramura. 1998. It's Not Over: Vari Hall as Contested Academic Space at York University. *Canadian Journal of Urban Research* 7(1):47–71.

Rogers, Barbara. 1979. *The Domestication of Women: Discrimination in Developing Societies*. New York: St. Martin's Press.

Rohde, J. E. 1982. Mother's Milk and the Indonesian Economy: A Major National Resource. *Journal of Tropical Pediatrics* 28:166–174.

Romalis, Shelly, ed. 1981. *Childbirth, Alternative to Medical Control*. Austin, TX: University of Texas Press.

Rosaldo, Renato. 1980. *Ilongot Headhunting 1883–1974: A Study in Society and History*. Stanford, CA: Stanford University Press.

Roscoe, Will. 1991. *The Zuni Man-Woman*. Albuquerque, NM: University of New Mexico Press.

Roseman, Marina. 1987. Inversion and Conjuncture: Male and Female Performance among the Temiar of Peninsular Malaysia. In *Women and Music in Cross-Cultural Perspective*. Ellen Koskoff, ed. Pp. 131–149. New York: Greenwood Press.

Rosenberg, Harriet G. 1988. *A Negotiated World: Three Centuries of Change in a French Alpine Community*. Toronto: University of Toronto Press.

Rosenberg, Harriet G. 1996. Determination/Despair: Agunot Speak about Their Chains. *Canadian Woman Studies/Les Cahiers De La Femme* 16(4):69–73.

Rosenberger, Nancy. 1992. Images of the West: Home Style in Japanese Magazines. In *Re-made in Japan: Everyday Life and Consumer Taste in a Changing Society*. James J. Tobin, ed. Pp. 106–125. New Haven, CT: Yale University Press.

Rosenblatt, Paul C., Patricia R. Walsh, and Douglas A. Jackson. 1976. *Grief and Mourning in Cross-Cultural Perspective*. New Haven, CT: HRAF Press.

Rouland, Norbert. 1994. *Legal Anthropology*. Philippe G. Planel, trans. Stanford, CA: Stanford University Press.

Roy, Arundhati. 1999. *The Cost of Living*. New York: The Modern Library.

Rubel, Arthur J., Carl W. O'Nell, and Rolando Collado-Ardón. 1984. *Susto: A Folk Illness*. Berkeley, CA: University of California Press.

Rubin, Gayle. 1975. The Traffic in Women: Notes on the "Political Economy" of Sex. In *Toward an Anthropology of Women*. Rayna R. Rapp, ed. Pp. 157–210. New York: Monthly Review Press.

Rylko-Bauer, Barbara, Merrill Singer, and John van Willigen. 2006. Reclaiming Applied Anthropology: Its Past, Present, and Future. *American Anthropologist* 108:178–190.

Sachs, Aaron. 1996. Dying for Oil. *WorldWatch* June:10–21.

Saggers, Sherry, and Dennis Gray. 1998. *Dealing with Alcohol: Indigenous Usage in Australia, New Zealand and Canada*. New York: Cambridge University Press.

Sahlins, Marshall. 1963. Poor Man, Rich Man, Big Man, Chief. *Comparative Studies in Society and History* 5:285–303.

Said, Edward W. 1979[1978]. *Orientalism*. New York: Vintage Books.

Saitoti, Tepilit Ole. 1986. *The Worlds of a Maasai Warrior*. New York: Random House.

Salam, Nawaf A. 1994. Between Repatriation and Resettlement: Palestinian Refugees in Lebanon. *Journal of Palestine Studies* 24(1):18–27.

Salamandra, Christa. 2004. *A New Old Damascus: Authenticity and Distinction in Urban Syria*. Bloomington, IN: Indiana University Press.

Salisbury, Richard. 1983. The Social Structure of an Unorganized Society: Beyond Intentions and Peripheral Boasians. In *Consciousness and Inquiry: Ethnology and Canadian Realities*. Frank Manning, ed. Canadian Ethnology Service, Paper No. 89e. Ottawa: National Museum of Man.

———. 1986. *A Homeland for the Cree: Regional Development in James Bay, 1971–1981*. Montreal and Kingston: McGill-Queen's University Press.

Salzman, Philip Carl. 2002. On Reflexivity. *American Anthropologist* 104:805–813.

Sanday, Peggy Reeves. 1973. Toward a Theory of the Status of Women. *American Anthropologist* 75:1682–1700.

———. 1986. *Divine Hunger: Cannibalism as a Cultural System*. New York: Cambridge University Press.

———. 1990. *Fraternity Gang Rape: Sex, Brotherhood, and Privilege on Campus*. New York: New York University Press.

———. 2002. *Women at the Center: Life in a Modern Matriarchy*. Ithaca, NY: Cornell University Press.

Sanders, Douglas E. 1999. Indigenous Peoples: Issues of Definition. *International Journal of Cultural Property* 8:4–13.

Sanders, William B. 1994. *Gangbangs and Drive-Bys: Grounded Culture and Juvenile Gang Violence*. New York: Aldine de Gruyter.

Sanjek, Roger. 1990. A Vocabulary for Fieldnotes. In *Fieldnotes: The Making of Anthropology*. Roger Sanjek, ed. Pp. 92–138. Ithaca, NY: Cornell University Press.

———. 1994. The Enduring Inequalities of Race. In *Race*. Steven Gregory and Roger Sanjek, eds. Pp. 1–17. New Brunswick, NJ: Rutgers University Press.

———. 2000. Keeping Ethnography Alive in an Urbanizing World. *Human Organization* 53:280–288.

Sankoff, D., and S. Laberge. 1978. The Linguistic Market and the Statistical Explanation of Variability. In *Linguistic Variation: Models and Methods*. D. Sankoff, ed. Pp. 239–250. New York: Academic Press.

Satsuka, Shiho. 1997. Re-Creation through Landscape: Subject Production in Canadian Cottage Country. M.A. Thesis, Department of Anthropology, York University.

Saugestad, Sidsel. 2001. *The Inconvenient Indigenous: Remote Area Development in Botswana, Donor Assistance, and the First People of the Kalahari*. Uppsala, Sweden: The Nordic Afrika Institute.

Saul, John Ralston. 1997. *Reflections of a Siamese Twin: Canada at the End of the Twentieth Century*. Toronto: Viking.

Sault, Nicole L. 1985. Baptismal Sponsorship as a Source of Power for Zapotec Women of Oaxaca, Mexico. *Journal of Latin American Lore* 11(2):225–243.

———. 1994. How the Body Shapes Parenthood: "Surrogate" Mothers in the United States and Godmothers in Mexico. In *Many Mirrors: Body Image and Social Relations*. Nicole Sault, ed. Pp. 292–318. New Brunswick, NJ: Rutgers University Press.

Savishinsky, Joel S. 1974. *The Trail of the Hare: Life and Stress in an Arctic Community*. New York: Gordon and Breach.

———. 1991. *The Ends of Time: Life and Work in a Nursing Home*. New York: Bergin & Garvey.

Schaft, Kai, and David L. Brown. 2000. Social Capital and Grassroots Development: The Case of Roma Self-Governance in Hungary. *Social Problems* 47(2):201–219.

Scheper-Hughes, Nancy. 1990. Three Propositions for a Critically Applied Medical Anthropology. *Social Science and Medicine* 30(2):189–197.

———. 1992. *Death without Weeping: The Violence of Everyday Life in Brazil*. Berkeley, CA: University of California Press.

———. 1993. *Death without Weeping: The Violence of Everyday Life in Brazil*. Reprint ed. Berkeley, CA: University of California Press.

Schlegel, Alice. 1995. A Cross-Cultural Approach to Adolescence. *Ethos* 23(1):15–32.

Schlegel, Alice, and Herbert Barry III. 1991. *Adolescence: An Anthropological Inquiry*. New York: Free Press.

Schmid, Thomas J., and Richard S. Jones. 1993. Ambivalent Actions: Prison Adaptation Strategies of First-Time, Short-Term Inmates. *Journal of Contemporary Ethnography* 21(4):439–463.

Schneider, David M. 1968. *American Kinship: A Cultural Account*. Englewood Cliffs, NJ: Prentice Hall.

Schrauwers, Albert. 2000. *Colonial 'Reformation' in the Highlands of Central Sulawesi, Indonesia, 1832–1995*. Toronto: University of Toronto Press.

Scott, Colin. 2001. *Aboriginal Autonomy and Development in Northern Quebec and Labrador*. Vancouver: University of British Columbia Press.

Scott, James C. 1985. *Weapons of the Weak: Everyday Forms of Peasant Resistance*. New Haven, CT: Yale University Press.

———. 1998. *Seeing Like a State: How Certain Schemes to Improve the Human Condition Have Failed*. New Haven, CT: Yale University Press.

Scrimshaw, Susan. 1984. Infanticide in Human Populations: Societal and Individual Concerns. In *Infanticide: Comparative and Evolutionary Perspectives*. Glenn Hausfater and Sarah Blaffer Hrdy, eds. Pp. 463–486. New York: Aldine Publishing Company.

Scudder, Thayer. 1973. The Human Ecology of Big Dam Projects: River Basin Development and Resettlement. *Annual Review of Anthropology* 2:45–55.

Sen, Amartya. 1981. *Poverty and Famines: An Essay on Entitlement and Deprivation*. New York: Oxford University Press.

Senghas, Richard J., and Leila Monaghan. 2002. Signs of Their Times: Deaf Communities and the Culture of Language. *Annual Review of Anthropology* 31:69–97.

Sentumbwe, Nayinda. 1995. Sighted Lovers and Blind Husbands: Experience of Blind Women in Uganda. In *Disability and Culture*. Benedicte Ingstad and Susan Reynolds, eds. Pp. 159–173. Berkeley, CA: University of California Press.

Shahrani, Nazif M. 2002. War, Factionalism, and the State in Afghanistan. *American Anthropologist* 104:715–722.

Shankman, Paul, and Tracy Bachrach Ehlers. 2000. The "Exotic" and the "Domestic": Regions and Representations in Cultural Anthropology. *Human Organization* 59:289–299.

Sharff, Jagna-Wojcicka. 1995. "We Are All Chickens for the Colonel": A Cultural Materialist View of Prisons. In *Science, Materialism and the Study of Culture*. Martin F. Murphy and Maxine L. Margolis, eds. Pp. 132–158. Gainesville, FL: University Press of Florida.

Sharp, Lesley. 1990. Possessed and Dispossessed Youth: Spirit Possession of School Children in Northwest Madagascar. *Culture, Medicine and Psychiatry* 14:339–364.

Sheriff, Robin E. 2000. Exposing Silence as Cultural Censorship: A Brazilian Case. *American Anthropologist* 102:114–132.

Shibamoto, Janet. 1987. The Womanly Woman: Manipulation of Stereotypical and Nonstereotypical Features of Japanese Female Speech. In *Language, Gender, and Sex in Comparative Perspective*. Susan U. Philips, Susan Steel, and Christine Tanz, eds. Pp. 26–49. New York: Cambridge University Press.

Shifflett, Peggy A., and William A. McIntosh. 1986–1987. Food Habits and Future Time: An Exploratory Study of Age-Appropriate Food Habits among the Elderly. *International Journal of Aging and Human Development* 24(1):2–15.

Shik, Angela W. Y. 1995. Visa-00000 Students from Hong Kong: Adaptation and Mental Health. Master of Science dissertation. University of Toronto.

Shipton, Parker. 2001. Money. In *The Dictionary of Anthropology*. Thomas Barfield, ed. Pp. 327–329. Oxford, UK: Blackwell Publishing.

Shore, Bradd. 1998. Status Reversal: The Coming of Age in Samoa. In *Welcome to Middle Age! (And Other Cultural Fictions)*. Richard A. Shweder, ed. Pp. 101–138. Chicago: The University of Chicago Press.

Short, James F. 1996. Gangs. In *The Social Science Encyclopedia*. Adam Kuper and Jessica Kuper, eds. Pp. 325–326. New York: Routledge.

Shostak, Marjorie. 1981. *Nisa: The Life and Times of a !Kung Woman*. Cambridge, MA: Harvard University Press.

Shu-Min, Huang. 1993. A Cross-Cultural Experience: A Chinese Anthropologist in the United States. In *Distant Mirrors: America as a Foreign Culture*. Philip R. DeVita and James D. Armstrong, eds. Pp. 39–45. Belmont, CA: Wadsworth Publishing Company.

Sidnell, Jack. 2000. Primus inter pares: Storytelling and Male Peer Groups in an Indo-Guyanese Rumshop. *American Ethnologist* 27:72–99.

Silva, Noenoe K. 2004. *Aloha Betrayed: Native Hawaiian Resistance to American Colonialism*. Durham, NC: Duke University Press.

Silver, Ira. 1993. Marketing Authenticity in Third World Countries. *Annals of Tourism Research* 20:302–318.

Simmons, William S. 1986. *Spirit of the New England Tribes: Indian History and Folklore, 1620–1984*. Hanover, NH: University Press of New England.

Singh, K. S. 1994. The Scheduled Tribes. In *Anthropological Survey of India, People of India, National Series Volume III*. K. S. Singh, ed. Delhi: Oxford University Press.

Skinner, G. William. 1993. Conjugal Power in Tokugawa Japanese Families: A Matter of Life or Death. In *Sex and Gender Hierarchies*. Barbara D. Miller, ed. Pp. 236–270. New York: Cambridge University Press.

Skocpol, Theda. 1979. *States and Social Revolutions: A Comparative Analysis of France, Russia, and China*. New York: Cambridge University Press.

Skrobanek, S., Nataya Boonpakdee, and Chutima Jantateero. 1997. *The Traffic in Women: Human Realities of the International Sex Trade*. London: Zed Press.

Slocum, Sally. 1975. Woman the Gatherer: Male Bias in Anthropology. In *Toward an Anthropology of Women*. Rayna R. Reiter, ed. Pp. 36–50. New York: Monthly Review Press.

Smart, J. 1994. Business Immigration in Canada: Deception and Exploitation. In *Reluctant Exiles: Migration from Hong Kong and the new Overseas Chinese*. R. Skeldon, ed. Armonk, NY: M.E. Sharpe.

Smith, Derek. 2001. "Policy of Aggressive Civilization" and Projects of Governance in Roman Catholic Industrial Schools for Native Peoples in Canada, 1870–95. *Anthropologica* 43(2):253–271.

Smith, Jonathan Z., ed. 1995. *The HarperCollins Dictionary of Religion*. New York: HarperCollins.

Smith, Laurajane, Anna Morgan, and Anita van der Meer. 2003. Community-driven Research in Cultural Heritage Management: The Waanyi Women's History Project. *International Journal of Heritage Studies* 9(1):65–80.

Smith, Yvonne Bobb. 1999. There Is No Place Like Home: Caribbean Women's Feminism in Canada. In *Emigre Feminism: Transnational Perspectives*. Alena Heitlinger, ed. Toronto: University of Toronto Press.

Snajdr, Edward. 2005. Gender, Power, and the Performance of Justice: Muslim Women's Responses to Domestic Violence in Kazakhstan. *American Ethnologist* 32:294–311.

Sobel, Elizabeth, and Gordon Bettles. 2000. Winter Hunger, Winter Myths: Subsistence Risk and Mythology among the Klamath and Modoc. *Journal of Anthropological Archaeology* 19:276–316.

Soh, Chunghee Sarah. 1993. *Women in Korean Politics*. 2nd edition. Boulder, CO: Westview Press.

Sperber, Dan. 1985. *On Anthropological Knowledge: Three Essays*. New York: Cambridge University Press.

Spilde Contreras, Kate. 2006. Indian Gaming in California Brings Jobs and Income to Areas that Need it Most. Indian Gaming. www.indiangaming.com/regulatory.view.?id=35.

Spiro, Melford. 1967. *Burmese Supernaturalism: A Study in the Explanation and Reduction of Suffering*. Englewood Cliffs, NJ: Prentice Hall.

———. 1990 On the Strange and the Familiar in Recent Anthropological Thought. In *Cultural Psychology: Essays on Comparative Human Development*. James W. Stigler, Richard A. Shweder, and Gilbert Herdt, eds. Pp. 47–61. Chicago: University of Chicago Press.

Spitulnik, Deborah. 1993. Anthropology and Mass Media. *Annual Review of Anthropology* 22:293–315.

Srinivas, M. N. 1959. The Dominant Caste in Rampura. *American Anthropologist* 1:1–16.

Staats, Valerie. 1994. Ritual, Strategy or Convention: Social Meaning in Traditional Women's Baths in Morocco. *Frontiers: A Journal of Women's Studies* 14(3):1–18.

Stack, Carol. 1974. *All Our Kin: Strategies for Survival in a Black Community*. New York: Harper & Row Publishers.

Stambach, Amy. 2000. *Lessons from Mount Kilimanjaro: Schooling, Community, and Gender in East Africa*. New York: Routledge.

Stanford, Craig B. 1999. *The Hunting Apes: Meat Eating and the Origins of Human Behavior*. Princeton, NJ: Princeton University Press.

Starr, June. 1978. *Dispute and Settlement in Rural Turkey: An Ethnography of Law*. Leiden, Netherlands: E. J. Brill.

Stein, Gertrude. 1959. *Picasso*. Boston: Beacon Press.

Stephen, Lynn. 1995. Women's Rights are Human Rights: The Merging of Feminine and Feminist Interests among El Salvador's Mothers of the Disappeared (CO-MADRES). *American Ethnologist* 22(4):807–827.

Stephenson, P. 1991. *The Hutterian People*. Lantham, MD: University Press of America.

Stillman, Amy Ku'uleialoha. 1996. Hawaiian Hula Competitions: Event, Repertoire, Performance and Tradition. *Journal of American Folklore* 109(434):357–380.

Stivens, Maila, Cecelia Ng, and Jomo K. S., with Jahara Bee. 1994. *Malay Peasant Women and the Land*. Atlantic Highlands, NJ: Zed Books.

Stocking, George W., Jr., ed. 1985. *Objects and Others: Essays on Museums and Material Culture*. History of Anthropology Series, 3. Madison, WI: University of Wisconsin Press.

Stocks, Anthony. 2005. Too Much for Too Few: Problems of Indigenous Land Rights in Latin America. *Annual Review of Anthropology* 34:85–104.

Stoler, Ann Laura. 1985. *Capitalism and Confrontation in Sumatra's Plantation Belt, 1870–1979*. New Haven, CT: Yale University Press.

———. 1989. Rethinking Colonial Categories: European Communities and the Boundaries of Rule. *Comparative Studies in Society and History* 31(1):134–161.

Stone, Linda. 1998. *Kinship and Gender: An Introduction*. Boulder, CO: Westview Press.

Storper-Perez, Danielle, and Harvey E. Goldberg. 1994. The Kotel: Toward an Ethnographic Portrait. *Religion* 24:309–332.

Story, G., W. Kirwin, and J. Widdowson, eds. 1982. *Dictionary of Newfoundland English*. Toronto: University of Toronto Press.

Strathern, Andrew. 1971. *The Rope of Moka: Big-Men and Ceremonial Exchange in Mount Hagen, New Guinea*. London: Cambridge University Press.

Stringer, Martin D. 1999. Rethinking Animism: Thoughts from the Infancy of Our Discipline. *Journal of the Royal Anthropological Institute* 5:541–556.

Stronza, Amanda. 2001. Anthropology of Tourism: Forging New Ground for Ecotourism and Other Alternatives. *Annual Review of Anthropology* 30:261–283.

Sullivan, Kathleen. 1992. Protagonists of Change. *Cultural Survival Quarterly* 16:4(Winter):38–40.

Sundar Rao, P. S. S. 1983. Religion and Intensity of In-breeding in Tamil Nadu, South India. *Social Biology* 30(4):413–422.

Susser, I., and Z. Stein. 2004. Sexuality and Women's Agency in the Prevention of HIV/AIDS in Southern Africa. In *HIV and AIDS in Africa: Beyond Epidemiology*. E. Kalipeni, S. Cranddock, J. Oppong, and J. Ghosh, eds. Oxford, UK: Blackwell Publishing.

Suttles, Wayne. 1991. The Traditional Kwakiutl Potlatch. In *Chiefly Feasts: The Enduring Kwakiutl Potlatch*. Aldona Jonaitis, ed. Pp. 71–134. Washington, DC: American Museum of Natural History.

Tannen, Deborah. 1990. *You Just Don't Understand: Women and Men in Conversation*. New York: Morrow.

Tanner, A. 1983. *The Politics of Indianness*. St. John's, NL: Institute of Social and Economic Research, Memorial University of Newfoundland.

Tauli-Corpuz, Victoria. 2005. Indigenous Peoples and the Millennium Development Goals. Paper submitted to the Fourth Session of the United Nations Permanent Forum on Indigenous Issues, New York City, May 16–27. www.tebtebba.org.

Taussig, Michael. 2004. *My Cocaine Museum*. Chicago: University of Chicago Press.

Tennant, Paul. 1990. *Aboriginal Peoples and Politics: The Indian Land Question in British Columbia, 1849–1989*. Vancouver: University of British Columbia Press.

Tester, Frank James, and Paule McNicoll. 2004. Isumagijaksaq: Mindful of the State: Social Constructions of Inuit Suicide. *Social Science and Medicine* 58:2625–2636.

Thomas, Frédéric, Francois Renaud, Eric Benefice, Thierry de Meeüs, and Jean-François Guegan. 2001. International Variability of Ages at Menarche and Menopause: Patterns and Main Determinants. *Human Biology* 73(2); 271–290.

Thompson, Nile R., and C. Dale Sloat. 2004. The Use of Oral Literature to Provide Community Health Education on the Southern Northwest Coast. *American Indian Culture and Research Journal* 28(3):1–28.

Thompson, Robert Farris. 1971. Aesthetics in Traditional Africa. In *Art and Aesthetics in Primitive Societies*. Carol F. Jopling, ed. Pp. 374–381. New York: E. P. Dutton.

Tice, Karin E. 1995. *Kuna Crafts, Gender, and the Global Economy*. Austin, TX: University of Texas Press.

Tiffany, Walter W. 1979. New Directions in Political Anthropology: The Use of Corporate Models for the Analysis of Political Organizations. In *Political Anthropology: The State of the Art*. S. Lee Seaton and Henri J. M. Claessen, eds. Pp. 63–75. New York: Mouton.

Tinker, Irene. 1976. The Adverse Impact of Development on Women. In *Women and World Development*. Irene Tinker and Michele Bo Bramsen, eds. Pp. 22–34. Washington, DC: Overseas Development Council.

Toren, Christina. 1988. Making the Present, Revealing the Past: The Mutability and Continuity of Tradition as Process. *Man (N.S.)* 23:696–717.

Traphagan, John W. 2000. The Liminal Family: Return Migration and Intergenerational Conflict in Japan. *Journal of Anthropological Research* 56:365–385.

Trawick, Margaret. 1988. Death and Nurturance in Indian Systems of Healing. In *Paths to Asian Medical Knowledge*. Charles Leslie and Allan Young, eds. Pp. 129–159. Berkeley, CA: University of California Press.

———. 1992. *Notes on Love in a Tamil Family*. Berkeley, CA: University of California Press.

Trelease, Murray L. 1975. Dying among Alaskan Indians: A Matter of Choice. In *Death: The Final Stage of Growth*. Elisabeth Kübler-Ross, ed. Pp. 33–37. Englewood Cliffs, NJ: Prentice Hall.

Trigger, Bruce. 1969. *The Huron: Farmers of the North*. New York: Holt, Rinehart and Winston.

———. 1976. *The Children of Aataentsic: A History of the Huron People to 1660*. 2 volumes. Montreal and Kingston: McGill-Queens University Press.

———. 1996. State, Origins of. In *The Social Science Encyclopedia*. Adam Kuper and Jessica Kuper, eds. Pp. 837–838. New York: Routledge.

———. 1997. Loaves and Fishes: Sustaining Anthropology at McGill. *Culture* 17(1–2):89–100.

Trosset, Carol, and Douglas Caulkins. 2001. Triangulation and Confirmation in the Study of Welsh Concepts of Personhood. *Journal of Anthropological Research* 57:61–81.

Trotter, Robert T., II. 1987. A Case of Lead Poisoning from Folk Remedies in Mexican American Communities. In *Anthropological Praxis: Translating Knowledge into Action*. Robert M. Wulff and Shirley J. Fiske, eds. Pp. 146–159. Boulder, CO: Westview Press.

Trouillot, Michel-Rolph. 1994. Culture, Color, and Politics in Haiti. In *Race*. Steven Gregory and Roger Sanjek, eds. Pp. 146–174. New Brunswick, NJ: Rutgers University Press.

Tudiver, S. 1997. Depo-Provera. *Womanly Times* Summer/Fall:1–5,14.

Turner, Terrence. 2002. Representation, Politics, and Cultural Imagination in Indigenous Video: General Points and Kayapo Examples. In *Media Worlds: Anthropology on New Terrain*. Faye D. Ginsburg and Lila Abu-Lughod, eds. Pp. 75–89. Berkeley, CA: University of California Press.

Turner, Victor W. 1969. *The Ritual Process: Structure and Anti-Structure*. Chicago: Aldine Publishing Company.

Tylor, Edward Burnett. 1871. *Primitive Culture: Researches into the Development of Mythology, Philosophy, Religion, Art, and Custom*. 2 volumes. London: J. Murray.

Uhl, Sarah. 1991. Forbidden Friends: Cultural Veils of Female Friendship in Andalusia. *American Ethnologist* 18(1):90–105.

UNAIDS. 2004. AIDS Epidemic Update. Electronic document, http://www.unaids.org/wad2004/EPIupdate2004_html_en/epi04_00_en.htm, accessed November 8, 2005.

United Nations Development Programme. 1994. *Human Development Report 1994*. New York: Oxford University Press.

United Nations Environment Programme. 2002. *Impact of Global Warming on Mountain Areas Confirmed by UNEP-Backed Mountaineers*. News Release.

Uphoff, Norman T., and Milton J. Esman. 1984. *Local Organizations: Intermediaries in Rural Development*. Ithaca, NY: Cornell University Press.

Valentine, Lisa Philips. 1995. *Making It Their Own: Ojibwe Communicative Practices*. Toronto: University of Toronto Press.

van der Geest, Sjaak, Susan Reynolds Whyte, and Anita Hardon. 1996. The Anthropology of Pharmaceuticals: A Biographical Approach. *Annual Review of Anthropology* 25:153–178.

Van Esterik, John. 1996. Women Meditation Teachers in Thailand. In *Women of Southeast Asia*. Penny Van Esterik, ed. Dekalb, IL: Northern Illinois University.

Van Esterik, Penny. 1989. *Beyond the Breast–Bottle Controversy*. New Brunswick, NJ: Rutgers University Press.

———. 1992. *Taking Refuge: Lao Buddhists in North America*. Program for Southeast Asian Studies. Phoenix, AZ: Arizona State University.

———. 1995. The Politics of Breastfeeding: An Advocacy Perspective. In *Breastfeeding: Biocultural Perspectives*. Patricia Stuart-Macadam and Katherine A. Dettwyler, eds. New York: Aldine de Gruyter.

———. 1996. Laywomen in Theravada Buddhism. In *Women of Southeast Asia*. Penny Van Esterik, ed. Dekalb, IL: Northern Illinois University.

———. 2000. *Materializing Thailand*. Oxford, UK: Berg Press.

Van Gennep, Arnold. 1960[1908]. *The Rites of Passage*. Chicago: University of Chicago Press.

Van Maanen, John. 1988. *Tales of the Field: On Writing Ethnography*. Chicago: University of Chicago Press.

van Willigen, John. 1993. *Applied Anthropology: An Introduction*. Revised ed. Westport, CT: Bergin & Garvey.

VanWynsberghe, Robert M. 2002. AlterNatives: *Community, Identity, and Environmental Justice on Walpole Island*. Boston: Allyn & Bacon.

Velimirovic, Boris. 1990. Is Integration of Traditional and Western Medicine Really Possible? In *Anthropology and Primary Health Care*. Jeannine Coreil and J. Dennis Mull, eds. Pp. 751–778. Boulder, CO: Westview Press.

Vellinga, Marcel. 2004. *Constituting Unity and difference: the meaning of vernacular houses in a Minangkabau Village*. Leiden:KITLV Press.

Verdery, Katherine. 1996. *What Was Socialism, and What Comes Next?* Princeton, NJ: Princeton University Press.

Vickers, Jeanne. 1993. *Women and War*. Atlantic Highlands, NJ: Zed Books.

Vidal, John. 2006. Seizing the Sustainability Agenda. *Guardian Weekly*, April 28–May 4: 3.

Vincent, Joan. 1996. Political Anthropology. In *The Social Science Encyclopedia*. Adam Kuper and Jessica Kuper, eds. P. 624. New York: Routledge.

Wacquant, Loic. 2004. *Body and Soul: Notebooks of an Apprentice Boxer*. New York: Oxford University Press.

Wakin, E. 1992. *Anthropology Goes to War: Professional Ethics and Counterinsurgency in Thailand*. Center for Southeast Asian Studies, Monograph 7. Madison, WI: University of Wisconsin.

Waldram, James. 2004. *Revenge of the Windigo: The Construction of the Mind and Mental Health of North American Aboriginal Peoples*. Toronto: University of Toronto Press.

Waldram, J., A. Herring, and K. Young. 1995. *Aboriginal Health in Canada: Historical, Cultural and Epidemiological Perspectives*. Toronto: University of Toronto Press.

Walker, Marilyn. 1984. *Harvesting the Northern Wild*. Yellowknife, NWT: The Northern Publishers.

Wallerstein, Immanuel. 1979. *The Capitalist World-Economy*. New York: Cambridge University Press.

Walsh, Michael. 2005. Will Indigenous Languages Survive? *Annual Review of Anthropology* 34:293–315.

Warren, D. Michael. 2001. The Role of the Global Network of Indigenous Knowledge Resource Centers in the Conservation of Cultural and Biological Diversity. In *Biocultural Diversity: Linking Language, Knowledge and the Environment*. Pp. 446–461. Washington, DC: Smithsonian Institution Press.

Watkins, Ben, and Michael L. Fleisher. 2002. Tracking Pastoralist Migration: Lessons from the Ethiopian Somali National Regional State. *Human Organization* 61:328–338.

Watson, Rubie S. 1986. The Named and the Nameless: Gender and Person in Chinese Society. *American Ethnologist* 13(4):619–631.

———. 1997 Museums and Indigenous Cultures: The Power of Local Knowledge. *Cultural Survival Quarterly* 21(1):24–25.

Waxler-Morrison, N. J. Anderson, and E. Richardson. 2005. *Cross-Cultural Caring: A Handbook for Health Professionals in Western Canada*. Vancouver: University of British Columbia Press.

Websdale, Neil. 1995. An Ethnographic Assessment of the Policing of Domestic Violence in Rural Eastern Kentucky. *Social Justice* 22(1):102–122.

Webster, Gloria Cranmer. 1991. The Contemporary Potlatch. In *Chiefly Feasts: The Enduring Kwakiutl Potlatch*. Aldona Jonaitis, ed. Pp. 227–250. Washington, DC: American Museum of Natural History.

Weiner, Annette. 1976. *Women of Value, Men of Renown: New Perspectives in Trobriand Exchange*. Austin, TX: University of Texas Press.

Weismantel, M. J. 1989. The Children Cry for Bread: Hegemony and the Transformation of Consumption. In *The Social Economy of Consumption, Monographs in Economic Anthropology No. 6*. Henry J. Rutz and Benjamin S. Orlove, eds. Pp. 85–99. New York: University Press of America.

Werbner, Pnina. 1988. "Sealing the Koran": Offering and Sacrifice among Pakistani Labour Migrants. *Cultural Dynamics* 1:77–97.

White, Douglas R., and Michael L. Burton. 1988. Causes of Polygyny: Ecology, Economy, Kinship, and Warfare. *American Anthropologist* 90(4):871–887.

Whitehead, Tony Larry. 1986. Breakdown, Resolution, and Coherence: The Fieldwork Experience of a Big, Brown, Pretty-Talking Man in a West Indian Community. In *Self, Sex, and Gender in Cross-Cultural Fieldwork*. Tony Larry Whitehead and Mary Ellen Conway, eds. Pp. 213–239. Chicago: University of Illinois Press.

Whitehead, Tony Larry, and Mary Ellen Conway, eds. 1986. *Self, Sex, and Gender in Cross-Cultural Fieldwork*. Chicago: University of Illinois Press.

Whiting, Beatrice B., and John W. M. Whiting. 1975. *Children of Six Cultures: A Psycho-Cultural Analysis*. Cambridge, MA: Harvard University Press.

Whiting, Robert. 1990. *You Gotta Have Wa*. New York: Vintage Books.

Whyte, Martin King. 1993. Wedding Behavior and Family Strategies in Chengdu. In *Chinese Families in the Post-Mao Era*. Deborah Davis and Stevan Harrell, eds. Pp. 189–216. Berkeley, CA: University of California Press.

Wienand, A. 2006. *An Evaluation of Body Mapping as a Potential HIV/AIDS Education Tool*. Cape Town, South Africa: Centre for Social Science Research, University of Cape Town.

Wikan, Unni. 1977. Man Becomes Woman: Transsexualism in Oman as a Key to Gender Roles. *Man* 12(2):304–319.

———. 1982. *Behind the Veil in Arabia: Women in Oman*. Chicago: Chicago University Press.

———. 2000. Citizenship on Trial: Nadia's Case. *Daedalus* 129:55–76.

Williams, Brett. 1988. *Upscaling Downtown: Stalled Gentrification in Washington, D.C.* Ithaca, NY: Cornell University Press.

———. 1991. Good Guys and Bad Toys: The Paradoxical World of Children's Cartoons. In *The Politics of Culture*. Brett Williams, ed. Pp. 109–132. Washington, DC: Smithsonian Institution Press.

———. 1994. Babies and Banks: The "Reproductive Underclass" and the Raced, Gendered Masking of Debt. In *Race*. Steven Gregory and Roger Sanjek, eds. Pp. 348–365. Ithaca, NY: Cornell University Press.

Williams, Raymond. 1983. *Keywords: A Vocabulary of Culture and Society*. New York: Oxford University Press.

Williams, Walter. 1992. *The Spirit and the Flesh: Sexual Diversity in American Indian Cultures*. 2nd edition. Boston: Beacon Press.

Wilson, Richard. 1995. *Maya Resurgence in Guatemala: Q'eqchi' Experiences*. Norman, OK: University of Oklahoma Press.

Winans, Edgar V., and Angelique Haugerud. 1977. Rural Self-Help in Kenya: The Harambee Movement. *Human Organization* 36:334–351.

Winland, D. 1992. The Role of Religious Affiliation in Refugee Resettlement: The Case of the Hmong. *Canadian Ethnic Studies* 24(1):96–119.

Winthrop, Rob. 2000. The Real World: Cultural Rights/Animal Rights. *Practicing Anthropology* 22:44–45.

Wolf, Charlotte. 1996. Status. In *The Social Science Encyclopedia*. Adam Kuper and Jessica Kuper, eds. Pp. 842–843. New York: Routledge.

Wolf, Daniel R. 1991. *The Rebels: A Brotherhood of Outlaw Bikers*. Toronto: University of Toronto Press.

Wolf, Eric R. 1966. *Peasants*. Englewood Cliffs, NJ: Prentice Hall.

———. 1969. *Peasant Wars of the Twentieth Century*. New York: Harper & Row.

Wolf, Margery. 1968. *The House of Lim: A Study of a Chinese Farm Family*. New York: Appleton-Century-Crofts.

Woodrick, Anne C. 1995. Mother–Daughter Conflict and the Selection of Ritual Kin in a Peasant Community. *Anthropological Quarterly* 68(4):219–233.

Woolford, Andrew J. 2005. *Between Justice and Certainty: Treaty Making in British Columbia*. Vancouver: University of British Columbia Press.

Woolfson, Peter, Virginia Hood, Roger Secker-Walker, and Ann C. Macaulay. 1995. Mohawk English in the Medical Interview. *Medical Anthropology Quarterly* 9(4):503–509.

World Bank. 2003. *Roma Poverty Remains Key Hurdle to Shared Prosperity in Central and Eastern Europe*. Washington, DC: The World Bank. www.worldbank.org/roma.

Worldwatch Institute. 2003. *Vital Signs 2003: The Trends That Are Shaping Our Future*. Washington, DC: Worldwatch Institute/W.W. Norton.

Wormald, Tom. 2005. Visions of the Future: Technology and the Imagination in Hungarian Civil Society. *Anthropology Matters* 7(1):1–10. http://www.anthropologymatters.com.

Wright, Sue. 1998. The Politicization of "Culture." *Anthropology Today* 14:1, 7–15.

Wu, David Y. H. 1990. Chinese Minority Policy and the Meaning of Minority Culture: The Example of Bai in Yunnan, China. *Human Organization* 49(1):1–13.

Xenophanes. 1992. *Xenophanes of Colophon: Fragments: A Text and Translation with a Commentary*. James H. Lesher, trans. Toronto: University of Toronto Press.

Xizhe, Peng. 1991. *Demographic Transition in China: Fertility Trends Since the 1950s*. New York: Oxford University Press.

Yang, Mayfair Mei-hui. 1994. *Gifts, Favors and Banquets: The Art of Social Relationships in China*. Ithaca, NY: Cornell University Press.

Yawney, Carole D., and J. Homiak. 2001. Rastafari. In *Encyclopedia of African and African-American Religions*. Stephen D. Glazier, ed. New York: Routledge.

Yinger, John. 1995. *Opening Doors: How to Cut Discrimination by Supporting Neighborhood Integration*. Center for Policy Research, Policy Brief No. 3.1995. Syracuse, NY: Syracuse University, Maxwell School of Citizenship and Public Affairs.

Young, Michael W. 1983. "Our Name Is Women; We Are Bought with Limesticks and Limepots": An Analysis of the Autobiographical Narrative of a Kalauna Woman. *Man* 18:478–501.

Zaidi, S. Akbar. 1988. Poverty and Disease: Need for Structural Change. *Social Science and Medicine* 27:119–127.

Zarrilli, Phillip B. 1990. Kathakali. In *Indian Theatre: Traditions of Performance*. Farley P. Richmond, Darius L. Swann, and Phillip B. Zarrilli, eds. Pp. 315–357. Honolulu: University of Hawaii Press.

Zureik, Elia. 1994. Palestinian Refugees and Peace. *Journal of Palestine Studies* 24(1):5–17.

Index

Committee of Mothers and Relatives of Political
    Prisoners, Disappeared and Assassinated of El
    Salvador, 248
communication, 316
    see also language
    body language, 321–322
    critical discourse analysis (CDA), 329–331
    and cultural diversity, 326–331
    embodied communication, 319–322
    fieldwork challenges, 326–327
    formal properties of verbal language, 317–319
    frame analysis, 326
    gender in Euro-American conversation, 329
    gestures, 320
    greetings, 320, 322f
    and inequality, 326–331
    information technology, 322–323
    journalism, politics of, 323–324
    media, 322–323
    participant observation challenges, 326–327
    silence, 320–321
    styles, or registers, 329
    varieties of human communication, 316–325
    verbal communication, 316
    writing systems, 334–335
communion, 304
communitas, 303
community activism, 249
community-based credit system, 410–411
community-based schools, 158
community healing, 181–182
complex household, 218
comprehensive claims, 413–414
condensation, 53
condomblé, 308
confederacies, 263
conflict. *See* social conflict
conservative economists, 400
consultant, 56
consumerism, 95, 96
consumption
    and age, 102
    changing patterns of, 113–117, 385
    and class, 101
    consumption budgets, 99
    consumption categories, 101–102
    consumption fund, 97–99
    and culture, 94–103
    depersonalized consumption, 97
    forbidden consumption, 102–103
    and gender, 101–102
    Hong Kong Chinese, changing patterns of
        consumption, 385
    meaning of, 94–95
    mode of consumption, 94, 95–97, 95f
    personalized consumption, 97
    and race, 102
    theorizing consumption inequalities,
        99–102
consumption budgets, 99
consumption categories, 101–102
consumption fund, 97–99
consumption inequalities, 99–102
contact languages, 335–336
contagion, 178
contagious magic, 287
contemporary human biological variation, 6
contested sacred sites, 310
continuous observation, 49
coolness, 183
Cooper, Joe, 87
cooperatives, 237–238
core areas, 66–67
Cornish, 339
corporate farms, 81
corpse, treatment of, 168–169
corruption, 237
The Cost of Living (Roy), 378
Costa Rica
    Guanacaste National Park, 359
    hospital births in, 183
    map, 359f
    street prostitutes in, 187
cottage country in Ontario, 359

countercultural groups
    body-modification groups, 235–236
    motorcycle gangs, 235
    youth gangs, 233–235
country music, and globalization in Brazil, 350
courts, 271
cousin marriage, 213, 214, 214f
couvade, 166
covert or undercover research, 55
craft cooperatives, 237–238
Craik, Brian, 1
credit card debt, 115
the Cree
    Dunne-Za/Cree of North River region of British
        Columbia, 291
    Grand Council, 1, 416
    Great Whale Project, 1
    hunting, 414f
    James Bay Cree Project, 49, 414
    the Lubicon Cree of northern Alberta, 356
    miyupimaatisiiu ("being alive well"), 175
    New Relationship Agreement, 1
    technological changes, 113–114
    Western foods, adoption of, 114
    Windigo psychosis, 180–181
creole, 328, 336
creolization, 19
cricket, 360–361, 398
Crime and Custom in Savage Society
    (Malinowski), 269
Crimean Tatars, 387
critical cultural relativism, 25–26
critical development anthropology (CDA),
    407–408
critical discourse analysis (CDA), 329
    the Akwesasne Mohawks, and cueing, 331
    class and language, 329
    gay language and belonging in Indonesia, 331
    gender and politeness in Japanese, 329–330
    gender in Euro-American conversation, 329
    Kogals, 330, 330f
critical legal anthropology, 270
critical media anthropology, 323
critical medical anthropology, 187–188
critique, 26
cross-cousins, 214
*Cross-Cultural Caring: A Handbook for Health
    Professionals in Western Canada* (Waxler-
    Morrison, Anderson, and Richardson), 189–190
Cuba
    below-replacement-level fertility, 123
    development assistance, 403
cues, 331
cultural anthropology, 4
    anthropological life, 29
    biological determinism *vs.* cultural
        constructionism, 26–27
    brief history of, 10–14
    careers in, 27–29
    critique, 26
    cultural relativism, 25
    culture, concept of, 14–19
    described, 7–8
    distinctive features of, 24–26
    diversity, valuing and sustaining, 26
    ethnocentrism, 25
    ethnography, 24–25
    ethnology, 25
    feminist anthropology, 14
    and the future, 421
    gay and lesbian anthropology, 14
    graduate study in, 29
    growth of, 8, 13
    holism, 27
    human agency, 14
    individual agency *vs.* structural, 27
    interpretative anthropology, 13
    interpretive anthropology *vs.* cultural
        materialism, 27
    introduction to, 10–26
    key figures, 11f
    and linguistic anthropology, 6
    majoring in, 29
    vs. migration studies, 372–373

multiple cultural worlds, 19–26
new theoretical perspectives, 14
postmodernism, 13–14
research. *See* research
specialization, areas of, 8
symbolic anthropology, 13
theoretical debates, 26–27
cultural broker, 153
cultural change
    and cultural integration, 17–19
    cultural interaction and change, 19
    development. *See* development
    diffusion, 398
    directed change, 396
    invention, 397
    two processes of, 396–398
    variations in causes, processes, and outcomes, 396
cultural configuration, 149
cultural constructionism, 26–27, 161, 215–216, 327
cultural context, 326
cultural crossover, 19
cultural evolution, 11
cultural heritage
    cultural heritage preservation, 361–363
    and development, 420
    intangible cultural heritage, 295–296, 361–363
    material cultural heritage, 361
    people-first cultural heritage preservation, 363
cultural heritage preservation, 361–363
cultural imperialism, 26, 398
cultural integration, 17–19
cultural interaction, 19, 19f
cultural knowledge in conflict mediation, 153
cultural learning, 17
*Cultural Logics and Global Economics: Maya
    Identity in Thought and Practice* (Fischer), 54
cultural materialism, 13
    adolescence, and gender, 160
    culture, definition of, 14
    described, 27
    infrastructure, 27
    vs. interpretative anthropology, 27
    structure, 27
    superstructure, 27
cultural relativism, 11
    absolute cultural relativism, 25
    critical cultural relativism, 25–26
    cultural imperialism, 26
    described, 25–26
    and female genital cutting, 162
cultural resource management (CRM), 9
cultural stratification, and class, 20
Cultural Survival, 26
cultural tourism, 359
culture, 4
    adolescence, 23
    and adolescent stress, 28
    age, 23
    and art, 344–346
    characteristics, 15–19
    and class, 19–20
    and clothing, 321
    concept of, 14–19
    and consumption, 94–103
    cross-cultural communication and multicultural
        health settings, 189–190
    and cultural anthropology, 14
    cultural interaction, 19, 19f
    cultural learning, 17
    Culture and Personality School, 148–150
    and death, 135–143
    definitions of, 14
    diachronic approach, 396
    drinking, 16–17
    eating, 15–16
    and economies, 66–67
    elimination, 17
    enculturation, 17
    and entitlement, 99–101
    ethnicity, 21
    and exchange, 103–113
    expressive culture. *See* expressive culture
    and fertility, 127–134
    gender, 21–23

North American English, 337f
North American Free Trade Agreement (NAFTA), 339
North Sentinel Island, India, 72
Northwest Coast culture
  ethnographic films, 51–52
  great wooden houses, 352
  potlatch, 117
Norway
  below-replacement-level fertility, 123
  commercial whaling, 419
  the Saami. *See* the Saami of Finland, Norway, and Sweden
  same-sex marriage, 213
  untied aid, 402
Nottaway-Broadback-Rupert Project, 1
Nowell, Charles James, 157
nuclear household, 218
  the Nuer, of Sudan, 75, 273
  the Nuer language, 317
Nunavut, Canada, 415f
Nunavut land claim, 414
Nunavut Territory, 140
nurturant-responsible personality, 155
the Nuu-chah-nulth of Vancouver Island, 419

O
Oaxaca, Mexico
  children, preferences for, 129
  family farming, 79
  folk dancers, 3f
  Guelaguetza festival, 130f
  the Maya of Oaxaca, godparenthood in, 212
  migrant labourers from, 81
  products identified with, 110
  Shan-Dany museum, 421f
  susto (fright/shock disease), 177
Obeyesekere, Gananath, 48
observation. *See* participant observation
obstetrical training, 188
Official Development Assistance (ODA) (Canada), 402–403, 404f
Official Languages Act (Canada), 329
the Ogoni, Ogoniland, Nigeria, 419, 420f
Ohio, factory workers in, 89
the Ojibwa of northwestern Ontario, 149, 180–181, 184, 188, 259, 327
Ok Tedi mine, 249
"Old Hag," 180
Old Order Amish of the United States and Canada, 124, 124f
Old Silla Kingdom (Korea), 5
Oliver-Smith, Anthony, 100
Olt Land region, 83f
Olt Land region, Romania, 82
Oman
  hospitality rules in, 104
  male/female literacy rates, 158f
  map, 105f
  sexual orientation, 161
One-Child per Couple Policy, 112, 132
the Onge, 71
Ontario, Mennonites in, 37
"open" capitalist societies, 239
open-ended interview, 47
the Orang Asli of Malaysia, 182–183
orangutan research, 8–9, 9f
order, anthropology of, 269–270
organic solidarity, 240
the Oromo people, 415–416
ostracism, 270
Our Lady of Guadalupe, 299f

P
the Pacific
  see also South Pacific
  language extinction, 339
  and pigs, 103
  tribes, 259
Pacific Northwest culture
  elimination, 17
  male carvers and painters, 348

potlatch, 94
  social safety net, 94
Paine, Thomas, 247
Pakistan
  development project cycle, 406
  direct female infanticide, 137
  the Karan in the Punjab region, 41–42
  Muslims in, 305
  the Pathans, 406–407
  purdah, 265
  sex-selective abortions, 132
paleoanthropology, 5
paleopathology, 5–6
Palermo, Sicily, immigrants in, 390
Palestinian refugees, 374, 390–391
palm readers, 298
Palm Sunday, 303f
Pamir, Afghanistan, yurts in, 351f
Panama
  craft cooperatives in, 237–238
  Kuna region in Panama, 238f
Pappas, Gregory, 89
Papua New Guinea, South Pacific
  the Arapesh, New Guinea, 149
  Asmat culture, 345f
  big-man leadership, 260–261, 261t
  Christianity, 303
  community activism, 249
  elimination, 17
  gender, and deadly food, 101–102
  Goodenough Island, women on, 49
  high-status foods, 103f
  horticulture, and division of labour, 73
  intertribal warfare, 18
  Irian Jaya, 339, 414
  the Kaliai people of Papua New Guinea, 205
  male initiation, 160
  map, 18f
  moka, 260
  the Mundogumor, New Guinea, 149
  patrilineal descent, 205
  the Sambia. *See* the Sambia
  Sepik River, Papua New Guinea, 109f, 149
  sharing-based kinship, 210
  shell ornaments, 109f
  shell wealth, 105
  symbolic goods, exchange of, 106
  the Tchambuli, New Guinea, 149
  Tok Pisin, 336
  Trobriand Islands of Papua New Guinea. *See* Trobriand Islands of Papua New Guinea
parallel cousins, 214
Paramaribo, Suriname, women's clubs in, 233
parent, becoming a, 165–167
parent-infant contact, 153–154
Parker, Richard, 38
participant observation, 35
  combined with talking, 47–48
  communication challenges, 326–327
  continuous observation, 49
  described, 35, 46–47
  ethics, and sexual intercourse, 127
  "father" of, 35
  Hawthorne effect, 46
participatory research (PR), 409
Passover in Kerala, 303
pastoralism, 75
  age set, 230
  changing modes of production, 87–88
  consumption items, 97
  division of labour, 75–76
  dwellings, 351–352
  health status, 185
  the herders of Mongolia, 87–88
  movements, study of, 388–389
  property relations, 76
  as sustainable system, 76–77
  tribal organization, 259
paternal involvement, 166–167
the Pathans, 406–407
patrilateral parallel-cousin marriage, 214
patrilineal descent, 205
patrilineal extended household, 218

patrilocal residence, 209
patrimony, 210
Patterns of Culture (Benedict), 149
Payakan, Paul, 260f
peace movement, 278
peacekeeping operations, 142, 279
peasant agriculture, 77
Peccerelli, Fredy, 199
Pedelty, Mark, 323
Pelto, Pertti, 399
Penreath, Dolly, 339
pentacle, 287, 287f
people, exchange in, 107–108
people-first cultural heritage preservation, 363
People of the Longhouse, 74f
"pepsistroika," 114
perceptions of the body, 174–176
performance arts, 349–350
periodic market, 110
periodic rituals, 292
peripheral areas, 66–67
permanent markets, 110
person-centred ethnography, 151–152
personality, 148
  in adulthood, 165–169
  birth and infancy, 152–155
  and child-rearing, 149
  and class, 150–151
  cultural patterns and national character, 149–150
  and culture, 148–152
  Culture and Personality School, 148–150
  dependent-dominant personality, 155
  enculturation, 148
  formal schooling, 157–158
  formation of, 152–165
  informal learning, 157
  narcissistic personality, 156
  nurturant-responsible personality, 155
  person-centred ethnography, 151–152
  the self and selfhood, 152
personalized consumption, 97
Peru
  Inca empire, 335
  indigenous rights to land, 413
  mass killings in, 143
Pessar, Patricia, 384
Peterson, Hector, 241f
the Peyizan yo of Haiti, 405
the Philippines
  the Agta of eastern Luzon, the Philippines, 70
  Basic Ecclesiastical Community (BEC) movement, 404
  Christianity, 303
  co-headship, 219
  emigrants, high proportions of, 375
  farmers' groups, 237
  the Ifugao, in Luzon, Philippines, 410, 418
  Ilongot people, Philippine highlands, 274
  love songs, 335
  map, 177f
  the Moros of southern Philippines, 414
  nurturant-responsible children, 156
  refugee camps in, 385
  safety in the field, 58
  the Subanun people, in Mindanao, Philippines, and health problems, 176
  women, as migrant workers, 377
Phillips, Lynne, 409
philologists, 7
phonemes, 317
photography, 34f, 51–52, 53f
phuuchai, 164
phuuying, 164
physical anthropology, 4
  see also biological anthropology
pibloktoq, 180
pidgin, 336
piercing studios, 235–236
Pigg, Stacey, 193
pilgrimage, 294–295
pilot study, 47
Pinter, Harold, 364

Western Samoa, 28f
Western Wall, Jerusalem, 302–303
wet rice agriculture, 79
wet rice cultivation, 138
We'wha, 164f
the Weyéwa, Sumba, Indonesia, 15, 16f
whale hunting, 419
the Whapmagoostui Cree, 175
"white immigration," 373
white weddings, 223
Whorf, Benjamin, 327
Wicca, 287
widow ghost attack, 180
widow(er)hood, 18f, 221
wife killing, 141–142
Wilson, Daniel, 13, 13f
Wilson, Margo, 135–136
Windigo psychosis, 180–181
Winland, Daphne, 37
witches, 298
Wolf, Daniel, 24, 235
Wolf, Margery, 205–206
Woman the Gatherer model, 70
women
    abused women, 141
    activist groups, 248–250
    African-American women and hairstyles, 35, 35f
    age, and status, 23
    Asian women, as migrant workers, 377
    the Bedouin, women's stories, 53
    Buddhism, religious roles in, 301
    chiefs and rulers, 262
    child care hypothesis, 78f
    Chinese women's movement, 247–248
    and collective farm labour, 82
    as cooperative speakers, 329
    deadly food in Papua New Guinea, 101–102
    decline of political status, 263
    and development, 409–412
    division of labour. See division of labour
    domestic violence, 220
    dowry death, 141–142
    and excessive daytime sleepiness (EDS), 17
    exclusion from politics, 265
    "fat-talk" among adolescent girls, 330
    female body ideals, 175
    female genital cutting (FGC), 161
    female puberty rites, 294, 294f
    femicide, 142
    "feminization of agriculture," 409
    food-processing hypothesis, 78f
    gender segregation, and research, 43
    the get, or Jewish divorce document, 44–45
    girls' groups, 237
    on Goodenough Island, Papua New Guinea, 49
    as heads of state, 265
    Hindu women and karma in Britain, 300

in India, 142
as indirect speakers, 329
maternal roles, 165
matriarchy, 263
menarche, 127
menopause, 127, 167
Muslim women, and khatam quran, 291
as new immigrants, 382
as objects of exchange in marriage, 107
organizing for change, 410–412
politicians in Korea, 257
pregnant women, 165
prisoners in North America, 23
property control, exclusion from, 80
public leadership positions, 207
as refugees, 377–378
sati (suicide of widows), 137
schoolgirls and stress, 381
and schooling, 157
tag questions, 329
toxic shock syndrome, 190
in Trobriand Islands, 39
veiling/head covering, 321–322
Venus figurines, as self-portraits, 348f
violence against, 410
virginity of the bride, 127
war practice of raping women, 276
white sari, and widowhood, 18f
and widowhood, 221
wife killing, 141–142
Woman the Gatherer model, 70
women's clubs, 233
women's work groups, 220
women-headed households, 219–220
Women of Value, Men of Renown
    (Weiner), 39
women's clubs, 233
Women's World Banking, 410
work group, 237
working class, 20
working-class employment, 235
working-class racism, 390
Working Group of Indigenous Minorities in
    Southern Africa (WIMSA), 22
working in the field, 39–45
World Alliance for Breastfeeding Action
    (WABA), 250
World Bank, 130, 364, 369, 378–379,
    400, 402, 418
World Breastfeeding Week, 250
world economy, 66–67
world food supply, 100
World Health Assembly, 250
World Health Organization (WHO),
    114, 153, 195
World Heritage List, 361
world order, maintenance of, 278–279

world religions, 298
    African religions, 307–308
    Buddhism, 300–301
    Christianity, 303–305
    Hinduism, 299–300
    Islam, 305–307
    Judaism, 301–303
    population distribution of major world
        religions, 298f
    proselytizing, 299
World War I, 142
World War II, 142, 149, 269
worldview, 286
Wounded Knee, 309
Wovoka, Paiute prophet, 309
wrestling in India, 357–358
writing about culture, 54–55
    see also ethnography
writing systems, 334–335
Writing Women's Worlds, 53

X
Xenophanes, 290
Xi'an, in China, 306f

Y
yaks, 75
the Yanomami of the Brazilian and Venezuelan
    Amazon
    conflicts with outsiders, 142
    and division of labour, 73
    informal learning, 156f, 157
    kinship terminology, 204
Yanomami region in Brazil and Venezuela, 74f
yDgDl, 257
yoik, 338
the Yoruba of Nigeria, aesthetic guidelines
    of, 345–346
the Yorùbá revivalist religion in United States, 308
Yoruba women, and iyalode, 262
Yoruba wood carving, 346f
youth gangs, 23, 233–235, 234
youth work groups, 237
Yugoslavia. See former Yugoslavia
yurts, 351–352, 351f

Z
Zaire. See Democratic Republic of Congo
Zambia, 293
the Zapotec Indians of Mexico, gender
    division of labour and, 79
Zawiya, Morocco, 127
the Zinacantáns of Mexico, 88–89
zoomorphic, 290
the Zuni, and two-spirit persons, 164f
Zuni potters, 348